CW00703914

RECORDS OF THE
BOROUGH OF LEICESTER

RECORDS
OF THE BOROUGH
OF LEICESTER

Volume VII
JUDICIAL AND ALLIED RECORDS 1689–1835

Edited by
G. A. CHINNERY
KEEPER OF ARCHIVES, LEICESTER MUSEUMS

With a commentary on Volumes V to VII by
A. N. NEWMAN
READER IN HISTORY, UNIVERSITY OF LEICESTER

Published under the Authority of the
Leicester City Council

LEICESTER UNIVERSITY PRESS
1974

First published in 1974 by Leicester University Press

Distributed in North America by
Humanities Press Inc., New York

© LEICESTER CORPORATION 1974

Set in Monotype Imprint
Printed in Great Britain at
The Broadwater Press, Welwyn Garden City

ISBN 0 7185 1092 5

PREFACE

THIS volume is the third in the present phase of publication of Leicester's records. The hope expressed in Volume V has, therefore, been fulfilled and the records of the old unreformed Corporation have now been published. Those of the rapid expansion of the town after 1835 do, we know, contain a vast amount of information of vital importance, not only to local studies but also to the national picture of town growth during the period when the country was ceasing to be rural and agrarian and was becoming urban and industrial. By 1835, Leicester had emerged as a manufacturing centre but its great growth was still to come. The new hope is that these records, too, can be brought into print.

The present volume contains the judicial records of the Corporation from 1689 to 1835. In addition, certain other information is included from the town's records and elsewhere highly germane to all the other material published but normally extremely difficult of access.

The City Council have again been pleased to be able to collaborate with the University of Leicester in this publication, and wish in particular to acknowledge the help and advice received from Professor Jack Simmons and from the University Press.

CONTENTS

INTRODUCTION

THE core of the records published in this volume is formed by the Quarter Sessions of the town in the eighteenth century. Leicester had received a separate court of Quarter Sessions as early as the fifteenth century, by Letters Patent of Edward IV dated 24 August 1464. These had determined the constitution of the Commission as the Mayor, Recorder, and four of the discreeter comburgesses who, in practice, were the four who had most recently passed the mayoralty; death of one of these four in office involved an extended term for the next in line. The sixteenth-century Sessions records have vanished, and much of the seventeenth-century Sessions material was, in the nineteenth century, incorporated in the Hall Papers Bound series. At the other end of the period, not much survives after 1800 until the new Grant of Sessions in 1836 following the Municipal Reform Act. The bulk of the material is, therefore, eighteenth-century. It is almost entirely legal or judicial in character. These records became subject to Crown Copyright by an Act of 1958, and material is reproduced here by permission of the Controller of Her Majesty's Stationery Office.

Apart from the legal side of presentment of defective highways and some poor-law matters, most of those things which in a county fell to be done by the Justices of the Peace, in Leicester fell within the province of the town's wider governing body, the Corporation. There already existed not only an administrative structure but also, in the Mayor's Court, judicial machinery for settlement of certain cases. Unfortunately the records of the Mayor's Court have almost completely disappeared, and a note in the only surviving volume, for 1609/10, may also give a clue to gaps in the Quarter Sessions records.

Jan. 26 [19]33.

This volume of record of cases before the mayor's court Leicester for the 7th year James I was given me by the late George Toller about 30 years ago. He said that when they were sending a lot of old papers to the destructor this fell off and got kicked into his office. Evidently the rest were all destroyed. His father was clerk to the peace.

Harry H. Peach

Thus no Sessions Order Books have survived, though a reference in *Blankley* v. *Winstanley* makes it clear that Sessions Books which recorded the process of cases were in fact kept.

Whether it is safe to argue from the placid nature of Leicester's Sessions that it was an extremely orderly and law-abiding community is doubtful. The regularity with which the Ward Constables present some variations of "omnia bene" is, after all, widespread across the country, but the generally small number of cases and amount of business transacted at a Sessions do suggest that minor matters might have been settled out of Sessions. However, every now and then there is a sudden rise of one particular class of document at a particular Sessions: in January 1797, for instance, there is a large group of prosecutions of pawnbrokers; in May and September 1709, several Constables' Presentments for pavement repair; and so forth. Recent Acts of Parliament are, as in the case of the pawnbrokers, often relevant, but no certain explanation is forthcoming which covers others.

The method adopted in this volume for presenting the Sessions Rolls is to try to eliminate 'common form' as far as possible but to give the rest of the information which each document contains. Exemplars of forms of documents are given in a preliminary section, then the content of the Rolls themselves. Slight changes of wording occur fairly frequently in the documents represented by each exemplar. Only major variations can, therefore, be noted, e.g. in the Writ of Summons, while for others the date of introduction of a printed form is recorded. Direct quotation is indicated in diamond brackets thus ⟨ ⟩. For identification each Roll has been given its sub-number from the main series of the City's records.

After much consideration it was decided that the Calendar of Justices which occurs almost every Sessions could not be printed. The names of the Justices of the Peace for each year are already printed in Volume V, as are those of the Mayors, Recorders, Bailiffs, Coroners, and Chamberlains. The Jury Lists, also, have not been printed for reasons which are discussed below. However, most Sessions had a Writ of Summons and this is noted as it gives the date for the Sessions. In the earlier part of the period it is always dated from the previous Sessions, and though its issue was presumably part of the business of the earlier Sessions it has seemed more sensible to attach the Writ to the Sessions it calls into being. Later, the Mayor issues the Writ of Summons and it is dated only one to three weeks before the Sessions. Monday was the usual day of the week chosen for holding the Sessions. One other convention requires comment. Where a Constable's Presentment is used as an indictment it has, nevertheless, been left amongst the Constables' Presentments and not moved into the Indictment section, but the comment "indicted" is added.

Clearly it is not possible to give the contents of an 'average' Sessions Roll; no Roll has all types of documents in it and no document appears in every Roll; even the summoning Writ has sometimes gone astray. However, most Rolls do contain the Writ of Summons, a list of Justices and their officers, and two Jury Lists, Grand and Petty, with the names of those actually impanelled noted. As the Grand Jury was, in the words of the Municipal Corporations Commissioners' Report, "invariably taken from the Common Council exclusively.... They attend as corporators in their robes of office", it has, therefore, been thought unnecessary to print either the Grand or the Traverse Jury Lists. Except for the procedural Writs, all other documents which do, in fact, occur in any Roll have been fully noted.

In general there are few indications of the process of a case; po. se (agrees to plead), culp. (guilty), flag. (to be whipped) occasionally appear, but more usually there is nothing and the lack of Order Books leaves the position obscure. Where the notes do occur they are given. If they are not given there are none.

After the Sessions Rolls it has seemed relevant to print firstly a number of items from the City's records which do not fall into a series, and secondly a number of official reports and returns which are closely connected with the town's growth but which are not, archivally speaking, part of the City's own records.

The first section includes important legal cases which the Corporation fought in order to retain or extend its privileges and jurisdictions. In Green's case, which lasted over a long period, 1740-9 (see Volume V, index), the Corporation attempted to maintain control of trading within the town and was defeated. Although Throsby in his *History and Antiquities of the Ancient Town of Leicester* (1791), p. 152, states that he had "not less than 60 Quarto pages in MS. of the transactions", practically no details have survived. Some legal opinions in the case are preserved in Bodl. MS. Eng. misc. e. 55, fo. 79 and are printed here by permission of the Bodleian Library. In *Blankley* v. *Winstanley*, 1789, the Corporation disputed the concurrent jurisdiction of the County Justices in the Liberties near the Borough, claiming exclusive rights. Judgment went against it after some interesting legal argument. Sergeant Yorke's opinion of 1766 had earlier seemed to be in the Corporation's favour. Finally, in *Bates* v. *Winstanley*, 1815, the Corporation attempted to resist the County Justices' rating of the suburban areas growing up in the recently enclosed Southfield. Again it was defeated, and the Borough rate continued to fall exclusively on the old Borough which contained a diminishing proportion of the population.

The Draft Bill for Watch and Ward relates to the attempt to improve conditions in the mid-eighteenth century. Though it is undated it is proposed in the Common Hall Minute of 1 December 1749 (see Volume V, No. 732), and the Accounts for 1749-50 record "Paid Edward Say for printing a Bill brought into parliament £6."

The relations of the Corporation with the Vestries of the town's constituent parishes are also illustrated. In Leicester neither central body nor parish body was dominant, and so there was room for a good deal of friction. This shows up occasionally in the official records, but it seemed proper to print the parish side of the case too. Much of the trouble arose over poor-relief and Borough rates. Publication of the rate figures was forced from the Corporation at last in 1817, pursuant to 55 Geo. III, c. 51, and thereafter appears as an annual insertion in the *Leicester Journal* with the exception of 1826. The normal date fell that year into the time of a disputed election campaign and publication was possibly held to be impolitic. In Volume VI it was noted that the rate was levied by the Justices demanding orally a certain portion of each parish's Poor Levy. This was handed over to the Treasurer by the Overseers. "It was not made by the Borough Justices at their Sessions, only by verbal order or warrant to the Chief Constable out of Sessions."

The Vestry Minutes of All Saints and St Mary de Castro occur, by some obscure chain of circumstances, amongst the records of the City Treasurer's Department, but I am indebted to the Provost for permission to quote from the Vestry Minutes of St Martin's, then the principal town church, now the Cathedral, to the Vicar of St Nicholas's for permission to quote from his records, and to the Select Vestry of St Margaret's likewise.

The end of the old Corporation was prefaced by the Report of the Commissioners on Municipal Corporations and achieved by the Reform Act of 1835. It has, therefore, seemed relevant to reprint both the Report of the Municipal Corporations Commissioners and that of the Municipal Boundaries Commissioners. The former begins uncompromisingly: "The Report on this Corporation has been rendered less complete than it should have been, by the refusal of the corporation, after the inquiry had proceeded to a certain extent, to furnish further information." Their version of the dispute follows and compares interestingly with the Corporation's own Minutes (see Volume V, No. 1611). The Town Clerk evidently fought a determined delaying action on the Corporation's behalf, and he remained to be a thorn in the side of the new Corporation when it took office. His account of the administrative practice of the old regime in his Examination throws a flood of light on the conditions the reformers objected to.

The Census Abstracts start in 1801, and the increase in population they show in 1811, 1821, and 1831 helps to explain the changing nature of the town which the old Corporation's administration, rooted more in the seventeenth than in the eighteenth century, was no longer adequate to control. The population grew between 1801 and 1831 from just under 17,000 to just under 40,000. The information required at each census may be outlined as follows:

1801: At this census, returns of baptisms, marriages, and burials at various earlier dates were called for (Table I), and the numbers of houses, persons, and occupations in the town (Table II).

1811: Baptisms, marriages, and burials were required for each year since

1801 (Table III), and the numbers of houses etc. as before (Table IV).

1821: The information required was the same as in 1811 (Tables V and VI).

1831: In addition to the information as before (Tables VII and VIII), the second of which was much expanded, a further return gave trades in the town (Table IX).

The returns which form part of the House of Commons Sessional Papers give details of the Borough Rates, receipts and expenditure, for a different though overlapping period from those supplied in the newspapers. In some years where the overlap occurs the figures given to Parliament and to the press do not tally. It has therefore seemed better to print both.

On a final political note, it is possible in this volume to print the lists of proposed Honorary Freemen, which had to be omitted from Volume V for lack of space. These Honorary Freemen were intended to pack the electoral lists in the 1768, 1777, and 1822–4 crises. Of the 2,000 proposed in 1822 only 800 actually took up their freedoms, but the rest provide almost a directory of Tory sympathizers, both local and country-wide.

References and Location

The Sessions Rolls form section BR iv/1 of the City's records. The Corporation cases, other than Green's, are in section BR iv/9 of the City's records. The Watching and Lighting Bill is BR ii/3/9. Vestry minutes in the Leicester Museums Archives Department form part of collections 21D51, 11D62, and 18D62. The Borough Rates were published in the *Leicester Journal*. The Examination of Burbidge is 49 L 1961 in the Archives Department Library. The lists of those to whom Honorary Freedoms were offered are in the Hall Books BR ii/1.

Acknowledgements

This third volume in the series represents the resolution of the City Council to continue the policy of publication, despite the difficulty that it seems always to coincide with times of national economic stress. Mrs M. M. Clarke has done the initial transcriptions, and has typed, proof-read, and indexed, so that to a considerable extent the substance of the book is her work. Mr T. A. Walden and Professor Jack Simmons have again given valuable encouragement, while discussions with Dr Newman about his Commentary have been unvaryingly stimulating and helpful. All hope that this publishing venture can be carried forward to chart the town's phenomenal growth during the second part of the nineteenth century.

G. A. C.

COMMENTARY ON VOLUMES V TO VII

MUNICIPAL Corporations in the eighteenth century were not the focal points of political activity that they had been in the seventeenth, and in consequence the pattern of municipal history changes. The earlier century to a large extent had been taken up with long struggles between various factions for control of the Corporation, or attempts by the Crown to secure that control for itself by replacing one set of charters by another. There are indeed eighteenth-century Corporations where these things happen as ferociously as they had earlier,[1] but these are the exceptions and there are no parallels to the *Quo Warranto* proceedings which play so important a part in municipal history under Charles II and James II, and which are amply evidenced in the volume of the *Records of the Borough of Leicester* covering the years from 1603 to 1688. Instead the Corporations were left very much to their own devices, administering their estates and properties as they saw fit, with the central government paying as little attention to them as possible and intervening only when the needs of the maintenance of law and order seemed to require it. So long as those rare occasions were not of immediate importance the Corporations could be left safely to go their own way. It follows of course, almost as an essential corollary, that the Corporation authorities restricted themselves to their own local concerns and displayed little initiative outside these concerns. They busied themselves largely with their own properties and estates, so that even at times of such intense national political agitation as that over the Excise schemes of 1732–3 the Hall Books for the borough of Leicester intersperse comments about petitions to be forwarded by the Corporation with instructions to the Corporation officers to take action to secure the return to one of the borough's Aldermen of a cow illegally taken as toll by another borough. There is certainly no feeling of high political excitement in Leicester.

This turning inwards reflects the changing place of the municipal Corporation in national politics and administration. Helen Stocks, in her Introduction to the *Records of the Borough of Leicester*, 1603–88, indicated the beginnings of this in the latter part of the seventeenth century, and the factors mentioned there continued to play their part in this period too. In all save a few of the larger urban centres the Corporation as such displayed no initiative in national affairs, and even when the parliamentary representatives of a borough played any significant part in national politics they did not do so in the name of the borough itself. Studies of parliamentary

---

1. Maidstone, in Kent, is an outstanding example.

boroughs in the eighteenth century have emphasized over and over again how rare it was for national issues to play any part in the election of members of parliament for the boroughs of England, and this was as true of Leicester as it was elsewhere. For most of the period under review the Corporation was genuinely independent, that is, not bound to any particular political 'interest'; all the electoral lists of this century numbered the borough among those that were so classed.[1] On the other hand, the Corporation was well known to have a large influence over the elections, and it was this which, in the early years of the nineteenth century, led to intensive disputes within the borough. For long it was rare for the elections to be seriously contested, and despite the differences between the county and borough Justices the M.P.s tended to be country gentry – such as Sir George Beaumont, or James Wigley. So long as parliamentary politics themselves were as narrow and restricted as they had been during most of the eighteenth century this situation had suited many. It was almost as if there were three different levels of political life – parliament, the country gentry, and the municipal Corporations – and none impinged on any other. Even though the Corporation lost its undisputed position at the election of 1768, an eventual compromise led at last to a general support of the younger Pitt. It was however as a result of this that the reformers in the borough, antagonistic to the old oligarchs in control of the Corporation, linked hands with those political radicals who were opposed in national politics to Pitt and his successors, so that increasingly opposition to the members put forward by the Corporation became identified with opposition to the oligarchy itself. Once the national struggles in Parliament became intense, attention turned back once again to the parliamentary municipal Corporations for the same reasons that had compelled such attention in the seventeenth century. Once again it became necessary to gain control of these bodies, 'remodelling' them if that was the only way, so that through their parliamentary representatives support could be secured in the House of Commons for measures which might otherwise not be carried. Thus there developed in the early nineteenth century that revival of interest in all the activities of municipal government which culminated in the political manœuvrings of the period between 1816 and 1828, as demonstrated in the Leicester Hall Books and the investigations of the Municipal Commissioners. This is not a pattern peculiar to Leicester. What is peculiar to Leicester however is the way in which these factors operate, and this is the story revealed in these three volumes.

These records of the borough of Leicester during the years 1689 to 1835 offer a great deal to the historian of municipalities. They contain more than merely corroborative details for that series of books dealing with the history

1. See *The History of Parliament,* those volumes covering the years 1715 to 1754 and 1754 to 1790.

of Leicester during its last century and a half of 'unreformed' existence, of which the latest have been those of Professor Greaves and Professor Patterson,[1] and they represent much more than another set of municipal records to add to the still all-too-meagre list of municipal records covering the eighteenth century. A comparison of records of Leicester with these others shows clearly both what is common to municipal Corporations generally in this period and also what is peculiar to Leicester, giving chapter and verse for the rather unusual situation in which Leicester found itself in the early nineteenth century. It is however particularly unfortunate that because of the lack of sufficient published records for other boroughs of a similar size it is virtually impossible to make all those comparisons in depth which otherwise would have enlightened our understanding of English municipalities at that particular juncture.

The government of the borough of Leicester remained firmly in the hands of the Mayor, Aldermen, and Common Councillors, a body which was 'close' at the outset and became even more restricted as the years went on. Since both the Council of Forty-Eight and the Bench of Twenty-Four were self-perpetuating there developed dangerous divergences between them and the much larger body of townsmen, divergences which were to show themselves eventually in a series of disputes which disturbed the politics and the administration of the borough. The basis of these divergences was to be found in the related questions of composition and functions of the Corporation. It was not that there was great competition to be selected for the Common Council; there was not often a full complement for it, and there are sufficient cases of persons who had to pay comparatively heavy fines to escape having to serve or as penalty for having missed a meeting to show this point. This levying of fines was never, however, carried to the extremes of the City of London where the fines were intended to pay for the new Mansion House. In extenuation of those who paid a 'fine' in lieu of service it must be added that the service of the Corporation could be consuming in terms not merely of time but of money, and that a comparatively large number of members of the Corporation seem to have found themselves in financial difficulties after having held office. Nonetheless there was little attempt to recruit the Corporation widely and membership was of course restricted to those prepared to conform to the practice of the Church of England. Perhaps the surest indication of the groups from which the Corporation was recruited can be found in an analysis of those who held office as Mayor in this period.[2] The Mayor holding office in 1688 was a mercer, that in 1834–5 was a hosier, and in between appear such

1. R. W. Greaves, *The Corporation of Leicester, 1689–1836* (1939, reprinted Leicester University Press, 1970); A. Temple Patterson, *Radical Leicester. A History of Leicester, 1780–1850* (Publications Board, University College, Leicester, 1954).

2. Henry Hartopp (ed.), *Roll of the Mayors of Leicester* (1946).

varied occupations as baker, grocer, inn-keeper, and woollen draper, as well as less frequent instances of printer, architect, and even "gentleman". But the balance amongst the most frequent occupations swings away from such as mercer (eight till 1749), chandler (six until 1777), and inn-keeper (12 till 1799) towards woollen-draper (nine after 1702 but the bulk coming after 1764), hosier (22 after 1742 but the bulk after 1780) and other small manufacturers. Nonetheless, despite these shifts, which reflect the change in Leicester from being a market town serving the needs of a prosperous countryside to a centre of growing industries, there were still greater changes in the industrial pattern of Leicester which find little reflection in the Corporation; as the Municipal Commissioners reported, "the governing body, taken in the aggregate, . . . is not composed of the most eligible persons, either as regards intelligence or station."

The census of 1831, taken together with the reports on the parliamentary borough's new boundaries of 1833, probably gives the best analysis of the population at this time. The population had risen from a little over 17,000 in 1801 to nearly 39,000 in 1831, but the increase was neither regular nor evenly distributed. It was St Margaret's parish which had the greatest increase, hardly surprising with the land available for expansion within its physical boundaries. The population of the parish rose fourfold within 30 years; as the 1831 Census noted, "the great increase of Population (8928 Persons) is attributed to the extension of Factories" although of course not all the factories lay in that one parish. The analysis in that census showed a wide variety of occupations, but included in the borough a range of activities associated still with country life – cattle-doctor and cowkeeper – as well as dyer, ironfounder, and even pawnbroker. The breakdown given in the Report by the Commissioners for dividing the borough into new wards tends however to disprove the idea that the old borough was being deserted by the leading merchants and gentlemen. If St Margaret's was the largest parish in the number of rated houses (6,030) and assessed rental (£43,058), it possessed only 195 ratepayers paying above £30 in annual rates, while St Martin's parish had a much higher density of these wealthier ratepayers – 559 houses, £14,071 in assessed rentals, and 161 wealthy ratepayers. It had not been surprising therefore that St Martin's parish took the lead in many of the actions of the last years of the unreformed Corporation, but if many of the leading radicals lived in St Martin's, many of the Mayors seemed to have lived there as well.

The office of Mayor may indeed have been highly desirable for social reasons, but it was certainly not to be desired for itself. It involved considerable expense, and there were some who, having held the office, found themselves bankrupt or reduced to living off a pension provided by the Corporation. The Mayor's salary increased from £40 to £240 in these years, and there were perquisites as well, but this was obviously insufficient even though it was apparently a little more generous than that provided by some other boroughs.[1] To offset this salary, there was a considerable expense of time not only during the actual year of office, but also as an *ex officio* magistrate during the four succeeding years. Moreover, despite the prestige of the office, it was not above the hurly-burly of local argument, and there were several attempts made to curb the mayoral discretion. Indeed, on one occasion,[2] the Corporation records show his colleagues displaying their dissatisfaction with the Mayor's conduct over apprenticeships by ordering the withholding of one-third of his official salary. There were several disputes over the extent of the Mayor's powers of appointment and dismissal. On several occasions there were queries about the appointment of masters in the grammar school (e.g. 24 January 1714), but the last time there was any discussion about this was in March and April 1746, when a party of Aldermen unsuccessfully disputed rights with the Mayor. The Hall Books thereafter record clearly that new headmasters were appointed by the Mayor and the past Mayors. And while it is not strictly true that any Mayor was actually killed as a result of riots during his term, one of them, Robert Dickinson, was so severely manhandled as to die shortly after the ending of his period of office. These disputes between the Mayor and Aldermen were reflected in the general working of the Corporation. It might have been expected that Leicester would have evolved a system of standing committees to which the functions of the Corporation would have been delegated, but in fact there was no such systematic approach during most of this period. The charter of James I in 1609[3] had created a body of commissioners for letting the town lands, and this group was composed of the Aldermen and the 24 most senior members of the Common Council, but their powers were rigidly confined to the stated purpose. Occasionally other committees were set up, but they tended to wither away from lack of continued business and were rarely heard of again, neither making progress nor submitting any final report. Even *ad hoc* committees had no machinery for replacing members who had died and so at last they often surrendered their authority back to the Corporation.

Even so, these were hardly committees dealing with the major items of Corporation business. It may well be that the reasons for this paucity of committees are to be associated with the difficulties of keeping the Corporation up to its full size, and that in practice the corporate body itself seems to have been small enough to fulfil its duties quite competently on

---

1. Sidney and Beatrice Webb, *The manor and the borough* (*English local government from the Revolution to the Municipal Corporations Act*, vols II and III), vol. II (1908, reprinted 1963), 315–16, state that other boroughs provided lower salaries for their mayors, but do not give the information on which their comparisons could be based.

2. 18 March 1698.

3. *Records of the Borough of Leicester*, vol. IV, xxxiii, 80–1.

its own. This is suggested, for example, by the resolution of the Corporation to form itself into a committee to revise its standing orders which added that "not less than five members" should constitute a quorum.[1] It was not until 1795 that a quasi-permanent committee was set up, and that was for the purpose of regulating the enclosure and letting of the great South Field. That committee remained more or less in being until 1812, becoming in many respects an executive committee of the Corporation, and there are quite a number of instances of work not concerning the South Field being referred to it. At the same time it would seem that in addition to the unpopularity of committee work the machinery for keeping committees in being was far from sophisticated. A committee "appointed to conduct the Sale of the old Houses belonging to the Corporation" reported on 30 June 1806:

> This Committee, tho' not now consisting of the number competent to transact business agrees to make the following Report, the Mayor having summoned the Members of it yesterday as well as this Morning and having failed both times, owing to the large proportion of Members dead since the establishment of it – this Committee being assisted at this Meeting by the advice of the South field Committee. . . Your Committee also recommend to the Hall to transfer the powers they are entrusted with to the South field Committee – they suggest this from the difficulty which has been found in raising a sufficient number of this Committee reduced as it now is by the death of several of its Members.

On the other hand, great jealousy arose between the South Field committee and the 'Lands Commissioners' set up under the charter, and this was not settled until 29 July 1812, when the two were amalgamated. The minute is highly illuminating:

> Your Committee beg leave to report that they have taken into their consideration the present reduced Number of Members comprising this Committee – and they have been anxious to frame their report to meet as far as practicable the wishes of the Individuals who have expressed their sentiments upon this subject and at the same time to consult what regards the Honour and interests of the Corporation. . . Your Committee would beg to recommend to the Hall to try the expedient of appointing the Members of that Commission for the time being to be the South Field Committee, 5 of them to be a quorum – Your Committee feels *no* confidence that this system will better, if so well, promote the despatch of business, but if inconvenience should be felt it will be competent to them afterwards to make a further report.

Despite this rather ludicrous ending of the separate existence of the South

1. 16 February 1784. Cf. also 21 September 1786.

Field committee, it may have been as a result of its establishment that the last years of the eighteenth century did at last see the growth of a number of permanent or quasi-permanent committees, such as that set up to regulate the repair of the pavements or those periodically re-established to examine the Corporation's accounts or to work out a way to reduce the Corporation's expenditure. None of these was strong enough to assert an extensive authority within the Corporation, and sometimes the Corporation itself undermined the delegated authority of its own committee. When, for example, it set up a select committee to superintend Alderman Newton's Trust, the minute added that "it is understood that every Member of the Corporation shall have authority to attend and vote at their Meetings and is requested to do so."[1] Even though, as is shown later, the Leicester bench of Justices began to emerge as a quasi-executive body this came too late to effect much alteration in the Corporation's routine. Another pointer to the Corporation's procedures is to be found in the order of 26 August 1815 that in future the "minutes" of the previous Hall be read before business could begin.

As a result it was perhaps inevitable that power should go increasingly to the paid officials of the Corporation, principally to the Town Clerk. The early Town Clerks were not necessarily men of high distinction, and certainly not of high salary; John Boley, Town Clerk between 1702 and 1715, was paid £5 during his last illness and was buried at the expense of the Corporation, and it was not until 1811 that the official salary (as distinct from the various fees the Town Clerk received from legal business) was raised to £200. Between 1745 and 1813 the office was held by three members of one family – Thomas Herrick, his "kinsman" John Heyrick, and then John's son William – and after that by Thomas Burbidge who had been originally a pupil of William Heyrick. The extent of the power of the early Town Clerks is not clear; the Heyricks, however, made their office socially acceptable, while it was Burbidge who managed to accumulate so many powers that he appeared at times as the evil genius of the Corporation. Certainly he added to that office many others, such as Town Solicitor, parish clerk to several of the Leicester parishes, and Clerk to the Governors of Sir Thomas White's and Alderman Newton's charities. Less perhaps of a rogue than he is often portrayed, he none the less dominated the last years of the unreformed Corporation.

The other main executive officers of the Corporation were the two Chamberlains, elected annually by the Corporation. The place of Chamberlain, as Professor Greaves has pointed out, was "not, as in London, a place of profit to be competed for, but a place of labour to be avoided if possible." Yet for those who wished to advance in the affairs of the Corporation it was essential to have served as Chamberlain, and only a handful

1. 5 January 1809.

of Mayors had not served earlier in this office. As Mr Chinnery has pointed out,[1] the least experienced members of the Corporation usually had this labour thrust upon them. There was some alleviation of their burdens from 1796, when the Corporation employed a full-time Steward of Estates, with the responsibility of supervision of "the whole of the Property of the Corporation."[2] This appointment merely balanced the vast increase of work thrust upon the Chamberlains as a consequence of the development of the Corporation's estates. The result of the general over-work and lack of experience of the Chamberlains will be seen in the chaotic nature of the accounts. It was not that they were dishonest, but that by the eighteenth century the system no longer worked in a satisfactory manner. Again to quote Mr Chinnery: "The Chamberlains seem to have done their best, but the growing complexities of their job during the period, combined with its amateur status, its short duration, and their junior position in the Corporation, led to a chaotic situation." He doubts whether, by 1835, their accounts "represent anything like a full picture of the Corporation's financial activity, its resources or its indebtedness."[3] His admirable schematic analysis of the finances of the Corporation itself makes this abundantly clear, for it demonstrates the stereotyped nature of the Chamberlain's accounts as well as emphasizing that it was only through that very formalism that the Chamberlains could ever have produced anything like an annual balance. The traditional receipts and payments represented a virtual 'ossification', so that new sources of income and new expenditures each could well have represented a considerable strain on the time, energies, and presumably the capacities of the Chamberlains. Changes were certainly not impossible; for example, new headings of accounts were opened in 1824. But it could well be argued that in fact radical alteration was impossible.

The account books as presented would certainly show that until the last quarter of the eighteenth century the Corporation's finances were apparently in good condition. In this, however, as in many other directions, the political, economic, and social changes of the period began to be felt; certainly by the end of the century the finances of the Corporation were coming under considerable strain, and by 1830 the situation had become well-nigh desperate. A considerable element in the financial difficulties of the Corporation was undoubtedly the cost of the 1826 election, but it could well be pointed out that in 1790 the Corporation had paid comparatively substantial sums towards the election expenses of favoured candidates so that no new principle had appeared. Nor had the crisis of 1826 suddenly blown up; discontents had earlier been expressed and a committee set up to consider the income and expenditure of the Corporation. This was on 26 November 1810, and three months later it reported:

1. *Records*, vol. VI, vii.   2. Greaves, *op. cit.*, 13. Hall Books, 14 July 1796.
3. *Records*, vol. VI, viii.

The want of money, which the Corporation has, for the last four or five years, experienced, has (not unnaturally) led to an enquiry, amongst persons unacquainted (as some of the younger members of the body must necessarily be) with the Corporation accounts, how its revenues are disposed of?

The Committee declared itself satisfied with the way in which the revenues had been administered, but it needs little reading between the lines to see in the establishment of a 'committee of accounts' and in the restriction of the powers of expenditure of the Mayor and Chamberlains to a limit of £30 a recognition of some financial weaknesses. Despite rapid growth of some sources of income – such as the rents for the enclosed South Fields – the expenditure of the Corporation was again to exceed its income, and on these further occasions finance committees were again established to review the Corporation's expenditure. The failure of these committees to make any serious impact is, in itself, a further mark of the weakness of the Corporation's committee structure.

The account books do not, however, give a complete picture of the finances, for they do not include reference to the various rates levied within the borough, such as the poor-rate, the borough-rate, and the gaol-rate. Their details are still highly obscure, not so much the authority by which they were levied as the organization by which they were collected and the ways in which they were spent. In Leicester these various rates became highly controversial, and the documents which have been printed in this volume illustrate the considerable controversy surrounding them. Continual reference in the House of Commons during and after 1828 is evidenced by various official returns laid before Parliament. There are no references to these in the account-books or in the 'ordinary' finances of the Corporation, for these rates were not in any way 'Corporation' revenues. The revenue from the various rates was considerable, coming virtually to the same figure as the rents and other Corporation revenues. When it is remembered that these totals were raised by a verbal demand from the magistrates out of sessions on the parish officers, it becomes clear that opportunities for peculation were considerable. When, in addition, the Borough Treasurer was also the Town Clerk, he becomes even more the object of attack.

The report of 1811 threw considerable light on the office of Town Clerk, if only by inference. There appear in it a defence of the size of the bills presented by the Town Clerk for "solicitor's work", as well as a spirited defence of William Heyrick's integrity, all implying that he had come under considerable criticism. He retired within two years, and was succeeded by Thomas Burbidge who was later to be the target for much of the reformers' animosity. Many of the charges rested on accusations of having misused his official position. The evidence is conflicting, and it is at times difficult to untangle his conduct before his loss of office in 1836 from that afterwards.

Burbidge, born in 1786 and thus only 50 when he was forced out of office in 1836, had begun as his predecessor's clerk, became the Deputy Town Clerk, and eventually Town Clerk. The usual picture of him is of the scoundrel portrayed by the reformers' onslaughts and by the Report of the Commissioners who visited the unreformed borough, while the pamphlet which reproduced the proceedings on his claim for compensation for loss of office also gives an unfavourable representation, showing Burbidge accumulating a number of minor offices à la Pooh-Bah and presenting accounts for payment which could not be substantiated in detail. A slightly different impression is given, however, by the minutes of the various parish vestries and select vestries with which Burbidge was associated. Time and time again the vestries had to press him to present accounts, securing them only when it was made clear that unless they could be produced more or less on time they would not be paid. It might well seem that there was an inefficiency in his office arrangements rather than a deliberate attempt to pad his bills. The confusions over the details of the various rates, for example, had begun long before Burbidge had taken up his appointment; it is surely relevant that he had been brought up in Heyrick's office and therefore not unlikely that he continued inefficient methods of his mentor. Nor are there any details of the numbers employed in his office, but certainly a considerable amount of routine business – such as the conveyance of South Field lands – was transacted through him. Discrepancies in his accounts and statements undoubtedly there were, but whether they arose from deliberate intent or from incompetence must remain 'not proven'.

One other branch of the Corporation had administrative functions. This comprised the magistrates of the borough, the municipal Justices of the Peace. For many purposes Leicester was less a corporate body than a collection of parishes under the overall jurisdiction of a number of Justices of the Peace. Much of town government was in reality parish government, so that the problems of the Leicester Justices were not at all unlike those of county magistrates dealing with their own parish authorities. The borough magistrates were not, of course, from the same social class as those for the county, nor did they hold their office on the same kind or length of tenure. In the borough the magistrates consisted of the Mayor and Recorder *ex officio* and those four Aldermen who had most recently themselves served as Mayor; any vacancies were filled by the Common Council from amongst the Aldermen. Their powers were not, however, at all dissimilar from those of county magistrates, and the effect which the powers of the magistrates had upon the development of the borough is obviously important. This century was the one in which the Justice of the Peace reached the highest point of his administrative as well as judicial importance, the period in which the will of the Justice was untrammelled by the interposition of any central authority save that of the courts of law, and their delays were proverbial. As a consequence, this century saw a steady increase in the responsibilities of magistrates, and the clearest illustration of this comes in the growth of size of Justices' manuals. Until the middle of the eighteenth century, Michael Dalton's *The Country Justice*, first published in 1618, was the main guide, but in 1755 was published Richard Burn's *The Justice of the Peace and Parish Officer*, in two volumes. By 1766 it had gone into 10 editions and had been extended into four volumes, and the 21st edition, published in 1810, "with many corrections, additions, and improvements" extended to five volumes; the 26th edition appeared in 1836.

The activities of the Quarter Sessions are more important than the comparatively fragmentary nature of the sessions rolls would seem to indicate, and indeed these rolls throw light not merely on the judicial work which might have been expected to be found there. Certainly the petty crimes of the borough pass in review before the Justices, but the changing trades of those indicted give an indication of the changing social and industrial status of the inhabitants as do the crimes themselves of which many are indicted. Under the same formula however appear indictments for failure to maintain the roads and pavements within the borough, and the procedure of indictment and presentation – of individuals or indeed of the Corporation itself – leads to further action being taken. The Grand Jury itself is shown, through these rolls, as playing a significant part in administration; in 1705 it was a Grand Jury recommendation that led to the appointment by the Corporation of two Bellmen, while there was a wholesale condemnation in 1714 of almost every Constable when they themselves were formally "presented" for having neglected their duties of presenting "offences and matters presentable (as appeared to us upon our own view)". The office of Constable was certainly no sinecure, and men of considerable standing in the community are found filling it; the name of Gabriel Newton, for example, appears as Constable the year before he became a member of the Common Council, and in this he is not unique.

The sessions rolls show that a considerable part of the Justices' work was administrative, and the administrative activities of the Justices fall into two main categories, those in which the Justices exercised an originating function and those, by far the majority, in which they supervised activities which were the responsibility of the parish. There was indeed a great deal for which the parish was responsible, whether it was part of a borough or not. There were the problems of the poor-law; there were the problems of cleaning and maintaining the highway; and there were the general problems of the maintenance of law and order in the localities. In all these the

Justices had the task of ensuring that the parishes were performing their tasks adequately, of approving or disapproving the nominations of the various parochial officers, and of being a first court of appeal from the decisions of these officers. A certain amount of this work was done through the machinery of the Quarter Sessions Court, but a great deal was done outside, and the possibility of action by one or two Justices on their own meant that they had considerable authority which they were not in general slow to use. The history of the relations between the Corporation of Leicester and the various parishes in Leicester demonstrates this. These activities had also a further consequence. Since the Corporation as a body could not exercise any direct control over the Justices as such it tended to be pushed further and further into the administrative background, thus emphasising even more the 'closed-in' nature of the Corporation. The Webbs, discussing this in general terms for the country at large, commented:[1]

> It was to the Borough Justices, and not to the Corporation that the Privy Council and the Secretary of State came increasingly to look for the peace and good order, and freedom from sedition, of their respective boroughs. It was to the Borough Justices that any warnings were addressed and any communications as to the regulation of liquor licensing, the management of the gaols, or the prevention of vagrancy, were made. Then the Borough Justices, besides sitting on the judicial bench, silently developed into an important legislative and executive authority for their town, more or less distinct from the Corporation as such; tending to become, in fact, an influential private committee of the little group of leading members of the Corporation, which in nearly all matters wielded in the Borough the real power of government.

It is doubtful whether, in the light of current knowledge of eighteenth-century municipal government, these arguments could be maintained as a general rule. The Justices' records here printed are too fragmentary to throw much light on this problem, but there are certainly hints that it was not until late in the eighteenth century that in Leicester the Justices began to act as an executive committee. For example, the order given in 1774 by the Mayor and Justices for the removal of the Cattle Market, and renewed in 1789,[2] would seem to have derived from their normal authority. In 1800[3] however, the Justices had extended their responsibility for keeping the peace to the wider issue of trying to alleviate the causes of possible disorder by the purchase of wheat and flour. In 1805 it was to a committee of the Mayor and Justices that the inspection of the accounts of Alderman

1. *op. cit.*, 389–90.
2. See J. Thompson, *Leicester in the Eighteenth Century* (1871), 154, and Temple Patterson, *op. cit.*, 4–5.
3. 15 September 1800.

Gabriel Newton's Charities was referred.[1] But in the 1820s the Justices emerge much more openly as the executive branch of the Corporation, being empowered to order the installation of such gas lamps to be paid for by the Corporation "as they shall think proper",[2] and being directed to act as a political committee in relation to the general election of 1826.[3] Certainly evidence for the pattern of relationships between the central government and the Justices, and between the Justices and the Corporation as such, would imply that the Webbs' statements need a good deal of modification.

Relations between the central government and the municipalities in the eighteenth century were much less close than they had been in the seventeenth. The comparative instability of the period immediately after the 1688 Revolution was not unnaturally marked by a fear of 'Jacobitism', and Leicester had its own share of government interest, alarums, and excursions; a number of government troops were, for example, quartered in the borough. By 1722, however, disturbances had become very minor, so that investigations in that year by the Secretary of State, Lord Townshend, into accusations of rampant disloyalty in the borough were not initiated by the government but by the country gentry, and represented in fact a further attempt by the county to exercise the same sort of control over the borough of Leicester as they exercised over the other boroughs in the county. These investigations, then, concerned central government far less than they did local rivalries and differences. The charters of the corporation, and a reluctance by the Secretary of State to intervene in the affairs of boroughs, saved Leicester from any action in 1722; in the same way, similar accusations were parried in 1738 and in 1744. At the same time, however, the Mayor and Corporation were quick to send loyal addresses to the king to demonstrate their loyalty in case there should be any suspicion of it.

This attitude of passivity by central government continued throughout the rest of the century, and it became rare for the central government to take any initiative itself in dealings with the local authorities. The issue is slightly clouded by the blurring of authority between the Corporation and the Justices of the Peace, but even during the disturbances in the 1790s the initiative for action seems to come always from the magistrates or from the Mayor as an *ex officio* Justice. It was for the Justices to decide, for example, whether local detachments of soldiers should be called out to keep the peace, and the most that the central government did was to pass on various reports received from spies or *agents provocateurs* together with the promise that sufficient troops would be made available locally for the purposes of law and order. Not that these soldiers were always necessary; in 1792 food riots were dispersed without the soldiers being called out. When soldiers were used, the central government had to receive a report by the officer

1. 19 December 1805.   2. 29 August 1821.   3. 30 August 1825; 5 September 1826.

commanding on the circumstances in which his men were used. Again, in the aftermath of the Napoleonic Wars, at a time of disturbance and riots, it was for the local authorities to act and to ask for help if necessary, and not for the central government to impose help, or even suggest it, where the magistrates were happy in their own minds.

There seems to be only one exception to this rule of passivity by the central government, certainly so far as Leicester is concerned. One of the Secretaries of State in 1766, Lord Shelburne, took an initiative in asking for information and hinting at possible action, writing to the Mayor of Leicester:[1]

> In consequence of the general accounts from Leicester of the riotous dispute which has lately appeared in your town and neighbourhood, and of the commitment of several persons on account thereof, I must desire that you will send up the several examinations of the persons so committed, taken upon oath, fixing the crimes of each offender, circumstantially and accurately, in order to be laid before the King, that his Majesty may judge what further steps may be proper to be taken to secure the obedience due to Law and Government, and to prevent such acts of outrage for the future.

Little response seems to have been evoked by this letter, which was sent also to the Mayors of Gloucester, Nottingham, and Oxford. Indeed, these actions by Shelburne are so completely out of character for a Secretary of State at this time that reasons for his initiative are more likely to be found in a study of him than in any study of local government in this period.

The pattern seems clear therefore. The eighteenth-century municipality, or even its bench of Justices, was not likely to be affected by a series of demands made upon it by the central government for action of any sort. Even when there were dangers of riot and disturbance the central government left matters in the hands of the municipalities, sometimes perhaps directly strengthening the local forces but never wishing or even able perhaps to intervene on its own account. The action therefore of setting up in 1833 a Commission to investigate the municipal corporations created a sense of interference and an even greater feeling in many places, not only in Leicester, that there should be no co-operation in such a flagrant breach of municipal privilege.

The basic problem facing the Corporation between 1689 and 1835 arose however not so much from weaknesses and difficulties in its own internal organization, or of interference by the central government, but rather from the absence of any real authority over various competing jurisdictions. Two other sets of authorities disputed the right of the Corporation to exercise

1. Secretaries' Letter Books, Public Record Office, S. P. Dom. 44, vol. 141. 14 October 1766.

its own jurisdiction in various parts of the built-up area, and the consequent conflict among these three accounts for a great part of the weaknesses exposed by the Commissioners investigating municipal Corporations in 1833. These other authorities were the county magistrates and the officers of the various parishes situated either wholly or partly within the borough, and the reasons why Leicester was so vulnerable to these rivals are to be found partly in its municipal geography. Leicester was not unique, of course, in having several parishes within its municipal boundaries, for it was usual for a borough of its antiquity and prosperity to contain several parishes or extra-parochial areas. The complications did not lie in the number of its parishes, for York or Norwich for example had many more, Norwich indeed having over thirty separate parishes. But these parishes were small in population and weak in parish income, so that there could be no effective competition between them and municipal authorities. In Leicester, where there were six parishes and two extra-parochial areas, four of its parishes were strong enough to resent bitterly the activities of the Corporation and to act as focal points for opposition. As a consequence, those elements in Leicester who, as shown above, found themselves excluded from active participation in municipal affairs through membership of the Corporation itself were able to capture the machinery of parish government and use it as a weapon against the municipal oligarchy. To add to these complexities three of the parishes, those of St Mary, St Margaret, and St Leonard, lay partly beyond the boundaries of the borough and thus partly outside the Corporation's authority, and there were three major liberties, the Castle View and Newarke Liberties and the Bishop's Fee, which were within the built-up areas of the borough but outside municipal jurisdiction, thus coming directly under the county magistrates. It was after 1689 that difficulties started becoming acute over these conflicting jurisdictions, and by 1835, as will become obvious, these difficulties had appeared over and over again in all the activities of the Corporation. Whatever the Corporation tried to do was hampered or even brought to a standstill by one or other of these rivals.

The first set of disputes, not finally settled until 1815, was between the borough and the county magistrates, and concerned the limits of their respective jurisdictions. On three occasions the county magistrates tried to assume authority over the borough, in 1722, 1738, and 1744. None of these attempts succeeded, and it is clear that the issue involved was basically the jealousy felt by the county magistrates of the borough's independence.[1] This jealousy was not one-sided; although at times the county magistrates were prepared to allow the borough magistrates to exercise a 'concurrent' jurisdiction with them in those liberties and built-up areas of the town lying outside the formal boundaries of the Corporation, the

1. See Secretaries' Letter Books, S. P. Dom. 44, vols. 123, 130, 229, 230, and 340.

borough magistrates consistently fought for their own exclusive jurisdiction over these same areas. The progress of these claims, and their fate, were marked by a series of law suits. The charters of the Corporation, particularly that of 1599, had granted an exclusive authority to the borough's magistrates in the borough itself, and permitted them to exercise authority in the liberties – the Bishop's Fee, Castle View, Wood Gate, the Newarke, and Bromkinsthorpe – without prejudice to any rights granted to any other persons or bodies corporate. In the course of a dispute in 1765 the county magistrates sought legal advice, and counsel, Charles Yorke, gave as his opinion that the borough had made out its case, and that the borough magistrates had exclusive jurisdiction over these 'extra-mural' areas. The county magistrates consequently withdrew until 1789 when in a further test-case, *Blankley v. Winstanley*, the decision was handed down that jurisdiction was after all concurrent in the liberties, and that the county magistrates could exercise a control there.

The second issue involved not legal jurisdiction but the borough rate. Until 1815 the borough rate was levied in full, through the parish organization, on those parts of the parishes which lay outside the jurisdiction of the Corporation. In 1811 however a case was begun by the overseers of St Mary's parish to have this point determined, and in the case of *Bates v. Winstanley*, heard in 1815, it was made quite clear that these portions of the three parishes which lay outside the Corporation paid rates not to the borough but to the county alone. The urban developments of the early nineteenth century made these disputes the more serious; the censuses and some other contemporary surveys show clearly the patterns of development and how the population moved to the areas outside the control of the Corporation and outside the area which the borough could claim to rate. The borough sought, and the county resisted, rating authority over these new wealthy areas, and in measure as the borough failed the wealthier borough inhabitants sought to move out of the borough and escape their municipal obligations. It was not merely because of rates alone that many moved; the nuisance of living in areas that were in the process of industrialization and sheer snobbery played their parts too, but once the process was begun it developed its own momentum, and was one factor in the growing impoverishment of the borough and the physical expansion of the built-up areas.

The other series of conflicts assumed its greatest significance in the last fifty years of the unreformed Corporation's existence. For many purposes, during the eighteenth and nineteenth centuries, the basic unit of local government in England was less the county or the borough than the parish, of course, under the general supervision of the Justices of the Peace. On issue after issue that arose in Leicester during this period, the parish officers were able to block the activities of the Corporation without necessarily being able, or even wishing, to undertake any activity themselves. On the other hand, the Corporation had a certain degree of control over the parishes in that it was the borough magistrates who could exercise magisterial control and it was the borough magistrates who had the power of levying a parochial rate for purposes approved by the bench. Various acts during the seventeenth century had permitted the levying of occasional rates for purposes such as scavenging, the repayment of constables' expenses incurred in dealing with vagrants, and, of course, the poor. Two statutes in 1739 and 1740 made the Justices' power of imposing a general rate much more specific[1] and in 1759 the Corporation approved a by-law authorizing the imposing of a pump-rate to meet the cost of providing a water supply in each ward. A further act in 1784 gave general authority to Corporations like Leicester, having Courts of Quarter Sessions, to levy a prison-rate, so that by the end of the eighteenth century the burden represented by the 'borough rate' could be quite substantial. The level of the rate was laid down by the Corporation, but levied on each parish by the parish officers along the lines of the poor-rate, and as the parishes grew more populous the parochial officers grew more and more restive under the Corporation's demands. The geographical situation of three of the parishes became a further complication; it was in those parishes which lay partly within and partly without the borough that the great bulk of early nineteenth-century building and development occurred. In 1824, as the vestry minutes of one parish record, "out of about 3,000 houses in [St Margaret's parish] . . . not 900 of them" were in the borough; only one of the parish officers lived within the borough and was thus amenable to effective control by the Corporation. Increasingly therefore the parochial officers resented the claims of the Corporation and its magistrates, and it was in this manner that there began that series of conflicts between parish and borough which characterizes the early nineteenth-century history of the Corporation.

Thus the freedom of action of the Corporation was restricted from both sides. It was little wonder perhaps that increasingly the Corporation came to consider that its primary purpose was to concentrate on the maintenance of its private interests and corporate properties. But although eighteenth-century Corporations did tend to look inwards, these narrow ends were not the sole objects of municipal concern. A high proportion of the members of these Corporations resided within their own municipalities, so that they were as concerned as anybody else over such problems as paving, lighting, policing, and cleansing, and over the country as a whole there was a great development of such aspects of municipal life. On the other hand, it was not necessarily the municipality which initiated these developments, nor was it the normal responsibility of the Corporation itself to participate in

1. 12 George II, c 29; 13 George II, c 18.

them, although on occasion in fact it did so. More commonly, the body responsible for urban improvements would be either a section of the corporate body established by statute as an improvement commission or an *ad hoc* statutory body of improvement commissioners largely independent of the Corporation. These however only became common after the passage in 1748 of an act giving general powers to the Corporation of Liverpool, and indeed did not really become widespread until after 1763. It has, however, been estimated that by the beginning of the nineteenth century over 200 bodies of improvement commissioners had been established in urban districts outside the metropolitan areas of London; they "far outweighed in importance, from the point of view of activity and expenditure in local government, the old Municipal Corporations that, in over a hundred cases, existed alongside them."[1] The mere existence of these various approaches to problems of municipal administration resulted in that vigour of municipal life which carried over beyond the Municipal Corporations Act of 1835 into the new municipal bodies of the nineteenth century.

If this is the general pattern it must however be made clear that it is one in which Leicester by no means participated. The Corporation itself was not prominent in initiating any large measures of municipal improvement, save for the development of the New Walk area of the borough; in 1792 an attempt was made to develop a new town centre and in 1814 a further unsuccessful attempt was initiated to build a new town hall. It was for this purpose that it was proposed that some of the South Field building lands should be sold, and Alderman Firmadge was even commissioned to draw up plans for which he was later paid, even though the scheme fell through. Nonetheless, the Corporation was largely unsuccessful in these schemes, while, as has been pointed out, Leicester was "one of the only four considerably large municipal towns without improvement commissioners, necessary though these were."[2] It was not that the Corporation were unaware of any need for improvement, but rather that there were tremendous problems of finance and of jurisdiction, and these were, in the last resort, one aspect of the central and continuing dilemma of the Leicester Corporation. Responsibility for maintenance of streets and pavements, for cleansing, and for watch and ward was divided between the parish and the borough, or, more specifically, between the parish and the wards into which the borough was divided. Constables of wards presented deficiencies under these heads to the borough magistrates in the same way as they presented any other offences under their jurisdictions, and if blame could not be attached directly to any individual the parish could be compelled to

1. Sidney and Beatrice Webb, *Statutory authorities for special purposes* (*English local government from the Revolution to the Municipal Corporations Act*, vol. IV) (1922, reprinted 1963), 243.
2. Greaves, *op. cit.*, 34.

make up for this failure. For their part the Justices, who were themselves members of the corporate body and thus had the responsibility of keeping down the expenses of the Corporation which was a property owner and liable as such to a parish rate or indeed to being presented in its turn, had a vested interest in making sure that others performed their share of the work.

Attempts were made by the Corporation to make some 'improvements'. Fire engines were provided for the town, and sheds were built to accommodate them. Officials were appointed to meet some of the needs of the community. Thus, in 1688, a "Bellman" was appointed, and this was followed in 1705 by a Grand Jury recommendation for the number to be increased to two, a recommendation put into effect in October 1706 when the two Bellmen were provided with uniform and bell. The Beadle had to ensure that the streets for which the Corporation was responsible were kept swept; the Town Crier had regularly to draw the attention of the inhabitants to an order issued by the Mayor during the reign of James I for the cleansing of the streets; there was a scavenging service for which a special rate was levied; and the Chamberlains had the duty of viewing the streets and preventing any building encroachments upon them. But basically even when the Corporation regulated these services and standards it made no attempt to pay for them out of Corporation funds, except where the Corporation was directly involved as an owner of property. This becomes obvious from a closer examination of two crucial aspects of town life – the provision of water, and the paving, lighting, and policing of its streets.

Although the Corporation regarded itself as largely responsible for the upkeep of the main conduit, repairing it as and when necessary with little argument, it treated the provision and maintenance of wells and pumps as the responsibility of each individual ward, and the Justices were not at all dilatory either in ensuring the prosecution of anyone for neglect or in strengthening the hands of the well-reeves. Indeed, the only by-law recorded in this 150 years of the Corporation's history was one of 25 November 1759, which ordered the erection of pumps in every ward, the choosing of pump-reeves, and the levying of a pump-rate parallel to the parish poor-rate.

More difficult to regulate was the condition of the streets and pavements, for here it was always much less easy to allocate responsibility for repairs. A series of highway acts from the middle of the sixteenth century had laid down that the responsibility for the upkeep of roads lay primarily with the property-owners adjoining the road, or in their default with the parish, and the Justices had the power to ensure the repair of such roads as were presented to them by the constable and to compel the parish to complete the work. The Corporation as such had no responsibility for anything other than the bridges within its boundaries or for those parts of the road where its property lay, but its own Justices superintended within the borough the work of the parishes, and ensured that highway overseers were appointed. Throughout these years the Corporation books record the attempts by the Corporation to ensure that everyone else did his work adequately. The Constables were urged to walk the streets, the Aldermen reminded of their duty to inspect their own wards, and the Chamberlains instructed to view the streets and report any encroachments. When it began to be necessary to provide street lighting the Corporation ordered six lights to be installed, and when gas came to Leicester authority was given to the magistrates to order gas lights for various public buildings "and in such other situations (if any) as they may think ought to be lighted by the Corporation."[1] Nor was the Corporation unmindful of its responsibility for the removal of traffic bottle-necks. It made attempts in this direction by the decision to remove the town gates and by another decision to contribute £100 towards the cost of improving Applegate Street by demolishing some houses there. On 14 September 1789 the Corporation agreed to pay towards the cost of clearing some obstructions on the condition that the ground be left "as part of the publick Street". As an owner of properties, the Corporation set a good example; the Chamberlains were constantly being instructed to have pavements put into good repair, and they had to maintain a list of those parts of roads and pavements for which the Corporation was responsible. In 1800 a Pavements committee was established, and it was given authority to spend a maximum of £150 a year to supervise these repairs. At other times the Corporation ordered the expenditure of quite large sums for laying out new streets or for repair of old, although it must be borne in mind that very often this was on condition that the parish would thereafter accept responsibility for upkeep. In the last resort, however, the Corporation had to fall back on its powers of compulsion, and the Justices were not slow to order the prosecution of offenders. The Sessions Rolls report repeated indictments of individuals and groups for failing to meet their responsibilities, and as late as the end of the eighteenth century the state of New Street was argued in a law suit as far as the court of King's Bench. This case, incidentally, seems to indicate yet another instance of perpetual squabbles between Corporation and parish, for although nominally the disagreement lay between the householders and St Martin's parish – a case lost by the parish – the majority of those householders seem to have been members of the Corporation.

None of this could meet the essential needs of the borough, and the Corporation itself was well aware of the problem. After an attempt in the winter of 1748–9 to improve the policing of the borough by increasing the number of the watchmen and ordering the payment to each of them of one

1. 29 August 1821, 28 August 1822.

shilling a night, the Corporation promoted in the winter of 1749–50 an act along the lines of the Liverpool Act for the appointment of improvement commissioners. An appropriate petition was presented to the House of Commons on 15 January 1750 and reported on favourably by a Select Committee; the two county members and one of the borough members were given formal instructions to introduce a bill. Under the draft bill the Mayor, Recorder, and Justices, i.e. the Quarter Sessions for the borough, were to be Improvement Commissioners with power not only to 'improve' the borough but also to levy a rate on the householders within the borough and "the parts thereunto adjoining". These powers would certainly have enabled the Corporation to undertake a substantial measure of improvement and the bill indicates that the Corporation was prepared to initiate changes, if the money could be found. But the bill was lost in Committee, so decisively that no reason for this can be traced, and this failure was followed by no renewed measure of improvement. There were the piecemeal improvements already mentioned, but it was not until 1820 that a further improvement measure was put forward. On 4 October 1820 the Corporation formally agreed to constitute itself as an open committee "to take into consideration the propriety of applying to Parliament for an Act to light, pave, or otherwise improve the approaches to and internal parts of the Town." Less than a year later, on 24 August 1821, the Committee had agreed to promote an Act for these purposes. A private company had also been set up to bring gas-lighting to Leicester and on 29 August 1821 the Corporation was empowered to order gas lights from this company. The opposition of the gas company placed obstacles in the way of projected Corporation improvements; although several members of the Corporation were among the shareholders of the company, the directors of the company were associated with the opposition to the Corporation. The arguments came to a head in the winter of 1821–2. A public meeting of householders was held at which the radicals insisted that any improvements should be paid for not out of a rate specially collected for that purpose but from the Corporation's own endowments. A subsequent meeting of the Corporation, on 16 January 1822, resolved that in view of "the very serious expence which would be entailed upon the inhabitants . . . and that a considerable portion of such expence will have to be borne by a great number of persons who have *no property to watch*, are of opinion that the expence . . . ought to be borne by the wealthier part of the Inhabitants *exclusively*." It is to be supposed that the radicals greeted the suggestion that they themselves ought to pay for the watching and lighting with mixed feelings.

The defeat of the Corporation's scheme was followed by that open conflict between municipal and parish authorities which dominated the Corporation's last years. Nominally the fight concerned the prison and the control of poor-law expenditure; in practice what was at stake was the extent to which the parishes could make themselves independent of the authority of the Corporation and the Justices. It is significant that the defeat of a final improvement plan in 1831 was followed by the establishment of an independent lighting and watching scheme by the parishes of All Saints, St Martin's, St Margaret's, and St Mary's, but that this in its turn was followed by the reform of the Corporation and the grant to it of much wider powers.

The dispute over the Leicester prison began in 1823 with a general prisons' act moved in the House of Commons by the Home Secretary, Sir Robert Peel; this act enabled seventeen specified local authorities, including Leicester, to improve their gaols. The borough Justices were authorized to levy an additional borough rate for this purpose, but of course after the judgements of 1815 this rate could only be levied on the restricted borough itself, and this not unnaturally caused discontent amongst the parishes within the borough's boundaries. The lead was taken by All Saints' parish, whose officers drew up a petition signed by the officers of almost all the parishes lying inside the Corporation's control. Only St Margaret's was not included for by now its main population lived outside the borough. As the minutes of the vestries demonstrate, particularly those of All Saints', the agitation was particularly violent before and after the parliamentary election of 1826. The attack was led by the parish officers who demanded to see details of how the borough rate was levied and spent. In an extremely full reply Burbidge explained why these records could not be made available; however, at a slightly later stage Burbidge gave to a delegation from St Martin's vestry some details of the rate's expenditure. During the progress of the election the agitation quietened, but a renewed attempt in 1827 to levy a rate for a new prison led to renewed attacks. On this occasion the attack was conducted by M.P.s; detailed questions and demands for returns to the House produced details to illustrate how the money had been raised and spent. If the agitation dropped when the Justices substituted for the scheme to construct a new prison the purchase of the old county gaol, now surplus to the county's needs, the whole series of events marked a further decline in the Corporation's prestige.

Similarly the poor-rate and the question of the poor-law were the occasion for bitter recriminations, sometimes between the Corporation (or more especially the magistrates) and the parish officers, and sometimes between the parishes themselves. The problems of the poor-law were almost endless. Each parish was responsible for the maintenance of its own poor, for the levying of its own poor-rate, and for the appointment of parish overseers of the poor, but the Justices had the task of exercising a general supervision of the operation of the poor-law. The records show also the activities of the Justices as auxiliaries to the parish officers; bastardy orders laying down the amount to be paid by the putative father had to be made by those Justices resident in the parish and are to be found in the parish records. Another aspect was the determination of the parish of 'settlement'; each parish tried desperately hard to lessen the burden on it of poor-relief, keeping out of the parish anyone likely to become a charge upon it unless that person could prove a legal right to establish a 'settlement'. The determination of the responsibility of one parish as against another was an important part of eighteenth-century Quarter Sessions work, and many cases were taken on appeal as far as the House of Lords. Once 'settlement' had been determined it was for the Justices to order the removal of any individual from one parish back to his place of origin.

The detailed operation of this law could, however, become unwieldy and even harsh and unfair in a borough such as Leicester, where the difficulties of finding work could become even more complicated by the virtual impossibility of moving from one urban parish to another. It was therefore not long before the churchwardens had developed a scheme to alleviate this problem; the minute book of St Martin's vestry records as early as 1691 that although various inhabitants of other parishes had come into St Martin's the parish of their legal settlement still accepted responsibility for taking them back if they ever needed poor relief. Nonetheless, problems remained, and one obvious way of avoiding them would have been the bringing together of all the parish workhouses into one united building. On four separate occasions – 1708, 1792, 1804, and 1810 – this was attempted, but at each time the attempt failed, the last two because of a refusal by St Margaret's vestry to participate, that parish having only recently built for itself a new workhouse, and also possibly because of the support for the union scheme expressed by the Corporation. The difficulties over the poor-rate usually showed themselves in the willingness of the borough magistrates to order relief from parish funds to applicants appealing from decisions of the parish overseers, so that in consequence the parish constantly strove to free itself from any supervision by the magistrates, attempting to appoint overseers without need for magisterial approval and when this proved insufficient, seeking even further independence. Of particular interest are the reactions of two of the parishes, St Margaret's and St Martin's, this latter having, as early as 1692, got rid of the attendance of the magistrates. In 1806 St Martin's appointed a permanent, salaried assistant overseer of the poor, and in 1812 removed poor-law administration altogether from the immediate control of the magistrates by adopting Gilbert's Act and appointing salaried poor-law guardians.

St Margaret's parish was far more extreme in its opposition, partly because the burden on it of the poor-law increased very rapidly as a result of an intense depression in the hosiery industry following the end of the Napoleonic Wars and of the rapid increase in population in the parish. Although earlier it had wished to have nothing to do with the schemes of the other parishes, in 1819 it had, in conjunction with All Saints' and St Mary's, adopted the Sturges Bourne Act which permitted the establishment of an elective select vestry and thus put the conduct of the affairs of the parish into the hands of its principal residents. It has often been implied that one reason was the desire to escape from control by the Corporation and its officials, but from the beginning Thomas Burbidge, the Town Clerk, offered his services to the new vestry, an offer graciously received and accepted. Friction did develop over his bills for legal business, less it would seem about the scale of his charges than his dilatoriness in submitting them. Constantly he had to be asked to render them quarterly, and eventually, in 1829, the vestry had to decide "that in future some other Attorney be employed to conduct the parish business". It took five more years before his bills were finally discharged.

The differences between the magistrates and the officers of the parish of St Margaret's came to a head between 1823 and 1827; the expansion of the parish necessitated the building of an additional church in the parish, St George's, a chapel of ease. In the process it was discovered that one of the churchwardens, Alderman James Rawson, had been guilty of peculation, collecting discounts from various tradesmen and charging the parish for the full amount of the contractors' bills. Little could be done at that stage, but in the next year, 1829, exception was taken by the vestry to the accounts as presented by the parish overseers. These accounts should normally have been approved at a parish meeting, but instead, fearing considerable opposition at such a meeting, the overseers forbade its being held, and had their accounts approved by the borough magistrates, amongst whom was James Rawson, now Mayor of Leicester. The course of the dispute, as recorded in the minutes of the vestry and select vestry of St Margaret's, illustrates clearly why the parish decided finally to remove all control over the parish's finances from the borough magistrates and instead elect all its own officials. A draft bill was promoted under which a new select vestry of Vicar, churchwardens, overseers, surveyors of highways, and twenty ratepayers would be elected by members of the parish. In face of considerable opposition, not only from the magistrates but also from all those who feared for the poor if the manufacturers controlled poor-relief, it was finally agreed between 1831 and 1832 that a total of 30 be nominated by the vestry, from whom the magistrates were to select 20. At the same time the parishes in the borough, with the exception of St Nicholas, adopted for themselves the provisions of a general act "to make provision for the lighting and watching of parishes". In other words, since the Corporation was not to be trusted by the parishes with powers of improvements the parishes now themselves took over power to do the task instead. In fact, of course, it was to be only a few years before a reformed Corporation resumed these powers for itself.

To the members of the old Corporation the coming of the Municipal Commissioners meant the collapse of the old order and the disappearance of the old landmarks, and the last entries by Thomas Burbidge in the Hall Books reflect this concept of impending doom. The truth nonetheless was that the new oligarchy which emerged and took power after the reform of the Corporation made possible the substantial developments of the nineteenth century. For, ironically enough, the new Corporation was vested with those powers which its predecessor had sought so long and had been taken over by the parishes. Those members of the various vestries which had taken powers for making improvements found themselves better able to secure those very improvements once they could use the authority of the Corporation for their implementation. In the long duel between parish and Corporation, the Corporation had won, at the cost of seeing itself taken over by the individuals who had been fighting on behalf of the parish. Similarly, these same individuals now found themselves exerting, and indeed increasing, the authority of the Corporation very often at the expense of the parish authorities whose powers now tended to dwindle away, and whose very territories were to be swallowed up by the revived borough.

This is the pattern revealed by the records of the borough of Leicester in the years between 1689 and 1835. But it would, of course, be wrong to look at those records as telling the entire story of Leicester in these years. There are many aspects of the life of the borough not at all mentioned. The coming of the canal to Leicester transformed many aspects of the economic life of the borough. A sub-committee of the Union Canal Company greatly eased the progress of the canal's work in Leicester; of its seven members, six were Aldermen or Common Councillors and five either had been or became Mayors.[1] Later, on 2 April 1830, the Hall Books record the agreement of the Corporation to support the construction of the Leicester and Swannington Railway, but make no mention of its opening, nor of the fact that by the early 1830s there were about 25 steam engines at work in the town. The general industrial developments of the early nineteenth century and the emergence of new classes of industrialists find little direct mention and are to be deduced only by implication, and this in a sense is a mark of the widening gulf between the Corporation and the borough's growing life. Future generations controlling the municipality would not be able in a similar fashion to keep their eyes averted from the problems which these developments would create for the borough or from the need to find urgent solutions to them.

1. See P. A. Stevens, *The Leicester Line* (1972), 28–9.

Acknowledgements

In the course of writing, I have incurred many debts to my colleagues who have been invariably helpful in response to a myriad of requests for either information or ideas, but particularly it is to Professor Jack Simmons that I owe most, not least because it was he who was responsible for the original invitation to study these records and to write a commentary on them. Like Mr Chinnery, I have welcomed the interest shown by Mr T. A. Walden, the former Director of the City of Leicester Museums, and like him I hope that there will be a continuation of publication of records to cover the growth of nineteenth-century Leicester. Both Mr Chinnery and I would wish to place on record our appreciation of the technical skill and advice of Mr Peter Boulton, the Secretary to the Leicester University Press. Above all, however, I have welcomed the continuous opportunity this work has afforded of close collaboration with Mr G. A. Chinnery, whose learning and infectious enthusiasm inspire all those who come into contact with him.

A. N. N.

EXEMPLARS OF DOCUMENTS

EXEMPLARS OF DOCUMENTS

All documents are hand-written unless otherwise indicated.

87   *Writ of Summons*

⟨George the second by the Grace of God of Great Britain France and Ireland King Defender of the faith and so forth To the Bayliffe of the Liberty of the Borough of Leicester Greeting   Wee Command you that you Omitt not by reason of any Liberty in your Bailiwick but enter the same and cause to come before the Keepers of our peace of our said Borough at the Guild Hall of the said Borough on Monday the Seventh day of October next comeing Twenty four good and lawfull Men of the Body of the said Borough to enquire and do such things on our part as shall be then and there Enjoyned them And Also that you make known to all Coroners Stewards and Constables in the same Borough, and the Constable of the Bishopps Fee near the said Borough that they be then and there to do and perform all things which by reason of their Offices are to be done, and that you make proclamation in all convenient places in your Bailiwick that the General Quarter Sessions of the peace the day and at the place aforesaid is to be held And that you be there to do and perform such things which appertaineth to your Office, And have the Names as well of the said Justices Coroners Stewards and Constables as of the Jurors aforesaid Witness Thomas Marten Esq Mayor of the said Borough at the Guild Hall of the said Borough the fifteenth day of July In the Twenty fifth Year of our Reign.

Herrick⟩

From 1765 onwards, the Writ of Summons appeared in a different form.

198   *Writ of Summons*

⟨Borough of Leicester   We Hamlett Clark Esquire Mayor of the said Borough Edmund Wigley Esquire Recorder of the same and William Dabbs Esquire Justices of our Sovereign Lord the King assigned to keep the Peace of our said Lord the King in the said Borough And also to hear and determine divers Felonies Tresspasses and other Misdeameanors in the said Borough committed (and two of us of the Quorum) To the Bailiff of the said Borough greeting On behalf of our said Lord the King we command you That you cause to come before us and others our Fellows Justices assigned to keep the peace of our said Lord the King in the said

3

Borough and also to hear and determine divers Felonies Tresspasses and other Misdemeanours in the said Borough committed on Monday in the Week next after the Feast Day of Saint Michael the Archangel, to wit, the second day of October next at ten of the Clock in the Forenoon of the same Day at the Guildhall in the said Borough Twenty four honest and lawful Men of the said Borough then and there to enquire present do and perform All and singular such Things as on behalf of our said Lord the King shall be enjoined their And also twenty four other good and lawfull Men of the said Borough to enquire between our said Lord the King and the Prisoners at the bar And also that you make known to all Justices of the Peace Coroners Stewards Keepers of Gaols and Houses of Correction within and for the said Borough that they be then and there present to do and perform those things which by reason of their respective Offices shall be to be done And moreover that you cause to be proclaimed through the Borough aforesaid in proper places that the aforesaid Sessions will be holden at the time and place aforesaid and be you then and there present to do and execute those things which belong to your Office And have you there then as well the names of the Justices of the peace Coroners Stewards Constables Serjeants at Mace as also this precept Given under our Hands and Seals at the Borough aforesaid this twentieth Day of September in the year of our Lord One thousand Seven hundred and ninety seven.

> H. Clark Mayor
> Edmund Wigley Rec.
> Will. Dabbs⟩

145   *Calendar of Justices*

⟨Borough of ⎫ A Calendar of the Names of the Mayor Justices of the
Leicester to wit ⎬ peace Coroners Steward Bailiff and other Officers sum-
            ⎭ moned to be and appear at the General Quarter Sessions
of the peace to be held at the Guildhall in and for the said Borough the Eleventh day of April in the year of our Lord 1774.

Richard Roberts Drake Esquire Mayor ⎫
William Burleton Esquire L.LD Recorder ⎬ of the said Borough.

Joseph Chambers ⎫
James Cooper ⎪
John Cartwright ⎬ Esquires Justices of the peace for the said Borough.
Robert Peach ⎭

William Mason ⎫
Samuel Jordan ⎬ Gent. Coroners of the said Borough.

Samuel Topp Esquire Bailiff ⎫
William Tilly Gentleman Steward ⎬ of the said Borough.

James Bishop ⎫
James Oldham ⎬ Chamberlains of the said Borough.

4

Joseph Hall
Michael Staples
John Throsby ⎬ Serjeants at Mace in the said Borough.
Lawrence Read
Robert Smith

Henry Coulson Keeper of the Goal and Bridewell in and for the said
Borough.

The Constables Names

William Wood
Thomas Langton
John Wright
Alexander Forrester
Joseph Haseldine
Thomas Brown
William Loseby
William Turner
John Wheatley
Joseph Springthorpe
William Dalby
Robert Aumey of the Bishop's Fee
Temple Sutton of the Newark
George Bramley of the Abby & Wood Gates
William Cook of the Braunston Gate

Samuel Topp Esquire Bailiff⟩

The Recorder is first included in 1694, the Sergeants-at-Mace in 1765, and
the Chamberlains in October 1770; the others occur throughout. The
Keeper or Keepers of the Gaol etc. are included only occasionally. The
Constable of the Bishop's Fee is indicated, rather intermittently, from the
first, but the Constables of the other Liberties are not included until 1767.
Very occasionally, the Constable of the Castle View is named.

126 *Indictments*

⟨Borough of Leicester to wit   The Jurors for our Lord the King upon their
oath present That Thomas Tompson late of the parish of Saint Nicholas in
the said Borough Taylor on the Third day of August in the Fifth year of the
Reign of our Sovereign Lord George the third now King of Great Britain
and so forth with force and Arms in the Parish of All Saints in the said
Borough in and upon one Samuel Brown Gentleman one of his Majestys
Justices of the Peace for the said Borough in the Peace of God and our said
Lord the King then and there being did make an Assault and him the said
Samuel did then and there beat wound and ill treat so that his Life was

5

greatly despaired of and other wrongs to the said Samuel then and there did to the great Damage of the said Lord the King his Crown and Dignity.⟩

198

⟨Borough of Leicester (to wit)   The Jurors for our Lord the King upon their Oath present That from the time whereof the Memory of Man is not to the Contrary there was and yet is a Common and Ancient Kings Highway leading from a certain Street called Horspool Street in the Parish of Saint Mary in the said Borough towards & unto a certain other Street called Gallowtree Gate in the Parish of Saint Margaret in the said Borough & the Libertys thereof used for all the liege subjects of our said Lord the King and of his Predecessors with their Horses Coaches Carts and Carriages to go return pass ride and labour at their free will and pleasure And that a certain part of the same Kings Common Highway situate lying and being in a certain Street or Lane called Millstone Lane in the said Parish of Saint Mary in the Borough of Leicester aforesaid to wit the Causeway and Pavement before the front of part of a certain Yard in the occupation of Mary Pratt of the said Borough Spinster containing in length Ten Yards & in breadth five yards on the twenty ninth Day of September in the thirty seventh year of the Reign of his present Majesty and continually afterwards until the day of the taking this Inquisition was and yet is in great Decay for want of due reparation and Amendment of the same So that the liege Subjects of our said Lord the King passing and travelling through the same with their Horses Coaches Carts and Carriages could not during the time aforesaid nor yet can go return pass ride and labour without great Danger To the great Damage and Common Nuisance of all the liege subjects of our said Lord the King passing through Way and against the Peace of our said Lord the King his Crown and Dignity And that the said Mary Pratt by reason of her tenure & occupation of the said part of the said Yard the same Common and ancient King's Highway so as aforesaid being in Decay ought to repair and amend when and so often as it shall be necessary.⟩

198 *Recognizance*

⟨Borough of Leicester, To wit. Be it remembered, that on the eighth day of August in the 37th Year of the Reign of our Sovereign Lord George the third of Great Britain, France, and Ireland, King, Defender of the Faith, &c. John Holyland of the said Borough Chandler & John Dale of the same Frameworkknitter personally came before me one of the Justices of our said Lord the King, assigned to keep the Peace within the said Borough, and acknowledged themselves to owe to our said Lord the King the Sum of Ten pounds apiece of good and lawful Money, of Great Britain, to be made and levied of their respective Goods and Chattles, Lands and Tenements, to the use of our said Lord the King, his Heirs and Successors, if the said John Holyland shall make default in the Condition under written.

The Condition of this Recognizance is such, that if the above-bounden John Holyland do and shall appear at the next general quarter session of the peace to be holden for the said Borough, and then and there answer to all such matters of Misdemeanors as shall be objected against him, and in the mean time keep the peace towards all his Majesty's liege subjects and especially towards Richard Poole Constable of Mr Alderman Drake's Ward in the said Borough and not depart the Court without leave, then the said Recognizance to be void, or else to remain in its force.

H. Clark Mayor⟩

The Condition frequently varies, notably in a Victualler's Recognizance or a Bastardy Recognizance. Printed Recognizances first appear in 1765 and are nearly always used after that date.

72 *Removal Order*

⟨Burg Leic   To the Churchwardens and Overseers of the Poor of the parish of Saint Margarett in the Burrough of Leicester in the County of Leicester And alsoe to the Churchwardens and overseers of the poor of the parish of All Saints in the Burrough of Leicester aforesaid.

Whereas Complaint hath been made by you unto us whose Hands and Seals are hereunto set two of his Majesties Justices of the Peace (Quorum unus) for the Burrough aforesaid, that John Freestone Sarah his wife and Elizabeth their daughter have lately intruded themselves into your said parish of St Margarett there to inhabit as your Parishioners contrary to the Laws relating to the Settlement of the Poor, and are there likely to become Chargeable, if not timely prevented. And whereas upon due Examination and Enquiry made into the Premisses and upon the oath of the Said John Freestone it appears unto us, and we accordingly Adjudge, That the said John Freestone Sarah his wife and Elizabeth their daughter are likely to become chargeable, and that their last legal Place of Settlement was in the parish of All Saints in the Burrough of Leicester aforesaid.

These are therefore in his Majesties Name to Order and Require you the said Churchwardens and Overseers of the Poor of St Margarett aforesaid, That you or some of you do forthwith remove and convey the said John Freestone Sarah his wife & Elizabeth their daughter from your said Parish of St Margarett to the Parish of All Saints aforesaid, and them deliver to the Churchwardens and Overseer of the Poor there, or some or one of them, together with this our Warrant or Order, or a true Copy hereof, whereby they are likewise required in his Majesties Name, and by Virtue of the Statutes in such Case made, forthwith to receive the said John Freestone Sarah his wife & Elizabeth their daughter into their said Parish of All

Saints and Provide for them as their own Parishioners. Given under our Hands and Seals, the three and Twentyeth day of March Anno Regni Domini Nostri Georgi Regis nunc Magnae Britanniae, &c. quinto Annoque Domini 1718.

Charles Tuffley Mayor   discharged
Arthur Noone⟩

The use of a printed Order first occurs in 1703, but it is by no means always used after this.

122   *Sacramental Certificate*

⟨Borough of Leicester to wit   We the Minister and Church Warden of the Parish and Parish Church of Saint Martin in the said Borough Do hereby Certify That Richard Beale Esq Mayor of the said Borough on Sunday the thirtieth Day of September did receive the Sacrament of the Lord's Supper in the Parish Church aforesaid immediately after Divine Service and Sermon according to the Usage of the Church of England In Witness whereof we have hereunto subscribed our Hands the said 30 Day of September 1764.

Thomas Haines ⎰ Minister of the Parish and
⎱ Parish Church aforesaid

John Gregory ⎰ Church Warden of the said
⎱ Parish and Parish Church

Thomas Hackett & Robert Whiteing Do severally make Oath That they did see the said Richard Beale Esq Mayor in the abovewritten Certificate named And who now present hath delivered the same into this Court Receive the Sacrament of the Lord's Supper in the Parish Church aforesaid And that they did see the said Certificate subscribed by the said Minister and Church Warden.

Thomas Hackett
Robert Whiting⟩

They are usually printed.

87   *Oath of Allegiance and Abjuration*

⟨Borough of Leicester to wit   At the General Quarter Sessions of the Peace of our Lord the King held within the said Borough at the Guild Hall of the said Borough on Monday the Seventh day of October in the Twenty fifth year of the Reign of our Sovereign Lord George the Second by the grace of God of Great Britain France and Ireland King Defender of the faith and so forth and in the year of our Lord One Thousand Seven Hundred and Fifty One Before Samuel Simpson Esquire Mayor of the said Borough William Wrighte Esquire Recorder of the said Borough and Thomas Marten Gentleman Justices Assigned to preserve the peace and to hear and determine several Felonys trespasses and other Misdemeanours committed in the said Borough.

I A.B. do sincerely promise and swear that I will be faithfull and bear true Allegiance to his Majesty King George the second.

So help me God.

I A.B. do swear that I do from my heart abhor detest and abjure as impious and heretical that Damnable Doctrine and position that Princes Excommunicated or deprived by the Pope or any Authority of the See of Rome may be deposed or Murthered by their subjects or any other whatsoever, And I do declare that no foreign prince person, prelate State or Potentate, hath or ought to have any Jurisdiction, Power, Superiority, preeminence or Authority Ecclesiastical or Spiritual within this Realme.

So help me God.

I A.B. do truely and Sincerely acknowledge profess testifie and declare in my Conscience before God and the World that our sovereign Lord King George the Second is lawfull and rightfull King of this Realme and all other his Majestys Dominions and Countrys thereunto belonging, And I do solemnly and sincerely declare that I do believe in my Conscience that the person pretending to be prince of Wales during the Life of the late King James and since his decease pretending to be and taking upon himselfe, the Stile and Title of King of England by the name of James the third, or of Scotland by the name of James the Eighth or the Stile and Title of King of Great Britain hath not any right or Title whatsoever to the Crown of the Realme or any other the Dominions thereto belonging, And I do renounce refuse and abjure any Allegiance or Obedience to him, And I do Swear that I will bear faith and true Allegiance to his Majesty King George the second and him will defend to the utmost of my power against all Traiterous Conspiracies and Attempts whatsoever which shall be made against his person Crown or Dignity, And I will do my utmost endeavour to disclose and make known to his Majesty and his Successors all Treasons and traiterous conspiracys which I shall know to be against him or any of them, And I do faithfully promise to the utmost of my Power to support maintain and defend the Succession of the Crown against him the said James and all other persons whatsoever which succession by an Act intituled An Act for the further Limmittation of the Crown and better securing the rights and Libertys of the subject is and stands limmitted to the Princess Sophia Electoress and Dutchess Dowager of Hannover and the Heirs of her Body being protestants, And all these things I do plainly and sincerely acknowledge and swear according to these express Words by me spoken and according to the plain and common Sence and understanding of the same words without any Equivocation mentall Evasion or secret Preservation whatsoever And I do make this Recognition acknowledgement abjureation

9

Renunciation and promise heartily willingly and truely upon the true faith of a Christian.

So help me God.

S. Simpson
Joseph Taylor
John Winter
Joseph Treen
Thomas Thornton
John Pocklington
Jonathan Hartell
John Field

I A.B. do declare that I do believe that there is not any Transubstantiation in the Sacrament of the Lords supper or in the Elements of Bread or Wine at or after the Consecration thereof by any person whatsoever.

S. Simpson
Joseph Taylor
John Winter
Joseph Treen
Thomas Thornton
John Pocklington
Jonathan Hartell
John Field⟩

The first and second promises first appear in 1715. The fourth promise, whether by accident or design, is not always included.

III   *Convictions*

⟨Borough of Leicester to wit   Be it Remembered that on the fourth day of March in the first year of the Reign of our sovereign Lord King George the third Francis Porter was convicted before me one of his Majestys Justices of the Peace for the said Borough of curseing Two profane Curses in the Parish of Saint Mary within the said Borough Given under my hand and Seale the day and Year aforesaid.

Edmund Ludlam⟩

The first printed one appears in 1770 but they are not always used.

⟨Borough of Leicester   Be it remembered That on the seventh Day of February in the Year of our Lord One thousand seven hundred and ninety two Elizabeth Palmer of the Borough of Leicester aforesaid Widow was convicted before us Joseph Neal esquire Mayor of the said Borough and John Dalby Esquire two of his Majesty's Justices of the Peace in and for the said Borough of having at several times within the last Six Months preceding the said seventh Day of February at the said Borough bought and received of and from Mary the Wife of Joseph Watson of the said Borough Tanner different Quantitys of Wool combed but not spun She the said Elizabeth Palmer then and there knowing the said Mary Watson to be a Person hired or employed to prepare or Work up the Woollen Manufacures & not having first obtained the consent of the Person or Persons so hiring or employing her the said Mary Watson contrary to the form of the Statutes in that Case made & provided Given under our hands and seals the Day and Year first above written.

Jos. Neal Mayor   John Dalby⟩

61   *Bastardy Order*

⟨Burg. Leics. The Order of John Cooper Esquire Mayor of the Burrough of Leicester aforesaid & Edward Hood of the Said Burrough Gentleman two of her Majestys Justices of the Peace for the said Burrough One whereof is of the Quorum, and both now Residing within the Limitts where the Parish Church of St Mary in the Burrough of Leicester aforesaid Standeth made the Seventh Day of February in the year of our Lord 1712 according to the Forme of the Statute in that case made & provided, concerning a Male Bastard Child lately born in the said Parish of St Mary of the body of Sarah Walker of the Parish of Saint Mary in the Said Burrough Singlewoman; Which Bastard Child hath been ever Since its birth & is Still Chargeable to the said Parish & is likely so to continue.

First Upon Examinacion of the Cause & Circumstances of the premises taken upon Oath before us & due Consideracion thereof being likewise had by us, We do adjudge John Kellett of the said Burrough of Leicester Bricklayer (who hath been already Charged by the said Sarah Walker upon her Oath to have begotten the said Child on her body) to be the Father of the said Bastard Child; And We do also Order that as well for the Relief of the said Parish of Saint Mary As Also for the Provision and Maintenance of the said Bastard Child: that He the said John Kellett shall Weekly and every Week from the Date of this present Order And so long as the said Male Bastard Child shall be chargeable to the said Parish of St Mary And untill the said Child shall Attain the Age of Tenn Year's pay or cause to be paid unto the Churchwarden's or Overseer's of the Poor of the Parish of Saint Mary aforesaid And their Successor's for the time being the Summe of One Shilling for & towards the Maintenance of the said Child And shall likewise pay or cause to be paid unto the Churchwarden's or Overseer's of the Poor of the Parish of St Mary aforesaid for the time being the Summe of Four Pounds within One Month after the said Bastard Child shall attain his Age of Tenn Year's for & towards the putting forth the said Child to be an Apprentice: And farther We Order that the said John Kellett do upon Notice of this Our Order, forthwith give Sufficient Security to the Churchwarden's & Overseer's of the Poor of the Parish of St Mary aforesaid well and truly to perform the same. Given under our hands & Seales the Seventh Day of February Anno Domini 1712.

John Cooper Mayor
Edward Hood⟩

170   *Certificate of Road or Pavement Repair*

⟨Borough of Leicester to wit I Hamlett Clark Esquire one of his Majesty's Justices of the Peace for the said Borough do hereby certify That on the thirty first day of March instant I viewed a certain part of the King's common Highway situate lying & being in the parish of Saint Margaret in the said Borough in a certain Street there called North gate Street without, to wit the Causeway & Pavement before the Front of a certain Messuage and dwelling house there in the occupation of Thomas Richardson of the said Borough Cordwainer containing in length fifteen feet and in breadth nine feet (On account of which said part of the Kings common Highway being out of repair the said Thomas Richardson of the said Borough Cordwainer now stands indicted) And that the same now is well & sufficiently amended & repaired with Stone & Gravel. Given under my hand this thirty first day of March 1788.

H. Clark⟩

164a   *Certificate of Removal of Obstruction*

⟨Borough of Leicester to wit I William Burleton Esquire LLD Recorder of the said Borough do hereby certify, That I have this day viewed the Kings common Highway leading from out of the Hangman Lane in the parish of Saint Margaret in the Borough aforesaid into the public Turnpike road in the parish and Borough aforesaid from Leicester to Harborough; for having had a great quantity of Timber and Wood in the said Common Highway William Dalby of the parish aforesaid Carpenter now stands presented: And that the said Timber and Wood is now removed and the Nuisance abated. Given under my hand this twenty seventh day of April 1786.

Will. Burleton Rr.⟩

189   *Process Paper*

⟨Borough of Leicester, to wit, Be it remembered That at the General Quarter Session of the Peace of our Sovereign Lord the King holden at the Guildhall in and for the said Borough on Monday in the Week next after the Close of the Feast of Easter, to wit, the Twenty eighth Day of April in the Thirty fourth Year of the Reign of our Sovereign Lord George the Third by the Grace of God of Great Britain, France and Ireland King Defender of the Faith and so forth And in the Year of our Lord One thousand seven hundred and Ninety four Before John Mansfield Esquire Mayor of the said Borough Edmund Wigley Esquire Recorder of the same

12

and Henry Watchorn John Eames Joseph Neal and Joseph Burbidge Esquires Justices of our said Lord the King assigned to keep the Peace of our said Lord the King in the said Borough And also to hear and determine divers Felonies Trespasses and other Misdemeanours in the said Borough committed upon the Oath of William Bellamy James Mallett John Saywell James Cook Edmund Swinfen Joseph Johnson the Younger William Hall James Cort Michael Miles Thomas Read John Stevenson and Mark Oliver Gentlemen good and lawful Men of the said Borough then and there sworn and charged to enquire for our said Lord the King and the Body of the Borough   It is presented as follows (that is to say) "Borough of Leicester The Jurors for our Lord the King upon their Oath present That Thomas Plowright late of the Abbey Gate in the Parish of Saint Leonard and within the Liberties of the Borough aforesaid Dyer on the tenth Day of April in the Thirty fourth Year of the Reign of our Sovereign Lord George the Third now King of Great Britain and so forth with Force and Arms at the Abbey Gate in the Parish of Saint Leonard and within the Liberties of the Borough of Leicester aforesaid in and upon one Abraham Anderson in the Peace of God and our said Lord the King then and there being did make an Assault and him the said Abraham Anderson then and there did beat wound and illtreat so that his Life was greatly despaired of and other Wrongs to him the said Abraham Anderson then and there did To the great Damage of the said Abraham Anderson and against the Peace of our said Lord the King his Crown & Dignity" And the said Thomas Plowright cometh and defendeth the force and injury when and so forth and every Contempt and so forth and whatsoever and so forth And having heard the said Indictment read he saith he is not guilty thereof and thereupon he putteth himself upon the Country And William Heyrick Gentleman Clerk of the Peace of the Borough of Leicester aforesaid who for our said Lord the King in this Behalf prosecuteth doth the like Therefore let a Jury thereupon come before the Justices of our said Lord the King assigned to keep the Peace of our said Lord the King to be holden at the Guildhall in and for the said Borough of Leicester by whom the Truth of the Matter may be better known and who are of no Affinity to the said Thomas Plowright to try upon their Oath whether the said Thomas Plowright be guilty of the Premises aforesaid or not, because as well the said William Heyrick who for our said Lord the King in this Behalf as the said Thomas Plowright have put themselves upon that Jury The same Day is given as well to the said William Heyrick who for our said Lord the King in this Behalf prosecuteth as to the said Thomas Plowright.⟩

Judgement

This is similar in form to the Process Paper but with additions. An example can be found in **IIIC.I** at the end of the Quarter Sessions Rolls.

Precept to Constables

⟨To Edward Springthorp Constable of Mr John Roberts Ward or to his lawfull Deputy.

These are in his Majesties name to command you to make diligent Serch after all Rogues Vagabonds and Idle Wandring Beggars And you shall enquire if Huy and Cry have beene duly persued as the Law requires And what Strangers are come in to your Ward and endeavour to settle themselves there not being duly qualified as the Law directs And if any persons Sell Ale without Licence or keepe disorderly houses or suffer unlawfull Games to be used in their houses Yards or Backsides And all other offences Committed or done within your Liberty contrary to the Lawes and Statutes of this Realme You are to present unto me and the rest of the Justices of this Burrough upon Friday next at two of the Clock in the After noone of the same Day at the Guild hall of the said Burrough And that you yourselfe be then and there personally present to make returne of this Precept As you will Answer the Contrary at your Perrills Dated the 27 day of August Anno Domini 1696.

John Pares Maior⟩

The precepts do not form part of the Sessions Rolls at present. They appear to have been dissociated in the nineteenth century, and now occur in the Hall Papers Bound series in the City records.

QUARTER SESSIONS ROLLS

18.1 *Writ of Summons*

Dated 8 July 1689 for 3 October 1689.

18.2 *Constables' Presentments*

Twelve Constables present "omnia bene".

18.3 *Case*

Indictments of William Gregory, gent., and Edward Hoskins for using a false declaration, in the names of the Mayor and a Justice of Liverpool, as a licence to beg. Hoskins guilty.

Text of the forged declaration:

⟨Learepoole in the County of Lancaster. To all and Singuler his Maiestys officers and loveing Subiects To whome these presence may Concerne Greetting whearcas the Bearer heare of Thomas Morton and his wife and family beinge Outtward bound from the Kingdome of England to America In A shipe Called the John Loaden with Marchants Goods the Saide shipe beinge unfortunately Cast Away neare this our Coaste of England by Gods Greate providence most of theire Lives was saved with the Loss of foure hundred and sixty pounds and upwards of theire own proper Goods As was playnely made Appeare they Comminge before mee the Maior and one other of his Maiestys Justises of the peace of the saide towne And County As Afforesaide and most humbly disired the saide Certificate for theire most saffe and secure way to travell to severall places And ports In this Kingdome wheare they had formerly some Trade these are therefore to disire you that are the Cunstables And Churchwardens or theire depewties to Afforde them Reliefe and Lodging in dew season to Avoyd the danger of the Lawe Accordingly to her Condiction being with Childe for the space of seaven months and noe Longer Given under our hands and seale with the seale of office dated this tenth day of september In the first yeare of our Soveraing Lord Kinge William And Queene Marie by the Grace of God England scottland france And Ireland defender of the faith etc in the yeare of our Lord 1689.

Thomas Rodgers maior   Edward Harris⟩

19.1 *Writ of Summons*

Dated 3 October 1689 for 13 January 1689/90.

19.2 *Case*

The Grand Jury present William March, Whetstone, Leics., labourer, for picking a pocket.   Ignored.

Information of Jonathan Drayton, Atherstone, Warwicks., tanner, taken 16 November 1689:

⟨This Informant Saith That he came from Atherston aforesaid about Twelve or one of the Clock this morneing with two horse Load of Tanned Calves skins for one Samuel Shipley of the Said Burrough Currier & Saith that he brought Twenty Shillings with him & borrowed four pounds more of one Mr Heathcock being then in the Said Burrough to pay the Butchers for hides which this Informant had bought of them and goeing to the house of Margarett Shuttlewood being the Signe of the Bull head in the Said Burrough where he used to Inne being in a roome called the shop fell asleep two persons came into the Said Roome one being William March the younger of Whetston in the County of Leicester Labourer who lately lived with one Mr Faulkingham minister of Glenfeild & the other Thomas Gumley miller of Glenfeild aforesaid in the said County of Leicester as they owne them selves, Elizabeth Toby Apprentice and Servant to the Said Margarett Shutlewood told her that as she [was] rocking a Child in the next roome lookeing through a Crack in a board in the Roome where the said Jonathan Drayton was asleep did see the said March sitting next to this Informant to take his hand out of this Informants pockett and did see the said March look of some silver which he had in his hand, upon which she told her Mistress & her Mistress the said Margarett Shuttlewood wakened this Informant and told him his pockett was Picked & bid him look for his money which this Informant did and missed all but Seaventeene Shillings and Six pence which was left in his Pockett.⟩

Information of Elizabeth Toby, spinster, taken 16 November 1689:

⟨This Informant Saith That one Jonathan Drayton a guest to this Informants Mistress house Margarett Shuttlewood widow being in a roome called the shopp in the said house a sleep and this Informant being in a roome next to the shop rocking one of her Mistress Children she looked through a Crack of a board in the wall of the said roome did see a man sitting next to him draw his hand out of his pockett & looked upon some silver piece of money and presently went out of the said roome & this Informant presently acquainted her Mistress therewith whereupon her Mistress steped out of the Daore into the streete & espied the said person neare the shambles not far from this Informants Mistress house called him back againe & then wakened the said Drayton & bid him looke in his Pockett for his money for she was afraid his Pockett was Picked or words to that effect.⟩

19.3 *Discharged Recognizances*

William March, Whetstone, Leics., labourer, to appear.

Jonathan Drayton, Atherstone, Warwicks., tanner, to appear and prosecute William March.

20.1   *Writ of Summons*
Sessions held 28 April 1690. No writ survives.

20.2   *Constables' Presentments*
Thomas Hartshorne (Mr Nobles Ward) presents Edward Hueit, reputed papist, for not attending church.

Robert Heyrick (Mr Deans Ward) presents Elizabeth Smith, widow, for a breach of the peace, and John Truss for assaulting the constable.

John Vaux (Mr Bents Ward) presents John Hueit, reputed papist, for not attending church. Indicted.

John Palmer (Mr Goodals Ward) presents Edward Joans for keeping a public house unfree.

William Harte (Mr Abneys Ward) presents Frances Creacroft for selling ale without a licence.

William Burton (Mr Southalls Ward) presents Edward Melborne, reputed papist, for not attending church.

20.3   *Discharged Recognizances*
Thomas Ward, brasier, to appear and give evidence against Isabella Headley.
John Cracroft, apothecary, to appear to prosecute and give evidence against Isabella Headley.

20.4   *Indictments*
Joseph Cozens, fellmonger, on presentments of Samuel Holmes and John Pratt, aletaster, for keeping an unlicensed alehouse and selling ale without a licence.

Edward Joanes, labourer, on presentment of John Pratt, aletaster, for selling ale without a licence. Joanes states:
⟨That hee doth keepe a Common Alehouse, and that hee hath kept the same three [months] and upwards without License from any Justices of the peace of the said Burrough, And further saith that hee believes dureing that time hee has received of Mr John Pratt of the said Burrough Common Brewer twenty Kinderkins of Ale over and above what hee spends & consumes in his owne house for his family And that the Said John Prat did promise this Informant That if hee would take ale of him hee would secure him from the Penalty of the Lawe or any damage that he should sustaine there by.⟩

Isabella Headley, widow, for stealing a pewter basin from John Cracroft.
Pleads guilty.

20.5 *Petitions*

⟨These are to informe you that Ann Swartemon Latly turnd out of Al
Saints Parish was formerly in habbited in St Martines Parish and was by
the Last overseers of the poore taken Care of by then in that parish and
since thay was out of place where shee was thay have turned her the said
Anne Swaitmon out of doors and shee is not able to mentaine her selfe and
child and Cannot com to speech of honer but would houmbly desier you
would be pleased to grant Anne order for the overseers now in place to take
Care of her for they say they Cannot doe it with out your order.
Ordered that Swetman shalbe sent to the house of Correction for six
months.⟩

Laurence Cooper & his wife:
⟨Humbly sheweth That your petitioners are both ancient people past their
labour & they have a Son that is struck lame by the hand of God who is
unable for any worke toward geting any thing to Sustaine his life & he is
also very much afflicted Falling fits & doth very often fall into much danger
of his life by fire or water and its the care of your petitioners to looke after
the preservation of his life & to mentaine him they are in no wayes capeable
to do it by reason of the age & poverty your petitioners crave your worships
favour as to moove in there in necesity this assessions to the Right worshipfull the Major & the rest of the Justices that your petitioners may have an
Order granted to them for the charitable Releife of them as also their Lame
& deseased Son according as their worships do truly understand their
necessity the premises considered & an order granted your most humble
petitioners shalbe bound to pray for your worships prosperous Eastate.⟩

Bartholomew Hewett, labourer:
⟨Sheweth That your Petitioner by vertue of a Capias issueing out of their
Majesties Court of Common Bench at Westminster and of a warrant thereupon direted to the Bayliffe of this Burrough was taken to prison and hath
there remained one yeare & an halfe and haveing satisfied your Peticioners
adversary of what was against him, is now by John Gassaway late Keeper
of the said Prison deteyned by vertue of a Capias issueing out of their
Majesties Court of Record for this Burrough at the suite of John Gassaway
late Keeper of the Said Goale for his lodgeing which is reckoned after two
shillings & foure pence the weeke, your Peticioner being informed that the
Keeper of the Towne Goale for this Burrough hath never beene paid after
that rate. But that upon Complaint of such poore Prisoners as your Peticioner now is the Justices of the peace for the Said Burrough have modera-
ted the same, and allowed such reasonable weekly payment for such hard

& poore lodgeing as in their wisdomes they conceive meete & requisite. Your poore Peticioner therefore humbly prays your good worships to commisserate your Peticioners sad & deplorable Condicion and give releife against these excessive Fees which your Peticioner is not able to satisfie, nor the Gaoler deserves for such meane lodgeing soe that your Peticioner may obteyne his liberty and worke forthe mainetenance of himselfe & distressed family. And your Peticioner shall ever pray etc.

Ordered that the Peticioner pay Mr Gassaway & Mr Topotts & shall pay to the Bayliffe after one shilling & 2d aweeke for his lodging dureing the time of his imprisonment.〉

21.1   *Writ of Summons*
Dated 28 April 1690 for 25 July 1690.

21.2   *Constables' Presentments*
John Page (Mr Southwells Ward) presents Edward Heuitt, reputed papist, for not attending church.   Indicted.

James Ludlam (Mr Bents Ward) presents Edward Melburne for not attending church.   Indicted.

John Pollard (Mr Bents Ward) presents John Hewit for not attending church.   Indicted.

21.3   *Case*
Indictment of William Stretton, Willoughby Waterleys, Leics., yeoman, for sedition.
Information of Michael Bonshaw, maltster, and John Parker, labourer, taken 26 May 1690:
〈These Informants say That they being at William Pages house at the signe of the Sarisons head within the Said Burrough Inholder did heare one William Stretton of Willowby waterleyes in the County of Leicester yeoman, say that I had a King of my owne nameing King James and said I will fight for King James soe long as I have breath to draw And these Informants Say that when they tould him they would have him before Mr Maior he clap't his ha[n]d on his breach and said he would stand for King James.〉

21.4   *Discharged Recognizances*
Christopher Stubbs, cordwainer, and his wife to appear and keep the peace towards Elizabeth, wife of William Mitchell.
Robert Cooke, husbandman, and his wife, Elizabeth, to appear and keep the peace towards Elizabeth Tayler.
Elizabeth Tayler, spinster, to appear and keep the peace towards Elizabeth Cooke.

Mary Low, widow, to appear and give evidence against Robert and Elizabeth Cooke.

Michael Bonshaw, maltster, and John Parker, labourer, to appear and give evidence against William Stretton.

21.5 *Petitions*

William Spencer, butcher:

⟨Whereas your poor Petitioner haveing beene in Prison for debt almost twelve Months, and haveing onely a Mother and a sister who are not able to add any releife to your poore Petitioner in this his great necessity, And whereas your poore Petitioner hath a wife and a Child who are in as great wants as your poore Petitioner himselfe Therefore your Poore Petitioner humbly desireing your worshipps to order your poore Petitioner the allowance bread for the releife of your poor Petitioner in this his Extreame want not haveing anything to subsist with, nor any freind to releive him or his wife and Child in this their great necessity And hopeing that your worshipps will be pleased to take into consideration the great necessity of your Poore Petitioner and humbly desireing to grant his request to order him the allowance bread Your poore Petitioner will be ever bound to pray etc.⟩

William Spencer, butcher:

⟨In all humility Sheweth that a warrent was granted by the now major in place to presse a mare of his which executed by William Hart Constable your petitioners mare served The now King Williams service to that speedy imploy to Harborow & had her there doth not send nor take care for the said petitioners major comeing home but hath enforsed him to be accosts to pay for her hay & corne he your petitioner prayeth that the said William Hart constable may have your order forthwith that he may have sufficient allowance to pay the charges he wanteth for the use of the mare being in the Kings service forthwith & by him to be paide for the saide service with out delay which granted your petitioner in all due respects shall be ever Bound for to pray for your worships prospereous Estate etc.⟩

John Heptonstall:

⟨This Affter the tender of my Humble Servis to your Worshipp [blank] Aqaint your Worship with the Misarable poore Condition of me And my poore famyly occationed by Wantt of Imploye in hiss Lawfull Calling And have bene Continged A prissonor In your Comon Goale the spaise off 29 Weakes or uppwards nott Haveing Any thing to helpe my selfe or famyly with butt whatt is ordered by your Worshipp And the Restt of the parishonor's Which is soe small that we are nott Able to subsistt therefore I mostt Humbly Reqestt your Worshipps Asistance by Letter of Reqestt to Gather the Charyty of well Disposed peopell towards my Relefe And my Loss nott qestoneng by the favorable Asistance of your Hand And Incoragement I maye gaine my Dischairge with owtt which I Cann nott And soe I qeston nott to Ease the parish of my Charge your Worshipp was pleased to grant me the liberty to take the Charyty of Good people butt I Cann gett noebody to goe with owtt your Hand. I have A bowtt fowretene or fivetene shillings In Mr Newtons Hands towards my Release therefore I Desire your Worshipp would be pleased to Consider my Condition whether In this or Any other Method that will tend to my Release By Doeing of which you will bind your poore Servant to praye for your Worships Health And Hapynes. from the Goale In Lester this 25th of July 1690.⟩

21.6   *Removal Order*
Eleanor Burgesse, widow, to be removed from St Martin's to St Mary's, 18 July 1690. ⟨This order is discharge by the Court upon the Peale of the Parishiners of St Maries.⟩

22.1   *Writ of Summons*
Dated 25 July 1690 for 6 October 1690.

22.2   *Prisoners*
Peter Smith
Elizabeth Jackston
Lydia Wheeland

22.3   *Constables' Presentments*
John Page (Mr Southwelles Ward) presents John Norres, gent., and George Boyar, cordwainer, for neglecting to Watch.   Indicted.

Richard Orton (Mr Mayors Ward) presents John Willows for not being a freeman.   Indicted.

John Pollard (Mr Hoods Ward) presents John Hewit, Roman Catholic, for not attending church, and Thomas Penford for trading unfree.   Indicted.

22.4   *Discharged Recognizances*
William Pollard, barber surgeon, and Elizabeth, his wife, to appear.
Susanna Followes, widow, to appear to prosecute and give evidence against William Smith.
Elizabeth, wife of Thomas Greene, labourer, to appear to prosecute and give evidence against William Smith.
Bartholomew Hawkins to appear and prosecute Lydia Wheland.
Elizabeth Grace, widow, to appear and answer charges.
Edward Melliburne, joiner, to appear and answer charges.
James Armeston, Kilby, Leics., yeoman, to appear and give evidence against Edward Melliburne.

Mary, wife of George Horner, to appear and keep the peace towards Hannah, wife of William Coley.

22.5   *Case*

Indictment of Edward Melliburne, joiner, for sedition.

Information of James Armeston, Kilby, Leics., yeoman, taken 3 October 1690:

⟨This Informant Saith That he being at the house of Francis Cracroft of the said Burrough Inholder last night about Nine of the Clock One Edward Melliburne (a Roman Cartholick) of the said Burrough being in this informants Company he said here is King James health but this informant remembers not whether he did drink it or not but said I will fight for King James & afterwards drank King Williams health & the prosperity to the Church of England.⟩

Information of William Porter taken 6 October 1690:

⟨This Informant Saith That he being at the house of Francis Cracroft of the said Burrough Inholder on Thursday night last about nine of the Clock did heare one Edward Melliburne (a Roman Cartholick) say here is a health to King James or God blesse King James & which at this time he cannot tell & upon some of those words he drank & afterwards drank King William and Queen Maries health & the prosperity to the Church of England.⟩

22.6   *Case*

Indictment of Lydia (Elizabeth) Wheeland, Chester, for stealing an apron from Bartholomew Hawkins.   Pleads guilty, whipped.

Information of Elizabeth Grace, widow, taken 3 October 1690:

⟨This Informant saith That one Wednesday last about Three of the Clock in the after noone their came unto her a woman whose name is since knowne to be Elizabeth Wheland & told this informant she was very necessitous & wanted money to pay for her lodgeing offered this Informant an apron to sell & this Informant asked her whether she came honestly by it & she said yes she did or els she would not sell it.⟩

22.7   *Presentment*

The Grand Jury present William Smith, Misterton, Leics., labourer, for theft of a pocket from Susanna Followes.   Ignored.

22.8   *Indictments*

Thomas Redley, on presentment of John Broom and John Wellinger, for trading as a smith unfree.

Mary, wife of George Horner, for assaulting Hannah, wife of William Coley.

22.9 *Informations*

Elizabeth, wife of John Bent, hosier, taken 5 August 1690:

⟨This Informant saith That on wensday last she being in the shopp of one William Pollard of the said Burrough Barber Chyrurgion the said William Pollard told this Informant that he said to Mr Newton of the Burrough of Leicester & vicar of St Martins the french were landed & the said Mr Newton replied & said God Speed them And further saith that the aforesaid William Pollard said Mr Newton was a hollowhearted and deceatefull man & Severall other Raileing words he gave against the said Mr Newton but at this time she doth not remember them And this Informant further Saith that on Sabath day last after dinner She goeing downe to her father in Law Thomas Bent & passing by the doore of the said William Pollard his wife called this Informant & asked her whether Mr Newton had spoken to her about goeing before Mr Maior & She this informant answear'd yes & asked this informant whether it was her or her husband tha spoak the said Words and this Informant replied & said it was her husband but the said Mrs Pollard said it was herselfe.⟩

Mary Newton, spinster, taken 5 August 1690:

⟨This Informant Saith That She being told by one Elizabeth the wife of John Bent that William Pollard said he told Mr Newton her father the french were landed and the said Mr Newton replied & said God Speed them And the said Mrs Bent alsoe told this Informant that the said Pollard said Mr Newton was a hollowhearted and deceatefull man, Mrs Newton this Informants mother heareing of this sent this Informant to the said William Pollard to know the reason why he had abused her husband in such a manner in his absence And the said William Pollard said he had forgott whether he had said the words to the said Mrs Bent or noe but said that he told Mr Newton the french were Landed and swore the said Mr Newton replied & said God Speed them And this Informant Saith She told him if her father had been at home he would have made him an example And the said William Pollard called her damned Bitch & said her father might kiss his Arce and the said Pollards wife comeing over the way the said Pollard told her, this Informant came to know whether he had said the words afore said or not & the wife of the said Pollard replied that the said Mr Newton did say the said words & would justify the same if it might be the last word she might speak but said she beleived the said Mr Newton spoke the said words in jest.⟩

22.10 *Petition*

John Heptonstall:

⟨Humbley Sheweth Wheareas Your Petitionor by wantt of Imploy in his Lawfull Calling being with his famly brought Low in the World And my selfe throwne In your Common Goale wheare I have Continied prisonor

c

A bove three qarters of A yeare nott haveing heare Any Imploye to gett A peney And since that by fire Lostt those few goods I had In soe much that I and my famly is Redused to that nesesitie to Lie on A wadd of straw And forsed to be Chairgeable to the parish which is A greate greefe to your petitioner. Whearefore Wee your poore petitionor Most humbley beseching your worships to Consider our Destresed and Most Deploarable Condition by your Spedie Relefe ether towards my Release or towards the Relefe of my poore Chillderen haveing but sixpence A weeke Alowed for fowre of them by which Alowance thay are nott Able to subsist I have throwgh your worship And some other good Cristian neibors gathered tow And fortie sillings which is in Mr Newtons hand towards my Relese which if your worships would be soe Gratiousely pleased to Asist me with A small Asistance to that I might gaine my Dischairge throwgh the Asistance of allmigtie god I qeston nott butt to Ease the parish boath of the Chairge of my selfe and famly Soe Begging your worships favor in this by your spedie Asistance Wee shall as Ever bownd in Dewtie praye for your worships Healths & hapienes. from the Goale in Lester this 6th of October 1690.⟩

23.1   *Writ of Summons*
                        Dated 17 July 1691 for 5 October 1691.

23.2   *Constables' Presentments*
Thomas Cartwright (Mr Bentes Ward) presents John Udging for not Watching.   Indicted.

George Harthorn (Mr Ludlams Ward) presents ⟨the town Lane next the But close for a newsence Being there.⟩   Indicted.

23.3   *Presentment*
The Grand Jury present Mary Low, widow, for trading as a chandler unapprenticed.   Ignored.

23.4   *Petition*
William Lander:
⟨Humbly Petitioneth That your Worships would be pleased to grant me an order that I may have something from the Parrish of St Margarets to help me in this my time of need, for I was wounded in the head on the 8 day of September Last past, in Dense Medow by Richard Poole, & have not been able to do a days work since, but I have been under the Syrourgions hand ever since, & am not cured as yet, & I have been forced to Pawn my Goods to maintain my Familie, & have made shift as long as I can, because I was not willing to be troublesom untill I could not help it, & am not able to pay the Syrourgion except I have some help from the parrish, I humbly beseech

your Worships to Grant this my humble petition, & your Humble Petitioner Shall ever Pray.

John Major Esquire Steward of the Court of Record for this Burrough is desired to speake to the overseers of the Poore of the Parish of St Margarett for some relief for the Peticionor.⟩

24.1 *Writ of Summons*

Dated 11 January 1691/2 for 4 April 1692.

24.2 *Constables' Presentments*

John Sutton (Ald. Abneys Ward) presents John Page for not repairing his street according to Mr Mayor's order.   Indicted.

Thomas Cartwright (Mr Bents Ward) presents Mr Wright, Recorder, for not repairing the street at the Parrot.   Indicted.

Matthew Sheffeild (Mr Bentlys Ward) presents Richard Palmar for keeping an unsealed measure. ⟨William Winkells hath inform against him.⟩ Indicted.

24.3 *Removal Orders*

Henry Yates and his wife and family and George Bates and his wife and family to be removed from St Mary's to St Nicholas', 22 January 1691/2. ⟨This warrent is vacuated & discharged etc.⟩

George Walker and his wife and family to be removed from St Mary's to St Martin's, 22 January 1691/2.   ⟨This order to be discharged & to Continue in the parish of St Mary.⟩   Endorsement: ⟨George Walker was Apprentice in St Martins parish with Abstinence Pougher for 7 years which Ended about 6 years since and then he went to live in St Maries parish & hath there beene ever since. He voted for Burgesses and he was told that his name was in the parish booke. He was Thirdborow for the Ward he lives in when John Holmes was Constable. He hath received Charity both bread & money severall times from the Overseers for 3 years last.⟩

25.1 *Writ of Summons*

Dated 16 April 1694 for 1 October 1694.

25.2 *Constables' Presentments*

Richard Blackborne (Ald. Southwells Ward) presents Ald. Southwell for not repairing the pump near the Gainsborough.   Indicted.

Thomas Hichcock (Mr Ludlams Ward) presents Thomas Brooke for not repairing the street in front of his door ⟨haveing Nottice Severly Times⟩. Indicted.

25.3 *Discharged Recognizances*

William Davis, hosier, to traverse an indictment.

Anna Dickins, Loughborough, Leics., spinster, Richard Blackburne, surgeon, Robert Page, joiner, and Elizabeth Tayler, spinster, to appear to prosecute and give evidence against Elizabeth, wife of William More.

Elizabeth Moore alias Groocock to appear and answer charges and obey the Court.

John Birstall, barber surgeon, to appear.

Sarah, wife of John Birstall, to appear and keep the peace towards Hannah, wife of Thomas Smeeton.

25.4 *Informations*

Anna Dickinson, late of London, spinster, taken 29 June 1694:

⟨This Informant saith shee comeing from London with Robert Page one of the Carriers of Leicester the last Thursday to Leicester and did lye all that night at Mrs Newtons house, and this morneing shee missed out of a paper box shee brought with her two pieces of Flanders lace, one holland shift one paire of Gorge Ruffles edged with a bone lace edging, one paire of sleeves one quoyfe a poynt lace and a Ribbon; parte of which things were found in a roome in the said house of the said Robert Page where Elizabeth wife of one William Moore & now servant to the said Robert Page doth lye.⟩

Robert Page, carrier, taken 29 June 1694:

⟨This Informant saith that one Anna Dickins comeing downe from London in his wagon last Thursday, came this morneing for two boxes shee brought downe with her, and opening her paper box missed severall Lynins, And there upon this Informant did search in severall roomes in his house, and goeing into the roome of Elizabeth moore his now servant did finde under the said Elizabeths Cloathes that did lye upon an other bed in the said roome one paire of lynnen sleeves & one quoife, which the said Anna Dickins owned to be her lynnins that was in the said paper box.⟩

Richard Blackburne, surgeon, taken 29 June 1694:

⟨This Informant saith hee being one of their majesties Constables for the said Burrough was Commanded to bring a servant of one Robert Page of the said Burroug called by the name of Elizabeth Groock before their majesties Justices of the Burrough of Leicester and as hee was bringing her along the streete hee did see the said Elizabeth turne her shoe and there fell out a piece of Ribon which one Anna Dickins ownes to be hers.⟩

Elizabeth Tayler, spinster, taken 29 June 1694:

⟨This Informant saith shee had a kinswoman that came from London called Anna Dickins which sent for this Informant and acquainted her shee had lost some things out of a paper box, and suspecting Robert Pages Servant one Elizabeth moore had obteyned a warrant to bring her before Edmund Johnson Esquire mayor & John Goodall Gent two of their majesties Justices of the peace for the Burrough of Leicester and comeing along the streete this Informant did see the said Groocock alias Moore shuffell out of her shoe a peice of poynt lace wrapped about with a Ribon of severall Colours, which the said Anna Dickins ownes to be hers & which was in the said box.⟩

25.5   *Petitions*

Mary Cox, All Saints', widow:
⟨Humbley sheweth that your poore petetioner is Aged and paste hir labor and that shee oweth thurtey shilings and three for Rente nether is your pore petetioner any way able to pay it and I tould the overseers my pore condetion but thay would yeeld me no releefe and making my appeale to the Right worshipfull Mr Recorder his Worship sente me to the overseers to tell them from his Worship that they should give me sumthing that was fiting but the overseers refusing I am constraned to appeale this worshipfull Bench. May it plese your Worships to way me pore condetion my labors are paste my lims being wekened in so much as I am not able to helpe my selfe to alow me sumthing what your worships shall thinke meete and your worships pore petetioner as in dutey bound shall always pray for your worships health and prosperetye.⟩

William Headley, St Margaret's:
⟨Humbley sheweth that at the laste setions your worships did order the oversears of the saide parrish to take Care and provide for my wyfe and my dafter in regard of there not being able to healpe them sealfes and accordingly they did alow them twelfe pence a weeke for seaven weeks or neare upon and then they tooke it away from them as also I lay sicke Eight weeks in the Chife time of summer and in that time the oversears gave me Eighteene pence. May it plese your worships to way the premises and what your worships shall thinke meete to be dunn in this my pore condetion I will willingly excepte and allways as in dewty bound pray for your worships health and prosperitye.
Peticioner to have 12d. a weeke untill further order.⟩

Elizabeth Newton, St Margaret's:
⟨Sheweth unto your worships that your humble petitioner being left with 6 small Children in a very poore Condition and your poor petitioners husband being gone for a souldier your petitioner and family of Children are in Extreame great wants, your petitioners Children wanting Clothes and your petitioner haveing noe fuell is in a most distressed Condition and cannot any longer subsist without your worships will bee pleased at this time and place to order some releife and maintenance for your poor petitioner and family of Children weekely from the said Parish of St Margaretts untill such time as your poor petitioners husband shall returne

back to your poor petitioner & family of Children which your petitioner hopes will bee in a short time, Your petitioner haveing made suite to the Overseers of the poore of the said Parish of St Margaretts but can have noe help nor releife therein nor shall have none, unlesse your worships will bee pleased to order some releife at this time for your poor petitioner & family of small children who are in excessive wants And hopeing and humbly intreating the favour of your worships to comisserate the poore estate & condition that your poore & humble petitioner & family of Children are in for want of releife & maintenance and to order that your petitioner & Children may at this time have some weekely allowance made according as your worshipps shall thinke fitt, And your petitioner shall bee ever bound to pray for your worshipps etc.⟩

25.6 *Removal Order*

William Carter, labourer, and his wife and family to be removed from All Saints' to Knighton, 27 January 1693/4.

26.1 *Writ of Summons*

Dated 27 March 1695 for 1 April 1695.

26.2 *Indictment*

Mary Cramp, Thurcaston, Leics., widow, for stealing a pewter plate from William Savage.   Guilty.

26.3 *Informations*

Richard Vaux, woolcomber and hosier, taken 22 February 1694/5:
⟨This Informant saith That one John Dorman Apprentice with Nicholas Alsop of the said Burrough stockin weaver brought unto this Informant at severall times stockins & yarne to sell telling this Informant they were his owne, And the first time hee gave this Informant two paire of welted Rolling Jersie hose for men, which hee sold to one John Birstall of the said Burrough Barber Chyrurgion for Two Shillings and sixpence and a paire of gloves worth about one shilling or fourteene pence; out of which this Informant spent in the said John Birstalls house at that time two shillings, And the said John Birstall did at that time tell this Informant if hee would bring him more hee would give him ready money for them; And the second time the said Dorman brought to this Informant five parcells of marvill yarne and alsoe one paire of mens Rolling hose and one paire of youths hose which yarne and hose hee sold to the said John Birstall for four shillings and sixpence and one paire of gloves like the former, And the third time the said Dorman brought this Informant, two paire of fine welted rolling mens hose, and two paire of plaine mens rolling hose which hee sold to the said John Birstall for four shillings and sixpence.⟩

Thomas Wells taken 22 February 1694/5:
⟨This Informant saith That hee and the said John Birstall meeting to geather, The said John Birstall shewed this Informant four paire of mens welted rolling Jersie hose, and three paire more of mens playne rolling hose and one paire of youths hose, and asked this Informant what the said stockins were worth, And the said John Birstall told this Informant hee bought the said stockins of a Contrie Man.⟩

27.1   *Writ of Summons*
                Dated 7 October 1695 for 13 January 1695/6.

27.2   *Constables' Presentments*
Joseph Hall (Mr Southwells Ward) presents John Coates, baker, ⟨for part of a house which is A nusance joyning near the Satturday markett⟩, and John Norris ⟨for a heap of Stones which lyeth at the house of John withers Smith near the Canke well⟩.   Indicted.

William Dawson (Ald. Abneys Ward) presents James Orton for leaving a wagon standing in the street.   Ignored.

John Dallaway (Mr George Bents Ward) presents the well near the Town Hall which is out of repair.   Indicted.

27.3   *Discharged Recognizances*
Edward Burges, tallow chandler, to appear and keep the peace towards Henry Freestone.
Samuel Bloxom, gardener, to appear and keep the peace towards William Winckles.
Thomas Clark, Blaby, Leics., labourer, to appear and answer charges.
William Hall, glazier, to appear to prosecute and give evidence against Thomas Clark.
John Pulham, jersey-comber, to appear and keep the peace towards William Wells.
Richard Hunt, labourer, to appear and answer charges and obey the Court.

27.4   *Presentment*
The Grand Jury present Thomas Clark, Blaby, Leics., labourer, for stealing 15s. from William Hall.   Ignored.

27.5   *Indictments*
Anne Mercy, spinster, for stealing a piece of iron, 10 pieces of wood and 2 shafts from William Southwall, gent.   Pleads guilty, whipped.

Jane, wife of Charles Tuffley, baker, for assaulting Anne Chettle.

Samuel Marshall, mercer, for trading as a woolcomber unapprenticed.

28.1 *Writ of Summons*
Dated 26 April 1696 for 17 July 1696.

28.2 *Constables' Presentments*
Joseph Large (Mr Southwels Ward) presents John Watson for selling ale without a licence. Indicted.

Edward Laasbey (the late Mr Bentleys Ward) presents John Burditt, sen., ⟨for an incroachment upon the kings Highway in a teniment Late in the ocupation of margritt Heaselwood widow⟩.

28.3 *Discharged Recognizances*
John Moore, Braunstone, Leics., labourer, to appear and keep the peace towards Edward Burbage.
John Best, Nottingham, framework-knitter, to appear and answer charges.
John Burdett, gent., to appear and answer charges and obey the Court.
Samuel Marshall, mercer, to prosecute his traverses.

28.4 *Indictments*
Samuel Marshall, mercer, for trading as a woolcomber unapprenticed.

Elizabeth, wife of Daniel Carr, baker, for stealing a pewter pot from John Franklyn. Guilty.

28.5 *Debtors*
John Hurt:
Certificate to Ellin Thomlinson and Hurt's other creditors informing them of Hurt's coming discharge under two Acts entitled Acts for the Relief and Release of Poor Prisoners for Debt and an Act entitled An Act for Relief of Poor Prisoners for Debt and Damages. Notes of service of copies of the certificate on: Ellin Tomlinson of Ashburne in the Peake, Derbs., John Hallingsworth of the same, William Handley, and Mrs Susannah Heggs. Note of the Writ by Ellin Thomlinson under which Hurt is detained.

Samuel Haughton:
Certificate to Charles Burrodell and Haughton's other creditors informing them of Haughton's coming discharge under the above Acts. Notes of service of copies of the certificate on: David Deakens, jun., of Leicester, Mrs Wagstaffe, Mrs Martin, Mr Willkins, tailor, Mr Worall, Mr Walton, William Sheares, Daniel Simpson, Mr Cradocke, clothier, Mr Sutton, Godfrey Barradell, Mr Lee, Isaac Harrise, Richard Andrew of Swithland, Thomas Booley of the same, Thomas Duckett of Sileby, Elizabeth Noble of the same, Charles Barradell's Executrix of the same, Charles Smith of the same, Thomas Parsons of the same, John Chamberline of the same, Christian Leeson of Syston, John Ilson of Barkby, Thomas Winsor of the

same, Rebecca Woolhouse of the same, Nathan Knight of the same, and William Pratt of the same. Note of the Writs by Sarah Martyn, Thomas Duckett, Charles Barodell, and Sarah Wagstaffe under which Haughton is detained.

John Heward:
Certificate to George Bent and Heward's other creditors informing them of Heward's coming discharge under the above Acts. Notes of service of copies of the certificate on: George Bent, sen., John Pratt, Ann Townsend, Richard Townsend, and James Ludlam. Note of the Writ by George Bent and William Bent under which Heward is detained.

29.1 *Writ of Summons*
Dated 17 July 1696 for 5 October 1696.

29.2 *Discharged Recognizances*
Andrew Clark, gent., to appear and obey the Court.
Edward Melborne, joiner, to appear and answer charges and obey the Court.
John Fawkes, Lincoln, dyer, to appear and answer charges and obey the Court.

29.3 *Indictment*
William Higgs, butcher, Joseph Groce, carpenter, Benjamin Withers, butcher, and Richard Hunt, butcher, for assaulting John Stubbs a tithing man. Plead guilty, fined 1s. each.

30.1 *Writ of Summons*
Dated [damaged] for 12 April 1697.

30.2 *Constables' Presentments*
Nine Constables present "omnia bene".

John Barker (Mr Fredmans Ward) presents James Brian, currier, for selling ale without a licence. Indicted.

George Brown (Ald. Abneys Ward) presents Alderman Philip Abney for ⟨Theft Ruott knowing that James Peters & John Treene & John Yates stoule his Three Geese & did not prosicute them according to Law⟩. Indicted.

30.3 *Discharged Recognizances*
William Fox, labourer, to appear and keep the peace towards Mary, his wife.
Mary, wife of Richard Clay, labourer, to appear and keep the peace towards Mary Fox.

Peter Feild, currier, to appear and answer charges.

John Hewitt, jun., cooper, to appear and answer charges.

John Hodge, St Leonard's, labourer, to appear and prosecute Frances, wife of Edward Higgett, Markeaton, Derbs., labourer, for the felony of a pair of sheets.

30.4   *Indictment*

Frances, wife of Edward Higgett, Markeaton, Derbs., labourer, for stealing a pair of sheets from John Hodge.   Po se, guilty.

30.5   *Informations*

William Page, Saracen's Head, victualler, taken 4 January 1696/7:

⟨This Informant saith that upon the last day of December About Eight or Nine of the Clock in the Evening of the same day John Yates John Hewitt the Younger William Windsor & Peter Feild came into this Informants house and went into the Parlour and calld for a Tankard of Drink and the sayd William Windsor called this Informant into the said Parlour and the sayd John Hewitt & Peter Feild Drank the late King James's health and Sang Sungs and this Informant went afterwards into the Kitchin and heard the said health drank by them and told them that if they would Shunn trouble they should forbare.⟩

Captain John Blake taken 4 January 1696/7:

⟨This Informant Saith that on the 31th of December last betweene Eight and Nine of the Clock in the Evening of the same day John Yates John Hewitt the younger William Windsor and Peter Feild came into the said Captaines Lodging at the Saracens head in the said Burrough in a Riotous manner and entred the Roome where he was being the Kitchin but there being no Roome for them they went into the next Roome where they Imediatly began to Sing Songs that were seditious and Scandalous to the King and Government and then drank the late King James his health with a huzsay and called for the Maid Servant of the house in and would have had her to drink the said health as the said Maid informed him And further saith that this was the second or third Attempt they made upon him in the like nature. William Page the Master of the House went in unto them and told them Gentlemen if you will avoyd trouble forbare your ill practices or words to that purpose but instead of Stopping they sang louder At lenghth this Informant went into the Roome to reprove them upon which they fell upon him which he beleives was the designe of their comeing.⟩

30.6   *Removal Orders*

James Harrison and his wife and children to be removed from St Martin's to St Nicholas', 21 October 1696.   ⟨Discharged⟩

Richard Low and his wife and family to be removed from St Margaret's to Knighton, 16 December 1696. ⟨Confirmed⟩

31.1   *Writ of Summons*
Dated 4 October 1697 for 10 January 1697/8.

31.2   *Prisoner*
Richard Wilkins committed for a felony

31.3   *Discharged Recognizances*
Benjamin Alsop, needlemaker, to appear and give evidence against Jervace, Thomas Gulson, Luke Hodges, John Fish, and Joseph Dickman for riot.
William Jervace, jun., apprentice to William Jervace, sen., fellmonger, to appear and answer charges.
Thomas Gulson, apprentice to Anthony Groce, parchmentmaker, to appear and answer charges.
Luke Hodges, apprentice to William Hodges, framework-knitter, to appear and answer charges.
John Fish, apprentice to Joseph Parker, framework-knitter, to appear and answer charges.
Joseph Dickman, apprentice to Samuel Hammont, woolcomber, to appear and answer charges.
John Dash, apprentice to Samuel Hammont, to appear and answer charges.
Paul Walwyn, hosier, to appear and answer charges.
Robert Broadhurst, tailor, to appear and answer charges.
Joseph Bently, mercer, to appear to prosecute and give evidence against Richard Wilkins for a felony.
Sampson Goodall, gent., to appear and keep the peace towards Thomas Dring.
Thomas Dring, Thornton, Leics., gauger, to appear and prosecute Sampson Goodall for assault and battery.
The Rev. James Poole to appear and prosecute Ann Johnson.

31.4   *Presentment*
The Grand Jury present ⟨Thomas Toopots and Thomas Hastwell Senior for diging a gravill pit soe big that horse and man may bee spoyled at it and [torn] it to lie open it beeing in the free school laine [torn] side of my Lords place yard.⟩

31.5   *Indictments*
Anne Johnson alias Lydia Gent, Ipstones, Staffs., singlewoman, and Charles Ferney, Ipstones, Staffs., butcher, for attempting to father Anne's bastard child on the Rev. James Poole.   Guilty.

Richard Wilkins, labourer, for stealing a piece of painted callico from Joseph Bentley.   Guilty.   Wilkins states:
⟨That he upon the 18th day of this instant December did feloniously take one piece of Printed Callco out of the Shop Window of Mr Joseph Bently Mercer within the said Burrough.⟩

William Headley, carpenter, for trading as a woolcomber unapprenticed.

31.6   *Informations*

William Chaplin, servant to John Watson, victualler, taken 14 August 1697:
⟨This Informant saith that this present day About six or seaven of the clock in the morneing as soone as he had opened the Street Doore of his Masters house he saw Elizabeth Coleman come into the yard belonging to his said Masters house thorough the back Gates of the said house and went into the Garden of the said John Watson and then and there tooke away one Laced Handkercheife one Laced Pinner and Laced Coife the goods of Ellen Johnson the Wife of John Johnson a Dutch Souldier quartered there and that she values the said Severall pieces of Lynnen at Ten pence.⟩
Ellen, wife of John Johnson, taken 14 August 1697:
⟨This Examinant saith that the Laced Handkercheife and Coyfe and Pynner in the Informacion above mencioned are her owne Goods.⟩

31.7   *Petitions*

Susanna Royner, St Martin's:
⟨Sheweth unto your worshipps that your Poore and humble Petitioner hath but twelve pence a weeke allowance from the said Parish And being of the age of Fourscore yeares & upwards and not able to doe any thing to gett a Lively hood the said twelve pence a weeke is soe poor an allowance that your poor & humble petitioner is almost staved & pined and hopeing that your worships will be pleased to order your poor petitioner a better allowance She being forced to pay houserent out of the said Allowance of twelve pence aweeke & your Petitioner shall be Ever bound to pray for your worships etc.
Ordered six a weeke more.⟩

Edward Deacon, St Martin's:
⟨Sheweth unto your worships that your poore and humble petitioner is a very poore man and out of Imployment & he and his family are almost starved and pined And hath noe weekely allowance from the said parish of St Martins These are humbly to request your worships favour to order aweekely allowance for your poor & humble petitioner his wife and family who suffers much for want thereof and unlesse releived shall all Perish for want of maintenance And hopeing your worships will be pleased to consider the poor Condition your humble petitioner is in for want of releife &

by soe doeing your poor & humble petitioner will be Ever bound to pray
for your worships etc.
Ordered 18d per weeke till further order.⟩

31.8 *Removal Orders*

William Copson and [blank] Dickman and their wives and families to be
removed from St Martin's to St Margaret's, 7 January 1697/8. ⟨Ordered
that this Order be confirmed.⟩

Bartholomew and James Hawkins to be removed from St Margaret's to
St Martin's, 7 January 1697/8. ⟨Ordered that this Order be discharged.⟩

31.9 *Order*

⟨Whereas Complaint hath this Day been made unto us whose names are
hereunto subscribed two of his Majesties Justices of the Peace for the said
Burrough of Leicester upon the Oath of Maximilian Talbott of the said
Burrough of Leicester Gent That on the second day of November instant
he did seize Nineteene Hides of Leather in the possession of Samuell
Shipley of the said Burrough Currier for not being searcht and Sealed
according to an Act of Parliament made in the first yeare of the reigne of
our late Soveraigne Lord King James the first We doe therefore persuant
to the power given unto us by the said Act And of one other Act made in
the Eighth and Ninth yeares of the Reigne of our Soveraigne Lord King
William the third for Ascertaineing the Duty of Leather adjudge the said
Nineteene Hydes of Leather to be forfeited or the value thereof Given
under our hands and Seales the Tenth day of November in the Ninth yeare
of the reigne of our Soveraigne Lord William the third by the Grace of God
of England Scotland France and Ireland King Defender of the Faith &c
Annoque domini 1697.

Henry Pate Mayor
John Pares

This Judgment Vacated at a Sessions held the 10th of January Anno
domini 1697.⟩

32.1 *Writ of Summons*

Dated 10 January 1697/8 for 6 May 1698.

32.2 *Discharged Recognizances*

William Hewson, basketmaker, to appear and answer charges.
John Burdett, sen., to appear and prosecute William Hewson.
Samuel Shipley, currier, to appear and prosecute William Handy, Daniel
Carr, and John Taylor for assault and battery and a breach of the peace.
John Taylor to appear and answer charges and keep the peace towards
Samuel Shipley.

William Handy, tailor, to appear and answer charges and keep the peace towards Samuel Shipley.

Daniel Carr, baker, to appear and answer charges and keep the peace towards Samuel Shipley.

32.3 *Presentment*

The Grand Jury present William Handy, tailor, for breaking into Samuel Shipley's house and assaulting Thomas Hewson.   Ignored.

32.4 *Indictments*

William Hewson, basketmaker, for breaking into John Burdett's house and stealing 10d.   Pleads guilty, fined 2s. 6d.

William Handy, tailor, for breaking into Samuel Shipley's house and assaulting him.   Appears and pleads guilty, fined 26s.

Daniel Carr, baker, and John Taylor, woolcomber, for breaking into Samuel Shipley's house and assaulting Samuel Cooper.   Appear and plead guilty, fined 20s. each.

32.5 *Removal Order*

Ann Hewes to be removed from St Margaret's to Markfield, 15 January 1697/8.   ⟨Ordered to be Vacated.⟩

33.1 *Writ of Summons*

Dated 6 May 1698 for 15 July 1698.

33.2 *Discharged Recognizance*

Samuel Marshall, mercer, to appear and prosecute his traverse.

34.1 *Writ of Summons*

Dated 15 July 1698 for 6 October 1698.

34.2 *Discharged Recognizances*

Edward Springthorpe, baker, to appear.

Ann, wife of Edward Springthorpe, to appear.

Edward Burges, sen., labourer, not to keep an alehouse until licensed.

34.3 *Indictments*

John Harrison, gardener, on presentment of John Clay, gent., for stopping up a watercourse which runs from the yard of Clay's house in St Martin's through Harrison's yard to the street.

John Harrison, gardener, on presentment of John Clay, gent., for stopping up a doorway in a wall so that Clay and his family can no longer use it.

34.4 *Removal Order*

John Williams to be removed from St Mary's to St Martin's, September 1698. ⟨Vacated for defect of the words upon Oath.⟩

35.1 *Writ of Summons*

Dated 6 October 1698 for 9 January 1698/9

35.2 *Prisoners*

Robert Armston ⎱ committed for felonies
John Duckett ⎰

35.3 *Discharged Recognizances*

John Townesend, Aylestone, Leics., miller, to appear and prosecute Robert Armeson.

William Reeves, tailor, to appear and give evidence against Robert Armson for a felony.

John Yates, pipemaker, to appear and answer charges.

John West, miller, to appear and prosecute John Duckett.

35.4 *Indictments*

Samuel Marshall, mercer, for trading as a woolcomber unapprenticed.

Robert Armeson, labourer, for stealing 2½ measures of meal, a sacking bag, and a leather bag from John Townesend.   Po se, guilty.

John Duckett, labourer, for stealing 2 strikes of grain and 1 of masline, and a sacking bag, value 5s., from Thomas West.   Po se, guilty to the value of 10d.

35.5 *Sacramental Certificate*

St Martin's   Simon Barwell, gent.

36.1 *Writ of Summons*

Dated 9 January 1698/9 for 17 April 1699.

36.2 *Prisoner*

Walter Shotton alias Bates

36.3 *Discharged Recognizances*

James Orton, labourer, to appear and answer charges.

Humphrey Jackson, Grays Inn Passage, Holborn, woolcomber, to appear and answer charges.

William Flack, Whites Garden, Southwark, victualler, to appear and answer charges.

William Thorley, labourer, to appear and answer charges.

Thomas Reddall, Stoughton, Leics., labourer, to appear and answer charges.

David Clay, brewer, to appear and answer charges.

Samuel Marshall, mercer, to appear and answer charges.

Susanna Worth, spinster, to appear to prosecute and give evidence against Walter Shotton for a felony.

James Heymor, Butterworth, Lincs., husbandman, to appear and answer charges.

Stephen King, Keyham, Leics., yeoman, to appear for using an unlawful strike.

Robert Peake, Keyham, Leics., yeoman, to appear to prosecute and give evidence against John Gee for using an unlawful strike.

Stephen King to appear and give evidence against John Gee.

John Gee, jun., cooper, to appear and answer charges.

36.4   *Indictments*

John Gee, jun., for having an illegal strike. Submits to the Court and is fined 6s. 8d.

Elias Wallin, woolcomber, for assaulting Thomas Webster.

Elias Wallin, woolcomber, for assaulting Jane, wife of Thomas Webster.

Walter Shotton, labourer, for stealing a blue linen apron from Susanna Worth.   Pleads guilty.

36.5   *Order*

⟨To the Churchwardens and Overseers of the Poore of St Mary in the Burrough of Leicester.

Whereas Frances Neale hath Complained to us whose names are hereunto Subscribed two of his Majesties Justices of the Peace for the said Burrough (Quorum unus) that she is destitute of all manner of Releife for her bodily Sustenance and haveing declared unto us upon her Oath that she was bound an Apprentice to Thomas West of your Parish of St Mary Miller These are therefore to Order and require you to provide for and allow the said Frances Neale such Lodging and other necessarys as are convenient for her till further Order Given under our hands and Seales the three & Twentieth day of February Anno Domini 1698.

John Cracroft Mayor
John Pares

Vacated ex mocion Mr Barwell upon Complaint of the Overseers of St Mary.⟩

37.1   *Writ of Summons*

Dated 17 April 1699 for 14 July 1699.

37.2   *Prisoner*
John Smith on bail for a felony

37.3   *Discharged Recognizances*
Thomas Roberts, victualler, to appear and answer charges.
Matthew Cook, labourer, to appear and give evidence against Thomas
Roberts for ⟨deteyneng his wages from him⟩.
John Smith, Birstall, Leics., labourer, to appear and answer charges.
Elizabeth, wife of John Worthington, plasterer, tiler, and tallow chandler,
to appear and give evidence against John Smith for a felony.
John Lancaster, vintner, to appear and answer charges.

37.4   *Indictment*
John Smith, Birstall, Leics., labourer, for stealing a strike and a sacking
bag from Richard Croxall.   Po se, guilty.

37.5   *Apprenticeship Indenture*
[Fragment] William Cox bound to Edward Burgis.
⟨Ordered by the Court that this Indenture be vacated.⟩

38.1   *Writ of Summons*
                  Dated 14 July 1699 for 2 October 1699.

38.2   *Constables' Presentments*
Nine Constables present "omnia bene".

Francis Crecroft (Ald. Wilkins Ward) presents Mrs Coleman, widow, for
⟨refuseing to pay for her watch & Ward according to Custome⟩.   Indicted.

William Topp (Ald. Brooksby's Ward) presents William Biddle and
Thomas Chapman, jun., for neglecting the Watch.   Indicted.

38.3   *Discharged Recognizances*
Thomas Freer, labourer, to appear and answer charges.
Joseph Erp, jun., to appear and answer charges.
Robert Bates, weaver, to appear and answer charges.
John Treen, blacksmith, to appear and answer charges.
Elizabeth Walwyn, widow, to appear and answer charges.
Anthony Hill, pipemaker, to appear and answer charges.
Ann Belgrave, widow, to appear and answer charges and keep the peace
towards Grace, wife of Thomas Watson.
Alice Belgrave, spinster, to appear and answer charges and keep the peace
towards Grace Watson.

38.4 *Removal Orders*

Ann Smith to be removed from St Mary's to Lutterworth, 28 July 1699.

Jane Officer to be removed from St Martin's to St Margaret's, 9 September 1699. ⟨Ordered to be confirmed.⟩

39.1 *Writ of Summons*

Dated 2 October 1699 for 12 January 1699/1700.

39.2 *Prisoners*

Mary Cooper for the felony of 7 yds flannel from Richard Weston, gent. Elizabeth Coleman for the felony of a silver cup

39.3 *Constables' Presentments*

Ten Constables present "omnia bene".

39.4 *Discharged Recognizances*

Thomas Simpkins, Thurmaston, Leics., chandler, to appear and give evidence against Mary, wife of William Cooper, Rothley, Leics., miller, for a felony.
Richard Wilson, mercer, to appear and give evidence against Mary Cooper for a felony.
Richard Weston to appear to prosecute and give evidence against Mary Cooper for a felony.

39.5 *Indictments*

Mary, wife of William Cooper, Rothley, Leics., miller, for stealing 7 yards of dyed flannel from Richard Weston. Po se, guilty, ⟨Burnt in the Cheeke⟩.

Elizabeth Coleman, Desford, Leics., singlewoman, for stealing a silver cup from John Holmes. Po se, guilty, ⟨Burnt in the Cheek⟩.

39.6 *Petition*

⟨Gentlemen this is to Accquaint you of the poor Condition of William Garrat of St margrets parish haveing not where with all to subsist by reason of haveing no imployment. I have not had three day's work since Last Michallmas haveing three small Children & the parrish allows me Nothing & have made my applycation to them but never the better. I had three houses which I was forced to sell to maintaine my famely & am now reduced to great poverty pray Consider the Low Condition of poor William Garrat.
Ordered upon this Peticion that the Parish of St Margeret find him a house.⟩

39.7 *Removal Orders*

Elizabeth Darman to be removed from St Margaret's to Fleckney, 22 November 1699. ⟨This Order revoked & repealed.⟩

John Cart and his wife and family to be removed from St Margaret's to Ashby Parva. [Torn.]

40.1 *Writ of Summons*

Dated [damaged] for 4 October 1700.

40.2 *Discharged Recognizances*

Joseph Coulson, jersey-comber, to appear and answer charges and obey the Court.

Mary, wife of John Hose, to appear and answer for taking 5 or 6 parcels of thread out of the shop of John Burdett, sen., mercer.

John Burdett, sen., to appear to prosecute and give evidence against Mary Hose for a felony.

William Deane, apprentice, to appear and give evidence against Mary Hose for a felony.

William Holmes, woolcomber, to appear and answer charges *re* the bastard child of Ann Johnson.

James Richmon, victualler, to appear and answer charges.

David Clay, jun., to appear and answer charges and keep the peace towards [damaged], wife of William Sadler, baker.

The wife of Edward Springthorp, baker, to appear and answer charges and keep the peace towards Mary [damaged].

John Smith, butcher, to appear and answer charges.

Edward Bracebridge, sen., fellmonger, to appear and give evidence against James Richmon for extortion.

George Bent, jun., woollen draper, to appear and prosecute Dorothy Johnson for the felony of $2\frac{1}{2}$ yds striped linsey.

Francis Whips to appear and prosecute Dorothy Johnson, widow, for a felony.

Henry Clemenson, bodice-maker, and Mary Watts, spinster, to appear and give evidence against Dorothy Johnson for a felony.

Thomas Manning, Thrapston, Northants., glazier, to appear and prosecute Katherine Miles and Joseph Colson for trying to poison his sister Frances, wife of Joseph Colson.

John Adison, Oundle, Northants., victualler, and his wife, Philippa, to appear and give evidence that Katherine Miles gave Philippa some poisoned cakes to send to Frances Colson.

Thomas Lockington, Thrapston, Northants., basketmaker, and Stephen Checkly, Thrapston, Northants., labourer, to appear and give evidence of the poisoned cakes being brought to Frances Colson.

40.3 *Presentments*

The Grand Jury present William Sadler, baker, for assaulting David Clay, sen. Ignored.

The Grand Jury present Martha, wife of William Sadler, baker, for assaulting David Clay, jun. Ignored.

Thomas Hewson presents Samuel Shipley, currier, for theft.

40.4 *Indictments*

Mary, wife of John Hose, labourer, for stealing 5 or 6 parcels of thread from John Burdett.

James Richmond, labourer, Under Bailiff, for attempting to extort 16s. from Thomas Withers. Protests he is not guilty, but will not plead in court.

Katherine Smith, widow, for attempting to make converts to Roman Catholicism.

Katherine Miles for trying to poison Frances, wife of Joseph Colson, with ratsbane. Pleads guilty.

Joseph Colson for trying to poison his wife, Frances.

Dorothy Johnson, Clayton, Yorks., widow, for stealing 4 yds dyed linen from Francis Whipps. Not guilty.

40.5 *Removal Order*

John Lewin to be removed from St Mary's to Humberstone, 10 April 1700. ⟨This Order confirmed.⟩

41.1 *Writ of Summons*

Dated 28 April 1701 for 6 October 1701.

41.2 *Prisoner*

Henry Lunn for a felony

41.3 *Constable's Presentment*

Henry Garrat (Mr Pares Ward) presents John Gritland and Robert Loasby for selling ale without a licence.

41.4 *Discharged Recognizances*

John Colton to appear and answer charges and keep the peace towards Elizabeth, wife of Abraham Burrowes.
William Staples, glazier, to appear and answer charges.
John Lancaster, vintner, to appear and answer charges.

John Hunt, butcher, to appear and answer charges.
William Handy, tailor, to appear and answer charges.
Francis Nedham, yeoman, to appear and answer charges.
Roger Lewin, butcher, to appear and answer charges.
Mary, wife of John Cooper, glazier, to appear and answer charges.
Babington Bradley, gent., to appear and answer charges and keep the peace towards [blank] Coleman.
Thomas Coltman, Coleman Street, London, periwig-maker, to appear to prosecute and give evidence against William Harris and John Skeath for the felony of his watch.
William Harris, haberdasher of hats, to appear and answer charges.
John Skeath, periwig-maker, to appear and answer charges.
John Sylby, labourer, to appear and answer charges.
John Skeath to appear and prosecute his traverse.

41.5   *Indictments*

William Harris, hatter, and John Skeath, labourer, for stealing a watch from Thomas Coltman.

William Chesterton, labourer, for keeping a common alehouse and selling ale and beer without a licence.

42.1   *Writ of Summons*
Dated 8 October 1701 for 13 April 1702.

42.2   *Discharged Recognizances*
Babington Bradley, gent., to appear and answer charges.
Pettit West, miller, to appear and answer charges.
Elizabeth, wife of Thomas Orton, sen., victualler, to appear and answer charges.
Mary, wife of Valentine Kestian, victualler, to appear and answer charges.
Henry Coates, victualler, to appear and answer charges to be made by the Parishioners of St Margaret's.

42.3   *Attachment Order*
⟨It appearing to this Court that the Parish of St Margarett in the said Burrough of Leicester was then indebted unto Richard Orton late one of the Overseers of the Poor of the said Parish in the Summ of One Pounds and Nineteen Shillings upon the said Richard Ortons Account And that the Parishoners of the said Parish have refused to pay to the said Richard Orton the said One pounds and Nineteen Shillings And the said Richard Orton haveing made Oath this Day in this Court that he gave timely

notice to the present Overseers of the Poor of the said Parish of St Margarett that he intended to move this Court this present Sessions for the payment of the said One pound and Nineteene shillings to him It is therefore Ordered by this Court that the present Overseers of the Poor for the said Parish of St Margarett Doe forthwith pay to the said Richard Orton the said One pound and Nineteen shillings and all his reasonable charge etc about procureing the same.

Attachment order Against Arthur Noone abovesaid to appear at next Sessions to shew cause etc.⟩

43.1   *Writ of Summons*

Dated 13 April 1702 for 13 July 1702.

43.2   *Constables' Presentments*

Eight Constables present "omnia bene".

Abstinence Pougher (Ald. Bents Ward) presents Jonathan Mason, cordwainer, for ⟨Annoying the Neighborhood with an house of Easement or house of Office etc.⟩   Indicted.

William Chandler (Ald. Wilkines Ward) presents Joseph Earpe, sen., for selling ale without a licence.   Indicted.

John Brooks (Mr Pares Ward) presents John Gritland and Robert Loasby for selling ale without a licence.   Indicted.

43.3   *Discharged Recognizance*

John Coates, jun., baker, to appear and answer charges.

43.4   *Indictments*

Daniel (Dannett) Pollard, tailor, for trading as a barber on a Sunday unapprenticed.

Nicholas Swingler, labourer, for keeping a common disorderly alehouse.

43.5   *Debtors' Petitions*

Robert Withers, Leicester Gaol:

⟨Humbly Sheweth unto your worships That your Petitioner is a Prisoner in the said Goale for debt and soe hath beene for twelve months last past And therefore humbly beseeches your worships that your Petitioners Creditors may be summoned to shew cause why your Petitioner should not be discharged your Petitioner not really and bona fide being Indebted to any one of his Creditors in twenty pounds pursuant to an Act Intituled an Act for Releife of poor prisoners for debt and in order thereunto that your

worships would take such orders and give such directions [as to] you shall seem meet & your Petitioner as in duty bound shall ever pray etc.⟩
Account of debts due to Robert Withers:

	s.	d.
⟨Thomas Withers of the Burrough of Leicester . .	1	11
Christopher Sharpe of the same Burrough . . .		8
	2	7⟩

James Bryan, as Robert Withers', but term of imprisonment ⟨above a yeare⟩.
Account of debts due to James Bryan:
⟨Dew to me from Benjamin [damaged] for victualls & drink & money lent . . . . [damaged]
Dew from Solomon Bray for lent money . . . . [damaged]
Dew from Jonathan Woolfe of Hoby for leather . . 5 0 0
Dew from Thomas Pegg for Leather . . . 3 0 0

15 7 0⟩

Edward Burgis, as Robert Withers', but term of imprisonment ⟨above three yeares⟩.

43.6 *Sacramental Certificate*
St Martin's   Alderman John Burdett, mercer

43.7 *Removal Order*
John Leonard and his wife and 3 children to be removed from All Saints' to St Leonard's, 28 May 1702.   ⟨This ordered quashed for insufficiencie.⟩

44.1 *Writ of Summons*
Dated 11 January 1702/3 for 5 April 1703.

44.2 *Prisoners*
George Bates for begetting a bastard on Jane Bates
Henry Love

44.3 *Constables' Presentments*
Nine Constables present "omnia bene".

William Chauner (Ald. Wilkins Ward) presents Thomas Bland, tailor, for trading unfree.

William Clements (Mr Cradocks Ward) presents Jeremiah Read, tailor, for trading unfree.

44.4 *Indictments*

John Bland, labourer, for trading as a tailor unapprenticed.

Edward [damaged] for keeping a common alehouse without a licence. Guilty.

44.5 *Sacramental Certificate*

St Martin's   Simon Barwell, gent.

45.1 *Writ of Summons*

Dated 12 July 1703 for 4 October 1703.

45.2 *Prisoner*

Benjamin Underwood

45.3 *Constables' Presentments*

Ten Constables present "omnia bene".

John Jenins (Ald. Wilkins's Ward) presents ⟨an old Building of Mr John Fosters Attorney in Hinckley being dangerouly out of repaire for 6 months last past standing next to Mr Brougtons in the street cald the southgate street⟩, and Edward Burges, sen., for selling ale without a licence.   Indicted.

45.4 *Note for Recognizance*

Josiah Johnson and John Holmes to appear and keep the peace towards Francis Elliott.

45.5 *Presentment*

William Anslip, St Martin's, basketmaker, ⟨hath served seaven yeares to the same and is a freeman of the said Burrough And whereas there are severall persons in the said Burrough not being freemen of the said Burrough which doe follow the said trade and never served seaven yeares thereto and by soe doeing doe very much Indempnify me the said William Anslip & my family one of which is Robert Tugman who never served an Apprentiship thereto & opens shop windowes daily and on the Fair day last threw the goods of me the said William Anslip about the Cornewall & would not suffer me to stand in quiet with my goods, and the other are Thomas Hewson the Elder & Thomas Hewson the younger who follow the said trade not haveing served seaven yeares thereto And therefore humbly requests you to lett the said persons be Indicted for the same, for if such persons be suffered soe to doe I the said William Anslip and my family cannot live but have & must very much suffer, and therefore I doe hereby Indict the said Robert Tugman Thomas Hewson Senior & Thomas Hewson Junior and without care be taken herein I & my family cannot live.⟩

45.6 *Indictments*

John Holmes, Countesthorpe, Leics., weaver, and Josiah Johnson, Countesthorpe, Leics., tailor, for assaulting Francis Elliott.

Robert Pickard, labourer, for trading as a woolcomber unapprenticed. Not guilty.

Samuel [damaged], labourer, for trading as a woolcomber unapprenticed.

45.7 *Petitions*

John Cooper, St Martin's:
⟨Humbly Sheweth unto your worshipps That your Petitioner haveing a daughter the use of whose Limbs are taken away that she is not able to gett anything for a Liveing nor to dresse nor ondresse herselfe And hath been soe for many yeares last past and is not likely to be any otherwayes whilst she lives And your Petitioner being in a very poor & low Condition is not able to mainteyne her without the help and assistance of the said Parish of St Martin who doe refuse to help your Petitioner therein although your petitioner has addressed himselfe to the officers of the said parish of St Martin severall times And hopeing your worships will take it into consideration & order that your Petitioner may be releived herein And your Petitioner as in duty bound shall ever pray etc.⟩

Mary, wife of William Higgins, St Mary's:
⟨Sheweth unto your worships that your Petitioners husband being in the Queenes service and your Petitioner haveing two small Children to mainteyne and the youngest being about a yeare & halfe old and being a Child that is broke in his body and almost always sickly and badly that it is almost all your Petitioners worke to looke after & order the said child and your Petitioner is allowed but tenpence a weeke from the Parish which is soe small that your petitioner & Children are very much suffers thereby, and when att any time your poore Petitioner goes to the said Parishioners to complaine & desire a better maintenance their Answeare is take more off from her & pinch her belly & tells her that she must not attend nor hold that poor sickly child but lett it lye in a Cradle & sitt in a Chaire whilst your poor petitioner workes, and tho your worships orderd them last Sessions to be releived as other poor in the said Parish yett they refuse to doe it, & tells me ten pence a weeke is too much & that bread & water is the Parish allowance & will doe noe more which is very hard upon your poor petitioner & Children and without better allowance your Petitioner & children must

very much suffer And hopeing your worships will take it into consideration And your petitioner shall ever pray etc.

And Mr Wilkins says that the Recorders word or order of sessions signifyes nothing & that the will choose after one day whether they will obey it or not.⟩

Edward Burgis, debtor, Leicester Gaol:
⟨Whereas your Petitioner who now is and who the first day of January Anno Domini 1701 was a prisoner in the said Goale for debt and hath Petitioned the Justices of the said Burrough to have the benefitt of a certaine Act of Parliament made in the first yeare of the raigne of her present Majestye Queene Anne over England etc Entituled an act for the Releife of poor prisoners for debt And your Petitioner haveing summoned his Creditors to appeare att this Sessions to shew cause if they can why your Petitioner should not be discharged, These are therefore humbly to begg the favour of this Court that your Petitioner may be brought up to this Court and discharged from his said severall Creditors if noe cause by them be shewed to the contrary. And your Petitioner as in duty bound shall ever pray etc.⟩

William Pawley, prisoner in the Old Gaol, Leicester:
⟨Sheweth That James Richmond the Keeper of the said Gaol having for a Considerable time removed all his family there from & now Inhabitting soe farr distant from the said Gaol as the Belgrave gate in the said Burrough & verry little attending att the said Gaol as releife may be brought into your said poor Petitioner, Victuals which has been often sent to him by several good Charitable Minded people in Leicester to him by reason of the Gaolers absence has been taken back or lost & eaten by poor persons in whose hands itt has been left whilst your said poor Petitioner has wanted, who is in a most Miserable & sad Condition if Considered, for he is now liked to be the only Prisoner in the said Gaol & to remaine there all Winter without Company & fire in such a Naked Nasty dismal place as it now is is terrible to thinke off Your said Petitioner therefore most humbly prays your Worshipps will Consider his sad Case & suffer him to be removed to the other Gaol or grant that some person may constantly attend att the place where he is, as the Charity of good persons may come to him or else itt cann't be supposed he can live there this next Winter but must starve, and humbly prays that he may rather be removed than remaine there Your said Petitioner alsoe prays your Worshipps will be pleased to grant him the Common allowance Bread of the said Gaol which will much help him in his deplorable Condition for he often wants sustenance from his Relations & had itt not been for other good peoples releiving him he had perished before this And your said Petitioner will be ever bound to pray for Your Worshipps long lives good healths etc.⟩

⟨Wee whose Names are here under Written Inhabitants near the old Gaol for the Burrough aforesaid Doe hereby testify & declare that whats mentioned in the said Petition as to the Gaolers being much absent from the said Gaol soe that releife has been often taken back that has been brought for the Petitioner is true and had been starved before this, had not wee and others releived him And pray he may be releived in the premisses by your Worshipps. John Holmes. Francis Johnson.

As to what provision may have been returned which was sent to the Petitioner I know not But this I am sensible of That the said James Richmond hath been much absent from the said Goale of late. Thomas Davye. Edward Alsop.⟩

45.8   *Sacramental Certificates*
St Martin's   Richard Weston, Mayor
              Edmund Cradock, Justice
              Arthur Noone, Coroner
              Joshua Goodrich, Coroner
              John Cooper, Chamberlain
              Charles Tuffley, Chamberlain
              Benjamin Gutheridge, Common Councillor
              Augustine Hefford, Common Councillor
Oath of Allegiance and Abjuration signed by them all.

45.9   *Removal Order*
Robert Pickard and his wife and family to be removed from St Mary's to St Nicholas', 19 July 1703.   ⟨This warrent vacated.⟩

46.1   *Writ of Summons*
              Dated 4 October 1703 for 10 January 1703/4.

46.2   *Indictment*
Isaac Robinson, woolcomber, Thomas Lewitt, gardener, William Lane, maltster, William Hitchcocke, gardener, and Robert Warburton, cordwainer, for riot and assault on William Hamond.   Case against Robinson and Hitchcocke ignored.

46.3   *Sacramental Certificate*
St Martin's   John Rogers, Archdeacon of the Leicester Archdeaconry
Oath of Allegiance and Abjuration signed by him.

47.1   *Writ of Summons*
              Dated 10 January 1703/4 for 27 April 1704.

47.2   *Prisoners*
Elizabeth Greenaway
Jane Gilashby

47.3   *Constables' Presentments*
Six Constables present "omnia bene".

Clement Streatton (Ald. Woodlands Ward) presents "omnia bene" and adds 〈Many of the inhabitants of this ward have Repared their streets & the rest will do it with all speed possable.〉

John Jennings (Ald. Wilkins Ward) presents George Muson and Simon Digby for not attending church.

Thomas Worth (Mr Pares Ward) presents Benjamin Allen for selling ale and beer without licence.

47.4   *Presentments*
The Grand Jury present Robert Lord 〈for that he haveing a Silver tankard [stolen] & knowing the theef did not or hath not made any prosecucion against the felon to the encouragement of such like villanies.〉

The Grand Jury present Elizabeth, wife of George Groce, carpenter, 〈for that she did expose to sale melted Bulloin contrary to the Law in that Case made.〉

The Grand Jury present Robert Clayton, labourer, for trading as a woolcomber unapprenticed.   Ignored.

47.5   *Indictments*
Elias Wallin, St Mary's, yeoman, for trading as a woolcomber unapprenticed.

Elizabeth Greenaway, spinster, for stealing 2 aprons, a coif, and a hood from Thomas Hartshorne.   Pleads guilty.

Edward Noone, labourer, and John Oxon, labourer, for stealing a cock and a hen from Thomas Bayley.   Oxon pleads guilty, but Noone is found not guilty.

47.6   *Petitions*
Joshua Stears, St Martin's:
〈Sheweth that your poore Petitioner for my Conveniency of a Lively hood Removeing Into the parish of St Nicholas wher now I Reside & have Nothing but what I got by hard Labour & have Been a Long time of Late sick of an Ague & their they Tax me for a personall Estate both to Church

& Poore which I am utterly unable to pay haveing a wife & Children to Maintaine by my Labour. Wherfore I humbly beseech your Worships will be pleased to take my Condition In to your Pious Considerations & give orders that the said Taxes May be abated & quite take of from my Personall Estate which I never had & your Poore Petitioner will For ever Pray.⟩

Thomas Wattson, St Martin's:
⟨Sheweth That your Poore Petitioner am almost past my work & have 3 small Children Not able to dress them selves & Could not goe on with my Business without the Assistance & help of some good Gentlemen in town who are kinde & Lend me money to Imploy my self & without their assistance I am utterly unable to doe any thing in my trade which for my Conveniency I now follow In the Parish of St Nicholas in the Said Burrough Where the Officers Tax me for a Personall Estate both to Church & Poore which I am utterly unable to pay. Wherfore I Humbly Beseech & beg your Worships will be please to take my Poore Condition into Consideration & give orders that I may be Excused from paying the same or order the officers of St Martins Parish to whom I belong to Pay it for me & your Poore Petitioner will for ever Pray.⟩

48.1   *Writ of Summons*
              Dated 2 October 1704 for 8 January 1704/5.

48.2   *Constables' Presentments*
Eleven Constables present "omnia bene".

48.3   *Indictment*
Josiah Ashwell ⟨for that he ought to have prosecuted Tobias Marshall of this Burrough Gold Smith for selling and exposing Silver Buttons stuffed with Lead within this Burrough it being a great cheat and abuse to her Majesties Subjects.⟩

49.1   *Writ of Sessions*
              Dated 20 April 1705 for 13 July 1705.

49.2   *Constables' Presentments*
Nine Constables present "omnia bene".

Edward Bates (Ald. Southwells Ward) presents a pump by the Conduit which is out of repair.

John Turlington (Ald. Roberts's late Ward) presents William Page for trading as a weaver unfree.

49.3 *Recommendation*

The Grand Jury recommend that ⟨there shall be two Bellmen appointed to watch every night throughout the Year within this Borough⟩.

49.4 *Discharged Recognizance*

Peter Davie to appear and answer ⟨such matters that he hath written and published reflecting on Mr Richard Weston of this Burrough relateing to the last Elleccion of Burgesses for the said Burrough⟩ and keep the peace towards Richard Weston.

49.5 *Petition*

Mary Blacke, spinster:

⟨Humbly Sheweth unto your worshipps That your Petitioner is near sixty yeares of age and hath lived all her time in the Parish of St Martins in the said Burrough and has worked all her time and never bin troublesome to the Parish till through age and sicknesse & weaknes of body your Petitioner was forced to goe to the Parish and aske Assistance of them and they were pleased to allow your poor & humble petitioner but Twelve pence a weeke, which is soe small a maintenance that your petitioner being not able to gett a penny to help herselfe with, but what she has from the Parish, and if an order for a better allowance be not forthwith made your poor & humble Petitioner will be starved and pined to death, your Petitioner never receiveing any Collection but for the two weekes last past twelve pence a weeke in all her time, and six pence of it goes for your petitioners washing & lodgeing every weeke soe that the other six pence is but small Assistance for a person as is not able to gett a penny besides, And your petitioner has bin at the last parish meeting and two Neighbours in her behalfe to Mr Mayor but he was not at home for some better maintenance but all to noe purpose, If therefore your worships would be pleased to consider your petitioners poor Condition and make a strict order for a better maintenance that your Petitioner may live and not dye for wants which I hope your worships will take care to doe and your Petitioner as in duty bound shall ever pray for your worshipps etc.⟩

50.1 *Writ of Summons*

Dated 5 October 1705 for 1 April 1706.

50.2 *Constables' Presentments*

Eight Constables present "omnia bene".

Edward Bates (Ald. Southwells Ward) presents William Page and Joseph Savige for selling ale in unsealed measures.

Charles Wagstaff (Ald. Willkins Ward) presents Frances Crecraft for selling in an unsealed measure.

Saul Brodast (Mr Pares Ward) presents Ralph Bottom for selling ale without a licence.

50.3 *Presentment*

⟨We being Informed that the well called the Gainsborough well in Alderman southwells ward lying very dangerosly onley haveing some rotten boardes nailed over it: it haveing been often presented, but no care haith been taken to repaire it: it its desiered that this sessions four persons may be Chosen well reeves to erect A new well or pump over it.⟩

50.4 *Petitions*

Samuel Bayley, St Margaret's, carpenter:

⟨Humbly Sheweth unto your worshipps That your Petitioner hath layen in a very poor & Lame Condition and hath lost the use of his Limbs ever since Michaelmas last soe that he is not able to help himselfe noe manner of way nor can he doe any thing to gett a penny to mainteyne himselfe his wife & family, And further Sheweth unto your worships That your Petitioner doth sell Ale for a little livelyhood & maintenance for his wife and family, But soe it happened that the last Sessions the Constable of the Ward wherein your petitioner lives came & called for a pint of drinke and because it was not filled either in pewter or sealed measures the Constable hath brought an Indictment against your petitioner although the said measure held a full pint, And your petitioner being poor is not able to pay the Fine that will be laid upon him in this matter And therefore humbly desires your worships to take it into your considerations and to mitigate the said Fine as your worships shall thinke fitt And your petitioner as in duty bound shall ever pray etc.⟩

Mary Coe, St Margaret's, widow, ⟨on the behalfe of herselfe and two small Children⟩:

⟨Humbly Sheweth unto your worshipps That your Petitioner is a very poor Widdow and hath two Children to mainteyne one of the age of 5 yeares & upwards and the other 4 yeares And alsoe Sheweth unto your worshipps that the said parish of St Margarett did allow your poor petitioner Eighteene pence a weeke which was but very small to mainteyne two small Children in Victualls & Clothes but however your poor Petitioner was content therewith, but the last weeke the said parish tooke off six pence a weeke from your poor petitioner And your petitioner has been at the officers of the said Parish to have the whole Eighteen pence to be allowed againe but cannot prevaile with the said officers to doe the same, nor will not be allowed except the same be ordered to be done in this place, & without which your poor petitioner & small Children will be almost starved & pined to death And hopeing your worships will be pleased to Consider the poor Condition of a poor widdow & Children and order her the Eighteen pence a weeke againe which is all your poor petitioner doth desire And your petitioner as in duty bound shall ever pray for your worships etc.⟩

Anne Johnson, widow, and Sarah Walker, widow, St Margaret's:
⟨Humbly Sheweth unto your worshipps That your poor & humble petitioners haveing each of them a child which are poor sickly & distempered children & the said Anne Johnson hath but four pence a weeke allowed and the said Sarah Walker but six pence a weeke allowed which is soe very small releife that your poor petitioners & children are almost starved & pined to death for wants And your poor petitioners have often been with the officers of the said Parish of St Margaretts both the old officers & alsoe the new officers for to desire & intreat for a further & better maintenance but all to noe purpose And your petitioners being in extreame wants & can have noe redresse except in this place Your petitioners hopes your worships will be pleased to take into your considerations the poor Condition your petitioners are in and make your poor & humble petitioners a further & better maintenance And your poor & humble petitioners as in duty bound shall ever pray for your worshipps etc.⟩

Elizabeth Garrett, St Margaret's, widow:
⟨Humbly Sheweth unto your worshipps That your Petitioner is a poor widdow and hath Three children and is allowed but six pence a weeke from the said Parish of St Margarett and which six pence a weeke doth just pay your Petitioners rent of a house your Petitioner lives in, and nothing to spare, soe that your petitioner has nothing out of that towards a maintenance of herselfe and children, And further sheweth unto your worshipps That your Petitioner has been with the officers of the said Parish of St Margarett severall times desireing and intreating them to make an allowance further and better unto your petitioner but all to noe purpose And therefore your poor & humble petitioner hopes to have a redresse therein from your worshipps for without a further & better allowance from the said Parish your Petitioner & family cannot subsist, And hopeing your worships will be pleased to order your poor & humble Petitioner a further & better maintenance to help her & her Children in her great wants & necessity And your poor & humble petitioner as in duty bound shall ever pray for your worshipps etc.⟩

Mary Hickambotham, St Margaret's, widow:
⟨Humbly Sheweth unto your worshipps That your Petitioner is aged seaventy yeares and upwards & in a manner blind and in such a poor Condition with Lamenes That she can neither dresse nor undresse herselfe and haveing noe freinds that is able to help her is in a very poor & Lamentable Condition, And it was heretofore ordered by the Sessions to

allow your poor petitioner Eighteene pence a weeke & which was duly paid your petitioner till the last weeke and then your Petitioner was reduced to twelve pence a weeke, And further sheweth that your Petitioner made very hard shift with the Eighteene pence a weeke which is but small for a maintenance washing & lodgeing & shifts & stockins and other things to be provided out of it, & now to be brought to twelve pence a weeke will pine & starve your petitioner to death And hopeing you will consider your poor petitioners Condition & order the Eighteene pence to be paid her againe, & your petitioners as in duty bound shall ever pray etc.⟩

Frances Fawsitt, St Margaret's, widow:
⟨Humbly Sheweth unto your worshipps That your petitioner is a poor widdow and soe hath been this Fifteene yeares and is of the age of 57 yeares & upwards and is lame of one Arme and her Eye sight very bad and almost past her Labour soe that your petitioner is in a very low & poor Condition And further sheweth that the said Parish did allow your poor petitioner four pence a weeke which was but very small to mainteyne a poor widdow with and last weeke the Parish tooke it off, And your petitioner has been with the officers of the said Parish to have the same allowed againe but all to noe purpose And can have noe redresse Except it be done in this place, wherefore your humble petitioner desires your worships will be pleased to consider a poor widdowes Condition and order her to have the four pence a weeke againe which is all your poor & humble petitioner desires And your petitioner as in duty bound shall ever pray for your worshipps etc.⟩

50.5 *Sacramental Certificate*
St Martin's   Alderman John Ludlam, Coroner
Oath of Allegiance and Abjuration signed by him.

50.6 *Examination*
George Johnson taken 5 March 1705/6:
⟨The said George Johnson saith that he was hired to Henry Coulson senier at Martlemas for one yeare to come, But the said George Johnson falling lame & not fitt for his service, went a way in or a boute July fallowing, 2dly the said Henry Coulson hired the aforesaid George Johnson, from the next Candlemas untill Martlemas following & he lived with him all that time, And then Henry Coulson hired the aforesaid George Johnson untill Harborrow faire following & he lived with him as a hired servant all the time of the aforesaid two hireings.⟩

50.7 *Removal Orders*
Elizabeth Smalley, widow, to be removed from St Margaret's to Barsby, 13 March 1706.

George Johnson and family to be removed from St Mary's to All Saints', 30 March 1706. ⟨Reversed⟩

William Pilkington and family to be removed from St Mary's to St Martin's, 30 March 1706. ⟨Reversed⟩

51.1 *Writ of Summons*
Dated 15 July 1706 for 11 October 1706.

51.2 *Constables' Presentments*
Nine Constables present "omnia bene".

James Norris (Ald. Woodlands Ward) presents Jonathan Gee and William Sturges for encroachment.

John Hardy (Mr Wilkins Ward) presents Joseph How for an encroachment.

51.3 *Sacramental Certificates*
St Martin's George Bent, Mayor
             Thomas Bradley, Coroner
             William Hammond, Chamberlain
             Matthew Judd, Chamberlain
St Mary's   Thomas Hartshorne, Justice
             Alderman William Bunney, Coroner
St Margaret's Thomas Ayres, jun.
Oath of Allegiance and Abjuration signed by them all.

51.4 *Removal Orders*
Ann Dash to be removed from St Martin's to All Saints', 13 June 1706. ⟨This ordered is quashed.⟩

William Lewin and his wife to be removed from St Martin's to St Nicholas', 13 June 1706. ⟨This order quashed for want of forme.⟩

Grace Redley, spinster, to be removed from St Martin's to St Nicholas', 29 August 1706. ⟨This ordered is quashed.⟩

52.1 *Writ of Summons*
Dated 11 October 1706 for 21 April 1707.

52.2 *Constables' Presentments*
Nine Constables present "omnia bene".

Thomas Lambert (Ald. Abney's Ward) presents Robert Lord, gent., for ⟨An Incrochment upon the Queens highway by erecting a Porch to his house where he now dwells in a street called Gallow tree gate in the said Burrough.⟩

52.3 *Presentments*

The Grand Jury present Constables John Hardy (Ald. Willkis' Ward), James Norris (Ald. Woodlands Ward) and Thomas Lambert (Ald. Abneys Ward) for neglecting their office.

52.4 *Sacramental Certificate*

St Martin's   Zacharius Duckett, gent.
Oath of Allegiance and Abjuration signed by him.

52.5 *Removal Order*

John Gascoigne alias Gaskins to be removed from All Saints' to St Margaret's, 2 January 1706/7. ⟨Ordered to be Confirmed.⟩

53.1 *Writ of Summons*

Dated 12 April 1708 for 4 October 1708.

53.2 *Prisoners*

Elizabeth Newton
Jane Heyrick

53.3 *Constables' Presentments*

Five Constables present "omnia bene".

Timothy Sumpter (Ald. Southwells Ward) presents Thomas Skerth for trading as a barber unfree.

Jonathan Read (Ald. Bents Ward) presents Thomas Spence for trading as a tailor unfree.

John Robards (Ald. Brooksbys Ward) presents David Clay, sen., for not attending church.

Thomas Goodrich (Ald. Woodlands Ward) presents Thomas Onby and Daniel Pollord for not attending church.

Philip Draper (Ald. Townsends Ward) presents Nicholas Tebbott for trading as a tanner unfree.

53.4 *Indictment*

Elizabeth Newton, St Martin's, widow, for stealing 2 pairs of stockings from Henry Treen.   Pleads not guilty, found guilty, ⟨to be whipt⟩.

53.5 *Petition*

Ann Heggs, St Martin's, widow:
⟨Sheweth That your poore petitioner am in the Sixty Ninth year of my

Age and so lame on both my Armes And sorely Afflicted with severall other distempers that doe Comonly attend old age: That I am utterly unable to doe any thing to get a peney Towards my Maintanance. I have but one shilling a week Collection from the parish Which is so small that except I have a better Allowance from the parish I must of Nessesity perish for want of Nessesaries haveing no fewell to lay on my fire nor none I can gett for want of money. Wherfore I most Humbly beg and Beseech your Worships will be pleased to take my poore & deploreable Condition into your Pious Consideration & give orders for my Speedy Reliefe. And your poore petitioner will as in duty Bound for ever pray for your Worships prosperity in this world & ever lasting Glory in the next.⟩

53.6 *Sacramental Certificates*
St Martin's   James Annis, Mayor
           Alderman Thomas Hemsley
           Alderman John Pares
           Alderman John Ludlam
           Alderman Edmund Johnson
           Edward Palmer, Chamberlain
           Francis Coltman, Chamberlain
           Robert Reignolds, Common Councillor
Oath of Allegiance and Abjuration signed by them all.

53.7 *Removal Order*
Elizabeth, wife of John Marshall, cordwainer, and her 2 children to be removed from St Martin's to St Margaret's, 4 September 1708. ⟨confirmed⟩

54.1 *Writ of Summons*
Dated 4 October 1708 for 5 May 1709. Adjournment held 30 May 1709.

54.2 *Constables' Presentments*
One Constable presents "omnia bene".

Timothy Sumpter (Ald. Southwells Ward) presents ⟨the severall & respective persons here mencioned for not repairing the Pavements before their severall and respective houses in the said Burrough the same being out of repair:
from the Kings Head to the white Swann
Mr William Mellborn
freere Layne & next to the George
widow Rayor
Betwen the Shambles & stalls.⟩   Indicted.

Jonathan Reed (Ald. Bents Ward) presents

⟨Mr Simod Barwell
James Whatson
John Ward
Widdow Goude
Mr Tounsin
Mr P Dave
Mr Noble for the Back sid of the Freeers
for a Newsence for thaire streets.⟩
Indicted.

for not repairing their severall and respective Pavements in the open and common streets which belongs to them severally to repair being within the said Burrough and out of repair

Thomas Garrett (Ald. Wilkins Ward) presents

⟨Mr Lister for not Reparin his dore
mrs hartshorn for not Reparin
thomas padman for not Reparing

their severall & respective Streets before their houses and grounds in the said Burrough the same being out of repair

The hangman Lane end.⟩   Indicted.

John Roberts (Ald. Brookesby's Ward) presents
⟨william wood for not Repaireing his pavement belonging to his house
widow Challton for not Reparing her pavement to her house
mr Francis Coltman for his dore all in the said Burrough and out of repair.⟩
Indicted.

Hastwell Butcher (Ald. Pares Ward) presents
⟨Edward Noone ⟩ for not Repaireing their Respective pavement before
Henry Dawson ⟩ theire Doors in the said Burrough the same being out
John Astwell   ⟩ of repair
Mr Bent sen. for not Repaireing their Respective pavement before the
Doors that John Headley and John Lewitt liveth in.⟩   Indicted.

Thomas Goodrich (Ald. Woodlands Ward) presents David Gee, John Adcock, Mary Ruseell, widow, Samuel Marshall, Anthony Hill or Mr Franks, Edward Knight, John Savage, Widow Dare, William Hames and Benjamin Ashwell ⟨for nusnes not Reporeing the streets before their severall and respective houses in the said Burrough the same being out of repair.⟩   Indicted.

Thomas Wellinger (Ald. Abney's Ward) presents
⟨Mr Edward Palmer & Francis Coltman Chamberlins for nusones in not Reporeing the streets
the causeway by the three crowns belonging to the town within the said Burrough
Mr Benitt att the East gate
Germin Beg for the like of their doors

Mr Willose ⎫ over seres of Sant Margerts Parish fr not Repareing the
Mr John Nuter ⎭ hey wayes by horsors close side going up to the horse
fare.⟩   Indicted.

Philip Draper (Ald. Townsends Ward) presents Richard Winfeild ⟨for a
nusens for not Repareing the pavement before his dores in the said Burrough the same being out of repair.⟩   Indicted.

Samuel Jacome (Ald. Cradocks Ward) presents Thomas Withers, Cornelius White and Nathaniel Hews for not repairing the pavement before
their doors, and ⟨the holiboons to the perrish of Sinnick Liss⟩.   Indicted.

John Frisby (Ald. Westons Ward) presents ⟨The School belonging to the
town⟩, George Barwell and William Goollson for not repairing the streets
before their houses.   Indicted.

54·3   *Constables' Presentments from a Monthly Meeting*
Thomas Garrett (Ald. Wilkins Ward) presents Mary Brown and Joseph
Waggatt for not repairing the pavement before their doors.   Indicted.

Thomas Wellinger (Ald. Abneys Ward) presents Thomas Ward ⟨for not
Carrying away his Manure from before his Door⟩, Susanna Freeman ⟨for
not Repairing the pavement before her Door⟩, Jerman Pegg and Edward
Hood ⟨for Wood lying before their Doors⟩, William Slater and Widow
Barton ⟨for nusances in not repairing their streets and annoying the
Common Streets with Barrells & other Lumber⟩ and William Vann and
John Hook for not assisting the Constable in the execution of a warrant.
Vann and Hook indicted.

54·4   *Presentment*
The Grand Jury presents John Denshire, John Pratt, Robert Headley,
Thomas Ward and Henry Smith ⟨for non Appearance Accerding to
adjournment⟩.

54·5   *Indictment*
William Porter, apprentice to Bartholomew Hallam, Nottingham, fellmonger, for stealing a pair of breeches from Bartholomew Hallam.   Pleads
guilty.   Porter states:
⟨That on the 29th of Aprill Last past he this Examinant went thro' a
window in the night time into the house of the above named Bartholomew
Hallam (from whom he had been about a week) and then and there with a
scurer open a Box and took out of it twenty Shillings in money (vizt) Six
halfe Crowns and one Crown peice And one pair of Leathern Breeches out
of the same Room.⟩

54.6   *Sacramental Certificates*
St Martin's   Thomas Orme, apothecary
              William Page, hatter
Oath of Allegiance and Abjuration signed by them both.

55.1   *Writ of Summons*
              Dated 5 May 1709 for 3 October 1709.

55.2   *Constables' Presentments*
Three Constables present "omnia bene".

Joseph Hall (Ald. Southwells Ward) presents Edward Palmer and Francis Coltman, late Chamberlains, ⟨for not repairing the Causeway between the Kings head and the White Swan which belongeth to the Corporacion being now very much out of Repair⟩ and ⟨for not repairing the Causeway belonging to the Town lying next to the George Inne⟩, Ann Page, widow, Joseph Cradock, Widow Raynor, Zacharius Duckett and Twiggs Pilgrim for not repairing the causeways before their doors, Daniel Simpson and John Ravenscroft ⟨for a Nusance in building upon & Blocking upp the Queens high way⟩ before their doors, and Thomas Skeath for trading as a barber unapprenticed.   Indicted.

Nicholas Swingler (Ald. Ayres Ward) presents Alderman Townsend for not repairing the causeway before his door.   Indicted.

Thomas Iliffe (Ald. Wilkins Ward) presents Thomas Ward for ⟨not repairing his Causeway lying beyond Mr Abney's before his Barn being now very much out of Repair⟩, and Widow Heggs, Mary Brown, widow, and Edward Muxloe, gent., and John Muxloe, clerk, for not repairing the causeways before their doors.   Indicted.

Gabriel Newton (Ald. Woodlands Ward) presents ⟨the Water Course by the turn Pike leading to St Mary's Church being a great Annoyance to her Majesties Subjects that goe that way it being in very bad Order and within or near the Said Burrough of Leicester⟩.   Indicted.

George Hall (Ald. Abney's Ward) presents Edward Palmer and Francis Coltman, late Chamberlains, for ⟨not repairing the Causeway lying over against Mr Mayors by the Stocks being now very much out of Repair⟩, and Thomas Ward and Thomas Bennett for not repairing the causeways before their doors.   Indicted.

Charles Keen (Ald. Townsends Ward) presents Richard Winfeild, sen., Anne Morris and Widow Springthorpe for not repairing the causeways before their doors.   Indicted.

William Bellamy (Ald. Westons Ward) presents Samuel Cox for trading as a barber unapprenticed. Indicted. John Watts, gent., for the defence, and John Boley, gent., for the prosecution.

John Jefferys (Ald. Ludlams Ward) presents Edward Harman, William Goadby, sen., Job Withers, Henry Garrett, John Pare, sen., Henry Yates and Robert Bingley ⟨for not amending & Repairing the Lane lying against their severall & respective grounds going out of the Churchgate to the Bottom of the farm Orchard called the farms Lane which belongs to them to amend & repair the same being now very much out of Repair⟩. Indicted.

55.3 *Discharged Recognizances*

John Bodycott, miller, to appear and obey the Court.

William Pilkington, labourer, to appear and obey the Court and keep the peace towards his wife.

Samuel Frost, Queniborough, Leics., butcher, to appear and obey the Court and keep the peace towards Daniel Carr.

Thomas West, miller, to appear and obey the Court *re* the bastard child of Mary Mitchell, singlewoman.

John Browne, labourer, to appear and obey the Court.

Thomas Poiner, carpenter, to appear and obey the Court.

55.4 *Petitions*

William Launder, labourer:

⟨Humbly Sheweth unto your worshipps That your petitioner is of the age of Threescore and Ten yeares and upwards and is a broken man by a Rupture in his Belly soe that your poor & humble petitioner by reason of old age and weakenes in body is not able to worke for his livelyhood & maintenance and all as your poor petitioner desires from the Parish of St Margarett where your petitioner hath his settlement is only a habitation for himselfe and wife, your poor and humble petitioner haveing layen Seaven Nights in a Hay Rick, And further sheweth unto your Worshipps; That your poor petitioner & his wife though often has been with Robert Headley Butcher the present Overseer of the Said Parish of St Margarett humbly to desire a small habitation for your poor & humble petitioner and his wife but all to noe purpose, and unlesse speedily releived by your worshipps your poor & humble petitioner will be lost; Soe hopeing and humbly desireing that your worshipps will be pleased to take the poor Condition of your petitioner into your Considerations and be pleased to order that your poor & humble petitioner and wife may have a small habitation provided by the Said Parish of St Margarett that your petitioner may lye noe more out of doors And your Petitioner as in duty bound Shall ever pray for your worshipps etc.⟩

Anne Heggs, St Martin's, widow:
⟨Humbly Sheweth unto your worshipps That your poor & humble petitioner is of the age of Threescore and Nine yeares and upwards and has bin & now is very much afflicted by sicknes and distempers that your petitioner is troubled with whereby your poor petitioner through old age and Affliction is not able to gett any thing towards a lively hood. And your poor & humble petitioner is allowed by the said Parish but fourteen pence a weeke which is soe small an Allowance for one in soe poor & sickly Condition that poor petitioner will be lost for want of maintenance not being able to wash & order herselfe but what she hires to be done out of the said Fourteen pence a weeke, And further Sheweth unto your worshipps that your petitioner has bin severall times with Mr John Cooper the present Overseer of the poor of the said Parish of St Martin to Crave some thing of a better weekly allowance but all to noe purpose which makes your poor petitioner give your worshipps this trouble, And all that your poor & humble petitioner does Crave, to make your petitioners weekely allowance four pence a weeke more & that the same may be continued & to allow your poor petitioner some money to buy her a few Coles or otherwise your petitioner will be starved to death in winter & humbly beggs that your worshipps will be pleased to order the same, And by soe doeing your poor & humble petitioner as in duty bound Shall Ever pray for your worshipps etc.⟩

55.5   *Sacramental Certificates*
St Martin's   Edward Hood, Mayor
               Alderman William Goadby
               Thomas Bradley, Coroner
               William Bunney, Coroner
               Humphrey Chapman, Chamberlain
               Thomas Ayre, Chamberlain
               John Earpe, Common Councillor
               Thomas Goodrich, Common Councillor
In the handwriting of John Boley, Town Clerk, a list of the above, followed by the note: ⟨You need not untie them but turn them over one after another as Mr Cart & Mr Lee have signed them And then subscribe 'em yourselfes.⟩
Oath of Allegiance and Abjuration signed by them all.

56.1   *Writ of Summons*
               Dated 3 October 1709 for 9 January 1709/10.

56.2   *Constables' Presentments*
Six Constables present "omnia bene".

Nicholas Swingler (Ald. Ayres Ward) presents Thomas Noble for ⟨a causeway at his back gate along the Garden and the friers for not keeping it in repair & sweeping it clean⟩.   Indicted.

Gabriel Newton (Ald. Woodlands Ward) presents Samuel Holmes, Edward Mosely and John Brookes for ⟨driveing & useing water Carts with Iron bound Wheeles within the said Burrough⟩.   Indicted.

William Bellamy (Ald. Westons Ward) presents Henry Colson, sen., for ⟨not carrying away the Manneur before his Door⟩, and Thomas Richmond for ⟨not carrying away a Muckhill lying before his Door⟩.   Indicted.

56.3 *Removal Order*
John Stinson and his wife to be removed from St Margaret's to St Martin's, 8 December 1709.   ⟨This ordered confirmed.⟩

57a.1 *Writ of Summons*
Sessions held 17 April 1710. No writ survives.

57a.2 *Discharged Recognizances*
Leonard Burton, labourer, to appear and obey the Court *re* the bastard child of Mary Scoffeild, Bishop's Fee.
Samuel Jacomb, fellmonger, Jane, his wife, and Mary Boss, widow, to appear and obey the Court.
Thomas Chapman, hosier, to appear and obey the Court.
Osee Wagstaffe, widow, to appear and obey the Court.

57a.3 *Indictment*
John Jones, labourer, for trading as a tallow chandler unapprenticed.

57b.1 *Writ of Summons*
Dated 17 April 1710 for 2 October 1710.

57b.2 *Constables' Presentments*
Ten Constables present "omnia bene".

57b.3 *Discharged Recognizances*
John Withers, blacksmith, to appear and obey the Court and keep the peace towards Widow Hartshorne.
Henry Dawson, tailor, to appear and obey the Court ⟨concerning his refusing to Submitt to the ordinances of the Taylors trade⟩.

John Page, whitesmith, to appear and obey the Court concerning Thomas Page, his apprentice.

William Baker, labourer, to appear and obey the Court and keep the peace towards William White.

Simon Allen, woolcomber, to appear and obey the Court.

57b.4   *Conviction*

William Goadby, jun., maltster, for ⟨prophanely swearing two Oaths⟩.

57b.5   *Petition*

Mary Mason, widow:

⟨Humbly Sheweth unto your worshipps That your petitioners husband hath bin dead for two yeares & a halfe last past and left your poor & humble petitioner with four Children and some of them small not able to gett their Liveings And alsoe Sheweth unto your worshipps That the Overseers of the Parish of St Martins in the said Burrough hath paid your petitioners rent for a yeare & halfe after her husbands death and now there is 3 quarters of a yeares rent for your poor & humble petitioners house to pay, the present Overseers of the said Parish doe refuse to grant a bill or order for the payment thereof which comes to 19s & 9d, And alsoe sheweth unto your worships That there was Fifteen pounds left to my four Children by their Grand mother but times being hard and Corne dear by the consent of my Children & rather then to be more burthensome to the Parish have called the same in to help to mainteyne my selfe & children your petitioner being almost 3 score yeares of age and can doe nothing now but knitt stockings & cannot gett above one penny a day thereby, NOW your poor & humble petitioner humbly desires of the Honorable Bench to order her said rent that is behind to be paid And alsoe to pay the same for the time to come and alsoe to allow her some weekely maintenance your petitioner being old & past her worke cannot subsist without what your worships please to order & by soe doeing your poor & humble petitioner shall Ever pray for your worships etc.⟩

57b.6   *Sacramental Certificates*

St Martin's   Thomas Bradley, Mayor
              Alderman Charles Tuffley
              Thomas Helmsley, Coroner
              William Goadby, Coroner
              John Newton, Chamberlain
              Richard Wilson, Chamberlain
              Richard Jordan, Common Councillor
              Gabriel Newton, Common Councillor

Oath of Allegiance and Abjuration signed by them all.

57b.7 *Removal Order*

John Hunt to be removed from St Mary's to St Nicholas', 13 May 1710. ⟨This order vacated.⟩

58.1 *Writ of Summons*

Dated 9 April 1711 for 1 October 1711.

58.2 *Prisoner*

Mary Cox

58.3 *Constables' Presentments*

Five Constables present "omnia bene".

58.4 *Indictment*

Thomas Hall, Joseph Earp, John Astwell, John Worthington, Charles Wagstaff, Charles Preston, Richard Jordan, John Groce, Thomas Johnson, Joseph Atkins and Richard Tompson, Constables, ⟨for not presenting the streets within their severall Wards (being in the Queen's high way) the same being very much out of Repair & greatly decayed to the Annoyance of her Majesties Liege People that pass that way with their Carriages etc & for other offences & misdemeanors in neglecting their severall offices as Constables⟩; John Coates, sen., baker, John Coates, jun., baker, Joseph Atkins, baker, Thomas Goodrich, baker, William Tayler, baker, and John Turvill, Abbey Gate, ⟨for defect in the Weight of their bread the same being much lighter than Assised Bread by the Statute according to the rate of Corn⟩; and John Haslock, Beaumont Leys, ⟨for Encroaching upon the Queens high way with a pair of Gates & an hedge by him erected & now standing near or adioining to the South end of St Sunday's bridge the same being an annoyance to her Majesties Liege People that pass that way and within the said Burrough⟩.

58.5 *Discharged Recognizances*

Edward Moseley, jun., labourer, to appear.

Thomas Kirke, Syston, Leics., butcher, to appear and obey the Court *re* charges to be made against him.

William Beaumont, carpenter, to appear.

Pettit West, miller, to appear and ⟨preferr or cause to be preferred one or more Bill or Bills of Indictment against Mary Cox Spinster for the stealing & takeing and takeing away out of a Chest in the house of the said Pettit West two Shillings and two pence of the money of the said Pettit West And do prosecute the same with effect⟩.

58.6 *Sacramental Certificates*

St Mary's Edmund Johnson, Mayor
John Cooper, Coroner
Charles Tuffley, Coroner
Thomas Lambert, Chamberlain
Thomas Gamble, Chamberlain
John Duckett, ironmonger, Common Councillor
Godfrey Barrodale, mercer, Common Councillor
Oath of Allegiance and Abjuration signed by them all.

59.1 *Writ of Summons*
Dated 1 October 1711 for 28 April 1712.

59.2 *Constables' Presentments*
Seven Constables present "omnia bene".

Joseph Earp (Ald. Willkins Ward) presents ⟨the mayor ballis and Borgis of the borow of Leicester for the Cosey Leiding to the Chapill Close being the markit Rode being brokin up and out of Repare and the Cosey In the grange lane being brokin up and out of repear⟩, Mary Broune ⟨for her Cosee befor hear door being brokin up and out of repear⟩, and Ann Heyes for the same. Ignored.

Charles Preston (Ald. Abneys Ward) presents the Mayor, Bailiff and Burgesses of Leicester ⟨for not repairing the Cawse way att the uper End of Gallotree gatte within this Burrough the same being much out of repair⟩. Ignored.

John Groce (Ald. Cradocks Ward) presents Anne Coates, widow, Job Bentley, innholder, Sarah Smith, widow, John Jackson, innholder, Elizabeth Tompson, widow, and Joseph Burstall, butcher, ⟨for uttering & selling Ale within the said Ward & within the said Burrough in vessells not stamped or Marked to be of the Content of a full Ale Quart or Pint according to her Majesty's Standard and contrary to the Laws in that Case provided⟩. Indicted.

Richard Thompson (Ald. Ludlams Ward) presents the Mayor, Bailiffs and Burgesses of Leicester ⟨for the pavement in St Via's gate and Church gate⟩. Ignored.

59.3 *Discharged Recognizances*
Edward Biddle, blacksmith, to appear and obey the Court and keep the peace towards Thomas Parsons, combmaker.
Elizabeth, wife of Edward Biddle, to appear and obey the Court and keep the peace towards Thomas Parsons.

Elizabeth Biddle, spinster, to appear and obey the Court and keep the peace towards Thomas Parsons.

Richard Dalby, labourer, to appear and obey the Court *re* charges to be made against him.

Thomas Parsons, combmaker, to appear and obey the Court *re* charges to be made against him.

James Bainbrigg, labourer, to appear and obey the Court *re* charges to be made against him.

John Coates, jun., baker, to appear and obey the Court *re* charges to be made against him.

William Clements, woolcomber, to appear and answer charges and obey the Court.

George Gee, South Kilworth, Leics., weaver, to appear and obey the Court *re* charges to be made against him.

Edward Biddle to appear and obey the Court.

Elizabeth, wife of Edward Biddle, to appear and obey the Court *re* charges to be made against her.

Elizabeth Biddle, spinster, to appear and obey the Court *re* charges to be made against her.

John Biddle, labourer, to appear and obey the Court *re* charges to be made against him.

Thomas Helmsley, gent., to appear and obey the Court *re* charges to be made against him.

William Page, hatter, to appear and obey the Court *re* charges to be made against him.

Samuel Cart, jun., gent., to appear and obey the Court *re* charges to be made against him.

Isaac Norris, brazier, to appear and obey the Court *re* charges to be made against him.

William Staples, plumber, to appear and obey the Court *re* charges to be made against him.

The wife of John Cox, woolcomber, to appear and obey the Court *re* charges to be made against her.

Henry West, gardener, to appear and obey the Court *re* charges to be made against him.

60.1 *Writ of Summons*
Dated 20 April 1712 for 6 October 1712.

60.2 *Constables' Presentments*
Nine Constables present "omnia bene".

William Sutton (Ald. Wilkins Ward) presents the Mayor, Bailiffs and

Burgesses of Leicester ⟨for the Cosey being the marcket rode that leds from the chappel close to the town being brocken up and out of repayr⟩. Ignored.

John Hastwell (Mr Mayors Ward) presents the Mayor, Bailiffs and Burgesses of Leicester ⟨for the Causway in Sanvey gate and Church gate being out of Repare⟩. Indicted.

60.3 *Discharged Recognizances*

Thomas Pochin, gent., to appear and obey the Court *re* the bastard child of Joyce Williams.

Anne Tayler, widow, to appear and obey the Court *re* charges to be made against her.

Edward Loasby, weaver, to appear.

Alice, wife of Thomas Green, labourer, to appear and obey the Court *re* charges to be made against her.

Thomas Darbyshire, framework-knitter, to appear and obey the Court *re* charges to be made against him.

Robert Brown, framework-knitter, to appear.

John Foxton, framework-knitter, to appear.

Richard Coleman, framework-knitter, to appear and keep the peace towards William Squire.

George Skellett, bricklayer, to appear and keep the peace towards Elizabeth, his wife.

60.4 *Petition*

Francis Lewin, John Denshier, Robert Headley, John Cooke and John Bellamy, butchers, sub-tenants of Twiggs Pilgrim for the shops and stalls in the Market Place:

⟨Humbly sheweth to your Worshipps that whereas by an order made at the last Sessions of the Peace held for this Burrough upon a mocion made by Twiggs Pilgrim tenant to the Corporacion for all the Shambles etc that the Subtenants to the Shopps etc might be severally taxed to the Church & Poor according to the Rates they severally pay for the same And your Peticioners or any of them haveing no notice of any such mocion to shew reasons why such taxes should not be charged upon them the said mocion was heard & an order made accordingly. Now So it is that your Peticioners are tenants to the said Pilgrim for the Shopps etc at a certain Rent which is now paid & for Ages Past hath been paid for the same And the Corporacion thinking those Rents sufficient have tyed the said Twiggs Pilgrim by a Covenant in his Lease not to raise any of them And the more to secure him from doing of it a Schedule of the Rents is annexed to the Lease to which your Peticioners referr And humbly lay before your worshipps what an

71

hardshipp it will be upon your Peticioners to bear such taxes their present Rents being now too high and contrary to the Covenant made by Mr Pilgrim And the great trouble the Officers will have to gather such taxes The premisses considered Your Peticioners hope for your redress And your Peticioners as in duty bound shall ever pray etc.⟩

Order referred to in the Butchers' petition:

⟨It is Ordered by this Court that Twigges Pilgrim ([who was] Assessed for the Stall's Scituate within the Shambles & Elsewhere within the Saturday Markett in the Assesments & Levy's made for the Parish Church And for the Releif of the Poor of the Parish of Saint Martin in the said Burrough) shall not at any time hereafter be taxed rated or assessed in any Assesments or Levy's to be made by the said Parish of Saint Martin either for the Church or Poor But that the Subtenants of the said Twiggs Pilgrim shall be taxed rated and Assessed in all Subsequent & future Levy's & Assesments for their Severall Stalls in the said Shambles & Saturday Markett And that the said Twigges Pilgrim shall give an Account to the Parishioners of the said Parish at a Generall Meeting of the said Parishioner's for raising & Assessing the Rates aforesaid of the names of Each & every of his Sub-tenants aforesaid whose said names shall hereafter be inserted in the said Assesments & Levy's And the summes charged on them for each and every their said Stalls shall be sett against their Severall and respective names And the same being lawfully taxed Rated & Assessed as aforesaid shall be (an Estreat Of the same being delivered to said Twigges Pilgrim) collected And Gathered upp by the said Twigges Pilgrim And the said Twigges Pilgrim to be accountable for the whole Summes by him Collected And to make due Payment of the same to the Overseers of the Poor or Collectors of the Poor's Rates for the said Parish for the time being And the said Overseer's or Collector's to Assist the said Twigges Pilgrim in Executing all such means as shall be needfull to Levy the same. At Sessions held 6th October. 1712. this order quashed.⟩

60.5	*Sacramental Certificates*
St Martin's	John Cooper, Mayor
	Alderman Matthew Judd
	Alderman William Wells
	Alderman William Hammond, Coroner
	Alderman Roger Lee, Coroner
	Edward Bracebridge, jun., Chamberlain
	Thomas Ludlam, Chamberlain
	Edward Noone, Common Councillor
	William Lewin, Common Councillor
	George Bent, jun., Common Councillor
	Henry Palmer, Common Councillor

Henry Payn, Common Councillor
William Cooke, Common Councillor
St Mary's   Alderman Robert Winfield
Oath of Allegiance and Abjuration signed by them all.

60.6   *Debtor*

Order to the Bailiff of Leicester to produce John Shilton, a prisoner, at Sessions so that he may be discharged under an Act for the Relief of Insolvent Debtors.
Certificate to John Wood, one of John Shilton's creditors, informing him of Shilton's coming discharge.
⟨A schedule of all the Estate goods Effects & debts belonging or oweing to John Shilton prisoner in her Majesties goale for the Burrough of Leicester. Estate He Saith He hath none nor any goods Effects or debts than as herein after is Expressed.

	s	d
Imprimis From Joyce Wallins of the Burrough of Leicester in the County of Leicester widow two shillings . . .	2	0
Item 2 from Humphrey Plumbtree of the Burrough of Leicester aforesaid tanner five shillings	5	0
Item 3 from Robert Pulin of the Bishopps Fee near the Burrough of Leicester aforsaid victular nine shillings	9	0
Summe totall	16	0⟩

60.7   *Removal Order*

John Billing and Sarah, his wife, to be removed from St Martin's to St Nicholas', 4 July 1712.   ⟨Upon heareing Councell on both sides this order was vacated & is by the Court vacated.⟩

61.1   *Writ of Summons*
                    Dated 6 October 1712 for 13 April 1713.

61.2   *Constables' Presentments*
Nine Constables present "omnia bene".

John Hastwell (Mr Mayors Ward) presents Henry Eatherington ⟨For not haveing his pavement before his house in repair it being much out⟩. Ignored.

John Jackson (Ald. Cradocks Ward) presents John Mawson for ⟨That part of Blue Bore Lane in the said Warde it Being very Dirty & the Pavement much out of repair against the house of the said John Mawson in the said Burrough⟩.   Ignored.

61.3   *Discharged Recognizances*

Mary, wife of William Handy, tailor, to appear and obey the Court *re* charges to be made against her.

William Marshall, hosier, to appear and obey the Court *re* charges to be made against him.

Henry Heaford, hosier, to appear and obey the Court *re* charges to be made against him.

John Worth, yeoman, to appear and obey the Court *re* charges to be made against him.

John Noone, baker, to appear and obey the Court *re* charges to be made against him.

Richard Marler, butcher, to appear and obey the Court *re* charges to be made against him and keep the peace towards Stephen Pool, his apprentice.

Nathaniel Norris, woolcomber, to appear and obey the Court *re* charges to be made against him *re* the bastard child of Elizabeth Holland, St Margaret's, singlewoman.

David Clay, ironmonger, to appear and obey the Court and keep the peace towards Elizabeth Johnson, widow.

Thomas Hall, innholder, to appear and obey the Court *re* charges to be made against him and keep the peace towards Frances, wife of Roger Lewin, butcher.

Samuel Marshall, woolcomber, to appear and obey the Court *re* charges to be made against him concerning James Allen, his apprentice.

Thomas Bradsworth, innholder, to appear and obey the Court *re* charges to made against him ⟨concerning his Refusing to Pay the Summe charged upon him towards the setting down a Pump in Mr Alderman Wilkin's Ward in the said Burrough by vertue of an Order of Session's⟩.

George Couzens, woolcomber, to appear and obey the Court *re* charges to be made against him of assault on Mary Wilson, spinster.

John Coates, jun., innholder, to appear and obey the Court *re* charges to be made against him and keep the peace towards Rebecca, wife of James Thornton, labourer.

John Kellett, bricklayer, to appear and obey the Court *re* charges to be made against him *re* the bastard child of Sarah Walker, St Mary's, singlewoman.

Alice, wife of John Schooley, carpenter, to appear and obey the Court *re* charges to be made against her.

John Davy, Bishop's Fee, labourer, to appear.

61.4   *Presentment*

⟨Wee whose names are here subscribed beg leave to acquaint you, that wee hear that Mr John Farmer for his own private advantage is endeavouring to fill up an Antient Well in the Gallowtree gate Street, in Mr Alderman

Hood Ward, which would be to the great prejudice of us the Inhabitants not haveing wells. Wee humbley request that the Said Well may be kept open & continued usefull for the bennefit of the Said Ward, as alsoe it may be further usefull in case of fire being in soe convenient a place in the Street.

Henry Vollentine	Thomas Penford	Robert Lord
Robert Rowlston	Samuel Tuckwell	[blank] Cramp
William Medburn	Edward Caulton	William Davie
Anthony Barton	Edward Biddle	John Clay
Edward Brightman	Thomas Parsons	Francis Fish
W. Slater	John [P]rice	Charles Wellinger⟩

61.5 *Indictment*

Robert Johnson, framework-knitter, for assaulting Anne Morris.

61.6 *Sacramental Certificate*

St Margaret's   John Farmer, Attorney-at-Law
Oath of Allegiance and Abjuration signed by him.

61.7 *Debtors*

Copy of *The London Gazette* for 3–7 March 1712/13, containing a notice that Thomas Hitchcock, Joshua Kirk, Thomas Goodrich and James Lepington, prisoners in Leicester Gaol, will, at the next Quarter Sessions, be discharged under the Act for the relief of insolvent debtors.

Order to the Bailiff to bring Thomas Hitchcock to the Quarter Sessions so that he may be discharged.
⟨A Schedule of all the Estate Goods Effects and debts belonging or oweing to Thomas Hitchcocke prisoner in the Goale for the Burrough of Leicester delivered at Easter Sessions held for the said Burrough anno Domini 1713 Estate he Saith he hath none nor any goods Effects or debts than as herein-after is Expressed

	£ s d
Imprimis from Theophilus Tebbs of Stamford in the County of Lincolne Laborer Thirty Shillings	1 10 0
Item from William Appleby of Burton upon Trent in the County of Stafford Gardener nine Shillings . . .	9 0
Summe Totall	1 19 0⟩

Order to the Bailiff and Lucy Topotts, the Keeper of the Gaol, to bring Joshua Kirk to the Quarter Sessions so that he may be discharged, and a notice of his coming discharge to Elizabeth Norris and his other creditors.

⟨A Schedule of the Estate Goods and Chattells belonging or oweing to Joshua Kirk prisoner in the Goale for the Burrough of Leicester and are as Followeth (vizt)

Estate he saith he has none

due from Thomas Oliver of Anstey	10	10
Benjamin Claxton of the Burrough of Leicester . .	5	0
William Harris of the said Burrough hatter . . .	4	6
	1 0	4⟩

Order to the Bailiff and Lucy Topotts, the Keeper of the Gaol, to bring James Leppington to the Quarter Sessions so that he may be discharged, and a notice of his coming discharge to Henry Potter and Thomas Roberts and his other creditors.

⟨A Schedule of all the Estate Goods Effects or debts belonging or oweing to James Leppington prisoner in the Goale for the Burrough of Leicester delivered at Easter Sessions held for the Said Burrough of Leicester Anno Domini 1713

Estate he Saith he hath none nor any goods Effects or debts than as herein-after is Expressed

	£ s d
Imprimis from Mr Caunt of Melton Moberey in the County of Leicester.	10 0
Item from Mr Moore of Kettleby in the Said County of Leicester	12 0
Item from Mr Watts of Wikin in the Said County of Leicester	10 0
Summe Total	1 12 0⟩

61.8   *Bastardy Orders*

Nathaniel Norris, hosier, having been adjudged the father of the bastard girl of Elizabeth Holland, St Margaret's, singlewoman, upon the evidence of Elizabeth and of the midwife, Mary Waggott, is ordered to pay a weekly maintenance of 1s. 6d. for the child until she is 10 years old, and then £4 for her apprenticeship.

John Kellett, bricklayer, having been adjudged the father of the bastard boy of Sarah Walker, St Mary's, singlewoman, is ordered to pay a weekly maintenance of 1s. for the child until he is 10 years old, and then £4 for his apprenticeship.

62.1   *Writ of Summons*
Dated 13 April 1713 for 5 October 1713.

62.2   *Constables' Presentments*

Eleven Constables present "omnia bene".

62.3   *Discharged Recognizances*

Joseph Hayes, Castle Yard, weaver, to appear and answer charges.

Mary, wife of John Maslin, Syston, Leics., to appear and answer charges.

Ann, wife of Joseph Hayes, to appear and answer charges of assault on Samuel Hall.

62.4   *Indictment*

Alice Pegg, widow, for trading as an upholder unapprenticed.

62.5   *Petitions*

William Lander, labourer:

⟨Humbly Sheweth That your peticioner Is a person of the age 69 years and in a manner [sick] and allowed only by the parish One Shilling by the weeke for his Subsistance and his wife being of Great Age can in noe manner assist him for maintenance Upon which your peticioner went into the Country to gett some Releife where one Thomas Lewitt mett with him One of the Overseers of the parish of All Saints in the Burrough of Leicester where he ordered him to be whipp'd And gave a shilling to see him soe Served Therefore your peticioner humbly Craves your Worshipps further Allowance for the better Support of your peticioner in order that he may not Travill the Country And Your Peticioner will ever pray etc.⟩

Hannah Tuffe, St Martin's, widow:

⟨Humbly Sheweth unto your worshipps That your poor and humble Petitioner is an Inhabitant belonging to the Parish of St Martin aforesaid and has been a poor Widdow this Nine yeares last past and is of the age of seaventy yeares and upwards and has lost the sight of one Eye by a fitt of fevor and has but a little sight of the other Eye soe that your poor and humble petitioner through old age badnes of sight and other Infirmityes is uncapable to gett a lively hood and maintenance and now cannot subsist without some Assistance from the said Parish And your poor petitioner has bin with the present Overseer of the said Parish by order from the worshipfull the Mayor to gett a little releife to help your poor and humble Petitioner in this her great wants but all to noe purpose for the present Overseer Mr Thomas Richmond doth refuse to assist & allow your poor Petitioner any maintenance in this her wants These are humbly to desire your worshipps to take the great necessity your poor petitioner is in into your considerations and order the said Parish to make your poor & humble Petitioner some allowance what your worshipps please to order that your poor petitioner be not pined & starved to death And your poor & humble petitioner shall ever pray for your worshipps etc.⟩

Mary Baxter, St Martin's, widow:
⟨Humbly Sheweth unto your worships That your Petitioner is a very poor Widdow and is very much disabled by the hands of God being struck with the dead Palsey soe that your petitioner hath lost the use of her limbs and is soe much disabled thereby that she is not able to gett soe much as a penny towards a lively hood & maintenance, And at the Sessions your worships were pleased to order your petitioner two shillings a weeke which they paid your poor petitioner for some time but Mr Cooper the late Mayor was pleased to take it off first to Eighteene pence a weeke and about Easter last to six pence a weeke and your petitioner has had noe more all summer then six pence a weeke whereby your petitioner has bin almost starved & pined, and about seaven weekes since which was the day & time that your worship the Recorder came to Towne the said Mr Cooper the late Mayor ordred the Overseer to allow your poor petitioner twelve pence a weeke which is soe small a maintenance that your petitioner cannot subsist with it to buy & provide victualls fuell and Clothes fuell & bread being now very dear & your Petitioner want shifts & Clothes to keepe her warme & shall be starved & pined to death this winter unless your worships will be pleased to order your poor & humble petitioner a better weekly maintenance And hopeing your worships will be pleased to consider a poor widdows Condition that is not able to gett one penny towards a lively hood & order her a better weekly maintenance & alsoe some necessaryes of Clothing to keep your poor & humble petitioner from being starved And your poor & humble Petitioner as in duty bound shall Ever pray for your worshipps etc.⟩

62.6   *Sacramental Certificates*
All Saints'   Arthur Noone, Mayor
              Alderman John Pratt, Coroner
              Joshua Goodrich, Coroner
              John Gutheridge, Chamberlain
              William Page, Chamberlain
              Thomas Johnson, Common Councillor
Oath of Allegiance and Abjuration signed by them all.

62.7   *Removal Order*
Anne Brookes, widow, to be removed from St Martin's to St Margaret's, 24 April 1713.   ⟨This ordered discharged.⟩

63.1   *Writ of Summons*
              Dated 5 October 1713 for 5 April 1714.

63.2   *Constables' Presentments*
Ten Constables present "omnia bene".

63.3   *Discharged Recognizances*

William Harris, hatter, to appear.

Thomas Hall, innholder, to appear.

Joseph Erpe, blacksmith, to appear and answer charges.

Dina, wife of Rowland Marler, butcher, to appear and answer charges.

Jacob Bottomley, blacksmith, to appear and answer charges.

Thomas Beasley, cordwainer, to appear.

63.4   *Presentment*

The Grand Jury present John Aslin, Edward Jones, William Frost, Henry Johnson, Thomas Moseby, Edward Barley, jun., Lemuel Leake and Widdow Wilson ⟨for that they & every of them severally have taken into their houses being private houses in this Burrough severall loose diss-orderly and vagrant persons to the disturbance of the neighbourhood⟩, Thomas Orton, sen., Thomas Barnshaw and Joan Wood for keeping dis-orderly public houses, and ⟨the highway lying next Mr Nobles garden as being out of repair⟩.

63.5   *Case*

Indictments of William Harris, hatter, and Thomas Beasley, cordwainer, for remaining 4 hours drinking in the alehouse of Joan Wood, widow. Both guilty.

Examination of William Wood, joiner, taken 4 March 1713/14:

⟨This Examinant uppon his oath sayeth that in the Bgining of January last William Harris of the said Burrough Hatter Thomas Beasley of the same cordwaner came to his mother woods house a Publique house a bout 9 a clock at night & Finding their Edward veasey, satt doune with him to drinck a glass of Ale and that a bout 2 houers after one William Pollard a Barber comeing in, the said Harris asked him to let him blood, which he did, & that Harris called For A glass & dranck som of his blood mixed with Ale, & that Beasley allso was let blood & dranck som of it & that som time after, Pollard let him selfe blood & Harris Dranck som of it allso, he allso sayeth that the Pretenders name was mentioned in that Company by the said Harris, but he can not say or remember that Harris or any of the Company did Drink the pretenders health but he beleives Harris might aske the Company if any of them durst drinck that Health or words to that Effect.⟩

Examination of William Pollard, barber, taken 5 March 1713/14:

⟨This Examinant upon his Oath saith that about the 13th of January last between the hours of Eleven & Twelve at night he went into the house of widdow wood at the Naggs head & Starr in Leicester to light his Candle where he found the above named William Harris Thomas Beasley & Edward Vesey drinking of Ale & they desired this Examinant to sitt down with 'em which he accordingly And after some time William Harris asked this Examinant if he was a Barber & he told him no he was a Shafster Harris asked him to Shave him And this Examinant told him twas to late to do it that night then Harris asked him if he would blood him which this Examinant told him he would And Vesey told Harris he durst not be blooded and threw a Shilling upon the table & said he would give that to pay the Surgeon for bleeding and imediately Afterwards did bleed Harris and as Harris was bleeding he said to lett you know I dare be blooded give me a Glass & you shall see me drink my blood And a glass was brought & a little blood taken in the bottom [torn] was filled upp with Ale & Harris drank it but without menconing any health [torn] presently afterwards Thomas Beasley was blooded And had a Glass & drank [torn] his own blood with Ale as Harris had done before. And this Examinant saith that [torn] Harris he drank his own blood in imitacion of Rochester And Harris answered [torn] he would drink any body's and told this Examinant he would drink his And to [torn] Examinant did bleed him self & tooke some little in a Glass which was filled upp with Ale & Harris drank it.⟩

63.6 *Sacramental Certificate*

St Mary's   John Clayton, clerk
Oath of Allegiance and Abjuration signed by him.

63.7 *Removal Orders*

Thomas Hardy to be removed from St Martin's to St Margaret's, 24 November 1713.   ⟨This order quashed by the Court.⟩

Robert Bagnall and his wife to be removed from All Saints' to Mountsorrel, 13 January 1713/14.   ⟨This order confirmed by the Court.⟩

64.1 *Writ of Summons*

Dated 5 April 1714 for 4 October 1714.

64.2 *Oath of Allegiance and Abjuration*

Signed by: John Pares, Mayor   James Wyatt
John Spicer   William Hollis
John Cooper   John Lenton
Thomas Helmsley   William Perfect
William Goadby   Ralph Ford
John Denshier   Henry Digges
Richard Wightman   Thomas Rice
Richard Jordan   James Guy
Joshua Goodrich   James Metcalfe
John Boley, Town Clerk   Thomas Griffiths
Humphrey Blowers   Jos. Ebrall
J. Gallimore   Francis Fish

64.3 *Discharged Recognizances*

William Harris, hatter, to appear.

Richard Tayler, woolcomber, to appear.

Rebecca, wife of James Thornton, labourer, to appear.

Hannah Harrison, spinster, to appear.

Mary Worth to appear.

Saul Broadhurst, tailor, to appear.

Henry Dawson, tailor, to appear.

Thomas Cartwright, framework-knitter, to appear.

64.4 *Presentments*

The Grand Jury present Constables Joshua Goodrich of Ald. [blank]'s Ward, Samuel Belton, woolcomber, of Ald. Brookesby's Ward, John Hartell of Ald. Johnson's Ward, James Orton, innholder, of Ald. Annis' Ward, Joseph Bunney of Ald. Cradock's Ward, William Duick, woolcomber, of Ald. Townsend's Ward, Edward Harrison of Ald. Wilkins' Ward, Edward Caulton, upholder, of Ald. Hood's Ward, Jonathan Ross, tailor, of Ald. Ayre's Ward, and John Lawrence, woolcomber, of Ald. Bradley's Ward, ⟨for that they and every of them severally & respectively have neglected their & every of their severall & respective duties in the Execucion of their severall & respective offices as Constables of the severall wards aforesaid in this Burrough in not presenting severall offences & matters presentable (as appeared to us upon our own view) in their several & respective Wards in this Burrough in the great neglect of their & every of their severall & respective duties and offices.⟩

The Grand Jury present Widow Worrall ⟨for makeing & continueing a Nusance against her house in the Highe Street in the said Burrough in the Kings high way by laying of trees and blockes in the said open Street to the hindrance & damage of Passengers with their Carts & Carriages And to the great prejudice of his Majesties Leige People⟩, Mary Brown, widow, Elizabeth Winters, widow, Widow Wells, and Richard Mawson, the Magazine, gent., ⟨for that they & every of them have neglected to pave the Streets against their severall & respective houses in the said Burrough the same being very much out of repair And belonging to them severally & respectively to repair⟩, Benjamin Hunt, cooper, ⟨for breaking the Pound in & belonging to the said Burrough of Leicester and takeing thence his Cattle impounded⟩, and Samuel Holmes, labourer, Edward Mosely, jun., labourer, and James Tucker, labourer, ⟨for that they and every of them have severally & respectively broken upp & damaged the pavements in severall streets in the said Burrough with their severall & respective Carts or Carriages with water commonly called Burn Carts by drawing the same with Iron bound wheels contrary to Law & the By Laws of this Burrough⟩.

Endorsement:
⟨24 of June 1714 William Blackwell there Sworn that his last legall Settlement was at Great Peatlin where he was hired for & lived one yeare with Robert Hull & received a yeares wages. Thomas Kilby Swore his Settlement in St Martins. Presentment Session 4 of October 1714 John Crooke turn'd over to Conyers White lived about 3 yeare and halfe there & then his master removed to St Martins where the Apprentice lived the remainder of his Apprenticeship which was from Mayday till about 3 weekes before Xmas.⟩

64.5   *Indictments*

William Slater, jun., woolcomber, for assaulting Richard Tayler.

Richard Tayler, woolcomber, for assaulting William Slater, jun.

William Davie, innholder, and Mary, wife of George Worth, cordwainer, for assaulting Mary, wife of John Pierce.

John Peace, cordwainer, for assaulting William Davey.

64.6   *Sacramental Certificates*

St Margaret's   John Pare, Mayor
                 John Boley, Town Clerk and Clerk of the Peace
                 Alderman John Denshire
                 Alderman William Goadby, Coroner
                 Richard Weightman, Coroner
                 Richard Jordane, Chamberlain
                 Joshua Goodrich, Common Councillor
                 Captain Humphrey Blowers
St Martin's   Alderman John Willows
                 Alderman Thomas Bradley
                 Alderman John Cooper
                 Alderman Thomas Hemsley, Coroner
                 Francis Fish, Common Councillor

64.7   *Removal Order*

Robert Brown and family to be removed from St Mary's to St Margaret's, 15 June 1714.   ⟨This order Confirmed.⟩

65.1   *Writ of Summons*

Dated 4 October 1714 for 25 April 1715.

65.2   *Constables' Presentments*

Four Constables present "omnia bene".

Samuel Belton (Ald. Brucksbeys Ward) presents John Harison ⟨for not Reparing his Cosway belongin to his house⟩.   Indicted.

John Hartell (Ald. Johnsons Ward) presents Thomas Ayers ⟨For nott Reparing the pavment att his Back door⟩.   Indicted.

Joseph Bunney (Ald. Cradock's Ward) presents ⟨the Drane or Watter Course Running under Mr Alderman Johnson house⟩.   Indicted.

Edward Harris (Ald. Wilkins Ward) presents Thomas Hall, Thomas Ward and William Suthell ⟨for marter lying in the sough gate streete⟩.

John Lawrance (Ald. Bradles Ward) presents ⟨the Cosway Lieng Against Mr Nobells Wall⟩.   Indicted.

65.3   *Discharged Recognizances*
Joseph Needham, Syston, Leics., butcher, to appear.
William Burton, Great Glen, Leics., butcher, to appear.
Thomas Briggs, labourer, to appear.
John Worthington, framework-knitter, to appear.
John Bodycott, miller, to appear.
Edward Hewett, framesmith, to appear.
Joseph Coates, baker, to appear.
Daniel Coates to appear.
William Harris, hatter, to appear.
Barbara, wife of John Ravenscroft, innholder, to appear.
John Noone, baker, to appear.
John Turvill, the Woodgate, baker, to appear.
Henry Smith, baker, to appear.

65.4   *Indictment*
Henry Smith, baker, John Noon, baker, and John Turvile, baker, for assaulting Thomas Johnson and damaging his periwig.   Case against Noon and Turvile ignored.

65.5   *Sacramental Certificates*
St Margaret's John Gallimore, Supervisor of Excise
               John Lenton, Supervisor of the Duty on Houses and
               Hides etc.
               William Hollis, Officer of the Duty on Hides etc.
               Josiah Ebrall, Gauger
               Thomas Griffiths, Gauger
               James Metcalfe, Gauger
               James Guy, Gauger
               James Wyatt, Gauger
               Ralph Ford, Gauger
               Thomas Rice, Gauger
               William Perfect, Gauger
               Henry Diggs, Gauger

65.6   *Removal Order*

John Squire to be removed from St Nicholas' to St Mary's, 29 December 1714. 〈confirmed〉

67.1   *Writ of Summons*

Dated 25 April 1715 for 3 October 1715.

67.2   *Discharged Recognizances*

Robert Hartshorne to appear and answer charges.

John Duckett, ironmonger, to appear and answer charges.

James Wood, silkweaver, to appear and answer charges.

Francis Fish, innholder, to appear and prosecute Samuel Stanley, labourer, for the felony of 2 geese.

Mary Darvell to appear and give evidence against Samuel Stanley for a felony.

67.3   *Sacramental Certificates*

St Martin's   Francis Lewin, Mayor
                Thomas Jordaine, Town Clerk and Clerk of the Peace
                Simon Martin, Chamberlain
                Benjamin Gutheridge, Chamberlain
                Joseph Bunney, Common Councillor
                William Brushfeild, Common Councillor
                Daniel Alcock, Common Councillor
                Captain Marcellus Laroon
                Captain David Marttell
                Lieutenant John Leighton
                Lieutenant Richard Grigson
                Lieutenant Robert Bransby
                Quarter-master Francis Gumbleton
                Quarter-master William Wallis
                Quarter-master Thomas Comings
                Quarter-master Daniel Garritts
                Quarter-master William Forrest
                Cornet Paul Stephen Husson
                Cornet George Barnard
                Cornet Henry Durell
                Cornet Tristram Stafford
                Cornet Andrew Robinson

St Mary's   Joshua Goodrich, sen.
                John Denshire

Oath of Allegiance and Abjuration signed by them all.

68.1   *Writ of Summons*

Dated 3 October 1715 for 13 January 1715/16.

68.2   *Oath of Allegiance and Abjuration*

Signed by: F. Lewin, Mayor

Edmund Johnson	Thomas Johnson
Arthur Noone	R. Turvile
Thomas Noble	William Topp
Edward Hood	E. Bracebridge
Robert Lees	John Gutheridge
Nathaniel Wright	Humphrey Chapman
William Hammond	John Newton
John Hungerford	Francis Coultman
T. Palmer, sen.	John Dawson
Thomas Bartishaw	Richard Wightman
Thomas Palmer, jun.	Thomas Jordaine
Thomas Lambert	Richard Townsend
Thomas Gamble	Simon Marten
William Page	Benjamin Gutheridge
Richard Roberts	George Bent, jun.
G. Barrodall	Thomas Orme
Joshua Goodrich	Thomas Ayre, jun.
Edward Noone	Thomas Willeas
John Earp	Samuel Simpson
Thomas Topp	James Norris
John Willows	Robert Headley
Charles Tuffley	John Lewin
John Pratt	Joseph Coates
Augustine Heafford	John Street
William Cooke	Edward Biddle
William Brushfield	John Hercourt
Daniel Alcock	William Cooke
Thomas [damaged]	Thomas Skeath
John Nickols	John Foxon
Thomas [damaged]	Robert Herricke
Michael Shipton	John Hackett, Curate of
William Wickes	All Saints'
Richard Goodfellow	John Clayton, Clerk
Thomas Turvile	Samuel Elly, Clerk
John Tufley	Thomas Adcock
Charles Goddard	Thomas Gee
John Topott	J. Greene
Simon Barwell	John Brookes upon his
	affirmacion being a quaker

Joshua Goodrich
John Denshier
Henry Treene
Thomas Davye
Gabriel Newton
Henry Smith
R. Reignolds
Francis Thickpeny
John Brokesby
James Annis
Robert Winfeild
John Payne
Joseph Bunney
John Kilbie, Vicar of
   St Margaret's
Edward Palmer
Thomas Ayre
Thomas Bradley
John Ayre
William Lewin
Samuel Carte, Vicar of
   St Martin's
William Fox, Vicar of
   St Mary's

Henry Palmer
Henry Payne
William Wells
Thomas Ward
John Abney, Curate of
   St Nicholas'
Jonathan Buckerfield
Edmund Cradock, sen.
Nathaniel Tyler
David Deakins
Thomas Standly
Richard Barrodall
Samuel Caulton
William Bass
Samuel Wood
Joseph Wilson
William Pollard
William Davey
John Harison
David Vallintine
Robert Harbrorn
Humphrey Blowers
George Anderson,
   Confrater

68.3   *Discharged Recognizances*

Benjamin Mugleston to appear and answer John Chiswell, mercer, for embezzling his goods.

John Chiswell, mercer, to appear and prosecute Benjamin Mugleston ⟨for Conveying away & Imbezzleing his goods and Lending his Money⟩.

William Harris, haberdasher, to appear and answer John Chiswell ⟨for receiveing goods from his Servant unknowne to the said John Chiswell⟩.

Ruth, wife of Richard Mason, to appear and answer charges to be made by John Chiswell, mercer, of ⟨receiveing goods from his Servant unknowne to the Said John Chiswell⟩.

Elizabeth, wife of John Campion, labourer, to appear and answer John Chiswell ⟨for receiveing Goods from his Servant unknowne to the said John Chiswell⟩.

Katherine, wife of George Rowe, gardener, to appear and answer John Chiswell, mercer, for receiving goods from his servant without his knowledge.

68.4 *Sacramental Certificate*

All Saints'   Robert Warbutton
Oath of Allegiance and Abjuration signed by him.

69.1 *Writ of Summons*

Dated 10 March 1716 for 9 April 1716.

69.2 *Constable's Presentment*

Richard Shipley (Ald. Bradleyes Ward) presents ⟨the parish [of] Saint Martins for a pavement that lyeth by Mr [torn]s walle over against the parrott for not being repaired⟩.

69.3 *Discharged Recognizances*

Elizabeth Orton, spinster, to appear and answer for the felony of a box of wares and merchandise from Joshua Steers.

Anne Orton, spinster, to appear and answer for selling goods supposed to be stolen from Joshua Steers.

Joshua Steers to appear and prosecute Elizabeth and Anne Orton for stealing and selling a box of wares.

John Wilkins, clockmaker, to appear and answer for ⟨not takeing the oaths to his Majestye⟩.

Thomas Roberts, innholder, to appear and answer for ⟨not takeing the oaths to his Majestye⟩.

Thomas Lewin, Syston, Leics., yeoman, to appear and answer for assaulting Francis Flude.

Francis Flude, North Kilworth, Leics., yeoman, to appear to prefer an indictment and give evidence against Thomas Lewin.

Abraham Banker, barber surgeon, to appear and answer charges to be made by Ann Windsor.

69.4 *Presentments*

The Grand Jury present Alderman Edward Hood and the Well Reeves ⟨for not keeping the well by the three Crownes in the said Mr Hoods ward in repaire the Same being now useless⟩, Thomas Gamble, Jonathan Gee, Joseph Large, and Benjamin Garland, Churchwardens and Overseers of St Martin's Parish, ⟨for not repaireing the Street or ground near the Dolphin in the Said Parish the Same being very much out of repaire⟩ and ⟨for not repaireing the pavement in the said Parish near the Parrott the Same being out of repaire⟩, and Joseph Hefford, John Noon, Edward Noon, and Thomas Willows, Churchwardens and Overseers of St Margaret's Parish, ⟨for not repaireing a Lane called Arch Deacon Lane in the said Parish the Same being out of repaire⟩.

The Grand Jury present Elizabeth Orton, spinster, for stealing a small metal box containing 20 yds caddis from Joshua Steeres, and Anne Orton, spinster, for being an accessary after the fact.   Ignored.

The Grand Jury present Elizabeth Orton, spinster, for stealing a flannel waistcoat, 3 linen aprons, and a pair of stockings from John Price.   Ignored.

69.5 *Removal Order*

James Freeston and Suzanna, his wife, to be removed from St Nicholas' to Burton Overy, 7 January 1715/16.   Discharged.

70.1 *Writ of Summons*

Dated 9 April 1716 for 1 October 1716.

70.2 *Discharged Recognizances*

Thomas Chamberlaine, gardener, to appear and answer charges.
Edward Groce, woolcomber, to appear and answer charges.
John Winkles, gardener, to appear and answer charges.
Edward Hewett, Bishop's Fee, framework-knitter, to appear and give evidence against John Loseby, Edward Groce, John Winkles, and Thomas Chamberlaine.

70.3 *Indictments*

The Inhabitants of St Margaret's Parish for not repairing Archdeacon Lane.

The Inhabitants of St Martin's Parish for not repairing the highway near Thomas Brace's house, 'The Dolphin'.

The Inhabitants of St Mary's Parish for not repairing Friar Lane.

70.4 *Sacramental Certificates*

St Margaret's   William Goadby, Mayor
Thomas Jordaine, Town Clerk and Clerk of the Peace
Alderman Thomas Ayre, Coroner
Augustine Heafford, Chamberlain
Thomas Orme, Chamberlain
John Noon, Common Councillor
Robert Lowe, Common Councillor
Joseph Kilbie, student at Emmanuel College, Cambridge
St Martin's   Humphrey Chapman, Coroner
Robert Hall, Common Councillor
John Cartwright, Common Councillor
Edward Bates, Common Councillor
Samuel Carte, jun., LL.B.
William Topp, gent.
St Mary's   Alderman John Wilkins
Oath of Allegiance and Abjuration signed by them all.

70.5 *Removal Orders*

John Morris, jersey-comber, Catherine, his wife, and Elizabeth, their daughter, to be removed from St Nicholas', Nottingham, to St Martin's, 26 July 1716.

John Morris, jersey-comber, Katherine, his wife, and Elizabeth, their daughter, to be removed from St Martin's to St Margaret's, 27 July 1716.

71.1 *Writ of Summons*
Dated 1 October 1716 for 29 April 1717.

71.2 *Prisoner*
William Wood

71.3 *Constables' Presentments*

Tobias Pickering (Ald. Willckins Ward) presents Widow Wells for not repairing the street belonging to her house, and John Jarvis for ⟨A Coman tresper In the Stretts with his Carts wagons and duingells⟩. Indicted.

George Fallowes (Ald. Noons Ward) presents Edward Noone, framework-knitter, John Astwell, John Hedley, John Lewitt, and Widow Scarbrough for not repairing the streets belonging to their houses. Indicted.

71.4 *Discharged Recognizances*

George Hartshorne, cordwainer, to appear to prosecute and give evidence against William Wood for the felony of 3 dressed calf skins.
William Hunt, butcher, to appear and answer charges.
John Martin, Whetstone, Leics., to appear and answer charges.
William Wrest, Fleckney, Leics., yeoman, to appear to prosecute and give evidence against John Martin for the felony of 2 strikes of barley.
Edward Paine, labourer, to appear and answer charges.

71.5 *Indictments*

William Wood, labourer, for stealing 3 dressed calf skins from George Hartshorne. Po se, guilty.

John Martin, Whetstone, Leics., baker, for stealing 2 strikes of barley from William Wrest. Po se, not guilty.

71.6 *Sacramental Certificate*
St Martin's   Thomas Brace, innholder
Oath of Allegiance and Abjuration signed by him.

71.7 *Removal Orders*
Ann, wife of Joseph Lee, to be removed from St Margaret's to Melbourne, Derbs., 7 January 1716/17.

E

Thomas White and his wife and family to be removed from St Nicholas' to All Saints', 17 January 1716/17.

72.1 *Writ of Summons*
Dated 6 October 1718 for 6 April 1719.

72.2 *Constables' Presentments*

John Leacey (Ald. Wilkins Ward) presents John Farmer for not mending the pavement against Mr Fox's house, Marmon Gee and Thomas Page for not mending the pavement by their houses, and John Hunt of Friar Lane and John Jarvis for leaving timber, wood, wagons, and carts in the streets. Indicted.

Thomas Bent (Ald. Tounsends Ward) presents Edward Holmes ⟨for keeping of An unLawfull house & Entertaing of tradesmen srvants att unLawfull times⟩. Indicted.

William Huftton (Ald. Annis Ward) presents John Hungorford for not repairing the causeway leading to his stable in Free School Lane, ⟨A Vatte from the presbiterian metting house which thay forse downe the Comon Shore In to Church Gate⟩, and John and Thomas Ludlam Co., partners, ⟨for their Tubbs and other said vesels standing in the cross to the anoyance of the market peeple upon wensday and friday markets⟩. Indicted.

Thomas Ward (Ald. Bradles Ward) presents George Chiselldine for not repairing the causeway by his house, and Mr Nedham for leaving his carts and wagons in the street. Indicted.

Stephen Bennett (late Ald. Jonsons Ward) presents ⟨the streets in My warde are in good repare⟩ and Samuel Newton for leaving his carts and wagons in the street. Indicted.

Thomas Garrett (Ald. Pars Ward) presents John Jackson for not repairing the causeway by his house. Indicted.

72.3 *Discharged Recognizances*

William Crawford, printer, to appear and answer charges.
Ann Johnson, spinster, to appear and give evidence against William Crawford for assault and abuse.
Thomas Springthorpe, woolcomber, to appear and answer charges.
Charles Fox, Burton Lazars, Leics., gardener, to appear and answer charges.
William Harris, hatter, to appear and answer charges.

72.4 *Indictments*

Thomas Springthorpe, woolcomber, for trading as a smith unapprenticed.

William Harris, haberdasher of hats, for assaulting Mary Coltman. Guilty.

72.5 *Sacramental Certificates*

All Saints'   John Brown, hosier
                Thomas Bent, fellmonger
St Martin's   Robert Anderson, clerk

Oath of Allegiance and Abjuration signed by them all.

72.6 *Removal Orders*

[Fragment] William Alsopp, Mary, his wife, and William and John, their children, to be removed from St Margaret's to St Martin's.

Thomas Brown and Agnes, his wife, to be removed from St Mary's to St Martin's, 23 March 1718/19. ⟨discharged⟩ Endorsement: ⟨Thomas Brown the Apprentice bound to Robert Brown his Brother by Indenture dated the 3d of October 1711 assigned over to [torn] Preston by an Indorsement on the said Indenture dated the 19th day of [torn].⟩

John Freestone, Sarah, his wife, and Elizabeth, their daughter, to be removed from St Margaret's to All Saints', 23 March 1718/19. ⟨discharged⟩

73.1 *Writ of Summons*

Sessions held 7 October 1745. No writ survives.

73.2 *Discharged Recognizances*

James Shearson, framework-knitter, to appear and answer charges *re* the bastard child of Elizabeth Turner, All Saints', singlewoman.
Amey Allen to appear and answer charges of assault on Ann, wife of Richard Sharpe, labourer.
Andrew Anderson, corporal, Maj.-Gen. Bragge's Regiment of Foot, to appear and answer charges *re* the bastard child of Sarah Hickling, widow.
Thomas Briggs, oatmeal man, to appear and answer charges of assaulting and threatening Jane Hardy.

73.3 *Sacramental Certificates*

St Martin's   Joseph Denshire, Mayor
                William Whatton, gent.
                William Higginson, gent.
                Robert Belton, gent.
All Saints'   Thomas Herricke, gent.
St Margaret's   Robert Hall, gent.

Oath of Allegiance and Abjuration signed by them all.

74.1   *Writ of Summons*
Dated 7 October 1745 for 13 January 1745/6.

75.1   *Writ of Summons*
Dated 14 July 1746 for 6 October 1746.

75.2   *Constable's Presentment*
Thomas Smith (Ald. Ludlams Ward) presents the Inhabitants of All
Saints' Parish for not repairing Bridewell Lane alias Corsby Lane.
Indicted.

75.3   *Presentment*
Samuel Simpson, Churchwarden of St Martin's, and Joseph Hall, Overseer of St Martin's, members of the Grand Jury, present Samuel Harrison,
gardener, ⟨for Lodgeing Strangers and Strolling People in his house
sictuate and being in the Parish aforesaid and for suffering more families
than one to dwell therein⟩.

75.4   *Indictment*
Samuel Harrison for keeping an illegal lodging house.

75.5   *Sacramental Certificates*
St Martin's   Thomas Topp, Mayor
                Thomas Phipps, gent.
                Thomas Marten, gent.
                Nicholas Throseby, tailor
                John Ward, barber
                John Westley, joiner
St Nicholas'   Joseph Newton, gent.
Oath of Allegiance and Abjuration signed by them all.

76.1   *Writ of Summons*
Sessions held 16 January 1746/7. No writ survives.

76.2   *Discharged Recognizances*
Arthur Watson, Belgrave, Leics., carpenter, to appear *re* his exercising his
trade within the Borough unfree.
Thomas Waine, innholder, and William Withers, butcher, to appear and
answer charges of assault on Benjamin Thorpe, butcher, at Thomas
Waine's house.
Thomas Taylor, victualler, to appear *re* the bastard child of Christian
Jones, widow, prisoner in Leicester Gaol.
Ann Roddle, singlewoman, to appear to prosecute and give evidence
against John Winsley, currier, for stealing a blue and white linen apron.

76.3   *Indictments*

The Inhabitants of All Saints' Parish for not repairing Bridewell Lane alias Corsby Lane.

John Winsley, currier, for stealing a blue and white linen apron from Ann Roddle.

John Winsley, currier, for stealing a holland shirt and 2 long neckcloths from Ellis Shipley, currier.

William Toone, labourer, for keeping an unlicensed alehouse.

77.1   *Writ of Summons*

Dated 16 January 1746/7 for 27 April 1747.

77.2   *Prisoner*

Mary Roberts

77.3   *Constable's Presentment*

Jonathan Simons (Ald. Hauckens Ward) presents Austen Heaford and Thomas Johson for putting rubbish in Millstone Lane.   Indicted.

77.4   *Indictment*

Mary Roberts for stealing a bundle of pictures from the shop of Thomas Marten, stationer.   Guilty.

78.1   *Writ of Summons*

Dated 13 July 1747 for 7 October 1747.

78.2   *Sacramental Certificates*

St Martin's   John Smalley, Mayor
              Thomas Marten, gent.
              Thomas Ludlam, gent.
              Samuel Olliver, innholder
              Samuel Brown, cutler
Oath of Allegiance and Abjuration signed by them all.

79.1   *Writ of Summons*

Dated 9 October 1747 for 11 January 1747/8.

79.2   *Constable's Presentment*

John Waring (Ald. Ludlam's Ward) presents ⟨the Lane Leading from the Town Goal to the Meeting House belonging to the Parish of All Saints⟩. Indicted.

79.3 *Indictment*

Francis Davis, farmer and grazier, for assaulting Robert Pull.

79.4 *Insolvency Assignment*

⟨Whereas Newton Chapman, late of the Burrough of Leicester Wool-Comber, A prisoner for Debt, and in Custody in the Goal for the said Burrough: On or about the third Day of October 1743, at the General Quarter Sessions of the peace, then held, in and for the said Burrough, Took the Benefit of the act of parliament, then lately passed, for the Relief of Insolvent Debtors, at Which time the said Newton Chapman, Delivered in his schedule, by him Signed, and otherwise Conformed to the Direction of the said act: Now We, whose hands are hereunder written, being the then Creditors of the said Newton Chapman (yet unpaid) Doe hereby apply for an assignment; and pray, that, by order of the next General Quarter Session of the peace, to be held, in and for the said Burrough, the Clerk of the peace in and for the said Burrough, may make an assignment, of the said Schedule, and all real, and personal Estate, therein mentioned, Unto Mr Robert Iliffe, and Elizabeth Orton, Two of the Undernamed Creditors; in Trust, for themselfes, and the rest of the said Creditors; as witness our hands, this Seventh Day of January In the year of our Lord, 1747.

> Robert Iliff
> Elizabeth Orton
> Mary Johnson
> Joseph Whattan
> Joseph Fossett⟩

80.1 *Writ of Summons*

Dated 18 April 1748 for 15 July 1748.

80.2 *Indictment*

The Inhabitants of All Saints' Parish for not repairing Bridewell Lane which runs from the Town Gaol to the Meeting House.

81.1 *Writ of Summons*

Dated 15 July 1748 for 3 October 1748.

81.2 *Indictments*

Mary Heaford for keeping an illegal lodging-house.

Humphrey Boot for keeping an illegal lodging-house.

Thomas Throseby, woolcomber, for keeping a dangerous black and white spaniel dog which bit William Brown in the leg.

81.3 *Sacramental Certificates*

St Martin's   Joseph Tayler, gent.
William Birstall, gent.
Samuel Simpson, gent.
Tyrringham Palmer
John Cooper

St Margaret's   Robert Hall, Mayor
Richard Beale
Henry Gutheridge
John Hunt Worrall

All Saints'   James Cooper
Edward Buswell

St Nicholas'   Edmund Johnson, gent.

Oath of Allegiance and Abjuration signed by them all.

82.1 *Writ of Summons*

Dated 3 October 1748 for 9 January 1748/9.

82.2 *Indictments*

Thomas Daft, yeoman, for trading as a clockmaker unapprenticed.

Thomas Tayler, victualler, and John Smith, Tilton, Leics., yeoman, for assaulting Thomas Franklin and imprisoning him for 6 hours.

83.1 *Writ of Summons*

Dated 9 January 1748/9 for 3 April 1749.

83.2 *Indictments*

Thomas Daft, yeoman, for trading as a clockmaker unapprenticed.

Thomas Dawson, tailor, William Dale, Sileby, Leics., framework-knitter, and John Ward, Sileby, Leics., framework-knitter, for assaulting Joseph Sanderson.

84.1 *Writ of Summons*

Dated 10 July 1749 for 6 October 1749.

84.2 *Discharged Recognizance*

Thomas Carr, woolcomber, to appear and obey the Court *re* his assault on Rachel Bird.

84.3 *Indictments*

Martha Sanders, widow, for stealing 3 pewter plates from Frances Bassett, widow.

Benjamin Thorpe, butcher, for assaulting Samuel Newton, jun.

Edward Veasey for keeping an unlicensed alehouse.

84.4 *Sacramental Certificates*
St Martin's   Thomas Phipps, Mayor
                John Winter, gent.
                Samuel Simpson, gent.
                John Wigley, hatter
                Anthony Ward
St Nicholas'   Joseph Newton, gent.
St Margaret's Richard Denshire, gent.
Oath of Allegiance and Abjuration signed by them all.

85.1 *Writ of Summons*
Dated 6 October 1749 for 8 January 1749/50.

85.2 *Discharged Recognizance*
John Baresby, barber and periwigmaker, to appear *re* the bastard child of
Elizabeth Hinman.

85.3 *Indictments*
John Holmes for keeping an illegal lodging-house.

William Gray for keeping an illegal lodging-house.

Thomas Carte, jun., Syston, Leics., yeoman, for trading as a butcher
unapprenticed.

Rowland Siddons, Ratby, Leics., labourer, for trading as a butcher unapprenticed.

85.4 *Sacramental Certificate*
St Martin's   James Bates, glover and breechesmaker
Oath of Allegiance and Abjuration signed by him.

86.1 *Writ of Summons*
Dated 15 April 1751 for 15 July 1751.

86.2 *Discharged Recognizances*
John Stanley, tailor, to appear and answer charges of assault on Thomas
King, the Bishop's Fee, tailor, at the "Turk's Head".
Robert Turlington, cordwainer, to appear and answer charges of assault on
Sarah, his wife.
William Coleman, framework-knitter, to appear and answer charges of
assaulting Francis Oswin, jun., framework-knitter, with a stick and laming
him.

86.3 *Sacramental Certificate*
St Mary's   William Bickerstaffe, schoolmaster
Oath of Allegiance and Abjuration signed by him.

87.1 *Writ of Summons*
Dated 15 July 1751 for 7 October 1751.

87.2 *Constable's Presentment*
John Hague (Ald. Ludlams Ward) presents Rogers Rudings ⟨for Not
Keeping in Rapair A Cartain Lane Called Friars Lane Leading from the
North Gates to a Cartain Lane Called Bulls Lane⟩.   Indicted.

87.3 *Discharged Recognizance*
John Payne, jun., staymaker, to appear and answer charges of assault on
John Dennis, gardener.

87.4 *Indictment*
Nicholas Richmond, framework-knitter, for illegally lodging John Keen in
his house.

87.5 *Sacramental Certificates*
St Martin's   Samuel Simpson, Mayor
John Field, cooper
John Pocklington, mercer
Joseph Tayler, barber
Joseph Treen
Thomas Thornton
John Winter
St Margaret's   Jonathan Hartell, woolcomber
Oath of Allegiance and Abjuration signed by them all.

88.1 *Writ of Summons*
Dated 13 January 1752 for 6 April 1752.

88.2 *Discharged Recognizance*
Thomas Underwood, Syston, Leics., butcher, to appear to prosecute and
give evidence against Thomas Leeds, labourer, for stealing a joint of beef.

88.3 *Certificates of Pavement Repair*
The following have repaired the pavements in front of their houses:
Mrs Basett.
Mrs Orton in Northgate Street.
John Hunt Worrall in Belgrave Gate.

88.4 *Presentment*

William Wrighte, Recorder, presents Thomas Pares, gent., ⟨for laying Wood and Muck on the West side of a certain street in the said Borough called the Belgrave Gate and on the East side of his Barn and ground there (near to the Sign of the fighting Cocks) being part of the Publick Highway leading from the said Borough to Loughborow in the County of Leicester⟩.

88.5 *Sacramental Certificates*

St Margaret's   John Lee, B.A., clerk
                John Bass
All Saints'   William Herrick, gent.
Oath of Allegiance and Abjuration signed by them all.

89.1 *Writ of Summons*

Dated 13 July 1752 for 2 October 1752.

89.2 *Constable's Presentment*

William Weldon (Ald. Miles Ward) presents ⟨the Widow Armston Causeway in the Church Gate⟩.   Indicted.

89.3 *Sacramental Certificates*

St Margaret's   Richard Denshire, Mayor
                John Miles, hosier
                Richard Roberts, barber
St Martin's   William Birstall, gent.
                William Day, mercer
St Mary's   Thomas Chapman, maltster
Oath of Allegiance and Abjuration signed by them all and
                Edmund Johnson
                Edward Howkins

90.1 *Writ of Summons*

Dated 2 October 1752 for 8 January 1753.

90.2 *Constables' Presentments*

John Lacey (Ald. Cartwrights Ward) presents the Mayor, Bailiffs and Burgesses of the Borough of Leicester for not repairing Grange Lane.

Jonathan Chettle, Thirdborough (Ald. Beltons Ward), presents Thomas Pares, sen., gent., and Elizabeth Bonner, widow, ⟨for not repairing a certain Pavement between the dwelling house of John Flower on the one side the way, and [blank] Bonner Daughter of the above named Elizabeth Bonner on the other side the way which said Pavement leads to the West Bridge in the said Borough and to the Castle Mill in or near the said Borough⟩.   Indicted.

90.3   *Certificate of Removal of Obstruction*
Thomas Pares has removed the wood and muck from Belgrave Gate.

90.4   *Sacramental Certificates*
St Mary's   Edmund Johnson, gent.
St Margaret's Edward Howkins

91.1   *Writ of Summons*
Dated 7 October 1751 for 13 January 1752.

91.2   *Prisoners*
William Smith
Thomas Mash

91.3   *Constables' Presentments*
George Bates (Ald. Lamberts Ward) presents Mrs Bassett ⟨for not re-
parring her pavement before her door⟩.   Indicted.

James Banks (Ald. Bass Ward) presents John Hunt Worral ⟨for Not keeping His Causey in Re pare⟩.   Indicted.

William Palmer (Ald. Lees Ward) presents Widow Orton ⟨for not repareing her Causway⟩.   Indicted.

William Robarts (Ald. Miles Ward) presents William Douse ⟨for Laying
Stones and Plaster In the Comman Street being A Nuscance⟩, and
Alderman Lee and William Green ⟨for Not Paveing Thayer Lemited
Bounds⟩.   Indicted.

92.1   *Writ of Summons*
Sessions held 30 April 1753. No writ survives.

92.2   *Discharged Recognizance*
William Greaves alias Graves, clockmaker, to appear and answer charges of
assault on Elizabeth Broughton whilst she was pregnant.

92.3   *Indictments*
William Greaves, clockmaker, for assaulting Elizabeth, wife of William
Broughton, labourer.   Fined 1s.

Richard Harting, yeoman, for assaulting William Stafford.

[Separate roll but for same Sessions as **92** above.]

93a.1   *Sacramental Certificate*
St Mary's   William Brushfield
Oath of Allegiance and Abjuration signed by him.

For **93b** see after **147a**.

94.1   *Writ of Summons*
Dated 1 October 1753 for 14 January 1754.

94.2   *Discharged Recognizances*
William Wilson, woolcomber, to appear and answer charges of assault on
John King, framework-knitter.
Joseph Sands, cordwainer, to appear and answer *re* the bastard child of
Elizabeth Sprigg, Glooston, Leics., singlewoman.
William (Wingiam) Yates, grazier, to appear and answer *re* the bastard
child of Sarah Webster, singlewoman.

94.3   *Sacramental Certificate*
St Martin's   Rev. Thomas Haines, clerk
Oath of Allegiance and Abjuration signed by him.

95.1   *Writ of Summons*
Dated 26 April 1754 for 15 July 1754.

95.2   *Discharged Recognizances*
Samuel Gutteridge, carpenter, to appear and answer charges of threatening
Richard Norton, jun., framework-knitter.
Henry Watkinson to appear and answer charges of felony of a hen from
William Pegg, blacksmith.

95.3   *Certificate of Road Repair*
For Grange Lane.

96.1   *Writ of Summons*
Dated 15 July 1754 for 7 October 1754.

96.2   *Discharged Recognizance*
Catherine Gamble alias Ratt to appear and answer charges of threatening
Margaret, wife of William Bagnall, tailor, ⟨and Mobbing her along the
Street⟩.

96.3   *Sacramental Certificates*
St Martin's   William Lee, Mayor
                   John Winter
                   John Hammond
                   William Orton

Thomas Dyson
James Sismey
John Coleman
Joseph Hall
John Cartwright
St Margaret's William Holmes
Oath of Allegiance and Abjuration signed by them all.

97.1   *Writ of Summons*
Sessions held 13 January 1755. No writ survives.

97.2   *Discharged Recognizances*
John Kellitt, bricklayer, to appear and answer charges of assault on Ann,
wife of John Walton, framework-knitter.
Samuel Goodrich, carpenter, to appear and answer charges of assault on
John Paling, carpenter, and William Laugton, gardener.
Edward Daws, woolcomber, to appear and answer *re* the bastard child of
Mary Goodfellow, St Margaret's.

97.3   *Indictment*
Joseph Thornton, framework-knitter, for illegally lodging Eleanor
Stephens, a common stroller, in his house.

98.1   *Writ of Summons*
Dated 13 January 1755 for 14 July 1755.

98.2   ·   *Discharged Recognizances*
William Earpe, woolcomber, to appear and answer *re* the female bastard
child of Eleanor Hawkins.
John Stokes, baker, to appear and answer *re* the bastard child of Mary
Loseby, singlewoman, and obey the Court.
Samuel Brookes, needlemaker, to appear and answer *re* the male bastard
child of Mary Farrow, St Margaret's, singlewoman.

98.3   *Sacramental Certificates*
St Martin's   Major John Jennings
              Lieutenant Teavil Appleton
Oath of Allegiance and Abjuration signed by them both.

99.1   *Writ of Summons*
Sessions held 10 October 1755. No writ survives.

99.2 *Sacramental Certificates*

St Martin's   James Sismey, Mayor
John Hammond, farrier
Samuel Jordan, hosier
Thomas Harris, grocer
John Hopkinson, druggist
Nicholas Throseby, tailor
Robert Belton, hosier
William Clarke, glazier
Thomas Stretton, tallow chandler
St Mary's   Temple Sutton, scarlet dyer
Francis Warberton, hosier
Oath of Allegiance and Abjuration signed by them all.

100.1 *Writ of Summons*
Sessions held 12 January 1756. No writ survives.

100.2 *Sacramental Certificate*
St Margaret's   Benjamin Sutton, hosier
Oath of Allegiance and Abjuration signed by him.

101a.1 *Writ of Summons*
Dated 12 January 1756 for 26 April 1756.

101b included with **57a**.

102.1 *Writ of Summons*
Dated 26 April 1756 for 12 July 1756.

102.2 *Application for Certificate for Dissenters' Meeting House*
⟨We whose names are hereunto Subscribed do hereby Certify that a certain Messuage or Bay of Building scituate in the Horsepool Street within the said Borough and now in our occupation is intended to be made use of as a Meeting house for Protestant Dissenters according to the Statute in that Case made and provided and we humbly pray that this our Cirtificate may be Recorded by this Court. Witness our hands this 12th Day of July in the Year of our Lord 1756.

Benjamin Withers
Jonathan Dawson⟩

103.1 *Writ of Summons*
Dated 12 July 1756 for 4 October 1756.

103.2   *Sacramental Certificates*

St Martin's   Edmund Ludlam, Mayor
               Nicholas Throseby, tailor
               John Westley, joiner
               John Gamble, grocer
               Cornelius Norton, grocer

Oath of Allegiance and Abjuration signed by them all.

104.1   *Writ of Summons*

Dated 19 April 1757 for 11 July 1757.

104.2   *Discharged Recognizance*

Thomas Thorpe, labourer, to appear and answer charges of assault on Thomas Andrews.

104.3   *Convictions*

Job Boots for cursing 1 profane curse.
Thomas Andrews for swearing 1 profane oath.

105.1   *Writ of Summons*

Sessions held 3 October 1757. No writ survives.

105.2   *Constables' Presentments*

Joseph Nicholson (Ald. Ayers Ward) presents William Rice ⟨for negleting his ofis as hedburow⟩.   Indicted.

Joseph Gilbert (Ald. Lee's Ward) presents Josiah Steans, woolcomber, for not repairing the pavement in front of his house.   Indicted.

John Harvey (Ald. Newtons Ward) presents John Newby ⟨for washing his Turd Cowls at the Cank Pump⟩.   Indicted.

105.3   *Indictments*

William Harris, victualler, for keeping a disorderly house.

Katherine Hurst for stealing a scarlet cloak from Martha Jenkinson. Offence acknowledged.

105.4   *Convictions*

John Burbage for cursing 6 profane curses.
Corporal James Ridgeway, Lieu.-General Bland's Regiment, for swearing 1 profane oath.

105.5 *Sacramental Certificates*
St Martin's   Joseph Hall, Mayor
John Winter, gent.
William Birstall, gent.
Richard Gamble
John Coxe Brown
St Margaret's William Holmes
Oath of Allegiance and Abjuration signed by them all.

106.1 *Writ of Summons*
Dated 3 October 1757 for 9 January 1758.

107.1 *Writ of Summons*
Dated 9 January 1758 for 3 April 1758.

107.2 *Certificate of Pavement Repair*
Josiah Steans, woolcomber, has repaired the pavement in front of his house.

107.3 *Examination*
Ann Ward, All Saints', singlewoman, taken 17 January 1758:
⟨This Examinant says she is with Child which Child when born will be a Bastard, Says that Thomas Cooper of the Borough aforesaid Framework knitter is the only father of such Bastard Child whereof she this Examinant is now pregnant and goeth with for that he the said Thomas Cooper had Carnal knowledge of her this Examinants Body the begining of May last at the house of John Adams in the Causey Lane in the Parish of All Saints aforesaid Framework knitter and two or three times since, And this Examinant further says the said Thomas Cooper is the only father of such Bastard Child whereof she this Examinant is now pregnant and goeth with no other Person whatsoever having had Carnal knowledge of her body And this Examinant further says the said Child when born is likely to become Chargeable to the Inhabitants of the Parish of All Saints aforesaid.⟩
Endorsement: ⟨Thomas Cooper is Convicted of being the father of the female Bastard Child born on the body of Ann Ward is ordered to pay 35s for the time she lay in & for the time since is ordered to pay 1s a Week so long as the Child is Chargeable.⟩

107.4 *Sacramental Certificates*
St Martin's Major William Eustace, 5th Regiment
Lieutenant Bennett Cuthbutson, Adjutant, 5th Regiment
Lieutenant John Smith, 5th Regiment
Lieutenant John Bailie, 5th Regiment
Ensign Gilbert Warman, 5th Regiment

Ensign Robert Palmer, 5th Regiment
Ensign Anthony Neugent, 5th Regiment
James Inglis, surgeon, 5th Regiment
Oath of Allegiance and Abjuration signed by them all.

108.1 *Writ of Summons*

Dated 3 April 1758 for 10 July 1758.

108.2 *Discharged Recognizances*

William Greaves, clockmaker, to appear and answer charges of assault on
Sarah Middleton at Samuel King's house.
Thomas Hardy, Gaddesby, Leics., butcher, to appear to prosecute and
give evidence against Elizabeth Proo for stealing a breast of veal.

108.3 *Case*

Indictment of Elizabeth Proo for stealing a breast of veal from Thomas
Hardy, Gaddesby, Leics., butcher.
Information of Thomas Hardy taken 27 May 1758:
⟨This Informant says between twelve and one of the Clock this day the
Woman now present who says her name is Elizabeth Proo feloniously
stolen, One breast of Veal off of his Stall standing in the Markett place
within the said Borough, and took away the same, That this Informant
followed her about twenty yards from his Stall and caught hold of her and
asked her what she was going to do with the breast of Veal, she had taken
from his Stall the said Elizabeth Proo denyed her having any breast of Veal
That this Informant took her back to his Stall and took the Veal from her,
and the breast of Veal now produced and shewn is this Informants property
and was Stole by the said Elizabeth Proo off of his Stall as aforesaid.⟩

108.4 *Sacramental Certificates*

St Margaret's William Stephens, grocer
                James Davis, woolcomber and hosier
St Martin's   Samuel Woodford, currier
Oath of Allegiance and Abjuration signed by them all.

109a.1 *Writ of Summons*

Dated 10 July 1758 for 2 October 1758.

109a.2 *Constable's Presentment*

William Mattock (Ald. Newtons Ward) presents Mrs Jane Mason for not
repairing her pavement.   Indicted.

109a.3   *Indictment*

John Foster, framework-knitter, for stealing ½ cwt Derbyshire coals from John Hunt.

109a.4   *Convictions*

John Burton for swearing 30 profane oaths.
Sarah Booth for swearing 2 profane oaths.

109a.5   *Sacramental Certificates*

St Martin's   Robert Belton, Mayor
               William Tilly, Coroner
               Samuel Jordan
               Nicholas Throseby
               Samuel Brown
               John Ward

Oath of Allegiance and Abjuration signed by them all.

For **109b** see after **110**.

110.1   *Writ of Summons*

Dated 2 October 1758 for 8 January 1759.

110.2   *Discharged Recognizances*

George Croxton, victualler, to appear and answer charges of assault on Samuel Tupman, a soldier.

John Chesson, jun., woolcomber, and William Allen, woolcomber, to appear and answer charges of riot, disturbing the peace, and assault on Robert Belton, Mayor.

Edward Wrighte, apprentice to William Hose, blacksmith, to appear and answer charges of assaulting Thomas Adcock and his wife and breaking their door.

110.3   *Case*

The Grand Jury present Margaret Turner for stealing a little leather purse, containing 3 guineas and 2 half guineas in gold, and 6s. in silver, from John Barsby.   Ignored.

Information of John Barsby, Billa Barrow, Stanton-under-Bardon, Leics., weaver, taken 11 October 1758:

⟨This Informant says the Person now present who says her Name is Margaret Turner feloniously stole out of his Breeches Pockett in the Markett place within the said Borough this day One little Leather Purse with the following pieces of money therein (that is to say) three Guineas in Gold, two halfe Guineas in Gold, and six shillings in silver, And further

says he Catched her with her hand in his Pockett and upon searching his Pockett missed the above purse and money upon which he Immediately apprehended her.⟩
Note—⟨John Barsby in £20 to Prosecute & give Evidence at the next Sessions.⟩

110.4   *Case*
Indictment of Thomas Taylor, labourer, for stealing a saddle from William Wilson. Po se.
Information of William Willson, the Bishop's Fee, mercer, taken 8 December 1758:
⟨This Informant says upwards of Twelve Months since a Saddle the property of this Informant was stolen out of his Stable near to the three Crowns within the said Borough, And says on Wednesday the sixth instant he found the same Saddle in the Custody and possession of Thomas Taylor of the Said Borough Yeoman And further says not.⟩
Note—⟨William Willson in £5 to Prosecute & give Evidence next Sessions.⟩

110.5   *Conviction*
John Chesson, jun., and William Allen for swearing 5 profane oaths.

110.6   *Information*
Samuel Tupman, sergeant, Col. John Boscawen's Regiment of Foot, taken 11 October 1758:
⟨This Informant saith that he being yesterday about noon at the House of George Croxton commonly known by the Sign of the Fish and Quart in the Churchgate in the Borough of Leicester aforesaid, after he had drank three mugs of ale there and paid for them, the Landlord Croxton going cross the Room, this Informant asked him how he did, & the said Croxton answered him with ill Language and soon after gave him a violent Stroke upon the side of his head with his fist.⟩

109b.1   *Writ of Summons*
                 Dated 8 January 1759 for 23 April 1759.

109b.2   *Discharged Recognizance*
Thomas Bates, yeoman, to appear and answer *re* the bastard child of Elizabeth Hawkins.

111a.1   *Writ of Summons*
               Sessions held 9 July 1759. No writ survives.

111a.2 *Sacramental Certificate*

All Saints'   John Jackson, jun.

Oath of Allegiance and Abjuration signed by him.

For **111b** see after **114**. For **111c** see after **202**.

112.1 *Writ of Summons*

Dated 9 July 1759 for 1 October 1759.

112.2 *Presentment*

Edmund Ludlam, Justice, presents Thomas Burgess, victualler, for encroaching upon the Highway by building the front of his house on it.

112.3 *Conviction*

John Bodicote for cursing 2 profane curses.

112.4 *Sacramental Certificates*

St Martin's   Nicholas Throseby, Mayor
              Alderman William Higginson
              Alderman William Birstall
              Alderman Samuel Oliver
              Alderman Henry Gutheridge
              Thomas Astle
              Benjamin Sutton
              John Poynton

St Margaret's   William Mason

Oath of Allegiance and Abjuration signed by them all.

113a.1 *Writ of Summons*

Dated 1 October 1759 for 14 January 1760.

113a.2 *Discharged Recognizances*

Thomas Stretton, tallow chandler, to appear to prosecute and give evidence against, and Robert Cooke, yeoman, to appear and give evidence against, Elizabeth Geary for stealing a wedge of soap from Thomas Stretton.

Elizabeth, wife of Thomas Geary, Thornton, Leics., farmer, to appear and answer charges to be made by Thomas Stretton.

John Lawrence, Excise Officer, to appear and answer *re* the female bastard child of Mary Bilson, singlewoman.

Mary Gibson, singlewoman, to appear and answer charges to be made by Mary Lee ⟨Touching and Concerning the said Mary Gibson dressing herselfe in a dress called a Masquerade dress and exposeing herselfe in such dress whereby the said Mary Lee was affrighted in such manner as caused her to fall into Fits⟩.

113a.3 *Case*

Indictment of Elizabeth Geary for stealing a wedge of soap from Thomas Stretton, tallow chandler. Discharged.

Information of Thomas Stretton, tallow chandler, taken 11 October 1759: ⟨This Informant saith about six of the Clock this Night the Person now present who says her Name is Elizabeth Barber feloniously stole from off the Window place belonging to the Shop of this Informant the Wedge of Soap now produced and shewn, And further says he first missed the Soap and then charged the said Elizabeth Barber with the stealing thereof and upon bringing her back she dropped the Soap which she has Confessed before Mr Mayor but refused to sign her Confession.⟩

113a.4 *Sacramental Certificate*

St Martin's   Henry Earpe

113b.1 *Writ of Summons*

Sessions held 14 April 1760. No writ survives.

114.1 *Writ of Summons*

Sessions held 14 July 1760. No writ survives.

114.2 *Discharged Recognizances*

John Wright, victualler, to appear and prosecute Henry Holmes ⟨on a Violent Suspition of his ripping off or pulling off a Silver Tankard Lid from a Tankard belonging to him the said John Wright last Night at his house in the same Borough of Leicester and feloniously stealing and taking away the said Silver Tankard Lid from his dwelling house as aforesaid⟩.

Elizabeth Ansty, spinster, Richard Ball, framework-knitter, and Anthony Parker, the Newarke, framework-knitter, to appear and give evidence against Henry Holmes.

John Parr, cordwainer, to appear and answer charges of keeping a disorderly house to be made by the Churchwardens and Overseers of St Nicholas' Parish and Anne, wife of William Lee, labourer.

114.3 *Presentment*

The Grand Jury present Henry Holmes, framework-knitter, for stealing a silver tankard lid from John Wrighte. Ignored.

114.4 *Indictments*

William Mortimer, framework-knitter, for keeping a disorderly house. Guilty.

Josiah Rice, framework-knitter, for keeping a disorderly house. Guilty.

John Parr, cordwainer, for keeping a disorderly house. Guilty.

114.5   *Sacramental Certificates*
St Martin's   John Lewin
               Richard Beale
               Clement Stretton, jun.
               Joseph Johnson
               Birkhead Bracebridge
Oath of Allegiance and Abjuration signed by them all.

111b.1   *Writ of Summons*
           Sessions held 2 April 1761. No writ survives.

111b.2   *Discharged Recognizance*
John Gilbert, framework-knitter, to appear and answer *re* the bastard child
of Mary Richmond, All Saints'.

111b.3   *Conviction*
Francis Porter for cursing 2 profane curses.

111b.4   *Sacramental Certificate*
St Martin's   John Gregory

115.1   *Writ of Summons*
           Sessions held 5 October 1761. No writ survives.

115.2   *Constables' Presentments*
Aaron Warren (Ald. Newtons Ward) presents the pump in the market
place.

John Coltman (Ald. Chapmans Ward) presents ⟨The Fryars Lane Leading
from the Northgate to Sycermore Lane from the Top Down to the place of
Cover for Cattle Rogers Rudins Gent Landlord⟩, and ⟨John Coltman for
the Other Side of the Said Lane from The Top Down to Samuel Brown
Esq. Mayor Orchard⟩.

115.3   *Discharged Recognizances*
Francis Tanzer, baker, to appear and answer charges to be made by
Richard Kind of ⟨Secreting from and defrauding the said Richard Kind
of the Sum of Six Pounds thirteen Shillings and Six Pence on the fifth day
of July in the year One Thousand Seven hundred and Sixty which he the
said Richard Kind had left on the Dough Trough in the Bakehouse of him
the said Francis Tanzer⟩.

Richard Kind, Hinckley, Leics., setter up of frames, to appear and prosecute Francis Tanzer.

Robert Bonner, baker, Sarah Cox, spinster, and Thomas Goodman, miller, to appear and give evidence against Francis Tanzer.

115.4 *Indictment*

Francis Tanzer, baker, for defrauding Richard Kind of £6 13s. 6d., consisting of a 36s. gold coin, a gold moidore value 27s., 3 gold guineas, and some silver coins, when Kind was in his bakehouse.

115.5 *Sacramental Certificates*

All Saints'   Samuel Brown, Mayor
     John Cooper, Chamberlain
     John Poynton, Chamberlain
     William Simpson, hosier
     William Brown, barber
St Martin's   William Higginson, Coroner
     John Wigley, Coroner
     Edward Hextall, Common Councillor
     John Hartell, Common Councillor

Oath of Allegiance and Abjuration signed by them all.

115.6 *Insolvent Debtors*

Gaoler's Oath:

⟨I Charles Coulson upon my Corporal Oath in the presence of Almighty God do solemnly swear profess and declare That all and every person and persons whose name or names are inserted and contained in the List by me now delivered in and subscribed to the best of my knowledge and belief have since the Twenty fifth day of October One thousand seven hundred and Sixty been Committed to the Gaol or prison of the Borough of Leicester at the suit or suits of the several person or persons therein respectively mentioned and that all and every of them whose name and names is and are contained in the said List to the best of my knowledge and Belief since the said Twenty fifth day of October have been really and truly Committed and that none of such prisoners to my knowledge or with my privity have voluntarily or with design or in Expectation to take any Benefit from or under any Act of parliament to be made for Relief of Insolvent Debtors been Committed to the said prison of the Borough of Leicester or got his her or their name or Names entered as prisoner or prisoners in the Books of the said Prison or since their Commitment have to my knowledge or with my privity resided out of the said prison of the Borough of Leicester.

So help me God.⟩

⟨An Alphabetical List of the Prisioners Confined for Debt in his Majesties Goal for the Borough of Leicester Comitted since the 25th October 1760.
Michealmas Sessions 5th October 1761.

Hudson Robert John	Brought in Custody by Capias July 11th 1761 at the Suit of Valentine Pyne Gentleman for a Debt of Two Pounds Seven Shillings & Sixpence	2	7	6
also August 31 1761	a Detainer of Execution at the suit of Valentine Pyne Gentleman for Three Pounds Seventeen Shillings and Ten pence	3	17	10
	Godfary Serjant			
Harvey John August 31st 1761	Brought in Custody by Capias July 6th 1761 at the Suit of Daniel Alcock for a Debt of Three Pounds Six Shillings & also under Execution at the Suit of Daniel Alcock for 7.6.8	7	6	8
	Laurence Read Serjant			
Ross John the Younger September 19th 1761	Brought in Custody by Capias at the Suit of Thomas Stretton for a Debt of Two Pounds Eight Shillings	2	8	0
	Godfary Serjant			
Ross John the Younger September 26 1761	Brought in Custody by Capias at the Suit of John Ross the Elder for a Debt of Three Pounds Ten Shillings	3	10	0
	Thomas Vann Serjant			
Wright John September 12th 1761	Brought in Custody Under Execution By Warrant from a Writ Directed from the Sheriff of the County of Leicester To the Bailiff of the Borough of Leicester returnable on the Morrow of all Souls Vizt. 3d November 1761 For Twenty Seven Pounds	27	0	0

Thomas Herrick Gentleman Bailiff of the Borough of Leicester

Charles Coulson Goaler⟩

Copies of notices from Valentine Pyne to Robert John Hudson, painter, and the Keeper of Leicester Gaol informing them of his intention to compel Hudson to produce a Schedule of his goods and effects.

'Compulsive Oath' of Robert John Hudson:

⟨I Robert John Hudson upon my Corporal Oath, in the Presence of Almighty God, do solemnly swear, protest and declare. That the Schedule now delivered in, and by me subscribed, doth contain, to the best of my Knowledge, Remembrance and Belief, a full, just, true, and perfect Account and Discovery of all my real Estate, either in Possession, Reversion, Remainder, or Expectancy, and of all the Goods, Chattles, and Personal Estate, which I, or any in Trust for me, or for my Benefit, or Advantage now have, or am intituled to; and of all Debts as are to me owing, or to any Person or Persons in Trust for me; and of all the Securities and Contracts whereby any Money now is, or will, or may hereafter become payable to, or any Benefit or Advantage may accrue to me or to my Use, or to any Person or Persons in Trust for me; and the Names and Places of Abode of the several Persons from whom such Debts are due and owing; and of the Witnesses that can prove such Debts or Contracts; and also a true Account of all Books, Papers, Decrees, Writings and Evidences relating thereto in my Custody or Power; and that neither I, nor any Person or Persons in Trust for me, have, to my Knowledge and Belief, any Lands, Money, Stock, or other Estate, real or personal, in Possession, Reversion, or Remainder, other than what is, or are in the said Schedule contained, except the Wearing Apparel, Bedding for myself and Family, Working Tools, and necessary Implements for my Occupation and Calling, and these in the Whole not exceeding the Value of Ten Pounds; and that I have not, or any Body for me, hath directly or indirectly sold, lessened, or otherwise conveyed, disposed of in Trust or concealed, all or any Part of my Messuages, Lands, Money, Goods, Chattles, Stock, Debts, Securities, Contracts or Estates, real or personal, or any Books, Papers, or Writings, concerning the same, whereby to secure the same, or to receive or expect any Profit or Advantage to myself or my Family, or with any View or Design to defraud or deceive any Creditor or Cretors to whom I am Indebted, or was indebted when committed to Goal, in any wise howsoever.
So Help me GOD.⟩

⟨A True Schedule and account of all the Estate and Effects of me Robert John Hudson late of the Borough of Leicester in the County of Leicester Painter now a Prisoner in the Goal for the said Borough of Leicester charged in Execution therein at the suit of Valentine Pyne of the said Borough Gentleman which I or any Person or Persons in Trust for me or for my use benefit or advantage am is or are seized of interested in or intitled to Pursuant to an Act of Parliament passed in the First year of the Reign of his Present Majesty King George the Third Intitled an Act for Relief of insolvent Debtors.

In my late Dwelling House situate in the Parish of All Saints in the said Borough:

One bedstead, Cornice and curtain rod, Two feather beds two bolsters two pair of Blankets three Sheets one quilt one looking glass three small Tables Six comon chairs one Corner Cupboard one land Iron one fire shovell one pair of Tongs one Staffordshire Grate one pair of Bellows one pair of Candlesticks one Dutch Oven one pair of Glass Salts one pint Glass Decanter Six Cheaney tea cups and saucers one Tea pot one Sugar bason three small silver tea spoons one old tea Kettle one childs Cradle one childs chair Two smoothing Irons, A map of the World another Map of Leicestershire four Knives and five forks One wash Tub one pail an old Brush and Mop Three old Iron Bars.

The under written is an account of the names of several Debtors and where they did respectively live (I being at this time ignorant where any of them live or may be found) and the several Sums of money from them respectively owing and how the same respectively became due and are secured:

		£	s	d
1750 January 7th	Mr [blank] Crouch late of Southampton buildings in London upholsterer for Lodgings in our house by me rented in Southampton buildings aforesaid for which Debt I have no Security	1	16	0
	Mr William Brown late of Chancery Lane London Coachman for the like from July to December 1750 for which I have no Security	2	4	6
1751 June 7th	Paid for five Chaldron of Sea Coal for Mr William Edmondson late of the Queens head Brooks Market London at 32s per Chaldron for which I have no Security	8	0	0
	Richard Hudson late of the Strand London a Porter for money lent at different times from June 1750 to March 1751 for which I have no Security	9	15	0
		21	15	6

Note   None of the above Debts have been demanded since the year 1752. I am not seized or possessed of or intitled to any real Estate either in Possession Reversion Remainder or expectancy.

The above written is a true and full Schedule of all I am possessed of except the wearing apparel for myself and family Working Tools and necessary implements for my Occupation and Calling and these in the whole not exceeding the value of Ten pounds Witness my hand the 5th day of October 1761.

Robert John Hudson⟩

Notices from Daniel Alcock to John Hervey, innholder, and the Keeper of Leicester Gaol informing them of his intention to compel Hervey to produce a Schedule of his goods and effects.

'Compulsive Oath' of John Hervey (in form of Robert John Hudson's above).

⟨A true Schedule of all the Estate and Effects of me John Hervey late of the Borough of Leicester in the County of Leicester Innholder now a prisoner in the Goal for the Borough of Leicester aforesaid Charged in Execution therein at the Suit of Daniel Alcock of Enderby in the County of Leicester aforesaid Gentleman which I or any person or persons in Trust for me or for my use benefit or advantage am is or are Seized of interested in or intitled to pursuant to an act of parliament passed in the first year of the reign of his present Majesty King George the Third Intitled an Act for Releif of Insolvent Debtors.

In the Dwelling house of Joseph Veasey in Thornton Lane in the Borough of Leicester aforesaid:

Two Bedsteads two Woolbeds one Boulster two pillows four Blanketts Two Childrens Chairs one pewter plate two Delf plates six knives and forks and a Cradle.

I am not Seized possessed of or intitled to any Real Estate either in possession Reversion Remainder or Expectancy nor are there any Debt or Debts Sum or Sums of money due or owing to me from any person or persons whomsoever.

The above written is a true and full Schedule as aforesaid of my All Except Wearing Apparel of myself and Family which does not amount to the value of Ten Pounds. Witness my hand this Fifth day of October One thousand Seven hundred and Sixty one.

John Hervey⟩

116.1   *Writ of Summons*
Sessions held 4 October 1762. No writ survives.

116.2   *Sacramental Certificates*
St Margaret's   Samuel Oliver, Mayor
                 Alderman William Orton
                 William Stephens, Chamberlain
St Martin's   John Miles, Coroner
                 Clement Stretton, Coroner
                 Tyrringham Palmer, Chamberlain
Oath of Allegiance and Abjuration signed by them all.

117.1   *Writ of Summons*
Sessions held 10 January 1763. No writ survives.

117.2   *Sacramental Certificates*

St Margaret's   Alderman William Holmes
                 Robert Peach, Common Councillor
St Martin's   Thomas Cobley, Common Councillor
                 John Bracebridge, Common Councillor
St Mary's   Alderman John Fisher
All Saints'   William Hodges

Oath of Allegiance and Abjuration signed by them all.

118.1   *Writ of Summons*

Sessions held 11 April 1763. No writ survives.

118.2   *Sacramental Certificate*

All Saints'   John Jackson, Receiver of Stamp Duties for Leicestershire
Oath of Allegiance and Abjuration signed by him and Robert Burnaby.

119.1   *Writ of Summons*

Sessions held 9 January 1764. No writ survives.

119.2   *Constable's Presentment*

Thomas Tunney (Ald. Simpsons Ward) presents John Clark, carrier, ⟨For that on Sunday the 25th day of September last, about two of the Clock in the Afternoon of the same day, his Man William was making of Shoes, and shoeing the Horses of the said John Clark, And also that the Waggon of the said John Clark, was loaded with Goods on the same day, to the great prophanation of the Lords Day⟩, ⟨for letting his Waggon on Wednesday the 2d day of November last, stand in the open street called the Gallow tree Gate within the said Ward, loaded with Branches of trees, which stood loaded there five days and nights, was afterwards removed, and then was brought again to the said street, and stood there loaded in the same manner, for three more days and nights, which was a publick Nusance to the Inhabitants of the said Street, was greatly Complained of by the said Inhabitants, and was an Obstruction to the passing and Repassing of the said Street or publick Highway⟩, ⟨for that on Wednesday the 14th day of December last, his Waggon stood in the said Gallow tree Gate street, and a large quantity of Muck his property, lay on one side of the said Waggon, which together took up most part of the breadth of the said street, so that the same was a great Obstruction to the Inhabitants of the said street, in Passing and Repassing thereof, and in particular on the same day, to the Reverend Mr Bunby & Mr Semonds and the several persons attending then and there a Corpse, that was going to be Interred so that they could not pass without great difficulty and danger of falling into the Cellars hereinafter presented⟩, and ⟨for haveing two Cellar Windows belonging to his new dwelling house in Gallow tree Gate aforesaid, which project or extend into the said street from his said House, by the space of Eight Inches, to the great peril and danger of the said Inhabitants in passing and Repassing the said street, And likewise that the pavement before the windows of the House of the said John Clark in the said street, is very much out of repair⟩. Indicted.

119.3 *Discharged Recognizance*

Sergeant Edward Rowley, Leicestershire Militia, to appear and obey the Court *re* the bastard child of Jane Wilson, St Martin's, singlewoman.

119.4 *Presentment*

The Grand Jury presents the watercourse beside the Churchway in Causeway Lane, which the Inhabitants of All Saints' Parish have blocked up causing it to overflow on to and damage the footpath which runs beside the orchards of Henry Hitchcock and Thomas Herrick, gents. Ignored.

119.5 *Indictments*

James Tayler, dyer, for assaulting Charles Burdett.

Thomas Ward, labourer, for stealing a shoulder of mutton from Thomas Needham.

119.6 *Information*

Jane Wilson, singlewoman, taken 6 December 1753:
⟨This Examinant says she is with Child, which Child when born will be a Bastard, Says that Edward Rowley a Serjeant in the Leicestershire Militia is the father of such Bastard child whereof she this Examinant is now pregnant and goeth with for that he the said Edward Rowley had carnal knowledge of her this Examinants body on Wednesday in Whitsun week last past at a Room he the said Edward Rowley rented of John Davey of the parish of Saint Margarett in the Borough aforesaid Framework knitter, and several times since at one of which times he got her with Child as aforesaid, And this Examinant further says the said Edward Rowley is the only and true father of the said Bastard Child whereof she this Examinant is now pregnant and goeth with as aforesaid no other person whatsoever having had carnal knowledge of her body And this Examinant further says the said Child when born is likely to become chargeable to the Inhabitants of the parish of Saint Martin in the said Borough, And further says not.⟩

119.7 *Sacramental Certificates*

St Martin's   Henry Gutheridge, Mayor
               Robert Bakewell, Recorder
               Alderman Benjamin Sutton

Alderman Joseph Chambers
Robert Peach, Chamberlain
James Bates, Chamberlain
Henry Watchorne
Thomas Phipps, jun.
All Saints'   William Orton, Coroner
Oath of Allegiance and Abjuration signed by them all.

120.1   *Writ of Summons*
Sessions held 30 April 1764. No writ survives.

120.2   *Indictments*
Thomas Chester for stealing 6 pails from Richard Garle.   Guilty.

Gilbert Illsley for stealing a horseshoe from Jacob Bothomley.   Not guilty.

Elizabeth Drake for stealing a silver watch from John Hubbard's house. Guilty.

121.1   *Writ of Summons*
Sessions held 9 July 1764. No writ survives.

121.2   *Indictment*
Mary Wade for stealing a brass kettle from Christopher Brown.

122.1   *Writ of Summons*
Sessions held 1 October 1764. No writ survives.

122.2   *Discharged Recognizances*
William Dowse, sen., bricklayer, to appear and answer charges of assault on Tyrringham Foxton.
William Dowse, jun., framework-knitter, to appear and answer charges of assault on Tyrringham Foxton.

122.3   *Case*
Indictments of William Dowse, sen., bricklayer, and William Dowse, jun., framework-knitter, for assaulting Tyrringham Foxton.
Information of Tyrringham Foxton taken 28 July 1764:
⟨This Informant says that on Monday the 16th day of this instant July he was imployed as a watchman in Mr Alderman Olivers Ward in the said Borough and that about Eleven of the clock at night when he was upon his Duty William Dowse of the said Borough Bricklayer Assaulted this Informant by striking him and violently kicking him upon his right Shin

which has caused a great Sore upon his Leg, And this Informant further says that William Dowse the younger Son of the above named William Dowse did likewise several times Assault this Informant the same night.⟩ Endorsement: ⟨Tyrringham Foxton in £10 to prosecute & give Evidence against William Dowse Senior & William Dowse Junior for assaulting the said Foxton, who is to prefer Bills of Indictment against them at the next Sessions.⟩

122.4   *Sacramental Certificates*
St Martin's   Richard Beale, Mayor
               Alderman Thomas Thornton
               Richard Ogden, Coroner
               Thomas Lockwood, Common Councillor
               Samuel Woodford
               John Pocklington
All Saints'   Alderman James Cooper
St Margaret's   James Bishop, Common Councillor
Oath of Allegiance and Abjuration signed by them all.

122.5   *Examination*
Katherine Wincott, widow, taken 3 September 1764:
⟨This Examinant voluntarily and freely upon her said Oath says that on the Tenth day of August last past she was delivered of a Male Bastard Child begotten on her body about the middle of November last past by Richard Bassett of the said Borough Grazier, And this Examinant further says that the said Richard Bassett is the only and true father of the said Male Bastard Child she has been delivered of as aforesaid and no other person whatsoever and that the said Child was begotten on her body at the sign of the Turks Head in the said Borough, And this Examinant further says the said Child is now become chargeable to the Inhabitants of the parish of Saint Mary in the said Borough. And further says not.⟩
Note: ⟨Richard Bassett in £40 to appear at the next Sessions to answer what shall be laid against him by the above named Catherine Wincott taken 5 September 1764 before Mr Mayor.⟩

123.1   *Writ of Summons*
Dated 24 December 1764 for 14 January 1765.

123.2   *Constables' Presentments*
William Oldham (Ald. Phipps Ward) presents ⟨part of the Coursway at the back of the Sarresones head in Millstone Lane it being in very bad Repair⟩, and Augustin Heaford ⟨his Rubbish Lying in a very bad Manner⟩. Indicted.

Thomas Tunney (Ald. Simpsons Ward) presents John Clark, common carrier, ⟨for that on Monday the Twenty ninth day of october last a Broad Wheeled Wagon and a Cart the Property of John Clark was Brought into the open Street Caul'd the Gallow Tree gate in the Evening of the Same day and there Continued all night untill the next day⟩, ⟨for that on fryday the second day of November last a Waggon of the Said John Clark Stood in the Said Street Caul'd the Gallow Tree gate and there Continued all the night and was amended and Repair on the Said open Street on Saturday the Third day of November⟩, ⟨for that on fryday the Thirtieth of November last a Waggon of the Said John Clark Stood in the Street Caul'd the Gallow Tree gate and there Continued all night and was amended and Repair'd in the open Street on Saturday following to wit the first day of December⟩, and ⟨for Bringing into and letting a Cart of him the Said John Clark Remain in the said Street called gallow tree gate all the night of the fourteenth day of December last to the grate annoyance and Damages and Common Nusance of Divers of the Inhabitants of the Said Street⟩. Indicted.

123.3 *Discharged Recognizances*

Henry Erpe, grocer, to appear and prosecute Richard Stables for stealing 2 pieces of silver out of his shop.

John Bayley, the Woodgate, wheelwright, to appear and keep the peace towards John Throsby.

Grace, wife of Phinees Roberts, woolcomber, to appear and answer charges.

Mary Veasey, spinster, to appear and prosecute Grace Roberts.

John Stokes, woolcomber, to appear and keep the peace towards John Paling.

Private William Orton, Sir Charles Howard's Dragoon Regiment, to appear and prosecute Jeremiah Groce, victualler, for an assault.

Private William Orton to appear and prosecute Thomas Groce, labourer, for an assault.

Jeremiah Groce to appear and keep the peace towards Private William Orton.

Thomas Groce to appear and keep the peace towards Private William Orton.

123.4 *Indictments*

John Bayley, wheelwright, for assaulting John Throsby, Sergeant-at-Mace, when Throsby was serving a Writ of Capias on him.   Guilty.

Richard Stables, labourer, for stealing 2 pieces of silver from the shop of Henry Erpe, grocer.   Guilty.

Grace, wife of Phinees Roberts, woolcomber, for obtaining 3 lbs wool, the property of William and Nathaniel Simpson, hosiers, from Mary Veasey, spinster, under false pretences.   Not guilty.

Jeremiah Groce, victualler, for assaulting William Morton.   Guilty.

Thomas Groce, labourer, for assaulting William Morton.   Guilty.

John Kerr, labourer, for stealing 11 printed books from Robert Horsley's shop.   Guilty.

123.5   *Sacramental Certificates*
St Martin's   Captain Henry-William Guyon
               Cornet James Calderwood
               John Heyrick, gent.
St Mary's   John Dalby, hosier
Oath of Allegiance and Abjuration signed by them all.

124.1   *Writ of Summons*
                 Dated 30 March 1765 for 15 April 1765.

124.2   *Discharged Recognizances*
William Litherland, drover, to appear and answer charges and keep the peace towards Thomas Wood.
Richard Litherland, Rothley, Leics., butcher, to appear and answer charges and keep the peace towards Thomas Wood.
Thomas Wood, framework-knitter, to appear and prosecute William Litherland for an assault.
Thomas Wood to appear and prosecute William Litherland.
Thomas Wood to appear and prosecute Richard Litherland.
Benjamin Brewood, Earl Shilton, Leics., framework-knitter, to appear and prosecute Thomas Ross for an assault.
William Wilson, mercer, to appear and obey the Court *re* the bastard child of Sarah Glover, St Martin's, singlewoman.

124.3   *Presentment*
The Grand Jury present the Inhabitants of St Margaret's Parish for not repairing part of Millstone Lane.   Ignored.

124.4   *Indictments*
John Clarke, carrier, for obstructing Gallowtree Gate with an empty wagon and an empty cart.

Augustine Heafford, carpenter, for obstructing Friar Lane with 3 cart loads of dirt and rubbish.

William Litherland, drover, for assaulting Thomas Wood.　Guilty.

William Litherland, drover, for obtaining a pair of stockings from Thomas Wood under false pretences.　Guilty.

Richard Litherland, Rothley, Leics., butcher, for obtaining a pair of stockings from Thomas Wood under false pretences.　Guilty.

Thomas Ross, Countesthorpe, Leics., framework-knitter, for assaulting Benjamin Brewood.　Guilty.

125.1　　　　　　　　　*Writ of Summons*
Dated 1 June 1765 for 19 July 1765.

125.2　　　　　　　*Discharged Recognizances*
Samuel Marvin, Earl Shilton, Leics., victualler, to appear and answer charges and keep the peace towards Baxter York.
Samuel Johnson, labourer, to appear and answer *re* the bastard child of Prisca Jarvis.
Thomas Norman, framework-knitter, to appear and answer charges and keep the peace towards Lucy Ward, widow.
John Ellis, Kibworth Beauchamp, Leics., butcher, to appear and answer charges and keep the peace towards John Brooks.

125.3　　　　　　　*Sacramental Certificate*
St Martin's　William Tilly, gent.
Oath of Allegiance and Abjuration signed by him.

126.1　　　　　　　　　*Writ of Summons*
Dated 30 September 1765 for 7 October 1765.

126.2　　　　　　　*Discharged Recognizances*
Joseph Simpson, gent., to appear and answer charges and keep the peace towards John Fisher, gent.
Richard Youell, framework-knitter, to appear and give evidence against Frances Banger for a felony.
Mary, wife of Henry Bell, framework-knitter, to appear and prosecute Frances Banger for a felony.

126.3　　　　　　　　　*Indictments*
Thomas Tompson, tailor, for assaulting Samuel Brown, Justice.　Po se, guilty.

Frances Banger for stealing a woman's scarlet cloth cloak from Henry Bell's house.　Po se, guilty.

126.4 *Conviction*

John Fisher for swearing 1 profane oath.

126.5 *Petition*

Anne, wife of Thomas Mosely:

⟨In all humility sheweth that your petitioner husband being by a disastrious fall of Timber was so bruised lamed and lost much blood that hee is so weake that he is not in capacity to worke for his family (of which family there is sixe to mentaine) he was & your petitioner industrious to provide for them, by knitting trade which is so lowe that they are in great wants & not with out sad remorse to them selves to deplore their low condition, the whole family being in want of necessary lynens to keepe them in health & christian society humbly sheweth this their great sorrow, with their humble request to your worships That your favour may be granted to them weekly & for the overseers forthwith under your worships hands for lynens or utterly they must perrish etc. which granted your petitioner as in all duty shall pray for your worships.

Petitioner allowed 12d. a weeke untill furter order.⟩

126.6 *Sacramental Certificates*

St Martin's   Joseph Chambers, Mayor
                    John Gregory
                    Richard Roberts Drake
St Mary's   John Fisher, gent.
                    Samuel Tuffley
                    George Webb
St Margaret's William Holmes, gent.

127.1 *Writ of Summons*

Dated 28 March 1766 for 7 April 1766.

127.2 *Discharged Recognizances*

John Hubbard, perukemaker, to appear and answer charges and keep the peace towards Thomas Clay.

William Garratt, grocer, to appear and answer charges and keep the peace towards Henry Goulder.

John Brewin, apprentice or servant to Edward Harris, gunsmith, to appear and answer charges.

127.3 *Indictment*

William Cooper, hosier, for assaulting Robert Deakins.

127.4 *Conviction*

John Hubbard for swearing 4 profane oaths.

128.1 *Writ of Summons*

Dated 1 July 1766 for 14 July 1766.

128.2 *Oath of Allegiance and Abjuration*

7 October 1765. Signed by: Joseph Chambers, Mayor
John Fisher
William Holmes
Richard Roberts Drake
John Gregory
George Webb
Samuel Tuffley
13 January 1766. Signed by: John Davenport
William Mason
14 July 1766.   Signed by: William Burleton

128.3 *Discharged Recognizance*

Nathaniel Cooper, gent., to appear and answer charges and keep the peace towards Richard Clayton, apothecary.

128.4 *Indictment*

George Robinson, framework-knitter, for illegally lodging Mary Ball and her illegitimate son in his cottage.

128.5 *Conviction*

James Taylor for swearing 1 profane oath.

128.6 *Information*

Richard Clayton, surgeon and apothecary, taken 17 April 1766:
⟨Who upon his oath saith that this day at his own house in the Parish of Saint Martin in the said Borough he was assaulted by Nathaniel Cooper of the parish of All Saints in the said Borough Gentleman, Saith that the said Nathaniel Cooper came to him to his own house and made the assault aforesaid by holding up his hand in a violent and hostile manner and threatening him as otherwise by abusive and meanacing words.⟩

128.7 *Sacramental Certificate*

All Saints'   William Burleton, Recorder

129.1 *Writ of Summons*

Dated 9 September 1766 for 6 October 1766.

129.2 *Discharged Recognizances*

Daniel Walton, sadler, to appear and answer charges and keep the peace towards Stephen Bywater, jun.

Stephen Bywater, jun., scrivener, to appear and prosecute Daniel Walton for an assault.

Robert Flint, yeoman, to appear and answer *re* the bastard child of Elizabeth Loyley.

John Clarke, labourer, to appear and prosecute Richard Niftin for a felony.

Mary, wife of Samuel Watts, labourer, to appear and answer charges.

129.3 *Presentments*

Joseph Chambers, Justice, presents the Inhabitants of St Margaret's Parish for not repairing Humberstone Gate from the east end of St Margaret's Workhouse.

William Burleton, Recorder, presents the Inhabitants of St Mary's Parish for not repairing the piece of road between the end of Braunstone Gate and the start of the Turnpike Road to Hinckley.

129.4 *Indictments*

Daniel Walton, sadler, for assaulting Stephen Bywater, jun.

John Pearson, carpenter, for lodging Catherine, wife of [blank] Latham, who was pregnant, in his house in St Nicholas' Parish where the baby was later born, thus forcing the Parish to pay 12s. maintenance towards the mother and child even though Catherine had no legal settlement in the Parish.

Richard Niftin, labourer, for stealing 9 pieces of silver, 44 pieces of copper, and a hempen bag from John Clarke.   Guilty.

Mary, wife of Samuel Watts, labourer, for assaulting John Fisher and Joseph Cooper, Justices, ⟨with indecent and opprobrious Language and Gestures⟩, whilst they were executing their offices.   Pleads guilty.

129.5 *Conviction*

Robert Deakins, victualler, for cursing 6 profane curses.

129.6 *Sacramental Certificates*

St Mary's	John Fisher, Mayor
	John Coleman, Chamberlain
	Joseph Johnson, Chamberlain
	James Cooper, gent.
	Benjamin Sutton, gent.
St Martin's	John Cartwright, gent.
	William Oldham
St Margaret's	Thomas Barwell
	William Oliver

129.7   *Application for Certificate for Dissenters' Meeting House*

⟨I Humbly Certify unto your Worships that the Dwelling house of me The Under written John Cowdall Sittuated in the Parrish of Allsaints In the said Burrough is intened to be Used As A Meeting place for Protestant Decenters from the Church of England Call'd Anna Baptists For the worship of Allmighty God Wittness my hand John Cowdall

Wittness Robert Cowdall⟩

130.1   *Writ of Summons*
Dated 17 April 1767 for 27 April 1767.

130.2   *Discharged Recognizances*
Thomas Dunmore, labourer, and Elizabeth Ludlam, spinster, to appear and give evidence against John Bland.

Charles Hackett, victualler, to appear and answer charges and keep the peace towards John Ross.

Charles Burdett, scourer, to appear and answer charges and keep the peace towards John Edwards.

John Bland, framework-knitter, to appear and answer charges.

Thomas Conduit, labourer, and John Phipps, Hungarton, Leics., plasterer, to appear and give evidence against Thomas Goode.

Thomas Goode, Houghton-on-the-Hill, Leics., labourer, to appear and answer charges.

James Pank, druggist and grocer, to appear to prosecute and give evidence against Thomas Goode.

John Loseby, framework-knitter, to appear and prosecute George Hort.

130.3   *Victuallers' Recognizances*
William Almey is licensed to keep an Inn for a year provided he keeps good order.

Thomas Daniell is licensed to keep an Inn for a year, or until the next Licensing of Victuallers, provided he keeps good order.

130.4   *Indictments*
Thomas Goode, labourer, for obtaining 1 lb bohea tea, $\frac{1}{2}$ lb green tea, 7 lbs lump sugar, and $3\frac{1}{2}$ lbs currants from James Pank under false pretences.   Not guilty.

George Hort, framework-knitter, for stealing a hand vice from Joseph Loseby.   Po se, not guilty.

130.5   *Sacramental Certificates*
St Martin's   John Barfoot, gent.
Loughborough   John Kirkland, Loughborough, Leics., gent.

131.1 *Writ of Summons*

Dated 29 September 1767 for 5 October 1767.

131.2 *Discharged Recognizances*

Joseph Wrighte, Melton Mowbray, Leics., carrier, to appear and answer charges.

Eleanor, wife of William Turner, woolcomber, to appear and answer charges.

William Westley, framework-knitter, Job Dawson, framework-knitter, and John Brown, framework-knitter, to appear to prosecute and give evidence against Eleanor Turner.

William Turner, jun., woolcomber, to appear and answer charges and keep the peace towards Humphrey Winter.

John Edwards, 2nd Dragoon Regiment, to appear and answer charges.

Richard Parrott, Belgrave, Leics., blacksmith, to appear and obey the Court *re* the bastard child of Sarah Irish, widow.

William White, labourer, to appear and answer charges and keep the peace towards Robert Langton.

Aaron Stroud, labourer, and John Wrighte, labourer, to appear to prosecute and give evidence against Joseph Hurst for a felony.

131.3 *Presentments*

The Grand Jury presents Joseph Wright, labourer, for bringing Alice Russell into the Parish of St Margaret's where she had no legal settlement, so that the Parish was forced to pay £3 for her maintenance. Not found against him, ignored.

The Grand Jury present Joseph Johnson, joiner, for obstructing the Swines Market or High Street with a cart load of dirt and filth which he left there for 10 hours, and which contaminated the air with its obnoxious smell. Ignored.

131.4 *Indictments*

Eleanor, wife of William Turner, woolcomber, for keeping a disorderly house. Pleads guilty.

Joseph Hurst, framework-knitter, for stealing a stone bottle and 2 lbs quicksilver from John Trubshaw. Po se.

131.5 *Convictions*

John Oldham for swearing 3 profane oaths and 3 profane curses.

John Cooper for swearing 2 profane oaths.

Thomas Higgins, needlemaker, for swearing 1 profane oath.

John Hayward for swearing 2 profane oaths.

Edward Loseby for swearing 1 profane oath.

131.6   *Sacramental Certificates*
St Martin's   Henry Watchorn
                 John Lewin
                 Sampson Chapman
St Margaret's   William Holmes, Mayor
                 Alderman William Mason, gent.
St Mary's   Alderman Richard Ogden, gent.

132.1   *Writ of Summons*
                 Dated 3 April 1768 for 11 April 1768.

132.2   *Discharged Recognizances*

Charles Hackett, victualler, to appear and answer charges to be made by John Fenton.

Thomas Hackett, gent., to appear and answer charges and keep the peace towards John Fenton.

John Fenton, victualler, to appear to prosecute and give evidence against Charles Hackett.

John Fenton to appear to prosecute and give evidence against Thomas Hackett.

John Glover, Thurmaston, Leics., farmer, to appear and answer charges and keep the peace towards George Dumelow.

Suzanna Brugh, widow, to appear and answer charges.

Joseph Horton, maltster, to appear and answer charges and keep the peace towards Joseph Chambers.

Joseph Chambers, gent., to appear to prosecute and give evidence against Joseph Horton.

Andrew Ledbrooke, grocer and druggist, to appear and give evidence against Joseph Horton.

John Smith, woolcomber, to appear and answer charges and keep the peace towards Haddon Dand.

Christopher Statham, woolcomber, to appear and answer charges and keep the peace towards William Read.

Joseph Perkins, woolcomber, to appear and answer charges and keep the peace towards William Howell.

Thomas Needham, butcher, to appear and answer charges and keep the peace towards Mary Philipps.

Mary Philipps, widow, to appear to prosecute and give evidence against Thomas Needham.

Sarah Halford, spinster, to appear to prosecute and give evidence against Joseph Brookes.

John Clarke, carrier, to appear and answer charges and keep the peace towards John Wrighte.

John Wrighte, Birstall, Leics., carpenter, to appear to prosecute and give evidence against John Clarke.

John Webster, bricklayer, John Wrighte, sen., Birstall, Leics., carpenter, and Joseph Kilby, Birstall, Leics., labourer, to appear and give evidence against John Clarke.

Benjamin Cooke, framework-knitter, to appear and answer charges to be made by Thomas Whittingham.

Thomas Whittingham, carpenter, to appear to prosecute and give evidence against Benjamin Cooke.

Samuel Hackett, butcher, to appear and answer charges to be made by Samuel Roades, jun.

Thomas Higgins, needlemaker, to appear and answer charges.

Joseph Brookes, woolcomber, to appear and answer charges.

132.3 *Indictments*

John Clarke, carrier, for assaulting John Wrighte, jun.

Joseph Horton, maltster, for assaulting Joseph Chambers, Justice, whilst he was executing his office. Copy—original removed by Writ of Certiorari.

Thomas Needham, butcher, for assaulting Mary Philipps, widow.

Joseph Brookes, woolcomber, for breaking the glass windows of William Halford's house.

Benjamin Cooke, framework-knitter, for assaulting Thomas Whittingham.

132.4 *Conviction*

John Cox, woolstapler, for swearing 4 profane oaths, ⟨God damn you damn you damn you damn you⟩.

132.5 *Certificate under the Prevention of Corruption Act*

⟨I William Holmes Esquire Mayor of the Borough of Leicester do Solemnly Swear that I have not directly nor indirectly received any Sum or Sums of Money office place or imployment gratuity or reward or any Bond Bill or note or any promise or Gratuity whatsoever either by my self or any other person to my use or benefit or advanttage for making any return at the present election of Members to serve in parliament and that I will return such person or persons as shall to the Best of my Judgement appear to me to have the Majority of Legal votes.⟩

Certificate in same form as above for the Bailiff, John Kirkland, gent.

133.1 *Writ of Summons*
Dated 21 September 1768 for 3 October 1768.

133.2 *Discharged Recognizances*

Drummer Hector Munro and Sergeant John Emmerson, Leicestershire Militia, to appear and answer charges.

William Ridgeway, jun., woolcomber, to appear and answer charges to be made by Jane, wife of Henry Orton, gardener.

Charles Daws, woolcomber, to appear and answer charges to be made by Ann, wife of Thomas Tredgitt.

Joseph Daws, woolcomber, to appear and answer charges to be made by Catherine, wife of William Taylor.

Samuel Harding Bletsoe, framework-knitter, to appear and answer charges.

John Alsop, slater, to appear and answer charges to be made by John Page, jun.

Edward Kemm, labourer, to appear and answer charges to be made by Ann Cooper, spinster.

John Foster, framework-knitter, to appear and answer charges to be made by James Truman.

Thomas Tredgitt, woolcomber, to appear and answer charges and keep the peace towards Thomas Langton.

Jonathan Middleton, labourer, to appear and answer charges.

John Radford, carpenter, to appear and answer charges to be made by John Cooke.

Mary, wife of Henry Hasting, framework-knitter, to appear to prosecute and give evidence against Mary, wife of John Norman, for a felony.

John Foster, framework-knitter, to appear and answer *re* the female bastard child of Mary Liquorish, singlewoman.

133.3 *Presentment*

The Grand Jury present the Inhabitants of the Borough of Leicester for not repairing the Braunstone Gate Bridge.

133.4 *Indictments*

Jonathan Middleton, labourer, for assaulting Richard Moseby, carpenter, and kicking him on the right leg until it broke.

Mary, wife of John Norman, labourer, for stealing a red and white swanskin woman's petticoat from Henry Hastings.   Po se, guilty.

133.5 *Convictions*

John Cox, woolcomber, for cursing 5 profane curses.

Charles Burton, framework-knitter, for swearing 3 profane oaths.

William Green, jun., slater, for swearing 3 profane oaths.

Thomas Brown for swearing 4 profane oaths.

Thomas Cholmondely, cordwainer, for swearing 2 profane oaths.

133.6   *Sacramental Certificates*

St Martin's   Alderman Clement Stretton, gent.
                    Alderman John Gamble, gent.
                    Alderman John Cartwright, gent.
                    Richard Walker, hosier
                    Samuel Topp
                    Richard Beale, jun.
                    William Buckley
St Margaret's   John Westley, Mayor
                    William Simpson
                    William Brown
St Nicholas'   Alderman Hamlet Clarke, gent.

134.1   *Writ of Summons*
            Dated 25 March 1769 for 3 April 1769.

134.2   *Discharged Recognizances*

John Martin, labourer, to appear and answer *re* the bastard child of Elizabeth Whattoff, widow.
Thomas Glover, chimneysweep, to appear and answer charges.
Samuel Watts, labourer, to appear and answer charges.
Obadiah Emptage, framework-knitter, and Sarah, his wife, to appear and answer charges.
John Radford, carpenter, and Thomas Mason, scourer, to appear to prosecute and give evidence against Obadiah and Sarah Emptage.
Frances, wife of John Taylor, framework-knitter, to appear and answer charges of felony.
Olive, wife of William Lewitt, jun., gardener, to appear to prosecute and give evidence against Frances Taylor for a felony.

134.3   *Indictment*

Frances, wife of John Taylor, framework-knitter, for stealing a silver teaspoon from William Lewitt. Pleads not guilty, ⟨Jury say Guilty to 6d value⟩.

134.4   *Conviction*

Samuel Hollis als. Shock for cursing 6 profane curses.

134.5   *Petition*

William Fox, All Saints':
⟨Humbly Sheweth unto your worshipps That your Petitioner is of the age of Seventy years and upwards and in a very poor & low Condition and is alsoe very decripid and lame & not being able to dresse nor undresse him-

selfe without the Assistance and help of his wife for seaven years or more last past, and is and has bin past all manner of Labour to gett a penny towards a maintenance for these many years, And the said Parish does allow your poor and humble petitioner but twelve pence weekly Collection to mainteyne him which is soe small an Allowance that your poor petitioner is almost starved and pined for want of a better allowance bread and Coles being soe very dear as they are, These are therefore humbly to beg of your worshipps to take into your considerations your petitioners poor Condition for want of a better allowance & to order the present officers to give a better weekly pay what your worships please to order and your petitioner as in duty bound shall ever pray for your worshipps etc.⟩

134.6   *Sacramental Certificates*
St Martin's   John Gamble, Mayor
              John Heyrick, gent.

135.1   *Writ of Summons*
               Dated 4 August 1769 for 23 August 1769.

135.2   *Discharged Recognizances*
Jonathan Chettle, victualler, to appear and answer charges.
William Brunt, sawyer, to appear and answer charges.
Mary, wife of William Duneclift, brickmaker, to appear and give evidence against William Brunt.
Thomas Taylor, woolcomber, and Sarah Bray, spinster, to appear and give evidence against William Brunt.
Joseph Bromley, perukemaker, to appear and answer charges.
John Brookes to appear and answer charges.
Edward Lord, framework-knitter, to appear and answer charges.
Benjamin Withers, framework-knitter, to appear and answer charges.
Ann, wife of Benjamin Withers, to appear and answer charges.
Joseph Walker, labourer, to appear to prosecute and give evidence against Benjamin and Mary Withers.
Elizabeth, wife of Frederick Hall, framework-knitter, to appear to prosecute and give evidence against Benjamin and Mary Withers.

135.3   *Presentments*
The Grand Jury present William Brunt, sawyer, for keeping a disorderly house.   Ignored.

The Grand Jury present Benjamin Withers, framework-knitter, and Ann, his wife, for keeping a disorderly house.   Ignored.

136.1   *Writ of Summons*
               Dated 23 September 1769 for 2 October 1769.

136.2 *Presentments*

John Fisher and William Holmes, Justices, present the Inhabitants of St Margaret's Parish for not repairing the Pasture Lane leading from Church-gate and Sanvy Gate to St Margaret's Pasture.

The Grand Jury present the Inhabitants of the Borough of Leicester for not repairing the Common Gaol which ⟨is in great decay and ruinous and particularly that the Outward Walls thereof are in many parts feeble and weak and it would tend to the convenience and utility of the Goal or Prison to have the same repaired and also a separate building or room for the Debtors distinct from the Felons⟩.

136.3 *Conviction*

James Biggs for ⟨buying and receiving a pair of brown marvel worsted Stockings the property of Thomas Kestins of the Borough of Leicester aforesaid Hosier and by him delivered to John Oldham of the same Borough Framework-knitter to be manufactored⟩.

136.4 *Sacramental Certificates*

St Martin's	Joseph Chambers, Mayor
	Alderman John Cooper, gent.
	Alderman Tyrringham Palmer, gent.
	Thomas Phipps
	John Hartell
St Nicholas'	Alderman Hamlet Clarke, gent.
	Alderman James Cooper, gent.
	William Astle
	Thomas Throsby
St Mary's	James Oldham
St Margaret's	Edward Sutton

137.1 *Writ of Summons*

Dated 14 April 1770 for 23 April 1770.

137.2 *Discharged Recognizances*

William Thorpe, butcher, to appear and obey the Court *re* the bastard child of Sarah Matchett, singlewoman.

Thomas Waterhouse, dyer, to appear and obey the Court *re* the bastard child of Sarah Greasley, singlewoman.

George Ross, baker, to appear and obey the Court and keep the peace towards John Once.

William Taylor, carpenter, to appear and answer charges of felony.

Rebecca Harrison, widow, to appear and prosecute Thomas Dixon for a felony.

John Bateman, labourer, and Robert Oxon, labourer, to appear and give evidence against Thomas Dixon, perukemaker, for a felony.

John Paling, carpenter, to appear and prosecute Catherine Lyon, single-woman, for a felony.

Eleanor, wife of Robert Phipps, stonecutter, to appear and prosecute Catherine Lyon for a felony.

Isabella, wife of John Paling, to appear and give evidence against Catherine Lyon for a felony.

Sarah, wife of Joseph Tompson, tailor, to appear and give evidence against Catherine Lyon for a felony.

Joseph Perkins, woolcomber, John Phipps, plasterer, and Elizabeth Hardy, widow, to appear and give evidence against Catherine Lyon for a felony.

137.3   *Indictments*

William Taylor, carpenter, for stealing 2 lbs lead from William Rawstorne, clerk.   Guilty.

Catherine Lyon, singlewoman, for stealing a red and white printed linen handkerchief from John Paling.   Po se, guilty.

Thomas Dixon, labourer, for stealing a pair of curling irons, a pair of toupee tongs, a powder machine, a razor, a pair of scissors, a piece of black silk, a piece of white silk, a silk handkerchief, a linen shirt, a linen stock, and a piece of ribbon from Rebecca Harrison, widow.   Po se, guilty.

Catherine Lyon, singlewoman, for stealing a calamanco gown from Robert Phipps.   Po se, guilty.

James Stone, labourer, for stealing a pewter basin from John Bruin Johnson.   Po se, not guilty.

137.4   *Convictions*

Peter Warburton for cursing 1 profane curse.
William Plant, framework-knitter, for swearing 2 profane oaths.
Joseph Nadon, linen draper, for cursing 33 profane curses.
William Cave, woolcomber, for cursing 1 profane curse.
Thomas Dore for cursing 2 profane curses.
Bishop Nicks, cordwainer, for swearing 1 profane oath.

138.1   *Writ of Summons*
Dated 21 September 1770 for 1 October 1770.

138.2   *Discharged Recognizances*
Mary Bird, spinster, to appear and answer charges.
John Lingham, framework-knitter, to appear to prosecute and give evidence against Mary Bird.

Samuel Gutheridge, carpenter, to appear and answer charges.

Sergeant Sampson Skidmore, Leicestershire Militia, to appear and answer charges.

James Hallam, framework-knitter, to appear to prosecute and give evidence against Sampson Skidmore.

John Wright, victualler, to appear to prosecute and give evidence against Mary, wife of William Hudson, for a felony.

Mary, wife of John Gadsby, to appear and give evidence against Mary Hudson for a felony.

Sarah, wife of James Tyler, framework-knitter, to appear to prosecute and give evidence against Rebecca, wife of James Bown, for a felony.

John Wright, victualler, to appear and give evidence against Rebecca Bown for a felony.

William Alsop, carpenter, to appear and answer charges.

138.3 *Presentment*

William Burleton, Recorder, presents the Inhabitants of the Liberty of Bromkingsthorpe in St Mary's Parish for not repairing the piece of road between the end of Braunstone Gate and the start of the Turnpike Road to Hinckley.

138.4 *Indictments*

Mary Bird, spinster, for assaulting John Lingham.

Samuel Gutheridge, carpenter, for assaulting Benjamin Elliott.

Sampson Skidmore, labourer, for assaulting James Hallam.

Mary, wife of William Hudson, labourer, for stealing 3 pewter plates and a pewter dish from the room her husband had rented in John Gadsby's lodging house.   Po se, not guilty.

Rebecca, wife of James Bown, labourer, for stealing a child's white robe and a plaid handkerchief from James Tyler.

138.5 *Conviction*

Sergeant William Pratt, 11th Dragoon Regiment, for cursing 3 profane curses and swearing 1 profane oath.

138.6 *Sacramental Certificates*

All Saints'   James Cooper, Mayor
Alderman John Cooper, gent.
Alderman Tyrringham Palmer, gent.
Samuel Topp, Chamberlain
John Clarke, Chamberlain

139.1 *Writ of Summons*

Dated 28 September 1771 for 7 October 1771.

139.2 *Discharged Recognizances*

Edward Gregory, victualler, to appear and answer charges.

William Hulse, Anstey, Leics., farmer, and William Wilkinson, farmer, to appear and give evidence against Edward Gregory on charges to be made by Hulse.

Thomas Vesie, apprentice to Samuel Whittle, framesmith, to appear and answer charges.

Edward North, bagman, to appear and answer charges.

Richard Jesson, Swithland, Leics., farmer, to appear and answer charges.

John Hitchins, cordwainer, to appear and answer charges.

Stephen Johnson, Anstey, Leics., farmer, to appear and answer charges to be made by Robert Palmer.

Stephen Johnson to appear and answer charges to be made by John Wheatley.

Stephen Johnson to appear and answer charges to be made by Joseph Draper.

139.3 *Indictments*

James Vaughan, Doctor in Physic, for obstructing New Street with a cart load of rubbish and manure.

Richard Jesson, labourer, for assaulting John Kelly.

Stephen Johnson, labourer, for assaulting Robert Palmer.

Stephen Johnson, labourer, for assaulting John Wheatley, Constable, whilst in the execution of his office.

139.4 *Convictions*

George Curry for swearing 2 profane oaths.

Edward North, victualler, for ⟨buying and receiving several pairs of worsted Stockings the property of John Cartwright the Younger of the said Borough of Leicester Hosier Of James Juba of Ibstock in the County of Leicester frameworkknitter, the materials of which the said Stockings were made the said John Cartwright delivered to the said James Juba to be manufactored⟩.

Edward North, bagman, for ⟨buying and receiving several pairs of worsted Stockings the property of Pitts Ward of the said Borough Hosier Of John Shenton of Whetstone in the County of Leicester frameworkknitter, the materials of which the said Stockings were made the said Pitts Ward delivered to the said John Shenton to be manufactored⟩.

139.5 *Sacramental Certificates*

St Margaret's John Cartwright, Mayor
Thomas Barwell
William Taylor
St Martin's Samuel Topp, Bailiff
St Mary's Richard Ogden, Coroner
St Nicholas' Hamlet Clark, Coroner

140.1 *Writ of Summons*

Dated 20 April 1772 for 1 May 1772.

140.2 *Discharged Recognizances*

John Bonner, framework-knitter, to appear and obey the Court *re* the bastard child of Elizabeth Miller, singlewoman.

William Keates, woolcomber, to appear and answer charges.

John Kirk, framework-knitter, to appear and answer charges.

Robert Barnett, framework-knitter, to appear and answer charges and keep the peace towards Eleanor, wife of Thomas Loseby, woolcomber.

Elizabeth, wife of Abraham Bunney, labourer, to appear to prosecute and give evidence against Mary Morley, singlewoman, for a felony.

Frances, wife of Samuel Harding Bletsoe, framework-knitter, to appear to prosecute and give evidence against Mary Morley for a felony.

Mary Summerfield to appear to prosecute and give evidence against Mary Morley for a felony.

John Wright, pawnbroker, to appear and give evidence against Mary Morley for a felony or felonies.

Richard Ringrose, cordwainer, to appear and answer charges.

George Measures, woolcomber, to appear and answer charges.

Robert Sleath, baker, to appear and answer charges and keep the peace towards John Iliff, baker.

Joseph Turner, framesmith, to appear and answer charges.

Walter Stonehouse, framework-knitter, to appear and answer charges and keep the peace towards Charles Mason.

William Sharpe, Groby, Leics., collarmaker, to appear and answer charges and keep the peace towards Gowen Scott, husbandman.

Mary, wife of William White, brickmaker, to appear and answer charges.

Richard Steines, victualler, to appear to prosecute and give evidence against Mary White for a felony.

Lydia, wife of John Burgess, needlemaker, to appear and give evidence against Mary White for a felony.

Thomas Ludd, Oadby, Leics., framework-knitter, to appear and answer charges and keep the peace towards William Coleman, victualler.

Samuel Clark, framework-knitter, to appear and answer charges.

Jeremiah Hughes, victualler, to appear and prosecute George Godwin for a felony.

Sarah, wife of Jeremiah Hughes, to appear and give evidence against George Godwin for a felony.

John Wright, pawnbroker, to appear and give evidence against George Godwin for a felony.

Samuel Keen, framework-knitter, to appear to prosecute and give evidence against Jonathan Seal, Maria, his wife, and Elizabeth Bullus, widow.

John Springthorpe, victualler, to appear to prosecute and give evidence against Jonathan and Maria Seal and Elizabeth Bullus.

Elizabeth Robinson, singlewoman, to appear and give evidence against Jonathan and Maria Seal and Elizabeth Bullus.

Thomas Clareson, dyer, and Sarah, his wife, to appear and answer charges.

140.3 *Indictments*

Mary Morley, singlewoman, for stealing a napkin and a pillow drawer from Abraham Bunney. Pleads not guilty, po se, found guilty.

Mary Morley, singlewoman, for stealing a flaxen shift from Mary Bletsoe. Pleads not guilty, po se, found guilty.

Mary Morley, singlewoman, for stealing a shift from William Summer-field. Pleads not guilty, po se, found guilty.

Mary, wife of William White, brickmaker, for stealing a copper saucepan from Richard Steines. Pleads not guilty, found guilty.

Robert Sleath, baker, for assaulting John Iliffe.

George Godwin, woolcomber, for stealing 2 sheets and a blanket from the room he had rented in Jeremiah Hughes' lodging-house. Pleads not guilty, found guilty.

Jonathan Seal, carpenter, and Maria, his wife, for keeping a disorderly house. Plead not guilty, found guilty.

Elizabeth Bullus, widow, for keeping a disorderly house. Po se, not guilty.

140.4 *Convictions*

Richard Haywood, Groby, Leics., farmer, for cursing 9 profane curses.

John Clark, Stanton-under-Bardon, Leics., farmer, for cursing 2 profane curses.

Joseph Whatton, jun., framework-knitter, for cursing 4 profane curses.

140.5   *Sacramental Certificates*

St Martin's   Alderman Richard Roberts Drake, gent.
                John Eames
St Mary's   Joseph Neal
St Margaret's Thomas Oliver

141.1   *Writ of Summons*

Dated 4 April 1772 for 7 August 1772.

141.2   *Discharged Recognizances*

Thomas Spalding, labourer, to appear and obey the Court *re* the bastard child of Sarah Parker, singlewoman.

William Mastin, Countesthorpe, Leics., farmer, to appear and answer charges.

John Haimes, Geddington, Northants., farmer, to appear and answer charges.

John Ashby, Weekley, Northants., farmer, to appear and answer charges.

Private John Hape, Royal Horse Guards Regiment, to appear and obey the Court *re* the bastard child of Mary Gibson, All Saints', singlewoman.

141.3   *Subscription to the 39 Articles*

⟨John Lloyd a Minister to a protestant Dissenting Congregation of the Baptist Denomination meeting in Thornton Lane in the said Borough: has Appeared this day before the Court desiring to take the Oaths and to make and Subscribe the Declaration enjoined by the Act of Tolleration in order to his being regularly quallified as a protestant Dissenting Minister and doth hereby declare his Sincere belief assent and Consent to the Articles of Religion commonly called the Thirty Nine Articles as being Agreeable to the holy Scriptures: except the Thirty fourth Thirty fifth and the Thirty Sixth and also that part of the Twentieth which saith: The Church hath power to decree Rites or Ceremonies and Authority in Matters of Faith: and that part of the Twenty Seventh which saith: "The Baptism of Young Children is in any Wise to be retained in the Church as most Agreeable with the Institution of Christ—Which are particularly allowed by the Act of Tolleration to be excepted in the Subscription enjoined upon all protestant Dissenting Ministers. And in Testimony of the Truth and Sincerity of this Declaration the said John Lloyd has hereunto Subscribed his Name.

John Lloyd⟩

141.4   *Insolvent Debtors*

⟨An Alphabetical List of the Debtor Prisoners in Leicester Borough Gaol Intended to be delivered Account of at Thomas a Beckett Sessions 1772 who were Prisoners on or before the 1st day of January 1772.

Prisoners Names		when received in prison	at whose Suit	The Debt			
Arnold Allen Robert		16th November 1771	Robert Cowdell	11	0	0	Died 30th July 1772
Do.	Do.	Do.	Thomas Jee	25	8	9	
Do.	Do.	Do.	John Plesto	9	11	6	
Do.	Do.		Joseph Smith	32	0	0	
Graham Mark		November 26th 1771	Samuel Thornton	7	4	0	

Newland Thomas	4th July 1772	James Whiteman	6	1	10

I Henry Coulson upon my corporal Oath in the presence of Almighty God do solemnly swear profess and declare that all and every Person and persons whose Name or Names are inserted or Contained in the first part of the List by me now delivered in and subscribed was and were to the best of my Knowledge and Belief upon the First Day of January One thousand Seven Hundred and Seventy two really and truly Prisoners in actual Custody in the Prison or Gaol of the Borough of Leicester at the Suit or Suits of the several persons there respectively mentioned and also that all and every person and persons whose Name or Names is or are inserted or contained in the Second Part of the said List now by me delivered in and subscribed as aforesaid have since the first Day of January One Thousand Seven hundred and Seventy two been Committed or Surrendered to the said Gaol or Prison of the Borough of Leicester at the Suit or Suits of the several person or persons therein respectively mentioned [Except] such persons as are therein particularly mentioned and described to have died in such Prison since the First Day of January one Thousand Seven hundred and seventy two and that all and every of them whose Name and Names is and are contained in the first part of the said List except as before excepted to the best of my knowledge and Belief have really and truly Continued in actual Custody in the said Gaol or prison of the Borough of Leicester ever since the first Day of January One thousand Seven hundred and Seventy two and that the said List is a true exact perfect and just List of all such Persons as were really and truly prisoners in actual Custody in the said Gaol or Prison of the Borough of Leicester on the said first Day of January One Thousand Seven hundred and Seventy two and who since the first Day of January One Thousand Seven hundred and Seventy two have been really and truly Committed or Surrendered to the said Gaol or prison of the Borough of Leicester (except as before excepted) to the best of my knowledge and Belief and that none of such prisoners to my knowledge or with my privity have voluntaryly or with Design or in Expectation to take any Benifit from or under any Act of Parliament to be made for relief of Insolvent Debtors Surrendered or been committed to the said prison of the Borough of Leicester or got his her or their Name or Names entered as Prisoners in the

Books of the said Prison or since the Commitment have to my knowledge or with my privity resided out of the said Prison of the Borough of Leicester.

H. Coulson Goaler⟩

Oath of Mark Graham:

⟨I Mark Graham upon my Corporal oath in the presence of almighty God do Solemnly Swear protest and Declare that on the First day of January One thousand Seven hundred and Seventy two I was a prisoner in the Goal or prison of the Borough of Leicester and that I was actually arrested before the said First day of January 1772 in the Action or Suit in which I was Committed as aforesaid to the said Goal or prison and that I have ever Since my said Committment continued a prisoner within the said prison in the actual Custody of the Goaler or keeper of the said prison or within the Liberties thereof at the Suit of Samuel Thornton and without any fraud or Collousion whatsoever and that the Schedule now Delivered by me . . .⟩ [continues as "Compulsive Oath" **115.6**]

⟨[torn] Account of me Mark Graham late of the Parish of All Saints in the Borough of Leicester wool comber, Now a prisoner in his Majesties Goal for the Said Borough Containing the whole of my Personal Estate (Except Wearing Apparel and Bedding for myself and Family, Working Tools and Necessary Implements for my Occupation and Calling and These in the whole not Exceeding the Value of Twenty Pounds) I having no real Estate for the benefit of my Creditors.

The Schedule or account above referred to

Five Gallons of Combers Oil, a fire Grate, Four Old Chairs, one Oval Table, One Square Table, Two Boxes, a Brass Pot, Ten tops of Coarse wool, Twenty Four pounds of Coarse wool and the Sum of One pound two Shillings and Seven pence half penny due to me from William Pearson of Stamford in the County of Lincoln Frameworkknitter for Worsted.

Mark Graham⟩

142.1 *Writ of Summons*

Dated 26 September 1772 for 5 October 1772

142.2 *Constable's Presentment*

John Springthorp (Ald. Fisher's Ward) presents the Inhabitants of St Mary's Parish ⟨for not repairing a stone footbridge situate in the Horsepool street in the said Parish & near to a certain place there called the Horsepool⟩. Indicted.

142.3 *Indictments*

William Mastin, labourer, for assaulting John Wright.

Robert Peak, butcher, for assaulting John Carter.

142.4   *Process Paper*

Robert Sleath, baker, having been indicted for assaulting John Iliffe, has pleaded "Not Guilty" and is to be tried.   Not guilty.

142.5   *Conviction*

John Billings, woolcomber, for cursing 18 profane curses.

142.6   *Sacramental Certificates*

St Martin's   Robert Peach, Mayor
                Edward Price
                William Oldham
St Mary's   Alderman Benjamin Sutton, gent.
                John Cooper
All Saints'   Alderman William Orton, gent.
St Margaret's   Alderman John Coleman, gent.
St Nicholas'   Hamlet Clark

143.1   *Writ of Summons*
                Dated 10 April 1773 for 19 April 1773.

143.2   *Discharged Recognizances*

John Holmes, Wigston Magna, Leics., framework-knitter, to appear and obey the Court *re* the bastard child of Ann Wright.
Colwell Langdon, woolcomber, to appear and answer charges.
John Hind, scourer, to appear to prosecute and give evidence against John Simpson, cordwainer, for a felony.
Suzanna, wife of Benjamin Mitchell, to appear and give evidence against John Simpson for a felony.

143.3   *Presentment*

Robert Peach, Mayor, and William Burleton, Recorder, present The Inhabitants of the Liberty of the Newarke for putting posts and chains across ⟨a certain Common highway in the Liberty of the Newark in the Borough of Leicester aforesaid in a certain place near to a certain new erected Messuage or tenement belonging to and in the tenure of Mr William Mason leading from a certain Street or Lane in the Parish of Saint Mary in the said Borough called South gate street into and over the Liberty of the Newarke aforesaid across a certain Lane in the Liberty of the Newarke aforesaid called Mill Lane into a certain other Lane in the said parish of Saint Mary and in the said Borough called Grange lane⟩. Copy—original removed by Writ of Certiorari.

143.4 *Indictments*

The Inhabitants of St Mary's Parish for not repairing the footbridge near the Horsepool in High Street or Southgate Street.

George White, jun., labourer, for stealing a hen from Francis Needham. Po se.

John Simpson, cordwainer, for stealing a pair of worsted stockings from John Hind. Po se.

George White, jun., labourer, for stealing 10 lbs tallow and 1 lb tobacco from William Lamb.

John Wolfe, labourer, for obstructing Coal Hill with 2 cartloads of dirt and filth.

Charles Freeman, carrier, for assaulting John Throsby, Sergeant-at-Mace, whilst Throsby was serving a Writ of Capias on Freeman.

143.5 *Judgements*

George White, jun., labourer, having been indicted for stealing a hen from Francis Needham, pleaded "Not Guilty", was tried, and found "Guilty". He was sentenced to ⟨be transported to some one of his Majestys Plantations in America for the Term of seven Years⟩.

George White, jun., labourer, having been indicted for stealing 10 lbs. tallow and 1 lb. tabacco from William Lamb, pleaded "Not Guilty", was tried, and found "Guilty". He was sentenced to ⟨be transported to some one of his Majestys Plantations in America for the Term of seven years⟩.

143.6 *Sacramental Certificate*

St Martin's   Alderman Samuel Jordan, gent.

144.1 *Writ of Summons*

Dated 24 September 1773 for 4 October 1773.

144.2 *Discharged Recognizances*

Thomas Webster, victualler, to appear ⟨and prosecute with effect against a Judgment of Robert Peach Esquire Mayor whereby he is adjudged to forfeit twenty pounds for receiving six pairs of Marble Stockings⟩.

Thomas Lockwood, mercer, to appear to prosecute and give evidence against Sarah Hall for a felony.

Hannah, wife of John Berridge, to appear and give evidence against Sarah Hall for a felony.

144.3 *Indictments*

Sarah Hall alias Hannah Oakley alias Hannah Parker, widow, for stealing 2 silk and cotton handkerchiefs from Thomas Lockwood.   Po se, guilty.

William Davenport, labourer, for stealing a coat, a waistcoat and a pair of breeches from Matthew Jarvis.   Po se, not guilty.

144.4 *Convictions*

John Carter for cursing 1 profane curse.

John Munton for cursing 1 profane curse.

Thomas Webster for ⟨buying and receiving six pairs of Marble Stockings of John Howkins of the said Borough frameworkknitter and which were made up & manufactored by him out of a quantity of worsted the property of Messieurs Thomas Fielding and Joseph Stafford both of the said Borough Hosiers & Partners who delivered the same worsted to the said John Howkins to be manufactured⟩.

144.5 *Judgement*

Sarah Hall alias Hannah Oakley alias Hannah Parker, widow, having been indicted for stealing 2 silk and cotton handkerchiefs from Thomas Lockwood, pleaded "Not Guilty", was tried, and found "Guilty". She was sentenced to ⟨be publickly whipped next Saturday and discharged⟩.

144.6 *Certificate of Road Repair*

For the road in the Liberty of Bromkingsthorpe.

144.7 *Sacramental Certificates*

St Margaret's   Richard Roberts Drake, Mayor
William Mason, Coroner
Samuel Jordan, Coroner
James Oldham
James Bishop
Thomas Topham

145.1 *Writ of Summons*

Dated 4 April 1774 for 11 April 1774.

145.2 *Discharged Recognizances*

William Kirby, Gumley, Leics., farmer, to appear and obey the Court *re* the bastard child of Elizabeth Lewitt, singlewoman.

Joseph Whatton, jun., framework-knitter, to appear and obey the Court *re* the bastard child of Mary Thorpe, singlewoman.

Edward Robinson, framework-knitter, to appear and answer charges.

William Gutheridge, carpenter, to appear and answer charges.

William Welton to appear and answer charges.

William Gutheridge, carpenter, to appear and obey the Court *re* the bastard child of Ann Newbold, singlewoman.

145.3 *Conviction*

William Smith for cursing 1 profane curse.

146.1 *Writ of Summons*

Dated 21 July 1774 for 8 August 1774.

146.2 *Discharged Recognizance*

John Christian, labourer, to appear and answer charges.

147a.1 *Writ of Summons*

Dated 29 September 1774 for 3 October 1774.

147a.2 *Discharged Recognizances*

Thomas Wood, jun., Sapcote, Leics., labourer, to appear and ⟨answer in a matter of Bastardy⟩.

Samuel Bunney, innholder, to appear and answer charges and keep the peace towards Henry Thorpe.

Henry Thorpe, Uppingham, Rutland, stonecutter, to appear to prosecute and give evidence against Samuel Bunney.

John Cooper, hosier, to appear and answer charges and keep the peace towards Elizabeth Bankart, spinster.

147a.3 *Conviction*

William Turner for cursing 1 profane curse.

147a.4 *Sacramental Certificates*

St Margaret's	Samuel Oliver, Mayor
	John Coleman, gent.
	John Parsons
	Sampson Chapman
St Martin's	Thomas Fisher Cooper
	Joseph Burbidge
St Mary's	Joseph Johnson, gent.

93b.1 *Writ of Summons*

Dated 3 January 1775 for 9 January 1775.

93b.2 *Discharged Recognizances*

John Billing, woolcomber, to appear and answer charges and keep the peace towards Robert Pindar.

Joseph Heard, hosier, to appear and answer charges and keep the peace towards John Jones.

John Smith, victualler, to appear and answer charges and keep the peace towards John Jones.

147b.1 *Writ of Summons*
Dated 20 April 1775 for 24 April 1775.

147b.2 *Discharged Recognizances*
Edward Harrison, innholder, to appear and obey the Court *re* the bastard child of Elizabeth Tomlin, widow.
Samuel Bankart, woolstapler, to appear and answer charges on two counts.

147b.3 *Indictments*
George Booth, labourer, for assaulting William Lewitt.   Pleads guilty.

Samuel Bankart, woolstapler, for assaulting Thomas Jeffcutt.

Samuel Bankart, woolstapler, for assaulting Henry Jeffcutt.

147b.4 *Sacramental Certificate*
St Martin's   Alderman John Pocklington, gent.

148.1 *Writ of Summons*
Dated 29 September 1775 for 2 October 1775.

148.2 *Discharged Recognizances*
William Lewitt, gardener, to appear and answer charges.
John Clark, victualler, to appear and answer charges.
Thomas Chester, linen draper, to appear and obey the Court and keep the peace towards Sarah, wife of James Wing.
John Johnson, bricklayer, to appear and answer charges.

148.3 *Indictment*
The Inhabitants of St Margaret's Parish for not repairing the Welford Road between Millstone Lane and Hangman Lane.

148.4 *Process Papers*
Samuel Bankart, woolstapler, having been indicted for assaulting Thomas Jeffcutt, has pleaded "Not Guilty" and is to be tried.

Samuel Bankart, woolstapler, having been indicted for assaulting Henry Jeffcutt, has pleaded "Not Guilty" and is to be tried.

148.5 *Sacramental Certificates*
St Mary's   Joseph Johnson, Mayor
             William Astle
             Hamlet Clark
St Martin's Alderman John Gregory, gent.
             Alderman John Pocklington, gent.
             Clement Stretton, Coroner

St Margaret's   Benjamin Gregory
John Mansfield
Robert Dickinson

149.1   *Writ of Summons*
Dated 8 April 1776 for 19 April 1776.

149.2   *Discharged Recognizances*
George Ramsden, innholder, to appear and obey the Court and keep the
peace towards Daniel Curisen, Excise Officer.
William Harrison, Stocking Farm, Leics., farmer, to appear and obey the
Court and keep the peace towards Henry Kirk.
Henry Kirk, Cropston, Leics., labourer, to appear and prosecute William
Harrison.
Samuel Hulse alias Howse, Anstey, Leics., farmer, to appear and answer
charges.
William Arnold, baker, to appear and answer charges of assault to be made
by Daniel Palmer.
William Arnold, baker, to appear and answer charges of assault to be made
by Thomas Bollard.

149.3   *Presentments*
The Grand Jury present the Mayor, Bailiffs, and Burgesses of the Borough
of Leicester for not repairing Churchgate.

The Grand Jury present Francis Harris, labourer, for not repairing the
pavement outside his house in Churchgate.

The Grand Jury present Robert Sleath, baker, for obstructing the road
opposite his house, ⟨a certain Common Kings highway leading from the
Parish of Saint Leonard in the said Borough through the Parish of Saint
Margaret⟩, with a ⟨cart load of Dung and other filth⟩.

The Grand Jury present George Ingram, labourer, for putting posts, rails,
and ditches across Humberstone Gate by St Margaret's Workhouse.

149.4   *Indictments*
John Bass, farmer, for obstructing the Welford Road where it adjoins
Gallow Field with a wagon load of dung and filth.

Daniel Woodland for not repairing Back Lane where it runs beside his
orchard or garden. Copy—original removed into the Court of King's
Bench by Writ of Certiorari.

150.1   *Writ of Summons*
Dated 31 March 1777 for 7 April 1777.

150.2   *Discharged Recognizances*
John Gizborne, framework-knitter, to appear and answer charges.
Jemima Hague, spinster, to appear and give evidence against John Gizborne.
George Horner, labourer, to appear and obey the Court *re* the bastard child of Suzanna Alfray.
Joanna, wife of John Elliott, to appear to prosecute and give evidence against George Cox.

150.3   *Presentment*
William Burleton, Recorder, presents the Inhabitants of the Liberty of Bromkingsthorpe for not repairing the Hinckley Road between Braunstone Gate and the Turnpike Road.

150.4   *Indictments*
John Gizborne, framework-knitter, for keeping a disorderly house.

George Cox, labourer, for assaulting Joanna, wife of John Elliott.   Guilty.

150.5   *Conviction*
George Sarson, framework-knitter, for cursing 4 profane curses.

150.6   *Sacramental Certificates*
St Martin's   Alderman Thomas Phipps, gent.
               Samuel Jordan
St Mary's   Edward Burton, Excise Officer

151.1   *Writ of Summons*
Dated 29 September 1777 for 6 October 1777.

151.2   *Discharged Recognizances*
William Murden, Croft, Leics., drover, to appear and answer charges of assault to be made by John Page, jun.
John Page, jun., perukemaker, to appear to prosecute and give evidence against William Murden.
William Radford to appear and answer charges to be made by Joseph Simpson.
Joseph Simpson, gent., to appear to prosecute and give evidence against William Radford.
Thomas Coleman, hosier, to appear to ⟨prosecute his appeal against a Conviction⟩.

Richard Weat, framework-knitter, to appear to prosecute and give evidence against James Lester for a felony.

William Harrison, Stocking Farm, Leics., grazier, to appear and answer charges.

151.3 *Indictments*

Francis Nedham, yeoman, on the presentment of William Burleton, Recorder, for erecting a building which encroaches on Humberstone Gate. Copy—original removed by Writ of Certiorari.

William Radford, carpenter, for assaulting Joseph Simpson.

Thomas Williams alias James Hawkins, labourer, for stealing a silk handkerchief, an India shawl, and a hanger from Nathan Wright, Esq. Po se.

James Lester, labourer, for stealing a striped linen and silk handkerchief from Richard Weat. Po se.

The Inhabitants of St Margaret's Parish for not repairing Humberstone Gate.

151.4 *Convictions*

Joseph Berridge, framework-knitter, for ⟨embezzelling a quantity of worsted the property of Thomas Topham of the said Borough Hosier before the first day of July last past⟩.

Thomas Coleman for ⟨buying a number of Stockings made of white worsted and amounting in weight to fourteen pounds in the Borough aforesaid before the first day of July last past which said worsted was the property of John Coltman of the Newark of Leicester Hosier and was delivered to Joseph Berridge of Great Wigston in the County of Leicester Frameworkknitter to be manufactured⟩.

151.5 *Sacramental Certificates*

St Margaret's	John Coleman, Mayor
	Peter Oliver, gent.
	Joseph Neal
	Thomas Bass Oliver
St Martin's	Thomas Phipps, Coroner
	Henry Watchorn, Coroner

153.1 *Writ of Summons*

Dated 11 October 1777 for 27 April 1778.

153.2 *Discharged Recognizances*

George Groce, woolcomber, to appear and answer charges.

John Smeeton, jun., Kibworth Beauchamp, Leics., weaver, to appear and obey the Court *re* the bastard child of Elizabeth Green, singlewoman.

Peter Oliver, wine merchant, to appear to prosecute and give evidence against John Howell for a felony.

153.3   *Indictments*

Thomas Johnson, woolcomber, for assaulting George Groce.

George Groce, woolcomber, for assaulting Thomas Johnson.

George Groce, woolcomber, for assaulting Eleanor, wife of Thomas Johnson.

Elizabeth, wife of Thomas Flower, labourer, for stealing a flowered cotton gown from Richard Smith.   Pleads ⟨not guilty, po se⟩.

John Howell, labourer, for stealing 2 quart glass bottles from Peter Oliver. Pleads ⟨not guilty, po se, Jury say Guilty⟩.

154.1   *Writ of Summons*
Dated 30 March 1780 for 7 April 1780.

154.2   *Discharged Recognizances*

William Robotham, journeyman hatter, to appear and ⟨prosecute his appeal against a Conviction⟩.

James Farmer, journeyman hatter, to appear and ⟨prosecute his appeal against a Conviction⟩.

John Tundley, journeyman hatter, to appear and ⟨prosecute his appeal against a Conviction⟩.

James Axson, journeyman hatter, to appear and ⟨prosecute his appeal against a Conviction⟩.

John Clark, framework-knitter, to appear and answer charges and keep the peace towards Jane, his wife.

154.3   *Information*

Jane, wife of John Clark, framework-knitter, taken 18 January 1780:
⟨Who saith that about four years ago when she lived with her said Husband he beat her violently, that afterwards they seperated by consent That she is afraid her said Husband will do her some bodily hurt by beating her unmercifully and that she has Just cause for being so afraid and therefore she prays Sureties of the Peace against her said Husband & that she does not require such Sureties out of Malice or for vexation.⟩

154.4   *Convictions*

William Robotham, journeyman hatter, for ⟨having entred into a Contract

Covenant Agreement By law Ordinance Rule or order of an illegal Club
Society or Combination or presuming or attempting to put an illegal agreement By law Ordinance Rule or order in execution contrary to the Statutes
in such Case made and provided or one of them⟩.

James Farmer, journeyman hatter, as for Robotham above.

John Tundley, journeyman hatter, for ⟨having demanded in the said
Borough a Sum of money of Thomas Cannam a Journeyman Hatter for the
use of an unlawfull Club Society or Combination contrary to the Statutes
in such Case made and provided or one of them and of having threatned
the said Thomas Cannam That he the said Thomas should have no more
work after he should have quitted the Service of Edward Harris in whose
service the said Thomas Cannam was employed as a Journeyman Hatter
Contrary to the statutes in such case made & provided or one of them⟩.

James Axson, journeyman hatter, as for Tundley above.

154.5   *Sacramental Certificates*

St Martin's   John Heyrick, Under Sheriff of the County
                 Thomas Jeffcutt, Common Councillor
                 Daniel Walton, Common Councillor
                 James Mallett, Common Councillor

St Margaret's   Alderman James Bishop, gent.
                 William Bishop, Common Councillor

155.1   *Writ of Summons*

Dated 21 April 1781 for 23 April 1781.

155.2   *Discharged Recognizances*

Thomas Jaques, labourer, to appear and answer charges.

John Pears, brickmaker, to appear to prosecute and give evidence against
Hannah Glazebrook for a felony.

Elizabeth, wife of John Pears, to appear and give evidence against Hannah
Glazebrook for a felony.

155.3   *Indictment*

Hannah Glazebrook, spinster, for stealing a striped cotton gown, a pair of
stays, a red frieze cloak, a pair of black worsted stockings, a striped muslin
apron, and a linen shift from John Pears. Po se, guilty of the shift and
shoes[?].

155.4   *Certificates of Road and Pavement Repair*

The Inhabitants of the Liberty of Bromkingsthorpe have repaired the
Hinckley Road between Braunstone Gate and the Turnpike Road.

The following have repaired the pavements in front of their houses:

William Bradsworth in Southgate Street.

Ann Pratt, spinster, in Millstone Lane.
Jeremiah Porrett in Millstone Lane.
Edward Davie, gent., by his garden in Southgate Street.
John Norman, woolcomber, in Deadman's Lane.

155.5   *Certificates of Removal of Obstructions*
Francis Nedham, yeoman, has removed the hovel from Humberstone Gate.
Francis Nedham, yeoman, has removed the hedges, walls, stakes, rails, posts, boards, and quicksets from Humberstone Gate.

156.1   *Writ of Summons*
Dated 29 September 1781 for 1 October 1781.

156.2   *Discharged Recognizances*
James Vaughan, Doctor in Physic, to appear and answer charges and keep the peace towards Richard Beale, gent.
Thomas Lane, Somerby, Leics., farmer, to appear and obey the Court and keep the peace towards Samuel Berry, Oxon, Northants., common carrier.
Joseph Parker, needlemaker, to appear and obey the Court *re* the bastard child of Elizabeth Hopkinson, singlewoman.
Charles Vaissiere, currier, to appear and answer charges.
James Smith, framework-knitter, to appear and prosecute Charles Gibbins for a felony.
Hannah, wife of James Smith, to appear and give evidence against Charles Gibbins for a felony.

156.3   *Indictments*
Thomas Lane for assaulting Samuel Berry.

Charles Gibbins, labourer, for stealing a piece of silver from James Smith. Po se, guilty.

Charles Vaissiere, currier, for assaulting Sarah Richardson, widow.

156.4   *Certificate of Pavement Repair*
Henry Smith has repaired the pavement in front of his house in Southgate Street.

156.5   *Sacramental Certificates*
All Saints'   Thomas Barwell, Mayor
              Tyrringham Palmer, Coroner
              James Bishop, Coroner
              Thomas Jeffcutt, Chamberlain
              James Willey, Chamberlain

157.1   *Writ of Summons*

Dated 30 September 1782 for 7 October 1782.

157.2   *Indictment*

John Cracroft, labourer, for stealing a linen table cloth from Richard Kinton.   Po se.

157.3   *Process Paper*

John Cooper, scourer, having been indicted for assaulting Thomas Ellis, has pleaded "Not Guilty" and is to be tried.

157.4   *Sacramental Certificates*

St Margaret's   James Bishop, Mayor
                William Bellamy, Chamberlain
                William Bishop, Chamberlain
                John Bass Oliver, Common Councillor
St Martin's   Tyrringham Palmer, Coroner
                James Cooke, Common Councillor
                John Slater, Common Councillor
                John Saywell, Common Councillor
St Mary's   Alderman Benjamin Sutton, Coroner

158.1   *Writ of Summons*

Dated 25 April 1783 for 28 April 1783.

158.2   *Discharged Recognizances*

James Darbyshire, jun., cordwainer, to appear and obey the Court *re* the bastard child of Mary Broughton, singlewoman.

Robert Weston, 87th Regiment of Foot, to appear and obey the Court *re* the female bastard child of Ann Ward, singlewoman.

John Martin, framework-knitter, to appear and answer charges and keep the peace towards William Hill.

William Harrison, Stocking Farm, Leics., grazier, to appear to prosecute and give evidence against William Langham, Robert Weston, George Wetherell, and William Harbutt for a felony.

Elizabeth Harrison, spinster, and Suzanna Tilson, spinster, to appear and give evidence against William Langham, Robert Weston, George Wetherell, and William Harbutt for a felony.

Francis Hickley, Primethorpe, Leics., carrier, to appear to prosecute and give evidence against William Smith for a felony.

Thomas Lockwood, mercer, William Fletcher, Mountsorrel, Leics., servant, John Derry, Mountsorrel, Leics., framework-knitter, and John Throsby, innholder, to appear and give evidence against William Smith for a felony.

158.3   *Indictments*

William Langham, labourer, Robert Weston, labourer, George Wetherell, labourer, and William Harbutt, labourer, for stealing 4 silver shillings, 2 silver sixpences, a red and white linen handkerchief, 3 iron keys, a brass key, and an iron tobacco box from William Harrison.   Po se, all guilty.

William Smith, labourer, for stealing a piece of white bleached linen cloth called "Russia Duck", 1 lb coloured thread, and 1 lb white thread from Francis Hickley.   Po se, guilty.

158.4   *Certificate of Road Repair*

For Church Gate.

158.5   *Certificate of Removal of Obstruction*

James Darbyshire has removed the bricks, sand, and wood from Hangman's Lane.

158.6   *Sacramental Certificate*

St Martin's   Alderman John Parsons

158.7   *Appeals against Poor Rate*

⟨To the Churchwardens and Overseers of the Poor of the Parish of Saint Mary within the Borough of Leicester in the County of Leicester.
Gentlemen
Take Notice That I Do Intend at the next General Sessions of the Peace to be holden at Leicester in and for the said Borough of Leicester to Appeal Against so much and such Part of the Last Levy Rate or Assessment made by You some or one of You for the Relief of the Poor of the said Parish of Saint Mary for this Present Year, whereby I am Rated too much, because You have Rated me in Respect of my House at more than its Annual Value and higher in Proportion than the Houses of Doctor Arnold, Mr Unwin, Mr Henry King, Mr Henry Wood, Mr Christopher Noble, Messrs. Harris and Leach, and several other Persons in the said Parish, And also Against so much and such Part of the said Levy, Rate or Assessment wherein the said Doctor Arnold, Mr Unwin, Mr Henry King, Mr Henry Wood, Mr Christopher Noble, Messrs. Harris and Leach and others are Charged too little, because each of them is Charged under the Annual Value of his House, and less in Proportion than I am, And also against such Part of the said Levy Rate or Assessment, wherein the House in the said Parish in the said Levy Rate or Assessment Mentioned to be in the Occupation of John Wood is not Rated or Assessed at all, And also against the said Levy Rate or Assessment because the several Tradesmen and others in the said Parish are not therein Rated in Respect of their Stock in Trade And because the said Levy is Oppressively Partial and upon the whole unequal and made by

no kind of Rule but Irregularity. And you the said Churchwardens and Overseers of the Poor are hereby Required to Produce on the Hearing of the said Appeal, the said Levy Rate or Assessment as well as all Former Rates, and the Books wherein the same are from Time to Time Entered And also the Vestry Books and all other Books Papers and Writings in Your any or either of Your Custody or power Relating thereto. Dated this Nineteenth day of April 1783. I am Gents Yours etc. John King.⟩

Similar appeal by Samuel Bankart.

159.1 *Writ of Summons*
Dated 1 January 1784 for 16 January 1784.

159.2 *Constable's Presentment*
William Ridgeway (Ald. Drakes Ward) presents the Inhabitants of St Margaret's Parish for not repairing St Margaret's Church Lane. Indicted.

159.3 *Discharged Recognizances*
John Jarvis, woolcomber, to appear and obey the Court *re* the bastard child of Elizabeth Olive, St Margaret's, singlewoman.
Robert Johnson, framework-knitter, to appear and answer charges.
Eleanor Eddinburg, spinster, to appear to prosecute and give evidence against Jane, wife of Francis Dawes, for a felony.
William Roberts, victualler, to appear to prosecute and give evidence against Henry Brown for a felony.
Private Matthew Udall, 26th Regiment of Foot, and Esther Bright, singlewoman, to appear and give evidence against Henry Brown for a felony.

159.4 *Indictments*
James Kenny alias Patrick Hoy, labourer, for stealing a canvas purse from Richard Parrott. Po se.

Jane, wife of Francis Dawes, labourer, for stealing a blue and white striped Manchester cotton gown from Eleanor Edinburgh. Po se.

John Kettleby, brazier, for obstructing Westons Lane with a cart load of dung and filth.

Henry Brown, labourer, for stealing a pair of worsted stockings from William Roberts. Po se.

159.5 *Certificate for Removal of Obstruction*
William Oldham, Esq., has removed the timber or wood from the Holy Bones.

159.6   *Sacramental Certificates*

St Martin's   William Oldham, Esq.
               Richard Beale, gent.
               John Parsons, gent.
               Edward Harris
               John Bass Oliver
               Edmund Swinfen
               John Peter Allamand
               William Parsons
               William Watts

160.1   *Writ of Summons*

Dated 1 April 1784 for 19 April 1784.

160.2   *Discharged Recognizances*

James Windram, dyer, to appear to prosecute and give evidence against, and William, his son, to appear and give evidence against, Moses Beeby for a felony.

Jane Lilley, widow, to appear and give evidence against Moses Beeby for a felony.

John Mortimer, Anstey, Leics., butcher, to appear to prosecute and give evidence against, and Richard Loseby, his apprentice, to appear and give evidence against, John Richardson for a felony.

Ann, wife of John Coulson, to appear and answer charges of felony and misdemeanour.

160.3   *Presentment*

The Grand Jury present Ann, wife of John Coulson, for aiding and abetting her husband's escape from the County Gaol, where he was awaiting the execution of a sentence of death passed on him at the Assizes for a felony, by smuggling in to him 2 knives, a saw, a steel, and an iron crow.   Ignored.

160.4   *Indictments*

The Inhabitants of St Margaret's Parish for not repairing St Margaret's Church Lane.

Moses Beeby, labourer, for stealing a Manchester velveret cotton waistcoat from William Windram.

John Richardson, labourer, for stealing a piece of pork from John Mortimer.   Po se.

160.5   *Certificate of Removal of Obstruction*

John Kettleby has removed the nuisance for which he was indicted.

161.1 *Writ of Summons*

Dated 29 September 1784 for 4 October 1784.

161.2 *Discharged Recognizances*

Michael Staples, victualler, to appear and answer charges.

Job Dawson, framework-knitter, to appear to prosecute and give evidence against Michael Staples for an assault.

Isaiah Banner, framesmith, to appear and prosecute William Stephenson for a felony.

Benjamin Cooke, framework-knitter, to appear and answer charges of felony to be made by John Valentine.

John Valentine, maltster, to appear to prosecute and give evidence against Benjamin Cooke for a felony.

John Witherbed, framework-knitter, William Cope, framework-knitter, and Francis Barfoot, woolcomber, to appear and give evidence against Benjamin Cooke for a felony.

William Chaplain, Newtown Linford, Leics., carpenter, to appear and answer charges of felony to be made by William Oldham.

William Oldham, Esq., to appear and prosecute William Chaplain for a felony.

Joseph Bown, jun., bricklayer, to appear and give evidence against William Chaplain for a felony.

Edward Smith, framework-knitter, to appear and answer charges.

161.3 *Indictments*

Benjamin Cook, framework-knitter, for stealing a cock from John Valentine. Po se, not guilty.

William Stephenson, 1st Dragoon Regiment, for stealing a silver watch from Isaiah Banner.

William Chaplain, Newtown Linford, Leics., carpenter, for stealing 2 oak boards from William Oldham, Esq.

161.4 *Sacramental Certificates*

St Martin's Joseph Chambers, Mayor
　　　　　　Benjamin Sutton, Coroner
　　　　　　Edward Price, Coroner
　　　　　　William Watts, Chamberlain
　　　　　　Abel Webster, Chamberlain

162.1 *Writ of Summons*

Dated 2 April 1785 for 4 April 1785.

162.2   *Discharged Recognizances*

William Middleton, needlemaker, to appear and obey the Court *re* the bastard child of Jane Corner.

John Carr to appear and answer charges of felony to be made by Samuel Webster.

Samuel Webster, Loughborough, Leics., carrier, to appear and prosecute John Carr for a felony.

John Webster and William Dabbs, hosier, to appear and give evidence against John Carr for a felony.

Isaac Wright, framework-knitter, to appear and obey the Court *re* the bastard child of Ann Oram.

Richard Smith, cordwainer, to appear and answer charges to be made by Elizabeth Hutchinson.

William Stubbs, Quorndon, Leics., carpenter, to appear and obey the Court *re* the bastard child of Dorothy Massey, singlewoman.

162.3   *Indictment*

John Carr, framework-knitter, for stealing a hemp bag and some paper shavings from Samuel Webster.

162.4   *Convictions*

George Ramsden, innholder, for swearing 6 profane oaths.

Thomas Mash, labourer, for swearing 10 profane oaths.

163.1   *Writ of Summons*

Dated 29 September 1785 for 3 October 1785.

163.2   *Discharged Recognizances*

Thomas Knight, framework-knitter, to appear and answer charges to be made by Jonathan Bott and Mary, his wife, and keep the peace towards them.

William Biggs, framework-knitter, to appear and answer charges to be made by Jonathan Bott and Mary, his wife, and keep the peace towards them.

John Foulds, carpenter, to appear and answer charges to be made by William Darman and keep the peace towards him.

John Goodess, bricklayer, to appear and answer charges to be made by William Darman and keep the peace towards him.

Thomas Issitt, tailor, to appear and answer charges to be made by Mary, wife of Thomas Fisher Cooper, perukemaker, and keep the peace towards her.

Robert Bruce, victualler, to appear and answer charges to be made by Thomas Wesson and keep the peace towards him.

Thomas Gadsby, labourer, to appear and obey the Court *re* a bastardy case.

William Ingle, apothecary, to appear and answer charges and keep the peace towards Robert Bree, Bachelor of Physic.

Joseph Simpson, gent., to appear and obey the Court.

163.3 *Presentment*

William Burleton, Recorder, and Joseph Chambers, Justice, present William Dalby, carpenter, for obstructing ⟨the Kings Common highway leading from out of the Hangman lane into the public Turnpike road from Leicester to Harborough in the said County⟩ with timber and wood.

163.4 *Indictments*

Thomas Issitt, tailor, for assaulting Mary, wife of Thomas Fisher Cooper.

Robert Bruce, victualler, for assaulting Thomas Weson.

Joseph Simpson, gent., for assaulting Joseph Withers.

William Ingle, apothecary, for assaulting Robert Bree, Bachelor of Physic, with a whip. Copy—original removed by Writ of Certiorari.

163.5 *Process Paper*

Robert Bruce, victualler, having been indicted for assaulting Thomas Weson, has pleaded "Not Guilty" and is to be tried.

163.6 *Certificate of Road Repair*

For St Margaret's Church Lane.

163.7 *Sacramental Certificates*

St Martin's   William Burleton, Esq.
            John Parsons, Esq.
            Tyrringham Palmer, gent.
            Hamlet Clark, gent.
            Edward Marston
            James Mallett
            John Peter Allamand
            Thomas Chatwyn
St Mary's   William Orton, gent.

164a.1 *Writ of Summons*
Dated 17 April 1786 for 24 April 1786.

164a.2 *Discharged Recognizances*

Richard Firmadge, plasterer, to appear and prosecute John Spence for an assault.

John Spence, victualler, to appear and answer charges of assault to be made by Richard Firmadge.

William Ingle, surgeon and apothecary, to appear and obey the Court and keep the peace towards Thomas Arnold, Doctor of Physic.

John Mortimer, Anstey, Leics., butcher, to appear to prosecute and give evidence against James Cart for a felony.

John Vice, tallow chandler, to appear and give evidence against James Cart for a felony.

Edward Webb, tallow chandler, to appear and give evidence against James Cart for a felony.

Richard Springthorpe, Anstey, Leics., framework-knitter, to appear and obey the Court *re* a bastardy case.

John Cooper, framework-knitter, to appear and obey the Court *re* a bastardy case.

Thomas Brown, labourer, to appear and answer charges to be made by Matthew Parker and keep the peace towards him.

Richard Creswell, framework-knitter, to appear and prosecute John Bollard for an assault.

164a.3   *Indictments*

The Inhabitants of St Mary's Parish for not repairing Southgate Street and Hangman's Lane. Copy—original removed by Writ of Certiorari.

The Inhabitants of St Mary's Parish for not repairing the road which runs from the West Bridge to a ford in the River Soar (and which then runs into Red Cross Street). Copy—original removed by Writ of Certiorari.

Thomas Brown, labourer, for assaulting Matthew Parker.

164a.4   *Certificate of Removal of Obstruction*

William Dalby, carpenter, has removed the timber and wood from ⟨the Kings common Highway leading from out of the Hangman Lane into the public Turnpike road from Leicester to Harborough⟩.

For **164b** see after **165a**.

165a.1   *Writ of Summons*

Dated 3 July 1786 for 21 July 1786.

165a.2   *Discharged Recognizances*

Robert Woollett, Peckleton, Leics., labourer, to appear and answer charges of felony.

William Goodrich, Wigston Magna, Leics., fellmonger, to appear to prosecute and give evidence against, and Thomas, his son, to appear and give evidence against, Robert Wollett for a felony.

William Turner, whitesmith, to appear to prosecute and give evidence against Richard Edmonds for a felony.

Thomas Bown, innholder, to appear and answer charges and keep the peace towards Jabus Dry.

William Woodcock, baker, to appear to prosecute and give evidence against John Greenwood.

John Greenwood, slater and plasterer, to appear and answer charges and keep the peace towards William Woodcock.

Samuel Matthews, mercer, to appear to prosecute and give evidence against Ann, wife of Peter Frecknall, for a felony.

John Jackson, mercer, to appear and give evidence against Ann Frecknall for a felony.

John Fancott, framework-knitter, to appear and answer charges and keep the peace towards Francis Cross, framework-knitter.

165a.3   *Indictments*

Robert Woollett, labourer, for stealing a sheepskin from William Goodrich. Po se, guilty.

Richard Edmonds, labourer, for stealing an iron stand and an iron fender from William Turner.   Po se, guilty.

Ann, wife of Peter Frecknall, labourer, for stealing a piece of muslin from Samuel Matthews.   Po se, guilty.

164b.1   *Writ of Summons*
            Dated 29 September 1786 for 2 October 1786.

164b.2   *Discharged Recognizances*

William Fox, labourer, to appear and answer charges and keep the peace towards William Swanson.

Lieutenant William Paul Cerjat, Royal Horseguard Blues Regiment, to appear and answer charges and keep the peace towards John Nedham.

Cornet John Ashton, Royal Horseguard Blues Regiment, to appear and answer charges and keep the peace towards John Nedham.

164b.3   *Indictments*

William Paul Cerjat, Esq., for assaulting John Nedham, woolstapler, with a whip. Copy—original removed by Writ of Certiorari.

John Ashton, Esq., for assaulting John Nedham, woolstapler, with a stick. Copy—original removed by Writ of Certiorari.

164b.4   *Sacramental Certificates*
St Martin's   Robert Peach, Mayor
               Tyrringham Palmer, Coroner
               John Freer, Common Councillor
St Nicholas'   Hamlett Clark, Mayor
               John Slater, Chamberlain
               John Saywell, Chamberlain
St Mary's   William Orton, Coroner

165b.1   *Writ of Summons*
Dated 5 March 1787 for 6 March 1787.

165b.2   *Discharged Recognizances*
Edward Smith, Tugby, Leics., labourer, to appear and prosecute William Smith for a felony.
Robert Flower, miller, to appear and prosecute Thomas Thurman for a felony.
Thomas Haddon, Mountsorrel, Leics., bricklayer, to appear and give evidence against Thomas Thurman for a felony.
Thomas Thurman, miller, to appear and answer charges of felony.
Thomas Holt, cordwainer, to appear and answer charges and keep the peace towards Ann, his wife.
Matthew Parker, blacksmith, to appear and answer charges and keep the peace towards Mary, his wife.
Thomas Cooley, cordwainer, to appear and answer charges and keep the peace towards Mary, his wife.
John Wood, cordwainer, to appear and answer charges and keep the peace towards Lucy, his wife.
John Tomlisson, carpenter, to appear to prosecute and give evidence against William Abbott for a felony.
George Green, carpenter, to appear to prosecute and give evidence against William Abbott for a felony.
John Satchell, carpenter, to appear and give evidence against William Abbott for a felony.
John Payne, woolcomber, and William Robinson, labourer, to appear and give evidence against William Abbott for two felonies.

165b.3   *Victualler's Recognizance*
Thomas Tarry is licensed to keep an alehouse ⟨for one Year, or until the next general licencing of Victuallers⟩.

165b.4   *Indictments*
William Smith, labourer, for stealing a woollen waistcoat from Edward Smith.   Po se, not guilty.

Thomas Thurman, miller, for stealing 80 lbs flour from Robert Flower. Po se, not guilty.

William Abbott, carpenter, for stealing a compass saw from John Tomlisson. Po se, guilty.

William Abbott, carpenter, for stealing an iron hatchet from George Green. Po se, not guilty.

165b.5 *Sacramental Certificates*
St Margaret's   Alderman Peter Oliver, gent.
St Mary's   William Harrison, jun.

166.1 *Writ of Summons*
Dated 7 April 1787 for 16 April 1787.

166.2 *Discharged Recognizances*
Henry Parsons Hillhouse, hosier, to appear and answer charges and keep the peace towards Elihu Samuel Fellows.
Elihu Samuel Fellows, hosier, to appear to prosecute and give evidence against Henry Parsons Hillhouse for an assault.
John Springthorpe, victualler, to appear and answer charges and keep the peace towards Samuel Simmons.

166.3 *Victualler's Recognizance*
John Howitt is licensed to keep an alehouse ⟨for one Year, or until the next general licencing of Victuallers⟩.

166.4 *Presentment*
The Grand Jury present the Inhabitants of the Borough of Leicester for the Gaol and the House of Correction which ⟨were and yet are in great decay and ruinous, and particularly That it would tend to the Convenience and Utility of the said Goal or Prison and House of Correction if certain Alterations and Additions were made to the same respectively for the better seperation of the Debtors and Criminals therein confined respectively⟩.

166.5 *Indictments*
Francis Asher, Costock, Notts., hosier, late Constable, for conveying John Tyler to St Martin's Parish, Leicester, where he had no legal settlement, so that the Parish was forced to expend 20s. for his maintenance.

Henry Parsons Hillhouse, hosier, for assaulting Elihu Samuel Fellows.

166.6 *Conviction*
George Dare, labourer, for swearing 5 profane curses ⟨to wit Damn you, Damn you, Damn you, Damn you, Damn you⟩.

166.7 *Sacramental Certificates*
St Martin's   Edmund Wigley, Recorder
St Margaret's   Alderman Robert Dickinson, gent.

167.1 *Writ of Summons*
Dated 28 June 1787 for 9 July 1787.

167.2 *Discharged Recognizances*
William Clarke, Bruntingthorpe, Leics., framework-knitter, to appear and answer charges and keep the peace towards Richard Broughton.
William Jackson, blacksmith, to appear and answer charges of felony.
Thomas Chatwyn, miller, to appear and prosecute Mary Bunney.
Lydia Preston, spinster, and Sarah Harris, spinster, to appear and give evidence against Mary Bunney.
Martha Cooper, singlewoman, to appear and give evidence against Mary Bunney.
Francis Barfoot, woolcomber, to appear and answer charges to be made by Mary, wife of John Kinderley.
Isaiah Banner, framesmith, to appear and answer charges to be made by William Calladine.
John Mortimer, Anstey, Leics., butcher, to appear and prosecute Thomas Gibson for a felony.
John Cox, cordwainer, and Joseph Read, Anstey, Leics., butcher, to appear and give evidence against Thomas Gibson for a felony.
John Allen, framework-knitter, to appear and answer charges to be made by Joseph Withers and keep the peace towards him.
William Springthorpe, framework-knitter, to appear and answer charges to be made by Joseph Withers and keep the peace towards him.
George Harris, labourer, to appear and answer charges to be made by Joseph Withers and keep the peace towards him.

167.3 *Victualler's Recognizance*
John Vernon is licensed to keep an alehouse for one year.

167.4 *Presentment*
The Grand Jury present Thomas Jackson, blacksmith, for stealing an iron hammer, an iron plow hatchet, an iron plashing hatchet, an iron stocking axe, 3 iron wedges, and an iron gorse hook from William Wood.   Ignored.

167.5 *Indictments*
Francis Barfoot, woolcomber, for assaulting Mary, wife of John Kinderley.

Thomas Gibson, labourer, for stealing a piece of beef from John Mortimore.

John Spencer, labourer, John Allen, framework-knitter, William Spring-thorpe, framework-knitter, and George Harris, labourer, for assaulting Joseph Withers, framework-knitter, whilst he was executing his duty as Watchman for Alderman Coleman's Ward, and freeing Spencer whom Withers had arrested for misbehaviour.

168.1   *Writ of Summons*

Dated 21 September 1787 for 1 October 1787.

168.2   *Discharged Recognizances*

Edward Berry Freckleton, innholder, to appear and answer charges.
William Bates, victualler, to appear and answer charges.
William Turner, whitesmith, to appear and answer charges and keep the peace towards William Woodcock.
John Orton, labourer, to appear to prosecute and give evidence against John Powell for a felony.
Thomas Frith, labourer, and George Hall, framework-knitter, to appear and give evidence against John Powell for a felony.

168.3   *Indictments*

George Ingram, labourer, for leaving a quantity of dung in High Cross Street which has polluted the air with its smell.

John Powell, labourer, for stealing a man's leather glove from John Orton. Po se, guilty.

168.4   *Conviction*

John Sherrard, framework-knitter, for swearing 6 profane oaths ⟨to wit "God damn you", "God damn you", "God damn you", "God damn you", "God damn you", "God damn you"⟩.

169.1   *Writ of Summons*

Dated 21 December 1787 for 14 January 1788.

169.2   *Discharged Recognizances*

John White, jun., framework-knitter, to appear and obey the Court *re* a bastardy case.
James Vaughan, Doctor of Physic, to appear and answer charges and keep the peace towards Septimus Sutton, apothecary.
John Mann, labourer, to appear and answer charges and keep the peace towards Robert Drake, gent.
Thomas Staughton, labourer, to appear and answer charges and keep the peace towards Elizabeth, wife of John Taylor, innholder.

Joseph Whetstone, woolcomber, to appear to prosecute and give evidence against Robert Burrows for a felony.

George Croxton, labourer, to appear and give evidence against Robert Burrows for a felony.

169.3 *Victualler's Recognizance*

Thomas Withers (Glaziers Arms) is licensed to keep an alehouse for one year ⟨or until the general licensing of Victuallers⟩.

169.4 *Indictments*

James Vaughan, Doctor of Physic, for assaulting Septimus Sutton.

William Perdie, labourer, for stealing a woollen waistcoat from Edward Smith.   Po se, guilty.

Robert Burrows, labourer, for stealing a wooden tub from Joseph Whetstone.   Po se, not guilty.

Thomas Staughton, labourer, for assaulting Elizabeth, wife of John Taylor.

John Allen, framework-knitter, for riotous assembly. [The Whetstone riots.]   Not guilty.

The following are indicted separately for not repairing the pavement in front of their houses in Northgate Street:
George Plant, dealer in cheese.
William Rice, victualler.
Ambrose Hayfield, labourer.
William Horner, labourer.
John Beeby, gardener.
Samuel Holmes, flaxdresser.
Edward Phipps, framework-knitter.
Robert Grice, cordwainer.
Joseph Bennett, woolcomber.
Mary Fielding, widow.
Joseph Gilbert, yeoman.
William Crawley, parchmentmaker.
John Townsend, labourer.
Robert Rider, framework-knitter.
Robert Benson, framework-knitter.
John Mason, tailor.
William Why, framework-knitter.
Robert Watts, flaxdresser.
Joseph Drake, woolcomber.
Thomas Fowkes, labourer.

John Hughes, framework-knitter.
Joseph Whetstone, woolcomber.
William Spawton, framework-knitter.
Nathaniel Marvin, patternmaker.
Thomas Richardson, cordwainer.
Elizabeth Turlington, spinster.

John Iliff, tanner, for not repairing the pavement in front of the Tan Yard, Northgate Street.

Henry Johnson, victualler, for not repairing the pavement in front of the Countesses Close, Northgate Street.

The Mayor, Bailiffs, and Burgesses of the Borough of Leicester for not repairing the middle causeway and pavement at the junction of Northgate Street and Sanvey Gate.

The following are indicted separately for not repairing the pavement adjoining their land in Waterlag Lane:
John Emmerson, victualler.
William Hudson, hosier.
Welles Orton, Esq.
Robert and William Hartshorn, woolcombers.

169.5	*Sacramental Certificates*
St Margaret's	Robert Dickinson, Mayor
	James Cook, Chamberlain
	Thomas Peach, Chamberlain
St Mary's	Alderman William Orton
	Thomas Jelf, Excise Officer
	William Williams, Excise Officer

170.1   *Writ of Summons*
Dated 12 March 1788 for 31 March 1788.

170.2   *Discharged Recognizances*
Robert Spencer, woolcomber, to appear and answer charges and keep the peace towards Welbourn Owston.
Joseph Miles, victualler, to appear and answer charges and keep the peace towards Welbourn Owston.
John Burton, carpenter, to appear and answer charges and keep the peace towards John Foulds, carpenter.

170.3   *Indictments*
The Inhabitants of All Saints' Parish for not repairing Carts Lane. Copy —original removed by Writ of Certiorari.

James Cart, labourer, for stealing 2 lbs beef suet from John Mortimer. Po se, guilty.

Joseph Miles, victualler, for assaulting Welbourn Owston.

Robert Spencer, woolcomber, for assaulting Welbourn Owston.

William Burley, yeoman, for obstructing Applegate Street with a wagon loaded with dirt, which he left standing there for 3 hours.

170.4 *Process Paper*

James Vaughan, Doctor of Physic, having been indicted for assaulting Septimus Sutton, has pleaded "Not Guilty" and is to be tried.

170.5 *Certificates of Pavement Repair*

The following have repaired the pavement in front of their houses in Northgate Street:
William Rice, victualler.
Thomas Richardson, cordwainer.
Mary Fielding, widow.
Joseph Bennett, woolcomber.
The Mayor, Bailiffs, and Burgesses of the Borough of Leicester have repaired the middle causeway and pavement at the junction of Northgate Street and Sanvey Gate.

170.6 *Sacramental Certificate*

St Margaret's   Alderman Peter Oliver

171.1 *Writ of Summons*

Dated 29 September 1788 for 6 October 1788.

171.2 *Discharged Recognizances*

Hannah, wife of Thomas Litler, victualler, to appear and answer charges and keep the peace towards Katherine, wife of Richard Taylor Barnacle.
Private George Fletcher, 29th Regiment of Foot, to appear to prosecute and give evidence against Esprée Bullard for a felony.
Michael Buswell, framework-knitter, to appear and answer charges and keep the peace towards John Jordan.
William Stevenson, Glenfield, Leics., farmer, to appear and answer charges and keep the peace towards Mary Hobell, widow.
George Batty, Falstone, Northumb., labourer, to appear and answer charges and keep the peace towards John Peet.
John Peet, Countesthorpe, Leics., labourer, to appear to prosecute and give evidence against George Batty.

George Batty, Falstone, Northumb., labourer, to appear and answer charges and keep the peace towards John Sherwood.

John Sherwood, framework-knitter, to appear to prosecute and give evidence against George Batty.

Richard Halford, stocking trimmer, to appear and answer charges and keep the peace towards Robert Cowdall.

Edward Langley, Clipston, Northants., farmer, to appear and answer charges and keep the peace towards Junius Baker.

Thomas Willowes, clerk, to appear and give evidence against William Pettifer, victualler, for contravening the conditions of the Victualler's Recognizance.

William Kemp, labourer, to appear and give evidence against William Pettifer, victualler, for contravening the conditions of the Victualler's Recognizance.

John Valentine, framework-knitter, to appear to prosecute and give evidence against John Park.

Edward Harrison, jun., gent., to appear and answer charges to be made by James Darbyshire, carpenter, and keep the peace towards him.

171.3 *Indictments*

Esprée Bullard, labourer, for stealing a silver hatband from Richard Spencer Schutz, Esq.

Robert Cowdall, labourer, for assaulting Richard Halford. Cowdall states: ⟨That on Saturday the tenth day of June last Richard Halford of the Borough aforesaid Stocking trimmer at All Saints parish in the said Borough advanced towards me with his Hand held up in a threatning manner damned me for an old Rogue, & threatned that he would do for me, from which Expression I verily believe I fear that the said Richard will either kill me, or do me some bodily hurt; therefor I pray of this Court that the said Richard Halford may find Sureties for the peace & good behaviour towards me, which I do not through hatred or malice which I bear towards the said Richard, but merely for the protection of my person.⟩

Edward Langley, farmer and grazier, for assaulting Junius Baker.

John Parks, framework-knitter, for assaulting John Valentine.

Edward Harrison, jun., gent., for assaulting James Darbyshire.

171.4 *Certificates of Pavement Repair*

The following have repaired the pavement in front of their houses in Northgate Street:
Robert Grice, cordwainer.
John Townsend, labourer.

William Why, framework-knitter.
Robert Benson, framework-knitter.
John Mason.
Edward Phipps, framework-knitter.
John Beeby, gardener.
William Horner, labourer.
Samuel Holmes, flaxdresser.
Joseph Drake, woolcomber.
Thomas Fowkes, labourer.
William Spawton, framework-knitter.
John Hughes, framework-knitter.
Joseph Whetston, woolcomber.
Robert Watts, flaxdresser.
Robert Rider, framework-knitter.
William Crawley, parchmentmaker.
Joseph Gilbert, yeoman.
John Iliff, tanner, has repaired the pavement in front of the Tan Yard, Northgate Street.
Henry Johnson, victualler, has repaired the pavement in front of Countesses Close, Northgate Street.
Robert and William Hartshorn, woolcombers, have repaired the pavement adjoining their land in Waterlag Lane.

171.5   *Sacramental Certificates*
All Saints' Henry Watchorn, Mayor
             William Parsons, Chamberlain
             Edmund Swinfen, Chamberlain
St Mary's   William Orton, Coroner

172.1   *Writ of Summons*
             Dated 7 January 1789 for 12 January 1789.

172.2   *Discharged Recognizances*
Thomas Stone, baker, to appear and answer charges and keep the peace towards Edward Daniel, baker.
William Hudson, hosier, to appear and answer charges and keep the peace towards Joseph Slater, hosier.
William Humberstone, framework-knitter, to appear and answer charges and keep the peace towards Samuel Bankart, woolstapler.

172.3   *Indictments*
Thomas Stone, baker, for assaulting Edward Daniel.

John Cobley, grocer, for not filling in a hole, 3 ft deep and 18 ft in circumference, by his house in Gallowtree Gate.

172.4 *Process Papers*

Edward Langley, farmer and grazier, having been indicted for assaulting Junius Baker, has pleaded "Not Guilty" and is to be tried.

Robert Cowdall, hosier, having been indicted for assaulting Richard Halford, has pleaded "Not Guilty" and is to be tried.
⟨Robert Cowdall of the Borough of Leicester in the County of Leicester Gentleman and Noblet Barker of the said Borough and County Surgeon and Apothecary Severally Make Oath and Say and First the Deponent Robert Cowdall the above named Defendant for himself Saith that Elizabeth Stray of the said Borough and County Spinster is a material Witness for him this Deponent in this Cause and without whose Testimony he this Deponent cannot safely proceed to Trial And this Deponent Noblet Barker for himself Saith that he has attended the Said Elizabeth Stray for several days last past as her Apothecary during her Indisposition And this Deponent further Saith that the said Elizabeth Stray is at this time so ill that she is not capable of attending to give Evidence without great danger of her life.

Robert Cowdall
Noblet Barker⟩

173.1 *Writ of Summons*
Dated 11 April 1789 for 20 April 1789.

173.2 *Discharged Recognizances*

John Flude, woolcomber, to appear and answer charges and keep the peace towards Mary, wife of James Armes.
John Howse, victualler, to appear and answer charges.
Joseph Hopewell, butcher, to appear to prosecute and give evidence against John Kirk for a felony.

173.3 *Indictment*

John Kirk, framework-knitter, for stealing a shoulder of mutton from Joseph Hopewell. Po se, guilty.

173.4 *Conviction*

William Burdett for swearing 6 profane oaths.

173.5 *Certificate of Pavement Repair*

Ambrose Hayfield, labourer, has repaired the pavement in front of his house in Northgate Street.

174.1   *Writ of Summons*
Dated 4 July 1789 for 13 July 1789.

174.2   *Constables' Presentments*
William Freer (Mr Mayor's Ward) finds no cause of presentment.

William Darman (Ald. Chamber's Ward) presents the Inhabitants of St Martin's Parish for not repairing the pavement in New Street.   Indicted.

174.3   *Discharged Recognizances*
James Dowley, hatmaker, to appear to prosecute and give evidence against Mary Godfary, singlewoman.
Tabitha, wife of William Bishop, innholder, to appear and give evidence against Mary Godfary.
Giles Hayes, Derby, woolcomber, to appear and obey the Court *re* the bastard child of Mary King.
Thomas Bramley, butcher, to appear to prosecute and give evidence against Francis Barfoot.

174.4   *Indictments*
Francis Barfoot, woolcomber, for assaulting Thomas Bramley.

Francis Barfoot, woolcomber, for assaulting John Wood.

Joseph Nicholson, tailor and broker, for allowing a hole, 6 ft deep, 12 ft in circumference, and covered with 12 iron bars, to remain in Gallowtree Gate beside his house.

174.5   *Complaint*
⟨I Sarah Johnson, the Wife of Joseph Johnson of the said Borough Cabinetmaker make oath and say That Thomas Holt of the said Borough Cordwainer did, on the twenty seventh day of April last, at the parish of All Saints in the said Borough & in my dwelling house there strike me a violent Blow on the Head which occasioned me to be senseless, and threatned to do me (meaning, as I verily believe, to do me mischief) So that I am afraid he will maim, wound or kill me—And therefore I pray that this Court will make him find sufficient Sureties to keep the peace towards me; And I do further swear That I do not require such Sureties out of malice or for Vexation, but merely for the Security of my person.
Sarah Jhonsn⟩

174.6   *Recommendation*
⟨We whose names are under written being Wool-growers do recommend the Bearer Samuel Cornmell, of Leicester to the Justices of the Peace as a

Person qualified to be Sworn as a Wool-winder, according to the directions of an Act of Parliament passed last Sessions.

May the 20, 1789.

John Iliffe
Samuel Bishop
Thomas Underwood
Joseph Iliffe⟩

174.7   *Sacramental Certificates*

St Martin's   Alderman John Eames
              John Fox, Common Councillor
              Thomas Read, Common Councillor
St Mary's   Alderman Joseph Neal
              Joseph Johnson, jun., Common Councillor
St Margaret's   Alderman Joseph Burbidge

175.1   *Writ of Summons*
Dated 29 September 1789 for 5 October 1789.

175.2   *Discharged Recognizances*
Joseph Bennett, worstedmaker, to appear to prosecute and give evidence against Mary Digby for a felony.
Elizabeth Keen, singlewoman, to appear and give evidence against Mary Digby for a felony.

175.3   *Presentment*
The Grand Jury present The Inhabitants of St Martin's Parish for not repairing the middle pavement in New Street.   Ignored.

175.4   *Indictment*
Mary, wife of William Digby, labourer, for stealing 2 ozs worsted yarn from Joseph Bennett.

175.5   *Conviction*
John Carr for swearing 2 profane oaths.

175.6   *Process Paper*
John Cobley, grocer, having been indicted for not filling in a hole, 3 ft deep and 18 ft in circumference, by his house in Gallowtree Gate, has pleaded "Not Guilty" and is to be tried.

175.7   *Gaoler's Certificate*
⟨The Certificate of William Loseby Goaler, in persuance of the Statute in this Case, made and Provided respecting the Goal of the said Borough.

Felons & Debtors Kept   ⎱   The Felons and Debtors are Kept Seperate
Separate   ⎰   at Nights but their is only one Yard to Air in.

Spirituous Liquors	No Spirituous Liquors Suffered to go into the Prisoners.
A Copy of the above Clauses & two others Mention'd	Their is a Coppy of the three Clauses hung up in the said Goal.
Copy of the Fees Payable By Debtors, & Orders for the Government of the Goal	There is a Copy of the Fees Payable by Debtors, and Orders for the Government of the Goal hung up in a Conspicuous Place in the Goal.
Clergyman	A Clergyman is Provided to Officiate on Particular Occasions in the said Goal.
Fees	No Fees Taken on Persons Acquited or Discharg'd upon Proclamation or Prosecution.
The Walls & Cielings of the Cells to be scraped & White-wash'd once in the Year	The Walls and Cielings of the Cells are scraped and White-washed once in the Year, the Cells are Kept Clean, and well supplied with fresh Air.
Sick	Their are Two Rooms set apart for the Sick.
Baths or bathing Tubs	Not Provided.
Surgeon & Apothecary	A Surgeon and A Pothecary is Appointed for the said Goal.

William Loseby Gaoler⟩

175.8 *Sacramental Certificates*

St Margaret's John Dalby, Mayor
Alderman John Mansfield
Edward Marston, Chamberlain
Thomas Chatwyn, Chamberlain
Samuel Clark, Common Councillor
Thomas Copson, Common Councillor
St Martin's John Eames, Coroner
Thomas Wright, Common Councillor
William Firmadge, jun., Common Councillor
St Mary's Joseph Neal, Coroner

176.1 *Writ of Summons*

Dated 1 January 1790 for 14 January 1790.

176.2 *Discharged Recognizances*

William Thompson, Groby, Leics., cordwainer, to appear and obey the Court *re* the bastard daughter of Ruth Frost, St Mary's, singlewoman.

John Grocock, labourer, to appear to prosecute and give evidence against John Gadesby for a felony.

William Stableford, carpenter, to appear to prosecute and give evidence against John Whattoff for a felony.

William Darman, Constable, to appear and give evidence against John Whattoff for a felony.

John Shergold, woolstapler, to appear and answer charges and keep the peace towards Jacob Sapcote, baker.

John Smith, gardener, to appear and answer charges and keep the peace towards Mary Walker.

Mary Walker, singlewoman, to appear to prosecute and give evidence against John Smith.

William Wood, innholder, to appear and answer charges and keep the peace towards Edward Bird, brazier.

Robert Braunstone, gardener, to appear and answer charges and keep the peace towards George Luck, tailor.

John Dale, framework-knitter, to appear and prosecute Joseph Willes for a felony.

William Dale, framework-knitter, to appear and give evidence against Joseph Willes for a felony.

Henry Johnson, framework-knitter, to appear to prosecute and give evidence against Joseph Thompson for a felony.

William Darman, Constable, to appear and give evidence against Joseph Thompson for a felony.

176.3 *Indictments*

John Gadesby, labourer, for stealing a velveret waistcoat and 2 pairs of worsted stockings from John Grocock.   Po se, guilty.

John Whattoff, framework-knitter, for stealing a piece of deal or wood from William Stableford.   Po se, not guilty.

Joseph Thompson, framework-knitter, for stealing 6 worsted pieces of stockings from Henry Johnson.   Po se, guilty.

176.4 *Conviction*

George Ramsden for swearing 5 profane oaths.

177.1 *Writ of Summons*
Dated 6 July 1790 for 15 July 1790.

177.2 *Discharged Recognizances*

Thomas Joffs, dentist, to appear and answer charges and keep the peace towards Elizabeth Langton, spinster.

John Wood, schoolmaster, to appear and answer charges and keep the peace towards John Jarvis, jun.

George Ramsden, innholder, to appear and answer charges and keep the peace towards John Lockwood.

Thomas Sanderson, butcher, to appear and answer charges and keep the peace towards William Weston.

Walter Dawson, needlemaker, to appear and answer charges and keep the peace towards John Richards.

Walter Dawson, needlemaker, to appear and answer charges and keep the peace towards Benjamin Coltman.

John Ingram, framework-knitter, to appear and answer charges and keep the peace towards Sarah, his wife.

Alexander Dudgeon, Castle View, woolcomber, to appear and answer charges and keep the peace towards John Hood.

John Hood, Kirkby Mallory, Leics., miller, to appear to prosecute and give evidence against Alexander Dudgeon.

John Hood, Kirkby Mallory, Leics., miller, to appear and answer charges and keep the peace towards Thomas Slater.

Private Thomas Slater, Leicester Militia, to appear and prosecute John Hood.

John Linthwaite Hill, framework-knitter, to appear and answer charges and keep the peace towards Robert Ryder.

Robert Ryder, framework-knitter, to appear to prosecute and give evidence against John Linthwaite Hill.

John Adcock, Syston, Leics., butcher, to appear and obey the Court *re* the bastard child of Elizabeth Lodge, St Margaret's, singlewoman.

Mary Ann Veasey, spinster, to appear to prosecute and give evidence against John Shea for an assault.

177.3 *Indictments*

Walter Dawson, needlemaker, for assaulting John Richards.

Walter Dawson, needlemaker, for assaulting Benjamin Coltman.

John Hood, Kirkby Mallory, Leics., miller, for assaulting Thomas Slater.

Alexander Dudgeon, woolcomber, for assaulting John Hood.

William Harris, labourer, for stealing a silk handkerchief from Joseph Bull. Po se, guilty.

John Linthwaite Hill, framework-knitter, for assaulting Robert Ryder.

John Shea, cordwainer, for assaulting Mary Ann Veasey, spinster.   Po se.

177.4 *Certificates of Removal of Obstruction*

John Cobley, grocer, has removed the hole in Gallowtree Gate.

Joseph Nicholson, tailor and broker, has removed the hole, covered by iron bars, 2¾ ins apart, from Gallowtree Gate.

178.1   *Writ of Summons*

Dated 29 September 1790 for 4 October 1790.

178.2   *Constable's Presentment*

Daniel Loyley (Ald. Fisher's Ward) presents the Inhabitants of St Mary's Parish for not repairing Horsepool Street between the Horsepool and the Pinfold.   Indicted.

178.3   *Discharged Recognizances*

Charles Rozzell, framework-knitter, to appear and answer charges and keep the peace towards Alderman John Fisher.

James Fossett, woolcomber, to appear and answer charges and keep the peace towards Ann, his wife.

Thomas Thornelowe, victualler, to appear and prosecute John Eden for a felony.

Elizabeth, wife of Thomas Thornelowe, victualler, and Hannah, wife of Benjamin Lewitt, pawnbroker, to appear and give evidence against John Eden for a felony.

James Tacey, Barrow-upon-Soar, Leics., framework-knitter, to appear and answer charges to be made by John Banner.

John Banner, hosier, to appear to prosecute and give evidence against James Tacey.

Edward Pendleton, framework-knitter, to appear and give evidence against James Tacey.

James Tacey, Barrow-upon-Soar, Leics., framework-knitter, to appear and answer charges to be made by Thomas Jeffcutt.

Thomas Jeffcutt, hosier, to appear to prosecute and give evidence against James Tacey.

Richard Luck, apprentice to Thomas Jeffcutt, hosier, to appear and give evidence against James Tacey.

178.4   *Indictments*

Charles Rozzell, framework-knitter, for assaulting John Fisher, gent.

James Tacey, framework-knitter, for obtaining 10 lbs worsted (the property of William and Thomas Smart, carpenters) from William Smart, under false pretences.

James Tacey, framework-knitter, for obtaining 6 lbs worsted from Thomas Jeffcutt, under false pretences.

John Eden, framesmith, for stealing a silk handkerchief from Thomas Thornelowe. Po se, guilty.

Francis Hall and John Lawson, framework-knitter, for stealing 2 gals brandy, 2 qts gin, 1 qt red port wine, a brass tea kettle, an iron corkscrew, 2 pewter liquor measures, 2 glass decanters, and 3 glass beakers from Francis Polack.

John Lawson, framework-knitter, for assaulting Daniel Loyley, Constable. Po se, not guilty.

178.5 *Process Papers*

Walter Dawson, needlemaker, having been indicted for assaulting John Richards, has pleaded "Not Guilty" and is to be tried.

Walter Dawson, needlemaker, having been indicted for assaulting Benjamin Coltman, has pleaded "Not Guilty" and is to be tried.

178.6 *Sacramental Certificates*

St Martin's	John Eames, Mayor
	Thomas Wright, Chamberlain
	John Freer, Chamberlain
	William Hall, Common Councillor
St Margaret's	Alderman Benjamin Gregory
	Joseph Burbidge, Coroner
	Mark Oliver, Common Councillor
	John Stevenson, Common Councillor
St Mary's	William Orton, Coroner
	Samuel Townsend, Common Councillor

179.1 *Writ of Summons*

Dated 18 April 1791 for 6 May 1791.

179.2 *Discharged Recognizances*

Ann, wife of William Thorpe, cordwainer, to appear and answer charges and keep the peace towards Elizabeth, wife of Thomas Brown.

Benjamin Walker, framework-knitter, to appear and answer charges and keep the peace towards Ann Boulter, singlewoman.

Jonathan Phillips, framework-knitter, to appear and answer charges and keep the peace towards Ann Boulter.

John Cowdall, labourer, to appear and answer charges and keep the peace towards Ann Boulter.

Thomas Gilbert, framework-knitter, to appear and answer charges and keep the peace towards Ann Boulter.

John Goddard, woolcomber, to appear and answer charges of felony to be made by James Fenton.

James Fenton, common carrier, to appear to prosecute and give evidence against John Goddard for a felony.

John Lomas, woolstapler, to appear and give evidence against John Goddard for a felony.

Robert Edwards, Thringstone, Leics., woolstapler, to appear and give evidence against John Goddard for a felony.

John Groocock, Whetstone, Leics., framework-knitter, to appear and give evidence against John Thorpe, victualler, for contravening the conditions of the Victualler's Recognizance.

William Clarke, Belgrave, Leics., framework-knitter, to appear and answer charges and keep the peace towards Ann, wife of William Cornish, victualler.

Private George Harrold, Leicestershire Militia, to appear to prosecute and give evidence against James Burnett for a felony.

Edward Agar, broker, to appear and give evidence against James Burnett for a felony.

John Thomas, woolcomber, to appear and give evidence against James Burnett for a felony.

179.3 *Indictments*

John Goddard, labourer, for stealing 10 lbs wool from James Fenton. Po se.

James Burnett, labourer, for stealing a pair of leather breeches and a cotton waistcoat from George Harrold. Po se, guilty.

180.1 *Writ of Summons*

Dated 29 September 1791 for 7 October 1791.

180.2 *Discharged Recognizances*

Thomas Goodwin, carpenter, to appear and answer charges and keep the peace towards Ann, wife of William Whiting, framework-knitter.

Edward Keys, gardener, to appear and answer charges and keep the peace towards Samuel Woodford, currier.

Samuel Miles, framework-knitter, to appear and answer charges and keep the peace towards Robert Swann, framework-knitter.

Thomas Turpin, needlemaker, to appear and answer charges and keep the peace towards Robert Swann.

Joseph Bills, jun., framework-knitter, to appear and answer charges and keep the peace towards Robert Swann.

John Brookes, framework-knitter, to appear and answer charges and keep the peace towards Robert Swann.

James Wheatley, framework-knitter, to appear and answer charges and keep the peace towards Robert Swann.

Robert Swann, framework-knitter, to appear to prosecute and give evidence against William Horner, jun.

William Horner, jun., needlemaker, to appear and answer charges and keep the peace towards Robert Swann.

Henry Adcock, framework-knitter, to appear and answer charges and keep the peace towards Robert Swann.

William Fancote, jun., framesmith, to appear and answer charges and keep the peace towards Robert Swann.

Onesiphorous Parkin, framework-knitter, to appear and answer charges and keep the peace towards Robert Swann.

Richard Walker, jun., Stanford-upon-Soar, Notts., farmer, to appear and answer charges and keep the peace towards Suzanna Wood, widow.

Richard Phillips, Bishop's Fee, bookseller, to appear and answer charges and keep the peace towards John Kettleby, brazier.

180.3 *Indictments*

Edward Keys, gardener, for assaulting Samuel Woodford.

William Horner, needlemaker, for assaulting Robert Swann.

Elizabeth Bailey, widow and victualler, for obstructing Humberstone Gate with 10 cart loads each of dung, muck, straw and rubbish.

Richard Phillips, bookseller, for assaulting John Kettleby.

180.4 *Gaoler's Certificate*

William Loseby's return under the Statute (same as **175.7**).

180.5 *Application for Certificate for Dissenters' Meeting House*

⟨I, the Reverend Henry Chappell of the Borough of Leicester Priest, do hereby certify to His Majesty's Justices of the Peace for the said Borough, assembled at the General Quarter Session of the Peace for the said Borough this Day, That the Dwelling-house of Elizabeth Wilkins Widow situate in the Causeway Lane & Parish of All Saints in the said Borough is intended to be used as a Place of Congregation or Assembly for religious Worship, by Persons professing the Roman-Catholick Religion, in persuance of the Statute made in the thirty first year of his present Majesty's Reign—Dated this seventh Day of October 1791.⟩

180.6 *Sacramental Certificates*

St Mary's	Joseph Neal, Mayor
	William Orton, Coroner
	Thomas Read, Chamberlain
	Samuel Clarke, Chamberlain
St Margaret's	John Mansfield, Coroner
St Martin's	William Heyrick, gent.

181.1   *Writ of Summons*

Dated 19 December 1791 for 13 January 1792.

181.2   *Discharged Recognizances*

Gilbert Hole to appear and answer charges and keep the peace towards Samuel Moore, woolcomber.

Thomas Hole, jun., to appear and answer charges and keep the peace towards Samuel Moore.

Ann Haymes, singlewoman, to appear and answer charges and keep the peace towards Elizabeth Lester, singlewoman.

Alice Wheatley, widow, to appear and answer charges of felony to be made by Thomas Chapman.

Thomas Chapman, maltster, to appear to prosecute and give evidence against Alice Wheatley for a felony.

Private James Harryman, 35th Regiment of Foot, to appear and give evidence against Alice Wheatley for a felony.

John Groocock, labourer, to appear to prosecute and give evidence against James Tring for a felony.

William Phipps, tailor, to appear and give evidence against James Tring for a felony.

David Webster, labourer, to appear to prosecute and give evidence against James Rogers.

William Richmond to appear and give evidence against James Rogers.

Suzanna, wife of Thomas Pegg, to appear to prosecute and give evidence against Mary Silvester, spinster, for a felony.

Elizabeth Moore, widow, to appear and give evidence against Mary Silvester for a felony.

Sarah, wife of John Satchell, sawyer, to appear to prosecute and give evidence against Jane Jackson, widow, for a felony.

William Newton, framework-knitter, to appear and give evidence against Jane Jackson for a felony.

William Wakeman, dyer, to appear to prosecute and give evidence against William Harrison for a felony.

Elizabeth, wife of Thomas Hudson, miller, to appear and give evidence against William Harrison for a felony.

181.3   *Presentment*

Edmund Wigley, Recorder, presents the Inhabitants of the Borough of Leicester for the House of Correction, which ⟨hath been and is inconvenient and insufficient for the proper and safe Custody of Offenders and Prisoners therein and is in want of great additions repairs and alterations thereto and should be enlarged⟩.

181.4   *Indictments*

Ann Haymes, singlewoman, for assaulting Elizabeth Lester.

John Wilson, butcher, for forcibly ejecting James Stretton from his lodging-room, and preventing him from returning.

Sarah Gibson, widow, for illegally lodging Mary Thompson, singlewoman, in her cottage.

Elizabeth Stevens, widow, for keeping a disorderly house.   Not guilty.

Alice Wheatley, widow, for stealing 2 pieces of wood from Thomas Chapman.   Po se, not guilty.

James Tring, labourer, for stealing a leather pocket book, 5 linen shirts, 2 cloth coats, a velveret waistcoat, an indianet waistcoat, a cotton waistcoat, and a pocket handkerchief from John Grocock.   Po se, guilty.

James Rogers, labourer, for assaulting David Webster.   Po se, guilty.

Mary Silvester for stealing 4 yds white lace edging and 18 yds brown satin ribbon from Ellis Shipley Brewin.   Po se, guilty.

Mary Silvester, singlewoman, for stealing a piece of silk, a piece of muslin called a neck cloth, and a piece of cambric called a handkerchief from James Vaughan.   Po se, not guilty.

Mary Silvester, singlewoman, for stealing 2 muslin handkerchiefs, a piece of white satin, a piece of muslin, 2 pieces of green ribbon, 2 pieces of spotted muslin, 2 pieces of black lace, 2 pieces of striped silk, 3 pieces of white ribbon, and a long piece of plain muslin from Thomas Pegg.   Po se, not guilty.

The Inhabitants of St Margaret's Parish for not repairing Millstone Lane from the Three Crowns Inn, occupied by William Bishop, to the house of William Ingle, surgeon and apothecary.

William Harrison, carpenter, for stealing a man's black coat from William Wakeman.   Po se, guilty.

Jane Jackson, widow, for stealing a black silk woman's hat and a woman's shawl from John Satchell.   Po se, guilty.

181.5   *Convictions*

Robert Atkins, Braunstone Gate, trimmer, for swearing 5 profane oaths. [blank] Bonner, framework-knitter, for swearing 5 profane oaths.

181.6   *Certificate of Removal of Obstruction*

Elizabeth Bailey, widow, has removed the 10 cart loads each of dung, muck, straw and rubbish from Humberstone Gate.

181.7   *Sacramental Certificate*

St Martin's   Thomas Watchorn, Common Councillor

182.1   *Writ of Summons*

Dated 31 March 1792 for 20 April 1792.

182.2   *Discharged Recognizances*

William Crawley, jun., framework-knitter, to appear and answer charges.

William Clarke, jun., bricklayer, to appear and answer charges.

John Kellett, framework-knitter, to appear and answer charges and keep the peace towards Samuel Cotes.

Thomas Brown, framesmith, to appear and obey the Court *re* the bastard child of Martha Keen, St Margaret's, singlewoman.

Richard Kinton, framesmith, to appear and answer charges and keep the peace towards Thomas Harris, labourer.

182.3   *Indictment*

Robert Swingler, labourer, for digging a hole, 5 ft long, 18 ins wide, and 9 ins deep, across the footpath running beside the Turnpike Road to Oadby.

182.4   *Convictions*

Sarah, wife of Richard Fossett, framework-knitter, for ⟨having at several times within the last Six Months bought & received of & from Mary the Wife of Joseph Watson of the said Borough Tanner different Quantitys of Wool combed but not spun She the said Sarah Fossett then and there knowing the said Mary Watson to be a Person hired or employed to prepare or work up the Woollen Manufactures & not having first obtained the Consent of the Person or Persons so hiring or employing her the said Mary Watson⟩.

Elizabeth Palmer, widow, for receiving combed wool from Mary Watson (as above).

183.1   *Writ of Summons*

Dated 1 June 1792 for 13 July 1792.

183.2   *Discharged Recognizances*

William Waite, needlemaker, to appear and answer charges and keep the peace towards James White, framesmith.

Thomas Abell, hosier, to appear to prosecute and give evidence against John Clarke for a felony.

Richard Mellows, sawyer, to appear and give evidence against John Clarke for a felony.

Thomas Swain, the Woodgate, labourer, to appear and obey the Court *re* the bastard child of Hannah Moore, All Saints', singlewoman.

Henry Jeffcutt, grocer, to appear to prosecute and give evidence against John Allen for riot and a misdemeanour.

Hugh Scott, grocer, to appear and give evidence against John Allen for riot and a misdemeanour.

Richard Measures, blacksmith, to appear and answer charges.

Benjamin Knowles, Bishop's Fee, blacksmith, to appear and answer charges.

Ann Boulter, singlewoman, to appear and answer charges and keep the peace towards Turlington Simpson, framework-knitter.

James Godfrey, butcher, to appear to prosecute and give evidence against John Ward.

183.3 *Indictments*

William Waite, needlemaker, for assaulting James White.

John Clarke, labourer, for stealing a pocket handkerchief and a pair of worsted gloves from Thomas Abell.   Po se.

John Allen alias Johnson, Bishop's Fee, labourer, for riotous assembly and assaulting William Richardson, Constable.   Po se, not guilty.

John Allen alias Johnson, Bishop's Fee, labourer, for riotous assembly and assaulting John Hall.   Po se, not guilty.

John Ward, framework-knitter, for assaulting James Godfrey.

183.4 *Certificate of Removal of Obstruction*

Robert Swingler, labourer, has filled in the hole across the footpath beside the Turnpike Road to Oadby.

184.1 *Writ of Summons*

Dated 19 December 1792 for 18 January 1793.

184.2 *Discharged Recognizances*

Richard Roddle, butcher, to appear and answer charges and keep the peace towards George Flude, jun.

Charles Perkins, Lutterworth, Leics., labourer, to appear and answer charges.

Thomas Gorden, carpenter, to appear and answer charges and keep the peace towards Mary, wife of William Richardson, carpenter.

Thomas Gorden, carpenter, to appear and answer charges and keep the peace towards Mary Hopkins, singlewoman.

William Holman, gardener, to appear and answer charges and keep the peace towards Sarah, wife of Thomas Carr, labourer.

John Carr, framework-knitter, to appear and answer charges and keep the peace towards Ann, his wife.

John Carr, framework-knitter, to appear and answer charges and keep the peace towards Mary Garner, singlewoman.

Thomas Poyner, Osbaston, Leics., farmer, to appear to prosecute and give evidence against John Gray and Ann, his wife, for a felony.

Robert Pindar, cordwainer, to appear and give evidence against John and Ann Gray for a felony.

Margaret, wife of Thomas Coleman, basketmaker, to appear and give evidence against John and Ann Gray for a felony.

George Heafford, framework-knitter, to appear and answer charges and keep the peace towards William Whileman.

Isaiah Banner, framesmith, to appear and answer charges and keep the peace towards Thomas Barras, framework-knitter.

Margaret, wife of Thomas Coleman, basketmaker, to appear and give evidence against Joseph Smith for a felony.

Mary Wall, singlewoman, to appear and give evidence against Elizabeth Peers for a felony.

Private George Beaumont, Royal Horse Guards Blue Regiment, to appear to prosecute and give evidence against John Clark for a felony.

William Dixon, postillion, to appear and give evidence against John Clark for a felony.

John Needham, ostler, to appear and give evidence against John Clark for a felony.

Samuel Knott, framework-knitter, to appear and answer charges and keep the peace towards Joseph Chamberlain, Esq.

Thomas Lovett, labourer, to appear to prosecute and give evidence against William Sanderson for a felony.

Thomas Morris, painter, to appear and give evidence against William Sanderson for a felony.

William Dorman, baker, to appear and give evidence against William Sanderson for a felony.

Thomas Johns, slater and plasterer, to appear to prosecute and give evidence against Elizabeth Peers for a felony.

184.3 *Indictments*

William Sanderson, labourer, for stealing a coloured silk handkerchief, a pocket knife, and a pair of men's leather gloves from Thomas Lovitt. Pleads not guilty, po se.

Elizabeth, wife of John Peers, brickmaker, for stealing a wooden tub from Thomas Johns. Pleads not guilty, po se.

John Clarke, labourer, for stealing a pair of leather breeches, a pair of shag breeches, a buff coloured cloth waistcoat, and a blue coloured cloth coat from George Beaumont. Pleads not guilty, po se, guilty.

184.4   *Indictments of Richard Phillips, bookseller, for selling*
seditious literature

⟨Borough of Leicester (to wit) The Jurors for our Lord the King upon their Oath present that Richard Phillips late of the Bishops Fee in the parish of Saint Margaret within the Liberties and Precincts of the Borough of Leicester aforesaid Bookseller being a wicked malicious seditious and evil disposed person and greatly disaffected to our said Lord the King and to his Administration of the Government of this Kingdom and wickedly maliciously and seditiously contriving devising and intending to stir up and excite discontents and Seditions amongst the Subjects of our said Lord the King and to alienate and withdraw the Affection Fidelity and Allegiance of his said Majesty's Subjects from his said Majesty's Person and Government and wickedly maliciously and seditiously to insinuate and cause it to be believed by all the liege Subjects of our said Lord the King that the Constitution of the Government of this Kingdom as by Law established is a System of Tyranny Injustice and Oppression and destructive of the Liberties and Happiness of his said Majesty's Subjects and thereby wickedly and seditiously to disturb and destroy the Peace good order Tranquility and Prosperity of this Kingdom on the Sixth day of December in the year of our Lord one thousand seven hundred and ninety two with force and arms at the Parish aforesaid & within the Liberties & Precincts of the Borough of Leicester aforesaid wickedly maliciously and seditiously did publish and cause and procure to be published a certain wicked malicious scandalous and seditious Libel of and concerning our said Lord the King and his Government of this Kingdom and also of and concerning the Constitution of the Government of this Kingdom intitled "The Jockey Club Part the Second" in which said Libel of and concerning the Government of this Kingdom and the Constitution of the Government of this Kingdom are contained divers wicked scandalous and seditious words according to the tenor following (that is to say) "The force of example operates with invincible effect and our cold-blooded A---t-c--tes (meaning Aristocrates) are well aware that when the Tumults which lately distracted France shall have wholly subsided and the Rebel Clan of Princes Priests and Nobles finding all further resistance vain shall have returned to their duty as Citizens and experienced the mercy of a sorely-abused but generous forgiving Nation that the inestimable Blessings of a free Constitution will be universally acknowledged and they anticipate with malignant Envy that G---t B-----n (meaning the Subjects of Great Britain) may be inspired with a Godlike Emulation to participate with their Neighbours in a more equal and extensive Enjoyment of Freedom foreseeing the event they shudder at the consequence and hence are straining every Nerve to eternize the reign of Ignorance Credulity and Misery" and in which said last mentioned Libel of and concerning our said Lord the King and his Government of this Kingdom and also of and concerning the Constitution of the Government of this Kingdom are contained divers other wicked scandalous malicious and seditious words according to the tenor following (that is to say) "Is the miserable Farce of R---l-y (meaning Royalty and also meaning thereby the Royal Office and Authority of our said Sovereign Lord the King) that p-l-t-c-l (meaning Political) H--b-g (meaning Humbug) to be ever kept up under such an infinity of discouraging examples to its present enormous Magnitude Is it not revolting that a People (meaning the Subjects of our said Lord the King) sinking under their Burthens should be so rooted in Apathy or so deluded by the fraud and Sophistry of their Rulers as to believe that there is virtue or wisdom in maintaining such infamous Establishments? In examining that Register of our Folly and Disgrace the C---l L--t (meaning the Civil List of our Lord the King) it strikes us as the strongest Libel on the Spirit and Understanding of Englishmen" And in which said last mentioned Libel of and concerning our said Lord the King and his Government of this Kingdom and also of and concerning the Constitution of the Government of this Kingdom are contained divers other wicked scandalous malicious and seditious words according to the tenor following (that is to say) Every event that tends to increase the above execrable L–st (meaning the Civil List of our said Lord the King) tends at the same time to impoverish and enslave themselves (meaning the Subjects of our said Lord the King) the real Dignity and Interests of a Nation consist in a System the very reverse of that which constitutes the spurious Dignity of a C---n (meaning Crown) in Cultivating the Blessings of Peace and Civilization not in extending the horrors of War and Destruction nevertheless the Dignity of the C---n (meaning Crown) forsooth eternally uppermost in the Mouth of P----es (meaning Princes) and their Sycophants is the plausible Engine in use to gull the People (little prone to Investigation) into a belief that this Visionary Dignity is immediately connected with their own happiness and glory Whereas in fact it forever militates against them usurping to itself the Fruits of their Industry and Labour to support a fascinating ruinous splendour that dazzles and confounds their Senses while it involves them deep in Calamity and ruin by the base and horrible uses to which they are perverted" And in which said last mentioned Libel of and concerning our said Lord the King and his Government of this Kingdom are contained divers other wicked scandalous malicious and seditious words according to the tenor following (that is to say) "Month after Month we continue the Savage Practice of immolating unhappy Men to the vices of G-v---m--t (meaning the Government of our said Sovereign Lord the King) without an effort made to remedy or even to palliate the evil To the great danger of subverting the Constitution of this Kingdom To the evil example of all others in the like case offending and against the Peace of our said Lord the King his Crown and Dignity And the Jurors aforesaid upon their Oath aforesaid do further present that the said Richard Phillips being such Person as aforesaid and again unlawfully wickedly malicously and seditiously devising contriving and intending as aforesaid afterwards, to wit, on the said Sixth day of December in the said year of our Lord one thousand seven hundred and ninety two with force and Arms at the Parish aforesaid within the liberties & Precincts of the Borough aforesaid wickedly maliciously and seditiously published and caused and procured to be published a certain other wicked scandalous malicious and seditious Libel of and concerning our said Lord the King and his Government of this Kingdom and also of and concerning the Constitution of the Government of this Kingdom Intitled "The Jockey Club Part the Second" in which said last mentioned Libel of and concerning our said Lord the King and his Government of this Kingdom and also of and concerning the Constitution of the Government of this Kingdom are contained divers wicked scandalous and seditious words according to the tenor following (that is to say) "The force of Example operates with invincible effect and our cold-blooded A---t-c--tes (meaning Aristocrates) are well aware that when the Tumults which lately distracted France shall have wholly subsided and the rebel clan of Princes Priests and Nobles finding all further resistance vain shall have returned to their duty as Citizens and experienced the Mercy of a sorely-abused but generous forgiving Nation that the inestimable Blessings of a free Constitution will be universally acknowledged and they anticipate with malignant Envy that G---t B-----n (meaning the Subjects of Great Britain) may be inspired with a Godlike Emulation to participate with their Neighbours in a more equal and extensive enjoyment of Freedom foreseeing the Event they shudder at the consequence and hence are straining every Nerve to eternize the reign of Ignorance Credulity and Misery (purporting and insinuating thereby that the Government of our said Lord the King is founded on Ignorance and Credulity and productive of Misery to the Subjects of our said Lord the King) And in which said last mentioned Libel of and concerning our said Lord the King and the regal power and Authority as by Law established in this Kingdom are contained divers other wicked scandalous malicious and seditious words according to the tenor following "Let us once again express an Anxious heartfelt hope that the reign of Ignorance and Delusion will soon expire and that finally mankind will rise and assert themselves (purporting and insinuating thereby that the existence of the regal Power and Authority as established by Law in this Kingdom was founded in Ignorance and Delusion and that it would be for the Interest and happiness of the Subjects of our said Lord the King that the regal

2d Count

Power and Authority of our said Lord the King should be abolished) In Contempt of our said Lord the King and his Government In open violation of the Laws of this Kingdom To the great danger of subverting the Constitution of this Kingdom To the evil example of all others in the like case offending and against the Peace of our said Lord the King his Crown and Dignity And the Jurors aforesaid upon their Oath aforesaid do further present that the said Richard Phillips being such Person as aforesaid and again unlawfully wickedly maliciously and seditiously devising contriving and intending as aforesaid afterwards to wit on the said Sixth day of December in the said year of our Lord one thousand seven hundred and ninety two with force and Arms at the Parish aforesaid & in the Liberties & Precincts of the Borough aforesaid wickedly maliciously and seditiously published and caused and procured to be published a certain other wicked scandalous malicious and seditious Libel Intitled "The Jockey Club; or a Sketch of the manners of the Age. I'll speak of them as they are, nothing extenuate nor set down ought in malice. Shaksp.—dicere Verum, Quid vetat?—part the Third." in which said last mentioned Libel of and concerning our said Lord the King and his most Christian Majesty are contained amongst other things divers wicked Scandalous malicious and seditious Words according to the tenor following (that is to say) "There is in many instances a striking resemblance in the Virtues of these two R-y-l (meaning Royal) Jockeys (meaning our said Sovereign Lord the King and his said most Christian Majesty) which supposing them to exist and it might be Treason on one side to doubt it are merely Negative no benefit from them having ever reached their Subjects and for all possible Injury effected by their Vices they have Cartes Blanches from the wise Decree established in favour of their Ancestors "That Kings can do no wrong". The History of their reigns (meaning the reigns of our said Lord the King and of his said most Christian Majesty) will best proclaim the Wisdom of this Decree and is calculated to raise Conjectures that as it was decreed "they could do no wrong" they (meaning our said Lord the King and his said most Christian Majesty) in return had formed the grateful Resolution "to do no good". And in which said last mentioned Libel of and concerning our said Lord the King and his Government of this Kingdom And also of and concerning the Constitution of the Government of this Kingdom are contained divers other Wicked Scandalous Malicious and Seditious words according to the tenor following (that is to say) In this Country (meaning the Kingdom of Great Britain) perhaps it is Ignorance and Fear rather than respect to the Law on which Government (meaning the Government of our said Lord the King) chiefly depends for submission since it would be an absolute Paradox to assert that LAWS (meaning the Laws of this Kingdom) founded in excessive unnatural Inequality the balance intirely on one side, Oppressive to the other can ever create voluntary and universal obediance

189

much less heartfelt reverence and affection, or that a Government (meaning the Government of our said Lord the King) thus constituted can possibly remain for any time together in a State of internal Tranquillity" And in which said last mentioned Libel of and concerning our said Lord the King are contained divers other Wicked Scandalous Malicious and defamatory Words according to the tenor following (that is to say) "His (meaning our said Lord the King's) Shining Qualities are Soberness Temperance and Chastity (not Charity as Panegyric is dumb on that Article)—a Piety that consists in the strictest observance of all the outward forms of Religion, A regular undeviating Œconomy that resists all the Vulgar claims of Humanity and a firmness of mind by envy miscalled obstinacy, that has ever shewn itself superior to Events neither to be admonished by advice or controuled by example" And in which said last mentioned Libel of and concerning our said Lord the King and his Government of this Kingdom And also of and concerning the Constitution of the Government of this Kingdom are contained divers other wicked scandalous malicious and seditious words according to the Tenor following (that is to say) "Here, we cannot resist the satisfaction of Transcribing the System above alluded to, (meaning the System of the Government of our said Lord the King) as described by the immortal Junius Twenty years ago, as also the Character of the Great Personage (meaning our said Sovereign Lord the King) who established, and still continues to conduct it, and we appeal to the Candour of our readers if the Character both of one and the other has not been uniformly preserved." Other Princes besides G---ge III (meaning George the third our said Sovereign Lord the King) have had the means of Corruption within their reach, but they have used it with moderation.—In former times, Corruption was considered as a Foreign Auxiliary to Government, and only called in upon extraordinary Emergencies. The unfeigned Piety, the unsanctified religion of his present M-j--ty, (meaning Majesty) have taught him (meaning our said Lord the King) to new model the Civil Forces of the State.—The natural resources of the Crown are no longer confided in. Corruption glitters in the Van,—collects and maintains a standing Army of Mercenaries, and at the same moment, impoverishes and enslaves the Country.—Some of his M-j--ty's (meaning Majesty's) Predecessors were Kings or Gentlemen, not Hypocrites or Priests.—They said their Prayers without Ceremony, and had too little Priestcraft in their Understanding to reconcile the Sanctimonious forms of Religion, with the utter destruction of the Peoples morality.—Even Charles the second would have blushed at the open Encouragement, at those eager, meretricious Caresses, with which every species of private Vice, public Prostitution, and Apostacy is received at St. James's (meaning the Palace of Saint James, one of the Royal Palaces of our said Lord the King) The unfortunate House of Stuart has been treated with an Asperity, which, if comparison be a

Defence, borders upon Injustice.—Neither Charles nor his Brother were qualified to support such a System of Measures, as would be necessary to change the Government and subvert the Constitution of England.—one of them was too earnest in his pleasures; the other in his Religion.—But the danger to this Country would cease, to be problematical, if the Crown should ever descend to a Prince, whose apparent Simplicity might throw his Subjects off their Guard who might be no Libertine in Behaviour, who should have no Sense of Honour to restrain him, and who with just Religion enough to impose on the Multitude, might have no scruples of Conscience to interfere with his Morality. with these honourable Qualifications and the decisive Advantages of situation, low Craft and Falsehood, are all the Abilities that are wanting to destroy the Wisdom of Ages, and to deface the Noblest Monument that human policy has erected. I know such a Man.' (meaning thereby our said Sovereign Lord the King) We cannot coincide with Junius in his Hyperbolical Eulogium on the English Constitution, but if such was the System, and such the Man, Twenty years ago, we believe that no Person will deny that the Character of both has been uniformly kept up, or that it still flourishes in all its original Vigour. In Contempt of our said Lord the King in open violation of the Laws of this Kingdom. To the great danger of subverting the Constitution of the Government of this Kingdom. To the evil example of all others in the like case offending and against the Peace of our said Lord the King his Crown and Dignity.⟩

⟨Borough of Leicester, to wit, The Jurors of our Sovereign Lord the King upon their Oath present that before the printing and publishing of the wicked malicious scandalous and seditious Libels hereinafter mentioned to wit on the twenty first Day of May in the year of our Lord one thousand seven hundred and ninety two to wit at Westminster in the County of Middlesex our said Lord the King by the advice of his Privy Council had Issued his Royal Proclamation whereby after Reciting that divers wicked and seditious Writings had been printed published and industriously dispersed tending to excite Tumult and Disorder by endeavouring to raise groundless Jealousies and Discontents in the Minds of his faithful and loving Subjects respecting the Laws and happy Constitution of Government Civil and Religious established in this Kingdom and endeavouring to vilify and bring into Contempt the wise and wholesome Provisions made at the time of the glorious Revolution and since Strengthned and Confirmed by subsequent Laws for the preservation and Security of the Rights and Liberties of his faithful and loving Subjects and that divers writings had been printed published and industriously dispersed recommending the said wicked and seditious publications to the Attention of all his faithful and Loving Subjects and that he had also reason to believe that Correspondences had been entered into with sundry persons in Foreign Parts with the view to forward the Criminal and wicked purposes above mentioned and that the wealth happiness and prosperity of this Kingdom did under Divine Providence chiefly depend upon a due submission to the Laws a just Confidence in the integrity and wisdom of Parliament and a Continuance of that Zealous Attachment to the Government and Constitution of the Kingdom which had ever prevailed in the Minds of the People thereof and that there was nothing which he so earnestly desired as to secure the publick peace and prosperity and to preserve to all his loving Subjects the full Enjoyment of their Rights and Liberties both Religious and Civil he therefore being resolved as far as in him lay to repress the wicked and seditious Practises aforesaid and to deter all persons from following so pernicious an example solemnly warned all his Loving Subjects as they tendered their own happiness and that of their posterity to guard against all such Attempts which aimed at the subversion of all regular Government within this Kingdom and which were inconsistent with the Peace and Order of Society and earnestly exhorting them at all times and to the utmost of their power to avoid and discourage all proceedings tending to produce Riots and Tumults and he did strictly charge and Command all his Majestrates in and throughout his Kingdom of Great Britain that they should make diligent enquiry in order to discover the Authors and Printers of such wicked and seditious writings as aforesaid and all others who should disperse the same and he did further Charge and Command all his Sheriffs Justices of the Peace Chief Majestrates in his Cities Boroughs and Corporations and all other his Officers and Majistrates throughout his Kingdom of Great Britain that they should in their several and respective Stations take the most immediate and effectual Care to suppress and prevent all Riots Tumults and other disorders which might be attempted to be raised or made by any person or persons which on whatever Pretext they might be grounded were not only contrary to Law but dangerous to the most important Interests of this Kingdom and he did further require and command all and every his Majistrates aforesaid that they should from time to time transmit to one of his Majesty's Principal Secretaries of State due and full Information of such persons as should be found offending as aforesaid or in any Degree Aiding or Abetting therein it being his Determination for the preservation of the Peace and happiness of his faithful and loving Subjects to carry the Laws vigorously into execution against such offenders as aforesaid And the Jurors aforesaid upon their Oath aforesaid do further present that after the said Proclamation had been issued and before the publishing of the wicked malicious scandalous and seditious Libels hereinafter next mentioned divers Addresses had on occasion of such proclamation been presented to his said Majesty by divers of his loving Subjects expressing their Loyalty and Attachment to his said Majesty and the Government and Constitution of this Kingdom to wit at Westminster aforesaid in the County of Middlesex aforesaid And the Jurors aforesaid on their Oath aforesaid do further present that Richard Phillips late of the Bishops Fee in the parish of Saint Margaret within the Liberties and Precincts of the Borough of Leicester aforesaid Bookseller well knowing the Premises but being a wicked malicious seditious and ill disposed person and greatly dissaffected to our said Lord the King and the Constitution and Government of this Kingdom and wickedly maliciously and seditiously contriving devising and intending to stir up and excite discontents and seditions among the Subjects of our said Lord the King and to bring the said Proclamation unto disregard and contempt amongst his Subjects and to alienate and withdraw the Affection Fidelity and Allegiance of his said Majesty's Subjects from his said Majesty's Person and Government and wickedly maliciously and seditiously to insinuate and cause it to be believed by all the Liege Subjects of our said Lord the King that the Constitution and Government of this Kingdom as by Law established is a System of Tyranny injustice and oppression and destructive of the Liberties and happiness of his said Majesty's Subjects and thereby to stir up and excite his said Majesty's Subjects to seditious Meetings and Conventions and wickedly and seditiously to disturb and destroy the peace good order and tranquility of this Kingdom on the Sixth Day of December in the Thirty third Year of the Reign of our Lord the now King with force and Arms at Parish aforesaid & within the Liberties & Precincts of the Borough aforesaid inlawfully wickedly maliciously and seditiously did publish and cause and procure to be published a certain wicked malicious scandalous and seditious Libel entitled "Letter addressed to the Addressers on the late Proclamation meaning his said Majesty's Proclamation (in which said Libel are contained amongst other things divers malicious scandalous and seditious matters of and concerning the constitution of this Kingdom according to the Tenor following that is to say) It is a good Constitution (meaning the Constitution of this Kingdom) for Courtiers Placemen Pensioners Borougholders and the Leaders of Parties and these are the Men that have been the active Leaders of Addresses (meaning the said Addresses so presented as aforesaid) but it (meaning the Constitution of this Kingdom) is a bad Constitution for at least Ninety nine parts of the Nation (meaning this Kingdom) out of an Hundred and this Truth is every Day making it's way it is bad first because it entails upon the Nation the unnecessary expence of supporting three forms and Systems of Government at once namely the Monarchical the Aristocratical and the Democratical, secondly because it is impossible to unite such a discordant composition by any other means than perpetual Corruption and therefore the Corruption so loudly and so universally complained of is no other than the natural consequence of such an unnatural Compound of Governments and in this Consists that excellence which the numerous Herd of Placemen and Pensioners so loudly extol and which at the same time occasions that enormous load of Taxes under which the rest of the Nation groans among the Mass of National Delusions calculated to amuse and impose upon the Multitude the standing one has been that of flattering them into Taxes by calling the Government (or as they please to express it the English Constitution) the Envy and the Admiration of the World scarcely an Address has been voted in which some of the Speakers have not uttered this hackneyed nonsensical falshood two Revolutions have taken Place those of America and France and both of them have rejected the unnatural compounded System of the English Government America has declared against all Hereditary Government and established the representative System of Government only France has entirely rejected the Aristocratical part and is now discovering the Absurdity of the Monarchical and is approaching fast to the representative System on what ground then do those Men continue a Declaration respecting what they call the Envy and Admiration of other Nations which the voluntary Practice of such Nations as have had the opportunity of establishing Government contradicts and falsifys will such Men never confine themselves to truth will they be for ever the deceivers of the People and in which said Libel are contained amongst other things divers other malicious scandalous and seditious matters of and concerning the Constitution of this Kingdom according to the Tenor following (that is to say) I have asserted and have shewn both in the first and second parts of Rights of Man that there is not such a thing as an English Constitution and that the people (meaning the people of England) have yet a Constitution to form and in which said Libel amongst other things are contained divers other malicious scandalous and seditious matters of and concerning the Constitution of this Kingdom according to the Tenor following (that is to say) It has ever been the Craft of Courtiers for the purpose of keeping up an expensive and enormous Civil List and a Mummery of useless and antiquated places and offices at the public expence to be continually hanging England upon some Individual or other called King though the Man might not have Capacity to be a Parish Constable the folly and absurdity of this is appearing more and more every Day and still those Men continue to act as if no Alteration in the public opinion had taken place they hear each others nonsense and suppose the whole Nation talks the same gibberish let such Men cry up the House of Orange or the House of Brunswick if they please they would cry up any other House if it suited their purpose and give as good reasons for it but what is this House or that House or any House to a Nation for a Nation to be free it is sufficient that she wills it her freedom depends wholly upon herself and not on any House nor on any Individual I ask not in what light this Cargo of Foreign Houses appears to others but I will say in what light it appears to me it was like the Trees of the Forest saying unto the Bramble come thou and reign over us and in which said Libel amongst other things are contained divers other malicious scandalous and seditious matters of and concerning the Constitution and Government of this Kingdom and the power and Authority of the Parliament thereof according to the tenor following (that is to say) I consider the reform of Parliament (meaning the Parliament of this Kingdom) by an application to Parliament (meaning the Parliament of this Kingdom) as proposed by the Society to be a worn out hackneyed Subject about which the Nation is tired and the parties are deceiving each other It is not a Subject that is cognizable before Parliament (meaning the Parliament of this Kingdom) because no Government has a right to alter itself either in whole or in part the right and the exercise of that right appertains to the Nation only and the proper means is by a National Convention elected for the purpose by all the people by this the Will of the Nation whether to reform or not or what the Reform shall be or how far it shall extend will be known and it cannot be known by any other means partial Addresses or separate Associations are not Testimonies of the general Will It is however certain that the opinions of Men with respect to Systems and principals of Government are changing fast in all Countries the alteration in England within the space of little more than a Year is far greater than could then have been believed and it is Daily and Hourly increasing it moves along the Country with the Silence of thought the enormous expence of Government (meaning the Government of this Kingdom) has provoked Men to think by making them feel and the Proclamation (meaning his Majesty's said Proclamation) has served to increase Jealousy and disgust to prevent therefore those Commotions which too often and too suddenly arise from suffocated Discontents it is best that the general will should have the full and free opportunity of being publicly ascertained and known and in which said Libel are contained amongst other things divers other malicious scandalous and seditious matters of and concerning the Representation by the Commons of Great Britain in Parliament assembled and of and concerning the power and Authority of the Parliament of this Kingdom according to the Tenor following (that is to say) I wish that Mr. Grey since he has embarked in the Business would take the whole of it into Consideration he will then see that the right of reforming the state of the Representation (meaning Representation by the Commons of Great Britain in Parliament assembled) does not reside in Parliament (meaning the Parliament of Great Britain) and that the only motion he could consistently make would be that Parliament (meaning the Parliament of Great Britain) should recommend the Election of a Convention by all the people because all pay Taxes but whether Parliament (meaning the Parliament of Great Britain) recommended it or not the right of the Nation would neither be lessened nor increased thereby and in which said Libel amongst other things are contained divers other malicious scandalous and seditious matters according to the Tenor following (that is to say) Instead then of referring to rotten Boroughs and absurd Corporations (meaning Boroughs and Corporations in this Kingdom) for Addresses or hawking them about the Country to be signed by a few dependent Tenants the real and effectual Mode would be to come at once to the point and to ascertain the sense of the Nation (meaning this Kingdom) by electing a National Convention (meaning a Convention of the People of this Kingdom otherwise than in Parliament assembled) to the great Damage of our happy Constitution and Government in Contempt of our said Lord the King and his Laws to the evil Example of all others in the like Case offending and against the Peace of our said Lord the King his Crown and Dignity.⟩ ⟨Borough of Leicester to wit The Jurors of our Lord the King upon their Oath present That Richard Phillips late of the Bishops Fee in the Parish of Saint Margaret within the Libertys & Precincts of the Borough of Leicester aforesaid Bookseller being a wicked malicious seditious and ill disposed Person and being greatly disaffected to our said Sovereign Lord the now King and to the Constitution and Government of this Kingdom and most unlawfully wickedly seditiously and maliciously devising contriving and intending to scandalize traduce and vilify our said Lord the now King and the Hereditary Succession to the Crown and Regal Government of this Kingdom as by Law established and to alienate and withdraw from our said present Sovereign Lord the now King the true and due Obedience Fidelity and Allegiance of his Subjects and wickedly and seditiously to disturb the Peace and Tranquility of this Kingdom on the Sixth Day of December in the thirty third year of the Reign of our said present Sovereign Lord the King with Force and Arms at the Parish aforesaid & within the Liberties & Precincts of the Borough aforesaid he the said Richard unlawfully wickedly maliciously and seditiously did publish and cause to be published a certain scandalous malicious and seditious Libel Intituled "Rights of Man Part the Second combining Principle and Practice by Thomas Paine Secretary for Foreign Affairs to Congress in the American War and Author of the Works Entitled Common Sense and the first part of the Rights of Man. London Printed for H. D. Symonds Paternoster Row 1792." In which said Libel are contained (amongst other things) divers scandalous malicious and seditious Matters of and concerning the Hereditary Succession to the Crown and Regal Government of this Kingdom as by Law established that is to say one part thereof according to the Tenor and Effect following (that is to say) "It cannot be proved by what right Hereditary Government (meaning amongst other things the said Hereditary Government of this Kingdom) could begin neither does there exist within the Compass of mortal Power a right to establish it (meaning such Hereditary Government) Man has no Authority over Posterity in Matters of Personal Right and therefore no Man or Body of Men had or can have a right to set up Hereditary Government" (meaning amongst other things the Government of this Kingdom) And in another part thereof according to the Tenor and

Effect following "Hereditary Succession (meaning amongst other things the said Hereditary Succession to the Government of this Kingdom) is a Burlesque upon Monarchy It puts it in the most ridiculous light by presenting it as an Office which any Child or Idiot may fill. It requires some Talents to be a common Mechanic but to be a King requires only the Animal Figure of Man a sort of breathing Automaton This Sort of Superstition may last a few years more but it cannot long resist the awakened Reason and Interest of Man" And in another part thereof according to the Tenor and Effect following (that is to say) "A Government calling itself free with an hereditary Office (meaning amongst other things the Government of this Kingdom with an hereditary Office of King thereof) is like a Thorn in the Flesh that produces a Fermentation which endeavours to discharge it" And in another part thereof according to the Tenor and Effect following (that is to say) The Hereditary System (meaning amongst other things the Hereditary System of Succession to the Crown of this Kingdom) therefore is as repugnant to Human Wisdom as to Human Rights and is as absurd as it is unjust" And in another part thereof according to the Tenor and Effect following (that is to say) "Whether I have too little Sense to see or too much to be imposed upon Whether I have too much or too little Pride or of any thing else I leave out of the Question, but certain it is that what is called Monarchy (meaning amongst other things the Monarchy of this Kingdom) always appears to me a silly contemptible thing I compare it to something kept behind a Curtain about which there is a great deal of Bustle and Fuss and a wonderful Air of seeming Solemnity but when by any Accident the Curtain happens to be open and the Company see what it is they burst into Laughter" And in another part thereof according to the Tenor and Effect following (that is to say) "That Monarchy (meaning amongst other things the Monarchy of this Kingdom) is all a Bubble a mere Court Artifice to procure money is evident (at least to me) in every Character in which it can be viewed" And in another part thereof according to the Tenor and Effect following (that is to say) "It can only be by blinding the understanding of Man and making him believe that Government is some wonderful mysterious thing that excessive Revenues are obtained Monarchy (meaning amongst other things the Monarchy of this Kingdom) is well calculated to insure this End It is the Popery of Government a thing kept up to amuse the Ignorant and quiet them into Taxes" In contempt of our said Lord the now King in open violation of the Laws of this Kingdom and to the great Danger of our happy Constitution To the Evil Example of all others in the like Case offending and against the Peace of our said Lord the King his Crown and Dignity.⟩

184.5 *Process Paper*

John Wilson, butcher, having been indicted for forcibly ejecting James

Stretton from his lodging-room and preventing him from returning, failed to appear at a previous Sessions, but has now pleaded "Not Guilty" and is to be tried.

184.6 *Certificate of Road Repair*
The Inhabitants of St Margaret's Parish have repaired Millstone Lane from the Three Crowns to the house of William Ingle, surgeon.

184.7 *Sacramental Certificates*
St Margaret's   Joseph Burbidge, Mayor
                 Benjamin Gregory, Coroner
                 Samuel Towndrow, Chamberlain
                 William Firmadge, Chamberlain

185.1 *Writ of Summons*
Dated 22 March 1793 for 12 April 1793.

185.2 *Discharged Recognizances*
Richard Toon, Bishop's Fee, victualler, to appear and answer charges and keep the peace towards John Weston, tailor.
William Hudson, Whitby, Yorks., merchant, to appear and answer charges.

185.3 *Process Papers*
Richard Phillips, Bishop's Fee, bookseller, having been indicted three times for selling seditious literature, has pleaded "Not Guilty" to all three and is to be tried.

185.4 *Application for Certificate for Dissenters' Meeting House*
We whose Names are hereunder written being Protestant Dissenters of the Church of England do hereby certify That a Building erected for a Place of public Worship in Millstone Lane in the said Borough of Leicester & known by the Name of The Millstone Lane Meeting House is intended as a Place of Meeting of Protestant Dissenters for religious Worship; And do hereby desire You to direct the Clerk of the Peace for the said Borough to register the same pursuant to the Statute in that Case made and Provided In Witness wherof we have hereunto set our hands the Eleventh Day of April 1793.

                                        James Clough
                                        John Rawson
                                        Richard Rawson
                                          Francis Rayns⟩

185.5 *Sacramental Certificate*
St Mary's   William Orton, Coroner

186.1   *Writ of Summons*

Dated 30 September 1793 for 14 October 1793.

186.2   *Discharged Recognizances*

John Paget, Brooksby, Leics., miller, to appear and answer charges and keep the peace towards John Simpkin, servant to the Rev. Mr Orton, clerk.

John Palmer, woolcomber, to appear and answer charges and keep the peace towards Francis Reynold, labourer.

John Clifford, Burton Overy, Leics., butcher, to appear and obey the Court *re* the bastard child of Ann Jelly, St Martin's, singlewoman.

Simon Richards, brickmaker, to appear and obey the Court *re* the female bastard child of Elizabeth Upton, St Margaret's, singlewoman.

George Slack, jun., framework-knitter, to appear and obey the Court *re* the female bastard child of Mary Jarvis, St Margaret's, singlewoman.

George Harley Vaughan, jun., schoolmaster at the Free Grammar School, to appear and answer charges.

186.3   *Indictment*

The Inhabitants of St Mary's Parish for not repairing the footpath from Wigston Magna to Groby between St Mary's Pinfold and the Horsepool.

186.4   *Indictment of George Harley Vaughan, schoolmaster, for distributing seditious literature*

⟨Borough of Leicester (to wit) The Jurors for our Lord the King upon their Oath present that before and at the time of the Publication of the printed Papers hereinafter mentioned a War was Prosecuted and carried on between our said Lord the King and the Persons exercising the Powers of Government in France (that is to say) at the Borough of Leicester aforesaid And the Jurors aforesaid upon their Oath aforesaid do further present that George Harley Vaughan late of Leicester aforesaid Schoolmaster being a malicious seditious and ill disposed person and wickedly and maliciously devising and intending to excite a spirit of sedition and discontent in the minds of the subjects of our said Lord the King and unlawfully to scandalize defame and to bring into hatred our said Lord the King and his administration of the government of this Kingdom and the Persons employed by him therein and to insinuate and cause it to be believed that the motives which had been declared and avowed by our said Lord the King and the said Persons to be the motives by which they were induced to enter into the said War were not the real and true motives by which they were induced to enter into the said War and also to insinuate and cause it to be believed that the said War had been entered into from wicked and unlawful motives and for unjust and oppressive purposes and that the same was prosecuted and carry'd on without any Just lawful or sufficient reason and that our said Lord the King and the Person employed by him in the

Administration of the said government of this Kingdom were ignorant of the situation and regardless of the distresses of the Subjects of this Country on the twenty sixth day of September in the year of our Lord One thousand seven hundred and ninety three with force and arms &c at the Borough of Leicester aforesaid and within the Jurisdiction of the Court of the said Borough of Leicester wickedly maliciously and seditiously publish'd and caused and procured to be published a certain printed Paper containing divers scandalous seditious and inflammatory matters and things of and Concerning the said War and of and concerning our said Lord the King and his administration of the Government of this Kingdom and the Persons employed by him therein that is to say in one part thereof according to the Tenor and effect following to wit War!!! "War is the Pharo-Table of Governments (meaning among others the government of this Kingdom) and Nations are the dupes of the Game" War's a Game, that were their Subjects wise, Kings would not play at "The ostensible motives by which government (meaning the government of this Kingdom) were induced to enter into a War with the French Republic (meaning the aforesaid War between our said Lord the King and the Persons exercising the Powers of Government in France) being so effectually removed that it is rediculous to entertain the Slightest apprehensions of their Relapse, it behoves every true Friend and well-wisher to the Happiness and Prosperity of this Country to inquire how far its continuance may be inimical or beneficial to either this duty is become more especially necessary as the object of the War is now changed and every rational and equitable end is acknowledged to be completely obtained by it And in another part thereof according to the Tenor and Effect following to wit If a decent subsistence cannot be obtained in time of Peace, but with unwearied labour and painful exertion, what is to be done when taxes increase, employment diminishes, wages Sink, and Provisions rise? Look to it Ye Loyal Addressers ye hood-winked half-witted Politicians for as your courtly effusions gave sanction to it, to you, and to you alone, the starving People will have a right to look for Subsistence And in another part thereof according to the tenor and effect following To wit Admitting that the motives which induced government (meaning the government of this Kingdom) to commence the War (meaning the aforesaid War) were laudable as it is now changed into a War of extermination against opinions it will vindicate any Atrocity that can be Committed, for if a difference of Opinion will Justify Nations murdering each other by thousands, it will Consequently justify individual Assassinations! Admitting that there was an unavoidable necessity for going to War, that necessity cannot exist now, as every rational Object is obtained, and the French have shewn unequivocal wishes for Peace! And in another part thereof according to the tenor and effect following To wit The Effects of War on the Poor. "These are the times that try Men's Souls" "Three days after the debate on the Kings Message I was walking from my Friend's House to the neighbouring Town to inspect the Printing of the preceeding Sheets, and on my way joined company with two Men of the Village who being employed by the Woolstaplers to let out Spinning to the Poor, had lately received orders to lower the price of labour—We were talking on this Subject when the exclamations of of a groupe of poor women going to market, over hearing our Conversation, made an impression on my mind which all the eloquence of the Houses of Lords and Commons cannot efface, We are to be sconced three pence in the shilling, let others work for me, I'll not. We are to be sconced a fourth of our labour, what is all this for? I did not dare to tell them what it was for, nor to add insult to misery. What was the beheading of a Monarch to them What is the navigation of the Scheldt to them? What is the Freedom of a Great Nation to them, but reason for joy? Yet the debating only on these Subjects has reached their Cottages, They are already sconced three pence in the shilling what must be their fate, when we suffer under the most odious scourge of the human race, and the accumulation of Taxes takes away half of that daily bread, which at present is scarce Sufficient for their Support? Oh! that I had the warning voice of an antient Prophet that I might Penetrate into the inmost recesses of Palaces and appal the haranguers of Senates; I would use no other Language than that of the Poor Market-Women; I would cry aloud in the ears of the first Magistrate (meaning our said Lord the King) we are Sconced three pence in the shilling, the fourth part of our Labour, for what? I would address myself to the deliberating bodies, we are Sconced Three Pence in the shilling the fourth part of our Labour for what? Is there a Man that could stand against this Eloquence? Yes, thousands. Three pence in the shilling for spinning conveys no Idea to them. They know not what a Cottage is; they know not how the poor live—how they make up their scanty meal—Perhaps there may be some one in the House of Commons whose Feelings are in Union with mine; communicate them to your Colleagues, impress them with the Horror attendant on their diliberations tell them what the deduction of three pence in the shilling occasions among the myriads of England. And should any grave Courtier pitying the distresses of the Poor, be anxious to relieve them, say to him, there is an easy method: Let the first Magistrate (meaning our said Lord the King) the Peers the Representatives of the People, the rich Men of the Nation all who are for War be sconced one fourth part of their annual Income to defray the Expence of it. Let them be the first sufferers, let the burden fall upon them, and not upon the Poor, Alas! my poor Countrymen, how many Years Calamity awaits you before a single Dish, or Glass of Wine will be withdrawn from the Tables of Opulence—At this Moment, perhaps, the Decree is gone forth for War. Let others talk of Glory, let others celebrate the heroes, who are to deluge the World with blood, the words of The poor Market Women will still resound in my Ears—We are sconced three-pence in the shilling, one fourth of our Labour—for what?" Because a set of Men (meaning the Persons employed by our said Lord the King in the Administration of the Government of this Kingdom) (more deserving the Name of Cannibals) who are interested in the continuance of the Abuses of the Constitution (meaning the Constitution of the Government of this Kingdom) wish to divert the Attention of the People (meaning the People of this Kingdom) from inquiring into and reforming them" In Contempt of our said Lord the King and his Laws To the evil and pernicious example of all others in the like case offending and against the Peace of our said Lord the King his Crown and Dignity And the Jurors aforesaid upon their Oath aforesaid do further present that the said George Harley Vaughan so being such Person as aforesaid and wickedly and maliciously devising and intending to excite a spirit of discontent and sedition in the Minds of the Subjects of our said Lord the King and to scandalize defame and bring into hatred our said Lord the King and his Administration of the Government of this Kingdom and the Persons employed by him therein and to cause it to be suspected and believed that the aforesaid War between our said Lord the King and the Persons exercising the Powers of Government in France was a cruel unjust and unlawful War on the part of our said Lord the King afterwards to wit on the said twenty sixth Day of September in the said year of our Lord one thousand seven hundred and ninety three with force and Arms &c at the Borough of Leicester aforesaid and within the Jurisdiction of the Court of the said Borough of Leicester wickedly maliciously and seditiously published and caused and procured to be published a certain other printed Paper containing certain scandalous seditious and inflamatory Matters and Things of and concerning the said War and of and concerning our said Lord the King and his Administration of the Government of this Kingdom and the Persons employed by him therein according to the Tenor and Effect following (that is to say) "Is it possible ye can have forgot the Streets filled with untenanted Houses; and Frames to Let staring ye in the Face, in every quarter of the Town, during the greatest part of the American War? What War occasioned then War (meaning the aforesaid War between our said Lord the King and Persons exercising the Powers of Government in France) may again occasion and again the prosperity of the Country may be put upon the cast of a Die! Will the murder of some thousands of Frenchmen be any Consolation under these Calamities? Will the cries of the many Widows and Orphans increase the numerous Felicities ye enjoy under our present Glorious and Happy Constitution? In Contempt of our said Lord the King and his Laws To the evil and pernicious example of all others in the like Case offending and against the Peace of our said Lord the King his Crown and Dignity And the Jurors aforesaid upon their Oath aforesaid do further present that the said George

Harley Vaughan so being such Person as aforesaid and wickedly and maliciously devising and intending to excite a spirit of discontent and sedition in the Minds of the Subjects of our said Lord the King and to scandalize and bring into Hatred our said Lord the King and his Administration of the Government of this Kingdom and the Persons employed by him therein and to insinuate and cause it to be believed that the said War had been entered into by the Government of this Kingdom against the Persons exercising the Powers of Government in France from wicked and unlawful Motives and for unjust and oppressive purposes on the said twenty sixth Day of September in the said Year of our Lord one thousand seven hundred and ninety three with Force and Arms &c at the Borough of Leicester aforesaid and within the Jurisdiction of the Court of the said Borough wickedly maliciously and seditiously published and caused and procured to be published a certain other printed Paper containing certain scandalous seditious and inflamatory Matters and Things of and concerning the said last mentioned war and of and concerning our said Lord the King and his Administration of the Government of this Kingdom and the Persons employed by him therein according to the Tenor and Effect following (that is to say) "At this moment perhaps the decree is gone forth for War, let others talk of Glory, let others celebrate the Heroes who are to deluge the World with Blood, the Words of the Poor Market-women will still resound in my Ears we are sconed three-pence in the Shilling, one fourth of our Labour—for what? Because a set of Men (meaning the Persons employed by our said Lord the King in the Administration of the Government of this Kingdom) (more deserving the name of Cannibals) who are interested in the continuance of the Abuses of the Constitution (meaning the Constitution of the Government of this Kingdom) wish to divert the Attention of the People (meaning the People of this Kingdom) from inquiring into and reforming them!" In Contempt of our said Lord the King and his Laws To the evil and pernicious Example of all others in the like Case offending and against the Peace of our said Lord the King his Crown and Dignity.⟩

186.5   *Sacramental Certificates*

St Margaret's   John Mansfield, Mayor
                 Alderman William Dabbs
                 Mark Oliver, Chamberlain
                 John Stevenson, Chamberlain
St Martin's   Alderman James Willey
                 Michael Miles, coachmaker
                 James Cort, ironmonger
                 John Walker, draper
St Mary's   William Orton, Coroner

187.1 *Writ of Summons*

Dated 10 December 1793 for 17 January 1794.

187.2 *Discharged Recognizances*

John Emmerson, yeoman, to appear and obey the Court *re* ⟨his appeal against a Conviction for selling Rum without a License⟩.

William Bates, victualler, to appear to prosecute and give evidence against Thomas Collingbourn.

William Bennett, carpenter, to appear and obey the Court *re* the bastard child of Dorothy Hand, St Margaret's, singlewoman.

Thomas Marvin, framework-knitter, to appear to prosecute and give evidence against William Phillips.

Thomas Rice, woolcomber, to appear to prosecute and give evidence against William Phillips.

Thomas Rice, woolcomber, to appear and give evidence against William Phillips.

Samuel Steads, gardener, to appear and give evidence against William Phillips on two counts.

187.3 *Indictments*

Thomas Collingbourn, woolcomber, for assaulting William Bates.

William Phillips, woolcomber, for assaulting Thomas Marvin. Po se, guilty.

William Phillips, woolcomber, for assaulting Thomas Rice. Po se, guilty.

188.1 *Writ of Summons*

Dated 10 April 1794 for 28 April 1794

188.2 *Discharged Recognizances*

William Thornelow, Newbold Verdon, Leics., butcher, to appear and answer charges and keep the peace towards John Wilson, Rearsby, Leics., woolcomber.

Edward Harris, gunsmith, to appear to prosecute and give evidence against John Hall for a felony.

James Caparn, brazier, to appear and give evidence against John Hall for a felony.

Eleanor, wife of Joseph Brewin, labourer, to appear to appeal against a conviction ⟨for having in her Possession embezzled unwrought yarn mixed & not giving an Account to the Satisfaction of the said Justices how she came by the same⟩, obey the Court and pay costs.

Thomas Plowright, the Woodgate, labourer, to appear and answer charges and keep the peace towards Abraham Anderson, labourer.

188.3 *Indictments*

John Hall, gunsmith, for stealing 2 lbs cast brass from Edward Harris.

Thomas Plowright, the Abbeygate, dyer, for assaulting Abraham Anderson.

188.4 *Process Paper*

George Harley Vaughan, schoolmaster, having been indicted for distributing seditious literature, has pleaded "Not Guilty" and is to be tried.

188.5 *Conviction*

Eleanor, wife of Joseph Brewin, labourer, for ⟨having received a Quantity to wit three Pounds of Mixed Yarn unwrought being Materials used in the Woollen Manufacture knowing the same to be purloined or embezzled⟩.

188.6 *Certificate of Repair*

The House of Correction has been repaired and enlarged.

188.7 *Sacramental Certificate*

St Martin's   Thomas Jeffcutt, hosier

189.1 *Writ of Summons*

Dated 9 July 1794 for 28 July 1794.

189.2 *Discharged Recognizances*

George Brown, surgeon, to appear and answer charges.
Robert Day, carpenter, to appear and answer charges and keep the peace towards John Cumberland, hosier.
Robert Day, carpenter, to appear and answer charges and keep the peace towards William Bell, jun., schoolmaster.
William Drothwaite, Excise Officer, to appear and answer charges and keep the peace towards John Hurst, woolstapler.

189.3 *Indictments*

Robert Day, carpenter, for assaulting John Cumberland.

Robert Day, carpenter, for assaulting William Bell.

189.4 *Process Paper*

Thomas Plowright, the Abbey Gate, dyer, having been indicted for assaulting Abraham Anderson, has pleaded 'Not Guilty' and is to be tried.

189.5 *Application for Certificate for Dissenters' Meeting House*

⟨We whose Names are hereunder written being Protestant Dissenters of the Church of England do hereby certify That a certain Building situate in

Redcross Street in the said Borough of Leicester and known by the Name of The Redcross Street Baptist Meeting House is intended as a Place of Meeting of Protestant Dissenters for religious Worship And do hereby desire you to direct the Clerk of the Peace for the said Borough to register the same pursuant to the Statute in that Case made and provided In Witness whereof we have hereunto set our Hands and Seals the Twenty fifth Day of July 1794.

> William Gill
> Benjamin Lewitt
> Richard Toone
> John Dewell⟩

190.1   *Writ of Summons*
Dated 30 September 1794 for 20 October 1794.

190.2   *Discharged Recognizances*

Jesse Goude, framework-knitter, to appear and obey the Court *re* the bastard child of Elizabeth Palmer, St Mary's, singlewoman.

Joshua Wardle, cordwainer, to appear and give evidence against Robert Spence.

Joseph Wright, cordwainer, to appear and answer charges.

William Wolf, cordwainer, to appear and answer charges.

Thomas Cooper, cordwainer, to appear and answer charges.

John Hopwell, cordwainer, to appear and answer charges.

John Chamberlain, cordwainer, to appear and answer charges.

Robert Mason, cordwainer, to appear and answer charges.

Robert Spence, cordwainer, to appear and answer charges.

Daniel Groom, cordwainer, to appear and answer charges.

David Hefford, cordwainer, to appear and answer charges.

John Chamberlain, cordwainer, to appear and answer charges and keep the peace towards Thomas Needham, Syston, Leics., cordwainer.

Thomas Cooper, cordwainer, to appear and answer charges and keep the peace towards Thomas Needham.

William Cooper, cooper, to appear and answer charges and keep the peace towards Thomas Needham.

David Hefford, cordwainer, to appear and answer charges and keep the peace towards Thomas Needham.

William Robotham, watchmaker, to appear and obey the Court *re* the bastard child of Margaret Potter, St Leonard's, singlewoman.

Thomas Atkins, cordwainer, to appear to prosecute and give evidence against Robert Spence.

Eleanor, wife of John Bateman, woolcomber, to appear to prosecute and give evidence against Robert Doubleday for an assault.

George Murray, cordwainer, to appear and answer charges.

Joseph West, hosier, to appear to prosecute and give evidence against Thomas Dawkins for a felony.

John West to appear and give evidence against Thomas Dawkins for a felony.

190.3 *Indictments*

The Inhabitants of St Martin's Parish, on the presentment of John Mansfield, Justice, for not repairing New Street. Copy—original removed by Writ of Certiorari.

Robert Mason, labourer, John Hopwell, labourer, Robert Spence, labourer, David Hefford, the Bishop's Fee, labourer, Joseph Wright, labourer, William Woolf, labourer, John Chamberlain, labourer, Freer Gee, labourer, Daniel Groom, labourer, George Murray, labourer, and Thomas Cooper, labourer, ⟨being Workmen or Journeymen in the Art Mystery & Manual Occupation of a Cordwainer and not being content to work and labour in that Art Mystery and Manual Occupation at the usual Rates and Prices for which they and other Workmen and Journeymen were wont and accustomed to work, but falsely and fraudulently conspiring and combining unjustly and oppressively to increase and augment the Wages of themselves and other Workmen and Journeymen in the said Art Mystery and Manual Occupation and unjustly to exact and extort great Sums of Money for their Labor and Hire in their said Art Mystery and Manual Occupation from their Masters who employ them therein with force and Arms on the same Day and Year aforesaid at the Parish of Saint Martin aforesaid in the Borough of Leicester aforesaid and within the Jurisdiction of the said Borough together with divers other Workmen and Journeymen in the same Art Mystery and Manual Occupation (whose Names to the Jurors aforesaid are yet unknown) unlawfully did assemble and meet together, and so being assembled and met did then and there unjustly and corruptly conspire combine confederate and agree among themselves that none of the said Conspirators after the same thirty first Day of July would work at any lower or lesser Rate than Two shillings and twopence for the making of every pair of Shoes and Six shillings for the making of every pair of Boots for or on Account of any Master or Employer whatsoever in the said Art Mystery and Manual Occupation To the great Damage and Oppression not only of their Masters employing them in the said Art Mystery and Manual Occupation but also of divers others of His Majesty's liege Subjects⟩. A case found against all except Cooper.

Elizabeth Bailey, the Bishop's Fee, widow and victualler, for obstructing Humberstone Gate with 2 cart loads each of dung, muck, straw and rubbish.

Robert Doubleday, framesmith, for assaulting Eleanor Bateman.

Thomas Dawkins, labourer, for stealing a pair of plaited silk and worsted stockings from Joseph West.

John Bardill, labourer, for stealing a silver spoon from Edward Chamberlain.

190.4 *Process Papers*

Robert Day, carpenter, having been indicted for assaulting William Bell, jun., has pleaded "Not Guilty" and is to be tried.

Robert Day, carpenter, having been indicted for assaulting John Cumberland, has pleaded "Not Guilty" and is to be tried.

190.5 *Sacramental Certificates*

St Margaret's   Benjamin Gregory, Mayor
John Walker, draper, Chamberlain
John Reynolds, grocer, Chamberlain
Robert Thompson, hosier
St Mary's   William Orton, Coroner

[Separate roll but for same Sessions as **190** above.]

191   *Warrant for the Release of Richard Phillips on Remission of Sentence*

⟨George R.

Whereas R. Phillips was at a Quarter Sessions of the Peace held at Leicester tried and Convicted of selling a Seditious Publication and was sentenced to be imprisoned Eighteen Calendar Months for the same And Whereas some favorable Circumstances have been humbly represented unto us in his behalf inducing us to Extend our Grace and Mercy unto him and to Remit unto him such part of his sentence of imprisonment as remains yet to be undergone and performed Our Will and pleasure therefore is that you cause him the said R. Phillips to be forthwith discharged out of custody and for so doing this shall be your Warrant Given at our Court at Saint James's the Twenty fifth day of August 1794 in the thirty fourth year of our Reign. To our Trusty and Welbeloved The⎫
Recorder of Leicester The Mayor of ⎮ By His Majestys Command
the said Town and all others whom ⎬   Portland⟩
it may Concern. ⎭

192.1   *Writ of Summons*

Dated 22 December 1794 for 12 January 1795.

192.2   *Discharged Recognizances*

William Entwistle, jun., to appear and answer charges.

Thomas Phillips, framework-knitter, to appear and give evidence against William Entwistle, jun.

192.3 *Process Paper*

Robert Mason, labourer, John Hopwell, labourer, Robert Spence, labourer, David Hefford, the Bishop's Fee, labourer, Joseph Wright, labourer, William Woolf, labourer, John Chamberlain, labourer, Freer Gee, labourer, Daniel Groom, labourer, and George Murray, labourer, all working as cordwainers, having been indicted for unlawful assembly and conspiracy to raise rates of pay, have pleaded "Not Guilty" and are to be tried.

192.4 *Certificate of Removal of Obstruction*

Elizabeth Bailey, the Bishop's Fee, widow, has removed the dung, straw, muck and rubbish from the street in the Bishop's Fee.

192.5 *Sacramental Certificate*

St Martin's   James Willey, grocer, Coroner

193a.1 *Writ of Summons*

Dated 4 July 1795 for 13 July 1795.

193a.2 *Discharged Recognizances*

Thomas Bruce, farmer, to appear and obey the Court *re* the bastard child of Sarah Briers, St Martin's, singlewoman.
William Burberry, jun., Coventry, butcher, to appear and answer charges.
Sergeant Frank Ludlam, Leicester Fencibles, to appear to prosecute and give evidence against William Burberry.
William Freer, jun., stocking-trimmer, to appear and obey the Court *re* the bastard child of Mary Whithers, All Saints', singlewoman.
John Greenshields, tailor, to appear and answer charges and keep the peace towards Edward Agar, tailor.
John Heyrick, jun., gent., to appear and answer charges and keep the peace towards William Kirk, gardener.
Francis Maples, framework-knitter, and Elizabeth, his wife, to appear and answer charges.
Sergeant Thomas Harpur, 15th Light Dragoon Regiment, to appear to prosecute and give evidence against Thomas Gray.
Sergeant Thomas Harpur, 15th Light Dragoon Regiment, to appear and give evidence against William Powney.
Thomas Gray, jun., to appear and answer charges.
William Powney to appear and answer charges.
Elizabeth, wife of William Grewno, victualler, to appear to prosecute and give evidence against John Brown for a felony.

Judith Allen, Loughborough, Leics., singlewoman, to appear and give evidence against John Brown for a felony.

Hugh Shelton, victualler, to appear to prosecute and give evidence against Mary Gibson.

Mary Gibson, singlewoman, to appear and answer charges and keep the peace towards Hugh Shelton.

Thomas Bankart, woolsorter, to appear and obey the Court *re* the bastard child of Catherine Clarke, St Martin's, singlewoman.

193a.3 *Presentments*

John Eames, Justice, presents the Inhabitants of the Borough of Leicester for not repairing the south end of St Sunday's (North) Bridge.

The Grand Jury presents John Brown, labourer, for stealing 2 linen shirts from William Grewno. Ignored.

193a.4 *Indictments*

William Entwistle, jun., framework-knitter, for obtaining 1s. from Sergeant Thomas Phillips, 79th Regiment of Foot, under false pretences, by enlisting as a soldier whilst apprenticed to [blank] Chambers, Nottingham, framework-knitter.

Thomas Gray, jun., watchmaker, for obtaining 40s. from Sergeant Thomas Harpur, 15th Light Dragoon Regiment, under false pretences, by enlisting as a soldier whilst apprenticed to John Wall, Coventry, watchmaker.

William Powney, watchmaker, for obtaining 1s. from Sergeant Thomas Harpur, 15th Light Dragoon Regiment, under false pretences, by enlisting as a soldier whilst apprenticed to John Wall, Coventry, watchmaker.

John Greenshields, tailor, for assaulting Edward Agar.

Ann, wife of William Loseby, woolcomber, for assaulting Esther Sermisher.

193a.5 *Notification*

⟨I Jonathan Foster Esquire Clerk of the Peace for the County of Leicester do hereby certify That at the General Quarter Session of the Peace of our Sovereign Lord the King holden at the Castle of Leicester in and for the said County on Tuesday the fourteenth Day of April last past John Heyrick late of Leicester in the County of Leicester Gentleman is and stands indicted by William Kirk of Leicester aforesaid gardener for an assault alledged by the said William Kirk to have been committed upon him by the said John Heyrick in the Liberty of the Braunstone Gate in or near the said Borough on the twenty second Day of March last past And that the said John Heyrick did at the same Sessions enter into Recognizance to be and appear at the next General Quarter Sessions of the Peace to be

holden for the said County and then and there plead to the said Indictment
And which Offence so charged in the said Indictment I believe to be the
same for which the said John Heyrick was bound to appear at the next
General Quarter Sessions of the Peace to be holden for the Borough of
Leicester. Dated the first Day of July 1795.

J. Foster
Clerk of the Peace⟩

193b.1 *Writ of Summons*

Dated 8 October 1795 for 19 October 1795.

193b.2 *Discharged Recognizances*

William Entwistle, jun., to appear and answer charges made against him at
the last Quarter Sessions.

Private Jeremiah Wise, Leicester Infantry, to appear to prosecute and give
evidence against Henry Asher and Henry Tims.

Sergeant William Welton, Loyal Leicester Volunteer Infantry Corps, to
appear and give evidence against Henry Asher and Henry Tims.

Henry Lingham, framework-knitter, to appear and answer charges and
keep the peace towards Sergeant William Welton.

John Ross, framework-knitter, to appear and answer charges and keep the
peace towards Private Jeremiah Wise.

Thomas Collins, framework-knitter, to appear and answer charges.

William Smith, woolcomber, to appear and obey the Court re the bastard
child of Mary Chapman, St Martin's, singlewoman.

Richard Beale, gent., to appear and answer charges and keep the peace
towards Benjamin Shelton, labourer.

John Greet, framework-knitter, and James Oldershaw, jun., gardener, to
appear to prosecute and give evidence against William Allen, Ann, his
wife, and Hannah Wale.

Sarah Burrows, widow, to appear to prosecute and give evidence against
Mary Phillips for a felony.

Nathaniel Woodcock, Headborough, Burbage, Leics., and Ann Briggs,
widow, to appear and give evidence against Mary Phillips for a felony.

William Allen, framework-knitter, to appear and answer charges.

Thomas Ryley, gardener, to appear and answer charges.

James Fenton, farrier, to appear and answer charges and keep the peace
towards William Peach, labourer.

193b.3 *Indictments*

John Ross, framework-knitter, for riot and assault on Jeremiah Wise.

Henry Asher, woolcomber, and Henry Tims, framework-knitter, for riot
and assault on Jeremiah Wise.   Po se, guilty.

James Fenton, farrier, for assaulting William Peach.

William Allen, framework-knitter, and Ann, his wife, for keeping a disorderly house.

Mary, wife of William Phillips, woolcomber, for stealing a pair of leather shoes from Sarah Burrows, widow.　Po se.

193b.4　　　　　　　　　　*Process Papers*

Thomas Gray, jun., watchmaker, having been indicted for obtaining 40s. from Sergeant Thomas Harpur, 15th Light Dragoon Regiment, under false pretences, has pleaded "Not Guilty" and is to be tried.

William Powney, watchmaker, having been indicted for obtaining 1s. from Sergeant Thomas Harpur, 15th Light Dragoon Regiment, under false pretences, has pleaded "Not Guilty" and is to be tried.

193b.5　　　　　　　　　*Sacramental Certificate*

St Margaret's　Alderman William Bellamy

194.1　　　　　　　　　　*Writ of Summons*
　　　　　　　Dated 29 February 1796 for 29 March 1796.

194.2　　　　　　　　*Discharged Recognizances*

John Clifford, Burton Overy, Leics., butcher, to appear and obey the Court *re* the bastard child of Ann Jolly, St Martin's, singlewoman.
Joseph Wills, framework-knitter, to appear and answer charges and keep the peace towards Mary Jordan, widow.
John Pegg, framework-knitter, to appear and obey the Court *re* the bastard child of Elizabeth Stanley, St Margaret's, singlewoman.
Robert Flower, jun., miller, to appear and answer charges and keep the peace towards Thomas Jackson, carpenter.

194.3　　　　　　　　　　*Indictments*

Joseph Wills, framework-knitter, for assaulting Mary Jordan.

Robert Flower, jun., Castle View, miller, for assaulting Thomas Jackson.

194.4　　　　　　　　*Sacramental Certificates*

St Martin's　　William Dabbs, Mayor
　　　　　　　　Thomas Jeffcutt, Coroner
　　　　　　　　Thomas Copson, Chamberlain
　　　　　　　　Charles Sansome, hosier
　　　　　　　　Robert Walker, hosier
　　　　　　　　John Nichols, grocer
St Margaret's　John Gregory, grocer

195.1 *Writ of Summons*

Dated 7 September 1796 for 3 October 1796.

195.2 *Discharged Recognizances*

George Gee, cordwainer, to appear and obey the Court *re* the bastard child of [blank], St Margaret's, singlewoman.

Edward Arnold, jun., to appear and answer charges.

Joseph Wood, tailor, to appear and answer charges and keep the peace towards William Beedells.

Welby King, jun., yeoman, to appear and answer charges and keep the peace towards Mary, wife of Francis Boot, yeoman.

Thomas Ferne, stonemason, to appear and obey the Court *re* the bastard child of Mary Smith, St Martin's, singlewoman.

Jonathan Gardener, trimmer, to appear and obey the Court *re* the bastard child of Elizabeth Lee, St Margaret's, singlewoman.

William Asher to appear and answer charges.

Elizabeth, wife of John Brotherwood, maltster, to appear and answer charges and keep the peace towards Elizabeth Grocock, spinster.

Joseph Gilbert, coal merchant, to appear and answer charges and keep the peace towards Ann, wife of William Rice, coal merchant.

Thomas Iliffe, framework-knitter, to appear and answer charges.

George Cooper, cordwainer, to appear and obey the Court *re* the bastard child of Frances Gamble, St Martin's, singlewoman.

Thomas Clarke, barber, to appear and answer charges and keep the peace towards Ann, wife of George Loseby.

John Cooke, framework-knitter, to appear and answer charges and keep the peace towards John Duneclift, grocer.

William Turner, whitesmith, to appear and answer charges and keep the peace towards Thomas Peet, blacksmith.

Welby King, jun., yeoman, to appear and answer charges and keep the peace towards Elizabeth Boot, spinster.

195.3 *Indictments*

Hugh Shelton, victualler, for refusing to watch with the Constable of Alderman Eames's Ward.

Elizabeth, wife of John Brotherwood, labourer, for assaulting Mary Grocock, spinster.

Welby King, jun., yeoman, for assaulting Elizabeth Boot, spinster.

Thomas Clarke, barber, for refusing to watch with the Constable of Alderman Eames's Ward.

Thomas Clarke, barber, for assaulting Ann Loseby.

The Inhabitants of All Saints' Parish for not repairing Elbow Lane.

Joseph Bryans, the Bishop's Fee, carpenter, for obstructing Humberstone Gate with wood and timber.

Francis Brathwaite, the Bishop's Fee, brickmaker, for blocking the watercourse in Granby Street with gravel, so that the water stagnated and polluted the air with its smell.

195.4 *Process Paper*

Robert Flower, jun., Castle View, having been indicted for assaulting Thomas Jackson, has pleaded "Not Guilty" and is to be tried.

195.5 *Sacramental Certificates*

St Martin's	Hamlett Clarke, Mayor
	Benjamin Sutton, Coroner
	William Hall, Chamberlain
	James Cort, Chamberlain
	Lieutenant James Edmond, 90th Regiment of Foot
	William Walker, merchant
St Margaret's	Alderman William Bishop
	William Bellamy, Coroner
	David Harris, Common Councillor

196.1 *Writ of Summons*

Dated 29 December 1796 for 9 January 1797.

196.2 *Discharged Recognizances*

James Edmonds, ⟨a Lieutenant upon half Pay in the 78th Regiment of Foot⟩, to appear to prosecute and give evidence against Edward Davis.

Edward Davis, apprentice to Henry Billson, Arley, Warks., tailor, to appear and answer charges.

John Flude to appear and answer charges and keep the peace towards Ann Palmer.

Joseph Bednell, labourer, to appear to prosecute and give evidence against Elizabeth Deakin for a felony.

Sarah Barsby to appear and give evidence against Elizabeth Deakin for a felony.

William Peet, tailor, to appear and give evidence against Elizabeth Deakin for a felony.

James Gibson, carpenter, to appear and answer charges and keep the peace towards Thomas Smith.

John Page Stringer, cordwainer, to appear and obey the Court *re* the bastard child of Mary Valentine, All Saints', singlewoman.

196.3 *Indictments*

John Flude, woolcomber, for assaulting Ann Palmer.

Elizabeth, wife of John Deakin, cordwainer, for stealing a flannel waistcoat and a pair of flannel drawers from John Edward Carter, Esq. Po se, guilty.

Charles Bollard, woolcomber, for not repairing the pavement in front of his house in Applegate Street.

[blank] Hill, tallow chandler, for not repairing the pavement in front of his house in Applegate Street.

Edward Davis for obtaining 1s. from Lieutenant James Edmond, 78th Regiment of Foot, under false pretences, by enlisting in the 90th Regiment of Foot whilst apprenticed to Henry Bilson, Arley, Warks., tailor.

196.4 *Process Papers*

Thomas Clarke, barber, having been indicted for assaulting Ann Loseby, has pleaded "Not Guilty" and is to be tried.

Elizabeth, wife of John Brotherwood, labourer, having been indicted for assaulting Mary Grocock, spinster, has pleaded "Not Guilty" and is to be tried.

Welby King, jun., yeoman, having been indicted for assaulting Elizabeth Boot, spinster, has pleaded "Not Guilty" and is to be tried.

196.5 *Convictions*

⟨Be it remembered That on the Eighteenth Day of November in the Thirty seventh year of the Reign of his present Majesty King George the third Hannah Lewitt of the Parish of Saint Mary in the Borough aforesaid Pawnbroker is convicted before me Hamlett Clark Esquire Mayor and one of His Majesty's Justices of the Peace for the said Borough of having on the fourteenth Day of September last at the said Parish of Saint Mary in the Borough aforesaid demanded received and taken from James Stallwood in the Names of James Taylor on redeeming the Pawn or Pledge hereinafter mentioned the Sum of One penny as and by way of Profit upon Three shillings theretofore, to wit, on the thirteenth day of the said Month of September at the Parish of Saint Mary aforesaid in the Borough aforesaid lent and advanced to him upon a certain Pledge or Pawn, to wit, a Gown the said Sum of One penny being more than after the rate of Four pence for the Loan of Twenty shillings for the Calendar Month including the current Month in which the said Pawn or Pledge was redeemed contrary to the Statute in such Case made And I the said Hamlett Clark do adjudge her the

said Hannah Lewitt to pay and forfeit for the same the sum of Five pounds
Given under my Hand & Seal the Day and year above written.

H. Clark   Mayor⟩

(Form as above) Ellis Mortin, St Margaret's, for charging 2d. interest on a
shirt.

(Form as above) Peter Colston, St Martin's, for charging 1d. interest on a
coat.

(Form as above) Richard Toone, St Mary's, for charging 1d. interest on a
shirt.

(Form as above) William Linthwaite, St Margaret's, far charging 1d. interest on a shirt.

(Form as above) Joseph Neal, St Martin's, for charging 1d. interest on a
coat.

197.1   *Writ of Summons*

Dated 10 April 1797 for 24 April 1797.

197.2   *Discharged Recognizances*

William Haddon, bricklayer, to appear and obey the Court *re* the bastard
child of Sarah Smith, St Margaret's, singlewoman.

George Page, labourer, to appear to prosecute and give evidence against
Jane Litchfield.

Joseph Page to appear and give evidence against Jane Litchfield.

John Highton, victualler, to ⟨try his Appeal to a certain Conviction of the
said John Highton of receiving a certain Quantity of Worsted of one John
Train knowing the same to be imbezzled and do & shall abide the Judgment
of & pay such Costs as shall be awarded by the Court⟩.

Ambrose Flewitt, carpenter, to appear and obey the Court *re* the bastard
child of Mary Berry, All Saints', singlewoman.

197.3   *Indictment*

Jane, wife of William Litchfield, framework-knitter, for keeping a disorderly house.   Po se, guilty.

197.4   *Process Paper*

Edward Davis, having been indicted for obtaining 1s. from Lieutenant
James Edmond, 78th Regiment of Foot, under false pretences, has pleaded
"Not Guilty" and is to be tried.

197.5   *Convictions*

John Highton for receiving 2 lbs worsted yarn from George Orton, who is
employed by Francis Burgess in woollen manufacture. He is fined ⟨the
sum of twenty pounds to be applied in manner following (that is to say) the

sum of Twenty shillings part thereof to be paid to the said Francis Burgess for the expences of the prosecution of the said John Highton the sum of Five shillings further part thereof to be paid to the said Francis Burgess as & for a Satisfaction for the said two pounds weight of Worsted yarn so bought received accepted & taken by way of Sale as aforesaid he being the party injured thereby the sum of Eight pounds & fifteen shillings further part thereof to be paid to the said Francis Burgess who informed us of the said offence of the said John Highton And the Sum of ten pounds the remainder of the said penalty to be paid to the Treasurer of the Leicester Infirmary for the use of a certain public Charity called the Leicester Infirmary⟩.

⟨Be it Remembered That on the Eleventh day of April in the thirty seventh year of the Reign of our Sovereign Lord George the third King of Great Britain and so forth at the Borough of Leicester aforesaid in the County of Leicester Joseph Farmer in his proper person came before me William Dabbs Esquire one of his Majesty's Justices of the Peace of the said Borough and complained to me upon his Corporal Oath then and there administered upon the Holy Gospel of God to him the said Joseph Farmer by me the said Justice That Jonathan Clarke of the Parish of Saint Margaret within the said Borough Cordwainer on the thirty first Day of March in the year aforesaid at the Parish aforesaid in the Borough aforesaid or within the Liberties thereof Did then and there attempt to take kill and destroy Fish in a certain River or Stream of Water called the River Soar situate and being in the Parish aforesaid in the Borough aforesaid or within the Liberties thereof without the Consent of Harry Earl of Stamford the sole and exclusive Owner of the Fishery of such River or Stream of Water against the form of the Statute in such Case made and provided (Such River or Stream of Water situate in the Parish aforesaid in the Borough aforesaid or within the Liberties thereof not being in any park or paddock or in any Garden Orchard or yard adjoining or belonging to any Dwelling-house but in other inclosed Ground which is private Property) And hereupon the said Joseph Farmer prays that the said Jonathan Clarke may be convicted of the said Offence and forfeit the Sum of Five pounds to be levied and paid according to the form of the Statute in such Case made and provided And that afterwards to wit on the Fifteenth day of April in the thirty seventh year aforesaid at the Borough aforesaid in the County aforesaid the said Jonathan Clarke having been previously in due manner summoned in pursuance of my Summons duly issued for that purpose to appear before me the Justice aforesaid at this time to answer the Matters of Complaint contained in the said Information, he the said Jonathan Clarke appeared before me the said Justice to answer and make defence to the same And having heard the same read he the said Jonathan Clarke is asked by me the said Justice if he can say Anything for himself why he should not be convicted of the Premises above Charged upon him in form aforesaid And thereupon he saith that he is Not Guilty of the said Premises Whereupon I the said Justice do now proceed to examine into the truth of the Complaint in the said Information mentioned in the Presence of the said Joseph Farmer and Jonathan Clarke And thereupon on the same day and year last aforesaid at the Borough aforesaid in the County aforesaid the said Joseph Farmer and one Thomas Measures being two Credible Witnesses in this behalf come in their proper persons before me the Justice aforesaid to prove the said Charges contained in the said Information against the said Jonathan Clarke and are now severally here by me the said Justice sworn; and do take their Corporal Oaths respectively upon the Holy Gospel of God to speak the truth and nothing but the Truth touching and concerning the matters contained in the said Information (I the said Justice having sufficient and competent power to administer such Oaths to the said Joseph Farmer and Thomas Measures) And the said Joseph Farmer being so sworn does on his said Oath depose and say in the presence and hearing of the said Jonathan Clarke that he the said Jonathan Clarke on the said thirty first day of March in the thirty seventh year aforesaid at the Parish of Saint Margaret aforesaid in the Borough aforesaid or within the Liberties thereof Did then and there attempt to take kill and destroy Fish in the said River or Stream of Water called the River Soar lying and being in the Parish aforesaid in the Borough aforesaid or within the Liberties thereof without the Consent of the Harry Earl of Stamford the Sole and exclusive Owner of the Fishery of such River or Stream of Water And that such River or Stream of Water situate in the Parish aforesaid in the Borough aforesaid or within the Liberties thereof is not in any Park or Paddock or in any Garden Orchard or Yard adjoining or belonging to any Dwelling house but in other inclosed Ground which is Private Property And the said Thomas Measures being so sworn as aforesaid does on his said Oath depose and say in the presence and hearing of the said Jonathan Clarke that he the said Jonathan Clarke on the said thirty first day of March in the thirty seventh year aforesaid at the Parish aforesaid in the Borough aforesaid or within the Liberties thereof Did then and there attempt to take kill and destroy Fish in the said River or Stream of Water called the River Soar lying and being in the Parish aforesaid in the Borough aforesaid or within the Liberties thereof And that such River or Stream of Water situate in the Parish aforesaid in the Borough aforesaid or within the Liberties thereof is not in any Park or Paddock or in any Garden Orchard or Yard adjoining or belonging to any Dwelling house but in other inclosed Ground which is Private property And the said Jonathan Clarke being asked by me the said Justice if he has got any Evidence to contradict the Proof aforesaid he the said Jonathan Clarke does not produce any Evidence to contradict the same nor does he shew any sufficient Cause why he should not be convicted of the

Premises aforesaid Whereupon it manifestly appears to me the said Justice that the said Jonathan Clarke is Guilty of the Premises charged upon him in and by the said Information therefore it is considered and adjudged by me the said Justice that the said Jonathan Clarke be convicted and he is by me accordingly convicted of the Offence charged upon him in and by the said Information And I do also adjudge that the said Jonathan Clarke for the said Offence hath forfeited the Sum of Five pounds to be levied and paid according to the form of the Statute in such Case made and provided And I do hereby order that the same be paid accordingly In Witness whereof I the said Justice to this Record of Conviction have set my Hand and Seal at the Borough aforesaid the said Fifteenth day of April in the thirty seventh year aforesaid.

William Dabbs⟩

197.6 *Certificates of Pavement Repair*

The following have repaired the pavement in front of their houses in Applegate Street:

Charles Bollard, woolcomber.

[blank] Hill, tallow chandler.

197.7 *Sacramental Certificates*

St Margaret's Henry Dalby, Steward to the Leicester Court of Record
St Martin's Jesse Berridge, surveyor

198.1 *Writ of Summons*

Dated 20 September 1797 for 2 October 1797.

198.2 *Discharged Recognizances*

William Palmer, framework-knitter, to appear and answer charges.

Elizabeth, wife of John Burton, to appear and answer charges and keep the peace towards Sarah, wife of James Ashwell, woolcomber.

John Walker, draper, to appear to prosecute and give evidence against Isabella Robinson for a felony.

John Corby, draper, to appear and give evidence against Isabella Robinson for a felony.

Matthew Watson Thomas, apprentice to John Walker, draper, to appear and give evidence against Isabella Robinson for a felony.

Isabella Robinson to appear and answer charges.

Simon Richards, brickmaker, to appear and answer charges and keep the peace towards Thomas Levis, labourer.

John Coltman, Wigston Magna, Leics., higgler, to appear and obey the Court *re* the bastard child of Hannah Harris, St Margaret's, singlewoman.

John Holyland, chandler, to appear and answer charges and keep the peace towards Richard Poole, Constable of Alderman Drake's Ward.

Thomas Hughes, print glazer, to appear and obey the Court *re* the bastard child of Judith Baggerly alias Mahone, St Martin's, singlewoman.

198.3   *Indictments*

Isabella, wife of Joseph Robinson, Rothley, Leics., framework-knitter, for stealing a piece of cotton or callico from John Walker.   Po se.

Simon Richards, the Bishop's Fee, brickmaker, for assaulting Thomas Lavis.

John Holyland, labourer, for assaulting Richard Pool.

Mary Pratt, spinster, for not repairing the pavement in front of her yard in Millstone Lane.

Joshua Sparrow, cooper, for not repairing the pavement in front of his house and yard in Millstone Lane.

The Inhabitants of St Mary's Parish for not repairing Grange Lane.

198.4   *Application for Certificate for Dissenters' Teacher*

⟨We whose names are under written Part of the Congrigation of Protestant Desenters Meeting in Redcross Street Within the Limits of the afforesaid Borough Request that you will please to grant to William Pearce of Applegate Street in the parish of St Nicolases Leicester your Licence as A Disenting teacher agreeable to the Act Made & provided in Such Case. Leicester October 1797.   John Wood
                                        Ebenezar Parr
                                        Thomas Billings
                                        William Snow
                                        William Atkins
                                        James Wright
                                        George Chamberlin⟩

198.5   *Sacramental Certificates*

St Martin's   Thomas Jeffcutt, Mayor
               Alderman William Watts
               James Willey, Coroner
               Michael Miles, Chamberlain
               Robert Walker, Chamberlain
               John Frewen Turner, Esq., Cold Overton
St Margaret's William Bishop, Coroner

199.1   *Writ of Summons*
              Dated 28 December 1798 for 16 January 1799.

199.2 *Discharged Recognizances*

John Bradley, victualler, to appear to prosecute and give evidence against John Harris for a felony.

Richard Jordan, Constable, to appear and give evidence against John Harris for a felony.

James Fenton, farrier, to appear and answer charges and keep the peace towards Richard Gostard, labourer.

Thomas Gee, labourer, to appear and obey the Court *re* the bastard child of Sarah Lane, St Margaret's, singlewoman.

John Abbott, Constable, to appear to prosecute and give evidence against John Lewin for a felony.

John Yates, miller, to appear to prosecute and give evidence against John Lewin for a felony.

Thomas Green, plumber, to appear and answer charges and keep the peace towards James Fenton, farrier.

Michael Thomas Jelf to appear and answer charges.

Ann, wife of William Rawlings, cordwainer, to appear to prosecute and give evidence against Michael Thomas Jelf for a felony.

Robert Pindar to appear and give evidence against Michael Thomas Jelf for a felony.

George Morris, the Stockingwood, Leics., labourer, to appear and answer charges and keep the peace towards Richard Wilson, victualler.

Edward Rice to appear and answer charges and keep the peace towards George Slack, victualler.

William Johnson, chimney-sweeper, to appear to prosecute and give evidence against William Lovett for a felony.

Mary Gibson, spinster, and Timothy and Thomas Broughton, labourers, to appear and give evidence against William Lovett for a felony.

Lucy, wife of Jonathan Atherstone, dyer, to appear to prosecute and give evidence against Jane Cooper for a felony.

John Sheldon, baker, to appear and answer charges and keep the peace towards Thomas Pretty, baker.

199.3 *Presentment*

The Grand Jury present Michael Thomas Jelf, cordwainer, for stealing a woollen shawl from William Rawlings.   Ignored.

199.4 *Indictments*

William Johnson, gardener, for obstructing the Market Place with a wooden stall.

James Cort, ironmonger, for obstructing the Market Place with 3 grinding stones.

Thomas Palmer, ironmonger, for obstructing Gallowtree Gate with 3 grinding stones.

Thomas Sutton, ironmonger, for obstructing Cheapside in the Market Place with 3 grinding stones.

William Parsons, ironmonger, for obstructing the Market Place with 3 grinding stones.

Samuel Taylor, grocer, for obstructing the Market Place with a large wooden hogshead.

Hugh Scott, grocer, for obstructing the Market Place with a large wooden hogshead.

James Fenton, farrier, for assaulting Richard Gostrich.

Mary Bird, widow, for illegally lodging Mary Issitt, singlewoman, in her cottage.

Edward Rice, labourer, for assaulting George Slack.

John Harris, labourer, for stealing a silver can from John Bradley.   Pleads guilty.

John Sheldon, baker, for assaulting Thomas Pretty.

William Lovett, labourer, for stealing a silver watch from William Johnson.

Jane Cooper, spinster, for stealing a pair of white silk stockings, a pair of white cotton stockings, and a pair of black silk gloves from Jonathan Atherstone.

199.5   *Sacramental Certificate*
St Martin's   Edward Price, Coroner

200.1   *Writ of Summons*
Dated 28 June 1799 for 17 July 1799.

200.2   *Discharged Recognizances*
Elizabeth Bird, widow, to appear and answer charges.
William Stanley to appear and answer charges and keep the peace towards Thomas Pole, framework-knitter.
William Lane, victualler, to appear and obey the Court *re* the bastard child of Elizabeth Castings, St Mary's, singlewoman.
John Robinson, labourer, to appear to prosecute and give evidence against Thomas Bell for a felony.
John Hand, glazier, and Joseph Smith, High Constable, to appear and give evidence against Thomas Bell for a felony.
John Carter, apprentice to John Hand, glazier, to appear and give evidence against Thomas Bell for a felony.

Thomas Pretty, baker, to appear and answer charges and keep the peace towards Henry Davies, lastmaker.

Francis Astill, woolstapler, to appear and answer charges and keep the peace towards James Fenton.

Samuel Beeby, gardener, to appear and answer charges and keep the peace towards Mary Belcher, singlewoman.

Richard Beale, gent., to appear and answer charges and keep the peace towards William Mitchell, worstedmaker.

Joshua Lokes, trimmer, to appear and obey the Court *re* the bastard child of Elizabeth Holt, St Martin's, singlewoman.

William Chamberlain, basketmaker, to appear and answer charges and keep the peace towards Joanna, his wife.

James Fenton, farrier, to appear and answer charges and keep the peace towards Mary Wood, widow.

Thomas Ward, stonemason, to appear to prosecute and give evidence against William Carnall for a felony.

Edward Harris, gunsmith, to appear and give evidence against William Carnall for a felony.

John Forryn, apprentice to Edward Harris, gunsmith, to appear and give evidence against William Carnall for a felony.

200.3   *Indictments*

John Haddon, framework-knitter, for not repairing the pavement in front of his house in Soar Lane.

Daniel Pegg, framework-knitter, for not repairing the pavement in front of his house in Soar Lane.

Robert Cowdall, hosier, for not repairing the pavement in front of his house in Soar Lane.

James Noble, worsted-spinner, for not repairing the pavement in front of his house in Soar Lane.

Elizabeth Bull, widow, for not repairing the pavement in front of her house in Soar Lane.

Thomas Bell, labourer, for stealing 3 pieces of lead from Thomas Buxton. Pleads not guilty, po se.

George Ingram, labourer, for leaving a quantity of dung in Canck Street (Weston's Lane) which polluted the air with its smell.

John Burton, labourer, Elizabeth Burton alias Harrison, and William Hinton for assaulting John Collison.

William Carnall, tailor, for stealing 2 iron chisels from Thomas Ward.

200.4 *Process Papers*

James Fenton, farrier, having been indicted for assaulting Richard Gostrich, has pleaded "Not Guilty" and is to be tried.

Edward Rice, labourer, having been indicted for assaulting George Slack, has pleaded "Not Guilty" and is to be tried.

John Sheldon, baker, having been indicted for assaulting Thomas Pretty, has pleaded "Not Guilty" and is to be tried.

200.5 *Sacramental Certificates*

St Martin's   Charles Parsons
Leire   Jonathan Glasby

201.1 *Writ of Summons*

Dated 1 October 1799 for 7 October 1799.

201.2 *Discharged Recognizances*

John Burton, carpenter, to appear and answer charges and keep the peace towards John Collinson, hardwareman.
Elizabeth Harrison alias Burton to appear and answer charges and keep the peace towards John Collinson.
Thomas Ludlam, woolcomber, to appear and answer charges of felony to be made by Thomas Hill.
Thomas Hill, woolcomber, to appear to prosecute and give evidence against Thomas Ludlam for a felony.
William Dorman to appear and give evidence against Thomas Ludlam for a felony.
James Jacques, labourer, to appear and answer charges and keep the peace towards James Fenton.
John Southwell Grimes, framework-knitter, to appear and obey the Court *re* the bastard child of Sarah Tresler alias Lee, St Margaret's, singlewoman.
Thomas Bankart, woolsorter, to appear and answer charges and keep the peace towards Francis Brown, carpenter.
James Fenton, farrier, to appear and answer charges and keep the peace towards Mary Wood, widow, and Thomas Read and Robert Rendar, Constables.

201.3 *Indictments*

Thomas Ludlam, woolcomber, for stealing 5 lbs unwrought wool from Thomas Hill.

James Fenton, farrier, for assaulting Thomas Read, Constable, and Mary Wood.

201.4 *Certificates of Removal of Obstructions*

James Cort, ironmonger, has removed his 3 grinding stones from the Market Place.

Thomas Palmer, ironmonger, has removed his 3 grinding stones from Gallowtree Gate.

William Parsons, ironmonger, has removed his 3 grinding stones from the Market Place.

Hugh Scott, grocer, has removed his hogshead from the Market Place.

William Johnson, gardener, has removed his wooden stall from the Market Place.

Thomas Sutton, ironmonger, has removed his 3 grinding stones from Cheapside in the Market Place.

Thomas Stevenson has removed his cart from Grange Lane.

201.5 *Certificate of Pavement Repair*

James Bunney, whitesmith, has repaired the pavement in front of his house in Bakehouse Lane.

201.6 *Sacramental Certificates*

St Margaret's	William Bishop, Mayor
	John Jackson, Chamberlain
	Francis Burgess, Chamberlain
	Isaiah Dixon
St Martin's	Alderman James Mallett
	James Willey, Coroner
St Mary's	Benjamin Sutton, Coroner

202.1 *Writ of Summons*

Dated 1 July 1800 for 14 July 1800.

202.2 *Discharged Recognizances*

John Holyland, chandler, to appear and answer charges and keep the peace towards Elizabeth, wife of William Derby, framework-knitter.

Thomas Woodford, Whetstone, Leics., butcher, to appear to prosecute and give evidence against William Weston.

Robert Price, Ellesmere, Salop, farmer, to appear to prosecute and give evidence against John Dakin for a felony.

John Iron, upholsterer, and John Abbott, Constable, the Bishop's Fee, to appear and give evidence against John Dakin for a felony.

William Weston, butcher, to appear and answer charges.

John Maule, surgeon, to appear and give evidence against William Weston.

Thomas Thornton, baker, to appear to prosecute and give evidence against Joseph Clay for a felony.

Thomas Swann, butcher, to appear and give evidence against Joseph Clay for a felony.

Hugh Phipps, woolcomber, to appear and give evidence against Joseph Clay for a felony.

Elizabeth Cave, singlewoman, to appear to prosecute and give evidence against Susanna Norfold for a felony.

Sarah, wife of Henry Smith, dyer, to appear and give evidence against Susanna Norfold for a felony.

202.3 *Presentment*

The Grand Jury present William Derby, framework-knitter, and Elizabeth, his wife, for assaulting John Holyland.   Ignored.

202.4 *Indictments*

William Weston, butcher, for engrossing 190 lbs beef bought from Thomas Woodford.

John Dakin, the Bishop's Fee, labourer, for stealing 2 glass bottles of wine from Robert Price.

Joseph Clay, labourer, for stealing 2 loaves of wheaten bread from Thomas Thornton.

Susanna Norfold, singlewoman, for stealing a cotton gown, a cotton handkerchief, and a cotton and linen apron from Elizabeth Cave.

202.5 *Certificates of Road Repair*

The following have repaired Grange Lane:
Robert Heggs, framework-knitter.
Mary Kirk, widow.
Robert Bales, framework-knitter.

202.6 *Sacramental Certificates*

St Mary's	Alderman John Slater, hosier
	James Mallett, jun., the Newarke, hosier
	Robert Johnson, hosier
St Martin's	John Sarson, grocer
	Thomas Miller, banker
	Isaac Lovell, draper
St Margaret's	William Heard, grocer
	James Bankart, woolstapler

IIIC.I *Judgements*

⟨Borough of Leicester

Be it remembered that at the General Quarter Session of the Peace of our Sovereign Lord the King holden at the Guildhall of the said Borough in and for the said Borough and the Liberties thereof on the twenty third day of April in the eleventh year of the reign of our Sovereign Lord George the Fourth by the Grace of God of the United Kingdom of Great Britain and Ireland King Defender of the Faith Before Isaac Lovell Esquire Mayor of the said Borough, Edward Goulburn, Esquire, Serjeant at Law Recorder of the same and Thomas Marston, Henry Wood, Mansfield Gregory and James Rawson Esquires Justices of our said Lord the King assigned to keep the Peace of our said Lord the King in the said Borough and the liberties thereof and also to hear and determine divers felonies trespasses and other misdemeanors committed within the same upon the oaths of Thomas Bryan, Richard Rawson, John David Jackson, William Kenworthey Walker, William Hackett, Willoughby James Bishop, William Gregory, Robert Parr, John Moore, Edward Staveley, Isaac Abell, John Fox Bell, John George White Young, John Garle Brown, Henry Cawood and Benjamin Payne good and lawful men of the said Borough then and there sworn and charged to inquire for our said Lord the King and the body of the said Borough it is presented as follows that is to say Borough of Leicester The Jurors for our Lord the King upon their oath present that George Hames late of the parish of Saint Martin in the Borough aforesaid Laborer and Charles Gostridge late of the same place Laborer on the fourth day of April in the eleventh year of the reign of our Sovereign Lord George the fourth now King of the United Kingdom of Great Britain and Ireland with force and arms at the parish of Saint Martin aforesaid in the Borough aforesaid One Saw of the value of Two shillings Two Moulding Planes of the value of Two shillings One pair of pincers of the value of Sixpence and one Chisel of the value of Sixpence of the goods and chattels of one Henry Sykes then and there being found feloniously did steal take and carry away against the peace of our said Lord the King his Crown and Dignity And the Jurors aforesaid upon their oath aforesaid do further present that the said George Hames was heretofore to wit at the General Quarter Session of the Peace holden in and for the said Borough and the liberties thereof on the twenty seventh day of April in the eighth year of the reign aforesaid duly convicted of felony And thereupon at the same Session before the said Justices of our said Lord the King severally came the said George Hames and Charles Gostridge under the custody of Thomas Jeffcutt, Esquire, Bailiff of the Borough aforesaid (in whose custody in the Gaol of our said Lord the King of and for the said Borough for the cause aforesaid they were before severally committed) and being brought to the bar here in their proper persons are severally committed to the said Bailiff And forthwith concerning the premises in the said Indictment above specified and charged on them as above, being severally asked in what manner they would be severally acquitted thereof the said George Hames and Charles Gostridge severally say that they are not Guilty thereof and

227

concerning this for good and ill they severally put themselves upon their Country Therefore let a Jury thereupon immediately come before the said Justices of our said Lord the King here by whom the truth of the matter may be better known and who are of no affinity to the said George Hames and Charles Gostridge or either of them to recognize upon their oath whether the said George Hames and Charles Gostridge or either of them be Guilty of the felony aforesaid or not And the Jurors of the said Jury by the said Bailiff to this matter impanelled and returned to wit John Brown, William Weston Stretton, William Iliffe, William Livens, Thomas Porter, Thomas Pollard, George Wykes, Richard Wilson, Joseph Pegg, Gabriel King, Benjamin Daws, and John Chatwin being called come who being chosen tried and sworn to speak the truth of and concerning the premises aforesaid say upon their oath that the said George Hames and Charles Gostridge are severally guilty of the felony aforesaid in the said Indictment specified and charged upon them above in manner and form as by the said Indictment above against them is supposed And upon this it is demanded of the said George Hames and Charles Gostridge by the Court here what they or either of them have or hath to say for themselves or himself why the Court here should not proceed to judgment concerning him upon the said Verdict and the said George Hames and Charles Gostridge having nothing to say why such judgment should not be proceeded in It is ordered and adjudged by the Court here that the said George Hames be imprisoned in the House of Correction for the said Borough of Leicester and kept to hard labor for the term of twelve Calendar months and that the said Charles Gostridge be imprisoned in the same House of Correction and kept to hard labor for the term of four Calendar months.

Thomas Burbidge
Clerk of the Peace⟩

(Form as above) John Brown, labourer, and William Dexter, labourer, having been indicted for stealing a purse containing 18 shillings, 1 sixpence, and 3 pennies from Henry Brown, pleaded "Not Guilty", were tried, and found "Guilty". Brown (who had a previous conviction for felony) was sentenced to transportation for life and Dexter to 6 months hard labour in the House of Correction.

(Form as above) Peter Hart, labourer, having been indicted for stealing a candlestick and 1 lb candles from Henry Marris, pleaded "Not Guilty", was tried, and found "Guilty". He was sentenced to 6 months hard labour in the House of Correction.

CORPORATION LEGAL CASES

CORPORATION LEGAL CASES

Green's Case [Bodl. Eng. misc. e. 55, fo. 79.]

Q. Whether the Corporation of Leicester can maintain an Action upon the Case upon the Custom above stated against Green (he not being a Freeman of the Borough) for using and exercising the Trade of a Clockmaker etc within the said Burrough of Leicester upon other days than Market days or fair Days held or kept within the said Burrough

Mr Bootle is of Opinion the Corporation may maintain an Action on the Case against Green for exercising his Trade within the Burrough not being a Freeman thereof contrary to the Custom, provided the Custom can be proved to the satisfaction of a Jury.

Q. Whether or no the Order made by the Mayor & Burgesses of the said Burrough in the 30 Year of Q. Elizabeth will be allowed as any Evidence of the said Custom & what other Evidence will be necessary to prove & Support the Custom

He does not think this Order will be any Evidence in support of the Custom, it will rather be an Evidence against it. The proper Evidence to prove the Custom is Instances of Strangers paying fines to the Corporation for Liberty of exercising their Trades there, that is to Say for their Freedom of the Corporation. And that as far back as you can go, And Instances of others having been refused to carry on their Trades there, who were not admitted.

N. The said Corporation commenced an Action against Green 3 or 4 years ago & Green thereupon making proposals to buy his Freedom the proceedings were dropt & Green then or some time after tendered £30 to the Mayor then being for his Freedom, which Sum was not then accepted, but since such Tender so made by Green, he has been requested by the Corporation to take up his Freedom upon payment of £30 but he now refuses to do so.

Q. Whether such Tender and refusal & request will be of any & what advantage or disadvantage to either party

This Tender and Refusal can be of no Disadvantage to the Corporation If any thing it is an admission of their Right by Green, for it cant be supposed, he would offer to pay such a Sum of Money in his own wrong, if he apprehended he had a right to carry on his Trade there without paying anything for it.

N. There are two women not free of the said Burrough & are neither Daughters or Widows of Freemen, who have carryed on the business of Milliners for the Space of 12 years last past and the Corporation having Respect to their Circumstances have not interrupted them therein.

Q. Will Proof of their carrying on their said Business quietly without any interruption by the said Corporation be of any detriment in maintaining an Action against the said Green

I dont think the Single Instance will be of any Avail against the Custom especially as the Corporation may in some Measure account for it in respect of their Circumstances as being a Case of Compassion. And if no other Instance can be produced it must be considered in this light & not on the Foot of their having a Right to Exercise their Trade there, not being Free.

Blankley v. *Winstanley*

IN THE KINGS BENCH

BETWEEN John Blankley . . . . Plaintiff
and
Clement Winstanley Esquire and ⎫
The Reverend Robert Burnaby Clerk ⎬ Defendants ⎭

FOR THE PLAINTIFF

LEICESTERSHIRE PLAINTIFFS DECLARATION SETS FORTH THAT Defendants heretofore to wit on the 21st day of October in the year of our Lord 1786 in the Parish of Saint Margaret in said County of Leicester with Force and Arms (to wit) with Swords Staves Knives and other offensive Weapons and with Fists Hands and Feet made an Assault upon Plaintiff and then and there beat bruised wounded and ill treated him and then and there imprisoned him and committed him, Plaintiff, to the House of Correction in and for the County of Leicester under and by virtue of a Warrant for that purpose there granted by Defendants as Justices of our Lord the now King assigned to keep the Peace of our Lord the now King in and for said County of Leicester and to hear and determine divers Felonies Trespasses and other misdeeds committed in the same and directed to the Constable of the Bishops Fee in the County of Leicester aforesaid and to the Keeper of the House of Correction of and for the County of Leicester aforesaid and under that Warrant and Commitment kept and detained Plaintiff in Prison there for a long space of time to wit from thence until the 5th day of November in the year aforesaid and caused and procured him under that Warrant and Committment to be corrected and held to hard Labour there under pretence that Plaintiff had been guilty of divers Misdemeanors miscarriages and ill behaviour towards one George White of the Bishops Fee aforesaid Framework-knitter his then Master by lying out on Nights and neglecting his Master's Business and disobeying his lawful Commands, they Defendants not having any such Jurisdiction over Plaintiff or any other Apprentices in the Bishops Fee aforesaid in as much as said Bishops Fee is within and under the exclusive Jurisdiction of the Magistrates of the Borough of Leicester and not under the Jurisdiction of the Justices of the Peace of the Body of the said County of Leicester

2d Count   AND ALSO for that Defendants heretofore vizt. on the same 21st day of October in the year aforesaid at the Parish of Saint Margaret in the County aforesaid with Force and Arms to wit with Swords Staves Knives and other offensive Weapons and with Fists Hands and Feet made another assault upon Plaintiff and then and there again beat bruised wounded and ill treated him and then and there imprisioned him and kept and detained him in prision there for a long space of time to wit for the space of two Months against his Will and without any legal Cause whatsoever and other Injuries to Plaintiff, Defendants then and there did against the Peace of our said Lord the now King and to the Damage of Plaintiff of 100£ and therefore he has brought this Action

PLEA   TO this Declaration the Defendants have pleaded the General Issue NOT GUILTY upon which Issue is joined.

CASE on Behalf of Plaintiff

In one of the Out Skirts of the Town of Leicester, and in the Parish of St Margaret, there is a certain District called The Bishops Fee, which comprizes one whole Street called Humberstone Gate, Part of another Street called Gallowtree alias Gartree Gate, and some particular Houses in a Place called Coal Hill and in a Street called Church Gate the whole containing 100 or more Houses; and this District is also supposed to extend over two or three hundred Acres of Field Land; and has usually been considered in the Hundred of Gartree in the County of Leicester, and not within the local Limits, or such Part of the Town as is known or distinguished by the Name of the Borough of Leicester, within which Limits the Residue of the said Parish of St Margaret confessedly is.

In and over this District or Place called The Bishops Fee till about the

Year 1765, the Justices of the Peace for the County of Leicester had, as long as any Person living remembers, usually exercised all Kind of Jurisdiction, and not the Magistrates for the Borough; except with Respect to the quartering of Soldiers, who were always billeted there by the Borough Magistrates, even when the Licenses for the public Houses were granted by the Justices for the County; and also except that the Borough Magistrates always it's supposed after the Charter of Elizabeth hereinafter stated appointed a Constable for that District, who formerly used to appear and make Presentments at the Borough Sessions, though that seems not to have been the Case for some years previous to 1765, since which Time or thereabouts he has regularly appeared there and exercised his Office fully; and also except that in Consequence of an annual Warrant from the Mayor to the Borough Chief Constable, he issues his Precepts to the petty Constables to summon all Persons using Weights and Measures to bring them for Trial at a certain Day to the Town Hall—this has always been complied with by the Residents in the Bishop's Fee (as well as the Rest of the Town) and for this Service the Trier, (who is the Mace Bearer) takes certain old accustomed Fees vizt. from those using only Weights or Measures 4d., from those who sell Ale & Liquors 8d., and those who sell Ale Wine & Liquors 1s.

The Bishop's Fee is a Manor of itself, and, either at the annual Court held for it, or by the County Justices, another Constable has regularly been appointed for this Place, who always has and still continues to pass all the Vagrants coming through the Town of Leicester. This District too always has, & still does, contribute towards the Land Tax and Window Tax for the County, as Part of the Hundred of Gartree. The Borough is assessed to these Taxes by itself, and is not considered to be within any Hundred, and has separate Commissioners: though formerly the Bishops Fee contributed with the Borough, and was taxed by the same Commissioners to the Subsidies Fifteenths and those Kinds of Taxes.

The Bishops Fee also contributes, and its supposed always has, to the County Rates, and it likewise does so to the Borough Rate; for, ever since that has been regularly established (which is about twenty Years) the Parish of St Margaret has paid its Proportion for the whole Parish to the Borough Treasurer, who has repaid to the Overseers what they have paid to the County Rate in respect of the Bishops Fee, which is very trifling in Comparison to its Proportion to the Borough Rate. Before the Borough Rate was established the Borough Magistrates at the End of each Year, used to issue their Warrant to the Overseers of the different Parishes to pay a Proportion of the Expences which the providing the Gaol Bread had amounted to the preceding Year, and also of transporting Felons when that happened.

It is understood that till about the said Year 1765, all parochial Levies &

other public Acts respecting the said Parish of St Margaret which required the Sanction of Magistrates, (except as to the said Contribution to the Gaol Bread &c) received such Sanction, as to the said Part called Bishop's Fee, from the County Justices, and as to the other Part thereof from the Borough Magistrates: and that till about that Period, the Officers of the Borough Court of Record, rarely, if ever (within Memory) attempted to serve or execute any Process of that Court within the said Bishop's Fee—but about the said Year 1765 the Magistrates for the Borough having determined to exercise Jurisdiction there, claiming it under the Charters hereinafter stated, which they insisted gave it to them in total Exclusion of the County Justices—and having at Thomas a Becket Sessions 1765 caused Extracts of the Charters of the 4th Edward 4th and 41st Elizabeth to be delivered to the Chairman of the County Sessions, the latter ordered a Case to be drawn by the Clerk of the Peace, and the late Mr C. Yorke's Opinion to be taken thereon for their Direction & Government—of which Case and Opinion the following is a Copy

"THERE are certain Places in the Skirts of the Town of Leicester called respectively the Bishops Fee, the Newark, the Castle View, Braunston Gate, Wood Gate, and Abby Gate, and these Places have been generally considered as only subject to the Controul of the County Justices, and not to be within or Parcel of such Part of the Town as is distinguished by the Name of the Borough of Leicester, or in any Degree subject to the Controul of the Magistrates for the Borough, (N.B. This was stated by the County Justices and as strongly in their own Favour as it could be and much more so than the Facts seem to warrant) save in respect to quartering Soldiers, in which Case Persons who keep public Houses in these Places, though their Licenses are from the County Justices, have submitted to the Borough Justices' Jurisdiction by receiving Soldiers upon their Ballotts or Orders for that Purpose; and all these Places contribute towards the Land Tax & other Rates for the County, and not for the Borough. The Bishop's Fee is considered as Part of the Parish of St Margaret in Leicester—The Braunston Gate as Part of the Parish of St Mary in Leicester—The Wood & Abby Gates as Part of the Parish of St Leonard in Leicester—and the Residue of the said several Parishes is in the Borough Part of Leicester; and all parochial Levies, and other public Acts respecting the several Places before particularly named, that required the Sanction of Magistrates, received such Sanction from the County Magistrates; and the other Parts of the Parishes of which these are Members have received the necessary Sanction from the Borough Magistrates: and such respective Places have been from Time to Time redressed in their Grievances by the Magistrates of those Places respectively—and as to the Newark and Castle View, their Constables and all other public Officers have been appointed by the

Magistrates for the County—as have the Constables and other Officers for the Bishop's Fee & the said other Places. WHEREAS the Constables & other Officers for such Parts of the said several Parishes as are in the Borough have been appointed by the Borough Magistrates. And the Bishop's Fee and other Places have been always considered as out of the Limits of the Borough; and there have not been above 3 or 4 Instances, if so many, 'till within this Year past, of any of the Mayor's Officers attempting to execute any Process out of the Mayor's Court in any of these Places; and though the Borough Justices have usually appointed a Constable for the Bishop's Fee, yet they have never required any Duty from him. WHEREAS now, the Magistrates of the Borough set up and exercise the same Right of Jurisdiction over the Bishops Fee as over the Rest of the Town; and insist they have a Right so to do, by Virtue of a Clause in a Charter granted to them by Queen Elizabeth and another of Edward 4th (both there stated).

A small Part of the Newark and in particular one House there is confessedly within the Borough, and such House is in the Parish of Saint Mary.

Qy. WHETHER the Borough Justices can justify exercising a Jurisdiction as such over the Bishop's Fee? And, if yea, whether exclusively or concurrently with the County Justices? And, if concurrently, who must grant the Licenses for selling Ale, and give the necessary Sanction to and inforce the Payment of the Parish Levies &c, and determine Grievances respecting the same?

Answer I think that the Words of Queen Elizabeth's Charter give a Jurisdiction to the Justices of the Borough throughout the several Parishes therein mentioned, as well in those Parts which are not within the Borough as in those which are. The same Charter speaks not only of the Borough but 'Precinctus et Libertates ejusdem' which Words may comprehend the Places in Question as Liberties or outlying Districts—and the former Charter uses the Word 'Precinctus'. I observe also that the Charter 4 Edward 4 contains negative Words to exclude the County Justices out of the Borough, but they are not expressly repeated in the material Clause of the Charter of Queen Elizabeth relating to the whole Circuit of these Parishes; at the same Time they may be considered as implied in the Words at the Conclusion 'qualia et que ac in tam amplis Modo et Forma prout iidem Major Balliui &c Virtute harum Literarum nostrarum Patentium aut aliorum Progenitorum nostri habere uri et gaudere possint aut debent &c'. These Words of Reference are sufficiently powerful (in my Opinion) to carry as well the negative Words of the Charter, for excluding the County Justices out of all Parts of these Parishes, as the affirmative Rights and Franchises conveyed by both Charters within the Borough itself, otherwise the Grant will not operate 'tam amplis Modo et Forma &c Virtute nostrarum Literarum Patentium aut aliorum Progenitorum nostrorum &c'. It is like Grants of Liberties by Words of Reference 'tot et talia' mentioned in the Abbot of Strata Marcella's Case 10 Co. Therefore upon the whole (as at present advised) I think that the Jurisdiction throughout all the Lands of the Parishes in Question is in the Borough Justices, exclusive of the County Justices; and that the concurrent Jurisdiction hitherto exercised (which must be disagreeable and inconvenient to the Inhabitants and to the Gentlemen composing both Jurisdictions) has been erroneously exercised by the County Justices, without due Warrant in Law—C. Yorke August 21st 1766."

In Consequence of this Opinion, so decidedly against the County Justices, they desisted from exercising any Jurisdiction in the Bishop's Fee (except that the Constable was appointed as usual either by them or at the Manor Court and passed the Vagrants as usual). And the Borough Magistrates exercised Jurisdiction in & over the Bishop's Fee, by granting the victualling Licenses and in all other Respects in the like Manner as they did within the Borough.

The Charters under which they claim and insist upon this Right are the following vizt.

[Recitation of Charters of:
24th August 4 Ed. IV
4th March 20 Hen. VII
1st June 41 Eliz.]

The County Justices having lately resumed their Claim to Jurisdiction in the Bishops Fee, and in several Instances exercised it, insisting they have at least a concurrent Jurisdiction with the Borough Magistrates; and having in October 1786 exercised it in the Instance complained of in Plaintiff's Declaration, by granting the Warrant stated below, under which the Plaintiff was committed and lay in Bridewell accordingly; the Plaintiff (nominally, but the Corporation really) has brought this Action against Defendants, the two County Justices who granted the Warrant, with the View & for the Purpose of having tried and decided this Question of Jurisdiction, which, as at present claimed and exercised is inconvenient & disagreeable, as well to the Inhabitants of the Bishop's Fee, as also to the Borough Magistrates & County Justices; and as the latter profess to defend it on the same Principles, it is hoped that Question will be fairly gone into, and Plaintiff not be turned round by any previous Quirk (such as Want of express Notice to Defendants the two Justices of the Charters or the like) and to avoid this, its submitted, whether it might not be proper on both Sides, to admit the several Facts necessary to bring the Question fairly before the Court.

The Warrant above mentioned is as follows vizt.

County of Leicester 〕 To the Constable of the Bishop's Fee in the said
     to wit 〉 County, and To the Keeper of the House of Correc-
         〕 tion of and for the County of Leicester aforesaid.

WHEREAS John Blankley Apprentice by Indenture to George White of the Bishop's Fee aforesaid Framework knitter was this Day brought before us two of his Majesty's Justices of the Peace for the said County of Leicester, and charged upon the Complaint on Oath of his said Master with having been guilty of divers Misdemeanors Miscarriages and ill Behaviour towards his said Master particularly by lying out on Nights and neglecting his Master's Business and disobeying his lawful Commands AND WHEREAS the said John Blankley hath not before us cleared himself of and from the said Complaint but on the contrary due Proof of the Truth thereof hath been made before us on Oath

THESE are therefore in his Majesty's Name to command you the said Constable forthwith to take and convey the Body of the said John Blankley to the abovesaid House of Correction for the said County and him deliver to the Keeper thereof together with this Precept and you the said Keeper are hereby required to receive into your Custody the Body of the said John Blankley and him safely keep & correct and hold him to hard Labour till the End of fourteen Days from the Date hereof. Hereof fail not respectively. Given under our Hands & Seals the twenty first Day of October in the Year of our Lord 1786.

C. Winstanley
R. Burnaby

OBSERVATIONS

That the Corporation do not found this Claim of Jurisdiction on any Idea that the Bishop's Fee is in the local Limits of the Borough, but only on the Charters, it is submitted, that the Land & Window Tax & County Rates do not relate to the Question.

That the same may be observed in respect to the Jurisdiction of the Borough Court.

That the Charter was accepted as to Jurisdiction, tho' perhaps not as to exclusive Jurisdiction 'till 1765.

That this Acceptance of Part was an Acceptance of the whole—Rex v. Amery Dwinford 575 Yarmouth Case cited in Rex v. Monday Cowp: 534.

That the Session held under it, and the Allocaturs are full Notice to the County Justices 2 Hale P.C. 25—4 Inst. 165—Bro: Abr: Comcon 6 Patent 111—Moore 187—Keilway 116—Abbott of St Alban's Case 20 H.7 8—Cromp: 8 & 181—Dalt. 24—Talbot v. Hubble 2 Strange 1154—Stat 2 & 3 P & M C. 18—notwithstanding the Doubts in 2 Hawk: P.C. c. 8—Lambert B. 1 C. 9—2 Hale P.C. C. 49 which all seem to arise on the Idea that as the Kings Commicion runs as well within Liberties as without the Justices

Acts are not void, but they are punishable for Contempt which is denied in the Authorities above, especially in the above Abbotts Case in the Year Book.

And—On the whole—That from the local Situation of the Place (all adjoining to, and Part intermixed with the Borough) the Peace of the Town at large will be much less likely to be preserved, under a distinct, than under one & the same Jurisdiction; not only as Offenders of every Description will be ready to take Advantage of the Distinction but as it will be (as it ever has been more or less) a Ground of Dispute & Disagreement between (and, as Mr Yorke very justly observed, inconvenient to) the Magistrates composing the different Jurisdictions. And, that nothing can be more clearly evident, than that the Charter of Elizabeth meant & intended to remedy these very Inconveniencies, if it had any Meaning at all; tho' probably it may be contended on the Part of the Defendants, that the Clause is void, from the Impropriety or Inaccuracy of describing the Bishop's Fee to be in the Borough, which, as to local Limits, we must admit is not the Fact; (Defendants will possibly produce old Title Deeds wherein it's almost universally called near the Borough) and indeed, had it been so, there then cou'd have been no Reason for the Clause so that the Nature of the Thing speaks for itself—that in must in this Place be construed to mean near, rather than that, from such an Inaccuracy as this (possibly a clerical one only) a Court shou'd be compelled to say that the Charter meant nothing, or intended to give nothing but what was given before.

AMONGST the many Instances of the Exercise of Jurisdiction within the Bishops Fee by the Borough Magistrates the undermentioned came particularly within the Knowledge and Observation of this Witness—M. Payne

BY THE JUSTICES ⎫
OF THE PEACE   ⎭

In licensing of Victuallers viz   At the Three Cranes—White Horse— Black Lyon—Turks Head—Blue Bell &c from 1766 for upwards of 12 or 14 Yeares

In billeting of Soldiers   For the whole of that Period—this Witness frequently making the Billetts

In bringing to Punishment

For Felonies   Thomas Bunney for stealing a Great Coat out of Three Cranes—The Indictment concerning which is in this Witness's Hand Writing—upon which Indictment Bunney was found guilty & ordered to be whipped at Epiphany Sessions 1766—as appears by Minute in Sessions Book—also

George White Junior for several Felonies—the Informations & Indictments concerning which are in this Witness's Hand Writing—George White was convicted and sentenced to be transported at Easter Sessions 1773

Riots   A violent one in 1766 in Humberstone Gate respecting the high Price of Cheese

For Nusances   Francis Nedham presented for a Nusance at Michaelmas Sessions 1777 (attested Copy of which is in this Witness's Hand Writing) also—indicted for erecting a Hovel—and for inclosing Part of a Highway in Humberstone Gate at Michaelmas Sessions 1780—which Indictments are of this Witness's Hand Writing

At Easter Sessions 1781—Nedham pleaded guilty and was fined —which Fine he paid—as appears by Minute in Sessions Book of this Witness's Hand Writing

4th May 1781—The above Nusances certified by a Borough Magistrate to be removed—Certificate of this Witness's Hand Writing

In appointing Constables viz   Robert Aumey and John Roe

In discharging Apprentices viz   Fenton & Fielders from Lakin who lived in Bishops Fee—Proceedings in this Witness's Hand Writing

BY THE CORONERS

In taking Inquisitions upon Persons who came to untimely Deaths viz George Marriott who was drown'd in a Brickkiln Pitt in April 1766 John Brierly who was shot near the Spittle House in 1779

PRIVILEGES   Besides the above the Court of Aldermen (Part of the Corporation) who have the Disposition of the 50£ of Sir Thomas Whites Charity which is given to Residents only—dispose of such Monies indiscriminately to the Inhabitants of the Bishop's Fee as well as to the rest of the Town—Instances of which in this Witnesses Knowledge & Memory are—Mr Allamand—Mr B. Gregory—Mr J. Mansfield and Charles Valentine.

Arguments on the Case

SUTTON for the Plaintiff said He should state the only Question to be whether under these Charters the Crown had granted an exclusive or only a concurrent Jurisdiction to the Borough Magestrates over the Bishop's Fee—because there was no Doubt but the Crown might create such an exclusive Jurisdiction—or annex an additional district to a Borough—Stran. 1154 Talbot v. Hubble ibid. 177 R. v. Inhabitants of Norwich—The two former Charters of Edward 4 & Henry 7 had expressly given such a Jurisdiction within the antient Borough And he contended that the Intent & Effect of the Charter of Elizabeth was to put the Bishops Fee on the same Footing—It is laid down in 9 Co. 30 "That when a Charter has general Reference to other Charters, it is as much in Law as if the other Charters had been recited—cited likewise 10 Co. 64a. It is the same thing then here as if the Charter of Elizabeth had recited that the former Charter excluded the County Justices & had granted that the Bishop's Fee should be under the exclusive Government of the Borough the Object of the Charter was to make a uniform Police throughout the Borough & Town and put the whole as it increased under the same Magistrates—The Petition is for an Entire Incorporation over the Borough with the addition of certain Liberties—makes the Mayor &c Justices within the Borough & Liberties—which last word was not in the former Charters—puts the new District under their Government Jurisdiction &c. And grants them within that District omnia singula & consimilia jura &c qualia & quae ac in tam amplo modo & forma prout iidem Major &c virtute harum literarum &c aut aliorum Progenitorum nostrorum &c They cannot have the same Power over the Bishop's Fee as they have within the antient Borough unless they have an exclusive Jurisdiction—And he stated the Inconveniencies of a concurrent & of course a clashing Jurisdiction.

It would he said be objected that the non-intromittant Clause being omitted in the Charter of Elizabeth the County Justices were not excluded —But that Doctrine did not apply here. The Jurisdiction given to the Borough Magestrates can be found only by Reference to the former Charters. This of Elizabeth only describes the District over which it is to extend—The words here Qualia & quae &c have been held sufficient to refer to the Particulars of other Charters as such as was now contended. For which he cited the Case of the Abbot of Strata Marcella 9 Co. 24—ibid 52 The Earl of Shrewsburys Case—10 Co. 64 John Whistlers Case— Plowd 12 & 130—Bro. Ab. tet Pat. pl. 31—1 Vent. 409 In the Case of Atkins v. Clare Lord Hale holds that such general words of Reference are sufficient to grant the Liberty of Retorna Brevium and he recognizes Amerydgths Case 9 Co. 29b. on which Sutton said he principally relied for that here as Lord Hale said of it in Ventris no Case could be fuller—King Henry 8 had granted to Queen Katharine within the Manor & Hundred of C. inter alia to be exempt from the Jurisdiction of the Admiral & to have Admiralty Jurisdiction—The Manor & Hundred descended to Queen Mary who granted them with the general Words tot talia eadem & hujus modi Libertates &c—And it was resolved that this general reference was to be applied to the Particulars of the former grant as much as if it had been recited—And in that Case too the Exemption & Grant of Admiralty Jurisdiction clearly depended on the Prerogative of the Crown as did likewise the Retorna Brevium in Sir Robert Atkins's Case & the Franchises in Other Cases.

The Saving Clause of all their Rights would have no Effect in the present

Case because of what follows, Aliter quam predicto Mason &c concessis—
2. As to the Effect of the usage stated. This he said may expound where
the Construction is doubtfull but the Jurisdiction in the present case is
clear, as derived from the former Charters—And the Reason why Usage
has this Effect is because it is the Exposition of Parties interested—But here
is nothing to infer that the Borough Magistrates had any Knowledge of the
Claim by the County Justices—Here is no adverse Exercise—The Borough
Magistrates were never interrupted—Nor is there any profitable Franchise
which has been taken by the County Justices.

COKE for Defendants said the Exclusive Jurisdiction of Corporation
Magistrates was not likely to be more beneficial or less corrupt than if the
County Jurisdiction concurred—That the usage for 200 Years would
certainly be immaterial if the Charter were clear but decisive if it were
doubtful—In this Case the Charter of Elizabeth he contended was clear the
other way—the utmost Effect of the Words quae & qualia ac in tam amplo
modo &c was to give the Borough Magistrates compleat Power to do in the
Bishop's Fee all that the County Justices might do—But not to exclude the
latter—Supposing a County Commission nearly exhausted, would a New
Commission to others tam amplo modo &c exclude the old remaining
Justices by that Clause—Then the saving Clause further explains it for
this is in as large Words—There is no doubt but the County Justices had a
Jurisdiction & even an exclusive & this cannot be taken away without
special words of exclusion—Lord Hales Authority is express on this point.
2 H.H.P.C. 47.

2. He denied that the Crown could grant such exclusive Jurisdiction by
Reference—Where he Acts by his Prerogative & makes a second Grant
with the strongest words of Reference this will not pass a Franchise without
special mention. The Cases on the other side related he said to Property
Such as subject may hold—And the Distinction he contended for was
this—Where the Crown acts as an Individual it may grant by Reference by
the Prerogative such grant will be void—Cited 12 Co. 2 2 Roll Ab 193 A.
pl. 2—The general Words tot talia &c were held not sufficient to grant
catalla felonum within a Manor which had come to the Crown—Cro.
Elizabeth 513 Lord Darcys Case—a General Grant of all Liberties and
Privileges which A. B. had by Charter or Prescription non-obstante abiquo
Statuto was held insufficient to grant a discharge from Purveyance, without
a particular Non abstante of the Stat. 27 Henry c. 24 by which this Liberty
had been resumed—And Lord Paget's Case is there cited to the same Effect
respecting Catalla Felonum—If the Crown meant to grant an exclusive
Jurisdiction to the Borough Magistrates [it] meant to take away that which
the County Justices had & this can only be by express Words.

There was he said Another Ground arising from the Usage. The
Borough might have made a bad use of their Jurisdiction which might have

been resumed and the Court may presume a different Grant on which the usage has proceeded—The Existence of this Charter is no obstacle to such Presumption Darwin v. Upton B. R. Michaelmas 1785.

And he mentioned by way of Illustration that Carte the Historian had left a Note which is preserved.

Saying that the concurrent Jurisdiction had Prevailed at Leicester because the saving Clause was thought to have prevented the exclusive Jurisdiction.

Both sides prayed another Argument.

L. KENYON Chief Justice—It is but Justice to say that Case has been extremely well argued on both sides. There is no Room to hope that further light would be thrown upon it by another Argument—I have no doubt now—Since the Time of Lord Hale it has been considered as a Cardinal Point in Corporation Law, that there must be special words in a Charter to exclude the County Justices—And it is founded in Reason. For without the least Reflection on this Corporation, Justice is not likely to be better administered in these limited Jurisdictions—In this particular Case, I should feel very reluctant to break in on a Custom which has subsisted for 200 Years. The concurrent Jurisdiction has been kept up without Inconvenience—The Crown has never been applied to—It is true that this will not do away the express Words of a Charter. No Usage or Invasion however sanctioned by Time can Overturn the clear Construction. But the Contemporanea Expositio is very Powerful where there is any doubt—And it is curious though not an Argument here that Carte has explained the usage by that Exposition.

I rely not at all on that, but on the Words of the Charter I am satisfied that this Bishop's Fee was not added to the Borough—It might be convenient that the Magestrates for the Borough might Act in this Neighboring District And that Power is given—But then comes the Saving Clause which shews that no Rights were to be disturbed by the Charter— It only confered on them the Power of Acting—There might have been a doubt if this District had been added to the Borough whether it did not become Subject in all Respects to the Jurisdiction of the Borough—It is not unusual that the Justices of a District should be Justices for the County at large. At Clithero the two Borough Justices may Act as one County Justice. However I find no Words to oust the County Justices here but the Contrary.

ASHURST Justice. It is a grant of a Concurrent Jurisdiction over a District not before Subject to the Borough Magistrates—The Clause does not expressly make it Part of the Borough or exclude the County Justices which is Necessary. And I do not agree that an exclusive Jurisdiction in Corporation Magistrates is most Convenient.

BULLER Justice. In a special Verdict we are bound to proceed on the

Facts stated. We cannot infer any Thing. I agree with the Doctrine in Darwin v. Upton which differs from this in the way in which it came before the Court. That was in a Motion for a New Trial which the Court Refused when the Evidence was such that the Jury ought to presume the Fact— Here the Verdict stated that the Bishop's Fee was no Part of the Borough at the Time of the Charter of Elizabeth.

1. Then on the Construction of that Charter It is clear that express Words are necessary to exclude the County Justices—It is material that the Bishop's Fee is not made Part of the Borough—The Clause which gives the Borough Magestrates a Power to act there could not exclude the County Justices And then the saving Clause makes this much stronger.

2. The usage which has prevailed for 190 Years I should think sufficient if the Words were more doubtful. I think there are Cases where the Court have admitted usage to controul the Apperent Sense of a Charter; in the Bewdley Case I think it was so held (v. 1 P. Wm. 223). There was another Case of Gape v. Handley B.R. Michaelmas 17 George 3—from the 16 Charles 2 The Mayor and Aldermen of St Albans had presented to a living the Grant of the Advowson appearing to be to the Mayor & Burgesses— The Court held the Right of Presentation to be in the former saying they would always pay the greatest Regard to Usage & though inclined to think that in a recent Case there might be another Construction. Yet after a Number of Years they would defer to the Usage. And I should think so here on the Words of the Charter alone.

GROSE Justice. Unless taken away the Power of the County Justices remained as before—Exclusive Jurisdiction is not expressly granted to the Borough Magestrates and the Charter of Elizabeth is just such as would have been drawn if the Intent was to grant a Concurrent Jurisdiction. When the Charter was first considered all Parties agreed in this Construction and have acted under it for 200 Years—The Case of Gape v. Handley is very Strong on this Point—Both on the Intention and Usage. I think the Case exceedingly clear.

Judgment for Defendants.

19 May, 1789.

Bates v. *Winstanley*

IN THE FIFTY-SIXTH YEAR OF GEORGE III.

Tuesday, Nov. 28th. 1815

BATES *against* WINSTANLEY and Another.

A charter granting jurisdiction to borough justices over a district not within the borough, without words of exclusive jurisdiction, does not exclude the county justices from rating the district to a county rate; therefore, where, by charters *Edw.* 4. and *H.* 7. to the borough of *Leicester*, the borough justices have exclusive jurisdiction within the borough, with a non intromittant as to the county justices; and by another charter, *Eliz.*, all houses, &c. within the parish of *St. Mary*, in *Leicester*, are put under the government and jurisdiction of the borough justices, saving to all persons their rights and jurisdictions: Held that the justices for the county of *Leicester* might well impose a county rate upon a part of the parish of *St. Mary*, which lies within the county, and not within the borough, although a rate in the nature of a county rate had been previously imposed for the same time by the borough justices; and although it appeared that in one instance only, in 1684, this part of the parish had contributed to the rate for the county at large, and that from 1768 to the present time rates in the nature of county rates had been assessed upon the parish at large by the borough justices; for before the charter *Eliz.* this part of the parish could not have been contributory to the borough rates, and must have been by law contributing to the county rates, and the charter did not vary the place to which it should contribute from the county to the borough; and though there was no poor rate, or petty constable, or other peace officer for this part of the parish, out of which the rate might be levied by stat. 12 *G.* 2. *c.* 29., yet the statute does not on that account transfer the right from the county to the borough justices, and the 44 *G.* 3. *c.* 34. *s.* 9. (local act) supplies any defect which there might be in 12 *G.* 2. *c.* 29. to warrant the levy.

TRESPASS against the defendants, justices of the peace for the county of *Leicester*, for causing the plaintiff's goods to be distrained for payment of a county rate imposed by the magistrates of the county upon certain lands called the *South Fields* in the parish of *St. Mary* in *Leicester*. Plea not guilty. At the trial there was a verdict for the plaintiff by consent, subject to the opinion of the Court upon the following case.

Leicester is an ancient borough and body corporate, and in the 4th *Edw.* 4. the king, by letters patent, granted to the borough (inter alia) That the mayor and four of the more discreet burgesses, together with the recorder, should be justices of the peace within the said borough, and the precincts and limits of the same, to hear and determine felonies, trespasses, and other misdemeanors, with a clause of non intromittant as to the justices of the county. In the 20th *Hen.* 7. the king, reciting by inspeximus the above charter, granted exclusive jurisdiction to the borough magistrates over the suburbs, in the same manner with a non intromittant clause. In the 41st *Eliz.* the queen granted a new charter to the borough, and extended the jurisdiction of the borough magistrates, and amongst other things granted, that the mayor, recorder, and four last aldermen who served the office of mayor, should be justices of the peace in the borough, and the liberty and precincts of the same, and should have power to hold sessions, &c. "*Et ulterius pro meliori regimine et gubernatione predicti burgi, ac omnium et singulorum burgensium, inhabitantium, commorantium, et residentium infra*

eundem burgum, volumus et concedimus quod omnia et singula domus, edificia,
messuagia, terras, tenementa, et hereditamenta quæcunque situata, jacentia,
vel existentia tam infra parochiam Sanctæ Margaretæ, &c. quam infra paro-
chias Sanctæ Mariæ, Sancti Leonardi, &c. in eodem burgo, per quodcunque
aliud nomen, vel alia nomina, vocantur sive nominantur, necnon omnes burgen-
ses, inhabitantes, commorantes, et residentes, in eisdem parochiis, et locis, sive
in eorum aliqua, pro tempore, et de tempore in tempus existentes, de cetero in
perpetuum sint, erunt, et reputabuntur fore, sub regimine, potestate, guber-
natione, jurisdictione, correctione, et coercione majoris, ballivorum, et burgen-
sium burgi prædicti, et successorum suorum, et quod major, ballivi, et burgenses
burgi predicti, et successores sui, deinceps in perpetuum habeant, gaudeant, et
utantur, omnibus et singulis eisdem consimilibus juribus, libertatibus, preemi-
nentiis, et jurisdictionibus, in omnibus et singulis eisdem parochiis Sanctæ
Margaretæ, Sanctæ Mariæ, &c. qualia et quæ, ac in tam amplis modo et
forma, prout iidem major, ballivi, et burgenses, virtute harum literarum nos-
trarum patentium, aut aliorum progenitorum nostrorum, habere, uti, et
gaudere possint, aut debent, in predicto burgo, aut in aliquo membro, parte, vel
parcella, ejusdem burgi. Ita tamen quod hæc præsens concessio nostra non sit ad
prejudicium nostrorum hæredum, aut successorum nostrorum, salvis etiam
omnibus et singulis corporibus corporatis et politicis, ac aliis personis quibus-
cunque, ac aliæ personæ cuicunque, omnibus juribus, libertatibus, preeminentiis,
et jurisdictionibus quibuscunque aliis quam predictis majori, ballivis, et bur-
gensibus (ut prefatum) concessis, quæ ipsi, aut eorum aliquis, jure et legitime
habuerint et gavisi fuerint ad confectionem, et tempore confectionis, harum
literarum nostrarum patentium, in tam amplo modo et forma, prout si hæ
nostræ literæ patentes nunquam habitæ vel factæ fuissent. The queen also
confirmed to the mayor, &c. all and singular *maneria, &c. libertates, liberas*
consuetudines, privilegia, franchesias, immunitates, exemptiones, et jurisdic-
tiones whatsoever, which the corporation theretofore had, or ought to have
enjoyed, within the borough, and the suburbs, limits, and precincts of the
same, by reason of any former charters or prescription. These charters were
accepted, and have been acted upon, and are still in force. The *South Fields*
are a part of the county of *Leicester*, and not within the borough, but are
within the parish of *St. Mary*, in *Leicester*, and have always been assessed
to the poor rates of that parish by the overseers appointed by the justices
for the borough, who have exclusive jurisdiction over the entire parish of
St. Mary, except the *South Fields*, and *Bromkinsthorpe*, and over the *South*
Fields, and *Bromkinsthorpe*, have a concurrent jurisdiction with the county
justices. The land-tax, and other parliamentary taxes, payable in respect of
the *South Fields*, have always been assessed by commissioners for the
county, and the entire proceedings in respect of such taxes have always been
with the commissioners of the county exclusively. There was no house
upon the *South Fields*, nor any inhabitant resident there, until the year

1804, nor has any constable or other parochial officer ever been appointed distinctly for the *South Fields*. Rates in the nature of county rates have been assessed by the magistrates of the borough at their general quarter sessions upon the parish of *St. Mary* from the year 1768 (when rates in the nature of county rates were first imposed in the borough) until the present time, and have been paid out of the poor's rates collected for the parish of *St. Mary* generally, to which poor's rate the *South Fields* have contributed. No rates in the nature of county rates have ever been paid to the county in respect of the *South Fields*, with this exception, that in 1684 the judges of assize imposed two several fines of 1000 marks, and 2000 marks, upon the inhabitants of the county, because there was no gaol, and such fines were apportioned and levied upon the several parishes and places in the county, and among the rest, 1*l*. 2*s*. was assessed upon the *South Fields*, and a special receiver of these fines was appointed by commissioners under letters patent of *Jac.* 2., which receiver duly accounted for the whole amount of them, and by order of the quarter sessions for the county paid the balance to the county treasurer. The case also stated the passing of 44 *G*. 3. *c*. 34. (local act), a copy of which was annexed, and that the justices of the peace for the county, at their general quarter sessions holden after *Easter* 1811, made one general rate, as and for a county rate, whereby they assessed every parish, township, liberty, and place, within the county, and, among others, the *South Fields*, and that the *South Fields* had before been rated by a rate made by the borough justices, in the nature of a county rate, for the same period of time for which the rate so assessed by the county justices was made (*a*). The plaintiff was one of the overseers of the poor of *St. Mary's*, and an occupier of land in the *South Fields*, and this distress was made upon him by virtue of a warrant granted by the defendants to levy the said county rate. If the Court are of opinion that the plaintiff is entitled, a verdict to be entered for 1*s*. damages, otherwise a nonsuit.

The question made upon this case was, whether the rate imposed by the county justices upon the *South Fields*, was lawfully imposed by them; which was argued by *Denman* for the plaintiff against the rate, and by *Reader* for the defendants in support of it. The argument for the plaintiff was in substance this:—The power of the county justices is not extended by 12 *G*. 2. *c*. 29. (general county-rate act) to such a district as this; for the act (*s*. 1.) directs the rate to be assessed upon every town, parish, or place; and (*s*. 2.) that it shall be paid out of the poor's rate; or (*s*. 3) if there be no poor's rate, shall be levied by the petty constable or other peace officer belonging to the same; so that the *South Fields* must be either a town, or parish, or a place having a poor's rate, or having a petty constable or other peace officer, in order to give the county justices jurisdiction. It is admitted that it is not a town or parish, nor a place having a petty constable or other officer; and

(*a*) It was agreed, upon the argument, that this fact should be inserted.

that it has no poor's rate out of which this rate may be levied, is plain from considering that the poor's rate is for the parish of *St. Mary's* at large, and not for the *South Fields*, and that the parish at large is not contributory to the county rate, but is, under the charter of *Eliz.* and by virtue of this act, explained by the 13 *G.* 2. *c.* 18. *s.* 7. to be assessed by the borough justices to a separate rate, in the nature of a county rate. And the jurisdiction of the county justices is not aided by the 44 *G.* 3. *c.* 34 (local act), because there is a saving in that act (*s.* 14.) of the jurisdiction of the borough justices as it stood before. 2dly, Granting that the county justices have a concurrent jurisdiction with the borough justices to rate the *South Fields*, yet the borough justices having already exercised it by imposing a rate for the very same period for which this rate is now imposed, the power of the county justices is for this time gone, according to the principle established in *Rex* v. *Sainsbury.* (a)

For the defendants it was answered, that if the borough justices had no jurisdiction to impose a rate, in the nature of a county rate, on the *South Fields*, the argument founded upon the priority of their exercise of it, was at an end. That the borough justices neither before nor since the 12 *G.* 2. *c.* 29. had any jurisdiction to impose this rate upon the *South Fields.* For the charter of *Eliz.* only gave them a concurrent jurisdiction in the commission of the peace with the county justices, but not to rate lands within the county which were not before rateable by them, but on the contrary were rateable by the county justices for several of the purposes now included in the county rate; as for repairing of bridges, by 22 *H.* 8. *c.* 5., and for relief of prisoners in the county gaol, by 14 *Eliz. c.* 5. Neither did the 12 *G.* 2. *c.* 29. enlarge their jurisdiction over these lands; for its intention was only to facilitate the assessing, collecting, and levying of county rates, and with this view to give power to the justices to consolidate under one assessment the several purposes for which before then several assessments used to be made; and it appears by 13 *G.* 2. *c.* 18. that the same power was intended to be given to the justices of liberties, &c. within the limits of their commission; but these lands never were within the limits of the commission of the borough justices to assess them for any of the purposes mentioned in the first act. This being so, it follows that they must be liable to be assessed by the county justices; and whatever difficulties might have existed in collecting or levying the rate under the 12 *G.* 2. are now removed by 44 *G.* 3. *c.* 34. (local act) *s.* 9.

Cur. adv. vult.

LORD ELLENBOROUGH C. J. on this day delivered the judgment of the Court.

This was an action of trespass against two justices of the county of

(a) 4 T.R.451.

Leicester, for distraining for a county rate, imposed by the county magistrates, upon certain lands in the parish of *St. Mary* in *Leicester*, called the *South Fields*; and the question was whether the county magistrates could impose the rate upon those lands. It was admitted in the argument, though not stated in the case, that the magistrates for the borough of *Leicester* had previously imposed a rate upon these lands in the nature of a county rate, for the same period of time for which the rate was levied by the county justices; so that the question is narrowed to this point, whether the county justices can impose the rate, after a previous rate imposed and levied by the borough. The *South Fields* are within the county of *Leicester*, but not within the borough; and the borough justices have a concurrent jurisdiction there with the county justices, but not an exclusive jurisdiction. By charters 4 *Ed.* 4. and 20 *H.* 7. the borough justices have an exclusive jurisdiction, with a non-intromittant as to the county justices, within the borough of *Leicester*, its precincts, limits, and suburbs, and by charter 41 *Eliz.* all houses, &c. within certain parishes including that of *St. Mary* are put under the rule, government, jurisdiction, &c. of the mayor, bailiffs, and burgesses, of the borough of *Leicester*, with a saving to all persons whatsoever of their rights, liberties, preeminences, and jurisdictions. The *South Fields* are within the parish of *St. Mary* in *Leicester*, and have always been assessed to the poor's rate of that parish, by the overseers appointed by the borough justices, and no parochial officer has ever been appointed distinctly for those fields. The only instance in which those fields ever contributed to the rate for the county at large, before the rate in question was imposed, was in 1684, when upon a fine on the county for want of a proper gaol, 1*l.* 2*s.* was assessed specifically upon these fields. There was no house upon the *South Fields* till 1804, and there were no rates upon the rest of the parish of *St. Mary* in the nature of county rates till 1768. From that time such rates have been assessed upon the parish by the borough magistrates. County rates are in general assessed in counties under the provisions of 12 *G.* 2. *c.* 29., and there is a special act in the present reign, 44 *G.* 3. *c.* 34., which contains some provisions for the county in question, the county of *Leicester*. The object of 12 *G.* 2. *c.* 29., was, not to impose new rates, but to facilitate the assessing, collecting, and levying those that were previously imposed; and for that purpose, instead of separate rates for the several purposes for which rates under former acts were imposed, there was to be one general rate to answer all the ends and purposes of former acts. There is no intention (in the act) to vary the obligation to pay, or the right to receive; the persons before liable to pay, were still to be liable to pay, and the persons entitled to receive, were still to be the persons so entitled. No part of the act implies a contrary intent. Two of the rates included in this consolidation, viz. the bridge-rate, and the rate for poor prisoners in gaols, were imposed by statutes of an earlier date than the charter which gave the borough justices a concurrent jurisdiction in the *South Fields*, viz. the former by 22 *H*. 8. *c*. 5. and the latter by 14 *Eliz*. *c*. 5. *s*. 37. The first of these statutes, that of *H*. 8., authorizes the taxation of every inhabitant; but 2 *Inst*. 702. is an express authority that the occupation of lands, without residence, is suffi- cient within this clause to make a man an inhabitant and liable as such. So that there can be no question but that before the charter of 14 *Eliz*. the occupiers of lands in these *South Fields* were liable to taxation in respect of county bridges. The stat. 14 *Eliz*. imposes the tax for poor prisoners upon every parish; and the statute for county gaols, 11 & 12 *W*. 3. *c*. 19. *s*. 1. upon the several hundreds, lathes, wapentakes, rapes, wards, or other divisions of the county, with an exception as to persons inhabiting in any liberty, city, town, or borough corporate having common gaols for felons, and commission of assize or gaol delivery of such felons; and 12 *Ann*. *stat*. 2. *c*. 23. (which is recited in 12 *G*. 2.) directs that the money to be raised under that act, shall be raised by such ways and means as money for county gaols or bridges. The money for county gaols therefore is assumed to be the subject of levy in the same manner as the money for bridges is, and which by stat. *H*. 8. is by taxation made upon every inhabitant within the county, and by construction upon occupiers of land, though not resident, as in- habitants. Before the charter of *Eliz*. therefore, these *South Fields* were liable in the hands of their occupiers to contribute in respect of bridges. There is nothing in this charter to vary their liability, nor is there any thing in this charter to exempt them from liability to the county in respect of those rates which were imposed between the charter and the 12th of *Geo*. 2. The charter does nothing more than entitle the borough justices to act as justices in a place in which before they could not have acted, but it does not make that place less a part of the county, nor does it contain a word which implies that that place is not still to be contributory to the county to the same extent as before, and it would be inconsistent with the saving in that charter of the rights of all persons whatsoever to hold that it entitled the borough to take away from the county its claim upon this place for contri- bution. The 12th *Geo*. 2. does not in express terms give any power to borough magistrates, and if it gave them any power by implication, it could only be to levy where they could before levy, and for sums to which they were before entitled. But the statute of the succeeding year 13 *G*. 2. *c*. 18. *s*. 7. throws great light upon this point. It recites that doubts had arisen whether 12 *G*. 2. extended to liberties and franchises not within the jurisdiction of the commissions of the peace for the counties in which such liberties and franchises were, and so never did nor were liable to contribute to the said county rates, and then it provides that where any liberties or franchises have commissions of the peace within themselves, and are not subject to the jurisdiction of the commissions of the peace for the counties in which they lie, and do not, nor did before 12 *G*. 2. contribute to the rates made for the said counties, the justices of the peace of such liberties and franchises within the respective limits of their commissions, may exercise the powers given by 12 *G*. 2. In such liberties and franchises therefore (in which a contribution to rates made for the counties existed before the 12 *G*. 2., and which liberties and franchises have only a concurrent, not an exclusive jurisdiction,) the justices of such liberties and franchises have no power under this latter act, inasmuch as these do not fall within the circumstances to which alone the proviso in the act is declared to extend. And where the jurisdiction is within certain limits exclusive, and in others concurrent only, the power of the justices of those liberties and franchises must be confined to those parts in which the jurisdiction is exclusive. The mischief of giving them the power where they had a concurrent jurisdiction only might in many cases be excessive; for if they had a concurrent jurisdiction over the whole county, they might, if the Plaintiff's argument were right in this case, anticipate and appropriate to themselves the whole county rate. The Plaintiff's argument is founded upon the supposition that the rate in respect of the *South Fields* must either be paid out of the poor's rate for the parish at large, which would be unjust, or that there was no mode of raising it under 12 *G*. 2., and that if it could not be raised for the county at large under 12 *G*. 2. it is not liable to be so raised under the 44th of *G*. 3. *c*. 34. We accede to the observation that it would be unjust to have the payment made out of the poor's rate, because that would be casting the burthen, not solely upon the *South Fields*, but upon that part of the parish which is within the borough and subject to the exclusive jurisdiction of the borough justices; and supposing it may be true that no rate could have been raised upon these *South Fields* under the provisions of 12 *G*. 2., because there is no petty constable, or other peace officer belonging to these *South Fields*, and the only mode of raising the rate, (where it is not to be paid out of the poor rates) pointed out by 12 *G*. 2., is under *s*. 3., by direction from the sessions to the petty constable, or other peace officer belonging to the place for which the rate is to be levied, which we are not satisfied is the case, inasmuch as the high constable might levy it; it does not follow, however, from this defect in 12 *G*. 2., if it be a defect, that the right is to be transferred from the county to the borough. There was no intention in 12 *G*. 2. to divest the county of any part of the rates which were before payable to it, and this supposed defect is not confined to these *South Fields*, but extends to every place within the county which had no poor rate, petty constable, or other peace officer, and this defect is completely remedied by the local act 44 *G*. 3. *c*. 34. That act sect. 9. expressly provides for assessing all estates, within all and every the parishes, townships, liberties, precincts, hamlets, extra-parochial and other places within the county; it directs the sessions to tax every parish, township, liberty, precinct, hamlet, extra-parochial place and other places within the county, according to the annual rent and value of the estates within the same, as they shall appear upon the returns under the property tax. It enacts that in any parish, &c. where there is no poor rate, the sessions may direct the sum to be rated and levied on the inhabitant or inhabitants, or occupier or occupiers of lands therein, (using terms in the singular number to include places in which there may not be more than one individual inhabitant or occupier,) and the chief constable is authorised, in case of non-payment, to levy the same by distress and sale of the goods and chattels of such inhabitant or inhabitants, occupier or occupiers; and it makes a similar provision (sect. 10.) though there is a poor rate, if it does not apply separately and distinctly to the place which is to pay the county rate. The proviso in this act that it shall not give jurisdiction to the county justices over any places within the borough, which before that act were subject to the rates in the nature of county rates imposed by the borough justices, falls in with the defendants' argument that these *South Fields* are to contribute to the county, because they are not within the borough, and because they were never by law subject to the borough rates. In as much therefore as before the charter of *Elizabeth* these *South Fields* could not have been contributory to the borough rates, and must have been by law contributory to the rates for the county; as that charter, if it could have varied the place to which they should contribute, from the county to the borough, does not appear to have had any such intention; as the 12th *Geo.* 2. could have had no such intention, and as the 44th *Geo.* 3. supplies any defect there might have been in 12 *Geo.* 2. to warrant the levy; we are of opinion that these *South Fields* were by law contributory, not to the borough, but to the county rate, and that the levy in question was therefore warranted by law, and consequently that there must be judgment of

Nonsuit.

WATCHING AND LIGHTING BILL

WATCHING AND LIGHTING BILL

A BILL for appointing a regular and able Watch in the Borough of Leicester, *and for enlightening and cleansing the Streets there, and for repairing the publick Pumps and Wells within the said Borough, and Parts thereunto adjoining.*

WHEREAS it would greatly tend to the Safety, Benefit, and Health of the Inhabitants of the Borough of *Leicester*, and Parts adjoining thereto, if Provision was made for maintaining an able and regular Watch therein, and for cleansing and enlightening the open Places, Streets, and other Passages within the said Borough, and Places thereunto adjoining, and for repairing the Pumps and Wells within the said Borough. And whereas the Laws now in being are insufficient for the Purposes aforesaid, may it therefore please your Majesty that it may be enacted, and be it enacted, by the King's most excellent Majesty, by and with the Advice and Consent of the Lords Spiritual and Temporal, and Commons, in this present Parliament assembled, and by the Authority of the same, That from and after (*space left blank*) the Mayor, Recorder, and Justices of the Peace of and for the said Borough of *Leicester* for the Time being, shall be, and they are hereby nominated, constituted, and appointed, Commissioners for the Intents and Purposes herein after-mentioned and declared. And that the said Mayor, Recorder, and Justices of the Peace for the said Borough for the Time being, shall and may, and they are hereby authorized and required to appoint a sufficient Number of able-bodied Men, not exceeding (*space left blank*) in the whole, from Time to Time, as the said Mayor, Recorder, and Justices of the Peace for the said Borough for the Time being, or any (*space left blank*) or more of them, shall think proper, to watch every Night within the said Borough, and Parts thereunto adjoining: And shall also appoint one or more Person or Persons to be Keeper or Lighter, or Keepers or Lighters, of the Lamps; and one or more Person or Persons to be Scavenger, Raker, or Cleanser, or Scavengers, Rakers, or Cleansers, of the Streets there: All which Persons so to be appointed, for the Purposes herein beforementioned, shall be (*space left blank*) chosen and appointed by the said Mayor, Recorder, and Justices of the Peace for the said Borough for the Time being, or any (*space left blank*) or more of them. And that it may be lawful to and for the Commissioners, so appointed and constituted as aforesaid, or any (*space left blank*) or more of them, to meet, and they are hereby authorized and required to meet and assemble together, at the Town-Hall within the said Borough, on the (*space left blank*) in order to put this Act into Execution; and shall and may, from and after that Time, by Adjournment, meet and assemble together there, or at any other convenient Place within the said Borough, as they, or any (*space left blank*) or more of them, shall appoint.

And be it further Enacted, by the Authority aforesaid, that all and every Person and Persons to be appointed and hired, pursuant to this Act, for the Duties and Services herein before and herein after-mentioned, any, or either of them, shall, from Time to Time, and at all Times, obey and observe, perform and duly execute, all such Orders, Directions, and Rules, as shall from Time to Time be made, or given, by the said Mayor, Recorder, and Justices of the Peace, and their Successors, or any (*space left blank*) or more of them, for and concerning the Duties, Services, Matters, and Things to be done, performed, and executed, for the Purposes aforesaid, or for the Purposes herein after-mentioned, according to the true Intent and Meaning of this Act, upon (*space left blank*) for every Offence, Refusal, or Neglect.

And be it further Enacted, by the Authority aforesaid, that all and every Person and Persons inhabiting within the said Borough and Town, shall, from and after the said (*space left blank*) sweep or cleanse, or cause to be swept or cleansed, all the Streets, Lanes, or publick Places, before their respective Houses, Buildings, and Walls, (*space left blank*) in every Week at least, that is to say, every (*space left blank*) or oftner if Occasion be, between the Hours of (*space left blank*) to the End the Dirt and Soil in the said Streets, Lanes, and publick Places, may be heaped ready for the Scavengers to carry away, upon Pain of (*space left blank*) for every Offence, or Neglect of sweeping as aforesaid. And no Person or Persons whatsoever shall throw, set, cast, or lay, or cause, permit, or suffer to be thrown, set, cast, or laid, any Coal-Ashes, Wood-Ashes, Rubbish, Dust, Timber, Dirt, Dung, Filth, Carts, Carriages, Tubs, Wood, or other Annoyances, in any open Street, Place, or Passage, or suffer the same to remain longer than the Space of (*space left blank*) in any open Street, Lane, or publick Passage, or Place, within the said Borough and Town, before or against his, her, or their Dwelling-House, or Houses, Buildings, or Walls, or those of his, her, or their Neighbour or Neighbours, or other of the Inhabitants there, or before or against any Church or Church-Yard, or other publick Place whatsoever, within the said Borough and Town, upon Pain of (*space left blank*) but such Inhabitant or Inhabitants shall, and he, she, and they, are hereby required to keep such Soil, Ashes, Rubbish, Dust, Dirt, Dung, and Filth, or cause the same to be kept, in their respective Houses, Backsides, or Yards, untill the Scavenger, or other Officer, or Person or Persons thereto appointed, shall come by or near their House or Doors, with his Cart, Wheel-barrow, or other Vehicle used for carrying away thereof; and then such Inhabitant or Inhabitants, who have not convenient Places in their Yards for keeping such Soil, Ashes, Rubbish, Dust, Dirt, Dung, and Filth, without being a

Nusance to the publick Streets or Places, shall, and is, and are hereby required, to carry and deliver such Soil, Rubbish, Dirt, Dung, and Filth unto the Scavenger as aforesaid, upon Pain of (*space left blank*).

And be it further Enacted, by the Authority aforesaid, that the Scavenger, or other Person or Persons, appointed or contracted with, in Pursuance of this Act, shall every (*space left blank*) or oftener if Occasion be, in every Week, bring, or cause to be brought, Carts, or other convenient Carriages, into the Streets, Lanes, and Places, within the said Borough and Town, where such Carts and Carriages can pass, and at or before their Approach, by Bell, Horn, or Clapper, or otherwise, or by a loud Voice or Cry, shall give Notice to the Inhabitants of their Coming; and give the like Notice in every Court, Alley, and Place into which the said Carts and Carriages cannot pass, and abide and stay there a convenient Time, so that the Persons concerned respectively may bring forth their Soil, Ashes, Rubbish, Dust, Dirt, Dung, and Filth, to the said Carts and Carriages; all which the said Scavenger, or other Officer, or Person or Persons, appointed or contracted with for that Purpose, shall, on the Days last before-mentioned, carry away, or cause to be carried away *gratis*, together with all the Sweepings of the said Streets and Lanes, upon Pain of (*space left blank*) for every such Offence or Neglect; except all such Rubbish, Earth, Dust, Dirt, Filth, and Soil, as shall be occasioned by building, rebuilding, repairing, or altering of any House or Houses, or any other Sort of Buildings, or digging up Ground, in the said Borough and Town, for such building, rebuilding, or altering, which said Rubbish, Earth, Dust, Dirt, Filth, and Soil, shall, within the Space of (*space left blank*) or other convenient Time, at the Direction of the said Mayor, Recorder, and Justices of the Peace, or any (*space left blank*) of them, assembled, or the (*space left blank*) Part of them present, be carried away by the respective Owners, or Occupiers, of such Houses, Buildings, or Ground, respectively, as aforesaid, upon Pain of (*space left blank*) for every such Offence, to be recovered, levied, and disposed of, as herein after is mentioned. Provided always, and it is hereby further Enacted, that it shall and may be lawful, to and for the said Mayor, Recorder, and Justices of the Peace, or such Number and *Quorum* of them as aforesaid, to purchase, rent, or hire such convenient Places, within the Limits of the said Borough of *Leicester*, or Parts thereto adjoining, to be used as and for Dung-hills, or Lay-stalls, and for laying and placing the said Soil and Dirt in and upon the same, until the same can conveniently be taken away by the said Scavengers, or Rakers, or other Person or Persons, so to be appointed or contracted with for that Purpose.

And be it further Enacted, by the Authority aforesaid, That it shall and may be lawful to, and for the said Mayor, Recorder, and Justices for the Time being, or such Number or *Quorum* of them so assembled as aforesaid; And they are hereby authorized and required to order, direct, and appoint what Number and Sort of Lamps, and how, and where they shall be set up, and to what House or Building, within the said Borough and Town, they shall be fixed, and where the same shall be placed, and for what, and how long Time, the same shall be, and continue lighted, so as in such Order and Direction, Care be taken in the first Place that the most publick, and most frequented Streets in the said Borough be first lighted, and afterwards the Places where the Persons inhabiting the same do contribute the greatest Share towards the Expence thereof. Provided always, and it is hereby Enacted, That all and every Person, Body Politick or Corporate, within the said Borough, who is or are obliged, or have been used to sweep or cleanse any Part of the said Streets, Lanes, or Passages, or other publick Places within the said Borough or Town, shall still remain chargeable with, and liable to sweep and cleanse the same, and shall be liable to the same (*space left blank*) for neglecting or refusing to sweep and cleanse those Parts of the Streets, Lanes, and Passages, or other publick Places within the said Borough or Town, which they have been used to sweep and cleanse, as the other Inhabitants are by this Act made liable unto, for not sweeping or cleansing the Streets, before their respective Houses, Buildings, or Walls.

Provided also, and be it further Enacted, That all and every Proprietor or Owner, Proprietors or Owners of any House, Building, or Edifice within the said Borough, which is not charged (or liable to be charged) to the Rates made to the Relief of the Poor, shall be obliged to enlighten such House, Building or Edifice, in such Manner as the said Mayor, Recorder, and Justices of the said Borough, or the major Part of them shall direct and appoint.

And be it further Enacted, that the said Mayor, Recorder and Justices for the said Borough, shall, and they are hereby impowered to order, direct, and appoint at what Places the said Watchmen shall respectively be stationed, and in what Manner, and how often they shall go their Rounds, and how they shall be armed, and how long they shall continue upon their Duty, and what Wages and Allowances shall be paid and given to such Watchmen, Scavengers, Rakers, and Cleansers of the Streets, Lanes, and publick Places, and to such Keeper and Lighter of Lamps, and shall and may, from Time to Time, make such Orders and Regulations as the Nature of each particular Service shall seem to them necessary and requisite.

And be it further Enacted, by the Authority aforesaid, that the said Mayor, Recorder, and Justices of the Peace for the said Borough, for the Time being, or any (*space left blank*) or more of them shall with all convenient Speed, cause a true Copy or Transcript of all such Orders and Regulations as shall be made from Time to Time concerning the said Watch, for the better Direction and Government of the Watchmen so to be appointed to be delivered to the Constables, for the Time being, of the said Borough, and to every of them; and that from and after the (*space left blank*) one or more of the said Constables of the said Borough for the Time being, or some Person to be procured by him with the Licence of the said Mayor, Recorder, and Justices, or one of them shall attend every Night by Turns, and shall keep Watch and Ward within the said Borough and Parts thereunto adjoining, at the Places which shall be respectively appointed as aforesaid, and during such Time and Times as shall be ordered and directed by the said Mayor, Recorder, and Justices, or the (*space left blank*) Part of them assembled as aforesaid, and so yearly and every Year afterwards, and shall in their several Turns or Courses of Watching, use their best Endeavours to prevent, as well all Mischiefs happening by Fire, as all Murders, Burglaries, and other outrageous Disorders, and to that End shall arrest and apprehend all Night-walkers, Malefactors, and suspected Persons, who shall be found wandering and misbehaving themselves, and shall carry the Persons who shall be so apprehended, as soon as conveniently may be, before the said Mayor, Recorder, or one of the Justices of Peace for the said Borough, to be examined, and dealt with according to Law. And shall (*space left blank*) or oftener, at convenient Times in every Night, go about the said Borough, and Parts thereunto adjoining, and take Notice whether all the Watchmen perform their Duty in their several Places or Stations, according to such Orders and Regulations as shall be made for that Purpose as aforesaid, and in case any such Watchmen shall misbehave themselves, or neglect their Duty, the said Constables, and every of them shall give Notice thereof to the Mayor and one other Justice of the Peace for the said Borough, who shall have Power to summon the Parties immediately before them, and upon hearing them, if they see Cause, may displace such Watchmen, and put another or others in his or their Stead till the next Meeting of the said Mayor, Recorder, and Justices, and (*space left blank*) such Offender in any Sum not exceeding the Sum of (*space left blank*) in order for the Punishment of such Offence.

And be it further Enacted, by the Authority aforesaid, That it shall and may be lawful for the said Watchmen, or any of them in the Absence of the Constable, and they respectively are hereby authorized and required in their several Stations, during the Time of their keeping Watch and Ward as aforesaid, to apprehend all Night-walkers, Malefactors, or Rogues, Vagabonds, and other disorderly Persons disturbing the Publick Peace, or any Persons who refuse to give a good Account of themselves, and to deliver the Person or Persons so apprehended, as soon as conveniently may be, to the Constable of the Night, to keep him, her, or them, in safe Custody for that Night, and who is hereby required to carry him or them, as soon as conveniently may be, the next Day, before the Mayor, Recorder, or one of the Justices of the Peace for the said Borough for the Time being, to be examined and dealt with according to Law. Provided always, and it is hereby declared, that no Person who shall be appointed or employed as a Watchman, by Virtue or in Pursuance of this Act, shall by Means or on Account of his being employed and acting in that Duty and Service gain, or be intitled to any Settlement in any Parish in the said Borough of *Leicester*.

And, for defraying the Charges and Expences of keeping such nightly Watch as aforesaid, and in cleansing the Streets, Lanes, and publick Places aforementioned, and for buying and setting up, and maintaining the said Lamps, and supplying the same with proper Materials, within the said Borough and Town as aforesaid, Be it further Enacted, by the Authority aforesaid, that from and after the said (*space left blank*) the said Mayor, Recorder, and Justices of the Peace, or such Number or *Quorum* of them so assembled as aforesaid, shall, and may under their Hands and Seals nominate and appoint (*space left blank*) Inhabitants or Residents of every Parish of the Borough aforesaid, to be Assessors in order to raise Money for the Purposes in this Act mentioned. And such Persons so nominated and appointed Assessors, are hereby impowered and required to make and settle (*space left blank*) or other Rate or Rates, Assessment or Assessments, by an equal Pound Rate upon all Owners or Occupiers of any Messuages, Houses, Shops, Warehouses, Malt-houses, Granaries, Buildings, and Yards, situate, lying, and being within the said Borough of *Leicester*, and Parts thereunto adjoining, not exceeding (*space left blank*) in the Pound, by the Year.—And also upon all and every personal Estate or Stock in Trade, as the same Premises were rated or assessed, by the last Assessment for the Relief of the Poor in the Year next preceding, such Rates and Assessments to be made by Virtue of this Act; which Rates and Assessments hereby directed to be made, as to such Parts thereof as lie within the said Borough, shall be allowed and signed by (*space left blank*) or more of the Justices of the Peace for the said Borough; and as to such Parts thereof which lie out of the said Borough, and in the County at large, the same shall be allowed and signed by any (*space left blank*) of his Majesty's Justices of the Peace for the said County; and after the Rates and Assessments so made and confirm'd, the said Mayor, Recorder, and Justices, or such Number and *Quorum* of them as aforesaid, shall have full Power, and they are hereby authorized and required to cause the same to be collected (*space left blank*) and to appoint (*space left blank*) or more Persons, to collect the same in each and every Parish within the said Borough, and Parts thereunto adjoining; and if any Person or Persons shall wilfully refuse or neglect to appear, assess or collect such Rates, or Assessments as aforesaid, being thereunto summoned and appointed as aforesaid, or refuse to be Sworn well and faithfully to execute either of the Offices of Assessor or Collector, which Oath the said Mayor or any one Justice of the said Borough is authorized to administer to any Person inhabiting within the said Borough; and any Justice of the Peace of the County, may administer the same to every such Person living out of the said Borough, every such Person or Persons shall, for every such Offence, forfeit and pay the Sum of (*space left blank*) to be (*space left blank*) of as herein after is directed. Provided always, that no Person or Persons shall be obliged to serve as Assessor or Collector of the Rates, by this Act imposed, more than (*space left blank*) in (*space left blank*) Years. And the said Rates and Assessments by this Act so to be made, shall be subject to, and chargeable with such Sum or Sums of Money, as shall from Time to Time be advanced, borrowed, raised, or received, for purchasing and erecting Lamps, and for carrying on the several Works hereby intended and directed to be done, which said Rates and Assessments shall be paid by the respective Tenants, or Occupiers, for the Time being, of the respective Premises, and by the respective Proprietors of their respective personal Estates or Stock in Trade so rated and assessed to the said Mayor, Recorder, and Justices, or such Number and *Quorum* of them as aforesaid, or to such Person or Persons, as they, or such Number and *Quorum* of them as aforesaid, shall order, direct and appoint. And in Case any Person or Persons so assessed, shall refuse, or neglect to pay such Rate or Assessment by the Space of (*space left blank*) next after Demand thereof made, it shall, and may be lawful to, and for the said Collectors respectively, by Warrant under the Hands and Seals of (*space left blank*) or more of the said Justices respectively, and which Warrant they are hereby authorized and required to grant to such Collector or Collectors applying for such Warrant to (*space left blank*) of the Goods and Chattels of the Person or Persons so refusing or neglecting to pay the same, rendering to such Person or Persons so refusing or neglecting the Overplus, if any be after the necessary Charges of making such (*space left blank*) being first deducted. Provided always, and be it further Enacted, That if any Difference or Dispute shall arise between the several Occupiers of the same Messuage, House, Shop, Warehouse, Malt-house, Granary, Building, or Yard, within the said Borough respectively rated or assessed for the Purposes aforesaid, touching or concerning their respective Proportions of any such Rates or Assessments be made by Virtue of this Act, then and in every such Cases, the said Mayor, Recorder, and Justices of the Peace for the said Borough for the Time being, or any (*space left blank*) or more of them, whereof the Mayor to be one, shall, and may hear, adjust and determine all, and every such Difference and Dispute, and in like Manner the Justices for the County at large, or any (*space left blank*) of them, shall adjust and determine all Differences and Disputes arising as aforesaid, where the Party shall live out of the said Borough. Provided also, That if any Person liable to pay the said Rates and Assessments by Virtue of this Act, shall remove from, or quit the House, Tenement or Premises, in Respect of which such Assessment, or Rate is made before the Assessment due from such Person shall be paid, it shall and may be lawful to, and for the said Collectors to (*space left blank*) in Case such

Person shall reside within the said Borough of *Leicester*, and a sufficient (*space left blank*) or otherwise, the Mayor of the said Borough for the Time being, shall, and may sue for, and recover the same by Action of Debt, Bill, Plaint, or Information, in any of the Courts of Record, at *Westminster*, with (*space left blank*) Costs of Suit.

And be it further Enacted, by the Authority aforesaid, that all and every Person and Persons who shall receive any Money, by Virtue of this Act, for the Purposes aforesaid, shall, from Time to Time, and as often as the said Mayor, Recorder, and Justices, or such Number or *Quorum* of them as aforesaid, at any Time assembled, shall require, make and render to the said Mayor, Recorder, and Justices, or unto such other Person or Persons as they shall appoint, a true and perfect Account, upon Oath; which said Oath may be taken in Writing, without any Stamp thereupon, before the Mayor, Recorder, or any one Justice of the said Borough, if the said Party lives within the said Borough, but, if such Person lives out of the said Borough, then before one Justice of the Peace for the said County, who are hereby respectively impowered and required to administer the same, of all such Sums of Money by such Person or Persons collected or received, or which shall have been rated and assessed, as aforesaid, and not received, and all other Matters and Things committed to their Charge, by Virtue and under the Authority of this Act, and pay and deliver unto such Person or Persons as the said Mayor, Recorder, and Justices, or such Number or *Quorum* of them, shall direct and appoint, all and every such Sum and Sums of Money, as shall remain in his or their Hands at the Time of such Account; and, if such Collector, or Collectors, shall refuse or neglect to account for and pay such Sum and Sums of Money accordingly, any (*space left blank*) or more of the said Justices respectively, shall and may cause the same to be (*space left blank*) upon the Goods and Chattels of such Collector or Collectors, rendering the Overplus to the Owner; and, in Case a sufficient (*space left blank*) cannot be found, then the said Justices respectively, or any (*space left blank*) of them, shall and may, by Virtue of this Act, (*space left blank*) such Person or Persons to (*space left blank*) of the said Borough of *Leicester*, if such Person shall be an Inhabitant of the said Borough, or to (*space left blank*) for the said County, if he shall live in the said County and out of the Borough, there to (*space left blank*) until he or they shall have made a true and perfect Account and Satisfaction, or Composition, to or with the said Mayor, Recorder, and Justices, or the (*space left blank*) Part of them, assembled as aforesaid, who are hereby authorized to compound the same, for so much as, upon the said Account, shall appear to be remaining in his or their Hands; and deliver all the Books of Accounts, and Papers, vouching or relating to the same, unto the said Mayor, Recorder, and Justices of the said Borough, or some or one of them.

And be it further Enacted, by the Authority aforesaid, that the Overseers of the Poor for the Time being, for the said Borough of *Leicester*, shall, and they are hereby required to make out and deliver, to the Assessors appointed by this Act as aforesaid, true Copies of the last Rate and Assessment which have been collected and levied, within the said Borough, for the Relief of the Poor thereof, in order to enable the said Assessors to make out such Rates as, by this Act, are directed to be assessed and made on the Inhabitants of the said Borough; and every such Overseer, or Overseers, who shall refuse or neglect to make out such Copy after Demand thereof made, as aforesaid, shall, for every such Offence, forfeit and pay the Sum of (*space left blank*) to be (*space left blank*) of the Goods and Chattels of such Offender, by Warrant under the Hands and Seals of any (*space left blank*) or more, of the said Justices respectively, rendering the Overplus to the Owner if demanded, after such (*space left blank*) the said Goods shall have been deducted and paid.

And it is hereby further Enacted, that, in Case any Money, received by any such Collector as aforesaid, shall be totally lost, the said Assessor, or Assessors, for the Time being, are hereby authorized and required, upon the Order, and by the Direction of the said Mayor, Recorder, and Justices respectively, or such Number and *Quorum* of them as aforesaid, to make a new or additional Assessment, for supplying and making Good such Deficiency, and the Charges occasioned by or on Account of the same.

And be it further Enacted, by the Authority aforesaid, that the said Mayor, Recorder, and Justices of the said Borough, or any (*space left blank*) or more of them, shall, by Writing under their Hands and Seals, from Time to Time, direct and appoint how, and in what Manner, all and every Sum and Sums of Money, collected and levied by Virtue of this Act, shall be applied and expended, for the effectual carrying of this Act into Execution.

And be it Enacted, by the Authority aforesaid, that the Right and Property of the Lamps, from Time to Time erected, or set up, by Virtue of this Act, shall be vested in the Mayor, Recorder, and (*space left blank*) senior Justices of the Peace of the said Borough for the Time being; who are hereby authorized and empowered to bring Actions, or prosecute Indictments, against any Person or Persons for stealing, taking away, breaking, extinguishing, or spoiling the same, in such Manner as is herein after-mentioned.

And be it further Enacted, by the Authority aforesaid, that it shall and may be lawful, to and for the said Mayor, Recorder, and Justices of the Peace, or such Number or *Quorum* of them as aforesaid, and they are hereby required to direct that a Book or Books shall be prepared and kept, wherein shall be fairly entered the Names of the Watchmen, Scavengers, and other Officers and Persons, employed to watch, and in cleansing the said Streets, Lanes, and publick Places, and the Keepers and Lighters of the Lamps, who shall be elected and appointed pursuant to this Act; and also the Names of the Persons herein after appointed to take Care of the publick Pumps and Wells, within the said Borough; and Copies of all Orders and Proceedings relating to the said Watchmen, Scavengers, and Lamps, and other Persons employed as aforesaid; and likewise an Account of all Sums of Money raised and paid, and how the same has been applied for and towards any of the Purposes in this Act mentioned; which Book, or Books, every Person or Persons contributing to the said Watch, Scavengers, and Lamps, or to and for any other Purposes in this Act mentioned, may from Time to Time, and at all convenient Times, resort, to peruse and inspect the same, without Fee or Reward.

And it is hereby further Enacted, that the Mayor, Recorder, and Justices for the said Borough or *Leicester*, for the Time being, respectively, shall and may, and they are hereby authorized and empowered, upon View or Information, to make such Orders for removing of Rubbish, and other Annoyances and Obstructions, out of the Streets, Lanes, and publick Places within the said Borough, or Parts thereto adjoining, as to them shall seem requisite and necessary.

And it is hereby further Enacted, that no Cart, Waggon, or other Carriage, shall be permitted to remain in the publick Streets or Passages, within the said Borough, any longer than is necessary for the loading or unloading the same respectively; and, if any Person making, or occasioning, any such Annoyance or Obstruction as aforesaid, upon Notice given by the said Mayor, Recorder, or Justices, or any one of them, as aforesaid, to remove the same, shall neglect or refuse so to do, within the Time limited and directed by such Notice, every Person in such Case offending shall, for every such Offence, (*space left blank*) to be recovered as herein after is mentioned and directed.

And be it further Enacted, that it shall and may be lawful, to and for the said Mayor, Recorder, and Justices, or such Number or *Quorum* of them as aforesaid, to contract with any Person or Persons, not being Mayor, Recorder, or a Justice of the said Borough, for a sufficient Number of Lamps, to be set up in the said Borough, and for Irons and Posts for fixing them on, and for finding and providing the said Lamps with all necessary Materials, and for lighting, attending, dressing, and repairing the same; and also to contract with and hire any Person or Persons to carry away the Dirt and Soil of the Streets, Lanes, and publick Passages of the said Borough, and Parts adjoining, according to the Tenor and Purport of this Act, for any Time not exceeding (*space left blank*) so that (*space left blank*) Notice at least be given, by Writing to be fixed up at the Town-Hall in the said Borough of *Leicester*, for all Persons willing to undertake the Lighting and Cleansing the Streets, according to the Tenor and true Meaning of this Act, to make Proposals for that Purpose, to be offered and presented to the said Mayor, Recorder, and Justices, at a certain Time and Place in such Notice mentioned.

And it is hereby further Enacted, by the Authority aforesaid, that if any Person or Persons shall willingly break, throw down, or extinguish any Lamp that shall be hung out, or set up, to light the Streets, Lanes, publick Places, or Buildings, or wilfully damage the Posts, Irons, or other Furniture thereof, every Person so offending, and being thereof convicted, by the Oath of one or more Witness or Witnesses, before the Mayor, Recorder, or any one or more Justice or Justices respectively, shall, for the first Offence, (*space left blank*) for every Lamp so broken, thrown down, extinguished, or otherways damaged, and for the second Offence the Sum of (*space left blank*) and for the third Offence the Sum of (*space left blank*) to be (*space left blank*) in such Manner as is herein and hereby after directed.

And be it further Enacted, by the Authority aforesaid, that it shall and may be lawful, to and for the said Mayor or Recorder for the Time being, or any one or more of the said Justices of the Peace respectively, to hear and determine any of the Offences which are made subject to and punishable by any (*space left blank*) and such Justices of the Peace respectively are hereby authorized and required, upon any Information exhibited, or Complaint made in that Behalf, within (*space left blank*) after such Offence committed, to summon the Party or Parties accused and the Witnesses on both Sides, and, after Oath of committing any of the Facts before-mentioned, by one or more Witness or Witnesses, to issue a Warrant or Warrants for apprehending the Party or Parties so offending, and upon the Appearance, or Contempt of the Party accused in not appearing, upon the Proof or Notice, to proceed to the Examination of Witness or Witnesses upon Oath, which Oath they are hereby authorized, empowered, and required to administer, and to give such Judgment, Sentence, or Determination, as shall be just and conformable to the Tenor and true Meaning of this Act; and where the Party accused shall be convicted of such Offence, upon such Information as aforesaid, or Confession of the Party accused, it shall and may be lawful, to and for such Justice to issue a Warrant or Warrants for the (*space left blank*) as are adjudged on the Goods and Chattels of the Offender, and cause (*space left blank*) tendering to the Party the Overplus, if any there be. And in Case any Person or Persons shall be convicted, in Pursuance of this Act, of breaking, throwing down, or extinguishing any Lamp to be hung or set up, as aforesaid, and no Goods or Chattels of any Person so offending can, at the Time of such Conviction, be found, then, and in such Case, it shall and may be lawful for such Justice or Justices of the Peace, before whom such Person or Persons shall be convicted as aforesaid, to (*space left blank*) respectively, there to be (*space left blank*).

And whereas there are several publick Pumps and Wells within the said Borough of *Leicester*, which would be of great Conveniency and Advantage to the Inhabitants thereof if the same were repaired and kept in good Order, but no Provision is made for that Purpose. Be it therefore enacted, by the Authority aforesaid, That from and after the (*space left blank*) The Mayor, Recorder, and Justices of the said Borough for the Time being, or any (*space left blank*) or more of them, shall, and may, and they are hereby authorized and required yearly, and every year, to nominate and appoint (*space left blank*) fit Persons in each Ward within the said Borough, by the Name of Pump-Reeves, or Well-Reeves, which said (*space left blank*) Persons so nominated and appointed, shall take Care that the said Pumps or Wells are duly repaired and kept in Order. And that the said Pump-Reeves or Well-Reeves shall, and they are hereby authorized and im-powered by, and with the Consent of the Alderman of their respective Ward for which they serve for the Time being, to make (*space left blank*) within each of their respective Wards, not exceeding (*space left blank*) in the Pound, by an equal Pound Rate, as they are assessed to the Poor Rates upon all dwelling Houses inhabited within the said Ward, which said (*space left blank*) shall be allowed by the Mayor of the said Borough, and the Alderman of each respective Ward, who are hereby severally authorized and required to allow the same; and the Money arising by (*space left blank*) shall be applied by the said Pump-Reeves and Well-Reeves, to defray the Expences of Repairing, and keeping in repair such Pumps and Wells within the said Borough, and to no other Use or Purpose whatsoever. And if any Person or Persons, being Occupier or Occupiers of any House or Houses within the said Borough shall refuse, or neglect to pay such (*space left blank*) it shall and may be lawful to, and for the said Pump-Reeves and Well-Reeves to (*space left blank*) of the Offenders Goods and Chattels, by Warrant under the Hand and Seal of the Mayor, or any other of the Justices of the Peace for the said Borough, which Warrant the said Mayor or Justice is hereby authorized and required to grant, returning the Overplus, if demanded, to the Owner, (if any) after deducting the Money due on the (*space left blank*).

And be it further Enacted, by the Authority aforesaid, That if any Person or Persons shall refuse to serve the said Office of Pump-Reeve or Well-Reeve, or being appointed to the said Office, shall neglect duly to execute the same, every such Person or Persons, so neglecting or refusing, shall for every such Offence (*space left blank*).

And be it further Enacted, by the Authority aforesaid, That if any Person or Persons shall wilfully break down, pull up, or otherwise damage the publick Pumps, or in any Manner prejudice the publick Wells within the said Borough, or the Works belonging to such Pumps or Wells, such Person or Persons, so offending, shall for every such Offence (*space left blank*).

And be it further Enacted, by the Authority aforesaid, That all (*space left blank*) by this Act to be incurred or imposed (the Manner of Recovering and Levying whereof is not otherwise hereby particularly directed) shall be (*space left blank*) of the Goods and Chattels of the Offender, or Offenders, living within the said Borough, by Warrant, or Warrants under the Hands and Seals of the Mayor, Recorder, and Justices for the Time being, or any (*space left blank*) or more of them, but if the Offender or Offenders lives in the said County of *Leicester*, out of the said Borough, then by Warrant under the Hands and Seals of (*space left blank*) or more Justices of the Peace for the said County, which Warrant, or Warrants they or any (*space left blank*) or more of them respectively, are hereby impowered and required to make, upon Information of one or more credible Witness, or Witnesses upon Oath, before them, or any (*space left blank*) or more of them, which Oath they or any (*space left blank*) or more of them, respectively, are hereby impowered and required to administer, and that all the (*space left blank*) when recovered, after rendering the Overplus (if any be) upon Demand, to the Party or Parties whose Goods or Chattels shall be so (*space left blank*) the Charges of such (*space left blank*) being first deducted, shall be paid and applied as follows; that is to say, (*space left blank*) thereof, shall go to, and be paid to the Informer, and the other (*space left blank*) shall be paid into the Hands of such Person or Persons, as the said Mayor, Recorder, or any (*space left blank*) or more of the said Justices shall appoint to receive the same, and be laid out, and applied to, and for such Uses and Purposes, as are mentioned in this Act, as the said Mayor, Recorder, and Justices, or such Number, or *Quorum* of them as aforesaid, shall under their Hands direct and appoint, and in Case no such (*space left blank*) can be had, then it shall, and may be lawful for the said Mayor, Recorder, and Justices respectively, or any (*space left blank*) or more of them, by like Warrant or Warrants to (*space left blank*) the Party, or Parties offending to the (*space left blank*) of the said Borough, or (*space left blank*) respectively, for the Space of (*space left blank*). Provided always, that it shall and may be lawful to, and for the said Mayor, Recorder, and Justices of the Peace respectively, or any (*space left blank*) or more of them, from Time to Time, where they see Cause, to mitigate, compound, or lessen, any of the (*space left blank*) aforesaid, as they in their Discretion shall think fit. So as such Mitigation or Composition do not extend to remit above (*space left blank*) and every such Mitigation or Composition shall be a sufficient Discharge for the Persons offending respectively, for so much of the said (*space left blank*) as shall be mitigated, lessened or remitted.

And, to prevent any vexatious Actions against the Collectors, or Receivers, be it Enacted, that where any (*space left blank*) shall be made for any Sum or Sums of Money justly due for the Purpose, in this Act mentioned, the (*space left blank*) itself shall not be deemed unlawful, nor the Party or Parties making it, be deemed a Trespassor, or Trespassors, on Account of any defect, or want of form in the Warrant, for the Appointment of such Collectors, or in the Rate or Assessment, or in the Warrant of (*space left blank*) thereupon, nor shall the Party, or Parties (*space left blank*) be deemed a Trespassor, *ab initio*, on Account of any Irregularity which shall be afterwards done by the Party or Parties (*space left blank*) but the Party or Parties aggrieved by such (*space left blank*) shall, or may recover (*space left blank*) for the special Damage he, she, or they shall have sustained thereby, and no more in any Action of Trespass, or on the Case at the Election of the Plaintiff or Plaintiffs: Provided always, That where the Plaintiff or Plaintiffs shall recover in such Action, he, she, or they shall be paid, his, her, or their (*space left blank*) Costs of Suit, and have all the like Remedies for the same, as in other Cases of Costs. But no Plaintiff, or Plaintiffs shall recover in any Action for any Irregularity as aforesaid, if Tender of Amends hath been made by the Party or Parties (*space left blank*) before such Action was brought. Provided also, That if any Person or Persons shall find him, her, or themselves aggrieved, or remain unsatisfied in the Judgment of the said Justices, or by any Rate or Assessment made in Pursuance of this Act, then such Person or Persons shall, and may, by Virtue of this Act, complain or appeal to the Justices of the Peace, at the next Quarter Sessions to be held for the Borough of *Leicester*, or at the next Quarter Sessions to be held at the Castle of *Leicester*, for the County of *Leicester*, at the Election of the Party aggrieved, who are hereby impowered to summon and examine Witnesses upon Oath, and finally to hear and determine the Matter of such Complaint or Appeal, and in Case of Conviction to issue a Warrant or Warrants for the (*space left blank*) by the Ways and Means before-mentioned, together with such Costs and Charges to the Party in whose Favour such Appeal shall be determined as the said Justices in their said Sessions, or the (*space left blank*) Part of them, then present, shall order and direct.

And be it further Enacted, That if any Action or Suit shall be commenced against any Person, for any Matter or Thing to be done, in Pursuance of this Act, then, and in every such Case, the Action, or Suit, shall be brought within (*space left blank*) next after the Cause of Action, shall arise, and not afterwards, and shall be laid, and brought, in the County of *Leicester*, and not elsewhere: And the Defendant or Defendants in such Action, or Suit, shall and may plead the general Issue, and give this Act and the special Matter in Evidence, at any Trial to be had thereupon, and if it shall appear to be done in Pursuance of this Act, or that such Action or Suit shall be brought after the Time herein before limited, in that Behalf, or shall be brought in any other County or Place than as aforesaid, then the Jury shall find for the Defendant, or Defendants: And upon such Verdict, or if the Plaintiff or Plaintiffs shall be nonsuited, or discontinue his, her, or their Action, or Suit, after the Defendant shall have appeared, or if upon demurrer Judgment shall be given against the Plaintiff or Plaintiffs, the

Defendant and Defendants shall, and may recover (*space left blank*) Costs, and have the like Remedy for the same, as any Defendant or Defendants hath, or have in other Cases by Law.

And it is hereby Declared, That this Act shall be taken and allowed in all Courts of Justice as a publick Act; and all Judges and Justices are hereby required to take Notice hereof as such, without specially pleading the same.

VESTRY MINUTES

VESTRY MINUTES

All Saints' Select Vestry Minutes

Select Vestry 4th November 1822
The accounts for the last four weeks was audited and other business disposed of.
This Meeting do adjourn to 18th instant.

J. Hudson

To Thomas Cook Esquire Mayor James Bankart Esquire George Ireland Esquire Aldermen and three of his Majestys Justices of the Peace for the Borough of Leicester.
I am directed by the select Vestry established for the Parish of All Saints in the said Borough humbly to represent to you the said Justices that previous to the complaint made to you by William Richards, no application had been made for Relief to the select Vestry, and the Select Vestry are advised that therefore the Order made by you on the first Instant in favour of the said William Richards is not by the Statute 59th Geo. 3 Cap. 12 Sect. 2 and that the Churchwardens and Overseers are not bound to obey such Order, or any subsequent orders which may be granted under similar circumstances.

J. W. Gillespie
Assistant Overseer

Copy

Leicester November 9th 1822

Sir
    I am directed by the Magistrates who signed the Order of relief in favour of William Richards's family on the 1st Instant to acquaint you in answer to your letter dated the 6th that it was given and signed by three of them (being the whole number present) for the purpose of shewing that the whole bench concurred in thinking that the circumstances in which the poor Woman and her children then were required the relief specified and that it was also given without taking the preliminary steps required by the select Vestry Act because I had understood you in a conversation some time ago that the select Vestry and Officers of your Parish would generaly defer to the opinion of the Magistrates on the complaints which might be made to them by the Poor. If I misunderstood you I am sorry for it. The other Parishes in Town who have placed themselves under the select Vestry Act seldom if ever resist the wishes expressed by the Magistrates who can have

no feeling on such subjects but an anxiety to act equitably and impartialy between the Parishes and the complainents. Richards's appeared to them to be a case of the most "urgent necessity" and they would therefore have been fully justified under the proviso at the end of the 2nd Section of the select Vestry Act, in ordering temporary relief to a larger amount than the aggregate of the four weeks for which their order was given.

I request you will communicate the contents of this Letter to your select Vestry at their next meeting and assure them at the same time that the suspision, which I have been given to understand exists, that the Magistrates and those connected with them have some hostile feeling towards the Parish of All Saints is quite unfounded.

I am Sir

Yours Obedient Servant

To Mr J. W. Gillespie   James Baines

Select Vestry 29th December 1823

To reconsider at the Next Vestry the propriety of having all the Houses numbered in the Parish—and that Mr Gillespie be requested to enquire the Probable expence.

It was ordered that the Clerk give notice on Sunday next in the Morning and also in the afternoon that the Levy laid at 2/– in the £ on the 23d December was 1/3 for the relief of the Poor and 9d for the Borough Rate; and that in future the particulars shall be thus stated. It was agreed—That Messrs. Forrester, Morris & Hudson be requested to wait upon the select Vestries of the other Parishes to consult what steps can be taken to prevent the Erection of a new Goal.

James Hudson

Select Vestry 12th January 1824

The Accounts were examined and pass'd and other Business disposed of. It was agreed that the Houses in the Parish should be numbered.

Select Vestry 26th January 1824

Ordered that the Parish of St Mary be repaid the 11/– for the Burial of George Sanderson.

Resolved that the parish do act in conjunction with St Marys or other Parishes in resisting the new settlement act from passing into a Law.

Resolved that the Memorial now read and Intended to be presented to the Majistrates on the subject of rebuilding the Borough Goal be laid before the Overseers and Select Vestrys of the other Parishes for their Signatures.

Resolved that Messrs. Miles be requested to draw a case to be laid before

Council to ascertain what power the Magistrates posess in Rating the Borough for supporting the Police and defraying other expences connected with that part of the Town within the liberties of the Borough.

To the Worshipfull the Mayor & Magistrates of the Borough of Leicester. Gentlemen

We the undersigned Parish offices and Members of Select Vestrys in the Borough of Leicester beg leave respectfully to call your attention to the serious, very alarming and increasing expenditure of the Borough Rate which now presses so heavily upon the Inhabitants of this Town. We contemplate with dread the overwhelming burden which must fall upon us if a new Goal be erected. We consider such a step unnecessary, and in that opinion we feel fully sanctioned by the determination of the Grand Jury of the late Michaelmas Sessions. We believe if this measure be proceeded with, that it will depreciate property within the Borough at least 25 per Cent, and will intail an increased Burden of at least 30 per Cent on the present parish Rates.

We respectfully request that you will take these statements into your serious considerations and pause before you attempt a measure which will it is feared have the effect of driving every respectable Inhabitant who can remove his business and habitation, out of the Borough, which will give most decided and unfair advantage to the Bishops Fee, the South Fields &c where persons will be able to live and carry on their business with every advantage, without being subject to these burdens.

Our resons for stating the erection of a New Goal to be unnecessary arise from the examinations of the Calenders printed at the Assizes and Sessions and a simular examination, if you will have the goodness to make it, would convince you that a large proportion of the prisoners committed to the Borough Goal are for offences in the Bishops Fee and South Fields, of which offences although you are obliged to take cognizance yet you must be well aware, you have the power of committing the offenders to the County Goal thereby considerably lessoning the present Borough Rate and rendering unnecessary the erection of a New Goal.

We beg leave to add, that in our official capacity we feel it our duty, as well as a pleasure, to Render every assistance in our power to the support of the Magistracy of the Borough in the execution of the Laws and we freely pay all necessary expences attending the same but at the same time, we must also in our Official capacity, beg leave respectfully to deprecate all unnessary expenditure of the public money and to express our confident expectation that whilst the Rate Levied for the maintenace of the poor, is by means of the laborious attention of the Select Vestrys, administred with the most rigid economy no waste will be permitted to exist in the expenditure of the Borough Rate.

At a special Vestry held on the 2nd February 1824
Resolved; that the Memorial agreed upon at the last Vestry and since
signed by the following Officers of other Parishes be presented to the
Magistrates by Mr Gillespie to-morrow.

James Morris   } Church Wardens
William Forrester } All Saints

Thomas Bowmar   }
John Yates   } Overseers
William Whetstone } of All Saints

John Coltman
John Sergeant
George Crosher
John Worthington
John Musson   } Select
John Hudson   } Vestry
Thomas Fielding   } of All Saints
John Pratt
John Jarvis
John Orton Garle

William Wheldale } Church Wardens
Thomas Watts   } of St Martins

W. Hacket   Visitor

W. Frisby
Robert Parr   } Guardians
John Cooper   } of St Martins
Stewart Mason

William Whitmore } Church Wardens
Thomas Stokes   } of St Nicols

William Larret } Overseers of Do.
S. Davis

Joseph Chamberlain } Church Wardens
John Baxter   } of St Mary

Thomas Wood Jun. } Overseers of St Marys
R. Rawson

William Dalton
Joseph Moore
Thomas Dexter
Walter Hall   } Select Vestry
Richard Hunt   } of St Marys
Samuel Kirby
Henry Wood
Richard Higginson

William Stretton   ⎫
Thomas Humberstone ⎪ Overseers of
John Mallet   ⎪ St Martins
Thomas Lockwood ⎭

No communications has been held with those Officers & members of Select Vestrys of the above Parishes not resident in the Borough.

The Officers of the Parish of St Margrets have not been consulted, only one residing in the Borough. We beg to call your attention to the fact that out of about 3,800 Houses in that Parish not 900 of them are in the Borough.

J. Hudson

Resolved, that the thanks of this meeting are due to Mr Hudson for drawing and procuring signatures to the before written memorial.

Select Vestry February 9th 1824

The Accounts where examined and pass'd.

At this Meeting it was Moved and seconded that a Copy of the reply received from the Mayor & Magistrates relative to the Petition against the erection of a New Goal be Inserted into the Minute Book of the Vestry.

Joseph Wright

Leicester February 5th 1824

Gentlemen

I am directed by the Mayor and Magistrates to acknowledge the receipt of the Memorial subscribed by yourselves and other Parish Officers and select Vestrymen of the Town, and to assure you that they are deeply impressed with the Importance of the subject to which you have directed their attention.

They will not fail to give every consideration to the points to which you advert and it will be with the most sincere satisfaction if they should find that they can consistantly discharge the duty which they owe to the Public without involving the Town in an expenditure of so onerous a nature as that which must ever attend (however economically managed) the erection of a new Goal.

The Magistrates are aware of the peculiar situation of Leicester, and how partialy the burthens of its general police are felt by the old part of the Town.

It has been, and will continue to be their study to alleviate this evil as far as it may be, but the effectual remedy for an injustice which saddles upon one part of the Town exclusively an expence occasioned, or in all events greatly augmented, by the other, is, they fear, only to be found in the sovereign power of the Legislature.

Whatever may be the conclusion to which the Magistrates may ultimately come you may be assured that they will arrive at it only after the most dispassionate consideration and that will always approach the subject

277

with every personal wish to avoid unnecessary expence, and to lay as little of burthen upon themselves and other Inhabitants of the Town as maybe consistant with the duty which they owe to the public at large.

I have the honor to be
Gentleman
Your most obedient & humble Servant
Thomas Burbidge
Town Clerk

To
Messrs. Morris, Forrester
and others.

Select Vestry 11th March 1824

It was Resolved that the petition now read be approved and sent round the Parish for signatures, and that the other parishes be requested to unite with us.

Resolved that this Meeting do adjourn to Saturday Evening at seven o'Clock.

To the Honorable the Commons of the United Kingdom of Great Britain and Ireland in Parliament assembled.

The humble Petition of the several persons whose names are hereunto subscribed on behalf of themselves and others Inhabitants of the Borough of Leicester in the County of Leicester.

Sheweth

That your Petitioners having learnt that a Bill has been brought into and is now pending in Your Honorable House to amend an Act passed in the last Session of Parliament for consolidating and amending the laws relating to the building repairing and regulating of certain Gaols and Houses of Correction in England and Wales they are induced humbly to represent to Your Honorable House the grievous hardships to which the Inhabitants of the ancient Borough of Leicester are subject by reason of the provisions of the said Act of the last Session having been extended to the Gaol and House of Correction of the said Borough, whereby although the object of the said Act appears to have been not to vary any liabilities that previously existed with regard to the expence of maintaining any Gaol or House of Correction in any City Town or Place to which the said Act extends, yet the Justices of the Peace of the said Borough are by the said Act authorized to raise on the said Borough all the expences of the several matters and things by the said Act directed to be done respecting Gaols Houses of Correction and Prisons and the support and maintenance of Prisoners confined therein without any clause or provision applicable to the special circumstances of the said Borough.

That the said Borough of Leicester hath had an exclusive jurisdiction for the trial of felonies or misdemeanors committed therein from a very ancient time but until the year one thousand seven hundred and sixty eight no Rates in the nature of County Rates were ever imposed on the Inhabitants of the said Borough of Leicester but the Gaol and Prisons were maintained at the expence of other funds by law applicable thereto.

That Leicester is an ancient Borough and Body Corporate and the Mayor Recorder and four last Alderman who served the Office of Mayor are His Majesty's Justices of the Peace in this Borough and have an exclusive jurisdiction with a Non Intromittent as to the County Justices within the old Town or ancient limits of the Borough And under a Charter of Queen Elizabeth the Borough Justices have also a concurrent Jurisdiction with the County Magistrates in other parts of the Town of Leicester not within the ancient limits of the Borough and at least one half of the Inhabitants reside in such concurrent jurisdiction wherein a great majority of the criminal offences arise.

That the Borough Justices are in the habit of committing Prisoners for offences which arise within such concurrent jurisdiction to the Borough Gaol or House of Correction notwithstanding it has been judicially decided that those parts in which the jurisdiction is concurrent are by law exempt from any Rate by the Borough Magistrates.

That unless some modification of the provisions of the said Act of the last Session shall take place not only will any proportion of the expences of maintaining the Gaol and House of Correction which was previously chargeable on other funds have been shifted on the Inhabitants of the Borough but also the Inhabitants within the ancient limits of the Borough, being not more than one half of the Town in extent, will have been rendered exclusively liable to the expence of providing and maintaining a Gaol and House of Correction sufficient for the extended classifications required by the said Act for those larger parts of the Town which are not contributory to the Borough Rate and in which a great majority of the criminal offences arise, which is manifestly unjust and oppressive towards the Inhabitants of the ancient limits of the Borough.

That the Borough Magistrates to whom a respectful Remonstrance was lately made upon the subject have expressed themselves to be aware of the peculiar situation of Leicester and how partially the burthens of it's general police are felt by the old part of the Town, and lament their inability to alleviate the evil, stating that "the effectual remedy for an injustice which saddles upon one part of the Town EXCLUSIVELY, an expence occasioned or in all events greatly augmented by the other is only to be found in the sovereign power of the Legislature".

Your Petitioners therefore humbly pray that sufficient clauses and provisions may be inserted in the said Bill now pending in Your Honorable

House not only for the purpose of relieving the Inhabitants of the Borough of Leicester from the hardships and injustice to which for want of proper modifications to meet the special circumstances of the said Borough they are liable under the said Act of the last Sessions, but also for securing and protecting the rights and interests of the said Inhabitants in any funds applicable by law towards maintaining the Gaol of the said Borough, and that they may have such relief in the premises as to this Honorable House shall seem meet.

And Your Petitioners shall ever pray &c.

At an adjourned meeting held March 15th 1824

The petition from the different Parishes accompanied with a letter to the Right Honorable Robert Peele was ordered to be forwarded and presented to the House of Commons.

Copy   Leicester March 15 1824
Sir

The Goal Act of the last Sessions having placed this Borough in a state of Great difficulty on account of the Special circumstances attending this place not having been provided for in the Act, and observing that you have introduced a bill for amending the Goal Act the Inhabitants of this Borough trust you will not only do them the favour to present their Petition to the House of Commons (of which a Copy is inclosed) but that you will not be averse to the introduction into your Bill for amending the Act, of a Clause or two for obviating the mischief.

The Inhabitants are far from disapproving of your excellent Goal Regulations provided their local Interests are properly protected and it is in the hope of your meeting this application with your known candor that we are induced to trouble you with our Petition instead of requesting our own Representitives to present it, wishing to avoid any semblance of opposition to your Bill.

I have the honor to Subscribe Myself
                    Sir
                        Your most Obedient humble Servant
                                Signed   William Forrester
To the Right Honorable   Chairman of the Select Vestry
Robert Peele M.P.   of the Parish of All Saints
P.S. We have taken the liberty of Addressing the Petition by the same Post to you Signed by 1630 Rated Inhabitants.

Select Vestry March 22nd 1824

Resolved, that Mr Hudson Mr Coltman Mr Forrester and Mr Morris be

Deputed to wait on Mr Mansfield respecting Mr Peele's Goal regulation Bill now pending.

Robert Birkley   Chairman

The Accounts were examined and pass'd.

Copy

Leicester March 22d 1824

Sir

By the Post of Monday last I took the liberty of addressing to you a Petition from the Inhabitants of this Borough relative to the Gaol Laws, and the Petitioners being naturally anxious upon the subject I trust Sir you will excuse my troubling you with a second Letter to ask whether the Inhabitants may hope for your favorable consideration of their case or whether it will be more agreable to you that they should adopt any other channel for bringing it before Parliament. I have the Honor to be Sir Your most Obedient Servant

The Right Honorable	signed William Forrester
Robert Peel M.P.	Chairman of the Select Vestry of
House of Commons	the Parish of All Saints
London	

Copy

Whitehall March 24th 1824

Sir

I beg leave to acknowledge the receipt of your letter, and to acquaint you that I will present the Petition of the Inhabitants of Leicester relating to the Prison Bill, to the House of Commons and I will move that it be referred for the Consideration of a Committee which is about to sit upon that subject.

I cannot pledge myself to any particular Proceeding with regard to the Prison of the Town of Leicester.

I am Sir Your most Obedient Humble
Servant

William Forrester	signed Robert Peel
Esquire	
Leicester	

Copy

Leicester 24th March 1824

Gentlemen

We beg leave to trouble you with a Copy of a Petition from the Inhabitants of the Borough of Leicester respecting the Prison Bill, which was lately transmitted to Mr Secretary Peel in preference to troubling yourselves, it being thought desirable to avoid any appearance of opposition to his Bill. We also send copies of the Letter that was addressed to Mr

L

Secretary Peel with the Petition, and of his Reply; from the latter of which you will observe that he has engaged to move that it be referred for the Consideration of a Committee which is about to sit upon the subject of Prisons.

Your active support of the object of the Petitioners is therefore most earnestly and respectfully solicited, and we shall be obliged by your informing us what Members compose the Committee, and at what time it would be necessary for the Petitioners to offer their Evidence.

The Subject is one of deep interest to the Inhabitants of the Old Town, and although the Petition did not by any means originate in any hostile feeling towards the Borough Magistrates, it is much to be regretted that the Corporation have not shewn any intention to favor the object of the Petitioners.

signed   James Morris, Churchwarden of All Saints
John Baxter Churchwarden of St Mary's
W. Hackett Visitor of St Martins
Thomas Stokes Churchwarden of St Nicholas

To John Mansfield Esquire M.P.
To Thomas Pares Esquire M.P.

All Saints' Vestry Minutes

All Saints Vestry May 6th 1824.

At a parish meeting held by special notice for the purpose of taking into consideration the propriety of uniting with the other parishes in the investigation of the expenditure of the Borough Rates it was resolved—
That this meeting fully approves of the resolutions entered into at the parish of St Martins and feel it their duty to unite with them in any measure that may be suggested by the united committee and that a proportion of the expence of such Investigation as the committee may adjudge shall be paid out of the poor Rates of this Parish.

St Martin's Vestry Minutes: No. 19

At a meeeting of Mr Mayor and Justices holden the fifteenth day of May Anno Domini 1691.

Whereas John Carr of the Burrough of Leicester Felmonger and Thomas Swingler of the said Burrough of Leicester Heelemaker late Parishoners to the Parish of Al Saints in the Burrough of Leicester aforesaid being settled Inhabitants therein did remove from thence in to the parish of St Martin within the Said Burrough, whereof the Overseeres of the Poore of the Said parish of St Martin takeing notice of their Settlement without delivering any Note in writeing of the number of their family's and the houses wherein they Intended to Inhabitt with their families as a late Act of Parliament in that case directs & appoints, And did thereupon procure warrants from the Justices of the peace for the said Burrough to remove the said John Car & Thomas Swingler into the Said Parish of All Saints to be settled there it being the parish wherein they had their last legall settlement, And for as much as It is the desire of us the Overseers of the poore of the Parish of All Saints aforesaid to avoid any future trouble concerning the removeing the Said John Carr & Thomas Swingler. Wee whose names are Subscribed the Overseers of the poore of the said Parish of All Saints doe as well for our Selves as on the behalfe of the Parishoners of the Parish of All Saints faithfully promise that if the Overseers of the poore of parish of St Martin aforesaid upon any just cause to us shewed that the said John Carr Thomas Swingler & their families or any of them are likely to be chargeable to the Said parish of St Martin we will receive the said John Carr Thomas Swingler & their families into our Said Parish & provide for them and Save & keep harmeles and Indempnified the said Parishoners of the parish of St Martin from all troubles expences charges & Damages whatsoever which shall happen or come to the Parishoners of the parish of St Martin aforesaid. In witnes whereof wee have hereunto put our hands the day & yeare aforesaid.

Witnes   David Deakin ⎫
   John Huckle   the mark of   ⎬ Overseers
   Bartholomew Sheares   Anthony Groce ⎭

At a meeting of Mr Mayor and Justices holden the Fifteenth day of May Anno Domini 1691.

Whereas Thomas Greene of the Burrough of Leicester Labourer late a parishoner of the parish of St Margaretts in the Burrough of Leicester aforesaid being a Settled Inhabitant therein did remove from thence in to the parish of St Martin within the said Burrough whereof the overseers of the poore of the said parish takeing notice of his settlement, whithout delivering a Note in writeing of the number of his family & the house wherein he Intends to Inhabitt with his family as a late Act of Parliament in that case directs and appoints did thereupon procure a warrant from the Justices of the Peace for the said Burrough to remove the said Thomas Greene into the said Parish of St Margaretts to be settled there it being the parish wherein he had his last legall settlement And for as much as It is the desire of us the Overseers of the Poore of the parish of St Margaretts aforesaid to avoid any future trouble concerneing removeing the said Thomas Greene. Wee whose names are subscribed the Overseers of the poore of the said parish of St Margarett Doe was well for ourselves as on the behalfe of the Parishoners of the Parish of St Margarett faithfully promise that if the Overseers of the Parish of St Martin aforesaid upon any just cause to us shew that the said Thomas Greene or his family is likely to be chargeable to the Said parish of St Martin wee will receive the said Thomas Greene & his family into our said Parish and provide for them and Save keep harmeles and Indempnified the said parishoners of the parish of St Martin from all troubles expences charges & Damages whatsoever which shall happen or come to the parishoners of the parish of St Martin aforesaid In witnes whereof wee have hereunto putt our hands the day & yeare aforesaid.

Witnes	William Sturton
John Huckle	Thomas Bass
Bartholomew Sheares	James Annis

Whereas William Tayler with his wife and family and Hannah Middleton widow and her Three Children both late of the Parish of St Margarett in the Burrough of Leicester being Settled Inhabitants in the Said Parish did remove from thence into the Parish of St Martin within the Said Burrough, whereof the Overseers of the Poore of the Said Parish of St Martin takeing notice of their Settlement without delivering a note in writeing to them of the number of their family and the houses wherein they intended to Inhabitt as the Law directs and did thereupon procure warrants from the Justices of the Peace for the said Burrough to remove the Said William Tayler his wife and family and the Said Hannah Middleton and her Three Children into the Said Parish of St Margarett to be settled there it being the Place wherein they had their last legall Settlement And for as much as It is the desire of us the Overseers of the Poor of the Said Parish of St Margarett to avoid any future trouble concerneing the removeing the Said William Tayler his wife and family and the Said Hannah Middleton and her Three Children. Wee whose names are Subscribed the Churchwardens and Overseers of the Poore of the Said Parish of St Margarett aforesaid Doe as well for our Selves and our Successors as on the behalfe of the Parishoners of the Parish of St Margarett aforesaid faithfully promise that if the present Churchwardens & Overseers of the said Parish of St Martin or their Successors upon any just cause to us or our Successors shewed That the Said William Tayler his wife or family are likely to be chargeable to the parish of St Martin or that the Said Hannah Middleton & her Three Children or any of them are likely to be chargeable to the said Parish of St Martin wee Or our Successors will receive the Said William Tayler his wife or any of his family and the said Hannah Middleton & her Three Children or any of them into our Said Parish of St Margarett and provide for them; and alsoe shall & will Save keep harmeles and Indempnifyed the said Parishoners of the Parish of St Martin aforesaid of and from all troubles charges expences & Damages whatsoever which at any time or times hereafter shall or may happen or come to the Parishoners of the parish of St Martin aforesaid for or concerneing the mainteyneing or provideing for the said William Tayler his wife and family or any of them or the Said Hannah Middleton & her Three Children or any of them. In witnes whereof wee have hereunto sett our hands the 20th day of March in the fifth yeare of the Reigne of King William and Queene Mary &c Annoque Domini 1692.

John Pears }
James Annis } overseers

Att a Parish meeting held this 12th day of August [1728] pursuant to publick notice given the Sunday before to consider about the repair of part of Fryar Lane and it appearing doubtfull whom it belong'd to it was agreed that if the Corporation would repair one half the Parish would repair the other part, So that the whole part of the lane which lyes within the Parish of St Martins may be repair'd at the joynt charge of the Parish and the Corporation, excepting Such part of the Said Lane as hath been Usually repair'd by Mr Noble and the other Land holders there.

At a Parish Meeting held the 24th Day of January in the Year of our Lord 1741 at the Parish Church of Saint Martin in the Burrough of Leicester by the Churchwardens, Overseers of the Poor and parishioners of the Said parish to Consider of Some good Course and most Necessary Order to be Taken for the Relief, Care, and Maintenance of the Poor of the Said Parish. It is ordered by the Churchwardens and Overseers of the Poor of the Said Parish (being the Greater part of the Said Officers now Assembled) and by the Parishioners now present (by and with the Assent and Consent of John Cartwright Esquire Mayor and William Lee Gentleman Justices of the Peace for the Said Borough (whereof one is of the Quorum) That George Green one of the present Overseers of the Poor of the Said Parish (Legally appointed) Do forthwith Demand, Collect and Receive the Monthly Rate and Assessment made upon the Inhabits of this Parish upon the Thirtieth day of December last And that the Said George Green Do apply and Dispose of all Such Money, which he Shall Collect and receive by Vertue of such Assessment, for and towards the Relief of the Poor in this Parish in such manner as he Shall be Directed and appointed by the Major part of the Churchwardens and Overseers of the Poor of the Said Parish, according to the Statute in the Case made and Provided And it is further Ordered that the Said George Green forthwith have Notice of this Order.

At A Parish Meeting held the First Day of February 1741 Pursuant to Publick Notice Given the Sunday Before to Cnsult of the repaires of the Old freeschool Lauft for to Make a Place Seprate for Mr Andrews scholars

Which was Agreed to. And Also Agreed at the same Time that Mr Brough-ton Shall Have an Umbrello as Cheape as may be and Also Agreed at the Same Time that there's Order thatt on the Neglect of Mr Green one of the Overseers of the poor in the Execution of his Office A Distress hath been taken upon his Goods by a Warrant from two Justices of the peace upon which he Hath given Notice to Appeal to the Sessions. It is Desired att this parrish Meeting to know what Method is proper to be taken in Respect of Such Appeal & also if the said Green shall proceed in the Execution of his said office According to the Usuall Costom of the said parrish & wether the parishoner's will stand by the said officers & in case any action att Law shall be brot against the said officers and it was put to the vote and voted that they would defray any Expence that might Ensue 70 against 45.

St Martin's Vestry Minutes: No. 21

At a Vestry Meeting of the Inhabitants of this Parish held on Tuesday the Sixteenth day of February 1795 Pursuant to Publick Notice given in Saint Martins Church the Sunday before to lay a levy for the Church It was agreed to lay such levy at Six Pence in the pound.

At this Meeting in pursuance of notice likewise given as above to take into Consideration what measures were proper to be taken by the Inhabitants of this Parish respecting the repairing of the Middle Causeway in the Newstreet within the said Parish now presented for want of repair—It was resolved that the Inhabitants of this parish will defend themselves against such presentment and that the Officers of the Parish do take such advise as they shall think proper for defending the same accordingly, & that all ex-pences attending such defence be paid out of the rates levied and collected within the said parish.

At a Vestry Meeting of the Inhabitants of this Parish held on Tuesday the fourth Day of May 1802 (pursuant to Public Notice given in the Church the Sunday before) to lay a Levy for the Poor to choose a Churchwarden and to consider of the Propriety of defending the Indictment of the New Street.

Resolved that the Presentment of the New Street be removed by Certiorari into the King's Bench & that it be brought to issue as soon as possible and that the Churchwardens & Overseers for the time being be appointed a Committee for the purpose of managing this defence.

At a Vestry Meeting of the Inhabitants of this Parish held on Wednesday the 20th July 1802.

Mr Sergeant Best & Mr Court having given their Opinion that the Parish were liable to repair New Street It was Ordered That the New Street be immediately repaired at the expense of the Parish and that the Indictment be withdrawn.

At a vestry meeting of the Inhabitants of this Parish held on Tuesday the third Day of July 1804 (pursuant to publick Notice given in the Church the Sunday before).
Ordered that a vestry meeting of this Parish be conven'd on Friday the 13th instant to take into consideration whether a House of Industry for the Town wou'd not lessen the rates & that the officers of the different Parishes in the Town be invited to call vestry meetings for the like purpose.

At a Meeting of the Inhabitants of the Parish held on Friday the 13th Day of July 1804 (pursuant to public notice given in the Church the Sunday before).
Resolved unanimously That this vestry approves of establishing a general Plan in the Town of Leicester for bettering the condition of the Poor.
That the Committee be empower'd to appoint any other Inhabitants of this Parish Members of the Committee.
That Copies of these resolutions be sent to the Minister & Officers of the different Parishes in the Towns.
That the Committee meet at this Vestry on Monday the 23d instant precisely at 10 o'Clock in the forenoon by which time it is presumed the Sentiments of the other Parishes will be taken upon the Plan.
That the Thanks of this Meeting be given to The Reverend Mr Vaughan, the Vicar, for having taken the Chair & for the propriety of his Conduct in it.
That the Thanks of this Meeting be given to Mr Cooke for his exertions in promoting the Plans.

Edward Thomas Vaughan
Chairman

At a Vestry Meeting of the Inhabitants of the Parish held on Thursday the first day of april 1824 at 10 O'Clock in the Morning pursuant to Notice to lay a levy for the Poor.
It was agreed to lay such Levy at Two Shillings and six pence in the Pound and the same is hereby laid accordingly.
Resolved that the Guardians and Overseers be requested to call a Meeting of the Inhabitants of this Parish, to take into consideration the propriety of instituting an enquiry relative to the Borough Rate.
And that the Guardians and Overseers be requested to call such Meeting

on Thursday next and to give Public Notice thereof in both the Leicester Papers.

At a Vestry Meeting of the Inhabitants of this Parish held on Thursday the eighth day of April 1824 at 10 o'Clock in the Morning pursuant to Notice, to take into consideration the propriety of instituting an enquiry relative to the Borough Rate.

Resolved that the Vestry Clerk of this Parish make a respectful application to the Town Clerk for a Copy of the Expenditure of the Borough Rate for the last year—offering to pay for it—And if he objects to furnish such Account then to take a Copy of the Orders made at the last Sessions.

Resolved that the thanks of this Meeting be given to the Chairman.

And that this Meeting be adjourned to this day Fortnight.

At a Vestry Meeting of the Inhabitants of this Parish held on Thursday the twenty second day of april 1824 at 10 o'Clock in the Morning pursuant to adjournment to take into consideration the propriety of instituting an enquiry relative to the Borough Rate.

Resolved That as the Town Clerk on behalf of the Magistrates has refused to give a Copy of the last year's account It is desirable to make a formal demand for inspecting all the Orders made at the last General or Quarter Sessions for payment of Money out of the Borough Rate And that the Vestry Clerk do make such formal Application this day; and obtain Copies of such Money Orders.

That a Vestry Meeting be called on Thursday the twenty Ninth Instant when the result of such application may be stated to the Vestry, and that in the Notice for calling such Vestry it be stated that a proposition will be then made for appointing of a Committee to consist of the Parish Officers with some other Parishioners for the purpose of taking such steps as may seem necessary for obtaining full Information as to the Application of the Monies raised upon the Inhabitants of this Parish in the nature of Borough Rates And that the Expenses that may be incurred in any proceedings sanctioned by such Committee, as necessary; be paid out of the Poor Rates of this Parish.

Ordered that the Town Clerk's Letter read at this Meeting be inserted in this the Minute Book.

Leicester
April 21 1824

Dear Sir,

In answer to your application to me on behalf of the Parish of Saint Martin for a copy of the Expenditure of the Borough Rate—I beg to state that the accounts and Vouchers relating to the Borough Rate are placed in my custody, as clerk of the Peace for the Borough, under the Provisions of the Statute of 12th Geo. 2d C. 29 which defines the purpose for which I am entrusted with them namely "to be inspected from time to time by any of the Justices as occasion shall require". Recent proceeding on this subject at Nottingham (where demands have repeatedly been made upon the Town Magistrates for copies of the accounts for the Parishioners at large) have developed the rights and duties of the respective parties and have led to the clear ascertainment of the fact that no such demand can be legally made or enforced—It would evidently be a breach of duty on my part to furnish such a copy without the order of the Magistrates, and even with such an order it is by no means clear that a clerk of the Peace would be warranted in such a proceeding—At the same time there exists no motive on the part of the Magistrates for desiring concealment and they seek none. This will be obvious from the fact that the Magistrates do direct a full abstract of the accounts to be published annually altho' the Statute (55th Geo. 3d C.51) is in its terms confined to Counties and Divisions of Counties (which Leicester is not) and consequently the Magistrates might have declined to order this publication. They thought, however, that the spirit of the act would justify, if it did not compel, them and they acted accordingly. If the Parish of Saint Martin will refer to that annual Abstract they will find every information which would seem to be necessary for shewing to them the purposes for which this Rate is usually expended. If indeed the object be, not to gain this general information, but to establish a controul over the detail of the expenditure, and to sit in Judgment upon each individual order of the Magistrates on the subject, it is sufficient to say that the Law does not authorize such an interference and the Magistrates would be ministering to their own degradation, and grossly compromising their own duties if they submitted to it. The increase of an expenditure of this description can scarcely be matter of surprise to any who reflect on the vast increase of our population, and on the amazing difference in the circumstances of the present times, as contrasted with former periods, in all those matters which occasion demands upon this fund. I would just mention that at Nottingham, where the population is not beyond all compare with our own, the expenditure (as appears from their published accounts) is about 7000£ a year whereas ours has never yet exceeded a rate of £600 a Quarter even in these days of our heaviest affliction. I think it right to add a word or two upon another branch of the subject. I allude to the mode in which the rate in question is raised—Much misconception seems to prevail on this point and I trust I shall stand excused in troubling you with this explanation, seeing that injustice may be effected by an unequal mode of assessment as well as by an unfaithful disbursement of the money when levied—After the trial which ended in taking away the Bishop's Fee, South Fields &c from contribution to the Borough Rate, a new assessment was made upon all the property situated in the Borough, and the annual value of this property was taken (as the Law authorized) from the Property tax assessments, which it was thought furnished the most satisfactory basis, in as much as the value therein affixed had the test of each individual's acquiesence in its accuracy—The result was that the whole of the Borough produced an annual value of £37,645. The separate value of each parish and district in the Borough was then extracted from the same Books, and the amounts were as follows

		annual value
St Martin's Parish .	. . . . . .	13,671 £
St Margaret's (the part in the Boro') .	. . .	6,884
St Mary's (Do.)	. . . . . .	5,089
St Nicholas .	. . . . . .	2,206
St Leonards .	. . . . . .	291
The Black Friars	. . . . . .	498
The white Friars	. . . . . .	414
		£37,643 [!]

The proportion of each Parish and District towards a £400 Rate (the usual amount at that period) was then ascertained by the Question If 37645£ are to pay £400 what must (the value of each parish) pay? and the answers were

		£		
St Martin's .	. . . . . .	145	5	0
St Margaret's	. . . . . .	91	5	6
St Mary's	. . . . . .	73	3	0
All Saints	. . . . . .	54	1	6
St Nicholas	. . . . . .	23	9	0
St Leonards .	. . . . . .	3	2	0
Black Friars	. . . . . .	5	6	0
White Friars .	. . . . . .	4	8	0
		£400	0	0

When the sum to be raised is £600 of course the contribution of each Parish and District is increased by one half, and thus St Martins parish has to pay to a £600 rate £217 17 6. It will be observed that this £600 rate amounts upon the whole property rated to about four pence in the Pound—(not quite so much) but what nominal Rate it may require in each Parish and District to raise its quota depends upon the proportion to the real value in which the property in such parish is usually rated for parochial purposes —As for instance in St Martin's the total value of the property (as originally ascertained by the Property Tax, perhaps increased or perhaps diminished since) was £13671. A rate of 4d in the Pound upon that value would raise £227 13s 6d being about 10£ more than St Martins contributes to a 600£ rate—How then can St Martin's pay 10d in the Pound (as is said) for its quota of the Borough Rate unless indeed the Property in the Parish be rated upon less than half its value.

I enclose you a copy of the last Abstract of the Borough Accounts
and am Dear Sir

To   Your most obedient Servant
Henry Dalby Esquire   Thomas Burbidge
    Vestry Clerk   Town Clerk

At a Vestry Meeting of the Inhabitants of this Parish held on Thursday the twenty ninth day of april 1824 at 10 o'Clock in the Morning, pursuant to Notice, to take into consideration the propriety of instituting an inquiry relative to the Borough Rate.

Mr James Neale was elected Chairman unanimously.

Resolved that the Magistrates having thought proper to refuse the respectful and unanimous request of the Inhabitants of this Parish to be furnished with a Statement of the particulars of the Borough Rate expenditure.

That the increased expenditure of the Borough Rate unrestrained as it has hitherto been by public Inspection, is the first cause of great uneasiness and apprehension in this Borough.

That from the great increase in the Suburbs of the Town and the limited extent of the Borough and the recent Law as to the extended classification of the Prisoners there appears to this Meeting no bounds to the future amount of this local but oppresive Tax.

That notwithstanding the late declaration of the Magistrates in their reply to the remonstrance of the Overseers and Select Vestries of the different Parishes respecting the erection of a New Gaol "that they felt personally the greatest anxiety to avoid the imposition of unnecessary taxation upon the Inhabitants of the Borough" it is the Opinion of this Meeting that the expenditure of the Borough Rate far exceeds any fair calculation for the ligitimate purposes.

That it is not only proper but legal that Offenders committing Offences out of the Precincts of the Borough, should be sent to the County Gaol, and that the Borough Gaol is both improperly and unnecessarily crowded with County Prisoners to the great oppression of the Inhabitants of the Borough and it is at least doubtful whether any part of the Expence occasioned by the Imprisionment of Debtors ought by Law to be paid from the Borough Rates, equally strong doubts exist as to the repairs of the Public Bridges and many other charges which prior to 1768 are supposed to have been defrayed by the Corporation.

That the Expence of the Police of the Borough only ought in justice and in Law to be laid upon the Inhabitants of the Borough, and that the Police of those parts adjoining to the Town but out of the Precincts of the Borough ought in Law and in Justice to be defrayed by the County Rate.

That in addition to the great and wanton extravagance in the expenditure of the Borough Rate this Meeting is by no means assured of the legal nature of all the different charges made upon the Borough Rate, and it is fully of Opinion that unless the Town adopt some speedy step either through the Courts of Law or by application to Parliament for obtaining Information as to the due application of the Money and so putting some limit to this alarming amount of local Taxation the consequences must be, most fatal and ruinous to this Borough.

Resolved that a Committee consisting of the following Gentlemen be appointed to consult with the other Parishes interested in this question as to what steps it may be expedient to adopt under the present alarming Circumstances, with power to appoint a Sub-committee to co-operate with any persons delegated from the other Parishes.

Mr. John Bankart	Mr. S. Miles
Mr. R. Miles	Mr. Nunneley
Mr. T. Lockwood	Mr. Stretton
Mr. P. Colston	Mr. Paget
Mr. Thomas Bankart	Mr. Shardlow

Report of Henry Dalby Vestry Clerk of the Parish of Saint Martins in Leicester in consequence of the resolutions of the Vestry Meeting held on the 22nd day of April 1824 directing the Vestry Clerk to make a formal demand for inspecting all the orders made at the last General or Quarter Sessions for payment of Money out of the Borough Rate and to obtain copies of such money orders.

On the 22nd April I applied at the Office of the Town Clerk and was informed he was from home. On Friday the following day I again attended at the Town Clerk's Office and demanded of him to inspect the above mentioned Orders, and to have copies of them and delivered my demand in writing (see Paper A) when the Town Clerk said he would see the Magistrates and give me an answer. On the same day he delivered his answer (vide Letter B). On that day I also attended the Magistrates at the Exchange when Mr Lovell and Mr Cook were present and delivered my demand in writing (vide Paper C) when they said they would consider of it and give an answer. On the same day I wrote to the Town Clerk the Note see paper D and sent it by a Clerk and received the following verbal answer "I decline complying with your request". On Monday not having received the Magistrates answer I went to enquire of the Town Clerk when I might expect it, who said the Magistrates would not meet till Thursday and no answer could be given. I the same day sent Copies of the demand as per paper C To the Mayor Mr Ireland & Mr Johnson who said in answer they should consider of it. On Tuesday I waited upon the Mayor and Magistrates individually for their answers to my written demand, when the answer given by each was, that the Magistrates would not meet till Thursday & would then send an answer and upon my demanding immediately to inspect or to give an order to the Town Clerk or proper officer, for me to inspect the before mentioned orders, The Mayor, and Magistrates, severally refused.

(A)

By Order of a Vestry meeting of the Inhabitants of the Parish of Saint Martin in the Borough of Leicester I do, as Vestry Clerk of the said Parish, demand of you to inspect all the orders made at the last General or Quarter Sessions of the Peace for the said Borough for payment of money out of the Boro' rate—And do also demand copies of such money orders, hereby offering to pay for the same.

To   H. Dalby
Thomas Burbidge Esquire
Town Clerk and Clerk of the
Peace for the Borough of Leicester

23rd April 1824 Duplicate delivered to Mr Burbidge and the demand made and Mr B. promised to see the Magistrates and give an answer verbal or written in the course of the day—William Weston.

(B)

Leicester
April 23 1824

Dear Sir,

As your demand to inspect "all the orders made at the last General or Quarter Sessions of the Peace for the Borough for payment of money out of the Borough Rate and of copies of all such orders" is made Officially as Vestry Clerk of Saint Martin's and in the exercise of an asserted claim of right I beg to request that the authority which is supposed to justify me in a compliance with this application may be pointed out and in the mean time you will consider me as declining to allow the inspection or give the Copies which you demand.

To Henry Dalby Esquire   Thomas Burbidge
Vestry Clerk of St Martins   Town Clerk

(C)

By Order of a Vestry meeting of the Inhabitants of the Parish of Saint Martin in the Borough of Leicester I do as vestry clerk of the said Parish hereby demand of you to inspect all the orders made at the last General or Quarter Sessions of the Peace for the said Borough for payment of money out of the Borough rate or to order the Town Clerk, Clerk of the Peace, or other proper officer in whose custody the same now are to permit me to inspect the same and to furnish me with copies of such money orders on my paying for the same.

To   H. Dalby

The Mayor & Magistrates

of the Borough of Leicester

    23rd April 1824 Delivered Duplicate to Isaac Lovell and Thomas Cooke Esquires who said they should consider of it—William Weston.

    26th April 1824 The like to Thomas Yates (Mayor) Robert Johnson & George Ireland Esquires who gave the like answers—William Weston.

    1824 April 27th waited upon Thomas Yates Esquire Mayor for his answer to this demand when he said the Magistrates would not meet till Thursday & would then give an answer. Then demanded that he would allow me to inspect or give me an order directing the Town Clerk or proper officer to let me inspect the within mentioned which he refused. H.D.

    Sameday The same application made to Mr Lovell Mr Ireland Mr Cook & Mr Johnson & the like answer given.

                                                       H.D.

(D)

Dear Sir,

    From the discussions which took place at the two late meetings, The inhabitants seemed to consider that the Records of the Borough Sessions are in the nature of a Public Document to which all persons interested in the subject matter of any orders of the Justices particularly those for the payment of money out of the Public Stock have a right to refer on paying the proper Fees And the Parish of Saint Martin having employed me to make the demand I have troubled you with, I can only state their view of the matter begging you will favour me with an explicit answer one way or the other in the course of tomorrow.

                          I am Dear Sir,

                               Your most Obedient Servant,

To Thomas Burbidge Esquire   H. Dalby

    Town Clerk   23rd April 1824

        24th April 1824

        Delivered Duplicate to Mr Burbidge who said my answer is I decline complying with the request—William Weston.

(E)

Leicester

April 29 1824

Dear Sir,

The demands which you have made upon the Magistrates have been taken into consideration, but I am not directed to add Any thing to the answers which have been already communicated.

I am your's very obediently,

To

Thomas Burbidge

Henry Dalby Esquire

Town Clerk

At a Vestry Meeting of the Inhabitants of this Parish held on Thursday the twentieth day of April One thousand eight hundred and twenty six at $\frac{1}{2}$ past eleven O'Clock Pursuant to Notice given in the Church the Sunday before for the purpose of considering certain matters relative to the Borough Rates.

Resolved unanimously that Mr Mansfield Gregory takes the Chair.

Resolved That Mr Miles report what has been furnished on the Writ of Mandamus.

Mr Miles having reported what had been furnished him—and This Meeting have heard read the Orders for payments out of the Borough Rate and the accounts for the two Quarters alluded to in the Writ of Mandamus, and although they are of Opinion that some of the Items may be of a questionable nature yet they are not influenced by any desire to open past transactions but that it is the hope of this Meeting that the Magistrates will take care that they order no payments out of the Borough Rate but what are warranted by Law and that the expression of this feeling be conveyed to the Magistrates to which the Town Clerk assured the Meeting the Magistrates would gladly pay every attention consistently with their duty to the Public —and the Town Clerk also assured the Meeting that the now overlooking the two Items of One hundred and fifty pounds each paid on account of the Costs of the Proceedings now pending in the Court of King's Bench shall not in any wise prejudice any question that may hereafter arise if any future orders shall be made for further payments on account of the Costs of such Proceedings.

Resolved that the thanks of this Meeting be given to the Committee for the trouble they have taken in the Business confided to them.

St Margaret's Vestry Minutes

Minutes of the 2nd meeting of the Select Vestry held September 26th 1820.

Mr Burbidge having addressed to the Vestry the following very handsome Letter offering his gratiutous assistance to the Vestry in case such assistance be thought necessary.

To the Chairman &c   (Copy)

Sir—Having been for so many years favoured with the confidence of St Margarets parish as their Solicitor in parish Affairs, I feel it incumbent upon me to offer my services to the Select Vestry without any expence to the Parish, If I can be of any use in Assisting them in the Office which they have undertaken.

It does not strike me that the constant attendance of a Vestry Clerk would be either necessary or desirable—But if the Vestry should think otherwise I shall be very happy to attend them by myself or my Clerks at all their meetings & to give them any other assistance in my power.

I beg the favour of you to make this
communication to the meeting
& remain Sir
Your obedient Servant
Th. Burbidge

Newstreet
September 26th 1820

Ordered That the Chairman be requested to communicate the thanks of this Vestry to Mr Burbidge for such Offer & to inform him that the Vestry are not aware of the constant attendance of a Clerk being necessary but should any such occasion occur, they will be happy to avail themselves of his Services.

At a Meeting of the Select Vestry held at the Committee Room 24th October 1820.
Order'd That Mr Burbidge be paid next week, his Account deliverd this Evening, amounting to £19 15s 6d.
Order'd That Mr Burbidge be requested to send his Account Quarterly.

At a Meeting of the Select Vestry December 26th 1820.
Order'd That Mr Burbidge be requested to send in his Account from Michaelmas last, to St. Thomas; immediately.

At a Meeting of the Select Vestry January 16th 1821.
Order'd That no further payments be made to Mr Burbidge until we have his Accounts up to St. Thomas 1820—& that the Chairman make the same Known unto Mr Burbidge by Letter or personally.

At a Meeting of the Select Vestry February 27th 1821.
Order'd That as the following Bills are now owing by the Parish;

Due to W. Jones & Sharpless	470. 2. 10
Amount of Bills &c	200. 0. 0
Owing to Mr Burbidge 1817	278. 3. 0
,, 1818	332. 18. 0
,, 1819	352. 2. 10
	1633. 6. 8

This Vestry strongly recommend that a Levy of 4s. in the pound be laid & notice given on Sunday the 11th for a parish Meeting the following Wednesday for that purpose.

At a Meeting of the Select Vestry March 13th 1821.
Order'd That Mr Burbidge's Bill be got & all others outstanding, to this day.
Order'd That Mr Burbidge's Letter of the 27th Ultimo be answered, stating that this Vestry have directed a Levy to be made which they trust will enable them to pay a part of his Bills.

At a Meeting of the Select Vestry held May 28th 1821.
Ordered That Mr Burbidges Bills be Taxed and that Mr J M Robinson be employed for the purpose.

At a meeting of the Select Vestry May 29th 1821.
Ordered That Mr Austin & Mr Marris be requested to wait upon Mr Robinson & explain respecting Mr Burbidges Bills.

At a Meeting of the Select Vestry, June 5th 1821.
Ordered That Mr Marris Mr Lockwood & Mr Inman be requested as a Select Committe to examine Mr Burbidges Bills.
Ordered That Mr Burbidge be requested to send in his Bills up to 25th March 1821.

Copy of the Report of Select Vestry presented at the Parish Meeting October 31st 1821.

Mr Burbidges Bills to Easter 1820	£963. 3. 10
to Michaelmas 1821	492. 8. 10
	1455. 12. 8

The Select Vestry beg further to state that since Michaelmas they have
paid off Mr Merrediths Account 118. 2. 6
and they have paid Mr Burbidge 354. 0. 0
in part of his demand against the Parish.

At a Meeting of the Select Vestry 11th December 1821.
Order'd On the Motion now made by Mr Austin, That a Special Meeting
of the Select Vestry, be called on Tuesday next for the purpose of appointing a Deputation, to wait upon the Mayor & Magistrates at the Exchange,
to obtain their sanction & Assistance for the more speedy Collecting of the
Poor Rates.

At a Meeting of the Select Vestry April 10th 1822.
Order'd That Mr Burbidge be requested to send in his demand upon this
Parish every Quarter.

At a Special Meeting of the Select Vestry February 10th 1824.
At this Meeting the Accounts were examin'd and found correct.
Resolv'd—That an Answer be sent to Mr Secretary Peel's Letter on the
Subject of the proposed Bill to amend the Laws relating to the Poor, and
that it advert to the Answer which has been sent by Saint Mary's Parish, &
express the particular Situation of St Margarets, expecially as to the number of small Houses and the confident belief of the Vestry that the Bill will
operate with gross injustice upon Manufacturing Districts, and upon the
Parish of St Margaret's in particular on account of its extent & its minute
subdivision amongst a large body of Proprietors who cannot regulate the
Population as is done in small Country Parishes, so as to proportion the
number of Inhabitants to the wants of the place, or to the Trade which is
carried on in it—and that the Letter specify such other Objections as may
occur to the measure.
Order'd—That this Meeting adjourn to the 24th Instant at six in the
Evening.

R. Austin   Chairman

At a Meeting of the Select Vestry held 7th April 1828.
Orderd that the Town Clerks Bill for 4 Years—from Easter 1824 to Easter
1826—amounting to £143. 12. 6—and the Balance of Law Bill to 1825
amounting to £40. 2. 2 be paid.
At this Meeting the Bills now owing to Mr Burbidge were examind and
enterd in the Ledger, amounting to £465. 6. 0—and the vestry are of
opinion that the whole of these Bills shoud be immediately paid.

At a Vestry Meeting held August 4th 1828.
Orderd that Mr Burbidg be paid 106. 11. 0 toward his Account and that the Chairman wait upon him and inform him that no more Money be paid untill he send in his last Quarters Account.

At a Vestry Meeting held September 22nd 1828.
Orderd that the following Bills be paid to Mr Burbidge and a Check given for this amount.

No. 9	29	2	1
12	10	18	2
13	35	3	10
14	4	15	6
15	10	17	2
16	3	19	10
17	24	5	4
18	7	14	8
19	11	.	6
£137	17	1	

At a Vestry Meeting held October 6th 1828.
Orderd that following Statement be presented to a Parish Meeting to be held October 9 1828.

The Treasurer has in hand	339. 2. 11½
Arears of Levys	279. 17. 8½
	619. 0. 8
Mr Burbidges Law Bills owing	69. 16. 2
Balance in favor of the Parish at this time	549. 4. 6

At a meeting of the Select Vestry held on Wednesday April 8, 1829.
Resolved That the report made by the committee and presented to this meeting be adopted and it is the unanimous wish of the present meeting that it should be printed and distributed through the parish and copied into this book.

Copy of Report.

The Select Vestry consider it their duty to state to the Parishioners the reason why they have not been called together, agreeable to Annual custom, to receive the report as to the state of the Parish Accounts and also to choose (if approved) a Select Vestry for the ensuing Year.

The new Overseers were chosen on Friday March 27th, next day the Vestry assembled, and come to the following Resolutions.

That Notice be given in the usual way, in St Margarets and St Georges Churches, for a Vestry Meeting to be held in St Margarets Church on Thursday April 9th at 10 o clock in the forenoon to receive the report of the Select Vestry, and also to appoint a Select Vestry for the ensuing Year. The Chairman signed it, who is an Officer, and Similar notices have been Signed in the same way ever since the formation of the Select Vestry in the Year 1820: when the above notice was presented by the Churchwarden (Mr Agar) the Vicar and Clerk had received the following Discharge.

To the Parish Clerk of Saint Margarets Leicester and to the Vicar of the said Parish.

We the undersigned being the Major part of the Churchwardens and Overseers of the said Parish do hereby discharge you from calling any Parish Meeting without the Authority in writing of the major part of the Churchwardens and Overseers of the said Parish of Saint Margaret. And we give you Notice in particular not to call a meeting for the appointment of a Select Vestry, until we have further considered the same.

Witness our hands the 28th day of March 1829.

Signed   James Rawson   Churchwarden
William Heard   Overseer
W. R. Griffen   Overseer
Edward Rawson   Overseer

The Vestry assembled again on Monday the 30th March and Ordered the following Notice to be drawn up and presented to the Officers for their Signatures.

Take Notice a Parish Meeting will be held in St Margarets Church on Thursday April 16th at 10 o clock in the forenoon in order to receive the report of the Select Vestry, and also to take into consideration the propriety of choosing a Select Vestry for the ensuing Year.

This Notice was signed by Mr Agar and Mr Heard, the other four Officers refused. Two of the Overseers stated they had no objection to sign it, providing the latter part was left out (that is of choosing a Select Vestry) not being able to obtain a majority of the Officers signatures the Vestry was again called together on Thursday April 2nd when they resolved to take Mr Denmans opinion upon the Legal mode of calling a parish meeting, which opinion they expect to receive in a few days.

At a Vestry Meeting held on Monday August 3rd 1829.

Order'd That the unusual course of verifying a swearing to accounts before two Magistrates as being correct, without having been previously examin'd & signed by the vestry, or having ascertained that they are correct, is consider'd by this vestry illigal, if done, to be taken, as passing the accounts & unnessarily dangerous to the overseers themselves, if thereby they have pergured themselves by swearing to what may be incorrect. JUDGE!!!

St Margaret's Select Vestry

At a Vestry Meeting held on Thursday June 5th [1828].
This Meeting do solemnly protest against Mr Rawsons Accounts and against the Manner in which Mr Rawson has obtained 4 Signatures to his own Account and that protest be enterd in the Parish Cash Book and Signd by the present Meeting and also in the Present Minute Book. Carried unanimously.

At a Vestry Meeting held on Thursday April 9th 1829:
1. Resolved that the Conduct of Mr Griffin the Acting Overseer is deserving severst censure in summoning and Subjecting a poor and industrious Parishioner with a Large family to the Expense of nine Shillings as costs for the payment of Levies dew the last Quarter and present Quarter amounting to only fourteen Shillings and this Meeting disclaims any participation in any oppressive and vindictive proceeding especially when so large a portion of the opulent in the Parish has not been applied to and paid the Levies dew the present Quarter.
2. Resolved that this Meeting claims the Right of every parishioner who pays Levies however humble his situation in Life to express his opinion upon the expenditure of Parochial Monies without being liable to persecution.
3. The first Person William Sutton (a Medical Practitioner) has a Wife and 8 Children, and the other Person John Harbutt a Butcher has a Wife and 7 Children.
This Meeting has subscribed the sum of 2£ for the former and 1£ for the latter as a Mark of their disaprobation of Mr Griffin Conduct.
4. Resolved that the thanks of this Meeting be given to Mr Agar Mr Bowater and those of the late Select Vestry who have so fearlessly, honorably and advantageously checkd and exposed the peculation of individuals in the management of the affairs of this Parish, and the present Select Vestry are requested to attentively watch over the proceedings of the present Overseers, whose Conduct in Refusing to call a Meeting for the purpose of choosing a Select Vestry at the usual time has Renderd them objects of suspicion, and unworthy the confidence of the Parishioners.
5. Resolved that it is the opinion of this Meeting that all unnessary legal proceedings in Regard to settlements wanton and interested expenditure

of public Money in parochial litigation should be scrupulously avoided.

6. Resolved that this Meeting is determined to support the Select Vestry in the prosecution of any individual guilty of a misapplication of the Parish funds, or abuse of his duties during the time of his office.

7. Resolved that the select Vestry, in all cases requiring legal advice, be Requested to consult Gentlemen whose character, integrity, and knowledge will be a guarantee for the faithfull and honest discharge of the trust confided to their care.

8. Resolved that it is the opinion of this meeting that the appointment of Overseers of the Poor ought to be vested in the Rate Payers and not subject to the exclusive controul of majistrates, whose interference, experiance has proved, has been generally hostile to the interests of the parishioners, and that the Select Vestry be authorised to communicate with Mr Otway Cave, to obtain an alteration in the election of Parish officers, by the insertion of a Clause or Clauses in an Act about to be brought before Parliment by Mr Hobhouse, entitled an Act for the Regulations of parish Vestrys, or in any other Act or Acts which may come before parliment, Relating to the management of Parish affairs.

9. Resolved that the Proceedings of the Meeting be enterd in the Parish Books, and Publishd in the Leicester Journal and Chronicle Newspapers.

10. Resolved that the thanks be given to the Chairman, Mr Agar, for his able and impartial Conduct.

At a Vestry Meeting held this 1st day of September 1831.

Report

The Committee appointed at the Vestry Meeting of the inhabitants of the Parish of St Margarets held on the 2nd of June last to superintend the preparation of a Bill for the better regulation & management of its affairs report to this Meeting that in pursuance of a resolution passed at the adjournd meeting of the 30th of the same Month they have continued their deliberations which have been carried on with great unanimity and with an anxious desire that the result may conduce to the good government of the Parish. Your committee have procured several acts of Parliament obtained within the last few years by other large & populous Parishes and propose to incorporate in the intended Bill such of the provisions as appears best adapted to the circumstances of this Parish and calculated to secure a faithfull administration of the Parochial funds. The general principles of the Bill being few & simple but its details necessarily long your committee have deemd it most eligible to present to this Meeting a concise view of its leading features.

The most important part of the Bill is that relating to the persons in whose hands the future government of the Parish should be placed and to the powers with which they should be intrusted. After mature consideration your Committee propose to constitute a Committee of Management consisting of the Vicar Churchwardens Overseers of the Poor & Surveyors of the Highways for the time being and Twenty Rate payers to be chosen anually by the inhabitants in Vestry assembled; and to vest in such Committee the full and complete superintendance management and disposition of all the affairs of the Parish with the exception of the application of the Church Rates over the expenditure of which the Parishoners already possess an effective control. As it will be necessary for accomplishing this object that the individuals composing such Committee should be clothed with very considerable powers it will be essential to a successfull application to Parliament that its constitution be such as to inspire confidence and afford security that their powers be not preverted or abused. On reference to similar Acts of Parliament your committee find that in all of them a certain annual assessment or the ownership of property has been renderd a necessary qualification for a Committeeman. After much deliberation your committee recommend that no person be eligible who shall be rated at less than ten pounds and that ten at least of the Committeeman be rated at fifteen Pounds or upwards. Your committee have had much difficulty in the formation of their judgment on this point having been most anxious to meet the views & wishes of all parties in this very important feature of the Bill; and they are convinced that the classification suggested will be most advantageous to the Parish by admitting nearly all who from their interest, intelligence, activity and habits of business would be its most usefull and efficient Servants; that it will be most in accordance with the general feelings of the inhabitants, and best calculated to secure the passing of the Bill. It is proposed that the Committee of Management should meet for the transaction of business once in evry fourteen days or oftener if necessary; and to prevent the inconvenience which would result from inattention to the duties of their office each Committeeman is required under a penalty to attend ten Committee Meeting at the least, during the year.

Your Committee further report that it will in their opinion be expedient to intrust to the Committee of Management so constituted the election and appointment of the treasurer and of all the paid officers and Servants of the Parish (except the Parish Clerks) and all the powers and authorities relating to the Poors Rates now vested in the Overseers (who from their office will be members of the Committee) together with the superintendence & control over the expenditure of the Highway Rate. To guard against any loss arising from the insolvency or dishonesty of any person employd as treasurer or collectors of money the committee are required to take security for the faithfull execution of their respective offices and are impowerd to call upon all officers of the Parish to account and produce vouchers for all payments when thereunto required.

Your committee consider that the minutes of the proceedings of the committee of management should be at all times open to the inspection of Rate payers and their accounts should be audited twice every year at a general vestry of the inhabitants and an abstract published.

Your Committee further report that considering it highly important that a good understanding should exist between the Overseers of the Poor and the committee of Management they have thought it desirable to introduce into the Bill a clause relative to the appointment of those Officers, and propose that the Committee should be directed to nominate annually Twelve inhabitant householders and to deliver a list of the names of such persons to the Justices of the Borough of Leicester from which they shall be required to elect four as Overseers. They recommend a similar provision respecting the appointment of surveyors or the Highways; the list to be deliverd to the justices to contain the names of Six Persons qualified as now by law required from which two are to be chosen as surveyors.

Your Committee further report that they have taken into their consideration the manner in which Rates are now laid and after attentively weighing the subject recommend all Parochial Assessments whatever to be made by the Committee of Management for the time being as most competant to estimate the Sums required to be raised and as a means of saving some expence in the collection. They apprehend that no evil can arrise from this provision as the Committee will be elected annually and as it is proposed that their accounts should be open to appeal.

It is thought expedient that the Committee should interfere with the expenditure of the church Rates but that the money collected by Virtue thereof should be paid over to the Churchwardens to be applied and accounted for as by law established.

Your Committee further report that in order to equalize the Parochial Rates and to remedy a greviance of which great complaint has been made they have introduced a clause empowering the Committee of Management to rate Landlords for all Houses & Tenements the annual assessment of which shall not exceed Six Pounds and giving to the committee to power of compounding with Landlords on such terms as they may think reasonable considering that all property in the Parish ought to contribute to its burdens they have thus extended the provisions of a recent Act of Parliament deeming it equally just in its principle and advantageous in its operation.

Your Committee further report that contemplating the possibility of a necessity arising for the erection of a new Workhouse in the Parish and being anxious to provide for every contingency they have introduced into the Bill certain clauses impowing the Committee of Management with the consent of the inhabitants of the Parish in Vestry assembled to build a Workhouse on part of the land now belonging to the Parish or on ground to be purchased for that purpose, and to employ the Poor that may be in the Workhouse in any work trade or manufacturer they may think proper.

Your Committee further report that the present laws as to calling Vestry Meetings appearing to them to be defective they have considerd it desirable to vest the Committee of Management the power of convening such meetings whenever they may deem it expedient.

Your Committee having thus stated the general purport of the Bill which has been prepared under their superintendence beg in conclusion to express their hope that it may receive the approbation of this meeting and of the Parish at large.

THE REPORT of the SELECT VESTRY OF ST. MARGARET, For the Year ending March 22, 1834.

In resigning their delegated authority, and passing their Accounts, the Select Vestry have great pleasure in stating that the parish is at length out of debt. (In the published Abstract of Accounts, the Parish appeared to be £433 17s. 11d. in debt; but this being only an Abstract of the Cash Account, it did not include Levies due, but uncollected, to the amount of £650, and other sums due to the Parish, which, if taken into the account, would have left a balance in its favour of £470.) The Attorney's Bills have been paid, debts of several years standing have been discharged, and the money advanced by many of the Parishioners for obtaining the new Act, has been returned to them; the rate-payers may in future, therefore, reasonably expect a considerable reduction in the Poor Rates.

The Select Vestry cannot but congratulate their fellow-parishioners on the restoration and continuance of peace in the Parish, and on the good feeling that now exists in its executive department. Vestry-men and Overseers now act together with the greatest cordiality, and though the Vestry is composed of individuals belonging to various religious denominations, and of different politics, party motives have not influenced their decisions; and in the choice of the servants of the Parish, fitness for the situation has been the sole object they have had in view; and the Select Vestry are convinced, from the experience they have already had, that in the management of the affairs of the Parish, all interests are best promoted by the total exclusion of party considerations, whether religious or political.

St Mary's Select Vestry Minutes

At a Meeting of the Select Vestry held at the poor house January 12 1824 by Special Notice.
Ordered That a checque be given for Forty pounds for payment of the poor for the Ensuing week.

The letter of Mr Secretary peel on the abstract of the amended Poor Law Bill as addressed to the Church wardens and overseers being laid before the Meeting:—

Resolved That an answer be prepared and that the Church wardens and overseers be requested with the assistance of any Gentlemen of this Vestry to draw up a Letter addressed to Mr Secretary peel objecting to the bill altogether and lay the Same before this Vestry at thier Next Meeting.

Oderd That this Vestry do adjourn to Monday the 19th Inst. at 6 oclock in the evening.

Joseph Chamberlain

At a Meeting of The Select Vestry held at the poor house January 26th 1824.

Resolved That the letter brought forward before the Select Vestry this evening in answer to Mr Peel's Letter on account of the Abstract Poors Law Bill be adopted, and a Copy of it be inserted in the Minutes.

Orderd That a check for Forty Pounds be given for the payment of the poor for the ensuing Week.

Orderd That this Vestry do adjourn to Monday Evening Next the 2nd February at 6 oclock.

William Haywood

We the Churchwardens and Overseers of the Poor of the Parish of St Mary in Leicester beg to acknowledge the Receipt of Mr Secretary Peel's polite Communication & to state the following objections to the proposed Bill for the Amendment of the Laws relating to the Settlement of the Poor.

The first Objection which occurs to us, is, that the proposed Bill if passed into a Law, would be a grievous Breach of public faith and would inflict a permanent and irreparable injury upon every description of real Property within the Limits of Manufacturing and Commercial Districts and Parishes. Houses and Lands in these Districts have been purchased upon the faith and well grounded expectation that no hasty or sweeping Alteration should be made in Laws which have regulated the affairs of the Poor for nearly 250 years. We submit that not only will such an hasty and sweeping Alteration be made if the proposed Bill be passed, but that the general principles upon which the Poor Laws of England were framed will be deserted, and the anomaly will be created of the greater portion of the Acts of Elizabeth and Charles still subsisting while the Principles upon which they were passed are exploded. It never was the intention of either of these Acts that the Poor of several Districts should be congregated into one Mass in any particular District and maintained or employed by the sole aid of that District; on the contrary, the Act of Charles contemplating the possibility of populous Districts being unable to maintain or employ the

306

Poor coming into them attempted to provide for their Dispersion in the adjacent Country in cases of Emergency (13 & 14 Chas. 2 C. 12). We trust we shall be able to shew, that the intended Bill is framed at direct variance with these principles and therefore, that if the Acts in question are to be retained, A Measure ought not to be engrafted upon them so contrary to their intention and spirit & which would have the effect of applying their Provisions to populous parts of the Empire, and abrogating them as to others less populous and therefore more capable of giving effect to them.

Our Second Objection, is, that the proposed Bill would be the absolute Ruin of certain Parishes in large Towns. We conceive that this would be the case with respect to the Parish with which we are connected, and we earnestly intreat the attention of Mr Secretary Peel to the following Statement. The Population of the Parish of St Mary in Leicester is about 7000 and the Parish contains:

			No.
Houses not exceeding	£5 per Annum Rental	845*
do	do	£10 per Annum Rental	183
do	do	£15 per Annum Rental	62
do	do	£20 per Annum Rental	20
do	do	£30 per Annum Rental	36
			1146

* N.B. Not one half of the Rates due from these can be obtained & they do not come within Mr Sturgis Bourne's Bill to rate the Landlords.

From this Statement it appears, that the Cheif Burthen of the Poors Rate necessarily falls upon the Land in the Parish and upon the higher description of Houses the proportion of which bears no comparison to the No. of Tenements in the Parish or to its population. Should the Bill be adopted we are confident it would have the effect of making Parishes similarly situated with our own nothing more nor less than large Workhouses; for the adjacent Country Parishes would immediately either purchase or rent small Houses within Parishes under the progressive operation of the Act. Houses of this description have already been taken by County Parishes for the purposes stated. This consideration is the more annoying, when it is recollected that a great majority of these small Houses contribute nothing to our Rates while they occasion our Parish expence in Bastardies and afford means of injury from the Country—consequences directly contrary to the intention of the Laws which compel relief. We contemplate that one principal ruinous effect of the proposed Bill, if passed, will be, the

Accumulation in our Parish of the Labourers of the surrounding Villages who will be thrown upon us for relief in Sickness or old age (vide our first objection on the other side of the sheet). Should the Bill be carried, we cannot contemplate less than £100 per week under our present Circumstances; Whereas our present payments are only about £30 per Week; and should a state of things occur similar to the Seasons of 1818–9, When our Payments were £100 and upwards per week, we conceive a weekly sum of £400 would not be sufficient to meet our Exigencies upon the Bill taking complete effect. Under such Circumstances what would the Land and higher rate of Houses be worth, and who would occupy either the one or the other.

The third Objection which strikes us, is, that the Bill would operate very partially, even in large Towns, In this Place it would benefit some Districts while it would ruin others. We beg to offer the following Statement in elucidation. The Parish of St Martin in Leicester is one of the most opulent in the place; in it reside a large proportion of the professional Men and wealthy Tradesmen. This Parish is thickly built upon—in the centre of the Town—and so encompassed with other Buildings as to be incapable of enlarging its number of Houses to any extent. Indeed so limited are its means of Accommodation, that it has been under the necessity of renting Houses for its Poor in the adjoining Parishes. We beg to refer you to the following Comparative Statement of the Houses in St Martin's and St Mary's Parishes and of their Rentals.

			St Martins	St Mary's
Houses not exceeding £ 5 per Annum Rental			159	845
do	do	£10	138	183
do	do	£15	125	62
do	do	£20	60	20
do	do	£20 & upwards	113	36
			595	1146

Thus it appears that in the Parish of St Martin's, not only are the No. of Poor comparatively few to those in St Mary, but the burthen of maintaining them is pretty equally apportioned amongst the Property, at the same time that effectual means are furnished to guard against any material increase of Poor except one occasioned by Servitude &c. Would it not be extremely unjust, that a Parish circumstanced like this should in process of Time be enabled to get rid of its Poor altogether, by sending them to reside in an adjoining and heavily burthened Parish. Would not this be the case should the proposed Bill be carried. We beg also to state, that we are unfortunately bounded on one side by an extra parochial Place whose Inhabitants have successfully resisted the Appointment of Officers and whose Sick and Poor having no one to whom they can apply, almost always fall casual upon us as their next neighbours.

Our fourth Objection to the proposed Bill, is, that it would occasion much litigation and thus defeat one of its avowed principal purposes. In making this Objection, we refer to the extreme uncertainty of the words in which such poor Person or Persons shall have been domiciled or resident principally each year &c. &c. which perpetually occurs in the Bill. Numberless questions would arise on these, & wherever a defective Residence was proved during the periods prescribed by the Bill, the old Law of settlement would come into play. We are of opinion in Parishes where any thing like management has taken place, the Law expences have not been so considerable as have been generally supposed. In this Parish, with a population of 7000 our Law Expences for the last four years have been as under.

	£	s	d
In 1820	77	1	8
,, 1821	16	3	4
,, 1822	19	14	8
,, 1823	26	15	0

In preceding years the Expences were certainly much more, and we attribute this diminution in a great degree to the Institution of a Select Vestry within our Parish, and feel very grateful for the politic and useful Act which gave rise to such method of conducting Parochial Affairs.

We feel convinced, that the Bill, if passed, would sooner or later be attended with a ruinous Re-action upon the general Property of the Country. The Manufacturing and populous Districts could not long sustain the pressure, and the evil of Removals would only give way to one of a more alarming, More extensive, and more afflicting Nature. From some Sources or others the Poor must be maintained in Seasons of Difficulty or Embarrassment, and after the most minute and attentive Consideration which we have been enabled to give the Subject; We are decidedly of opinion, that the Laws as at present subsisting, if properly Executed are fully competent to meet the Justice of the case, and that considering the length of Time they have existed and the Improvements made in them, We deem them the best which can be adopted under the endless Variety of conflicting interests and opinion attendant upon them.

We are
    Your Most Obedient
      Humble Servants
        Joseph Chamberlain⎫
        John Baxter   ⎬ Churchwardens

John Deakins ⎫
R. Rawson ⎪ Overseers
William Haywood ⎬
Thomas Wood ⎭

St Marys Leicester

N.B. This is a Copy of what was sent to Mr Peel, by Post, January 30th 1824.

At a Meeting of the Select Vestry held at the poor House May 3d 1824.
Ordered   That a cheque be given to Mr Haywood for Thirty pounds for the payment of the poor for the ensuing week.

That Mr Baxter Mr Frisby & Mr Hunt be Requested to Meet the Committee of St Martins Respecting the Borough Rates agreeable to the following application and Letter.

Gentlemen

At a Vestry Meeting of St Martins yesterday a Committee was appointed to take the Necessary Steps for obtaining information as to the due application of the Borough Rates, & at a Meeting of the Committe this day, I am requested to Make application to the Members of the Select Vestries and the parish officers of the Borough in order to invite thier coopperation with Such Committee in the objects delegated to it. As the Resolutions of the Vestry are printed in the Leicester Journal, and will appear in the Chronicle of to Morrow it is unnecessary to Send yo a copy. The St Martins Committee earnestly hope that each parish will Convene a Meeting by due Notice on Sunday Next for appointing delegates that the attendance of Such delegates is requested at St Martins Workhouse on Friday next the 7th of May at 11 Oclock in the forenoon when Material bisisness will be brought forwards.

I an Gentlemen
Your Most obedient Servant
April 30 1824   J. Bankart   Chairman

Resolved unanimously That Mr Sibson be requested to Collect the poor Rate, the Borough Rate, the Church Rate and no other.
Ordered That this Vestry do adjourn to Monday next May 10th at 7 oclock.

At a Select Vestry Meeting held at the Poor House of St Mary's the tenth day of May 1824.
Ordered that a Checque be given to Mr Haywood for payment of the Poor for the Sum of Forty Pounds for the ensuing week.
Resolved that the thanks of this Vestry be given to the Gentlemen who attended St Martins Committee agreeably to the Resolutions copied under-

neath but this Meeting cannot agree to any payment being made out of the Poors Rate as they consider such payment would be a misapplication.

7th May 1824

At a Meeting of the Committe.

Mr Forrester and Mr Hudson attended as delegates for the parish of All Saints.

Mr Stokes (Churchwarden) Mr Sheen and Mr Gardiner as delegates for the parish of St Nicholes.

Mr Baxter (Churchwarden) Mr Frisby (Churchwarden) elect and Mr Hunt overseer of the poor, delegates from the Select Vestry of St Marys. A Letter was read from Mr Jones one of the Overseers of St Margerets, Stating that they had no knowledge of the invitation to send delegates to this Meeting in time to Comply with the request.

Resolved   That it is expedient that the question whether the Inhabitants have or have not a right to inspect the orders of the Magistrates for the payment of Moncy out of the Borough rates be Judicially decided, and that in order to obtain Such decision an application be forthwith made on behalf of the Inhabitants to the Court of Kings Bench for a Mandamus.

Mr Dalby having Stated to this Committee that on account of his private connections it would be more agreeable to his feelings not to act professionally in the proposed proceedings. It was therefore resolved that Messrs. Miles Alston & Miles be employed as Soliciters to conduct the intended Buisness.

That in order to faciliate any points upon which the Soliciters may Stand in Need of Communication with the Committee the following Gentlemen be appointed a Sub Committee and any two of them Shall be Competent to act on any emergency.

Mr J. Bankart	Mr Hudson	Mr T. Lockwood
M. Baxter	Mr Rogers	Mr Frisby
Mr Colston	Mr Stokes	Mr Forrester
Mr Gardiner		

That the expences Shall be paid by the Several parishes of St Martins All Saints St Nicholes and St Marys in proportion to thier respective payments to the Borough Rate but as to the parish of St Marys as the poor rates extends beyond the Borough, thier Quota can only be raised by Voluntary Contributions and in case of any defalcation in St Marys Quota the deficiency Shall be made good by the other three parishes.

Resolved that the parish of St Margerets be Solicited to Cooperate on the same terms as St Marys.

John Bankart   Chairman

Resolved That this Meeting do adjourn to Monday evening Next May 17th at 7 oclock.

St Nicholas' Vestry Minutes

May 6th 1824

At a Vestry Meeting of the Parishioners of St Nickolas held this day for the purpose of taking into consideration the propriety of uniting with the other Parishes in this Town in the Investigation of the expenditure of the Borough Rate, Mr Thomas Stokes (Chairman) it was resolved

That this Meeting fully approve of the resolutions entered into by the Parish of St Martins and feel it their duty to unite in any measure that may be suggested by their Committee.

That a proportion of the expence of Such Investigation of the borough rate as this Committee may adjudge shall be paid out of the Poor Rates of this Parish.

That the Four following Gentlemen be appointed to represent this Parish in their Committee Mr Wilding Mr Stokes Mr William Gardiner and Mr Samuel Sheen and that two of them be competent to act.

BOROUGH RATES

M

Leicester Journal, 23rd May, 1817.

BOROUGH OF LEICESTER.

ABSTRACT OF THE TREASURER's ACCOUNT OF RECEIPTS AND EXPENDITURE,

For One Year, ending at Epiphany Session, 1817.

RECEIPTS.

	£.	s.	d.
BALANCE of last Year's Account in the Treasurer's Hands .	755	6	0
Borough Rates received Of the Receiver General .	1590	12	0
of Customs repayment for 52 Corn Returns	5	4	0

EXPENDITURE.

	£.	s.	d.
PAID Costs of Prosecutions of Felons, and Expences of apprehending Offenders and conveying them to Prison Expences of the Gaol, viz:—	306	0	5
Bread and Clothing for the Prisoners, Medicines, Repairs, Painting and Lime-washing, Levies and Taxes, conveying Transports to the Hulks, &c. . Salaries, viz:—	362	4	4½
Chaplain's, Treasurer's, Chief Constable's, Gaoler's, Inspector's of Weights and Measures, and incidental Expances .	242	4	9
Expences of Maintenance and passing of Vagrants .	133	0	4
For Returns of the Prices of Corn	6	10	0
To the Petty and Special Constables, for keeping Nightly Watch, and for attendance on several occasions, by order of the Magistrates .	176	5	6
For Constables' Staves .	17	18	4
For Coroner's Inquests .	27	2	0

	£	s	d
For Returns relative to the Expence of Maintenance of the Poor, &c.	4	10	0
For Repairs of Bridges	2	0	6
For Damage done by Rioters . . .	35	9	7
Towards Costs of Action respecting the County Rate lately made upon the South Fields, which had hitherto been rated to the Borough	200	0	0
Re-paid the Parish Officers of St. Mary so much of the Borough Rate paid by them as is now decided to belong to the County	48	0	0
Towards erecting Rooms at the Gaol for employing the Prisoners	531	16	1½
For Printing and Stationary . . .	3	7	6
Balance in the Treasurer's Hands . .	254	12	7
	£2351	2	0

£2351   2   0

The Accounts, of which the above is an Abstract, were audited by us,

THOMAS MILLER, MAYOR.
M. MILES.

315

Leicester Journal, 13th March, 1818.

BOROUGH OF LEICESTER.

ABSTRACT OF THE TREASURER'S ACCOUNT OF RECEIPTS AND EXPENDITURE,

For the Year ending at Epiphany Session—1818.

RECEIPTS.

	£.	s.	d.
BALANCE of last Year's Account in the Treasurer's Hands .	254	12	7
Borough Rates received .	1650	19	0
Of the Receiver General of Customs, re-payment for 49 Corn Returns .	4	18	0
Of Mr. M. Payne, late Treasurer, for Militia purposes, being a sum which had been deposited in his hands, to meet the current Payments, on account of the Militia when embodied .	100	0	0

EXPENDITURE.

	£.	s.	d.
PAID—Costs of Prosecutions of Felons, and Expences of apprehending Offenders, and conveying them to Prison .	284	13	11
Expences of the Gaol & House of Correction. viz:— Bread and Clothing for the Prisoners, Medicines, Repairs, Painting and Lime-washing, Levies and Taxes, conveying Transported Felons to the Hulks, &c. .	627	17	2
Salaries—viz:— Chaplain's, Treasurer's, Chief Constable's, Gaoler's, Inspector's of Weights and Measures, and Incidental Expences .	285	16	6
Expence of Maintenance and passing of Vagrants .	114	11	1
To Families of Non-commissioned Officers of Militia, employed on the Recruiting Service, and Treasurer's Salary .	28	19	0
For Returns of the Prices of Corn .	5	4	0
To the Petty and Special Constables, for keeping Nightly Watch part of the Year, and for Attendance on several Occasions, by Order of the Magistrates .	151	3	9
For Coroner's Inquests .	21	16	0
Remainder of Bills, &c. for erecting Room at the Gaol to employ the Prisoners .	193	6	11

To the Clerk of the Peace of the County, for taxed Costs, on the
Trial respecting the County Rate, made on the South Fields } . . . 200 0 0

Sundry small Payments, amounting to 33 7 2

Balance in the Treasurer's Hands 63 14 1

£2010 9 7

£2010 9 7

The Accounts, of which the above is an Abstract, were audited by us,

JOHN GREGORY, MAYOR.
M. MILES.

317

Leicester Journal, 22nd January, 1819.

BOROUGH OF LEICESTER.

ABSTRACT of the Treasurer's Account of Receipts and Expenditure, for the Year ending at Epiphany Session, 1819.

RECEIPTS.

	£.	s.	d.
Balance of last year's Account in the Treasurer's hands	63	14	1
Borough Rates received	1554	1	0
Of the Receiver General of Customs repayment for Corn returns . . .	5	0	0
Balance due to the Treasurer . .	85	17	8

EXPENDITURE.

	£.	s.	d.
Paid Costs of Prosecutions, expenses of apprehending Offenders, and conveying them to Prison, and other charges .	473	9	9
Expenses of the Gaol and House of Correction, viz:— Bread and clothing for the Prisoners, medicines, repairs, painting and lime-washing, levies and taxes, conveying transported Felons to the Hulks, &c. &c.	560	4	5
Salaries, viz:— Chaplains, Treasurer's, Chief Constable's, Gaoler's, Inspector's of weights and measures, and incidental expenses	275	16	1
Expenses of maintenance & passing of Vagrants	117	15	0
For returns of the price of Corn . .	5	4	0
To the Petty and Special Constables for keeping nightly watch part of the year, and for attendance on several special occasions by order of the Magistrates .	77	10	1

318

To the Petty Constables, & a large extra
number of Special Constables for atten-
dance at the time of the Elections   .   114 19   6

For Coroners' inquests   .   .   .   20   8   0
For Constables' staves, printing, advertise-
ments, and other incidental payments   63   5 11

£1708 12   9

£1708 12   9

The Accounts, of which the above is an Abstract,
were audited by

JAMES BANKART, Mayor.
M. MILES.
JOHN GREGORY.

319

Leicester Journal, 21st January, 1820.

BOROUGH OF LEICESTER.

ABSTRACT of the Treasurer's Account, of Receipts and Expenditure, for the Year ending at the Epiphany Sessions, 1820.

RECEIPTS.

	£.	s.	d.
BOROUGH RATES received . . .	1466	10	6
Of the Receiver General of Customs re-payment for Corn Returns . . .	5	4	0
Balance due to the Treasurer . . .	393	19	11

EXPENDITURE.

	£.	s.	d.
PAID Costs of Prosecutions, Expences of apprehending Offenders, and conveying them to Prison, and other Charges .	405	16	9
Expences of the Gaol and House of Correction, viz:— Bread and Clothing for the Prisoners, Medicines, Painting and Lime-washing, Levies and Taxes, conveying Transported Felons to the Hulks, &c. &c. .	461	3	1
For Alterations and extra Repairs at the Gaol	309	19	1
Salaries, viz:— Chaplain's, Treasurer's, Chief Constable's, Gaoler's, Inspectors of Weight & Measures, and incidental Expences .	288	19	6
Expence of maintenance and passing of Vagrants, up to the time of Establishing the Vagrant Office .	57	0	0
For Returns of the price of Corn .	5	4	0
To the Petty and Special Constables, for keeping Nightly Watch part of the Year, and for Attendance on several special occasions, by order of the Magistrates .	153	5	0

	£	s.	d.
For Coroner's Inquests	24	18	0
For Constables' Staves, Printing, Advertisements, & other incidental Expences .	73	11	4
Balance of last Year's Account, due to the Treasurer	85	17	8
	£1865	14	5

The Accounts, of which the above is an Abstract, were audited by us,

Thomas Miller.
John Gregory.

£1865 14 5

M*

BOROUGH OF LEICESTER.

Leicester Journal, 16th February, 1821.

Abstract of the Treasurer's Account of Receipts and Expenditure, for the Year ending at Epiphany Session, 1821.

RECEIPTS.

	£.	s.	d.
Borough Rates received . . .	1887	19	6
Of the Receiver General of Customs, repayment for Corn Returns . . .	5	0	0

EXPENDITURE.

	£.	s.	d.
PAID Costs of Prosecutions, Expenses of apprehending Offenders, and conveying them to Prison, and other charges . .	222	18	10
Expenses of the Gaol and House of Correction, viz:— Bread and Clothing for the Prisoners, Medicines, Levies and Taxes, conveying transported Felons to the Hulks, &c. &c. .	445	8	8
For Alterations, Painting, and Lime-washing and Repairs at the Gaol . . .	100	11	11
Salaries, viz:— Chaplains', Treasurer's, Chief Constable's, Gaoler's, Inspectors of Weights and Measures, and incidental Expenses .	285	8	6
Rewards for apprehending, and Expense of passing Vagrants . . .	6	10	6
For Returns of the Price of Corn . .	5	4	0
To the Petty and Special Constables, for keeping nightly watch part of the year, and for attendance on several special occasions, by order of the Magistrates . . .	231	11	2
For Coroner's Inquests . . .	42	11	6

	£	s	d
For Printing, Advertisements, and other incidental Payments	18	4	11
Balance of last Year's Account due to the Treasurer	393	19	11
For collecting Rates	42	0	0
Balance of this Account in the Treasurer's hands	98	9	7
	£1892	19	6

£1892 19 6

The Accounts, of which this is an
Abstract, were audited by us,

ISAAC LOVELL, Mayor.
JOHN GREGORY.

Leicester Journal, 3rd May, 1822.

BOROUGH OF LEICESTER.

Abstract of the Treasurer's Account of Receipts and Expenditure for the year ending at Epiphany Session 1822.

RECEIPTS. &c.

	£.	s.	d.
Balance of last year's Account in the Treasurer's hands . .	98	9	7
Borough Rates received . .	1867	4	6
Of the Receiver General of Customs repayment for Corn Returns . .	5	2	0
Balance due to the Treasurer . .	90	19	8

EXPENDITURE.

	£.	s.	d.
Paid Costs of Prosecutions, expences of apprehending Offenders and conveying them to Prison, and other charges .	306	9	4
Expence of the Gaol and House of Correction viz. Bread and Clothing for the Prisoners, Medicines, Levies and Taxes, &c. .	420	0	6
For conveying transported Felons to the Hulks	220	0	0
For alterations, painting, Lime Washing and repairs at the Gaol and House of Correction .	165	19	10
Salaries, viz. Chaplains, Treasurers Chief Constables, Gaoler's, Keeper of House of Correction, Inspectors of Weights and Measures, and incidental expences .	441	3	6
For conveyances of the Gaol and House of Correction from E. Wigley Esq. surviving Trustee	42	13	6
Town Clerk's bill of fees and for business done relating to the Borough Rate &c. .	122	17	4
Rewards for apprehending and expence of passing Vagrants .	10	8	0

	£	s.	d.
For returns of the price of corn . . .	5	4	0
To the petty and special Constables for keeping nightly watch part of the year and for their attendance at Assizes and Sessions and on several special occasions by order of the Magistrates	166	2	0
For Coroners Inquests	53	8	6
For printing, Advertisements and other incidental payments	46	1	3
For collecting Rates . . .	61	8	0
	£2061	15	9

The Accounts of which the above is an Abstract were audited by

Geo. Ireland, MAYOR.
John Gregory
James Bankart
Robert Johnson
Isaac Lovell.

325

Leicester Journal, 28th March, 1823.

BOROUGH OF LEICESTER.

Abstract of the Treasurer's Account of Receipts and Expenditure for the Year ending at Epiphany Session 1823.

RECEIPTS. &c.

	£.	s.	d.
Borough Rates received . . .	1981	2	6
Balance due to the Treasurer . . .	30	11	7

EXPENDITURE:

	£.	s.	d.
Balance of last year's Account due to the Treasurer . . .	90	19	8
Paid Costs of Prosecutions, expences of apprehending Offenders and conveying them to Prison, and other charges .	422	7	4
Expences of the Gaol and House of Correction (viz.) Bread and Clothing for the Prisoners, Medicines, Levies and Taxes &c.	304	8	3
For conveying Transported Felons to the Hulks .	160	0	0
For alterations, Painting, Lime Washing, &c. repairs at the Goal and House of Correction	112	5	9
Salaries (viz.) Chaplains, Treasurers Chief Constables, Gaoler's, Keeper of House of Correction, Inspectors of Weights and Measures, and incidental expences .	432	7	6
Expence of Vagrants and Rewards for Apprehending .	97	14	6
For Returns of the Price of Corn .	5	4	0

326

To the petty and special Constables for keeping nightly watch part of the Year, and for their attendance at Assizes and Sessions, and on several special occasions by order of the Magistrates . . . 131 14 5

For Coroners Inquests . . . 43 16 0

For Printing and Advertising . . . 11 7 0

For collecting Rates . . . 60 14 6

For Paving at and near the Public Bridges belonging to the Borough . . . 110 9 7

For Lamps and Lighting at the Bridges and Gaol . . . 28 5 7

£2011 14 1

£2011 14 1

The Accounts, of which the above is an Abstract, were audited by

Thos. Cook, MAYOR
Robt. Johnson
Isaac Lovell
Geo. Ireland.

N.B. The Magistrates request that all Tradesmen and others, having demands upon the BOROUGH RATE, will send their Bills and Accounts to the Treasurer quarterly previous to each Session, that they may be examined and discharged.

327

Leicester Journal, 14th May, 1824.

BOROUGH OF LEICESTER.

ANNUAL Abstract of the Receipts and Expenditure of the Treasurer of the Borough of Leicester, published pursuant to 55th Geo. 3d, Cap. 51.

THE TREASURER.

Dr. RECEIPTS.	£.	s.	d.
TO Borough Rates received .	2154	7	3
—Cash received of the Inspectors of Weights and Measures, being the amount of Fines imposed by the Magistrates upon persons convicted of having deficient weights and measures in their possession .	52	10	0
—Balance due to the Treasurer .	427	17	9

Cr. EXPENDITURE.	£.	s.	d.	£.	s.	d.
By Balance of last year's account due to the Treasurer .				30	11	7
—Repairs of Gaol and House of Correction, Iron work, painting whitewashing &c. .				145	18	6
Expences of Gaol and House of Correction viz:—						
—Gaoler's Salary and for Turn-key .	225	0	0			
—Keeper of House of Correction Salary and for assistant .	120	0	0			
—Chaplain of Gaol and House of Correction .	60	0	0			
—Surgeon & Apothecary for Medicines .	33	14	5			
—Bread for Prisoners .	185	4	3			
—Clothing & bedding &c. for ditto .	144	7	9			
—Levies and Taxes on Goal and House of Correction .	23	5	7			
—Conveying transports to the Hulks .	86	17	4			
—Incidents .	62	18	11			
				941	8	3

	£	s	d
Expences of apprehending Felons, conveying to prison, Costs of Prosecutions by orders of Court, Transport orders &c.	532	6	6
Sessions business and expences	161	17	0
Clerk of the Peace for miscellaneous business	64	12	10
Clerk of Assize, Marshall and Cryer, by orders	34	0	0
Coroner's Inquests	28	7	6
Repairs of Bridges, Paving and incidents	128	2	11
Inspector of Market for Corn Returns	5	4	0
Inspectors of Weights and Measures and incidents	42	19	0
Convictions, Commitments & Prosecutions of Vagrants, maintenance and passing, &c.	166	6	6
Advertisements, Printing and Stationary	35	17	10
Chief Constable's Salary, and for incidents	12	8	6
Collecting Rates	10	13	3
Chief and petty Constables, by order	203	9	6
Miscellaneous	69	11	4
Treasurer's Salary	21	0	0
	£2634	15	0

£2634 15 0

The Accounts, of which the above is an Abstract, were audited by

THOS. YATES, Mayor,
ROBT. JOHNSON,
ISAAC LOVELL,
THOS. COOK.

329

Leicester Journal, 22nd April, 1825.

BOROUGH OF LEICESTER.

ABSTRACT of the Treasurer's Accounts for the Borough of Leicester, of Receipts and Expenditure for the year ending Epiphany Session, 1825. Published pursuant to 55th GEORGE III, C. 51.

Dr.   THE TREASURER.   Cr.

RECEIPTS.

	£.	s.	d.
TO Borough Rates received, viz. £600, £600, £600, £800 .	2600	0	0
—Cash received of the Inspectors of Weights and Measures, being the amount of fines imposed by the Magistrates upon persons convicted of having deficient weights & measures in their possession .	45	5	0
—Cash arising from the sale of defective weights and measures . . .	4	2	4

EXPENDITURE.

	£.	s.	d.		£.	s.	d.
BY Balance of last year's Account due to the Treasurer . . .					427	17	9
—Repairs of Gaol and House of Correction, ironwork, painting, limewashing, &c. .					115	12	10
—Expences of Goal and House of Correction, viz							
—Gaoler's Salary and for Turnkey .	250	0	0				
—Matron's Salary .	20	0	0				
—Keeper of House of Correction's Salary, & for Assistant	120	0	0				
—Chaplain of Gaol & House of Correction .	60	0	0				
—Surgeon and Apothecary for medecines .	49	4	6				
—Bread for Prisoners .	192	6	11				
—Clothing. Bedding, &c. for ditto .	74	2	9				
—Levies and taxes on Gaol and House of Correction	25	8	3				
—Conveying Transports to the Hulks .	51	1	6				
					842	3	11

	£	s	d
Expences of apprehending Felons, conveying to prison, costs of prosecutions, by orders of Court, Transport orders, &c.	286	14	2
Sessions business, and expences incident thereto	87	8	10
Clerk of the Peace for miscellaneous business	179	7	4
Clerk of Assize, Marshall and Cryer by orders	17	9	8
Coroner's Inquests	33	5	6
Repairs of Bridges, paving and incidents	57	19	6
Inspector of Market for Corn Returns	5	4	0
Inspectors of Weights and Measures, and incidents	64	10	9
Convictions, commitments, and prosecutions of Vagrants, maintenance and passing, &c.	146	18	0
Advertisements, printing, and stationary	47	5	6
Chief Constable's salary, and for incidents	11	0	6
Collecting Rates	13	3	0
Chief and Petty Constables by order	216	6	6
Miscellaneous	3	10	0
Treasurer's Salary	21	0	0
Balance in Treasurer's hands	72	9	7
	£2649	7	4

The Accounts, of which the above is an Abstract, were audited by

CHARLES COLEMAN, Mayor.
ISAAC LOVELL,
GEORGE IRELAND.
THOMAS YATES.

331

Leicester Journal, 16th February, 1827.   BOROUGH OF LEICESTER.

ABSTRACT of the Treasurer's Accounts for the Borough of Leicester, of Receipts and Expenditure, for the Year ending Epiphany Sessions, 1827.

PUBLISHED PURSUANT TO 55th. GEO. 3d. c. 51.

The Treasurer.

Dr.   RECEIPTS.

	£.	s.	d.
To balance of last Account in the Treasurer's hands . .	186	0	8
To Borough Rates received, viz.			
Ordered at Epiphany Session 800			
Ordered at Easter Session 800			
Ordered at Midsummer Session 1200 }	2800	0	0
Cash received of the Inspectors of Weights and Measures, being the amount of Fines imposed by the Magistrates upon persons convicted of having deficient weights and measures in their possession . .	48	15	2
Balance due to the Treasurer . .	445	5	10½

EXPENDITURE.   Cr.

	£.	s.	d.		£.	s.	d.
Repairs of Gaol and House of Correction, iron-work, painting, lime-washing, &c. .					103	0	9½
Expences of Gaol and House of Correction, viz—							
Gaoler's Salary and for Turnkey .	250	0	0				
Matron's Salary . .	20	0	0				
Keeper of House of Correction's Salary and for Assistant .	120	0	0				
Chaplain of Gaol & House of Correction .	60	0	0				
Surgeon and Apothecary for Medicines .	34	0	7				
Bread for Prisoners .	201	19	7				
Clothing, Bedding, &c. for Ditto .	102	17	7				
Levies and Taxes on Gaol & House of Correction .	42	6	4¼				
Conveying Transports to the Hulks .	43	9	0		874	13	1½
Costs of Prosecutions . .					468	11	10
Repairs of Guardhouse . .					8	0	6

	£	s.	d.
Clerk of Assize, Marshall, Cryer, and Associate	45	9	10
Coroners Inquests	18	13	4
Repairs of Bridges, paving and incidents	211	2	3½
Inspector of Market for Corn Returns	7	16	0
Inspector of Weights and Measures and incidents	60	14	3
Maintenance and passing of Vagrants	120	0	0
Advertisements, Printing, and Stationary	8	11	0
Collecting Rates	13	17	6
Chief and Petty Constables	288	12	3
A new Fire Engine, with Pipes, &c.	122	15	6
For Standard Weights and Measures according to the New Act of Parliament	121	3	0
For Constables Staves	80	14	0
The High Constable, in part discharge of Special Order for extraordinary expences	700	0	0
For repairs of damages done by Rioters	63	18	0
Clerk of the Peace, Fees &c.	120	8	6
The Treasurer, 2 years Salary	42	0	0
	£3480	1	8½

February 9th. 1827,
Examined and allowed the foregoing Abstract,

HENRY WOOD, Mayor.
THOS. COOK.
THOS. YATES.
THOS. MARSTON.

Leicester Journal, 25th April, 1828.

BOROUGH OF LEICESTER.

ABSTRACT of the Treasurer's Accounts for the Borough of Leicester of Receipts and Expenditure, for the year ending Epiphany Sessions, 1828.

Published pursuant to 55th George 3d. c. 51.

THE TREASURER.

Dr.

RECEIPTS.

	£.	s.	d.
To Borough Rates received, viz— 4 Rates of £1200 each	4800	0	0
Cash received of the Inspectors of Weights and Measures, being the amount of Fines imposed by the Magistrates upon persons convicted of having deficient weights and Measures in their possession . . .	19	6	1
Balance due to the Treasurer . . .	2	13	11

Cr.

EXPENDITURE.

	£.	s.	d.	£.	s.	d.
By Balance of last year's Account .				445	5	10
Repairs of Gaol and House of Correction, Iron-work, Painting, Lime-washing, &c. . .				82	7	8
Expences of Gaol and House of Correction, viz.—						
Gaoler's Salary and for Turnkey .	250	0	0			
Matron's Salary . . .	20	0	0			
Keeper of House of Correction's Salary and for Assistant .	120	0	0			
Chaplain of Gaol and House of Correction .	60	0	0			
Surgeon and Apothecary for Medicines . .	35	5	0			
Bread for Prisoners . .	230	17	3			
Clothing, Bedding, &c. for do .	165	4	1			
Levies and Taxes on Gaol and House of Correction .	42	8	2			
Conveying transports to the Hulks	114	11	3			
				1038	5	9

	£	s.	d.
Costs of Prosecutions including prosecutions against County Gaoler and Treasurer .	891	16	4
Repair of Guardhouse .	9	2	7
Clerk of Assize, Marshall, Cryer and Associate .	19	15	10
Coroner's Inquests .	45	5	6
Repairs of Bridges, Paving, and Incidents .	106	14	6
Inspector of Market for Corn Returns .	10	8	0
Inspector of Weights and Measures and Incidents .	49	18	6
Repair of Fire Engine .	10	13	5
Maintenance and passing of Vagrants .	173	4	1
Advertisements, printing, and Stationary .	46	10	6
Constables and Police Expences .	370	11	3
The High Constable, remainder of special order for extraordinary expences .	643	0	0
Jury Box, Prisoners Box, and other preparations for Assizes & Sessions .	140	19	7
On Account of purchase for New Gaol and Interest thereof .	520	4	0
Clerk of the Peace, Fees, Returns, &c. .	173	0	8
Miscellaneous .	23	16	0
The Treasurer, one year's salary .	21	0	0
	£4822	0	0

April 24th, 1828—Examined and allowed the foregoing Abstract,

M. GREGORY, Mayor.
THOS. YATES.
THOS. MARSTON.

335

Leicester Journal, 8th May, 1829.

BOROUGH OF LEICESTER.

ABSTRACT of the Treasurer's Accounts for the Borough of Leicester, of Receipts and Expenditure, for the Year ending Epiphany Sessions, 1829, published pursuant to 55th Geo. 3d., c. 51.

The Treasurer.

RECEIPTS.

Dr.	£.	s.	d.
To Borough Rates received, viz. 4 rates at £1200 each	4800	0	0
Cash received of the Inspectors of Weights and Measures, being the amount of Fines imposed by the Magistrates upon persons convicted of having deficient weights and measures in their possession	6	19	7
By Rent of the land purchased for a New Gaol, to Michaelmas, 1827	22	0	0
By Cash received for fines imposed by the Magistrates for Assaults, &c,	2	9	0
By Cash received as a Deodand imposed by the Coroner's Inquest upon William Thorpe	2	0	0
By Cash received of C. Herbert, being in part of the purchase money of land on Welford Road, bought by the Borough, and re-sold to him	63	0	0
Interest thereon to Michaelmas	1	9	0

EXPENDITURE.

	£.	s.	d.		£.	s.	d.
By balance of last year's Account		2	13	11			
Repairs of Gaol and House of Correction, Iron-work, Painting, Lime-washing, &c.		128	15	1			
Expenses of Gaol and House of Correction, viz—							
Gaoler's Salary & for Turnkey	250	0	0				
Matron's Salary	20	0	0				
Keeper of House of Correction's Salary and for Assistant	120	0	0				
Chaplain of Gaol & House of Correction	60	0	0				
Surgeon and Apothecary for Medicines	43	11	9				
Bread for Prisoners	182	16	2				
Clothing, Bedding, &c. for ditto	92	19	0				
Levies and Taxes on Gaol and House of Correction	33	3	9				
Conveying transports to the hulks	89	14	11				
		892	5	7			

336

	£	s.	d.
Costs of Prosecutions and Law Expenses .	766	17	0
Clerk of Assize, Marshal, Crier, and Associate	25	11	6
Coroner's Inquests	31	3	0
Repairs of Bridges, paving, and incidents .	65	17	8
Inspector of Market for Corn Returns .	10	8	0
Inspector of Weights and Measures and Incidents	45	17	6
Maintenance and passing of vagrants .	135	5	5
Advertisements, printing, stationery, and miscellaneous	31	15	3
Constables and Police Expenses .	377	19	10
New Gaol Land payments . .	925	0	0
Parliamentary Returns . .	200	0	0
Clerk of the Peace, Bill of Fees, &c. .	185	18	8
The Treasurer one year's salary .	21	0	0
Balance in the Treasurer's hands .	1051	9	2
	£4897	17	7

£4897 17   7

April 30, 1829,—Examined and allowed the foregoing abstract,

JAS. RAWSON, Mayor.
THOS. MARSTON.
HENRY WOOD.
MD. GREGORY.

337

Leicester Journal, 7th May, 1830.

BOROUGH OF LEICESTER.

ABSTRACT OF THE TREASURER'S ACCOUNTS, FOR THE BOROUGH OF LEICESTER, OF RECEIPTS AND EXPENDITURE, FOR THE YEAR ENDING EPIPHANY SESSIONS, 1830,

Published pursuant to 55th Geo. III. cap. 51.

THE TREASURER.

Dr. RECEIPTS.

	£	s.	d.
To Balance of last account, in the Treasurer's hands . .	1,051	9	2
——Borough Rates received, viz. {£800, 800, 600, 600}	2,800	0	0
By Cash received for Fines imposed by the Magistrates for Assaults, &c. . .	7	19	9
——Cash received for Penalties imposed by the Magistrates for Offences against the Victuallers' License Act, .	5	10	0

EXPENDITURE. Cr.

	£	s.	d.
Repairs of Gaol and House of Correction, Iron-work, Painting, Lime-washing, &c. .	77	15	5
Expenses of Gaol and House of Correction, viz.—			
Gaoler's Salary, and for Turnkey, 250 0 0			
Matron's Salary . . 20 0 0			
Keeper of House of Correction's Salary, and for Assistant .	120	0	0
Chaplain of Gaol & House of Correction . .	60	0	0
Surgeon and Apothecary, for Medicines, . .	31	12	6
Bread for Prisoners, . .	241	12	9
Clothing, Bedding, &c. for ditto, 190 5 7			
Levies and Taxes on Gaol and House of Correction, . .	42	5	6

		£	s.	d.
Conveying Transports to the Hulks . . .		67	10	0
		1,023	6	4
Costs of Prosecutions, &c. . . .		947	15	4
Clerk of Assize, Marshal, Crier, and Associate .		15	4	6
Coroner's Inquests . .		52	4	2
Repairs of Bridges, Paving and Incidents .		14	18	0
Inspector of Market, for Corn Returns, .		10	8	0
Inspector of Weights and Measures, & Incidents, . . .		43	11	6
Maintenance and passing of Vagrants, .		166	12	10
Advertisements, Printing & Stationery, and Miscellanies, . .		32	19	6
Constables and Police Expenses, .		368	15	0
Repairs of Fire Engine, . .		13	16	2
Clerk of the Peace, Bill of Fees, &c. .		185	11	4
The Treasurer, One Year's Salary, .		21	0	0
Balance in the Treasurer's hands, .		891	0	10
		£3,864	18	11

£3,864 18 11

30th April, 1830.—Examined and allowed the foregoing Abstract.

ISAAC LOVELL, MAYOR,
THOMAS MARSTON,
MANSFIELD GREGORY,
JAMES RAWSON.

Leicester Journal, 15th April, 1831.

BOROUGH OF LEICESTER.

ABSTRACT of the TREASURER'S ACCOUNTS for the BOROUGH of LEICESTER, OF RECEIPTS AND EXPENDITURE,

For the Year ending Epiphany Sessions, 1831.
Published pursuant to 55th Geo. III. c. 51.

THE TREASURER.

Dr.	RECEIPTS.	£.	s.	d.
To Balance of last Account in the Treasurer's hands . . .		891	0	10
To Borough Rates received, exclusive of Gaol Rates, viz. { £400 600 600 600 }		2200	0	0
By Cash received for Fines imposed by the Magistrates upon persons having deficient weights and measures in their possession .		1	5	0

340

EXPENDITURE.					Cr. £. s. d.
Fitting up Gaol and House of Correction, Iron-work, Painting, Lime-washing, &c. .					292 18 9
Expenses of Gaol and House of Correction, viz.—	£.	s.	d.		
Gaoler's Salary . . .	250	0	0		
Turnkey, one quarter . .	13	0	0		
Matron's Salary . .	20	0	0		
Keeper of House of Correction's Salary . . .	120	0	0		
Turnkey . . .	17	0	0		
Surgeon and Apothecary, for Medicines . .	19	12	0		
Bread for Prisoners . .	175	12	2		
Clothing, Bedding &c. for ditto .	101	14	9		
Levies and Taxes on Gaol and House of Correction, .	35	14	7		
					752 13 6

	£	s.	d.
Chaplain of Gaol & House of Correction, .	60	0	0
Costs of Prosecutions, &c. .	384	17	2
Conveying Transports to the Hulks .	87	16	0
Clerk of Assize, Marshal, Crier, and Associate	22	6	6
Coroner's Inquests	27	7	0
Repairs of Bridges, Paving & Incidents, .	16	16	0
Inspector of Market, for Corn Returns, .	10	8	0
Inspector of Weights and Measures, and Incidents	44	18	0
Maintenance and passing of Vagrants .	177	7	11
Advertisements, Printing & Stationery, and miscellaneous	45	17	1
Night Watch and Police Expenses .	395	1	8
Repair of Fire Engines . . .	5	8	3
Clerk of the Peace, Bill of Fees, &c. .	194	1	2
The High Constable, in discharge of order for his extraordinary expenses, . .	225	0	0
The Treasurer, one year's Salary .	21	0	0
Balance in the Treasurer's hands .	328	8	10
	£3092	5	10

£3092 5 10

12th April, 1831.—Examined and allowed the foregoing Abstract.

JOHN BROWN, MAYOR.
MANSFIELD GREGORY.
JAMES RAWSON.
ISAAC LOVELL.

Leicester Journal, 13th April, 1832.

BOROUGH OF LEICESTER.

ABSTRACT OF THE TREASURER'S ACCOUNTS FOR THE BOROUGH OF LEICESTER, OF RECEIPTS AND EXPENDITURE,

For the Year Ending Epiphany Sessions, 1832.
Published Pursuant to 55th Geo. III. c. 51.

THE TREASURER.

Dr.   RECEIPTS.

	£.	s.	d.
To Balance of the last Account in the Treasurer's hands .	328	8	10
—Borough Rates received, exclusive of Gaol Rates, viz. £600 0 0 / 1,000 0 0 / 600 0 0 / 800 0 0	3000	0	0
By Cash received for Fines imposed by the Magistrates, upon persons having deficient weights and measures in their possession .	2	4	9

Cr.   EXPENDITURE.

	£.	s.	d.
Gaol and House of Correction, Ironwork, Painting, Limewashing, &c. .	271	10	5
Expenses of Gaol and House of Correction, viz.			
Gaoler's Salary . 250 0 0			
Turnkey . 55 5 0			
Matron 20 0 0			
Keeper of House of Correction . 120 0 0			
Turnkey . 52 0 0			
Surgeon and Apothecary, for Medicines . 35 7 6			
Bread for Prisoners . 166 14 3			
Clothing, Bedding, &c. for ditto . 102 17 7			
Levies and Taxes on Goal and House of Correction . 35 11 8	837	16	0
Chaplain of Gaol and House of Correction .	60	0	0
Prosecutions and Sessions business .	434	15	8
Conveying Transports to the Hulks .	32	14	4

	£	s	d
Clerk of Assize, Marshall, Cryer, & Associate	14	19	11
Coroner's Inquests	21	7	8
Repairs of Bridges, paving and incidents	11	17	6
Inspector of Market for Corn Returns	10	8	0
Inspector of Weights & Measures, & Incidents	[4]4	16	0
Maintenance and passing of Vagrants	104	12	11
Advertisements, Printing, and Stationery, and Miscellaneous	43	14	7
Night Watch and Police expenses	484	6	7
Repair of Fire Engines	4	12	6
Clerk of the Peace Bill of Fees, Law Charges	174	3	0
The High Constable, remainder of order for his extraordinary expenses in 1830	59	7	0
To him in discharge of Order for extraordinary expenses in 1831	204	17	6
For damage done by Rioters	20	5	6
For Constables Staves	15	0	0
The Treasurer, one years salary	21	0	0
Balance in the Treasurer's hands	458	8	6
	£3,330	13	7

£3330 13 7

10th April, 1832.—Examined and allowed the foregoing Abstract.

G. B. HODGES, Mayor.
Md. GREGORY.
JAMES RAWSON.
ISAAC LOVELL.
JOHN BROWN.

343

Leicester Journal, 19th April, 1833.

BOROUGH OF LEICESTER.

ABSTRACT OF THE TREASURER'S ACCOUNTS FOR THE BOROUGH OF LEICESTER,
OF RECEIPTS AND EXPENDITURE FOR THE YEAR ENDING EPIPHANY SESSIONS, 1833.

Published Pursuant to 55th. Geo. 3rd. c. 51.

THE TREASURER.

DR. RECEIPTS.

	£.	s.	d.
To Balance of last Account in the Treasurer's hands . .	458	8	6
To Borough Rates received, exclusive of Gaol Rates, viz.			
£800 0 0			
800 0 0			
600 0 0			
800 0 0	3000	0	0
By Cash received for Fines imposed by the Magistrates upon persons having deficient weights and measures in their possession .	3	1	7
By Cash received in respect of Fines imposed by the Magistrates under the Act of 7th, Geo. 4th	24	10	0

EXPENDITURE. CR.

	£.	s.	d.
Gaol and House of Correction, Ironwork, Painting, Limewashing, &c.	£191	9	2
Expenses of Gaol and House of Correction, viz.			
Gaoler's Salary .	250	0	0
Turnkey .	54	12	0
Matron .	20	0	0
Keeper of the House of Correction	120	0	0
Turnkey .	52	0	0
Surgeon and Apothecary for Medicines .	46	4	2
Bread for Prisoners .	206	3	5
Clothing, Bedding, Coals, Oatmeal, &c. for ditto .	223	7	5
Levies and Taxes on Gaol and House of Correction .	41	2	0
Sundries .	48	10	0
	1061	19	0
Chaplain of Gaol and House of Correction .	60	0	0

344

	£	s	d
Prosecutions and Sessions business	518	0	8
Conveying Transports to the Hulks	68	16	8
Clerk of Assize, Marshal, Cryer, & Associate	10	19	6
Coroner's Inquests	78	12	0
Repairs of Bridges, Paving and Incidents	..	..	..
Inspector of Market for Corn Returns	10	8	0
Inspector of Weights and Measures and Incidents	44	11	0
Advertisements, Printing, and Stationery, and Miscellaneous	38	12	3
For Constables, Night Watch, and other Police expenses	398	3	4
Repair of Fire Engines	19	3	6
Clerk of the Peace, Bill of Fees, and Law Charges for the year	185	12	2
Money returned to the Black Friars, being overpaid by them	10	16	3
Expense of valuing the Friars	19	11	6
The Treasurer, one year's Salary	21	0	0
Balance in the Treasurer's hands	748	5	1
	£3486	0	1

£3486 0 1

The Accounts, of which the above is an Abstract, were audited and allowed by us,

THOS. MARSTON. Mayor.
JAS. RAWSON.
ISAAC LOVELL.
JNO. BROWN.
G. B. HODGES.

Leicester Journal, 2nd May, 1834.

BOROUGH OF LEICESTER.

Abstract of the

TREASURER'S ACCOUNTS FOR THE BOROUGH OF LEICESTER,

of Receipts and Expenditure, for the Year ending Epiphany Sessions, 1834.

Published Pursuant to 55th. George III. c. 51.

THE TREASURER.

Dr.   Receipts.

	£.	s.	d.
To Balance of last Account in the Treasurer's hands . . .	748	5	1
To Borough Rates received, exclusive of Goal Rates, viz.			
£600 0 0			
1000 0 0			
600 0 0			
800 0 0	3000	0	0
By Cash received for fines imposed by the Magistrates upon persons having deficient weights & measures in their possession .	4	14	0
By Cash received in respect of Fines imposed upon Beer-sellers and others, under the Acts of 7th Geo. IV. and 1st Wm. IV. .	61	17	6

Cr.   Expenditure.

	£.	s.	d.	£.	s.	d.
Gaol and House of Correction, Ironwork, Painting, Limewashing, &c. .				233	16	8
Expenses of Gaol & Houses of Correction, viz.						
Gaoler's Salary . . .	250	0	0			
Turnkey . . .	54	12	0			
Matron . . .	20	0	0			
Keeper of the House of Correction	120	0	0			
Turnkey . . .	52	0	0			
Surgeon and Apothecary for Medicines . .	75	3	0			
Bread for Prisoners . .	229	5	3			
Clothing, Bedding, Coals, Oatmeal, &c. for ditto, and provisions for Prisoners in House of Correction .	223	10	3			
Levies and Taxes on Gaol and House of Correction .	39	2	4			
Sundries . . .	24	13	7	1088	6	5

346

	£	s	d
Chaplain of Gaol and House of Correction .	60	0	0
Prosecutions and Sessions business . .	596	6	0
Conveying Transports to the Hulks . .	98	15	6
Clerk of Assize, Marshal, Cryer, and Associate	28	6	8
Coroner's Inquests	69	16	0
Repairs of Bridges, Paving, and Incidents .	9	4	8
Inspector of Market for Corn Returns . .	10	8	0
Inspector of Weights and Measures, and Incidents	45	18	6
Advertising, Printing and Stationary, and Miscellaneous	31	0	6
Printing, &c. in respect of the Registration of Voters for the Borough . . .	29	19	0
For Constables, Night-watch, and other Police expenses	346	10	11
Repair of Fire engines	1	6	4
Clerk of the Peace's bill of fees and Law charges for the year	181	14	8
The high Constable, for a special order for extraordinary expenses in the execution of his office	378	14	0
The Treasurer one year's salary . .	21	0	0
Balance in the Treasurer's hands . .	583	12	9
	£3814	16	7

£3814 16 7

The Accounts, of which the above is an Abstract, were audited and allowed by us.

THOS. COOK, Mayor   G. B. HODGES,
ISAAC LOVELL,   THOS. MARSTON.
JNO. BROWN,

347

Leicester Journal, 1st May, 1835.

BOROUGH OF LEICESTER.

Abstract of the

TREASURER'S ACCOUNTS FOR THE BOROUGH OF LEICESTER,

of Receipts and Expenditure, for the Year ending Epiphany Sessions, 1835.

Published Pursuant to 55th, George III. c. 51.

THE TREASURER.

Dr.   Receipts.

	£.	s.	d.
To Balance of last Account in the Treasurer's hands . . .	583	12	9
To Borough Rates received, exclusive of Gaol Rates, viz. £800 0 0 / 800 0 0 / 800 0 0 / 600 0 0	3000	0	0
By Cash received in respect of fines imposed upon beersellers, and others, under the Acts of 7th Geo. IV. and 1st William IV. . .	26	5	6
By Cash received by sale of Registers of voters for the Borough . .	18	0	0

Cr.   Expenditure.

	£.	s.	d.
Gaol and House of Correction, Ironwork, Painting, Limewashing, &c. . .	110	18	11
Expenses of Gaol and House of Correction, viz.			
Gaoler's Salary . . .	250	0	0
Turnkey . . .	54	12	0
Matron . .	20	0	0
Keeper of House of Correction .	120	0	0
Turnkey . . .	52	0	0
Surgeon and Apothecary for Medicines . .	77	2	3
Bread for Prisoners . .	174	5	6
Clothing Bedding, Coals, Oatmeal, &c. for Ditto, and Provisions for Prisoners, in House of Correction . .	179	7	8
Levies and Taxes on Gaol and House of Correction . .	42	17	3
Sundries . . .	22	7	8
	992	12	4

348

	£	s	d
Chaplain of Gaol and House of Correction .	60	0	0
Prosecutions and Sessions' Business .	498	14	0
Conveying Transports to the Hulks .	97	3	7
Clerk of Assize, Marshall, Cryer & Associate	8	11	0
Coroner's Inquests .	59	19	0
Repairs of Bridges, Paving and Incidents .		—	
Inspector of Market for Corn Returns .	10	8	0
Inspector of Weights and Measures, and incidents .	43	8	0
Advertising, Printing and Stationary and Miscellaneous .	36	7	6
Printing &c. in respect of the Registration of Voters for the Borough .	27	12	0
For Constables, Night-watch, and other Police expenses .	320	6	10
Repair of Fire Engines .	1	7	5
Clerk of the Peace, Bill of Fees, and Law Charges for the year .	160	19	4
The Treasurer, one year's Salary .	21	0	0
Balance in the Treasurer's Hands .	1178	10	4
	£3,627	18	3

£3,627 18 3

The Accounts of which the above is an Abstract, were Audited and allowed by us,

R. RAWSON, Mayor.
JNO. BROWN.
G. B. HODGES.
THOS. COOK.

349

REPORT OF THE MUNICIPAL CORPORATIONS
COMMISSIONERS 1835

CONTENTS

N*

X. WORKING OF THE CORPORATE
   SYSTEM
Political Exclusiveness
Religious exclusion
Interference in Elections
Creation of Honorary
   Freemen
Election of 1826
   Payment of Election ex-
      penses out of Corporate
      Funds
   Conduct of Returning
      Officer
   Conduct of Parish Officers
   Conduct of Magistrates
Administration of Justice
Distrust of the Corporate
   Magistrates
Political choice of Parish
   Officers

Appointment of Police
Granting of Licenses
Distribution of Charities
Character of Corporate Au-
   thorities and Magistrates
Competency of Magistrates
Administration of Poor Laws
Collision with Select
   Vestries
Appointment of Overseers
Opposition to Local Bill
Administration of Revenues
   Corporate Funds
   Borough Rate
   Gaol Rate
State of party feeling
Effect of distrust on the Im-
   provement of the Town
Public Opinion

BOROUGH OF LEICESTER

I. THE Report on this Corporation has been rendered less complete than Preliminary Statement. it should have been, by the refusal of the corporation, after the inquiry had proceeded to a certain extent, to furnish further information. The circumstances under which this refusal took place are as follows:—

Shortly previous to our proceeding to Leicester, we had transmitted to the mayor and town clerk of the borough a copy of the printed circular furnished by the Board, pointing out the different heads on which we should require information at the time of holding our inquiry.

On our arrival at Leicester, the town clerk waited on us, and requested that we would postpone our proceedings for a few days, to enable him to take the opinion of the recorder of the corporation as to the line of conduct he should adopt, alleging that from a sense of the responsibility which he should incur on the one hand, in disclosing, as the officer of the corporation, any of the concerns of that body; or on the other, in refusing obedience to His Majesty's Commission; he was anxious to shelter himself in either case by acting under the sanction of the authority of the proper legal adviser of the corporation. We however deemed it our duty to decline to accede to this request on two grounds; 1st, because it was obvious that the town clerk might at once relieve himself from all responsibility by taking the sense of the corporation themselves, who were on the spot, instead of applying to the recorder, who was at a distance; 2d, because it appeared to us that it would be to compromise His Majesty's Commission to postpone the important duties which it committed to our charge, while the validity and extent of its authority should be submitted to the consideration of a third party, however eminent or learned. Finding us therefore determined to persist in proceeding at once with our inquiry, the town clerk thought it right not to take upon himself the responsibility of resisting our precept, and attended to give evidence before us.

The proceedings commenced on the 14th of September. The first and part of the second day were occupied in receiving the answers of the town clerk on the general subjects of inquiry, embracing the constitution, privileges, and existing state of the corporation. At the end of that time we postponed the further examination of that officer, in order to afford time for the completion of certain returns which we had demanded of him relative to the estates and expenditure of the corporation, and proceeded to receive

355

the testimony of such of the inhabitants as were desirous of giving evidence on the occasion.

We had in our first communication to the town clerk called on him for returns of the income and of the expenditure (in detail) of the corporation. The returns furnished to us in the first instance by the town clerk proved to be neither more nor less than mere abstracts. That which professed to be a return of the corporate expenditure for a specific period, was for the most part not a return of the actual expenditure, but consisted of mere averages, which the town clerk, on being questioned, admitted were founded not on actual calculation, but on estimates made by guess. It further appeared, that on the year's income there remained a balance of upwards of 800*l.* unaccounted for. Deeming this return therefore wholly unsatisfactory, we required that an amended one, containing the actual expenditure during a specified period, should be furnished to us. After the delay of an entire week and reiterated applications on our part, a few additional returns of expenditure were supplied, consisting of the details of which a few of the items contained in the first return were composed, but which threw no light whatsoever on the average estimates, and still left a large balance on the year's expenditure wholly unaccounted for. The whole of these additional returns might have been extracted from the corporation account books in a very short space of time, yet a week had been occupied in preparing them; and the town clerk declared that a considerable time would be further required to prepare those which yet remained to be furnished. It seemed manifest that the town clerk was trifling with the inquiry, and we could not therefore but infer that there existed some motive for concealment. Moreover, it had come to light in the examination of the town clerk, that the corporation had in the year 1823 paid the fees on the admission of 800 honorary freemen out of the corporate funds, and that in 1826 they had expended the sum of 10,000*l.* in a single contested election, which sum had been raised by the mortgage of part of the corporate estates. It also appeared that very considerable sales of corporate property had taken place. Under these circumstances it appeared to us highly important that the corporate accounts, over which the most complete obscurity had hitherto rested, should be examined. Being however impressed with a conviction that the production of any returns which we might call for would be delayed beyond the period to which our inquiry must be limited, or perhaps ultimately never be furnished at all, we considered that we should most effectually discharge our duty by calling at once for the accounts of the corporation and inspecting them ourselves. We therefore called upon the town clerk to produce for our inspection the account books of the corporation for the last ten years. The town clerk demanded that a pledge should first be given by us that the account books should be confined to our own inspection alone. This pledge we declined to give, observing however at the same time, "that it had not been our practice to read through aloud the accounts which he had hitherto furnished us with, but simply to seek explanation on points which seemed to require it; that consequently pursuing the same course, if the account books should require elucidation we should demand explanation from him in public as before, but should not debar ourselves, should circumstances render it necessary, from obtaining information from such sources as we deemed proper." At the same time that we called for the account books, we required to see the draft of the mortgage before referred to, and as it appeared that a record of all the proceedings of the corporation was contained in certain journals, called the Hall Books, we deemed it essentially our duty, after the evidence which had been given, to require these books for the last 20 years to be produced for our inspection, in order to ascertain whether other transactions of a like nature with those which had been brought to light had occurred during that period. The town clerk hereupon declared his intention to submit the question of the production of the accounts and the journals of the common halls to the consideration of the corporation, and to abide by their directions. This discussion took place on Monday, the 23d September, on which day Mr. Serjeant Goulburn, the recorder of the borough, first appeared before us, and claimed a right to advise the town clerk whether or not to answer questions put by us—a right which we refused to concede, considering that though the relation in which the learned recorder stood to the corporation might authorize him to advise the town clerk previous to his giving evidence, as to any course he should pursue, it was inconsistent with the respect due to the authority under which we acted, that any one should interfere with a witness while under our examination.

On the evening of the day in question, we caused the town clerk to be served with a notice to attend on us, and to produce all deeds, documents, accounts and books in his custody or possession, relating to the corporation, specifying more particularly the draft of the mortgage for 10,000l., the account books of the corporation for the last ten years, and the hall books for the last twenty years.

On the following day a common hall of the corporation was held, to take into consideration the course which should be adopted on the occasion. The following is a minute of the proceedings and resolutions of the meeting, an official copy of which was transmitted to us:—

"At a common hall, holden this 24th day of September 1833, Thomas Marston, esq. mayor, the town clerk reported to the hall, that on Saturday, the 14th day of September instant, he attended Richard Whitcombe and Alexander Edward Cockburn, esqrs. two of the Commissioners appointed to inquire into the state of Municipal Corporations in England and Wales, at the castle of Leicester, pursuant to their request, to be examined by them, by virtue of His Majesty's commission. That before he submitted to be examined, he requested the Commissioners to allow him time, until the following Monday, to consult the recorder of the borough, the legal adviser of the corporation, as to how far he (the town clerk) was justified in disclosing at a meeting, open to all the town, the detail of the private income and expenditure of the corporation, with which he becomes acquainted only in his official and confidential character of town clerk and solicitor to the corporation. That the Commissioners declined to comply with this request, and required him to enter upon his examination immediately. That in the absence of the recorder, and without other legal advice, he (the town clerk) proceeded to answer upon oath, to the best of his knowledge and ability, all questions put to him by the Commissioners, relative to the constitution of the corporation and to its income and expenditure. That such examination continued during the better part of two days, and closed apparently to the satisfaction of the Commissioners. That on the following Thursday and Friday and Monday he again attended the Commissioners, who required further returns from him, in addition to those already furnished by him; and also demanded to be delivered up to them the hall-books of the corporation for the last twenty years; the chamberlain's accounts for the last ten years, and many other documents, embracing the minutest details of corporation affairs, the particulars of the title by which the corporation held its land and other property, the particulars of mortgages and other securities for money, granted by the corporation or by individual members of it, together with other matters with which he (the town clerk) had become acquainted solely as the officer and solicitor of the corporation, and as solicitor of certain members thereof. That the Commissioners insisted that such books, papers, documents and information should be furnished to them in public, at meetings like that then assembled, which was open to all the town, and principally attended by violent political opponents of the corporation; and that such books, papers, documents and information should be there publicly examined and questioned, at the suggestion of any individual present. That he (the town clerk) distinctly inquired from the Commissioners whether such books, papers, documents and information, when furnished, would be confined to the Commissioners themselves, or submitted to the inspection of others; to which the Commissioners replied, that they would make no pledge upon that subject, and intimated that the utmost publicity would be given by them to such documents, accounts and information when furnished. That he (the town clerk) has been informed, and verily believes, that all the documents and accounts hitherto furnished by him to the Commissioners, have been by them handed over or shown to the political opponents of the corporation, and that occasion has been taken therefrom to assail the character and rights of the corporation. That upon the last occasion of his (the town clerk) being examined, the recorder, who was then present, interfered to desire him (the town clerk) not to answer a question put to him, involving the title of the corporation to certain property, whereupon the Commissioners declared that he (the town clerk) had no right, whilst under examination, to the advice of the recorder as to what questions he ought properly to answer. That from the mode in which the examination of him (the town clerk) and other witnesses, submitted by him to the examination of the Commissioners, on behalf of the corporation, has been conducted, his mind is impressed with the belief that the further prosecution of this inquiry cannot tend to an impartial elucidation of facts, but is calculated to hold up him (the town clerk) and the corporation to the obloquy and ill will of their political opponents. That at such meetings great excitement necessarily prevails, which the Commissioners have no power to repress; and that such excitement is quite inconsistent with the dispassionate investigation of truth. That under these circumstances the town clerk has felt it his duty to ask for the directions of the corporation in common-hall assembled, as to his further course of proceeding before the Commissioners; and whether it be their pleasure that he should deliver up to the Commissioners the documents last referred to, viz. those which are in his custody as the officer and legal adviser of the Corporation.

"Resolved, unanimously,—That the report of the town clerk be received, and entered upon the minutes.

"Resolved, unanimously,—That this corporation feels towards His Majesty's Commission the greatest possible deference and respect, and desires to yield obedience to it; but that they do not consider that it can form any part of the object of that Commission to assemble daily large meetings of the town, and to require the disclosure before them of all the private pecuniary affairs of the corporation, and of the titles by which they hold their property. That therefore this corporation, in common-hall assembled, is of opinion that the town clerk should not deliver up to the Commissioners the further books, papers, documents and accounts, which they have now required."

[The town clerk then produced to the hall a summons, which is copied underneath, and which was delivered to him last night, being since his last appearance before the Commissioners.]

"COPY SUMMONS

Which calls for all deeds, documents, writings, accounts, books, &c. relating to the estates of funds belonging to the corporation, or to the affairs of the corporation, particularizing the copy of a certain mortgage executed by the corporation, and all the chamberlain's accounts for the last ten years, and the hall-books for the last twenty years, &c.

"Resolved, unanimously,—That under the circumstances above detailed by the town clerk, this corporation does not feel justified in authorizing the town clerk to deliver to the Commissioners the documents specified in the said last-mentioned summons.

"Resolved, unanimously,—That the warmest thanks of the hall be given to Mr. Serjeant Goulburn, the recorder, for his prompt attendance at Leicester to sustain the rights and interests of the corporation, and for his valuable advice and assistance in the emergency in which they find themselves placed.

"Resolved,—That the thanks of the hall be given to the mayor for having called the hall on this important occasion.

(signed) "Tho. Burbidge, Town Clerk."

As the foregoing resolutions purported to be founded on the report made to the common hall by the town clerk, and as the two main statements contained in that report, namely, 1st, That the utmost publicity would be given to the documents called for; and 2dly, That great excitement prevailed at the proceedings of the Commissioners, were altogether at variance with the fact, we deemed it proper to transmit to the mayor, as the head of the corporation, a communication addressed to that body, in which the mis-statements contained in the report were pointed out, accompanied by a precept to attend before us with the documents which we had required. The following is a copy of the communication referred to.

"To the mayor, bailiffs and burgesses of the borough of Leicester: A copy of resolutions agreed to by the corporation in common hall, having been laid before His Majesty's Commissioners, which resolutions are prefaced by a report made to the corporation by their town clerk, the Commissioners feel it due to the members of the corporation to apprise them that such report is in many important particulars at variance with truth. The Commissioners make this communication from a feeling which it would be unfair towards the corporation not to entertain, that they would not have disobeyed a requisition made to them by virtue of His Majesty's Commission if they had not been misinformed; and the Commissioners have resolved to address a communication to the corporation in the present shape, as the only mode of guarding that body from a recurrence of misrepresentations, the perusal of the town clerk's report having convinced the Commissioners that they ought not in justice either to themselves or the corporation, any longer to place confidence in the channel through which their communications with the corporation have heretofore been conveyed. The Commissioners will not condescend to enter into any discussion on the opinions expressed by the town clerk as to the mode in which they have exercised the functions entrusted to them by the authority of His Majesty's Commission, but they think it right to disabuse the corporation as to the facts alleged in the report of the town clerk. The Commissioners deny, that at the meetings at which their inquiry has been carried on, any excitement or disorder has prevailed. On the contrary they assert that those meetings have been remarkable for order and propriety of behaviour on the part of those who have assembled to witness proceedings in which the inhabitants of Leicester must necessarily feel so deep an interest. The Commissioners however gather, that the resolutions of the common hall have been influenced principally by the statement of the town clerk, that the returns and other documents demanded by them were required to be produced in open court, and would be exposed by them to the utmost publicity. The Commissioners therefore deem it proper to announce to the corporation that the statement is altogether untrue. The Commissioners distinctly and repeatedly expressed to the town clerk that the documents required might be delivered to them wheresoever he thought proper, in the same manner as accounts and documents had formerly been delivered to them by that officer. They stated to the town clerk that if the documents demanded should prove satisfactory, they would not be publicly examined and questioned; but at all events, that publicity would not be given to such documents; that if explanations should be required on any particulars, these explanations would be called for from the town clerk or other officers of the corporation in the same open manner in which the Commissioners had conducted those previous examinations to which the town-clerk himself had already been a party. It is true that the Commissioners refused to pledge themselves, that the documents should, under all circumstances be confined to their own exclusive inspection; because they felt, that if necessary explanations as to the contents of those documents should by possibility be withheld on the part of the corporation, it must be left open to the Commissioners to have recourse to such other sources of information as the refusal of the corporation might render necessary for the attainment of the important objects of His Majesty's Commission. The Commissioners taking for granted, that the resolutions of the corporation were founded upon the erroneous representations of the town clerk, and having placed those representations in their true light, think right to renew their requisitions, as set forth in their former precept. Whether the required documents may render necessary the examination of any members of the corporation, will be matter of ulterior consideration. After the delay which has taken place, the Commissioners feel themselves compelled by their official duties elsewhere, to adjourn their inquiry into the affairs of the corporation of Leicester to the day specified in the inclosed precept. In resuming that inquiry they will be anxious to receive not only the documents referred to, but such other evidence as the corporation may feel inclined to submit to their consideration."

At the time this communication was made, in consequence of the delay which had occurred, the period at which, according to previous arrangements, our inquiry into the corporation of the city of Coventry was appointed to be held, had arrived. It became therefore necessary to adjourn our proceedings at Leicester for several days.

On the 7th October we resumed our inquiry at Leicester. On the morning of that day a common hall was held, the proceedings of which are recorded in the following resolutions:—

"Guildhall, Leicester. At a common hall holden on the 7th day of October 1833 (Thomas Cook, esq. mayor), the late mayor, Mr. Alderman Marston, produced to the hall a communication which he had received from the Commissioners for inquiring into Municipal Corporations, and a precept from them, requiring the production of certain books, papers and documents; and the same having been read,

"It was resolved, That this corporation discovers nothing in the communication to the late mayor just read, which differs in any material respect from the statement made to them by their town clerk at their last hall, or which tends to impair the confidence which they repose in that officer.

"Resolved, That such communication contains nothing from which this corporation can infer that the documents sought for by the Commissioners' precept will be confined for their inspection, or applied only to further the objects of His Majesty's Commission.

"That on the contrary, it is to be collected from that communication, that the Commissioners propose the same course with respect to the documents now required, which they have pursued towards those heretofore furnished; namely, to submit such documents, if they shall think fit, to other persons, and upon suggestions from any source, however hostile to the corporation, to subject its officers and members to public interrogations, so framed as to extract, if possible, grounds to assail their character and property, and to induce a false belief that they have betrayed the trust reposed in them.

"That it appears to this corporation, that His Majesty's Commission confers no power to assemble daily, within this populous town, large meetings of people, to select for inquiry before them topics of great local irritation, such as the merits of an election for Members of Parliament, warmly contested seven years since; and to call before such meetings the magistrates of the town and members of the corporation, in order to put to them questions which directly tend to impugn their conduct and motives, and thereby to degrade their authority, and destroy their influence in the town.

"That at such meetings the Commissioners are armed with no powers to preserve the peace, or restrain excitement, to what length soever it may be carried, or to protect individuals examined before them from present insult or future outrage.

"That at such meetings great temptation is held out to perjury, by inviting all persons of whatever class, character or conduct, to depose to matters criminating those in office and authority, without power to punish untruth, or any mode whereby the truth or falsehood of what falls from a witness may be fully and fairly sifted whilst his examination proceeds.

"That at such meetings no security exists that what passes there will be fully and fairly reported; nor have the Commissioners power to prevent statements going forth to the public, designedly false and garbled, and published with the express intention to asperse character, public and private, of which latter evil this corporation and its members have had, during the progress of the present inquiry, ample experience.

"That from meetings so convened and conducted persons of respectability and intelligence naturally shrink, unwilling to subject themselves to the clamour and expressions of ill-will, called forth by any statements which may not be in unison with the feelings of the assembled crowd, by which means an entirely false impression is conveyed of the sense of the town, and the testimony precluded of those most competent to speak to its real wishes and feeling.

"That the evils consequent on this course of proceeding would be aggravated to an intolerable degree, if such examinations should assume the appearance of being *ex parte*, and of being carried forward only to uphold one political party in the town against the other.

"That, influenced by these considerations, this corporation sees no ground to depart from the resolution adopted at its last hall, or to give to the town clerk or its officers any directions inconsistent therewith.

(signed)   *"Tho. Burbidge*, Town Clerk."

The above resolutions were sent to us, accompanied by the following note from the mayor:

"The mayor of Leicester begs to inclose to the Commissioners on Municipal Corporations, a copy of the resolutions adopted this morning at a common hall, the contents of which will sufficiently explain to the Commissioners the reasons why the documents, specified in their last precept, cannot be delivered up to them; and the Commissioners will also learn, from the reasons which led to that resolution, the grounds upon which the mayor and other magistrates of the town are forced to decline appearing before the Commissioners for public examination.—Leicester, October 7, 1833."

It would be altogether out of place to discuss here the grounds on which these resolutions are founded, or to maintain the propriety of the publicity given to our proceedings, in conformity with the unanimous resolution of the board, as the best security for truth, and the only effectual means of obtaining the full and accurate information, without which our inquiry would have been wholly nugatory. This opportunity is, however, taken to state, that the existence of any excitement or danger to the public peace, which is put forward by the Corporation as one of the grounds of their resolutions, is utterly at variance with the truth.

All classes of the inhabitants, it is true, appeared to take a deep interest in our inquiry, the progress of which considerable numbers of them attended at the county hall to witness; but not the slightest confusion or disturbance occurred to interrupt for a moment the order and regularity of the proceedings. The apprehension of insult or outrage expressed in the resolution is utterly unfounded, and can be considered in the light of pretext only. Equally untrue is it, that the examination of the officers and members was so carried on, "as to extract, if possible, grounds to assail their character and property, and to induce a false belief that they had betrayed the trust reposed in them," or "to impugn their conduct and motives, and thereby degrade their authority, and destroy their influence in the town." The sole object and effect of the interrogations was, to elicit full information as to the conduct of the corporation; and if the inquiry should have led to the consequences which are represented to have resulted from it, the fault is in the misconduct of the body whose transactions have been disclosed, and not in the manner of the inquiry by which those transactions were brought to light.

It is unquestionably true, that in this as in all other corporations which we visited, an opportunity was afforded to the inhabitants of the town to furnish information, or offer suggestions to serve as a guide in our examination of the corporate authorities. It is at once obvious, that being possessed of no local knowledge to direct our inquiries, if we had shut out the assistance of persons possessing such information, our investigation must have been comparatively useless, while to have had recourse to the corporate functionaries, whose conduct we were deputed to examine, to point out any abuses which might exist in the working of the local government, or any transactions which it would of course have been their interest to conceal, would have been altogether idle and absurd. At the same time it should be stated, that in no instance did we permit the conduct of the corporate body, or of individual members of it, to be called in question, without affording abundant opportunity to the parties to be present, or without immediately putting any questions which were suggested by way of cross examination to the witnesses by whom the conduct of the parties in question was impugned. Lastly, it is important to remark, as throwing light on the motives of the corporate body in refusing to attend to give evidence before us, that the mode of conducting our inquiry, and the circumstances attending on it, were the same from the commencement, but that no objection to attend or give evidence before us was made until we had emphatically declared our intention not to rest satisfied with the preliminary

evidence offered and the defective returns hitherto supplied, but to investigate thoroughly the political and pecuniary transactions of the corporation for the last ten or twenty years. Connecting a refusal made under
such circumstances with the disclosures previously elicited from the town
clerk, it appears impossible not to infer that there still remained other
transactions which the corporation were desirous should not be brought to
light, and rather than disclose which, they preferred to treat His Majesty's
Commission with disobedience and disrespect.

II. The Limits of the Borough of Leicester comprehend the parishes of Local Limits.
All Saints, Saint Martin and Saint Nicholas, parts of the parishes of Saint
Mary, Saint Margaret and Saint Leonard, and the White and Blackfriars,
which are extra-parochial.

The borough is by no means co-extensive with the town. The limits Borough.
appear to be well known for the purpose of rates, but are not laid down in
any official plan or document, nor are they ever perambulated.

The remainder of the town is comprehended in what is termed the Liberties not
included in
the Borough.
Liberties. The liberties comprise the parts of the parishes of Saint Mary,
Saint Margaret and Saint Leonard, not within the borough, and the hamlet
or township termed the Newarke, and include a part of the town called the
Castle View.

The limits are bounded by parish boundaries, which are well known and
defined, and are regularly perambulated at intervals of three years. The
liberties extend about half a mile round the town, and inclose it on all sides.
A considerable portion of the liberties is built over, and buildings are
rapidly extending in every direction. The population of this part of the
town nearly equals that of the borough.

The jurisdiction of the corporate magistrates extends over the whole Corporate
Jurisdiction.
town, with the exception of that part called the Castle View: it is exclusive
within the borough; but the magistrates of the county possess a concurrent
jurisdiction over the liberties.

The liberties, including the Castle View, have been added to the borough Parliamentary
Boundaries.
by the Boundary Act, as regards the return of members to Parliament for
the borough.

The following statistical details are collected from Returns made to Statistical
Details.
Parliament:

English statute acres	3,960
Population:	
1801	16,953
1811	23,146
1821	30,125
1831—Males, 18,958;—Females, 19,946;—Total, . .	38,904

Occupations; viz.

Families employed in agriculture	279
Ditto, trade, manufactures, &c.	6,951
Ditto, not comprised in above classes	1,465

Annual value of real property—
(1815) . . . . £. 58,108

Assessed Taxes for years ending—

	£.	s.	d.
5th April 1829	5,180	2	$-\frac{1}{4}$
— 1830	5,220	17	$-\frac{3}{4}$
— 1831	5,278	8	$6\frac{3}{4}$

Parochial Assessments for years ending—

	£.	s.	d.
25th March 1825	9,182	8	–
— 1829	13,464	8	–

Number of houses in 1830:

Assessed as £. 10 and under £. 20 rent	450
20 — 40	299
40 and upwards	106
	855

Number of electors registered under new Act in 1832:

Resident Freemen	1,569
Non-resident ditto	501
	2,070
£. 10 occupiers	1,200
Scot and Lot Voters	256
	3,526

Of these were registered in double characters . . .	463
Individual voters on the Register	3,063

HISTORY.

Charters,
1 John.

III. Leicester is a borough by prescription.

In the first year of King John, the king granted a charter to Robert Earl of Leicester, which granted exemption from the suits of shires and hundreds and aid to the sheriff, with a grant of sac, soc, and team, and infangthef, and quittance of toll, pontage and passage.

In the same year the burgesses obtained a further grant from the king, that all purchases and sales of their lands in the town of Leicester, made in the portman-mote, should be valid. Another charter was also granted on the same day to the burgesses, that they might freely traffic throughout the king's dominions with their merchandizes.

23 Henry III.

In the 23d Henry III. Simon de Montfort, Earl of Leicester, granted a charter to the burgesses, in which, after reciting that Robert, sometime Earl of Leicester, had enfeoffed by his charter to the burgesses of Leicester a certain pasture, called the Cowhaye, in the south fields of Leicester, he newly remised, released, and entirely from him and his heirs for ever, quitted claim to all right which he had to the said pasture, to the free burgesses of Leicester.

In the 53d of the same reign, the same king granted to the burgesses of Leicester, that neither their persons nor goods, in any place of the king's dominions, should be arrested for any debt, whereof they were not sureties or principal debtors, unless the debtors were of their community and under their power, having wherewith to satisfy the debts in whole or in part, unless it should be reasonably made to appear that the mayor and burgesses were deficient in doing justice to their creditors. *53 Henry III.*

In 49th Edward III. John of Gaunt, King of Castile and Leon, and Duke of Lancaster, by indenture, to farm let to the burgesses and commonalty of Leicester, the bailiwick of the town, suburbs and fields, with the appurtenances of the same, with all executions, profits of the port-mote courts, fair, markets, and all other courts, rents, farms, goods, chattels of fugitives, felons, forfeitures of waste, &c. deodands, treasure trove, with the keeping of all manner of prisoners, except the Castle of Leicester, the mill under the same, the rents and services by the porter at the castle, of old time accustomed, the court of the same, &c. And also granting to them and their successors sufficient timber in the woods of the manor of Leicester, for the repairing of all houses, shops, shambles, &c. *49 Edward III.*

King Richard II. in the second year of his reign, confirmed the charter of King John to the burgesses of Leicester, as to their sales in the portman mote. *2 Richard II.*

King Edward IV. in the fourth year of his reign, granted to the mayor and burgesses, and their successors for ever, that the mayor and four of the discreetest co-burgesses, with one person skilled in the laws, to be called the Recorder, should be justices, to keep and cause to be kept the statutes of servants, artificers and labourers. That the mayor and comburgesses, or any three or two of them, with the recorder, should have power to hear and determine all manner of transgressions, misprisions, extortions, and all other causes, complaints and misdemeanors within the town or borough, as fully as the justices in the county of Leicester, clipping of coin, &c. only excepted. *4 Edward IV.*

That no justice of the peace of the county, or other justice or commissioner of the king or his heirs, should intermeddle in any matter (except as before excepted).

That neither they, the mayor and burgesses, nor their successors, nor any constable of the town or borough of Leicester, nor any other person there commorant, should be bound to appear before any other justice of the peace, or any other justice or commissioner of the king, or his heirs, either within or without the said town, to inquire or do any thing in the matters aforesaid, happening in the town or liberties (except as before

excepted), save only before the mayor and four of the discreeter comburgesses, and their successors.

That if any mayor, burgess, constable or other person, within the town
or burgh abiding, should be summoned or impannelled, and refuse to
appear before any other justice about any such matter, or to swear or
inquire about any heads or articles thereunto belonging, that for such his
refusal, he should not be put in contempt, or incur any loss or penalty to the
king or his heirs.

That the mayor and the 24 comburgesses, (probably the grand jury)
should yearly upon the feast of Saint Matthew, elect four of the said 24, to
be justices of the peace for the year ensuing, and two of the said 24 to be
coroners, and no other coroner to intermeddle.

That they, the mayor, burgesses and their successors, should not be
impannelled on any assizes, juries, jurisdictions or recognizances, though
they concerned either the King or his heirs, or other of his liege people, or
be sworn or put upon the trial of any arraignment or assize before any
justice or commissioners of the king or his heirs, about any cause or matters
happening without the town or borough.

Bye-Law,
1 Richard III.
In an ancient book of the borough there appears the following entry:
"At a common hall holden at Leicester, the 7th April 1st Richard III., it
was ordained as follows: Whereas for the great rumour and slander that
runs upon the town of Leicester as well of divers evil disposed persons, as
of broken pavements, stones, timber and muck, to the great noysance of
the king's people and destruction of the said town, unless remedy be had:
it is, therefore, ordayned and established by the whole assent and agreement, as well as of the right honourable and worshipful John Roberts, esq.,
the then mayor and all his brethren of the same town, as by the worshipful
commonaltie of the same, that the said town shall be divided in 12 wards,
and in every of the said wards one of the mayor's brethren for the time
being dwelling within the same ward or next thereunto, be called an alderman, to have full power and authority to correct and punish all such people
at any time trespassing, after the quantity of his trespass." The ordinance
further provided, that "if any such person would not obey the correction
and punishment of the alderman, that then the alderman should show his
name unto the mayor, who, according to justice, was to correct and punish
the trespasser until he should submit himself unto his alderman." Also
"that every time it should happen any such alderman should decease, or be
mayor, that then at the next common hall to be holden after his decease,
one other of the mayor's brethren should be chosen an alderman and have
the power and correction, &c."

Mandate,
4 Henry VII.
In the 4th year of King Henry VII., a Mandate was directed by the king
to the mayor, bailiffs, comburgesses and burgesses of the town of Leicester;
reciting, that "forasmuch as at every election of a mayor or a burgess of the

parliament, or at assessing of any lawful imposition, the commonalty of the said town, as well poor as rich, have always assembled at the common hall; whereas such persons be of little substance or reason, and not contributors, or else fall little to the charge sustained in such behalf, and have had great interest through their exclamations and hedyness, to the subversion, not only of the good policy of the said town, but likely to the often breach of the peace and other inconveniences increasing, and causing the full misery and decline of our said town, and to the great discouragement of some of the governors there: For reformation whereof, and to the intent that good rule and substantial order may be had and entertained there from henceforth, the king strictly charges the said mayor, bailiff and twenty-four comburgesses of the said town now being, that at all common halls and assemblies thereafter to be holden there, as well for the election of the mayor, of the justices of the peace and burgesses of our parliaments, as also of passing any lawful impositions or otherwise, they jointly choose and call unto them the bailiff of the said town for the time being; and also 48 of the most wise and sad commoners, inhabitants there, after the discretions of the said commonalty, and no more; and there to order and direct all matters occurrent or supervening among you, as by the reason and conscience shall be thought lawful and most expedient. Given at our Palace of Westminster, under our seal of our said Dutchy the 2d day of August, 4th year of our reign. By Council of our said Dutchy of Lancaster."

It appears that the inhabitants were greatly dissatisfied at this deprivation of their ancient rights; and at the next election, after the promulgation of this decree, insisted on their former privileges in a tumultuous manner. An Act of Parliament, enforcing the provisions of the decree, was in consequence passed both as respects Northampton and Leicester. The Act was first passed as to Northampton, and its provisions were immediately afterwards extended to Leicester. It is as follows: [Stat. 4 Henry VII.]

"Forasmuch as of late divisions have grown, as well in the towns and boroughs of Northampton and Leicester, as in other towns and boroughs corporate among the inhabitants of the same, for the election and choice of mayors, bailiffs and other officers, by reason that such multitude of the inhabitants being of little substance, which oft in number exceed in their assemblies others that have been approved decent and well disposed persons, have by their multitude and headiness used in the assemblies caused great troubles among themselves, as well in the elections as in assessing of other lawful charges amongst them, to the subversion of the good rule of the said boroughs, and oft-times to the great breach of the king's peace within the same; For reformation whereof, and for the more quiet and restfulness of the king's subjects hereafter, and for the conservation of the king's peace, be it enacted by the advice and assent of the Lords and

Commons, &c. that from henceforth the elections of mayors, bailiffs and other officers, and also the assessing of all lawful charges that shall hereafter be made and had in the borough of Northampton, shall be had, made and used in the following manner; that is to say, the mayor and his brethren for the time being that there oft-times past have been mayors, or the more part of them, upon their oaths shall chuse 48 persons, of the most wise, discreet and best disposed persons of the inhabitants by their discretions, other than before that time had been mayors and bailiffs of the same; and the same persons, or part of them, from time to time hereafter to change when and as often as shall seem necessary; which persons, and the mayor and his brethren, and such persons there as have been mayors and bailiffs of the said town for the time being, or the more part of them, shall make yearly election of all the mayors and bailiffs; and the elections by them so made, to be effectual in like manner as if the elections were made by such form as aforetime hath been used: provided, that if in the elections or any of them, the voices be divided and equal for sundry parties, then the voice of the mayor for the time being to stand for two voices."

Charter,
20 Henry VII.

Henry the VII., in the 20th year of his reign, granted a charter to Leicester, confirming by inspeximus that of Edward IV., and giving exclusive jurisdiction to the justices of the borough, with the usual non-intromittant clause.

1 Edward VI.

In the 1st of Edward VI., there is a general confirmation of all the previous charters to Leicester; and the same occurs again in the 1st of Queen Mary, and the 1st of Queen Elizabeth.

Bye-law,
16 Eliz.

From an entry in the corporation books, dated 20th September, 16th Elizabeth, it appears that as regards the election of chamberlains, the ancient right of the burgesses to choose their own officers, had not in practice been altogether taken away by the statute 4th Henry VII.: for it was then ordained that "henceforth it should be lawful for the mayor elected to nominate and choose his chamberlain, and for the commonalty to choose and elect for their chamberlain, as well any such person as hath not before fined, as any such as have fined for the same, in order as they be most ancient in election. And if any of the aforesaid persons, inhabitants of the said town, so elected do obstinately refuse and will not serve in the office of chamberlain aforesaid; that"—here the document breaks off, and is followed by a blank leaf.

Charter,
31 Eliz.

In the 31st Elizabeth, the queen granted a charter to Leicester, which recites that the borough had existed corporate of one mayor and 24 aldermen, and one other society, commonly called the Forty-eight; and that the mayor and the said society had been incorporated by her progenitors. The queen then proceeds to create Leicester a body corporate and politic for ever, under the name of "Mayor and Burgesses of the town of Leicester;"

and grants that the corporation should be capable to hold and sell lands; to plead and be impleaded; that there should be one mayor, 24 aldermen and 48 burgesses of the inhabitants, and that one of the aldermen should be elected mayor every year; and that the mayor and burgesses, should enjoy all former privileges. The charter also contained a grant of the sheep-pens and shambles, and of various lands, &c., lately belonging to the four colleges in Leicester.

Queen Elizabeth, in the 41st year of her reign, granted another Charter of incorporation to the borough. It commences by reciting, "That the borough of Leicester, was an ancient and populous borough, and from ancient times was a borough incorporate, and the inhabitants and their predecessors had held hitherto divers liberties, franchises, privileges and immunities, by divers prescriptions and customs in the same borough from time of memory &c., and by divers concessions and grants from the Queen's progenitors." _{Charter, 41 Eliz.}

The charter then makes Leicester a free borough, and the burgesses and their successors a body politic and corporate, under the name of "Mayor, Bailiffs and Burgesses of the Borough of Leicester," with powers to sell and purchase lands, and to plead and be impleaded by their corporate name; and grants to the corporation, for the first time, a common seal. The charter also directed, that there should be a mayor and two bailiffs, and 24 honest and discreet men inhabiting and abiding within the borough, who should be called Aldermen of the Borough, and 48 other honest and discreet men inhabiting and commorant within the borough, commonly called the Company of Eight-and-Forty, but who in future should be called the Common Council of the Borough, as assistants of the mayor and aldermen; and it provided that the mayor and aldermen shall have power of making laws for the good government of the burgesses, artificers and inhabitants.

It further provided, that the mayor, recorder and the four aldermen who had last served the office of mayor should be justices of the peace for the borough; and it extended the jurisdiction of the Corporation over the parts of the parishes of St. Margaret, St. Mary and St. Leonard not within the borough, with a saving to all persons whatsoever of their rights, liberties, pre-eminences and jurisdictions; by which means a concurrent jurisdiction was preserved to the magistrates of the county: after which follows a grant of view of frankpledge of all the inhabitants and resiants within the borough, to be holden twice a year, before the mayor, bailiffs, stewards, &c. It also provided, that no foreigner should buy or sell any merchandize within the borough, except in gross, save in the time of fairs, markets, &c. It granted a market for wool, &c.; and confirmed all the former privileges and grants to the borough.

The foregoing charter was confirmed by a subsequent one of the 16th

Charles II. This, as well as all preceding charters, were surrendered in the 36th Charles II.; but eventually the charters were restored by the proclamation of 1688. The charter of 41 Elizabeth is considered the governing charter, by which the corporation is now constituted and regulated.

Ancient
Grants and
purchases of
property.

The burgesses of Leicester were possessed of property at an early period. The grant made by John of Gaunt, of the bailiwick of the town and its appurtenances, has before been mentioned. In the 7th of Henry VII. it appears, from the records of the corporation, that a view having been taken of the muniments of the corporation, there were found, *inter alia*, the deeds relating to tenements in Dede-lane, to lands and tenements in Wheston, Ratcliffe, Thrussington, and Cosington, and a tenement in Belgrave-gate, besides other tenements in the town.

The charter of the 31st Elizabeth before referred to, besides the municipal privileges it conferred, contained a very important grant of property. It grants the shambles and sheep-pens, divers lands specifically named, parcel of the town and manor of Leicester, and of the honour of Leicester, all which are said to be parcel of the lands and possessions of "our ancient duchy of Lancaster, in our aforesaid town of Leicester, and the suburbs of the same town;" the hospital of St. John and St. Leonard, and all the lands and tenements thereof; divers lands come to the crown by escheat, together with divers other lands specifically mentioned; all lands formerly belonging to the dean, prebendaries, and the choristers of the college aforesaid; the guild commonly called St. Margaret's Guild, with all lands, tenements and appurtenances; a late chapel called St. John's Chapel, a guild called the Corpus Christi Guild, the lands of the late College of the Blessed Virgin in Leicester, a close formerly parcel *Collegii novi operis*, to hold of the Queen in fee-farm, at a yearly rent of 123*l.* 13*s.*

The charter also contains a grant of the reversion of a moiety of an estate called the Grange. The other moiety of this estate appears to have been previously purchased by the corporation; and the fee of the moiety, the reversion of which was conveyed by the Queen's grant, appears to have been acquired shortly after. The following entries occur in the corporation records:—

"March 18th, 28 Eliz.—At a common hall agreed by the 24 and 48, to lend money till Christmas next towards paying 300*l.* which the town is indebted for the Grange, &c."

"May 2d, 1587,—At a common hall, for obtaining 400*l.* which is by covenant to be paid to Mr. Francis Hastings, the 12th May next, for the reversion of one moiety of the Grange, which he hath procured from her Majesty, it was agreed as followeth, viz.: Henry Biddel lent 50*l.*; Mr. Morton, 50*l.*; Mr. James Ellys, mayor, 30*l.*; Mr. William Noryce, 20*l.*; Mr. Thomas Clarke and Mr. Robert Heyrick, 100*l.*"

"Oct. 20.—At a meeting of the mayor, &c., agreed that a bond shall be made to Mr. Elcock, of London, from the mayor and burgesses, under the common seal, for the payment of 200*l.* owing to him, and the interest of the same, viz. 18*l.* per annum, so long as the 200*l.* is unpaid, and thereupon the lease lately made to him of the Grange, for 10 years, to be called in and cancelled, so as thereby the rent of the Grange be employed for the use of the town and paying of the preacher."

The lands called the South Fields, appear to have been purchased about the same period. In the 30th Eliz. the following entry occurs:

"February 21st, 30 Eliz. 1588.—Towards paying for the lands purchased in the South Fields of Mr. Wightman, the 24 lend 40*s.* each, and the 48, 20*s.* for six months."

Other entries show that various acquisitions of property were made about this period.

"March 26th, 1591.—Several papers relating to a bargain of Mr. George Tatam and Mr. Thomas Clarke of 600*l.*, giving account of indentures about houses and lands, sealed and delivered to several persons."

"January 11th, 36 Eliz. 1594.—The mayor to buy the windmill in the South Fields (the purchase whereof is 20*l.*) upon the town's bond."

"40 Eliz.—It appears that in this year the commonalty of Leicester were called upon to pay a portion of the town's debt, incurred by the corporation purchases and law expenses, towards which the aldermen paid 58*l.*, the 48 (common council) 39*l.* 15*s.* 6*d.*, and the commonalty 20*l.* 11*s.* 4*d.*"

"Sept. 29th. 1617.—Paid Lord Spencer by Mr. Woodland, the first payment for the land on the South Fields, which was purchased of him this year for 40*l.*"

In the course of our inquiry, it appearing that the property called the South Fields had been mortgaged by the corporation to defray the expenses of an election, an opinion was expressed by the town clerk, that this land was the absolute property of the corporation, altogether independent even of any moral obligation to apply it to the use of any other than the select body, on the ground that it had been originally purchased by the contributions of the body itself. It appears, however, from the entries relating to the purchase, which appear on the corporation records, that in the only three instances in which the governing body contributed, namely, on the 18 March 1586, 20 October 1587, and 21 Feb. 1588, they in the two first instances merely advanced money on loan, and in the third contributed a share only in conjunction with the commonalty. It appears that the corporation were previously entitled to many quit rents; and there is reason to believe that the latter were about this time disposed of, and the proceeds applied towards their purchases.

It is quite clear that during the whole of this period the corporation property was considered as strictly the property of the town. The following entries in the corporation books are material to this point:

"25th May 1490.—The chamberlayns were ordered to pay of their proper goods a certain sum, (viz. 10*l.* &c. for half a fifteenth) to the king in the name of the town, in like manner as other chamberlayns have done for such like charges and other charges to the said town appertaining, until such time as they may levy it again of the revenues and other receipts of the said town."

"22 May 7 Hen. 7.—The sheeps market shall be kept in the Saturday market, and the profits thereof be received for the use of the town by such persons as are deputed by the mayor and his brethren, &c. the mayor to forfeit 40*s.*, and every of his brethren 20*s.* if he attempt to break the said ordinance."

"That the sheeps market shall be henceforth holden still in the market place, and the profits to be to behoof of the town."

"Hen. 8.—Agreed that a subsidy of 21*l.* shall be levied and gathered within the town to content the town's debt; and there were assessors appointed for each of the twelve wards, and one collector with the constable in each ward."

"That the first Friday in clean Lent every mayor hold a common hall; and there the chamberlain's accounts to be shewed, that it may be known in what degree the town stands."

"Agreed, that when any venison comes to the 24 and 48 by gift of any nobleman or gentleman, it shall be eaten at the only costs of the said 24 and 48, and no part of the charge to be borne by the chamber of the town."

"22d November 6th Eliz.—At a common hall, the town stock having been decayed by great gifts, in country as well as town, to noblemen and women and others, as also at the banquets of venison; of gifts and rewards given to players, musicians, jesters, noblemen's bearwards and such like, it is enacted that from the said day no such great allowance shall be paid out of the town stock, but that the spenders thereof, as at the banquets of venison, plays, bear baitings, &c. every of the 24 and 48 being required by the commandment of Mr. Mayor to be there, shall bear every one his own portion."

"11th August.—At a common hall agreed that there shall be put into the general lottery ten lots, viz. 5*l.* out of the stock of the town, and if any of the said lots be returned with any gain it shall be put into the stock of the town, and if any part of the said lottery be lost in the adventure it shall be made up by the 24 and 48, half by one and half by the other company."

"13th Mar. 21 Eliz.—Item. It is agreed to buy the bailiwick to the use of the town, and Mr. John Stanford, who bought Mr. John Danet's patent, hath now sold it to the town for 4*l.* besides his charges; and the town must enter upon it at Michaelmas next so soon as the audit is finished."

"Oct. 21st, 1597.—The stewards of the fairs shall yearly make their accompt to the mayor, and pay the overplus to the chamberlains for the use of the town."

"40th Eliz.—In this year the commonalty of Leicester were called upon to pay a portion of the town's debt, incurred by the corporation purchases and law expenses, towards which the aldermen paid 58*l.*, the 48 (common council) 39*l.* 15*s.* 6*d.* and the commonalty 20*l.* 11*s.* 4*d.*"

"March 20.—Agreed that the chamberlains that hereafter shall be, shall collect all the town's rents whatsoever, and shall have yearly for their pains 20 nobles with their old fee."

"Dec. 1st, 1612, 10 Jac.—Agreed that the recorder shall have for his fee yearly 5*l.*, and at every assizes towards his charge 20*s.*, and the town to bear and pay his charge at his coming to Leicester at all times about the town's business. Agreed to write to Mr. Justice Nicholls, to desire him to acquaint Mr. Recorder elected, with this our order for his fee and other charges, in regard the town is now poor and indebted, and that our recorders in times past have only had 4*l.* fee per annum and less."

The following part of the oath taken by the chamberlains at this period deserves also to be mentioned:

"We shall improve the livelode belonging unto the commonalty of the town of Leicester to the most behove of the same town; and also the tenements thereof we shall well and sufficiently repair during our office. We shall endeavour also for to improve the Chapman Gilde to the uttermost of our powers. And moreover we shall well and truly charge and discharge ourself of all lands and rents belonging to the town and of the Chapman Gilde, and of all other money as shall come to our hands belonging unto the commonalty of this town and thereof a true account shall yield up to the auditors assigned in the end of our year."

IV. The Corporation consists of a mayor, 24 aldermen, (including the mayor,) 48 common councilmen, and an indefinite body of burgesses or freemen. *CORPORATION. Component Bodies.*

The title of the corporation is, "The Mayor, Bailiffs and Burgesses of the Borough of Leicester." *Style.*

The Governing Body of the corporation consists of the mayor, the 24 aldermen, and the 48 common councilmen, otherwise called "The Company of the Eight-and-Forty." *Governing Body.*

The Mayor is annually elected on St. Matthew's day, by the mayor, aldermen and common councilmen, out of the aldermen. *Mayor.*

The mayor is the head of the corporation, and an integral part of the common council. He is a magistrate by virtue of his office, and one of the quorum at the quarter sessions. He is also returning officer of the borough. He has a salary and various allowances from the corporation amounting to 240*l.* per annum.

Aldermen.

The Aldermen are elected for life, by the mayor and aldermen, out of the common council.

They form part of the common hall of the borough; they elect the common councilmen and the officers of the corporation. The four aldermen who have last served the office of mayor are justices of the peace for the borough. They have no peculiar privileges, nor any emoluments.

Common Councilmen.

The Common Councilmen are elected by the mayor and aldermen, out of the resident freemen.

Their functions are confined to deliberating and voting in the common halls of the corporation.

They have no peculiar privileges, nor any emoluments.

Amoveability.

Any member of these three integral parts of the governing body is amoveable in case of misbehaviour in his office, by that part of the body in whom the right of election is vested.

Common Halls.

The mayor, aldermen and common councilmen constitute what is called the Common Hall of the corporation. Each member has an equal voice. A majority of the whole body, not of each integral part, is required to constitute a legal meeting. They have the management of all corporate concerns, the control of the corporate revenues, and the power of creating of freemen. The appointment of officers is vested in the mayor and aldermen.

Bye-Laws.

A power of making Bye-laws for the government and regulation of the town, as well as for that of their own body, is vested by the charter in the mayor and aldermen. From the records of the corporation, it appears that this authority was exercised till late in the 17th century, as regards the trade and the general police of the town. This authority does not, however, as far as the town in general is concerned, appear to have been exercised in modern times.

Officers.

The Officers of the corporation are (besides the Mayor)—

> A Recorder,
> A Town Clerk,
> A High Bailiff,
> A Steward of the Borough Court,
> A Chamberlain,
> A Steward,
> A Mace-bearer,
> Four Serjeants-at-Mace,
> A Chief Constable,
> A Beadle, two Bellmen, and a Crier.

The Recorder is elected by the mayor and aldermen during good be- Recorder.
haviour. He is required by the charter to be learned in the law, and is in
practice always a barrister.

The recorder is a magistrate by virtue of his office, and a judge of the
Court of Record. He presides at the Quarter Sessions, which cannot be
held in his absence.

He has a salary of 100 guineas a year by an allowance from the corporation.

The present recorder does not reside, but he attends regularly at the
Quarter Sessions.

The Town Clerk is appointed during good behaviour by the mayor and Town Clerk.
aldermen.

His functions are, to act as general legal adviser and assistant to the
corporation; and to attend the corporate meetings and record their proceedings. He is also clerk of the peace for the borough; and in practice acts
likewise as under-bailiff, without any regular appointment. In practice he
is also, though not necessarily, solicitor to the corporation. He likewise acts
as clerk to the magistrates. He has a salary of 200*l.* a year from the corporation. In this salary are included all charges for attending the corporate
meetings: for business done as the corporation solicitor, he makes the
usual professional charges. He receives the ordinary fees as clerk of the
peace and clerk to the magistrates, and takes all fees accruing to the head
bailiff.

The High Bailiff is appointed in like manner. The duties of this officer High Bailiff.
are the same as those of the sheriff of a county. He appoints the gaoler, and
summons all juries, criminal and civil. The duties of the office are performed by the town clerk, who acts as under bailiff, and receives all fees
accruing therefrom. From a return of the corporation expenditure, it appears that the high bailiff receives a salary of 50 guineas, and in addition
thereto, a gratuity of 50*l.* a year. We were informed that this was paid to
the gentleman who lately held the office on account of his residing at a distance.

The Steward of the Borough Court is appointed in like manner, but at Steward of the
the pleasure of the mayor and aldermen. He presides in the Borough Court Borough
Court.
in the absence of the recorder.

The emoluments of the office consist of fees on business done in the
court: these fees average from 30*l.* to 40*l.* a year.

This office is at present held by the gentleman who holds the office of
town clerk. But he holds it *pro tempore* only till the appointment of another
person, who was under age at the time the town clerk was appointed, and to
whom all the emoluments are made over. This arrangement was made at
the wish and with the concurrence, if not by the express desire of the court
of aldermen.

Chamberlain and Steward.

The Chamberlain and Steward are appointed by the mayor and aldermen. Their duties are entirely confined to the collection of the corporate revenues. The steward for the most part receives the rents and pays them over to the chamberlain, who acts as treasurer and makes all payments. It does not appear from the returns of expenditure made by the corporation, that any salary is attached to the office of chamberlain. The steward has a salary of 100*l.* per annum.

Mace-bearer.

The Macebearer is appointed by the mayor and aldermen during pleasure. His duty is to carry the mace, and to be in attendance on the mayor and corporation. For this he receives a salary of 95*l.* a year. He is also one of the officers to execute process from the Court of Record, for which he receives the usual fees. He is always a constable, and when employed as such, is paid the usual fees. He is employed to serve all summonses and warrants.

Serjeants at Mace.

The Serjeants at Mace are likewise appointed during pleasure. They are assistants to the macebearer, and with him execute process from the Court of Record, and receive the fees thereon. They have each a salary of 20*l.* from the Corporation.

Chief Constable.

The Chief Constable is appointed by the magistrates from year to year. The police is under his management. He has a salary of 50*l.* a year paid out of the Borough rate.

Town Servants.

The Beadle and Crier have each 20*l.* a year: the two Bellmen 10*l.* each. These officers, who are usually termed the Town Servants, have also other small perquisites.

Freedom of the Borough.

The Freedom of the Borough is acquired, 1st, by birth; 2d, by servitude; 3d, by gift of the Corporation.

Freedom by Birth.

All the sons of a freeman born after the admission of the father are entitled to the freedom, whether born within the borough or without.

Freedom by Servitude.

Freedom by servitude is acquired by serving an apprenticeship for seven years to a freeman, provided the apprentice be bound by indenture, and the indenture enrolled before the mayor. The service need not be within the borough.

Freedom by Gift.

Freedom by gift of the corporation is conferred by a vote of the Common Hall. It may be conferred either on payment of a certain sum or gratuitously. In ordinary cases it is conferred on payment of money. The particular sum is voted in each case at the same time with the freedom; but there is usually a standard sum. That sum has often varied within living memory. It is now 35*l.*

The freedom has also at times been given without payment; but this has for the most part been for electioneering purposes. In a single instance, no farther back than the year 1823, the freedom was voted at once to no less than 2,000 persons, all strangers to the borough; and of these, 800 actually took up their freedom, the corporation paying the fees on their admission.

The circumstances under which this flagrant abuse of corporate privileges took place will be more particularly detailed hereafter.

The Fees paid on Admission to the freedom, besides the stamp duty, which for freemen by birth or servitude is 1*l.*, for freemen by gift or purchase 3*l.*, are as follows:

Fees on Admission.

By an Eldest Son:

	£.	s.	d.
To the Mayor	–	4	–
— the Town Clerk	–	4	6
— the Macebearer	–	6	–
— the Crier	–	4	–
— the Beadle	–	2	–
£.	1	–	6

By a Second Son:

	£.	s.	d.
To the Corporation	–	5	–
— the Mayor	–	2	–
— the Town Clerk	–	4	6
— the Macebearer, Crier, and Beadle	–	1	–
£.	–	12	6

By a Third or other Son:

	£.	s.	d.
To the Corporation	–	10	–
— the Mayor and other officers the same as the foregoing	–	7	6
£.	–	17	6

The fees paid on admission by right of apprenticeship, are the same as those paid by a third son, viz. . – 17 6

Freemen by Gift or Purchase, pay

	£.	s.	d.
To the Mayor	–	2	–
— the Town Clerk	–	4	6
— the Macebearer	–	–	6
— the Crier	–	–	4
— the Beadle	–	–	2
£.	–	7	6

The exact number of freemen resident and non-resident is not known. It is supposed to amount to from 4,000 to 5,000. The number of resident freemen registered in 1832 was 1,569; the number of those resident within seven miles, 561; making together 2,070.

Number of Freemen.

Privileges of Freemen.

Prior to the passing of the Reform Act, all freemen enjoyed the right of voting, in conjunction with the inhabitants paying scot and lot, for the election of Members to serve in Parliament for the borough.

Right of Trading.

Among other privileges enjoyed by the freemen, was formerly the exclusive right of trading within the borough, all foreigners being precluded by the charter from selling wares and merchandizes within the limits (except in gross, or at the time of the fairs) without the leave and license of the corporation. The exclusive right of trading has however long fallen into disuse, except as regards one particular branch of trade. Licensed victuallers, if not free of the borough, are still in all cases compelled to purchase their freedom before they are allowed to carry on business.

ADMINISTRATION OF JUSTICE.

Magistrates. Jurisdiction.

V. The Magistrates are the mayor, the recorder, and the four aldermen who have last served the office of mayor.

The jurisdiction of the corporate magistrates extends over the borough and liberties, with the exception of a small part of the latter, called the Castle View, from which it is excluded. The jurisdiction is exclusive within the borough. The magistrates of the county have a concurrent jurisdiction over the liberties.

Quarter Sessions.

The Court of Quarter Sessions for the borough is held regularly before the borough magistrates. Three of the five justices (of whom the mayor and recorder must be two) are required to constitute the court. The recorder always attends and presides. The jurisdiction of the court extends to all cases not touching life or limb; all felonies not capital consequently are tried before it.

Court of Record.

A Court of Record is established by the charter, in which real, personal and mixed actions may be brought to any amount. The judges are the mayor, the recorder, the bailiffs and the steward, before any one of whom the court may be held: it is directed to be held weekly, or oftener if need be. The practice is the same as that of the Court of King's Bench. New rules, assimilating the practice to the recent improvements in that court, had been lately framed, but had not as yet been adopted in practice. The steward's fee on issuing a writ is 10s. The average amount of costs in an action of debt, when judgment is suffered to go by default, is from about 7l. to 8l.: on a judgment after a writ of inquiry, about 12l.; and on a judgment after verdict, about 15l. or 16l. The court is little used. In cases where the debt is small, the amount of costs is sufficient to deter parties from proceeding; and where the debt is large, it is thought more advisable to bring the action in one of the superior courts, because in the event of the defendant's removing the cause by *certiorari* (which is usually done when the debt is of any magnitude), the proceedings must be commenced *de novo* in the court to which it is removed.

Juries.

The Juries at the quarter sessions and the court of record are selected by the high bailiff, or in practice more generally by the under bailiff, his deputy.

The grand jury at the sessions are invariably taken from the common council exclusively. There is no provision in the charter to that effect, but such has been the unvarying custom. They attend as corporators in their robes of office.

VI. The Police consists of a chief constable, 30 constables or head-boroughs appointed for particular wards, and from 37 to 40 general constables. They are all appointed annually by the magistrates. POLICE. Constables.

The town is not regularly watched by night. In summer no watchmen are employed; in winter the chief constable selects seven or eight of the ordinary constables who are willing to undertake the duty, and these to a certain extent keep watch in the town. Watching and Lighting.

The town is also not sufficiently lighted.

Two or three of the parishes have availed themselves of the provisions of the General Watching and Lighting Act, and have appointed a few watchmen and partially lighted the streets; but their powers and funds are found to be inadequate. Much inconvenience is said to be felt in consequence of the defective state of this branch of the police. In 1822 an attempt was made to unite the parishes in an endeavour to procure a local Act for the purpose of making suitable provisions on this head, but the majority of the inhabitants refused to consent to such a measure from a jealousy of the corporation, and a disinclination to vest further powers in that body.

On extraordinary occasions, such as elections, special constables are appointed in considerable numbers by the magistrates. This has formed a heavy item of expense to the borough. Special Constables.

The inhabitants as a body, except in one or two instances arising out of particular circumstances (which will hereafter be noticed), have been remarkable for peaceable and orderly conduct, even in times of great political excitement; a circumstance the more striking on account of the strong political and party feeling which divides and agitates the borough. Public meetings on political questions have been frequently held, but have been unaccompanied by disorder. In 1832, after the rejection of the Reform Bill by the House of Lords, a political union was established in the town which consisted of 5,000 members. Several public meetings, and in one instance a great procession took place; the popular feeling was highly excited, but no disturbance or breach of the peace occurred. The political union was dissolved in the following year. General State of the Town.

There is a Gaol, and a House of Correction, in the borough. The buildings are immediately contiguous. The gaol has been recently rebuilt, and the house of correction is likewise a modern building. After the passing of Gaols.

the General Gaol Act (4 Geo. IV. c. 64.), the former borough gaol, which had been built in the year 1791 at considerable expense, was found incapable of being adapted to the regulations prescribed by that Act. The borough magistrates accordingly determined on building a new gaol; they purchased land of the corporation for the purpose, at a cost of between 3,000*l.* and 4,000*l.* Before, however, they had begun to build, the magistrates of the county having erected a new gaol, the old county gaol became vacant. This the borough magistrates purchased from the magistrates of the county for the sum of 5,000*l.* They then enlarged and rebuilt the old county gaol, and built the new house of correction at a further cost of 8,000*l.* To meet this heavy expenditure, about 12,000*l.* has been raised on the credit of the rate; the remainder was defrayed out of the current borough rate, and by sale of part of the land bought of the corporation. The part thus sold fetched 1,200*l.*; the rest remains for sale, and at present produces a rent of only 6*l.* a year.

It unfortunately turns out, that the object for which this heavy expense has been incurred has altogether failed. All classification required by the statute remains as impracticable in the present gaol as in the former. We were informed by the gaoler, that both in the gaol and the house of correction, the only classification which could be effected was, the separation of women from men, and debtors from felons, which separation already existed in the old gaol. It is impossible to separate men from boys, or the convicted from the untried. The latter object is attempted to be accomplished as far as possible, by confining men under sentence in the house of correction only, reserving the gaol for the untried and the women. As regards the latter, no classification whatsoever can take place. We were assured by the gaoler, that a considerable enlargement and alteration of the gaol must take place, before the proper classification could be carried into effect.

The gaol is besides inadequate in point of space. It is calculated to contain forty prisoners; more are frequently confined in it, and it sometimes becomes necessary to confine in the treble cells two more persons than they ought to contain. Several of the cells are ill constructed and confined, and do not sufficiently admit of the light and air. The debtors ward is particularly inconvenient and confined.

The prison establishment consists of a gaoler, and a turnkey and matron for the gaol, a keeper of the house of correction, and a turnkey under him.

The gaoler has a salary of 250*l.* per annum. The salary of this office in 1812 was 120*l.*; it was raised in 1817 to 150*l.* on the occasion of the abolition of the fees previously taken by gaolers; and again in 1824 to its present amount, when the magistrates, instead of paying a fixed sum for the removal of transports, determined on paying only the actual expenses.

The keeper of the house of correction, who is the gaoler's son, has a salary of 120*l.* a year, and a residence. The turnkey of the gaol has a salary of 55*l.* a year; the turnkey of the house of correction one of 52*l.* a year. The matron has 20*l.* a year. A chaplain is also appointed to the gaol, with a salary of 60*l.* a year.

The gaol is not regularly visited. No visiting magistrates are appointed; all being considered liable to this duty. The magistrates seldom visit the gaol, unless the gaoler or keeper of the house of correction reports the necessity of their presence, or repairs are supposed to be required. No regular visitation takes place at the quarter sessions.

It is however due to the officers of this establishment to say, that, as far as the inadequate nature of the buildings would allow, it appeared to be well regulated, and conducted with every regard to health, cleanliness and order.

It has been determined by the Court of King's Bench, that the borough magistrates have a right to commit prisoners to the county gaol, for offences committed within the liberties, and to cause such prisoners to be brought before them for trial at the borough sessions.* Since this decision, which took place in 1826, the practice of the borough magistrates has been to commit all offenders from the liberties to the county gaol.

VII. The expenses of the administration of justice, the maintenance of the gaol, and the preservation of the public peace, are defrayed by a rate levied on the borough. The interest on the debt incurred in rebuilding the gaol and house of correction is defrayed by a gaol rate levied under the 4th Geo. IV. c. 64. VII. Borough and Gaol Rate.

The rate is levied on the borough alone, and does not extend to the liberties. The question as to the liability of the liberties to the rate was raised in the year 1815, when it was decided by the Court of King's Bench, that as the Charter of 41 Eliz. which first gave jurisdiction to the borough magistrates over the liberties had reserved the former jurisdiction of the county magistrates, the previously existing liability of the liberties to contribute to the rate for the county imposed by the latter magistrates, still continues.†

THE following is an Account of the Borough Rate for the year ending Epiphany Sessions 1833.

	£. s. d.	£. s. d.
RECEIPTS:		
To Balance of last Account in Treasurer's hands		458 8 6
	800 – –	
To Borough Rates received, exclusive of Gaol Rates .	800 – – 600 – – 800 – –	
		3,000 – –
Carried forward . . . . . . £.		3,458 8 6

* Rex *v.* Musson, 6 Barnw. & Cres. 74.   † Bates *v.* Winstanley, 4 Maule & Selw. 429

		£.	s.	d.
Brought forward . . . . . £.		3,458	8	6
By Cash received for Fines imposed by the Magistrates upon persons having deficient weights and measures in their possession . .		3	1	7
By Cash received in respect of Fines imposed by the Magistrates under the Act 7 Geo. 4.		24	10	–
£.		3,486	–	1

EXPENDITURE:

		£.	s.	d.			
Gaol and House of Correction, ironwork, painting and lime-washing					191	9	2
Expenses of Gaol and House of Correction; viz.							
Gaoler's Salary	250	–	–				
Turnkey	54	12	–				
Matron	20	–	–				
Keeper of the House of Correction . . .	120	–	–				
Turnkey	52	–	–				
Surgeon and Apothecary, for Medicines . .	46	4	2				
Bread for Prisoners	206	3	5				
Clothing, Bedding, Coals, Oatmeal, &c. for ditto .	223	7	5				
Levies and Taxes on Gaol and House of Correction .	41	2	–				
Sundries	48	10	–				
					1,061	19	–
Chaplain of Gaol and House of Correction					60	–	–
Prosecutions and Sessions' business					518	–	8
Conveying Transports to the Hulks					68	16	8
Clerk of Assize, Marshal, Crier and Associate . . .					10	19	6
Coroners Inquests					78	12	–
Repairs of Bridges, Paving and Incidents							
Inspector of Market for Corn Returns					10	8	–
Inspector of Weights and Measures and incidents . . .					44	11	–
Advertisements, Printing and Stationery, and Miscellaneous . .					38	12	3
For Constables, Night-watch and other Police Expenses . .					398	3	4
Repairs of Fire-engines					19	3	6
Clerk of the Peace, Bill of Fees and Law Charges for the year . .					185	12	2
Money returned to the Black Friars, being overpaid by them .					10	16	3
Expense of valuing the Friars					19	11	6
The Treasurer, one year's Salary					21	–	–
Balance in the Treasurer's hands					748	5	1
£.					3,486	–	1

The subject of these rates will be reverted to hereafter.

Management
of the Poor.
VIII. The Management of the Poor and the appointment of parish vestries, is in all the parishes of the borough, except Saint Margaret's, under the regulation of the general law, and of select vestries appointed under the statutes 58 Geo. III. c. 69, and 59 Geo. III. c. 85.

Local Act
relating to St.
Margaret's
Parish.
The parish of Saint Margaret's, dissatisfied with the mode in which the magistrates exercised their power of appointing overseers, and of interfering in the relief of the poor, have obtained a local Act (2 Geo. IV. c. x). Under this Act, the general parish vestry, constituted as before, annually return a list of 30 persons to the magistrates, who select 20 therefrom; and

these, with the vicar, the churchwardens, the overseers of the poor and the surveyors of the highways constitute the select vestry.

The select vestry return a list of 24 householders to the magistrates, who choose therefrom four persons to be overseers for the year. By the Act, all the functions of overseers and churchwardens as regards the relief of the poor, and the assessment of poor, church, and highway rates, is transferred from the parish officers to the select vestry, those officers being placed entirely under the control of the latter body.

IX. The present annual Income of the corporation applicable to their general purposes, as appears from a return delivered to us by the town clerk, is as follows: REVENUES.
Income.

	£.	s.	d.
Old Grange, South Fields, &c.	2,009	18	6
Other property acquired under charters and grants, consisting of lands, tenements and tolls of market	1,118	9	1
Modern purchases (including Freake's grounds, and new market) .	937	6	4
Fee-farm and chief rents	66	12	10½
Casual receipts, such as purchases of freedoms. &c. . . .	190	15	–
TOTAL . . . £.	4,323	1	9½

The first return made to us by the town clerk of the annual ordinary Expenditure of the corporation, was as follows: Expenditure.

				£.	s.	d.
Sums payable to charities out of corporation general revenue . .				202	7	11
Salaries and allowances to mayor, recorder, high bailiff, town clerk, steward, head schoolmaster, the vicars, organists, mace-bearer, serjeants-at-mace, town servants, &c.				1,125	11	8
Miscellaneous, but usual payments:	30	2	10			
	150	–	–			
	166	–	–			
	89	12	3½			
				435	15	1½
Other miscellaneous payments, including occasional grants for public charities				200	–	–
Interest payable				450	–	–
Town clerk's annual bills, say about				315	–	–
Expenses of managing estates, and repairs of houses, &c. . .				450	–	–
Levies and arrears, about				30	–	–
Salary of superintendent of market . . . £. 120	–	–				
Ditto of superintendent of new market. . . 80	–	–				
				200	–	–
			£.	3,408	14	8½

Not considering the above Return as sufficiently explicit, (for reasons which have been already set forth in a former part of this Report), we called for a more detailed return setting forth the details of all the foregoing items, with the exception of those relating to the allowance of the super-intendents of the market.

Additional returns were then furnished, containing the items included in the sum of 1,225*l.* 11*s.* 8*d.* classed under the head of Salaries; and those of the four sums, making together 435*l.* 15*s.* 1½*d.*, classed under the head of "Miscellaneous, but usual payments."

The payments enumerated in the first of these additional returns, under the head of Salaries, may be classed under the following heads:

	£.	s.	d.	£.	s.	d.
The Mayor's Salary:						
Ancient salary	13	6	8			
More out of the rent of the Gosling Closes, as allowed by order of hall	12	6	8			
More, being the additional salary to the Mayor in 1713	20	–	–			
More, by order of common hall in 1736	40	–	–			
More, by order of common hall in 1769	50	–	–			
More, by order of common hall in 1797	50	–	–			
More, by order of common hall in 1806	50	–	–			
More, being coal and capon money	5	11	6			
				242	4	10
The recorder's salary				105	–	–
High bailiff's ditto	52	10	–			
Also, a gratuity during pleasure	50	–	–			
				102	10	–
Town clerk's salary				200	–	–
Additional charges for stamps, &c.				15	1	2
Steward's salary				100	–	–
Mace bearer's ancient salary	7	9	8			
More, as inspector of the corn market, for one year	2	12	–			
More, his salary for the like	5	–	–			
More, additional salary, for rendering assistance to the chamberlain	20	–	–			
More, for two seals	–	2	–			
More, by order of hall, in lieu of boarding with the mayor	40	–	–			
More, additional salary, by order of hall	20	–	–			
				95	3	8
Four serjeants at mace, at 20*l.* each				80	–	–
Cryer and beadle, at 20*l.* each				40	–	–
Two bellmen, at ten guineas each				21	–	–
Six waits				30	–	–
Library keeper				5	–	–
Allowance to cryer and beadle, to prevent their going round with their Christmas-box				–	5	–
Payment to them on St. Thomas's day, which used to be paid them by the parishes				–	5	–
For a pair of shoes each, for the cryer and beadle				1	2	–
Mole catcher's salary				1	11	6
Allowance to a superannuated servant of corporation				10	10	–
				1,049	13	2
From which, deduct charges of town clerk for stamps, &c. not coming under head of salaries				15	–	–
which leaves a total of salaries, and allowances to officers and servants of corporation, of				1,034	13	2
Exclusive of the salaries of superintendents of the markets, which amount to 200*l.* a year more.						

To which must be added the following allowances:

	£. s. d.	£. s. d.
To the Rev. Mr. Erskine as lecturer of the Borough, yearly salary during pleasure	20 – –	
Ditto – as vicar of St. Martin's	10 – –	
Ditto – to the Rev. Dr. Fancourt as vicar of All Saints .	10 – –	
Ditto – to him as vicar of St. Mary's	10 – –	
Ditto – to the Rev. Mr. Davis as vicar of St. Nicholas .	10 – –	
Ditto – to the Rev. Mr. Irvine as vicar of St. Margaret's .	10 – –	
A yearly gratuity during pleasure to the organist of St. Martin's	10 – –	
Ditto – to the organist of St. Margaret's . . .	10 – –	
Ditto – to the organist of St. Mary's . . .	10 – –	
		100 – –

	£. s. d.	£. s. d.
To the head schoolmaster, his salaries and allowances, as under:—		
The Town's free gift during pleasure . . .	16 – –	
More, the Town's annual free gift during pleasure .	8 – –	
Ditto . . ditto	3 – –	
Ditto . . ditto	5 – –	
More, by order of hall, on condition of his taking boys free of entrance	5 – –	

N.B.—The five foregoing gifts were formerly paid to the head-master, and the head and under usher; but by order of hall, in July 1797, were all directed to be to the Rev. Mr. Heywick, on his being appointed sole master, and are now paid to Mr. Davies.

	£. s. d.	£. s. d.
More, the Town's free gift during pleasure, by order of hall, 1797	30 – –	
More, ditto by the like order, being the rent of a tenement in Sanvy-gate, and a garden in Elbow-lane .	8 18 6	
		75 18 6
Total allowances to clergymen, organists and schoolmasters . .		175 18 6
Making, together with the salaries, &c. to the officers and servants of the corporation, the total mentioned in the original Return; viz. .		1,225 11 8
To this must be added the salary of the superintendent of the market . . . . £.120 – –		
Ditto – of the new market . . . . . . 80 – –		
		200 – –
Making a total of salaries and allowances of . . . . £.		1,425 11 8

The first four items included under the head of miscellaneous but usual payments, may be reduced to the following heads:—

RENTS AND CHARGES:	£. s. d.
Chief rent out of Gainsboro' (land-tax deducted) . .	5 18 6
Fee-farm rent to the Earl of Pembroke, out of the South Field tithes	4 7 10
Year's rent to the Duchy of Lancaster for premises rented on lease, expiring 27th December 1858 . . .	15 1 –
Year's rent to Wigston's hospital for the new sheep market	1 13 8
Year's payment in lieu of tithes, issuing out of the Horsefair garden, to the prebendary of St. Margaret's, as by St. Margaret's award	1 5 1½
Rent of pews at St. George's church	10 10 –
Carried forward . . . . . £.	38 16 1½

	£.	s.	d.
Brought forward . . . . . . £.	38	16	1½

PUBLIC BUILDINGS, &c.

	£.	s.	d.	£.	s.	d.
Fires at Town-hall and Exchange . . .	17	18	3			
Sweeping chimnies at ditto	–	12	–			
Insurance	11	17	6			
Lighting public buildings	39	17	–			
Winding clock at Exchange	2	2	–			
Repairing ditto	1	11	–			
Parochial levies on free school	6	10	6			
For playing engines four times	10	10	–			
For cleaning and taking care of Town-hall and stoves .	10	–	–			
				100	12	3

CHARGES connected with CORPORATION ESTATES.

Receipt stamps for the rent days	5	18	3			
Annual allowance for expenses at the rent days . .	15	15	–			
Additional ditto	15	3	4			
				36	16	7

ENTERTAINMENTS, &c.

Allowance to the chamberlains for the auditor's dinners, by order of hall	10	10	–			
To the grand jury for four sessional dinners, at 5l. 15s. 6d. each; and additional by order of hall, at five guineas each sessions	44	2	–			
Paid Messrs. Carbonell for a pipe of wine . . .	97	14	–			
For carriage thereof	2	11	–			
				154	17	–
Allowance to mayor for postages	5	–	–			
For his Standard newspaper	14	16	3			
For the John Bull ditto	1	16	–			
For the Herald ditto	1	12	–			
				23	4	3

ALLOWANCES to CORPORATION SERVANTS.

Payment to mace-bearer and servants of fees for newly elected aldermen and two common councilmen .	–	16	–			
To the same, for attending on the fair and market days, to keep the cattle within the places allotted to them, in order to prevent the more public streets from being incommoded by them	11	5	–			
Allowance to mace-bearer, for what he paid for refreshments at the several sessions	10	1	1			
Ditto – at the assizes	2	9	5			
Ditto – for what he paid for cleaning knives . .	4	4	–			
				28	15	6

SUBSCRIPTIONS.

To the infirmary	10	10	–			
To the horse race, as increased by order of hall . .	21	–	–			
To the Waterloo soldiers and pensioners in Leicester, on the anniversary of the battle of Waterloo, by order, at 2s. 6d. each	15	15	–			
				47	5	–
Small miscellaneous payments	.	.		4	18	5
			£.	435	15	1½

The sum of 200*l.* included in the original return of the town clerk, under the subsequent head of miscellaneous payments, as well as the remaining sums comprised in the original return (with the exception of the 450*l.* for interest, and 200*l.* for the salaries of the superintendents of the markets) turned out on further inquiry to be average estimates only. And it was admitted by the town clerk that these averages were merely conjectural and not founded on arithmetical calculations. We were unable to obtain any explanation of the items of which those charges were composed.

The 200*l.* mentioned to be payable to charities is the interest of money vested in the corporation as trustees for the benefit of the several charities, and applied by them to the general purposes of the corporation.

The sum of 450*l.* included in the general account of expenditure under the head of interest, is the amount of interest payable on a sum of 10,000*l.* raised by the mortgage of a part of the corporation property called the South Fields, in the year 1829. The discreditable circumstances under which this debt was incurred will be hereafter narrated. It suffices for the present to state that the 10,000*l.* in question was raised in order to pay off a debt incurred by the corporation party for the expenses at the election in 1826. The mortgage bears date the 24th March 1829.

The expenditure accounted for by the table in the return referred to, amounts to 3,408*l.* 14*s.* 8½*d.*, while the income of the corporation has been stated to be 4,323*l.* 1*s.* 9½*d.*; 814*l.* 8*s.* 7*d.* [*sic*] therefore is still unaccounted for on the year's expenditure. The subsequent refusal of the corporation to submit to further inquiry prevented this subject from being investigated. *Expenditure not accounted for.*

Considerable alienations of the corporation property have taken place since the year 1810; but the amount of property disposed of is one of the points which the abrupt refusal of the corporation to submit to further investigation leaves involved in some degree of uncertainty. *Sales of Land.*

It happens, however, that in the year 1810 a committee was appointed by the common hall to take into consideration the income and expenditure of the corporation. Their report, which was furnished to us by the town clerk, shows what property had been alienated on the one hand and acquired on the other, at that period; besides which it contributes to throw light on the general financial state of the corporation: it will therefore be inserted here. It is as follows:

"Your committee having been summoned by the mayor to inquire into the matters referred to them, had laid before them, at three several meetings, all the accounts of the different chamberlains, during the last twenty years, ending with those of Messrs. Thompson and Burbidge, chamberlains, in the late mayoralty of Samuel Clarke, esq., being the last accounts which have been yet audited; for, although the order of hall under which your committee act, only directs them 'to prepare a statement of the income and expenditure of the corporation in such a shape as will show what portion of it is applicable to charitable purposes, and other obligatory payments, and what at the disposal of the corporation;' yet, in order to give the whole body a comprehensive view of its pecuniary affairs, and to satisfy the minds of those members, who, being unacquainted with the manner in which the accounts are kept and audited, might probably not be satisfied with the mere statement of the result, it appeared desirable to take a retrospective view, and to afford the opportunity to every individual member of satisfying his own mind, by an actual inspection of the documents from which that result should be produced. The want of money, which the corporation has for the last four or five years experienced, has (not unnaturally) led to an inquiry amongst persons unacquainted (as some of the younger members of the body must necessarily be) with the corporation accounts, how its revenues are disposed of. Every member is aware that within these few last years large sums have been raised by sales of part of the corporation property, but they are not all apprized of the manner in which those sums have been applied; it therefore appeared desirable to your committee to investigate that point; and they find that within the last ten years some old houses, and the horse-fair house and garden have been sold for the sum of 8,386*l.* 17*s.* which, together with the money arising from the sale of some funded property, appears to be duly accounted for from time to time in the chamberlain's accounts. In order to shew the advantages of these sales, they beg to state that the annual rents of the houses and lands which have been so sold, and produced this sum of 8,386*l.* 17*s.* amounted to 127*l.* 8*s.* 6*d.* only. With these purchase monies, added to the money arising from the sale of the property in the funds (making together about 10,000*l.*), it appears that the land-tax of the corporation estates (to the annual amount of 80*l.*) has been redeemed for the sum of £. 2,000 – –

The South Fields have been inclosed and subdivided at an expense of more than . . . . 4,700 – –

An annual rent of 141*l.* payable to the Duchy of Lancaster, and which incumbered the whole of the corporation estates, has been purchased at the price of . . . . 3,476 – –

And several small purchases of land have been made to the amount of more than . . . . 1,000 – –

£. 11,176 – –

Thus, is the money produced by the sales above alluded to much more than accounted for, without specifying many other large extraordinary payments which have also been made in the course of the last ten years. And it is with great satisfaction that your committee have to state, these difficulties have been surmounted without any retrenchment of the charities and liberalities of the corporation, which, on the contrary, have been greater than at any former period.

"It will be seen by the above statement, that by the purchase of the Duchy rent and the redemption of the land-tax alone, the corporation has acquired an additional annual income of more than 220*l*. But the great source of increase to its annual revenues arises from the inclosure of the South Fields and meadows. The total rental of that property in the year 1804, in its uninclosed state, was only 963*l*. 18*s*. 3*d*., whereas the net rental of it last year was 1,894*l*. 17*s*. 9*d*. being very nearly double."

In the same year a committee was appointed, to whom the sale of a part of the South Fields was committed by the common-hall: that committee, in the year 1814, reported as follows:—

"Your committee having sold as much of the South Fields as was necessary to answer the purposes for which those sales were directed, think it their duty to report to the hall the result of their proceedings.

"The quantity of land which has been sold, including the parts laid out for streets, is about five acres, which, previous to being sold, let at about 6*l*. per acre. The amount of the purchase monies arising from the sales is 6,577*l*. 16*s*. Out of this sum the corporation has been enabled to make the following payments, viz.

	£.	s.	d.
For houses in Southgate-street, bought of Mr. William Hall . .	650	–	–
— houses bought of Mr. William Hardy	460	–	–
— the Nag's Head Inn, bought of Mrs. Thornelve . . .	1,500	–	–
— building, &c. in the Sheep-market, bought of Mr. M. Reid and of the executors of Mr. Joseph Brown	590	17	–
— For ground bought of Mr. Miller, near the New Walk, in order to complete the new streets, &c.	627	15	–
To Messrs. Robys, a sum borrowed of them about seven years ago .	700	–	–
— Trinity Hospital, a sum which the corporation had retained on interest many years, but which is now invested in the funds .	210	10	2
— the returning officer's counsel at the last general election . .	320	–	–
A subscription in 1812 to the poor of Leicester	300	–	–
Ditto – to the Russian sufferers	105	–	–
Ditto – to the poor of Leicester, in 1813	210	–	–
Ditto – to the County School	105	–	–
Ditto – to the German sufferers	105	–	–
For erecting a new guard-house, engine-house, &c. . about	200	–	–
Making altogether . . . . . . £.	6,084	2	2

"The houses and buildings purchased as above stated, now let for 132*l*. per annum, exclusive of the guard-house and engine-house, which are appropriated to the public rent-free. Thus, the corporation will perceive, that by selling five acres of ground, which produced an income of no more than 30*l*. per annum, they have not only been enabled to make many large and extraordinary payments for public and charitable purposes, which the exigencies of the times called for, but have also acquired a considerable additional income. Several other extraordinary payments, besides those above enumerated, have indeed been made during the last four or five years; but your committee do not think it necessary to give to the hall more than a general statement, in order to account for the application of the purchase monies arising from the property, the sale of which was more immediately entrusted to them."

From the two foregoing reports it appears that between the years 1800 and 1814 there had been sold—

Prior to 1810:

	£.	s.	d.
Old Houses; and the Horse Fair House and Garden, producing together the sum of . . . . .£. 8,386 7 –			
Property in the Funds, about . . . . . 1,613 13 –			
Making together about . . .	10,000	–	–
Between 1810 and 1814:			
Five Acres in the South Fields	6,577	16	–
Producing in all . . . . . . £.	16,577	16	–

On the other hand, the Corporation estate, with the produce of the property sold before 1810, had been improved by the following outlay:—

	£.	s.	d.
By redemption of the land tax to the yearly amount of 80l. per annum, at a cost of	2,000	–	–
By redemption of an annual rent of 141l., to the Duchy of Lancaster at a cost of	3,476	–	–
By the inclosure and subdivision of the South Fields, whereby the annual rental of the same had been augmented 930l. 19s. 6d., at a cost of	4,700	–	–
By the purchase of land to the value of.	1,000	–	–
£.	11,176	–	–

Exceeding in the whole the sum raised by the sale up to that period by 1,176l.

With the produce of the sales between 1810 and 1814, a beneficial improvement had been effected:—

	£.	s.	d.
1st. By the purchase of land and houses, producing an increase of the annual rental of 102l. at a cost of	3,828	12	–
2d. By the erection of a new guard and engine-house, applicable to public purposes, at a cost of	200	–	–
3d. By the payment of two debts amounting to	900	10	2
£.	4,929	2	2
Besides other payments, amounting to	1,145	–	–
Making a total accounted for of . . . . £.	6,084	2	2
Thus leaving a Balance of . . . . . £.	493	13	10

for which the Committee do not think it necessary to account.

It was stated to us by the town clerk, in the course of the inquiry, that since he had been in office, a period of about 20 years, not more than 10 acres had been alienated, at the price of about 1,200*l.* per acre, which would consequently have produced about 12,000*l.* The town clerk at the same time stated that in the same period property had been acquired to the amount of about 5,000*l.*; he further stated that none could have been acquired without his knowledge. It will presently appear, that this statement has since turned out upon the town clerk's own showing, to have been altogether erroneous.

Having been informed that sales of land, to a far greater extent than what had been spoken to by the town clerk, had been made by the corporation, we expressed our intention of pursuing this subject of inquiry. The course suddenly adopted by the corporation rendered us unable further to examine the corporate officers on this important matter. Several highly respectable inhabitants of the town then came forward, and gave their evidence on the subject. They deposed, that within the last 20 or 25 years a considerable portion of the South Fields, which they remembered from their boyhood as forming part of the uninclosed Lammas land belonging to the corporation, had been sold by that body for the purposes of building. They enumerated to us, with great minuteness of detail, the various streets which had been built upon the land in question, which now forms an extensive portion of the suburbs of the town, and agreed that the quantity sold must have been from 25 to 30 acres. Mr. Lawrence, a land surveyor, having formed an estimate from a map made for the overseers of St. Mary's, and believed to be correct, stated the extent of land thus sold to be 26 acres, exclusive of the main streets, which were given in by the vendors, but inclusive of the smaller streets, which were paid for by the purchasers. The least valuable part of this land was stated to have been worth at least 5*s.* a yard to sell; some parts were stated to have been sold at 5*s.*, others at 6*s.* and 7*s.* the yard. The land was sold by the corporation by private contract. Members of the corporation were in more than one instance purchasers. A witness stated that he bought land of an alderman and common councilman (father and son) at 7*s.* 6*d.* and 8*s.* a yard within six months after they had purchased from the corporation, and that they had informed him that they had given 5*s.* a yard for it. The witness stated that there was nothing to prevent the corporation from obtaining the price he gave.

Assuming the estimate of the surveyor above referred to to be correct, and taking the corporation to have sold at 5*s.* a yard (which, upon the evidence, appears to be a very low rate) as the price of each acre would be 1,210*l.*, the total amount of sales may be stated at 31,460*l.*

The foregoing estimate relates only to the land sold on the South Fields; in addition to this Mr. Lawrence, the surveyor, stated, as within his knowledge, that two acres and a quarter of land, in what is called Freake's Ground, had been sold two years before, to a railway company, for 300*l.* an acre, making 675*l.*, and forming, therefore, with the price of the land sold in the South Fields, a total of 32,117*l.*

It has been mentioned, that the town clerk, in his evidence, stated, that since he had held his office, land to the amount of 12,000*l.* only had been alienated; and on the other hand, property to the amount of 5,000*l.* only had been acquired. After the facts above stated had been deposed to by witnesses whose station and character placed their veracity above all suspicion, it became highly important that the officers of the corporation should be further examined on the subject. But the course which the corporation thought proper to pursue rendered this impossible. Since our return to town, however, a statement has been transmitted to us by the town clerk, purporting to be an account of all property sold since the year 1810, and of the purposes to which the produce has been applied. It is obvious that such a document, furnished after the termination of our inquiry, instead of during its progress, whereby all opportunity of a more minute examination, and of putting the various questions to the corporate officers which such a statement would have suggested has been wholly avoided, must lose very much of the authority to which it would be otherwise entitled. Nevertheless, subject to this observation, the substance of the statement will be here set forth. It in the first instance refers to the sales included in the Reports of the Committees of 1810 and 1814; but the sales prior to 1810 are not material to the present question, as it will be remembered that the land referred to as sold, in the Report of 1810, formed no part of the South Fields. The statement estimates the land referred to as sold in the Report of 1814, at five acres. It goes on to state, that between 1814 and 1831 there had been further sold 13 acres and 328 yards, making, therefore, in all a total of 18 acres 328 yards sold from the South Fields, instead of 26 acres, as estimated by Mr. Lawrence, the surveyor, or from 25 to 30, as stated by other witnesses.

The account states that the 13 acres and 328 yards were sold at 5*s.* a yard, making, therefore . . . . . . £. | 15,812 – –

If, therefore, to this amount be added the value of the land referred to as sold in the Report of 1814; viz. . . . . . . | 6,577 16 –

The total value of land sold in the South Fields will be . . . . £. | 22,389 16 –

To this, according to the statement, is to be further added, for land sold in Leicester Forest . . . . . £. | 1,846 – –

Making the total amount of sales since 1810 . | 24,235 16 –
Ditto since 1814 . . . . . | 17,658 – –

The produce of the land sold prior to 1814 is accounted for by the committee of that year.

The statement then proceeds to account for the application of the amount thus raised subsequently to the year 1814, as follows:

	£.	s.	d.
Paid towards the purchase of the Bull's Head Inn, in the Market-place, Leicester	1,287	–	–
Laid out in building walls, &c. to fence in gardens near the New Walk, to preserve the walk from nuisances	303	–	–
To purchase-monies paid for purchase of land to make the new market, and paving and preparing the same	2,327	–	–
To purchase of land near Leicester, bought of Mr. Pares . .	1,987	–	–
To purchase of land near Leicester, bought of Mr. Ruding's trustees	1,082	–	–
To purchase of stalls, pens, &c. for the market when taken into the hands of the corporation, and in re-paving and improving the market-place	1,491	–	–
Expended in rebuilding and enlarging the North Mill, and in erecting a new house and out-buildings, &c.	2,858	–	–
Expended in rebuilding and enlarging the Swan's Mill, and building a new house, &c.	1,782	–	–
To money lent to Trinity Hospital, laid out in rebuilding some of their houses	690	–	–
To money lent towards erecting a steam engine at the North Mill .	200	–	–
To a fine paid on the renewal of a lease from the Duchy of Lancaster	339	–	–
Laid out in the purchase of oak boards	406	–	–
Laid out in the purchase of land connected with the formation of the new streets	326	–	–
Another purchase of land for the like	360	–	–
Expenses incurred in preparing ground for streets, and levelling and fencing, making culverts, agency for sales and expense of titles, &c.	1,816	–	–
Purchase-monies still due to the corporation, about . . .	2,000	–	–
By cash paid for the under-mentioned public subscriptions, besides those paid out of the annual income of the corporation, viz.:			
For the new church in St. Margaret's parish	210	–	–
Expenses incurred and paid by the corporation in the public celebration of the coronation of King George IV.	366	10	6
Subscription to the frame-work knitters	100	–	–
Subscription towards improvement at the West Bridge . . .	100	–	–
£.	20,030	10	6

Total amount from sales since 1814 and up to the end of 1831 . . £. 17,658 – –

Total amount appropriated as above in purchases, and in beneficial improvements of the corporation property, and for public purposes, as above specified . . . . } £. 20,030 10 –

If the foregoing statement had been submitted to us pending our inquiry, we should undoubtedly have deemed it our duty to institute further inquiries respecting many of the heads it embraces. We should have thought it necessary to institute the fullest inquiry as to the quantity of land sold, before we could have dismissed as inaccurate the testimony of the very respectable and competent witnesses who spoke positively to the fact of at least 25 acres having been disposed of. Moreover, it appears difficult to conceive that the whole of the land, which was sold at different times and in various lots, and appears to have been of different degrees of eligibility for the purposes of building, should have fetched throughout the same uniform price of 5s. a yard. We were assured that the least eligible was worth 5s. a yard, and were informed that some had been sold by the corporation at 6s. and 7s. a yard. Some land, not long after the original sale, was proved to have been resold by the purchasers at 10s. a yard. Some, within six months of the sale, has already been stated to have been resold at 7s. 6d. or 8s. a yard.

It appears, therefore, that either 5s. a yard cannot be the true price of the whole, or that the corporation must have sold great part of the land at much less than its real value. Both these inferences may, to a certain extent, be true; and we should therefore have thought it right to require strict proof as to the price for which each lot was disposed of, and to inquire in what instances the purchasers were or were not members of the corporation, as also whether the 2,000l. of the purchase money still remaining unpaid was due from any members of the body. Upon the mode in which the money has been applied inquiries might also have suggested themselves: at present the subject will be passed over without observation. It may, however, be remarked, though obvious, that the account is incorrect in stating the amount beneficially appropriated at 20,030l. 10s. 6d., inasmuch as from this must be deducted the 2,000l. still unpaid, which is one of the items included in the total alluded to.

The statement is also remarkable in another particular. In the application of the money, it accounts for 2,372l. 10s. 6d. more than the amount raised by the sales. From what source this overplus has been derived is not stated.

Accounts.

The revenues of the corporation are collected by the steward, and by him paid over to the chamberlain, who acts as treasurer.

Audit Committee.

An audit committee is annually appointed, consisting of four aldermen and eight common councilmen (who take the office in rotation), and of two additional members of the corporation, named by the chamberlain. To this body the duty of auditing the accounts of the corporation is committed. The general accounts are audited once a year; tradesmen's bills every six months. The material part of the trouble appears to devolve on the town clerk, who examines all accounts and vouchers, and makes out a general account, which is then submitted to the committee.

Accounts not published.

No publication of the corporation accounts is ever made, and the body of the freemen and inhabitants have hitherto been wholly ignorant of the amount of the corporate income, and the manner of its application.

The following is a TABLE of the CHARITIES of which the Corporation are Trustees:—

Nature of the Funds.	How acquired.	Purposes for which given.	Mode in which they are now distributed or applied.	Charities of which the Corporation are Trustees.
A rent-charge of 2*l.* per annum out of Rowlatt's Close, the gift of Mrs. Twigden.	by deed - - -	- - to three poor widows of St. John's Hospital, 10*s.* each to buy gowns, and 10*s.* amongst the six widows for coals.	- - as directed by the deed, namely, for gowns and coals.	
Land in the lordship of Enderby, in the county of Leicester, now let for 65*l.* per annum, the gift of Mr. Bent.	- - by the will of Alderman Bent, once mayor in the borough, dated in 1703.	- - to support four poor freemen's widows, in a hospital called Bent's Hospital.	- - in support of four widows in this hospital, and a nurse, at an increase of pay allowed by the state of the funds.	
A rent-charge of 3*l.* issuing out of the Tippett's, in St. Mary's parish, being Mr. Moreton's gift.	- - by will of Mr. William Moreton (one of the aldermen of the borough) dated 17th August 1620.	- - to six widows in St. John's Hospital, Leicester, 18*s.*, to buy them coals; and 2*l.* 2*s.* to seven poor housekeepers, freemen of the borough, 6*s.* each to buy coals.	- - the 18*s.* are paid to the widows of St. John's, and the residue is distributed amongst the poor, as part of the money called wood and coal money, annually.	
A rent-charge of 3*l.* out of the Duck Holmes, in St. Mary's parish, Mr. Ward's gift.	- - by Mrs. Elizabeth Ward (daughter of Alderman William Moreton) by deed, dated 18th June 1628.	- - to three widows of St. John's Hospital, alternately 10*s.* each, to buy gowns; for coals for them all 10*s.* To two alms women in Trinity Hospital 10*s*, and to the common box there 10*s*.	as directed by the deed.	
A rent-charge of 12*l.* out of the Leroes, in St. Margaret's parish, the gift of Mr. William Billers.	- - given by Mr. William Billers, one of the aldermen of the borough.	- - to uses for the benefit of two widows in Trinity Hospital, and a gown to one annually, and the remainder to buy oatmeal for the poor.	as directed by the will.	
A rent-charge of 10*l.* per annum out of divers premises in Leicester, called Blunt's gift.	- - by the will of Mr. Thomas Blunt, dated 13th January 1663.	- - to buy 40 pair of shoes for the poor of Trinity Hospital, annually, and widows of St. John's, on St. Thomas's day, and certain small sums to be paid to the mayor and town clerk, &c.	as directed by the will	
A rent-charge of 2*l.* 10*s.* per annum out of a house in Silver street, the gift of Mr. Bent.	- - by the will of Mr. George Bent (one of the aldermen) dated in or about 1735.	- - to be distributed amongst the poor widows of St. John's Hospital.	as directed by the will.	
A gift or rent-charge of 10*l.* out of the honor of Leicester, by the hands of the Receiver General of His Majesty's Duchy of Lancaster.	- - by the Crown, out of the revenues of the Duchy of Lancaster, originally granted by Queen Elizabeth.	- - for better maintaining the under usher of the free grammar school.	paid to the master of the free grammar school.	

Nature of the Funds.	How acquired.	Purposes for which given.	Mode in which they are now distributed or applied.
An annuity or rent-charge of 3*l*. 6*s*. 8*d*. out of the manor of Theddingworth, the gift of Sir Ralph Rowlatt.	by Sir Ralph Rowlatt	for the under usher of the grammar school.	paid to the master of the free grammar school.
An annuity of 3*l*. 6*s*. 8*d*. out of a close in Abbey Gate.	- - by Mr. William Norrice (one of the aldermen.)	for the head usher of the grammar school.	paid as above.
An annuity of 1*l*. payable out of the Waterlags, the gift of Thomas Clarke.	- - by Mr. Thomas Clarke (one of the aldermen.)	for the under usher of the grammar school.	paid as above.
A messuage and land at Whetstone, in Leicestershire, bought by the corporation with the money bequeathed by Christopher Tamworth, esq., now let at 60*l*. per annum.	- - by the will of Mr. Christopher Tamworth he gave 200 marks to the corporation to buy lands of the yearly value of 6*l*. 13*s*. 4*d*.; the corporation bought land at Whetstone, which now lets for 60*l*. per annum.	- - to pay to some one in holy orders to read divine service twice a day in St. Martin's church on work days, not to be attached to the vicarage of St. Martin, but the clergyman to be chosen by the mayor and aldermen.	- - now always paid to the vicar of St. Martin's parish, who performs divine service in the week day at stated times, but not daily.
Land in Leicester Forest, given by King Charles the First, for the poor of Leicester, let at 52*l*. per annum.	- - by King Charles the First, of ever blessed memory.	- - to the poor of the corporation (freemen) to buy them wood or coal.	- - it is distributed annually by the aldermen of wards, with other monies, and is called the wood and coal money.
An annuity or rent-charge of 10*l*., payable out of the manor of Cotes Deval, the gift of Mr. Poultney.	- - by the will of John Poultney, esq., who died on the 15th May 1637.	- - to be distributed by the mayor and justices at their discretion, amongst the poor of the different parishes in Leicester.	- - this is paid to the clerks of the different parishes on St. Thomas's Day, in certain proportions, to be given to the poor.
Land at Bushby, in Leicestershire, now let at 70*l*. per annum, the gift of Mr. Nidd.	- - Mr. Richard Nidd, of the city of London, by his will, dated 31st July 1617, gave 300*l*. to the corporation to be laid out in land of the yearly value of 15*l*.; the corporation purchased the estate at Bushby, which now lets for 70*l*. per annum.	- - for the poor of Mountsorrel, where the testator was born.	- - the whole rent is paid over to the parish officers of Mountsorrel, who distribute it, or it is supposed do so, amongst the poor.
An annuity or rent-charge of 9*l*. per annum, out of the manor of Asterby, in Lincolnshire, the gift of Mr. Acham.	- - by the will of Mr. Anthony Acham, of Holborn, London.	- - to be given in bread to the poor of Leicester, at the discretion of the corporation, viz. 30*s*. on the last Sunday of every alternate month.	- - it is now given in fourpenny loaves every other month, as directed by the will, and is sent to the churchwardens for distribution.

Nature of the Funds.	How acquired.	Purposes for which given.	Mode in which they are now distributed or applied.
An annuity or rent-charge of 2*l.* out of a house in St. Martin's parish, the gift of Mr. Hugh Botham.	by the will of Mr. Hugh Botham.	- - to be distributed to the parishes of St. Martin, St. Margaret and St. Mary, equally.	- - this is paid to the parish clerks of each of the parishes, for the poor.
Land at Allexton, for 32*l.* per annum, the gift of Mr. Hayne.	- - by the will of Mr. Thomas Hayne, of the parish of Christchurch, London, he gave to the corporation 400*l.* to be bestowed on lands or houses near Leicester, of the yearly value of 24*l.* The corporation bought the land at Allexton, which now lets for 32*l.* per annum. given in Leicester four years, and 20*s.* for a sermon yearly, and the remainder to the poor of Leicester, at the discretion of the mayor, aldermen and recorder.	- - to pay a schoolmaster at Thrussington to teach 10 poor children there 6*l.* per annum; to two scholars being and studying in Lincoln College, Oxford, 6*l.* yearly; to buy three bibles, yearly, 20*s.*, to be Thrussington one year;	- - the rent is now distributed as the will directs, except that when no scholars claim the exhibition money, it is kept in hand until some one who may be qualified does claim; and as to the residue of the rent it is paid thus: 10*l.* of it is distributed as part of the wood and coal money, and the remainder is given away in coals to the poor of the town at other times.
Houses in Causeway Lane, Leicester, built by 50*l.* given by Mr. Cammack, and 115*l.* received for the sale of St. John's Hospital garden.	- - purchased and built with monies belonging to St. John's Hospital.	- - towards the maintenance of the poor widows in St. John's Hospital.	- - in the maintenance of the widows of St. John's Hospital.
Estates at Barwell, Earl Shilton, Strettin and Bushby, of the yearly value of 517*l.*, and money in the funds, yielding an income of 214*l.* 14*s.* 4*d.*	- - by the gift of Alderman Gabriel Newton, by deeds of settlement made in the year 1760, and also by his will, dated 21st July 1761. residue to be employed in supporting and extending a school at Leicester, established by Alderman Newton, in which 35 boys were then educated and clothed, and in endowing schools in other places, should the income be adequate. ment and support of schools at those places, surplus rents by the corporation.	- - to pay certain annual sums towards the maintenance of schools at Bedford, Buckingham, Huntingdon, Hertford, Ashby-de-Zouch, St. Neots, Earl Shilton and Barwell, and the	- - in payment of the annual sums directed by the trust deed to the places therein mentioned, and in maintaining a school at Leicester, in which 100 boys are now clothed and educated, and in paying annual sums to Hinckley, Lutterworth, Claybrook and Lubenham, for the establishment, established out of the
An estate at Cadeby, in Leicestershire, of the annual value of 95*l.* and money in the funds, yielding an annual income of 63*l.* 10*s.* 10*d.*	- - by gift of Alderman Gabriel Newton, settled by deed, dated 27th August 1761.	- - to pay 26*l.* a year to Northampton corporation to establish a school there, and the residue towards apprenticing poor children of the town of Leicester.	as directed by the trust deed in all respects.

Nature of the Funds.	How acquired.	Purposes for which given.	Mode in which they are now distributed or applied.
Five-sevenths of the produce of some land at Leicester, sold under the directions of the Court of Chancery, but not yet in hand for the purposes of the trust, owing to another suit being instituted, which is now pending.	- - Mr. Elkington by his will, dated 29th May 1607, gave two sums of 50*l.* each to the corporation upon certain trusts, and these sums, with other monies belonging to the corporation, were laid out in the purchase of a close at Leicester, which close has since been sold, and produced upwards of 3,000*l.*, five-sevenths of which have been decreed to be for the purposes of the charity.	- - the trust was to lend out the principal in loans of 10*l.* to poor artificers of Leicester and Lutterworth for one year at interest at 5 per cent., and to apply the produce for the poor of St. Martin's, Leicester and Lutterworth, and a certain sum to the town clerk for preparing the bonds.	- - this trust fund is at present not applied at all, on account of a Chancery suit on the subject against the corporation being still pending; but the decree of the court in the former suit directed that it should be lent out in loans of 50*l.* for three years at 3 per cent., and the produce to be for the poor of Lutterworth and St. Martin's, and 5*l.* to the town clerk.
Money amounting to 15,000*l.* and upwards.	- - from the estates of Sir Thomas White, given to the corporation of Coventry some time before his death, which happened in 1566, upon trust every fifth year to pay a certain proportion to the corporation of Leicester.	- - to be let out in loans of 40*l.* and 50*l.* each to tradesmen, free burgesses of Leicester, for nine years, without interest, on sufficient security.	- - it is now let out in loans of 100*l.* under a decree or order of the Court of Chancery, made on the application of the corporation, on account of the funds being so much increased, and lent for nine years, without interest, to tradesmen resident in Leicester, being free burgesses of the town.
Two hundred pounds to be laid out in the funds, paid to the corporation in the year 1830.	- - given by the will of Alderman Thomas Reid, dated 30th June 1821.	- - the income to be applied in rewarding boys put out apprentice from Alderman Newton's school, if they conduct themselves well.	- - it has not yet been paid to any one.

Besides the above charitable funds in the order and disposition of the corporation the corporation pay to certain charitable uses upwards of 200*l.* per annum, which does not arise from, nor is issuing out of, any specific property; but is in the nature of a charge upon the general revenues of the corporation, as the trustees originally appointed for such purposes, arising out of funds placed in their hands when they accepted the trust.

Owing to the abrupt termination of our inquiry we had no opportunity of inquiring into the manner in which the charitable trusts of the corporation had been administered.

WORKING OF THE CORPORATE SYSTEM.

X. According to the constitution which has been described, the governing body of this corporation has been shown to be a self-elected, close, and irresponsible body. The results of this system have been highly unsatisfactory, and altogether incompatible with the legitimate objects of municipal government.

In no corporation has a more complete system of political exclusiveness existed than has prevailed in this. From the mayor to the humblest servant of the corporation, every office has been filled by persons of the corporation or, so called, Tory party, to the total exclusion of all who entertained different opinions, however wealthy, however intelligent, however respectable. Yet the persons entertaining different political opinions from the corporation, constitute, to say the very least, an equal proportion of the opulence and intelligence of the town, and unquestionably form a numerical majority of the population. In every department in which the corporate authorities exercise a power of appointment or patronage—in the appointment of the police; the nomination of parish officers; the distribution of public charities; the employment of tradesmen and the expenditure of the borough rate—the same rigid exclusion of all save one political party has been invariably adhered to. *Political Exclusiveness.*

Not only difference in political opinion however—diversity of religious faith has also formed an equal ground of exclusion. Dissenters are very numerous in Leicester; they constitute a large proportion of the wealth and respectability of the town, and at least one-third of the population. Since the repeal of the Test and Corporation Acts no dissenter has ever been elected into the corporation. Many of the dissenters belong to the poorer classes. None have been known to partake in the charities administered by the corporation. *Religious Exclusion.*

No corporation has interfered more extensively or more openly in elections. They have usually canvassed in a body, and the whole weight of their power and patronage has been unsparingly applied to the purpose of influencing the returns. *Interference in Elections.*

The political character of the body, and the extent of their interference in election politics, cannot better be illustrated than by a narrative of the proceedings connected with the election of members of parliament for the borough in the year 1826. Previously, however, to entering on this statement, it will be necessary to advert to a transaction which, though immediately connected with that election, somewhat precedes it in order of time. And lest the extraordinary nature of this proceeding might, by possibility, raise a doubt of the accuracy of these details, it may not be inexpedient to observe that the following statement is given on the evidence of the town clerk himself. In the year 1823, the corporation, in order to insure the return of members for the borough at the ensuing election, resolved on creating a multitude of freemen at once. With this object the freedom of the borough was voted to no less than 2,000 persons, consisting of country gentlemen, clergymen, and members of the legal profession, residing in various parts of the country and in the metropolis, all of them *Creation of honorary Freemen.*

strangers to the borough. To all of these the following circular was, by the direction of the Common Hall, addressed by the town clerk.

Sir, Leicester, Dec. 31, 1823.

I have the pleasure to acquaint you that the corporation of Leicester have unanimously elected you to be an honorary freeman of the borough. They are anxious to increase the number of freemen by the addition of gentlemen of sound constitutional principles; and they trust that as you cannot exercise the privileges of the office until twelve months after admission, you will do them the favour to take up your freedom at as early a period as possible. This may be done on any day, but it requires your personal attendance before the mayor.

The corporation will defray all fees and charges incident to the occasion; but you will have to pay a stamp duty of 3*l.* to the King, an expense to which they trust you will cheerfully submit, in support of a cause so identified with the best interests of the public.

I have the honour to be, &c.

To ——— (signed) *Tho. Burbidge*, Town Clerk.

Of the 2,000 honorary freemen elected as above mentioned, 800 actually took up their freedom, the corporation paying their fees to the town clerk on admission out of the corporate purse. Of those so admitted 445 voted at the ensuing election.

Election of 1826.

We now proceed with the election itself. A deputation of the corporation invited Sir C. Hastings, a gentleman of the county, to stand on the corporation interest. The invitation was accepted on the express understanding that Sir Charles should not be put to expense, beyond a stipulated sum, in securing his return. Sir Charles then made his public entry into the town, when the corporation went out in procession to meet him. Two other candidates appeared in the field: Mr. Evans in the interest of the Whig or anti-corporation party; and Mr. Otway Cave, whose avowed opinions, though not very explicitly expressed, approximated more nearly (except on the subject of Catholic Emancipation, on which he refused to give any pledge) to those of the corporation party, than to those of their opponents. In the month of May the following circular was addressed by the town clerk to the honorary freemen, who had taken up their freedom in the year 1823.

Sir, Leicester, 27 May 1826.

I am directed by the corporation to take the liberty of representing to you the present state of affairs with respect to the borough election. Sir C. A. Hastings, bart. comes forward on the invitation of the corporation and the True Blue interest, to support the King and constitution in church and state. He is an avowed opponent to what some call Catholic Emancipation, but what we call popish ascendancy. He is directly opposed to Mr. William

Evans, who stands forward on the low party and radical interest, and who is the champion of reform and the pretended liberalities of the day, and a decided friend to Catholic Emancipation. The third candidate is Mr. Otway Cave, whose family was originally staunch Blue. He says his mind is not made up on the Catholic question, and on that subject he will give no pledge. In other respects he professes to be Blue; and though an admirer of the new lights rather than the old, he is more decidedly Blue than Mr. Evans.

After this explanation, you will judge which candidate best claims your support; but the corporation trust that the old True Blue interest will not occupy the lowest place in your regard.

The committee will be much obliged by your exertions, and by any returns you can make them.

I am, Sir, very respectfully,

To ———   Your most obliged and humble servant,

(signed)   Thomas Burbidge, Town Clerk.

As the period of the election drew near, Mr. Otway Cave being more acceptable to the corporation party than Mr. Evans, a negotiation was set on foot between the friends of Mr. Cave and the corporation, for a coalition between him and Sir Charles Hastings. This was agreed to on the part of the corporation on two conditions; firstly, that the return of Sir Charles Hastings should be secured; secondly, that Mr. Otway Cave should pledge himself to vote against Catholic Emancipation—a pledge which that gentleman accordingly agreed to make in a handbill to be circulated for the purpose. These preliminaries being arranged, a meeting took place between the leading agents and friends of the two candidates, and three members of the corporation, when the following memorandum was drawn up:—

June 7, 1826.

The following propositions are agreed to on the part of Sir Charles Hastings and Mr. Otway Cave:—

The return of Sir Charles Hastings to be secured by the retirement of Mr. Otway Cave, if necessary. His retirement is guaranteed by the pledge of Colonel Evans and Colonel Cheney.

The expenses on both sides from the day of election to be shared equally; but in the event of Mr. Otway Cave retiring (from necessity), then Mr. Wood and Mr. Philips to decide whether any and what proportion of his share of the expenses from the election day shall be repaid to him. Such proportion to be in their discretion, but not to exceed one-third.

All expenses incurred by Sir Charles Hastings and Mr. Otway Cave prior to the day of election, to be shared in such way as Mr. Wood and Mr. Philips may decide to be equitable.

403

Upon these principles each party pledges himself to the other to give all the support in their power to secure the election of both.

This arrangement is made without the knowledge of the respective candidates, and is not to be communicated to them.

Tho. Burbidge.	*Edward Cheney.*
Wm. Dewes.	*D. L. Evans.*
J. Liptrott Greaves.	*Jos. Philips.*
Isaac Lovell.	
Henry Wood.	
Jas. Rawson, jun.	

The consequences which eventually resulted from this agreement deserve to be traced before we pass on to the actual proceedings at the election.

It may be noticed that the details which are here given are taken from a pamphlet published by the town clerk, with the authority of the corporation, in vindication of their claim on Mr. Otway Cave, after their rupture with that gentleman, and which was declared by the town clerk in his evidence before us to contain a true statement of the facts.

After the agreement above-mentioned the corporation party took on themselves all the heavy expenses of the election, relying on the agreement that all expenses should eventually be equally borne by both parties. "The poll commenced," says the pamphlet alluded to, "on the 13th June 1826, and continued ten days, at an immense expense to the corporation party, and all the heavy expenses of Mr. Otway Cave ceased. The corporation party gave the most zealous support to Mr. Otway Cave throughout the conflict, and in the end Sir Charles Hastings and Mr. Otway Cave were returned by a majority of 700."

In the beginning of 1827, the heavy election accounts being about to be paid, (the current and lighter payments having been made before), the accounts of the corporation party were made out. It was found that, including all monies which had been paid by them, as well as those which were outstanding, the total of their expenditure amounted to about 27,000*l.* Of this sum, 3,450*l.* had been received from Mr. Otway Cave:—950*l.* in various sums during the progress of the election; 1,000*l.* under the head of "secret service money" at the same period; and two sums of 1,000*l.* and 500*l.* immediately after the election was over. The sum actually expended by the corporation party amounted therefore to 23,550*l.* They gave credit to Mr. Cave for the 3,450*l.* above-mentioned, and they called upon him t contribute towards the general expense such a sum as, in addition to the sums which he had himself expended, would make his share of the expenses equal to theirs. The sum they claimed was 5,000*l.* As this sum would have reduced their outlay to 18,550*l.*, and as the expenses of both parties were to be equalized, it follows (though this is not distinctly expressed in the correspondence) that they gave credit to Mr. Cave for having himself expended (in addition to the sum paid to them) 10,100*l*. It also follows that the total aggregate expense of both parties amounted to 37,100*l*.

The demand of the corporation on Mr. Otway Cave not being acquiesced in, a lengthened correspondence took place between Mr. Burbidge the town clerk and Mr. Wood the then mayor, on the one side, and Mr. Otway Cave and Colonel Evans and Colonel Cheney on the other, which eventually led to a positive refusal on the part of Mr. Evans to pay the 5,000*l*. demanded. The only part of this correspondence which is material to the present purpose is the fact, that throughout the whole of it the claim was advanced and maintained—not on behalf of Sir Charles Hastings or his party, but on behalf of the corporation as a body; while the opposite party contended that they were not bound by the spirit of the agreement—because at the time it was entered into they had not been made acquainted with the stipulation subsisting between Sir Charles Hastings and the corporation, and had never contemplated the being involved in expenses beyond those actually sustained by Sir Charles Hastings;—nor by its letter, inasmuch as the corporation were not on the face of it parties to the agreement. These grounds of defence having been put forward by Mr. Otway Cave in a pamphlet published by him, a counter statement, bearing date 24 August 1827, and signed by the town clerk "on behalf of the corporation," was published in the Leicester newspapers. Upon the question whether the corporation were parties to the agreement, the statement alluded to contains the following passage:—"To put the point beyond doubt we assert that it was well and most distinctly understood that the corporation were, and were intended to be, substantially the parties to that agreement, and that Sir Charles Hastings was in fact a representative of them and of the interest of which they were the head, and we well remember the strongly expressed desire of the 'military gentlemen' (meaning Colonels Evans and Cheney) that the undersigned (meaning the town clerk) should affix his signature to the agreement as doubly binding Sir Charles Hastings and the corporation too; and let it further be remarked who were the persons distinctly and severally ratifying this agreement? Why Mr. Burbidge, Mr. Dewes, and Mr. Greaves, as the professional agents of Sir Charles Hastings; Colonel Cheney, Colonel Evans, and Mr. Philips, as the friends and sponsors of Mr. Otway Cave; and Alderman Lovell, Alderman Wood, and Mr. (now Alderman) Rawson, on behalf of the corporation."

It was afterwards agreed that the matter in dispute should be referred to the arbitration of two gentlemen. But the arbitrators were unable to agree as to the ground on which the discussion of the question should rest, —the arbitrator appointed by Mr. Otway Cave contending that the naked agreement must alone form the basis of their deliberations, while the arbitrator of the opposite party maintained that all the circumstances under which the agreement had been entered into ought also to be taken into consideration. The arbitration consequently went off on this preliminary point, and the matter was allowed to drop.

Payment of Election expenses out of Corporation funds. We now come to the issue of this remarkable transaction. Sir Charles Hastings had paid the full amount of the sum to which it had been stipulated that his expenses should be limited. On that gentleman, therefore, the corporation had no further claim. Bills to the amount of 10,000*l.* remained unpaid, one half of which the corporation must, under any circumstances, have borne, but the whole of which was now thrown on them in consequence of the refusal of Mr. Otway Cave to pay the 5,000*l.* demanded of him. The parties to whom the bills were due became pressing, and applied to the committee of the corporation party for payment. To get rid of the immediate difficulty, the necessary amount was raised on bonds given by different members of the corporation; and these bonds were afterwards paid off by the corporation, 10,000*l.* being raised for that purpose by a mortgage of part of the corporate estates. This statement rests on the evidence of the town clerk. It is established, therefore, beyond all controversy, that 10,000*l.* of the corporate funds have been sunk in a single election, the whole of which is irrecoverably lost to the corporation.

Secret Service Money. It remains only to explain that part of the foregoing expenditure which is included under the item of 1,000*l.* for "secret service money." In the letter published by the corporation in the newspapers, it is stated that this "was money advanced towards the expenses incurred in taking up freedoms, and was sent to the party making those payments by indirect channels, and for reasons obvious even to children, called secret service money. And thus," continues the statement, "this corrupt insinuation (alluding to certain observations made by Mr. Cave's party relative to this charge) is explained." In another part of the corporation pamphlet, it is stated that this sum was not paid by Mr. Otway Cave to the corporation party; but it is admitted that it was paid to "the individual who undertook to pay the expense of taking up freedoms for those who were friendly to the cause," as also that credit was given for it to Mr. Cave, as "a sum which he had disbursed (by his agents) and for which he was entitled to credit." It is clear, therefore, that the sum in question was expended for a common purpose, and considered part of the common expense: and whether, therefore, it came from the pocket of Mr. Cave or the corporation, must be matter of complete indifference.

Conduct of Returning officer. We now revert to the election, during the progress of which the conduct of the returning officer and the magistrates was marked by extreme partiality and injustice towards the party opposed to them.

A week before the election began, a correspondence took place between the agents of the several candidates relative to a requisition to the returning officer for the erection of hustings, and a contribution of the candidates for that object. Mr. Evans however refused to contribute unless the plan of the hustings should first be shewn to him. On the other hand, the returning officer refused to exhibit any plan, or even to cause a plan to be made, until the requisition had been signed by the candidates and their respective contributions had been paid. A correspondence hereupon took place between Mr. Evans's committee, and the town clerk, as the agent or adviser of the returning officer, and on the latter declaring that the returning officer would cause the booths to be erected in a manner which should not be prejudicial to any of the candidates, Mr. Evans contributed his share of the expense, at the same time expressing in writing his "dissent from the measure of polling by tallies, or from any arrangement in the construction of the hustings which would tend to produce a similar effect;"—the ground of the objection being a suspicion (which afterwards proved correct) of an intended coalition between the other candidates; in the event of which, the effect of voting by tallies would be to give two votes to each of those candidates for every one polled for Mr. Evans. Upon a perusal of the correspondence above referred to, it seems impossible to doubt that the town clerk had been consulted by and had advised the returning officer as to the course to be adopted. He was at the same time acting as the agent of one of the candidates, a character which appears by no means compatible with that of legal adviser to an officer in whom impartiality was so essential a qualification. Notwithstanding the recorded objection of Mr. Evans, and the fact of the coalition,—of which, as the corporation were parties to it, the mayor, who was the returning officer, must necessarily have been aware,—the hustings, which were not completed till the day preceding the election, (and till which time therefore Mr. Evans's friends were kept in ignorance of the arrangement,) were constructed in such a manner as that the votes should be taken in pens; the effect of which mode of polling (one vote being taken from each pen in succession) was precisely similar to that of voting by tallies, and of which, it must have been obvious to the most ordinary capacity, that the necessary consequence, where a coalition subsisted between two candidates against a third, must be to give to the one side two votes for every one polled by the other. Immediately on the opening of the poll an objection was taken by the legal agents of Mr. Evans to this mode of polling; upon which, counsel retired with the assessor and argued the point before him. It was stated to us by the recorder of the borough, Mr. Serjeant Goulburn, who acted as assessor at the election, that the ground of objection taken before him was, that the mode of polling objected to could only take place by consent of all parties, and that the popular party had a right to the advantage which their numbers and physical strength afforded them in obtaining the readiest access to the poll: he stated that the fact that two votes were being polled for one, was not brought to his attention, add-ing, that if it had been, he should at once, being aware of the coalition, have seen the impropriety of the system and have caused an alteration to be made. It appears however impossible to doubt that the recollection of the learned Serjeant, which proved to be imperfect on other subjects connected with the election,—such as the time when this objection was first taken, and whether the mode of polling by pens was adopted on the first or second day,—must necessarily have been inaccurate on this head. For it was dis-tinctly affirmed by several highly respectable members of Mr. Evans's committee, that the main, indeed the only ground of their objection to the polling by pens was the advantage it gave the other party of polling two votes to one; and it is therefore most improbable that their able counsel, Mr. Rolfe, should have omitted so important and cogent an argument. Indeed it was stated by Mr. Babington, a county magistrate and a member of Mr. Evans's committee, that he entertained not the least doubt that in some observations which Mr. Rolfe addressed to the assessor on the hust-ings, before he and the other counsel for Mr. Evans retired with that officer, Mr. Rolfe urged the impropriety of voting by pens, as giving the other party two votes to one. "I feel sure," added Mr. Babington, "that he said nothing about physical force." At all events it is certain that the opera-tion of the system was brought to the knowledge of the mayor—the respon-sible officer—as numerous complaints were made to him on the hustings, and a protest against the mode of polling, signed by several electors, was delivered to him. It was stated by the recorder, that the effect of the mode of voting complained of, or the fact of complaints having been made, was not communicated to him by the mayor.

The remonstrances of Mr. Evans's friends having proved unavailing, the voting went on. After about an hour and a half, Mr. (now the Lord Chief Justice) Denman was put in nomination, partly with a view of obtaining a second tally for the voters of Mr. Evans. Mr. Burbidge, the town clerk, then acting as one of the legal advisers of the returning officer and sitting im-mediately below him, (being at the same time known to be the professional agent of Sir Charles Hastings,) rose and proposed Mr. Cobbett, with a view, as he stated to us, of creating a doubt as to the nomination which had just been made being a *bona fide* one. Votes were then tendered for Mr. Denman, both from the outside of the pens and from Mr. Evans's pen, but were rejected, the returning officer refusing to allow Mr. Denman to have a turn. A Mr. Mitchell, one of Mr. Evans's committee, then climbed upon the rail of Mr. Evans's pen, and addressing the returning officer, demanded a pen for Mr. Denman's voters. Mr. Mitchell was well known to the mayor to be an elector. The assessor threatened to commit him if he did not im-mediately desist from interfering. The assessor had scarcely ceased ad-dressing him, when the chief constable, in the sight, as it was affirmed, of the mayor and recorder, struck Mitchell a violent blow with his staff, which caused him to fall to the bottom of the pen, whence he was carried away insensible. Several witnesses spoke to this transaction. One stated, that after Mitchell was struck down, several constables beat him with their staves while on the ground; and that he himself, on exclaiming "do you mean to murder the man," received a severe blow across the forehead. We were assured that the demeanor of Mitchell, though from the excitement of the moment certainly very energetic, was by no means insolent, and in no degree implied any threat or intention of violence; and that no impartial person could have supposed that he had any intention of creating a riot,— a fact which his subsequent treatment renders it material to notice.

The passions of the populace, already highly excited by the injustice done to the popular candidate, exasperated by this last act, now broke out into actual violence, and an attack was made on the hustings with a view to destroy the pens. Many persons left the hustings. The returning officer and the assessor retired into an adjoining room, and were followed by the counsel for Mr. Evans and Mr. Babington, a county magistrate, on the authority of whose evidence this statement is given. The assessor, some-what hurried, then asked "what was to be done?" Mr. Rolfe, on behalf of Mr. Evans, urged the injustice of this mode of polling by pens, and insisted on the duty of the returning officer to take the votes for Mr. Denman. It is beyond all question, that on this occasion the undue advantage afforded to the other party by the method of polling was clearly pointed out to the assessor. Mr. Babington, having had the evidence of Mr. Serjeant Goul-burn on this subject read over to him, swore positively to the fact as dis-tinctly within his recollection; and also stated, that the reason why Mr. Denman had been put in nomination was at the same time mentioned to the assessor. That officer however refused to take votes for Mr. Denman on that day, but promised that some arrangement should be made against the next. In the mean time the riot became greater, and to allay the tumult it was ultimately arranged that votes should be taken for Mr. Denman through Mr. Evans's pen.

During the progress of the polling gross partiality was practised by the parish officers who attended to check the votes of persons who had received parish relief. When voters in the interest of Mr. Evans, who had become incapacitated by receiving relief, came up to poll, the officers were in-variably active; but if voters, similarly circumstanced on the other side, were seen coming up, they absented themselves, and were no where to be found. Their conduct was repeatedly complained of to the returning officer; but the latter did not interfere, and no steps were taken to remedy the evil. It may be mentioned, that the conduct of these officers has been the same at other elections.

Conduct of Parish officers.

It being obvious that the polling by pens, which at once showed for whom a voter was about to poll, considerably facilitated the unfair practices of the parish officers, the people still continued strongly opposed to the pens. On the afternoon of the second day the popular clamour gradually increased to a serious tumult: still no violence was offered by the people, till the constables beginning to use their staves freely, a conflict took place, and stones were thrown into the hustings. The poll was then stopped, and the magistrates retired from the hustings to the Exchange, a building situated in the market-place, immediately contiguous to the hustings; and the Riot Act was soon after read. Several witnesses deposed, that after the magistrates had left the hustings, no violence was offered by the people, till stones were thrown among the crowd from the roof of the Exchange, which was occupied by the corporation party. It was sworn that the macebearer of the corporation threw the first stone. Other persons connected with the corporation were also seen engaged in like manner. A witness, a very respectable man, who remained during the day at Mr. Evans's committee room in the market-place, from an upper window of which he could overlook the Exchange, swore that previously to the magistrates coming to the Exchange, he saw vast quantities of stones carried up through a trap door, and placed on the top of the Exchange. He stated positively that these stones were not gathered from the street; they must, therefore, have been previously deposited in the lower part of the Exchange.

Stones having been thrown from the Exchange, the crowd from the market-place then began to throw in return, and the throwing of stones lasted for an hour and a half, till the arrival of the military, who had been sent for, suppressed a tumult which might otherwise have led to most disastrous results.

It seems impossible to doubt that the partiality of the returning officer, the unfairness of the overseers, and the violence of the constables, operating on the minds of the people already aggrieved by the unfair exercise of the corporation influence against the popular party, and always exciteable at the period of an election, led to the tumult and outrages which took place on this occasion, and for the quelling of which the magistrates afterwards charged 1,300*l.* on the borough rate.

Conduct of Magistrates.

One or two instances of magisterial misconduct, arising out of the election, and which form an apt appendage to the proceedings which have been detailed, will close this narrative. It has been stated, that on the first day of the polling a Mr. Mitchell was knocked down by a constable, while calling on the mayor to grant a pen for Mr. Denman. He was carried away insensible, and did not return till after all tumult had subsided.

At 11 o'clock on the night of the same day, the chief constable, with a posse of other constables, came to Mitchell's house and apprehended him. Being asked for his authority, he refused to produce it. Mitchell being aware that the magistrates were still sitting at the Exchange to grant freedoms, requested to be conducted thither, offering to give bail to any amount. The chief constable refused, saying that the offence was not a bailable one, and that his orders were to take him to prison. Mitchell was accordingly taken to the common gaol, and confined there for the night. In the morning he asked for pen and paper; but the constable said, that what Mitchell wrote, he (the constable) must see. At 11 o'clock Mr. Parkes, a solicitor, of Birmingham, visited him, and the magistrates afterwards came to the prison. A charge was then preferred against Mitchell of having been concerned in the riot. Mr. Parkes demanded to see the warrant on which he had been apprehended, but none was produced; Mitchell was, however, admitted to bail. At the sessions no charge was preferred against him; but he was made to pay a pound for withdrawing the recognizances. There appears to have been no shadow of a ground for preferring any charge against him.

Another case arising out of the election was that of a man named Clarke, a shoemaker. On the Saturday after the riot (which took place on the Wednesday) this man was apprehended and conveyed to the Exchange, where he was kept in custody two or three hours. From thence he was taken to the office of Mr. Cooke, one of the aldermen. The constable then took from his pocket a piece of paper, which he gave to the alderman, and the latter having looked at the paper, directed the constable to take Clarke to prison. Nothing was said to the prisoner, and no charge was preferred against him. The prisoner then demanded to know what he had done, to which the alderman's only answer was, that he would know another day. Clarke then observed, that he could find bail, to which the alderman replied "not to the amount we want," and added, that the bail must be the prisoner's own recognizance in 200*l.* and two sureties in 100*l.* each, and that such bail must be procured in ten minutes, or he must be taken to prison. Clarke's brother, who was waiting without, succeeded in procuring two sureties within the time prescribed. One of them desired to know what was the charge against the prisoner, but the alderman refused to inform him. The surety, thereupon observed, that the bail required was very heavy, and the charge might, for aught he knew, be very serious. The only reply of the magistrate was, "then if you don't like to be bail for him, he must go to prison." The bail was then given, without any charge being specified or any evidence being offered against the prisoner. At the ensuing sessions an alderman came to Clarke, and desired him to call on the town clerk respecting his trial. He did so, when the town clerk advised him not to let his lawyer bring his trial on that day, as if he did so, it was very likely he would be convicted, adding, "let it stand over till another sessions; it will die away." At the ensuing sessions the town clerk again told him, "he might go home, as his trial would not come on that sessions." At a third sessions he told him, "he might go home; he would hear no more about it." Clarke was afterwards compelled to pay 25*s.* for withdrawing his recognizances.

One of Clarke's bail, a master manufacturer and a most respectable man, stated to us that he had known him many years; that he was a poor man, with several children, and had always borne a good character as an honest and industrious man and a peaceable inhabitant. Clarke himself swore positively that he had not been in any way concerned, either in the attack on the hustings or the riot in the market-place. At the time of his apprehension he was actively engaged as an inspector of votes for Mr. Evans.

Administration of Justice.

The same spirit of political partizanship which is so strikingly manifested in the foregoing details, appears to have prevailed in every department to which the power of the corporate authorities extends. Even the most important of their functions, the administration of justice, has not been exempt from its influence.

Distrust of the Magistrates.

From a remote period there has existed among the inhabitants a widely spread and deep rooted suspicion of the integrity of the magistrates, in cases where political opponents are concerned, more especially in cases of a political complexion. It was stated to us by a county magistrate living within the liberties, that, in cases arising within the concurrent jurisdiction, application had several times been made to him for summonses, the parties alleging that they should not be fairly dealt with by the borough magistrates. "Knowing how the magistracy is constituted," added the gentleman in question, "I should in some cases think such an apprehension not an unreasonable one." The same feeling extends to the grand juries, who, as has already been mentioned, are composed of members of the common council, to the exclusion of all other inhabitants. In political cases, such as affrays or riots arising out of elections, it has been usual to remove the indictments by *certiorari* into the county.

The belief that a political opponent is not likely to obtain an equal measure of justice at the hands of the magistrates is universal among the party opposed to them. It is by no means uncommon among the dispassionate persons of their own party. "If," said Mr. Brown, a highly respectable solicitor of Leicester, a witness whose evidence becomes the more important from his agreeing with the corporation in politics,—"If I were on the other side in politics, I should not place confidence in some of the magistrates." Two cases were brought under our notice by this gentleman, in both of which he had himself been professionally concerned. In one of these a Mr. Robinson, a political opponent of the corporation, was charged with having sold coke with a false measure. It was proposed to try the measure by a standard measure ready filled with potatoes. This was objected to on behalf of the defendant, on the ground that potatoes might be unfairly packed. It was agreed to take a standard measure to the wharf, and to try the measures with coke. The informer and the defendant's attorney, accompanied by an inspector, then proceeded to the wharf: the trial was made, and the informer declared himself satisfied of the fairness of the measure. The parties returned to the magistrates, between whom and the inspector a conversation in whispers took place. The standard measure filled with potatoes was then brought into the room and the contents emptied into the disputed measure, which, according to this test proved to be too small. Upon this the magistrates exclaimed that it was "a hollow case" against the defendant. Mr. Brown declares himself convinced, that the measure, which had been filled out of the room, had been unfairly packed. He at the time protested strongly against this mode of measurement, to which he had objected from the first; and it was arranged that the case should be adjourned to give time for further inquiry. An arrangement was made, in the hearing of the magistrates, between the defendant's attorney and the town clerk, that in the interim, they, accompanied by a third party to prevent dispute, should again proceed to the wharf, and make the trial of the measures as before. This was done accordingly, and the town clerk and the person who accompanied them declared that they were satisfied. On the ensuing day Mr. Brown inquired of the town clerk, if the magistrates were satisfied? He answered that "they would convict, and that they were much displeased with him for having gone to the wharf." On behalf of the defendant evidence was also given by two competent persons who had ascertained the capacity of the measure in dispute by mathematical admeasurement. Both made it exceed the standard measure: nevertheless the defendant was convicted by a full bench of magistrates. During the proceedings the witnesses for the defendant were treated with unfairness. One of the magistrates stated that "nothing on earth should convince him that the measure was a right one." Mr. Brown declared it to be his deliberate conviction that in this case some of the magistrates were actuated by party feelings.

The other case spoken to by Mr. Brown was that of a Mr. Fielding, a master manufacturer of Leicester, who had taken an active part against the corporation in the election of 1826. In November 1830 a charge of larceny was brought against Mr. Fielding by a man named Higgs, who deposed that having taken to Mr. Fielding's warehouse a quantity of worsted yarn in parcels, which had been ordered of him by Mr. Fielding; he had seen Mr. Fielding, believing himself unobserved by Higgs, take a parcel of the yarn from a scale in which it had been placed for the purpose of being weighed, and secrete it. It is unnecessary to go at length into the evidence. It will be sufficient to state that the case rested on the testimony of the principal witness Higgs; that upon his statement much doubt was thrown in the first instance on his cross-examination by the defendant's attorney, and that at the subsequent trial he was positively contradicted by two witnesses, in a most important particular. Of Mr. Fielding's innocence no doubt can be entertained. He was acquitted at the trial, and the recorder, who tried the case, expressed his entire concurrence in the verdict of the jury. The particular in which the conduct of the magistrates was called in question, was their refusal to take bail, which was offered to any amount. The case excited a powerful interest in the town, and among all classes of the opposite party the refusal of the magistrates was ascribed solely to political motives. Some circumstances attending the examination before the magistrates tended to promote such a suspicion. In addition to the well known fact of Mr. Fielding being a warm political opponent, it appeared that one of the magistrates who took an active part in the examination, adversely to Mr. Fielding, had had a personal quarrel with that gentleman. After one witness had been examined for the prisoner the magistrates refused to hear further evidence, though it was expressly tendered with a view to induce them to take bail; declaring that the felony having been sworn to, the case was clear, and they should not take bail. An application was afterwards made to a judge of the Court of King's Bench to admit the defendant to bail; the application was immediately granted, and bail taken in half the amount which the defendant had come prepared with. There can be no doubt that the magistrates would have been justified in admitting to bail under the circumstances of the case. Nevertheless it is impossible to say that they may not have exercised an honest discretion in leaving the party to his application to the superior court. The case in question is precisely one of those which afford the most striking illustration of the evils of a political magistracy, in whom the exercise of all discretion in difficult cases, should their decision prove adverse to a political opponent, cannot fail to be attended with suspicion and a diminution of the confidence and respect so essential to their authority and character.

Political choice of Parish officers. In another department of the magisterial office—the appointment of Parish Officers—the political partiality of the magistrates has been equally conspicuous.

For many years they have, with a few solitary exceptions, appointed overseers exclusively from among their own party, more especially taking care to appoint staunch partizans at times when elections were expected, thereby securing a great advantage to their party in consequence of the unscrupulous conduct of these officers on such occasions. The collision of the magistrates with the select vestries on this and other subjects will be noticed hereafter.

Appointment of Police. The same spirit of exclusion and selection of political partisans has prevailed in the appointment of the police, more particularly in the choice of special constables at elections. "Every man of opposite opinions," said to us Mr. Paget, an influential gentleman of Leicester, "believes he sees in a peace officer an armed adversary." He further stated that at elections he had seen uncalled-for cruelty inflicted on the people by both special and regular constables. He himself, at the election in 1820, had been in personal danger from these men, and considered that in getting out of their hands without injury he had had a lucky escape.

Looking principally to their political conduct, the magistrates appear also to have been often culpably inattentive in inquiring as to the character of the persons appointed. Among other instances, one of the select vestry of the parish of St. Nicholas stated to us that a workhouse master and assistant overseer of that parish, who was also a headborough of his ward, had been dismissed by the vestry a year and a half before for embezzling the parish money. The parish forbore to prosecute, on the party signing an acknowledgment of his guilt and of their leniency. The facts were notorious, besides which, one of the magistrates was informed of them by an overseer of the parish. Nevertheless, the constable was continued in his office. He had always made himself active in electioneering on the corporation side.

The granting of licences has likewise been made subservient to political purposes. A particular case was brought under our notice. A worsted-spinner, named Cooper, a person against whose character there existed no objection, but who at a former election had voted against the corporation, in the year 1825 built a house in a part of the town called the Friars, for the purpose of getting it licensed. The neighbourhood was thickly inhabited, and there was no public-house within 150 yards of his. He mentioned to an alderman whom he supplied with worsted, that he wished to have a licence; the alderman replied, "that their rule was to grant favours to those from whom they received them." The licence was refused, the reason assigned being that there was no house wanted in the neighbourhood. The next year a licence was granted to a voter on the corporation side for a house situated within 50 yards of the former. No public-house had been closed between the former application and the grant of the licence. *Granting of licences.*

Nearly all the licensed victuallers are partisans of the corporation. The admissions on this head of Mr. Bond, a solicitor of considerable experience in elections, who came forward to speak in favour of the corporation, are deserving of attention. Being questioned on this subject, his answers were as follows: "I think the licensed victuallers are of course conservatives.— The number of them voting against the corporation is very small in proportion to those who support it.—I think they feel it their interest to support the corporation candidates.—I believe they support that political party because the corporate magistrates dispense licences." Private interest has not, however, been lost sight of. A large proportion of the public-houses belong to members of the corporation. A very unfair practice has prevailed of granting an undue proportion of the loans from Sir Thomas White's charity to licensed victuallers. It has been stated that every man, in order to carry on trade as a licensed victualler, if not already a freeman, is obliged to purchase his freedom, the customary price of which is about 35*l*. It has been usual to grant the loan at the time of enfranchisement to persons purchasing the freedom in order to become victuallers. Since 1800, 738 loans have been granted; of these, 203 have been to licensed victuallers; the total sum distributed amongst them since that time being 10,150*l.* Thus a means is found of putting money into the corporation purse, and, at the same time, of lightening the burden to the party who pays it, at the cost of other trades at least equally entitled to partake in the benefits of the charity.

Distribution of Charities.

It has been stated that the patronage of the corporation has been made subservient to political purposes. This has been particularly the case in the distribution of the charities of which the corporation are trustees. The evidence on this head was such as to leave room for no doubt whatsoever. Numerous witnesses stated the fact to be perfectly notorious; and several cases were brought under our notice which fully bore out the general impression. A charitable donation, called Coal and Wood Money, is annually distributed by the corporation. It is not applied for, but is carried round by the constables, one of whom, on giving it to a freeman for the first time, told him, "it was for their friends in the blue interest." Several freemen deposed that they had received this money regularly for several years, as long as they voted in the corporation interest, till on their giving a vote to the opposite party, the money was immediately withdrawn.

In one of these cases on the freeman inquiring of the constable why the money was not given to him as before, the constable answered "that none were to have it who had not voted for Hastings and Cave." A father and son lived in the same house; at the election in 1832 the son voted with the corporation, the father on the opposite side. The son received the money; it was refused to the father. In another case the wood money was actually promised by a mayor, when canvassing with a candidate, to induce a freeman to promise his vote. A witness who had lived in the service of one of the aldermen applied to him shortly after the election in 1826 to have his son put into the Newton's school. The alderman's answer was, "You know you did not poll blue at the last election, and therefore we shall look to our own friends first."

A similar principle has prevailed in the distribution of the loans of Sir Thomas White's charity. A freeman, named Scott, deposed, that on setting up in business in 1827, he applied for the loan. He had in the preceding year voted against the corporation. An alderman whom he canvassed said to him, "I would as soon have you as any of your party, but we must serve our own friends first." A like answer was made to Mr. George Billing, now a manufacturer in Leicester, who setting up in business applied for the loan in 1832, having voted against the corporation at the two preceding elections. From a Return made by the town clerk to the House of Commons of the persons who have received Sir Thomas White's charity, it appears that from 1822 to the time of this inquiry (September 1833,) there had been distributed 117 loans of 100*l.* each. On a comparison of this Return with the poll-books of the elections which had occurred in the interim, it appeared that of the 117 recipients 76 had voted for the corporation candidates, and only four against them; 36 had either not polled or had had no votes, and one to whom the loan was voted in 1824 never received the money; the last-mentioned freeman voted against the corporation in 1826. In the year 1832–33, 11 grants (forming part of the 117) had been made. Of the 11 persons who received the loans one had no vote; the remaining 10 voted at the election, in December 1832, for the corporation candidate.

From a return of the children admitted into the school belonging to Newton's charity, it appears that in the year 1832–33, the number of children admitted was 135. On reference to the poll-book of the election of 1832, it appears that of the fathers of these children the number who voted at that election was 47, and that of these 45 voted for the corporation candidate and only two against him. In many of these instances, several of the children belonged to the same father; in many of the other cases referred to in which the father did not vote, the grandfather or some near relative voted for the corporation candidate.

Practically speaking, as well as in a moral point of view, this mode of distributing charities cannot be considered otherwise than as a species of bribery. There can be no doubt that its effect is to give to the corporation an influence which they would not possess as members of society, and that it tends to destroy in the minds of the voters all sense of public spirit or political independence. We were assured by several witnesses who had taken part in the elections, that when canvassing they had repeatedly been told by the poorer voters that their wish was to vote for them, but that they were prevented from doing so by a fear of losing the corporation charities.

A serious practical evil resulting from the self-elective and exclusive system in this corporation is, that the governing body, taken in the aggregate, and in consequence the magistracy, is not composed of the most eligible persons, either as regards intelligence or station. Neither does it appear that in the selection of magistrates that attention to personal character has been invariably given which is essential to the dignity of the office. *Character of the corporate authorities and magistracy.*

An instance of this nature was brought before us, which, however painful as turning upon a question of personal misconduct, we felt it our duty to enter into, inasmuch as a public condemnation of the party, emanating from competent authority, had been immediately followed by his elevation to the highest corporate office. It is unnecessary to enter here into the merits of the case, and it will be gladly passed over as involving a question of private character. It is sufficient for the present purpose to state, that the individual in question (an alderman) had been, during the year 1828, churchwarden of Saint Margaret's parish; that on his quitting office, a committee was appointed by the vestry to examine his accounts, and that the committee in their report recommended that the accounts should be disallowed, particularly objecting to several items on the ground that the churchwarden had taken discount on paying the parish bills, but had charged the whole amount to the parish. Within two months after this report had been published, and before the matter had been in any way cleared up or the difference between the party and the parish adjusted, the alderman was elected mayor and served that office. The person in question had on all occasions distinguished himself as an active political partisan. Several members of the corporation are said to have resigned in consequence of his promotion to the mayoralty.

Competency of Magistrates. Several witnesses (some of them of the corporation party in respect of politics,) concurred in expressing an opinion unfavourable to the general competency of the magistrates as a body. A striking proof in confirmation of this opinion is to be found in the extreme disproportion which the number of prisoners convicted bears to the number of those committed by the borough magistrates. From a Return made to the House of Commons in 1827, it appears that the number of persons committed for trial to the borough gaol, between the years 1810 and 1827 (both inclusive) was 1,087. Of these, 30 were removed by habeas corpus to the county, and the result of their trials does not appear. Of the remaining 1,057, 589 only were convicted. The proportion of acquittals to convictions will consequently be within a mere trifle as 4:5.

Administration of Poor Laws. Independently of the distrust of the magistrates as administrators of justice in criminal matters arising from their known political bias, their conduct in the other branches of their authority has given great dissatisfaction to the town. This has been particularly the case in respect to the administration of the poor laws. The poor-rates of the borough of Leicester are extremely heavy, amounting annually to from 12 to 15 shillings in the pound. From the report of the commissioners on the poor laws it appears that the sum annually furnished by the six parishes of Leicester to the poor-rate had increased between the years 1825 and 1832 from 9,182*l.* to a sum little short of 14,000*l.*; and that from the statement of the overseers it appeared that a still further sum would be wanting for the ensuing year. "A state of things," continues the report, "upon which it is impossible to come to any other conclusion than that, if not checked by the timely interference of the legislature, this dreadful evil threatens, at no very distant period, to paralyse the industry and swallow up the property of the whole town." Upon the evidence adduced before us on this subject it is impossible to doubt that the evils of this system have been materially aggravated by the very injudicious interference of the borough magistrates in matters relating to the relief of the poor. Upon this point witnesses of all parties agreed. All attempts on the part of the select vestries to distinguish between the honest and industrious poor and the dissolute and worthless pauper appear to have been thwarted by the perverse determination of the magistrates to order relief in every case in which application was made to them.

Indeed, they seem to have considered the refusal of the vestry to grant relief as at once a sufficient reason for them to award it. Several cases of a startling nature were brought under our notice, but the details would swell to too large a size the bulk of this Report, and the agreement of so many witnesses of opposite parties on this subject renders it less necessary to enter into particulars.

On this and on other subjects the magistrates have brought themselves into open collision with the select vestries of the different parishes. About the year 1822 the inhabitants of All Saints parish placed themselves under the management of a select vestry and dismissed the town clerk from being their solicitor: their legal expenses had previously amounted to 160*l.* in two years; since that time they have averaged 11*l.* per annum. In the year 1826 the parish of Saint Margaret's adopted a similar course. *Collision with the Select Vestries.*

Both these parishes complain that from the date of the change referred to they have met with constant opposition from the magistrates.

The case has been the same in the parish of All Saints [*sic;* = St Mary's], which is also under the management of a select vestry. In this parish the select vestry made a rule to enforce the poor-rate on all houses assessed at 5*l.* and upwards. Summonses have been granted against persons neglecting to pay, but the magistrates, without assigning any reason, have refused to grant warrants to enforce the payment. There are many houses consequently on which the vestry have been unable to procure payment of the rates at all.

In the parishes which are under the management of select vestries it has been usual for the select vestries annually to return to the magistrates a list of twelve names from which to select the overseers, it being understood that the four names at the head of the list are the persons whom the parish desire to have chosen. Not only have the magistrates not appointed the persons at the head of the list, but they have (with very rare exceptions) appointed persons not on the vestry list at all, taking care invariably to select persons of their own party. In like manner, in the parishes not under select vestries, and in which the parish officers have returned the list to the magistrates, the overseers have always put on the list persons of the corporation party only. Thus, throughout all the parishes, the corporation have filled the parochial offices with their own partisans. These overseers have frequently set themselves in direct opposition to the vestries, have neglected to attend at the vestry meetings, and have disregarded the wishes of the vestries, making payments contrary to the votes of these bodies. In one instance the parish officers of Saint Margaret's, with the mayor, being churchwarden, at their head, signed an order to the vicar to annul a notice sent him by the vestry to call a parish meeting for the purpose of filling up several parish offices, in consequence of which the meeting was not held. *Appointment of Overseers.*

We were assured that in one parish, in frequent instances, the vestry and parishioners had been dissatisfied with the accounts of the overseers, yet no appeal against them had been made, because a belief existed that the magistrates would not afford redress.

Opposition to Local Bill. In the year 1832, the parish of Saint Margaret's, wishing to put an end to this state of things, applied to Parliament for a local Act, by which it was proposed that the appointment of the parish officers should be vested in a select vestry appointed by the general vestry, and that the parish officers should be placed entirely under the control of that body. At a public meeting, held at the church, the parishioners were unanimous in promoting this Act. The magistrates and parish officers held a private meeting to organize the opposition to the Bill, and afterwards, before a committee of the House of Commons, used their most strenuous exertions to defeat it. Captain Bowater, a gentleman of conservative politics, who was one of the committee appointed by the parish for promoting the Bill, declared to us that the opposition of the magistrates had been vexatiously conducted; Mr. Paget, the late member for the county of Leicester, who had been a member of the committee of the House of Commons on the Bill, in his evidence before us said, "I say advisedly, from my knowledge as a member of that committee, and on my oath, that the conduct of the magistrates was most vexatious;"— he further stated that the opposition appeared to the committee so frivolous and vexatious, that they were on the point of taking on themselves the responsibility of putting a stop to further proceedings, and at once reporting in favour of the Bill.

In the mean time, however, the parish, having been put to considerable expense, had consented to a compromise, by which it was agreed that the general vestry should annually return a list of 30 names, from whom the magistrates should choose 20 to constitute the select vestry; and that the select vestry should return a list of 24, from whom the magistrates should choose four to be overseers. The opposition to this Bill put the parish to heavy expense: their own costs amounted to 1,375*l.*; the cost of the opposition which they had also to pay, amounted to 600*l.* more.

The effect of these collisions between the magistrates and the vestries, has been the production of a degree of irritation and angry feeling, which cannot but be extremely prejudicial to the character and influence of the magistracy.

Previously to quitting this part of the subject, it may be satisfactory to observe that the collision of parties which some persons appear to anticipate from the abolition of the exclusive system, has not been found to exist in the select vestries of this town, which composed of persons of all parties, have been found to work excellently well without discord or disunion. Indeed, generally speaking, political considerations do not appear to have exercised any influence in the composition or working of these bodies; and if in any of them any traces of political feeling are to be found, it is to be entirely ascribed to the conduct of the magistrates, who in choosing the select vestrymen from the parish list of St. Margaret's, and in the appointment of overseers in the other parishes, still persist in being guided by their political predilections alone.

The evidence on the subject of the select vestry of St. Margaret's is extremely satisfactory, as showing the possibility of a complete amalgamation of parties in concerns of local interest. The following is an extract from the evidence of Mr. Hutchinson, a member of the Society of Friends, and one of the select vestry of St. Margaret's parish. "The election of the select vestry under the local Act, may be taken as a fair sample of popular election on an extended scale in Leicester. The select vestry is composed of Tories, Whigs, and Radicals. The two latter are a majority. Yet they have selected the parish solicitors, the parish treasurer, the surveyors, and one of the collectors, from the Tory party. The vestry act together with the greatest harmony, political considerations never entering into any matters that come before them. The political excitement and acerbity of feeling which existed before the passing of the Act, has been much softened down, and the vestry have given general satisfaction. There are several dissenters in the vestry, but this leads to no religious differences, neither do the churchmen and the dissenters take different sides. The mixing of the different religions has had the effect of producing union and good feeling between them."

It is complained by the inhabitants that the corporation as a body have taken pains to stifle and suppress the public feeling on matters of national concern; and as the organs of the borough have frequently misrepresented it to the government and the legislature. They have invariably refused to call public meetings of the inhabitants, though applied to for that purpose. They refused to call a meeting on the subject of the repeal of the Alien Act, on the amelioration of the Criminal Code, on the Catholic Question, and on various other subjects of national or public concern, notwithstanding that requisitions most respectably signed were presented to them for the purpose—assigning as a reason that the purposes of the proposed meetings were unconstitutional, or the meetings themselves dangerous to the public peace. In all such cases, however, meetings have notwithstanding been held, have been numerously and respectably attended, and accompanied by no disorder or disturbance of the public tranquillity. On the other hand the corporation on presenting addresses and petitions to the Throne and Legislature, purporting (according to the style of the corporation) to be on behalf of the mayor, bailiffs and burgesses, have never called meetings or taken any steps to ascertain the state of public opinion in the borough.

As administrators of public funds, it is impossible to speak of the corporate authorities except in terms of unqualified censure.

The Returns furnished to us will not allow of a complete analysis of their expenditure; but it appears clear that with an income exceeding 4,300*l.* a

Refusals to call Public Meetings.

Administration of Revenues.

Corporate funds.

year, they contribute little or nothing (with the exception of occasional subscriptions, the amount of which bears no proportion to their income) to the alleviation of the heavy local burdens, or to the public institutions or general improvement of the town; while on the other hand a sum exceeding 1,000*l.* per annum is divided in salaries among the officers of the corporation.

The sales of land have already been adverted to with such observations as the subject appeared to suggest. Upon the payment of the expense of the admissions of the 800 honorary freemen out of the corporate funds, and the squandering of 10,000*l.* on a single election, all comment would be utterly superfluous.

This opportunity may, however, be taken to state that the order for raising the 10,000*l.* by mortgage, to pay off the bonds entered into for the payment of election expenses, was carried in the Common Hall, without one dissentient voice.

Borough rate.

The borough rate has formed a subject of loud and reiterated complaint on the part of the rate payers.

This rate was first established in the year 1766, prior to which time it seems clear that the expenses to which it is now applied were defrayed out of the corporate funds. There can be no doubt that the bulk of that property was originally granted towards the payment of the general charges of the borough, and no record is to be found of the borough having been taxed prior to the period referred to, for the purposes to which the rate is applied. The rate was at first levied as part of the poor rate, and the sum raised was very small. The first rate imposed on the parish of All Saints, was 4*l.* 16*s.* In 1785, it was 7*l.*, while in 1827 it amounted to 684*l.* 15*s.*

From a Return made to the House of Commons in 1827, of the amount and expenditure of the borough rate, between the years 1810 and 1827, it appears that in 1810 the borough rate amounted to 730*l.* 5*s.*, and in 1811 to 508*l.* only. Since which time it has been gradually progressing, till in the year 1827 it had reached the sum of 4,800*l.* It now averages about 4,000*l.* a year, inclusive of the gaol rate, which amounts to about 800*l.* per annum. The rateable property of the borough was valued in 1824 at 22,983*l.* 11*s.* 4*d.*; the clear rental or effectively rateable property is said at the present time not to exceed 20,000*l.*

An account of the expenditure for the year 1833 has been given in a preceding part of this Report. The amount of rates levied for that year was 3,000*l.* which is rather under the average amount. This amount is exclusive of the sum raised to pay the interest on the debt incurred in rebuilding the gaol, usually termed the gaol rate. The accounts of the gaol rate are never published: till our inquiry the actual existence of the debt was not publicly known.

We had no opportunity of inquiring into the details of this expenditure.

It is certain that it has increased in modern times in a most extraordinary ratio. From the return to the House of Commons in 1827, it appears that in 1810 twenty-six prisoners were tried; the costs of prosecution were 41*l.* 7*s.* 4*d.* In 1827 the number of prisoners tried was 68; the costs of prosecution were 911*l.* 12*s.* 2*d.*, being an increase in the expense of prosecutions, in the ratio of more than eight to one. Other items of expenditure have increased in a like proportion, as will appear from the following Table taken from the above-mentioned Return.

	Gaoler's Salary.	Main-tenance of Prisoners.	Other Gaol Expenses.	Costs of Prosecu-tions.	Police Establish-ments, including Vagrants.	Militia, Paving, Treasurer and Law Expenses.	TOTAL EXPENSE.
	£. s. d.	£. s. d.	£. s. d.	£. s. d.	£. s. d.	£. s. d.	£. s. d.
1810 . .	70 14 8	94 18 7	46 2 11	41 7 4	145 17 3	95 11 8	494 12 5
1827 . .	390 – –	266 2 3	984 15 2	911 12 2	1,570 10 1	253 14 6	4,376 14 2
Increase £.	319 5 4	171 3 8	938 12 3	870 4 10	1,424 12 10	158 2 10	3,882 1 9

No proportionate increase of the population in the borough has taken place in the interim; and we were assured that on the other hand the value of rateable property had materially decreased.

The amount of the rate for the county, on an average of seven years, has been not quite 5½*d.* in the pound. In consequence of the great disproportion between this amount and that of the borough rate, the liberties being exempt from the heavy additional burden imposed on the borough by the higher amount of the rate, property in the borough has been materially depreciated. Many of the inhabitants have removed from the old borough into the new in order to avoid the rate; and among these have been many of the magistrates themselves. Of the 72 persons of whom the corporation is composed, 30 only are domiciled within the borough; the rest reside in the liberties. We were assured that many houses had been shut up, in consequence of the numerous removals from the borough into the liberties.

The borough was valued in 1824. It is much complained of that no revaluation has since taken place, though the value of property, as it is alleged, has materially altered, and some parishes are unfairly assessed.

The rate on account of the gaol forms a heavy additional item of expenditure. It has been before stated that a debt of 12,000*l.* has been incurred by the borough in the purchase and subsequent rebuilding of the old county gaol. The rate payers contend that this expense might have been entirely avoided, inasmuch as the magistrates, by availing themselves of a provision of the general Gaol Act, might have contracted with the county magistrates for the maintenance of their prisoners, and have sent the greater portion of the latter to the house of correction for the county. We were assured that the magistrates of the county had applied to those of the borough to know

Gaol rate.

if it was their intention to avail themselves of the provision referred to. In the month of January 1824, it being then known that the magistrates had it in contemplation to build a new gaol, a memorial was presented to them signed by upwards of forty parish officers and members of the select vestries of the different parishes, deprecating the intended measure, as entailing a heavy and wholly unnecessary expense on the borough. The magistrates, however, persevered in their design. The heavy expense thereby incurred appears to have been little better than an absolute waste of money. It has been shown that the new gaol is utterly inadequate to the purposes of an efficient or proper state of prison discipline. Even in point of room very little indeed has been gained. It seems impossible to doubt that the magistrates would best have consulted the interests of the borough by availing themselves, though at the sacrifice of their own patronage, of the provisions of the recent Gaol Act, to transfer their prisoners to the house of correction for the county; an arrangement from which no inconvenience could have resulted, the county prison being situated in the immediate vicinity of the town. At all events it is quite clear that the only objects which could have justified the erection of a new gaol and house of correction, have, as the matter now stands, been in no degree attained, while a debt of 12,000*l.* has been added to the burdens which already pressed so heavily on the capital and industry of the borough.

Under such circumstances it may not be improper to remark that one of the aldermen was employed as architect in rebuilding the gaol, and that the corporation steward was also employed in some part of the work.

State of party feeling.

It appeared to us impossible to doubt that the state of things which has been described in the foregoing details has had a most pernicious effect on the general tone of social feeling in this town.

The appropriation of all municipal authority by the one party, to the total exclusion of the other, and the application of the whole power and influence thus obtained to the furtherance of political purposes, have produced in the minds of the excluded party a sense of grievance and injustice by which the vehemence of party spirit has been materially aggravated, and a degree of bitterness and rancour has been infused into the conflicts of political opinion, such as the ordinary collision of parties, if left to a fair trial of strength, would not have been sufficient to engender.

Another mischievous consequence which has not failed to result from the present system, is the lessening the respect towards the magistrates and the diminution of their proper influence over the people. To use the forcible expression of Mr. Brewin, an enlightened and opulent inhabitant of Leicester, who gave evidence before us, "The system tends to engender a spirit of insubordination and of resistance to constituted authorities, far more than national grievances, greater but more distant, would do.—It is a sore always galling; a disease that visits us by our firesides."

The feeling of distrust and ill-will which subsists between the corpora-tion and the inhabitants has been attended with mischievous effects in preventing the combination of the inhabitants with the local authorities for undertakings of a public nature and the general improvement of the town. A striking instance of this sort occurred in the year 1822. The streets of the town were at that time in a very bad state from being insufficiently paved and drained. Much inconvenience was also felt from the town not being properly lighted or watched. The corporate authorities were desirous of obtaining a local Act, granting power to commissioners to provide for these important objects. A public meeting of the householders and proprietors of real property in the town having been held at the desire of a majority of the gentlemen whom it was intended to appoint as commissioners under the Act, in order to take the sense of the inhabitants on the proposed measure—owing, as it appears, to a disinclination to intrust any additional powers to the municipal authorities, and from a belief that public expenses of this nature ought to be defrayed out of the corporate funds, the proposal for a local Act was rejected by a large majority, and resolutions passed declaring "that the streets of the town were in a state of uncleanliness, filth and neglect, repugnant to every feeling of decency, destructive of the comfort, and injurious to the health of the inhabitants:" But "that the town then labouring under the severe pressure of poor rate, church rates and borough rates, as well as of other unavoidable imposts, no additional rate could be imposed without being severely and injuriously felt, or without trenching in numerous instances upon the funds immediately necessary to sub-sistence;" that on the other hand "the ample endowments of the corpora-tion were intended and ought to be made applicable to the purposes of general utility, and that they could not be more advantageously applied than in cleansing, paving and lighting and under-draining the streets of the town:" and that "it was not therefore expedient or proper to apply to Parliament for the proposed Act." The Act was in consequence dropped. Some of the parishes have taken measures under the General Lighting and Paving Acts in some degree to provide for the objects to which the proposed Act was intended to apply.

Effect of public distrust in the improvement of the Town.

The testimony of numerous witnesses, combining with first rate res-pectability and intelligence a thorough acquaintance with the town and its inhabitants, produced in our minds a conviction that a vast numerical majority of the inhabitants of the town, and a very large proportion of the opulence and intelligence it contains, are adverse to the existing system, and anxiously desire its reform. In the year 1833, a petition was presented to parliament strongly pointing out the alleged abuses of the corporation, and praying for the reform of that body. The petition was originally agreed to at a most respectable meeting convened on the occasion. It lay three days for signature. Care is said to have been taken that it should be signed by

State of Public opinion.

none but competent persons. It received the signatures of 5,000 persons, a number which may be taken to amount to five-sevenths of the adult male population of the town.

The feeling of dissatisfaction has also partially extended to the corporate body itself. Seven members of the body, an alderman and six common councilmen, have resigned within a recent period. One of the number being examined by us, stated that dissatisfaction at the system pursued by the corporation had been one of the leading motives which induced him to resign.

It would be, however, wrong not to state that many persons came forward on our inquiry to declare their confidence in the magistracy, and to express their own satisfaction, and their belief as to that of the public, in the existing system. But neither in numbers, station or weight, could these witnesses bear comparison with those who expressed an adverse opinion. Of the number of witnesses (fifteen in all) who declared themselves in favour of the corporation, seven were overseers of the poor, a class of men who have been shewn to be peculiarly under the influence of the magistrates;—one was a solicitor, who having volunteered on the corporation side at the registration in 1832, had been appointed a paid assessor at the ensuing election; and who having stated that the majority of the town were favourable to the corporation, admitted that his knowledge was derived, not from intercourse with the manufacturers and inhabitants in general, but from the members of the conservative club. Another was a solicitor who had been many years a managing clerk in the town clerk's office: others, with one or two exceptions, had either received favours from the corporation, or were evidently zealous partisans, who, probably from having been accustomed to associate the existing state of things with the ascendancy of their party, had conceived an opinion (which they did not hesitate to express), that the exclusive system was alone calculated to promote the welfare of the town—forming therein a strong contrast to the witnesses on the other side, who equally deprecated the idea of an exclusive magistracy, even though formed from the party to which they themselves belonged. It should be added, that the recorder, who appeared before us, gave evidence in favour of the existing authorities on two points;—1stly, As to the impartial manner in which the magistrates discharged their duties;—2dly, As to the efficiency of the police. But as regards the first point, he spoke only to the exercise of the judicial functions of the magistrates in quarter sessions, where their conduct does not appear to have been ever called in question, and where indeed his own presence and the publicity of the proceedings would naturally operate as a salutary restraint. As regards the second point, it appeared on further inquiry that the opinion of the recorder was not founded on any local knowledge, but on the absence of cases of riot at the trials at the quarter sessions. It is obvious that the same effect might result from the peaceable and orderly disposition of the people, to which indeed (with one or two exceptions arising out of peculiar circumstances) testimony has already been borne.*

On the whole, taking into consideration all the evidence adduced before us as to the state of public opinion—particularly the candid declarations of several highly respectable members of the conservative party who were examined by us on this subject—it appears quite impossible to doubt, not only that the bulk of the inhabitants, comprising all classes of the party opposed to the corporation in politics, are eager for the reform of the existing municipal institutions, but also that moderate and dispassionate men of all parties are sensible of the abuses to which the present system has led, and weary of the state of perpetual antagonism which has so long subsisted between the corporate authorities and so large a portion of the inhabitants, are desirous of substituting for a political magistracy chosen from among violent partisans, one which, combining the most competent and respectable men of all parties, may act without suspicion of partiality, and may acquire and preserve the respect and confidence of the public.

In conclusion, it may be observed, that all persons who expressed themselves desirous of an alteration in the constitution of the governing body, agreed in opinion that the election of the municipal authorities might safely be entrusted to the 10l. occupiers: some thought the suffrage might be still further extended. A few who appeared to have more maturely considered the subject, expressed a wish for the appointment of stipendiary magistrates.

A. E. Cockburn.

Documents herewith transmitted:

Copy of governing Charter.	List of Freemen.
Abstract of Corporation Income.	Table of Fees paid on Admission.
Returns of Expenditure referred to in Report.	Return of Recipients of Loans since 1823.
Rentals of Charity Estates.	List of Boys on Newton's Charity.
Return of Sales of Lands.	

---

* After the termination of our inquiry, several papers were transmitted to us, signed by inhabitants of Leicester amounting in the whole to about 1,200 persons, declaring that the parties in question were "perfectly satisfied that the magistrates of this borough administer justice to all parties with great impartiality, and discharge the duty they are called upon to perform with marked intelligence and discrimination. That they are at all times assiduous to preserve good order in the town," and that the parties signing these documents "can place implicit confidence in them."

We had no means of ascertaining in what manner the documents in question had been procured, a circumstance by which it is obvious that the weight of such declarations may be materially affected. But it would be wholly inconsistent with the power and influence which the corporation have been shewn to exercise, to suppose that they do not possess a numerous body of adherents in the town.

REPORT OF
THE BOUNDARY COMMISSIONERS
1837

LEICESTER.

REPORT upon the PROPOSED MUNICIPAL BOUNDARY and DIVISION into WARDS of the BOROUGH of LEICESTER.

THE ancient Borough of Leicester consists of the Parishes of All Saints, St. Martin's and St. Nicholas; parts of the Parishes of St. Mary, St. Margaret and St. Leonard, and the White and Black Friars, which are extra-parochial.

The Liberty, which comprises the remaining portions of the Parishes of St. Mary, and St. Margaret, and the Hamlet or Township of the Newark, have been annexed to the Borough by the Parliamentary Boundary Act, as has also the Castle View, which although included within the Limits of the Liberties, is not subject to Corporate jurisdiction. The Boundary of the new or Parliamentary Borough is well known and defined, and is perambulated once in three years. It embraces all the ground over which the Town is likely to extend for many years to come, and seems well adapted to form the new Municipal Limit.

The Population contained within the Parliamentary Borough amounted according to the Census of 1831, to 40,512, and is rapidly increasing.

The principal Manufacture carried on is that of Woollen Hosiery. The making of cotton or Berlin gloves is also an important branch of Industry. Coal is supplied at a reasonable rate by the Swannington and Leicester Railroad, and also by canal from the Derbyshire mines. A branch railway is in contemplation to connect Leicester with the London and Birmingham Line at Rugby, and to be extended to Derby and Nottingham. The trade of the Town was stated to be in a most prosperous state.

The Town is paved out of the Highway Rate.

The Parishes have lately combined and placed themselves, as far as regards the lighting of the Town, under the provisions of the general Act (3 & 4 Will. IV.)

The Police is complained of as very inefficient; there is no regular nightly watch, and in consequence burglaries and other serious offences are of frequent occurrence.

Water.

Water is plentifully supplied from pumps and wells.

DIVISION INTO WARDS.

Looking to the local arrangements of the Town, and the way in which the different classes of the Population are distributed, we recommend the following division into Seven Wards, as one which will distribute these classes in somewhat equal proportions to each of the Wards.

Boundary of Ward No. 1, or All Saints Ward.

No. 1; or, *All Saints Ward.*—From the Point at which St. Nicholas Street crosses the Boundary of the respective Parishes of St. Nicholas and St. Martin, Northward, along the Boundary of the Parish of St. Nicholas to the Point at which the same meets the River Soar; thence, Northward, along the River Soar to the Point at which the same meets the Boundary of the Parish of St. Leonard; thence, Westward, along the Boundary of the Parish of St. Leonard to the Point at which the same meets the Boundary of the Parish of St. Margaret; thence, Southward, along the Boundary of the Parish of St. Margaret to the Point at which the same meets the East Gate; thence along High Street to the Point at which the same meets High Cross Street; thence along High Cross Street to the Point at which the same meets St. Nicholas Street; thence along St. Nicholas Street to the Point first described.

Boundary of Ward No. 2, or St. Margaret's Ward.

No. 2; or, *St. Margaret's Ward.*—From the Point at which the Melton Road crosses the Boundary of the Parish of St. Margaret, Southward, along the Melton Road to the Point at which the same meets Belgrave Gate; thence along Belgrave Gate to the East Gate; thence, Westward, along the Boundary of the Parish of St. Margaret to the Point first described.

Boundary of Ward No. 3, or Melton Ward.

No. 3; or, *Melton Ward.*—From the Point at which the Melton Road crosses the Boundary of the Borough, Southward, along the Melton Road to the Point at which the same meets Belgrave Gate; thence along Belgrave Gate to the Point at which the same meets Humberstone Gate; thence along Humberstone Gate to the Point at which the same meets the Humberstone Road; thence along the Humberstone Road to the Point at which the same crosses the Boundary of the Borough; thence, Northward, along the Boundary of the Borough to the Point first described.

Boundary of Ward No. 4, or St. George's Ward.

No. 4; or, *St. George's Ward.*—From the Point at which the Humberstone Road crosses the Boundary of the Borough, Westward, along the Humberstone Road to the Point at which the same meets Humberstone Gate; thence along Humberstone Gate to the Point at which the same meets Gallowtree Gate; thence along Gallowtree Gate to the Point at which the same meets Granby Street; thence along Granby Street to the Point at which the same meets the London Road; thence along the London Road to the Point at which the same crosses the Boundary of the

Parish of St. Margaret; thence, Eastward, along the Boundary of the Parish of St. Margaret to the Point at which the same meets the Boundary of the Borough; thence, Northward, along the Boundary of the Borough to the Point first described.

No. 5; or, *Market Ward.*—From the Point at which the London Road crosses the Boundary of the Parish of St. Margaret, Northward, along the London Road to the Point at which the same meets Granby Street; thence along Granby Street to the Point at which the same meets Gallowtree Gate; thence along Gallowtree Gate to the Point at which the same meets High Street; thence along High Street to the Point at which the same meets Cheapside; thence along Cheapside to the Point at which the same meets Cank Street; thence along Cank Street to the Point at which the same meets Hotel Street; thence, Southward, along Hotel Street to the Point at which the same meets Market Street; thence along Market Street to the Point at which the same meets the Boundary of the Parish of St. Margaret; thence, Eastward, along the Boundary of the Parish of St. Margaret to the Point first described.

Boundary of Ward No. 5, or Market Ward.

No. 6; or, *Welford Ward.*—From the Point at which the London Road crosses the Boundary of the Parish of St. Margaret, Westward, along the Boundary of the Parish of St. Margaret to the Point at which the same meets Market Street; thence along Market Street to the Point at which the same meets Hotel Street; thence along Hotel Street to the Point at which the same meets Peacock Lane; thence along Peacock Lane to the Point at which the same meets Southgate Street; thence, Southward, along Southgate Street, to the Point at which the same meets Oxford-street; thence along Oxford Street to the Point at which the same meets the Welford Road; thence along the Welford Road to the Point at which the same crosses the Boundary of the Borough; thence, Northward, along the Boundary of the Borough to the Point at which the same meets the Boundary of the Parish of St. Margaret; thence, Westward, along the Boundary of the Parish of St. Margaret to the Point first described.

Boundary of Ward No. 6, or Welford Ward.

No. 7; or, *St. Mary's Ward.*—From the Point at which the Welford Road crosses the Boundary of the Borough, Northward, along the Welford Road to the Point at which the same meets Oxford Street; thence along Oxford Street to the Point at which the same meets Southgate Street; thence along Southgate Street to the Point at which the same meets Peacock Lane; thence along Peacock Lane to the Point at which the same meets Cank Street; thence along Cank Street to the Point at which the same meets Cheapside; thence along Cheapside to the Point at which the same meets High Street; thence, Westward, along High Street to the Point at which the same meets St. Nicholas' Street; thence along St. Nicholas' Street to the Point at which the same meets the Boundary of

Boundary of Ward No. 7, or St. Mary's Ward.

the Parish of St. Nicholas; thence, Northward, along the Boundary of the Parish of St. Nicholas to the Point at which the same meets the River Soar; thence, Northward, along the River Soar to the Point at which the same meets the Boundary of the Borough; thence, Westward, along the Boundary of the Borough to the Point first described.

Councillors. Each of these Wards will have Six Councillors.

Objections to Division by Revising Barristers. The accompanying Tables will show all the details relative to the rating of the different Parishes in the Borough, and will be explanatory of our reasons for objecting to the Divisions adopted by the Revising Barristers; for by reference to the Table it will be seen that Ward No. 1, comprising the Parish of St. Martin, contains a much larger amount of property, and at the same time a smaller number of Houses, than any of the other Wards, the proportion of the latter being very far inferior, not exceeding one-half of that in the smallest of the remaining Wards. This Ward, therefore, contains an undue proportion of the wealthier classes, and we have therefore proposed the above-described Division, which places the different Wards more nearly on an equality.

J. Hammill.
W. Denison.

ST. MARGARET'S.

NAMES OF STREETS.	Sides of Street.	Number of Inhabited Houses on each side of Street.	Amount of Assessed Rental on each side of Street.	Proportion to actual Rental.	Rate Payers, divided into Six Classes, as below:					
					At and under £. 5.	Above £. 5, up to £. 10.	Above £. 10, up to £. 20.	Above £. 20, up to £. 30.	Above £. 30, up to £. 40.	Above £. 40.
					1st.	2d.	3d.	4th.	5th.	6th.
			£. s. d.							
Horsefair-street	S.	4	428 5 –		–	1	1	1	–	1
Millstone-lane	S.	12	105 – –		4	4	2	1	–	1
Bowling Green-street	–	13	159 – –		1	6	5	1		
Market-street	E.	15	504 – –		–	–	3	7	–	5
Ditto	W.	20	385 – –		–	8	4	6	1	1
Pocklington's-walk	–	18	284 – –		6	1	8	2	1	
Marble-street	–	36	178 10 –		27	6	2	1		
Oxford-street	E.	5	60 – –		–	1	4			
Newark-street	N.	15	147 – –		7	4	3	–	–	1
Chancery-street	–	26	217 – –		3	19	4			
King-street	W.	1	15 15 –		–	–	1			
New-walk	E.	34	719 18 –		–	–	21	9	4	
Wellington-street	–	92	803 13 –		37	34	13	3	4	1
Elton-street	–	5	21 – –		5					
Ashwell-street	–	7	43 6 –		5	2				
Slawson-street	–	14	51 7 –		14					
East-street	–	18	98 6 –		14	4				
Albion-street	–	109	651 – –		75	28	5	1		
Stamford-street	–	55	208 – –		42	13				
Granby-street	W.	93	813 – –	Three-fourths.	65	12	9	1	–	6
Ditto	E.	96	1,289 – –		43	12	24	9	3	5
London-road	W.	35	675 10 –		8	12	3	4	4	4
Ditto	E.	41	1,076 – –		1	7	12	10	4	7
Bishop-street	–	8	149 10 –		–	1	5	1	1	
Belvoir-street	N.	32	579 16 –		15	4	3	1	4	5
Ditto	S.	21	377 – –		–	12	4	2	1	2
Chatham-street	–	69	455 10 –		26	34	9			
York-street	–	49	217 10 –		30	17	2			
Dover-street	–	99	433 5 –		59	34	5	1		
Calais-street, Dover-street	–	36	144 18 –		31	5				
London-road	–	7	117 – –		5	–	1			
Waterloo-street	–	54	226 – –		31	12	1			
Regent-street	–	6	97 10 –		–	2	3	1		
Cannon-street	–	2	24 – –		–	1	1			
Nelson-street	–	8	95 – –		–	4	4			
Evington-lane	–	3	56 5 –		–	–	2	1		
Mill Hill-lane	–	4	52 – –		1	2	–	1		
Marston's Mill-lane	–	3	78 10 –		1	–	1	–	–	1
Prebend-street	–	2	91 – –		–	–	–	–	–	2
Conduit-street	–	59	319 – –		36	16	7			

ST. MARGARET'S—*continued.*

NAMES OF STREETS.	Sides of Street.	Number of Inhabited Houses on each side of Street.	Amount of Assessed Rental on each side of Street.	Proportion to actual Rental.	At and under £. 5.	Above £. 5, up to £. 10.	Above £. 10, up to £. 20.	Above £. 20, up to £. 30.	Above £. 30, up to £. 40.	Above £. 40.
			£. s. d.		1st.	2d.	3d.	4th.	5th.	6th.
Glebe-street	–	11	96 15 –		2	8	–	1		
South Hanover-street	–	9	30 10 –		8	–	–	1		
Without name street	–	4	43 – –		–	3	–	1		
Upper Conduit-street	–	3	35 15 –		–	2	–	1		
Slate-street	–	8	37 10 –	Three-fourths.	4	4				
Hanover-street	–	13	48 10 –		12	1				
Newport-place	–	10	74 11 –		8	1	1			
Northampton-street	–	132	785 – –		70	56	6			
Foxe's-street	–	2	8 16 –		2					
St. George's-street	–	18	88 6 –		9	6	3			
Church-street	–	13	170 10 –		–	12	–	1		
Rutland-street	–	83	1,019 15 –		27	25	13	14	2	2
Upper Charles-street	–	115	528 10 –		81	31	2	1		
Colton-street	–	101	528 10 –		50	44	6	1		
Bosworth, Brick Yard-lane	–	2	7 – –		2					
Wigston-street	–	31	161 – –		22	7	2			
Yeoman-street	–	24	109 – –		17	7				
Yeoman-lane	–	14	59 10 –		9	5				
Yeoman-square	–	8	19 – –		8					
Charles-street	–	66	858 – –		14	26	11	9	4	2
Halford-street	–	38	559 10 –		2	6	24	6		
Free-lane	–	29	134 5 –		21	4	4			
Gallowtree-gate	E.	31	1,512 5 –		1	–	1	4	9	16
Humberstone-gate	S.	54	926 18 –		17	9	12	6	4	5
Ditto	N.	82	1,412 10 –		43	5	9	14	2	9
Fox-lane	–	10	101 5 –		7	3				
Nelson-square	–	38	146 10 –		37	–	1			
St. James's-place	–	19	81 15 –		13	6				
Sand Pit-lane	–	12	48 5 –		11	1				
Humberston-road	S.	19	372 5 –		3	5	9	1	–	1
Ditto	N.	54	739 5 –		17	18	9	5	2	3
Stanley-street	–	5	28 5 –		2	3				
Curzon-street	–	8	46 5 –	One-third.	4	4				
Brunswick-street	–	24	67 5 –		21	2	1			
Wharf-street	–	156	938 11 6		106	36	11	3		
Wheat-street	–	126	343 5 –		110	12	3	1		
Carley-street	–	52	222 – –		41	9	2			

ST. MARGARET'S—*continued*.

NAMES OF STREETS.	Sides of Street.	Number of Inhabited Houses on each side of Street.	Amount of Assessed Rental on each side of Street.	Proportion to actual Rental.	Rate Payers, divided into Six Classes, as below:					
					At and under £.5.	Above £.5, up to £.10.	Above £.10, up to £.20.	Above £.20, up to £.30.	Above £.30, up to £.40.	Above £.40.
					1st.	2d.	3d.	4th.	5th.	6th.
			£. s. d.							
Benford-street	–	48	153 15 –		45	3				
Metcalf-street	–	62	200 10 –		56	4	2			
Lewin-street	–	24	85 10 –		20	4				
Eaton-street	–	37	147 15 –		30	7				
Providence-place	–	15	69 10 –		13	1	1			
Brook-street	–	56	117 – –		51	5				
Goodacre-street		7	20 3 4		7					
Lead-street	–	18	73 5 –		13	5				
Denman-street	–	56	203 15 –		44	11	1			
Piccadilly	–	18	42 – –		18					
Bow-street	–	5	22 5 –		4	1				
Pike-street	–	15	49 15 –		14	–	1			
Milton-street, Wharf-street	–	18	83 15 –		13	3	2			
Fleet-street	–	36	146 16 –		31	4	1			
Alfred-street	–	3	19 – –		2	–	1			
Kenyon-street	–	18	81 15 –		14	3	1			
Eldon-street	–	24	183 16 –		20	2	–	2		
Camden-street	–	9	35 7 –		8	1				
Lord-street	–	8	35 16 –		8					
Earl-street	–	2	10 13 –		1	1				
Russel-square	–	35	158 11 –		28	2	4	1		
Russel-street	–	77	331 7 –		63	13	–	1		
Neal-street	–	23	88 16 –		20	3				
Milton-street, Russel-street	–	19	68 11 –	One-third.	17	2				
Bedford-street	–	2	14 16 –		–	2				
Mill-street	–	25	92 7 –		22	2	1			
Bridge-street	–	35	229 15 –		26	8	–	–	–	1
Nameless	–	3	9 13 –		3					
Brickhill-lane	–	2	7 5 –		2					
Rudkin-street	–	10	28 3 –		9	1				
Barkby-lane	–	170	506 4 –		159	9	–	2		
Lee-street	–	12	55 4 –		10	–	2			
Paradise-row	–	10	23 9 –		10					
Haymarket	E.	6	442 10 –		–	–	–	–	1	5
Ditto	W.	9	303 10 –		–	1	1	–	5	2
Belgrave Gate	E.	222	1,828 14 –		82	43	72	17	5	3
Ditto	W.	177	2,204 3 –		55	43	43	18	9	9
Bread-street	–	13	29 16 –		13					
Hill-street	–	11	58 14 –		9	2				
Grove-street	–	23	69 – –		21	2				
Lower Grove-street	–	23	64 3 –		21	2				

ST. MARGARET'S—*continued.*

NAMES OF STREETS.	Sides of Street.	Number of Inhabited Houses on each side of Street.	Amount of Assessed Rental on each side of Street.	Proportion to actual Rental.	Rate Payers, divided into Six Classes, as below:					
					At and under £. 5.	Above £. 5, up to £. 10.	Above £. 10, up to £. 20.	Above £. 20, up to £. 30.	Above £. 30, up to £. 40.	Above £. 40.
			£. s. d.		1st.	2d.	3d.	4th.	5th.	6th.
Grosvenor-street	–	62	190 – –	One-third.	56	5	1			
George-street	–	47	267 10 –		35	8	4			
Upper George-street	–	15	60 10 –		14	–	1			
Crabb-street	–	66	220 – –		60	5	1			
Wood Boy-street	–	76	281 5 –		63	9	2	1	1	
Britannia-street	–	83	297 5 –		72	10	1			
Belgrave-road	–	3	44 5 –		1	–	1	1		
Ditto–foot ditto	–	2	138 10 –		–	–	–	1	–	1
Abbey Meadow-lane	–	1	30 – –		–	–	–	–	1	
Hampden-street	–	19	94 2 –		18	–	–	1		
Wood-street	–	6	36 18 –		4	–	2			
Navigation-street	–	75	550 10 –		49	22	2	1	–	1
Orchard-street	–	40	124 5 –		34	5	1			
Garden-street	–	45	120 5 –		42	3				
Green-street	–	40	107 5 –		39	–	1			
Abbey-street	–	58	226 5 –		51	4	3			
Lower Green-street	–	9	22 6 –		9					
Ditto–Garden-street	–	7	14 5 –		7					
Mansfield-street	–	94	397 5 –		78	14	–	1	–	1
Upper Sandacre-street	–	31	129 10 –		30	–	–	1		
Lower–ditto	–	16	45 10 –		14	1	–	1		
Gravel-street	–	22	122 10 –		9	13				
Royal East-street	–	36	186 5 –		25	8	–	2	1	
Wood-street	–	20	50 10 –		20					
Public Wharf-yard	–	9	100 5 –		–	6	–	2	1	
Foundry-yard and Lane	–	23	264 15 –		11	11	–	–	–	1
Ditto–Square	–	8	66 10 –		3	3	2			
Queen-street	–	27	120 15 –		23	4				
Charlotte-street	–	35	129 9 –		31	4				
Caroline-street	–	36	109 – –		35	1				
Gas-street	–	26	272 15 –	Three-fourths.	13	8	–	4	1	
Thames-street	–	48	226 5 –		40	6	–	1	–	1
St. John's-street	–	20	101 15 –		20					
Burley's-lane	–	78	268 5 –		76	2				
Short-street	–	34	107 – –		32	2				
New-lane	–	7	30 – –		6	–	1			
Archdeacon-lane	–	80	380 15 –		64	11	5			

ST. MARGARET'S—*continued.*

NAMES OF STREETS.	Sides of Street.	Number of Inhabited Houses on each side of Street.	Amount of Assessed Rental on each side of Street.	Proportion to actual Rental.	Rate Payers, divided into Six Classes, as below: At and under £.5.	Above £.5, up to £.10.	Above £.10, up to £.20.	Above £.20, up to £.30.	Above £.30, up to £.40.	Above £.40.
					1st.	2d.	3d.	4th.	5th.	6th.
			£. s. d.							
Luke-street	–	10	39 5 –		9	1				
Grafton-place	–	7	42 10 –		5	1	1			
Canning-street	–	12	42 15 –	Three-fourths	12					
Friday-street	–	4	67 15 –		–	2	–	1	1	
Canning-place	–	11	149 5 –		2	2	5	2		
St. Margaret's-street	–	33	144 – –		27	4	2			
-street	–	8	62 10 –		7	–	–	1		
Devonshire-street	–	10	33 5 –		10					
Church-gate	E.	139	981 8 –		91	33	8	4	2	1
Ditto	W.	68	549 5 –		32	21	8	6	1	
Pasture-lane	–	75	294 5 –		55	15	5	–	–	1
Sanvey-gate	N.	89	352 10 –		65	16	3	4	1	
Keen's-yard ditto	–	20	37 15 –		20					
Needle-gate	–	28	60 6 –		20					
Craven-street	–	33	145 14 –		30	2	1			
Northumberland-street	–	23	81 1 –		23					
Hungerford-street	–	8	29 5 –		8					
Northgate-street	E.	52	191 16 –		44	6	1	1		
Northgate-street	W.	8	62 8 –		6	1	–	–	–	1
Old-mill lane and yard	–	16	44 – –		16					
Frog-island	–	7	344 10 –		–	–	1	2	4	
Pingle-street	–	11	119 10 –		8	1	–	–	2	
-street	–	9	35 10 –		9					
Soar-lane	–	1	43 – –		–	–	–	–	–	1
Butt-close-lane	–	8	37 – –		7	1				
TOTAL	–	6,030	43,058 1 10	–	3,965	1,140	498	213	86	109

Most of the Houses compounded 25 per cent., up to 3s. per week; above 3s., up to £.3. 10s. One-eighth instead of one-fourth.

Amount of Poor-rate for 1834 . . £.6,378.

Amount in the Pound on Valuation . . 2s. 9d.

Amount of Valuation upon which this is levied . . £.46,380.

Amount of Borough Rate . . £.1,262.; County Rate . . £.713. 17s.

Amount of Rate levied under Local Act (Public) for Paving, Lighting and Police, &c. . . .£.1,010.

Population in 1831 . . 24,000.

Population at present, about . . 28,000 or 29,000.

ST. LEONARD'S.

NAMES OF STREETS.	Sides of Street.	Number of Inhabited Houses on each side of Street.	Amount of Assessed Rental on each side of Street.			Proportion to actual Rental.	Rate Payers, divided into Six Classes, as below:						Number of Persons rated for Houses, Warehouses, Shops, and Counting-houses, and who were not excused on account of poverty in 1835.	
							At and under £.5	Above £.5, up to £.10.	Above £.10, up to £.20.	Above £.20, up to £.30.	Above £.30, up to £.40.	Above £.40.	Rated	House-holders.
			£.	s.	d.		1st.	2d.	3d.	4th.	5th.	6th.		
Wood Gate	1	24	123	18	4	Two-thirds.	21	–	1	2	–	–	23	24
Abbey Gate	2	30	145	–	8	–	25	2	1	–	–	1	21	30
Frog Island	2	56	241	6	–	–	46	6	4	–	–	–	32	56
TOTAL	–	110	510	5	–	–	92	8	6	2	–	1	76	110

	£.	s.	d.
Amount of Poor Rate for 1834	292	9	7
Amount in the Pound on Valuation	–	9	–
Amount of Valuation upon which this is levied	851	11	6
Amount of County Rate for 1834	13	10	–

Population in 1831 . . . . 444.

,, at present . . . . 451.

H. Stevenson, Overseer, St. Leonard's.

ALL SAINTS.

NAMES OF STREETS.	Sides of Street.	Number of Inhabited Houses on each side of Street.	Amount of Assessed Rental on each side of Street.	Proportion to actual Rental.	Rate Payers, divided into Six Classes, as below:					
					At and under £. 5.	Above £. 5, up to £. 10.	Above £. 10, up to £. 20.	Above £. 20, up to £. 30.	Above £. 30, up to £. 40.	Above £. 40.
					1st.	2d.	3d.	4th.	5th.	6th.
			£. s. d.							
Bond-street	All	113	799 17 6		59	37	11	5	–	1
Causeway-lane	–	40	382 – –		23	11	6			
Church-gate	W.	14	39 15 –		13	1				
Cumberland-street or Elbow-lane	All	91	419 17 6		80	8	2	1		
Free School-lane	S.	7	110 15 –		–	4	1	1	1	
Ditto	N.	15	220 17 6		1	5	6	2	1	
Friars'-road	All	9	63 15 –		8	–	–	1		
Friars' Causeway	–	8	172 17 6		1	2	3	1	–	1
Frog Island	E.	37	352 5 –		32	2	2	–	–	1
High Cross-street	E.	40	585 10 –		13	9	10	4	1	3
Ditto	W.	78	690 – –	Three-fourths.	38	20	9	6	4	1
North Gates	E.	5	22 2 6		3	2				
Ditto	W.	6	37 15 –		2	2	2			
North Gate-street	E.	58	300 7 6		49	2	5	–	1	1
Ditto	W.	74	432 15 –		54	14	4	1	–	1
Opening	–	10	38 12 6		10					
Quaker's-lane	–	6	17 5 –		6					
Saint Peter's-lane	S.	25	161 – –		17	7	1			
Ditto	N.	29	174 10 –		7	20	2			
Sanvy-gate	S.	78	392 10 –		60	12	5	–	1	
Simon-street	All	10	51 – –		8	2				
Soar-lane	–	28	145 12 6		23	3	2			
Swine's Market	–	4	42 7 6		–	2	2			
Union-street	W.	2	29 – –		–	–	2			
Ditto	E.	1	22 10 –		–	–	–	1		
Vauxhall-street	All	26	122 10 –		25	1				
TOTAL	–	814	5,827 7 6	–	532	166	75	23	9	9

	£.	s.	d.
Amount of Poor Rate for 1834	1,238	–	–
Amount in the Pound on former Valuation, 12s.; on present Valuation would be about 7s.	–	12	–
Amount of Valuation upon which this is levied	4,179	–	–
Amount of Borough and Gaol Rate for 1834	652	–	–
Amount of Rate levied under Local Act for Paving, Lighting and Police . .	80	–	–

Population in 1831 . . . . 3,284.

,, at present . . . . 4,034.

The Parish of All Saints has been re-valued this year, and is now rated at rack-rent, deducting one-fourth for repairs: it was in 1834 rated at two-thirds of the actual value. An assessment of about 7s. in the pound will now produce as much as 12s. did in 1834.

James Hudson, Overseer.

Q

ST. MARY'S PARISH.

NAMES OF STREETS.	Sides of Street.	Number of Inhabited Houses on each side of Street.	Amount of Assessed Rental on each side of Street.			Proportion to actual Rental.	Rate Payers, divided into Six Classes, as below:					
							At and under £5.	Above £5, up to £10.	Above £10, up to £20.	Above £20, up to £30.	Above £30, up to £40.	Above £40.
			£.	s.	d.		1st.	2d.	3d.	4th.	5th.	6th.
Welford-road	E.	68	677	19	4		17	30	12	7	2	
Regent-street	–	36	357	15	10		–	30	4	1	–	1
James-street	–	15	69	2	6		9	6				
Mill-street	–	14	64	10	–		8	6				
Marlborough-street	–	34	249	9	2		14	15	3	1	1	
Duke-street	–	73	472	19	10		44	27	1	1		
Marquis-street	–	8	46	2	6		3	5				
King-street	–	81	1,332	15	–		9	14	28	23	4	3
Princess-street	–	14	349	17	6		–	–	8	4	–	2
Wellington-street	–	32	246	11	9		18	9	3	–	–	2
Park-street	–	18	89	4	2		16	2				
New-walk	–	5	71	12	6		–	1	3	1		
London-road	–	12	111	4	2		6	2	3	1		
Welford-road	W.	99	806	13	2		68	17	3	2	4	5
Norton-street	–	16	63	–	–		14	2				
South Gate-street	E.	27	327	17	6	Three-fourths on Houses.—Rack Rent on land.	8	7	9	1	1	1
South Gate	–	4	66	7	6		–	–	3	1		
Friar-lane	–	44	387	14	11		22	15	1	4	1	1
Millstone-lane	–	21	104	8	4		16	2	1	2		
Newark-street	–	12	238	–	–		–	2	4	5	1	
Oxford-street	E.	159	756	18	4		120	25	7	4	2	1
York-street	–	71	391	4	2		44	19	7	–	1	
Upper Brown-street	–	41	252	18	4		30	4	6	–	1	
Lower Brown-street	–	15	65	–	10		14	–	1			
Oxford-street	W.	76	557	13	4		47	13	9	4	1	2
South Gates	–	16	105	3	4		9	3	4			
South-gate-street	–	53	466	15	10		27	11	9	5	1	
Grange-lane	–	87	352	18	10		75	9	2	–	–	1
Bonner's-lane	–	24	72	10	–		24					
Newarks	–	4	83	–	10		1	–	1	1	–	1
Castle-street	–	24	128	17	–		18	2	3	1		
Bakehouse-lane	–	65	219	4	4		59	5	1			
Redcross-street	–	115	724	11	8		84	23	6	1	–	1
The Hollow	–	4	194	2	6		–	1	1	–	–	2
Harvy-lane	–	14	115	–	–		10	2	2			
Applegate-street	–	6	102	17	6		1	2	–	2	1	
Bath-lane	–	6	36	15	–		4	1	1			
Bridge-street	–	38	700	1	10		21	7	6	2	2	
Dun's-lane	–	52	159	17	6		36	10	4	1	–	1
Braunstone-gate	–	87	650	17	2		68	12	6	1		
West-street	–	44	172	–	10		42	2				
Narborough-road	–	8	279	2	6		–	1	3	–	1	3
TOTAL	–	1,642	12,720	17	4	–	1,006	344	165	76	24	27

Total Number of Houses . . . . 1,642.
Population in 1831:
   St. Mary's 5,168
   Southfield 1,608
                                                ————
                                                6,776.
Present Population, nearly . . . . 8,000.
Annual Borough Rate, being 1s. 11d. in the pound . . . . . . £.668. 3. 4.

Poor Rates for 1834, at 2s. 10d. in the pound on 3-4ths of the value on Houses, and
   at the rack-rent on land . . . . £.2,558.

   Amount of Valuation on which this is levied:
      On Houses . . . . £.12,820
      On Land 5,230
                                             ————
                                          £.18,050.

      In the County, about   £.11,050 ⎫
      In the Borough, about . . . . . 7,000 ⎬ Rate at 2½d. is £.115. 2. 1.
                                              ⎭

Amount of Rate levied under Local Act for Paving, Lighting, Police, &c.:
   For Bromkinthorpe, at 8d. in the pound, per annum, on old assessment
      on 2,720l. . . . . £.90 13 4
   For Southfield, at 2½d. in the pound, per annum, on old assessment
      on 2,311l. 24 1 6
                                              ———— £.114. 14. 10.

       Bromkinthorpe and Southfield, all in St. Mary's Parish.

ST. MARTIN'S.

NAMES OF STREETS.	Sides of Street.	Number of Inhabited Houses on each side of Street.	Amount of Assessed Rental on each side of Street. £. s. d.	Proportion to actual Rental.	At and under £.5. 1st.	Above £.5, up to £.10. 2d.	Above £.10, up to £.20. 3d.	Above £.20, up to £.30. 4th.	Above £.30, up to £.40. 5th.	Above £.40. 6th.
Cank-street	–	17	289 10 –		–	5	7	4	–	1
Cart's-lane	–	8	63 15 –		–	8				
Church-gate	W.	14	92 8 6		4	6	4			
East-gates	–	9	416 5 –		–	–	–	3	2	5
Friar-lane	–	16	705 – –		–	–	4	3	1	8
Gallowtree-gate	W.	27	1,111 5 –		–	–	4	5	7	11
High-street	N.	53	1,235 – –		11	–	15	15	4	8
High-street	S.	51	1,312 7 6		6	6	12	13	6	8
High Cross-street	–	56	1,052 14 –		7	15	16	10	3	5
Horsefair-street	N.	4	170 – –		–	–	–	–	2	2
Hotel-street	–	15	538 10 –		–	1	2	6	1	5
Little-lane	–	18	76 1 –	Three-fourths.	14	4				
Loseby-lane	–	14	222 15 –		1	2	7	4		
Market-place	–	23	1,351 10 –		2	–	–	1	2	18
Cheapside	–	8	496 15 –		–	–	–	–	2	6
Conduit-row	–	10	431 5 –		–	–	–	3	–	7
Cornwall	–	16	797 5 –		–	–	1	2	2	11
Backside	–	9	380 5 –		–	–	2	1	–	6
Exchange-row	–	5	121 10 –		2	1	–	–	1	1
Poultry	–	14	574 10 –		–	–	2	4	-	8
Millstone-lane	N.	5	102 – –		–	–	3	2		
New-street	–	10	401 5 –		–	–	–	5	1	4
Peacock-lane	–	4	24 – –		–	4				
Saint Martin's-street	–	15	533 5 –		–	–	4	4	1	6
Saint Nicholas-street	–	6	27 – –		4	2				
South Gate-street	E.	5	140 5 –		–	–	2	2	–	1
Silver-street	–	28	469 2 6		9	7	5	2	1	4
Swine's-market	–	19	265 10 –		–	7	9	3		
Thornton-lane	–	31	177 17 9		17	13	–	1		
Townhall-lane	–	36	344 15 3		11	13	8	4		
Union-street	–	13	148 – 3		–	6	6	1		
		559	14,071 11 9	–	88	100	113	98	36	125

Amount of Poor Rate for 1834 . . £.3,798. 8s. 2½d. It was an unequal valuation in 1834; some being assessed at one-half, others at two-thirds of the actual rental. The parish has since been re-valued, and the whole assessment is at three-fourths, as in the preceding columns.

Amount in the Pound on Valuation . . 1st Quarter, 3s.; 2d Quarter, 3s.; 3d Quarter, 2s. 9d.; 4th Quarter, 2s. 6d.

Amount of Valuation upon which this is levied . . £.7,187. 5s.

Amount of County Rate for 1834 . . £.1,362.

Population in 1831 . . 3,034.

ST. NICHOLAS.

NAMES OF STREETS.	Sides of Street.	Number of Inhabited Houses on each side of Street.	Amount of Assessed Rental on each side of Street.	Proportion to actual Rental.	Rate Payers, divided into Six Classes, as below:					
					At and under £.5.	Above £.5, up to £.10.	Above £.10, up to £.20.	Above £.20, up to £.30.	Above £.30, up to £.40.	Above £.40.
					1st.	2d.	3d.	4th.	5th.	6th.
			£. s. d.							
Nicholas-street	N.	14	115 16 8		6	5	1	2		
	S.	31	228 13 4		14	9	7	1		
Thornton-lane	N.	34	91 8 8		34					
	S.	10	20 – –		9	1				
Harvey-lane	E.	6	17 10 –		6					
Nicholas-square	S.	10	47 – –		5	5				
	N.	16	83 – –		13	2	1			
Applegate-street	E.	11	26 4 –		9	2				
	W.	14	95 1 8	Two-thirds.	10	2	1	1		
Talbot-lane	W.	7	162 3 4		3	–	–	2	1	1
	E.	40	106 6 8		35	5				
Churchyard	–	7	28 6 8		4	3				
Jewry Wall-street	S.	25	66 3 4		24	1				
	N.	51	146 5 –		48	–	3			
Bath-street	E.	8	31 6 8		7	1				
Blue Boar-lane	S.	3	36 13 4		1	–	1	1		
	N.	13	30 10 –		13					
Sycamore-lane	E.	2	26 – –		–	–	2			
	W.	20	57 6 8		18	1	1			
Bath-lane	E.	17	32 6 8		17					
	W.	13	151 – –		3	4	4	1	–	1
Including Shops, &c.	–	352*	1,599 2 8	–	279	41	21	8	1	2

* This includes empty Houses, about 30.

Amount of Poor Rate for 1834:

      Poor Levies . . . . . . £.668 7 9½

      Borough, &c., Empty Houses deducted . 198 15 9

                                      £.469 12 –½.

Amount in the Pound on Valuation . . 9s. 6d.

Amount of Valuation upon which this is levied . . £.1,598.

Amount of Borough and Gaol Rates for 1834 . . £.198. 15s. 9d., which is included in the Poor Levies.

Population in 1831 . . 1,494.

Very little alteration in the Population at present.

445

AUGUSTINE, AUSTIN, OR WHITEFRIARS.

NAMES OF STREETS.	Side of Street.	Number of Inhabited Houses on each side of Street.	Amount of Assessed Rental on each side of Street.	Proportion to actual Rental.	Rate Payers, divided into Six Classes, as below:					
					At and under £. 5.	Above £. 5, up to £. 10.	Above £. 10, up to £. 20.	Above £. 20, up to £. 30.	Above £. 30, up to £. 40.	Above £. 40.
					1st.	2d.	3d.	4th.	5th.	6th.
Bridge-street, &c. &c. Including Empty Houses	N.	45	£. s. d. 328 – –	Two-thirds	31	8	2	3	–	1

Amount in the Pound on Valuation . . 3s.
Amount of Valuation upon which this is levied . . £.492.
Amount of Borough and Gaol Rates for 1834 . . £.38.
Population in 1831 . . 180.
Little Decrease in the Population at present.

Samuel Langton,
Assistant Overseer.

BLACKFRIARS.

NAMES OF STREETS.	Number of Inhabited Houses on each side of Street.	Amount of Assessed Rental on each side of Street.	Proportion to actual Rental.	Rate Payers, divided into Six Classes, as below:					
				At and under £. 5.	Above £. 5, up to £. 10.	Above £. 10, up to £. 20.	Above £. 20, up to £. 30.	Above £. 30, up to £. 40.	Above £. 40.
				1st.	2d.	3d.	4th.	5th.	6th.
Caroline-street	17	£. s. d. 72 10 –							
Friars, Open	7	15 10 –							
Alexander-street	56	75 15 –							
Ruding-street	74	129 5 –	One-third.	239	8	3	2	2	
Sarah-street	20	174 15 –							
Friar's Causeway	42	102 12 6							
Blackfriars-street	35	55 2 6							
Wharf-yard	3	14 10 –							
Factories and shops	4								
TOTAL	258	640 – –	–	239	8	3	2	2	

Amount of County Rate for 1834, £.142. 10.; 5s. in the pound on valuation.
Population in 1831 . . . 1,152.
Population at present . . . 1,152.

LEICESTER, DIVIDED INTO SEVEN WARDS.

NAMES OF WARDS.	Number of Inhabited Houses.	Amount of Assessed Rental	Rate Payers, divided into Six Classes as below:					
			At and under £. 5.	Above £. 5, up to £. 10.	Above £. 10, up to £. 20.	Above £. 20, up to £. 30.	Above £. 30, up to £. 40.	Above £. 40.
			1st.	2d.	3d.	4th.	5th.	6th.
DIVISION BY REVISING BARRISTERS.								
		£. s. d.						
Ward No. 1.	559	14,171 11 9	88	100	112	97	36	126
No. 2.	1,718	10,265 13 –	1,294	277	95	54	22	18
No. 3.	2,022	10,905 5 10	1,545	263	133	48	11	21
No. 4.	1,155	11,388 11 –	565	316	141	66	26	41
No. 5.	1,312	11,475 5 3	610	404	157	72	26	31
No. 6.	1,405	10,219 6 1	906	221	127	47	19	22
No. 7.	1,639	10,329 13 2	1,224	234	118	41	18	15
	9,810	78,755 6 1	6,232	1,815	883	425	158	274
PROPOSED DIVISION.								
No. 1, or ALL SAINTS WARD	1,406	11,329 13 3	931	214	135	60	27	30
No. 2, or ST. MARGARET'S WARD	1,718	10,265 13 –	1,294	277	95	54	22	18
No. 3, or MELTON WARD	2,022	10,905 5 10	1,545	263	133	48	11	21
No. 4, or ST. GEORGE'S WARD	1,155	11,388 11 –	565	316	141	66	26	41
No. 5, or MARKET WARD	1,044	13,586 – 6	472	245	113	56	33	96
No. 6, or WEL-FORD WARD	1,338	10,681 9 –	898	213	120	61	15	32*
No. 7, or ST. MARY'S WARD	1,127	10,597 17 4	527	287	146	80	24	36
	9,810	78,755 6 1	6,232	1,815	883	425	158	274

* The Newark and Castle View are included in this Ward.

SUMMARY OF THE SEVERAL PARISHES, &c.

NAMES OF PARISHES, &c.	Number of Inhabited Houses.	Amount of Assessed Rental.	Rate Payers, divided into Six Classes, as below:					
			At and under £. 5.	Above £. 5, up to £. 10.	Above £. 10, up to £. 20.	Above £. 20, up to £. 30.	Above £. 30, up to £. 40.	Above £. 40
			1st.	2d.	3d.	4th.	5th.	6th.
		£. s. d.						
St. Margaret's	6,030	43,058 1 10	3,965	1,140	498	213	86	109
St. Leonard's	110	510 5 –	92	8	6	2	–	1
All Saints	814	5,827 7 6	532	166	75	23	9	9
St. Mary's	1,642	12,720 17 4	1,006	344	165	76	24	27
St. Martin's	559	14,071 11 9	88	100	113	98	36	125
St. Nicholas	352	1,599 2 8	279	41	21	8	1	2
Whitefriars	45	328 – –	31	8	2	3	–	1
Blackfriars	258	640 – –	239	8	3	2	2	–
TOTAL	9,810	78,755 6 1	6,232	1,815	883	425	158	274

DIVISION of LEICESTER by the REVISING BARRISTERS.

WE divided the Borough into Seven Wards, and we have determined and set out the Extent, Limits, and Boundary Lines of the said Wards as follows:—The First Ward comprises the Parish of St. Martin, and is bounded by the Boundaries of that Parish. The Second Ward comprises that portion of the Parish of St. Margaret which (commencing at the East Gate) is situate West of Belgrave Gate and Belgrave Road, and is bounded by that Gate and Road on the East, on the North and West by the exterior Boundary of the said Parish to the Western Corner of St. Margaret's Pasture, and on the South by the Boundary between St. Margaret's Parish, and St. Leonard's All Saints, and St. Martin's Parishes to the East Gate. The Third Ward comprises that other portion of St. Margaret's Parish situate between Belgrave Gate and Belgrave Road on the West, and Humberstone Gate and Humberstone Road on the East, and is bounded by the said Gates and Road on the West and East respectively on the South by the East Gate, and on the North by the exterior Boundary of the Parish from the Humberstone Road to the Belgrave Road. The Fourth Ward comprises that other portion of St. Margaret's Parish situate between the Humberstone Gate and Road on the North, and Gallowtree Gate, Granby Street, and the London Road, as far as the Turnpike Gate on the South, and is bounded by the said Gates, Roads and Streets on the North and South respectively; on the West by the East Gate, and on the East by the exterior Boundary of St. Margaret's Parish, from the Humberstone Road to the

Boundary of St. Mary's. The Fifth Ward comprises that other portion of St. Margaret's Parish situate South of Granby Street and the London Road, and that portion of St. Mary's Parish situate East of the Welford Road, and is bounded by Granby Street and the London Road on the North, by Horsefair Street on the West, by Market Street and Welford Road on the South, and on the East by the exterior Boundary of St. Mary's Parish, from the Welford Road to the Boundary of St. Margaret's Parish. The Sixth Ward comprises the remainder of St. Mary's Parish, including the New-arke and Castle View, and that portion of St. Margaret's Parish situate South of Market Street, and is bounded on the East by Market Street and the Welford Road, on the South-west and North-west by the exterior Boundary of St Mary's Parish, and on the North by the Boundary between that Parish and the Black Friars, the Augustine Friars, St. Nicholas Parish and St. Martin's, and along Millstone Lane to its junction with Market Street. The Seventh Ward comprises the Parishes of All Saints, St. Leonard's, and St. Nicholas, together with the Black Friars, the Augustine Friars, and that detached part of St. Margaret's Parish called the Pingle, and all other places within the said Borough not included in any of the Wards before described, and the exterior Boundaries of the Parishes and places comprised in this Ward, constitute the Boundaries of this Ward.

We have assigned the number of Councillors to each Ward as follows: to the First Ward, Six Councillors; to the Second Ward, Six Councillors; to the Third Ward, Six Councillors; to the Fourth Ward, Six Councillors; to the Fifth Ward, Six Councillors; to the Sixth Ward, Six Councillors; to the Seventh Ward, Six Councillors.

Francis Curzon.
William Finelly.

Disapproved by His Majesty in Council.

Wm. L. Bathurst.

EXAMINATION OF THOMAS BURBIDGE

EXAMINATION

OF

THOMAS BURBIDGE, ESQ.

LATE TOWN CLERK

OF

THE BOROUGH OF LEICESTER,

BY

THE TOWN COUNCIL,

TOUCHING THE STATEMENTS MADE IN HIS

CLAIM TO COMPENSATION,

FOR THE LOSS OF HIS OFFICES OF TOWN CLERK, ATTORNEY
AND SOLICITOR OF THE CORPORATION, CLERK OF THE PEACE,
CLERK TO THE MAGISTRATES, STEWARD OF THE BOROUGH
COURT, UNDER BAILIFF OF THE BOROUGH, ASSESSOR TO THE
CORONERS FOR THE BOROUGH, AND CLERK TO THE VISITORS
OF THE LUNATIC ASYLUMS.

LEICESTER:
PRINTED BY JOHN HENRY DAVIS, MARKET PLACE.

1837.

EXAMINATION

OF

THOMAS BURBIDGE, ESQ.

————o————

TOWN HALL, WEDNESDAY, FEBRUARY 1, 1837.

————

PRESENT:

THOMAS PAGET, ESQ. MAYOR.

ALDERMEN.

MR. ROBERT BIRKLEY.
MR. SAMUEL CARTWRIGHT.
MR. JAMES CORT.
MR. DAVID HEFFORD.
MR. WILLIAM EVANS HUTCHINSON.
MR. JAMES RICHARDS.
MR. SAMUEL SPURRETT.
MR. HENRY HIGHTON.
MR. SAMUEL WATERS.
MR. JOSEPH WHEATLEY.

COUNCILLORS.

MR. JOHN ALLEN.	MR. SAMUEL HOW.
MR. ROWLAND AUSTIN.	MR. JAMES HUDSON.
MR. JOHN BANKART.	MR. CHARLES INMAN.
MR. JOHN BAXTER.	MR. JOHN KIRBY.
MR. JOHN BIGGS.	MR. JOHN MANNING.
MR. WILLIAM BIGGS.	MR. JOHN MOORE.
MR. ROBERT BREWIN.	MR. JOHN NICHOLS.
MR. THOMAS BURGESS.	DR. NOBLE.
MR. JOS. CHAMBERLAIN.	MR. JOHN OLDACRES.
MR. JOHN COLTMAN.	MR. WILLIAM ROWLETT.
MR. JOHN COOPER.	MR. JAMES SARGEANT.
MR. WILLIAM DALTON.	MR. ROBERT JOHN SMITH.
MR. WILLIAM DRAYTON.	MR. THOMAS STOKES.
MR. JOSEPH FIELDING.	MR. EDWARD WESTON.
MR. RICHARD HARRIS.	MR. THOMAS WHEELER.
MR. SAMUEL S. HARRIS.	MR. JOSEPH WHETSTONE.
MR. JOHN HOULDEN.	MR. JOSEPH F. WINKS.

454

MR. BURBIDGE EXAMINED BY THE
TOWN CLERK.

THE TOWN CLERK: Before proceeding, Mr. Burbidge, I have to state, that although the Council have thought it right to request your attendance here, to answer such questions as they may think it necessary to put to you, touching your claim to compensation, this inquiry must not be construed into an admission on their part that under the circumstances of the case you are entitled to any compensation whatever. In any course which they may adopt in reference to your claim, they do not consider themselves prejudiced by this investigation.

MR. BURBIDGE: I attend here, because the Act of Parliament gives you power to summon me to answer such questions as you may put to me concerning the things stated in my claim. I will thank you to inform me what form of oath you intend to administer?

TOWN CLERK: This is the form—"You shall true answers make to all such questions as shall be asked of you by any Member of this Council, touching the matters set forth in this statement subscribed by you, So help you God."

MR. BURBIDGE: Very well.

Mr. Burbidge having been sworn, the examination proceeded.

TOWN CLERK: When were you appointed to the office of *Town Clerk?*

MR. BURBIDGE: In September, 1813, I believe.

Was there any other appointment than that which appears in the Hall Book?

No, not that I am aware of.

On what day were you removed from the office?

When my successor was appointed, I consider. On the 1st of January, 1836.

When were you appointed *Clerk of the Peace?*

I consider at the same time that I was appointed Town Clerk.

There was no distinct appointment?

No, I believe not. I am not aware that there was.

Was it not customary in former years to make an express appointment to this office?

I am not aware that it was.

Perhaps you have not looked into the Hall Books to see whether it was so or not?

No, I never have.

Then you consider that you held the appointment in virtue of your office of Town Clerk?

Yes; at least, as an adjunct to it.

When were you removed from the office of Clerk of the Peace?

In May some time, I think. I don't exactly know the day: it was when Mr. Toller was appointed.

The 10th of May.—When where you appointed *Clerk to the Magistrates?*

Virtually when I received the appointment of Town Clerk. There was no separate appointment.

In fact, the only appointment you had to the office of Clerk to the Magistrates, was your appointment in the Hall Books to the office of Town Clerk?

Yes.

When were you removed from the office of Clerk to the Magistrates?

Sometime in May, I think. It was when the new Magistrates began to act.

In April, I think.

Oh, in April. Perhaps it was.

By whom were you removed?

I don't know. I ceased to act when another Clerk was appointed: it was under the authority of the new Magistrates, I suppose.

Not by the Council?

No, except so far as my removal from the office of Clerk to the Magistrates was included in the appointment of a new Town Clerk. I was virtually removed from the office when a new Town Clerk was appointed.

You received no notice from the Council that you had ceased to be Clerk to the Magistrates?

No, except that I regarded myself as virtually removed from the office when a new Town Clerk was appointed. I continued to act as Clerk to the old Magistrates for some time after the appointment of a new Town Clerk, but I certainly did not then hold the office on the same tenure as when I held the appointment of Town Clerk.

When were you appointed *Steward of the Borough Court?*

I can't say exactly: the Hall Books will show. It was in September, 1828, I think, when Mr. Dalby died.

When were you removed from the office?

In May, I think.

You held the office for the benefit of a third party?

Yes, for Mr. Henry Dalby, Jun. Legally, I held the office for my own benefit; but morally, and as a man of honour, I held it for Mr. Dalby.

There is a minute in the Hall Books to that effect, I believe?

Yes, I believe there is.

When were you appointed *Under Bailiff?*

I have acted as Under Bailiff ever since I was appointed Town Clerk.

Who appointed you to the office of Under Bailiff?

There was no deed of appointment: it was generally by direction of the Mayor. The business was conducted at my office.

Is not the right of appointment vested in the High Bailiff?

I don't know. For certain purposes it most likely was, but not for others: it might be for what concerned the duties of his office.

Is not the office of High Bailiff in a Borough analogous to that of High Sheriff in a County, and the office of Under Bailiff to that of Under Sheriff?

Yes; but there is a difference in their original constitution; the one being appointed under a charter, the other by the King.

But the duties are similar?

Yes, quite so.

There was no appointment, in your case, by the Corporation as a Corporation?

No, certainly not.

When were you removed from the office?

When Mr. Mellor was appointed. It was about May. I don't recollect the exact date: the books will show.

How did you know that you were removed?

When I heard that Mr. Mellor was appointed, I knew.

Then were you not the officer of Mr. Wright, the High Bailiff, and not of the Corporation?

Yes, certainly: that is, I consider he would have had the power of dispossessing me.

I understand you to say, that the power of appointment and removal rested in the High Bailiff?

Yes, but I consider that the office was virtually an adjunct to that of Town Clerk. Legally, the nomination would be in the High Bailiff.

When were you appointed *Assessor to the Borough Coroners?*

I have held the office ever since I became Town Clerk.

Is the office recognized by the Charter?

No, but by immemorial usage.

Would not the appointment be in the Coroners for the time being?

No; I should doubt whether they, as part of the Corporation, had the power of removal and appointment. The question never arose. As the Coroners were appointed yearly, I should not think that they had the power of removing the Assessor.

What were the duties of the office?

To take down the evidence at inquests, and sum it up to the jury: to act as Coroner, in fact.

Has there always been an Assessor?

In my day, always; and in the time of my predecessor. I have never known the time when there was not such an officer: of my own knowledge, the office has existed thirty-five years.

When did you cease to hold the office?

When Mr. Gregory was appointed Coroner under the new system, and the old Coroners ceased to act.

457

You were not removed by the Council?

No.

Is there such an office now?

No; the office of Coroner has been newly created by an Act of Parliament: in fact, it is not now considered a Corporate office.

When were you appointed *Clerk to the Visitors of the Lunatic Asylums?*

I have filled the office ever since I was Town Clerk.

Did you hold the office in virtue of a distinct appointment by the Magistrates, or under the Corporation?

There was no distinct appointment: the office devolved upon me as Town Clerk, according to the usual custom.—[Here Mr. John Gregory, jun. clerk to Mr. Burbidge, spoke to him in an under tone. Mr. B. then added,]—I am reminded by Mr. Gregory, that there was a formal entry of the appointment made by the Magistrates at Quarter Sessions, from time to time; but that was a mere matter of form. The office always devolved on the Town Clerk.

The duties are defined by the Act?

Yes.

When were you appointed *Solicitor to the Corporation?*

At the same time I was appointed Town Clerk: that is, I have always acted as Solicitor to the Corporation.

Has it been the usage of the Corporation to employ the same person as Town Clerk and Solicitor?

It was not formerly: they had a separate Solicitor for some, if not for all descriptions of business. Mr. Lowdham once acted as Solicitor.

Did not Mr. Lowdham continue to act in that capacity down to the year 1800?

No.

Do you know when he ceased to hold the office?

He was not the Solicitor of the Corporation after Mr. William Heyrick became Town Clerk, I believe. That was in 1791.

Was he not the Solicitor of the Corporation in 1796?

After he ceased to be the regular Solicitor of the Corporation, he continued to act in that capacity in a suit as to tithes in Saint Mary's Parish, which he brought to a close.

Can you state positively that Mr. Lowdham was not the Corporation Solicitor after the appointment of Mr. Heyrick as Town Clerk?

No, I cannot. During the whole of my time in Mr. Heyrick's office, he was not.

The offices were not distinct, then, before your time?

No, they were united when Mr. Heyrick was Town Clerk.

Previous to Mr. Heyrick's time?

I cannot say. I recollect Mr. Lowdham being Solicitor to the Corporation: I am not able to say whether the offices were distinct or united before his appointment.

You have not examined the Hall Books with a view to decide that question?

No, I have not.

Can you state whether the Solicitor's appointment was during pleasure?

No, but most likely it was, when the office was distinct from that of Town Clerk.

Are you not aware that till lately it was the custom for the two offices to be filled by different individuals?

No, except as to Mr. Lowdham. I don't mean to say that it was not so.

When was Mr. Lowdham appointed?

I don't know: I can't say, of my own knowledge, that he ever was appointed—I only know that at one time he held the office.

You know nothing as to his predecessor?

No.

[Here the Town Clerk read a list of the names of gentlemen who had filled the office of Solicitor, distinct from the office of Town Clerk, from the year 1681 down nearly to the close of the eighteenth century. The examination was then resumed.]

What documents do you produce, Mr. Burbidge, in support of the first item in your claim—£625 14s. 10d.?

My bill-books, which I have dissected and analyzed, so as to arrive at the amounts which I have received during the five years. The examination will involve long details, with which it would be tedious to trouble this meeting. If convenient, I will be glad to meet a Committee with all my books and papers, and give them every information.

Can't you give us copies of the bills and documents upon which your claim is founded?

I am not prepared to do so: I have got my books with me.

Will you furnish copies of the bills on which this first item is founded?

No; I don't see that I am called upon to comply with such a demand. I will meet a Committee, with my books.

Then do you object to furnish copies?

I have never thought of it: no application of the kind has ever before been made to me, and I have never considered the subject. Much of what is required consists of receipts, &c., dispersed through my cash-book, which I could not hand over to the Council.

Then am I to understand that you object to furnish the particulars for the first item?

My answer is, that as such a demand has not before been made, I must take time for consideration: I have had no previous intimation that the Council had such a wish.

459

You received a notice, calling upon you to produce all books, papers, and writings in your possession, relating to your claim?

And I am here ready to do so.

Then what documents do you produce in support of your claim as Town Clerk and Solicitor?

No documents: I have here my bill-books, with an analysis of the accounts under examination; and I am ready to go through them with the Council or a Committee.

Will you hand over the books and papers to the Mayor?

[Here Mr. Burbidge placed two bill-books in the hands of the Mayor; also, papers showing the various totals of the bills which went to make up the gross sums set down under the different heads of the claim.]

You have not got separate accounts?

No.

Where are the bills to which these papers refer?

In the books.

We must require a statement of each particular bill, with a copy?

You must give me time to consider whether I shall comply or not. The law, I think, does not require me to furnish copies.

Who has the custody of the bills made out from these books?

You, I believe.

No: are there no bills that you know of, except what I have got?

I don't know what bills you have received.

Who was the legal *custos* of the bills paid?

I cannot answer that question: I was not—the Corporation themselves, I suppose. The bills would be placed in the Charter House.

Where are the bills which were not sent to me, and which are not in the Charter House?

I cannot tell: I thought you had them all.

You say that the Corporation would keep the bills: was it the office of any particular member to do so?

I cannot say: they would be placed among the Corporation vouchers.

In the Charter House, or in your office?

Generally in the Charter House.

Those which are not in the Charter House and have not been sent to me, where would they be?

I fancied you had got the whole.

Whose duty was it to take charge of the bills?

That is a matter of judgment. You may suppose one person, I another. I cannot answer the question.

Who, as a matter of practice, kept the bills?

Generally speaking, after they were audited and passed, they were placed in the Charter House.

Was there any other officer but the Town Clerk who kept the bills?

I cannot say: it was not the office of the Town Clerk—they seldom remained in his possession except for the purpose of preparing the Borough Account.

Who paid the accounts?

Sometimes the Chamberlains, sometimes they were paid by orders of the Magistrates out of particular funds. The Chamberlains' bills were paid by the Chamberlains.

In whose hands were they left?

They were often left at my office for years, and then wrapped up and deposited in the Charter House. Sometimes bills were lodged in a portion of this building (the Town Hall).

The Magistrates' bills, where were they placed?

If they were Corporation bills, with the Chamberlains'.

Then there was no particular officer whose duty it was to have the custody of the bills?

Certainly.

To whom were bills originally presented for payment?

To the Corporation Auditors: they were audited, and paid by the Chamberlains afterwards.

Were the items in the claim made out from your cash book?

The bill books: some casual receipts come under other heads in the cash book.

[Here the inspection of the bills on which the claim was founded commenced, the Town Clerk reading the gross amount of each bill from the analysis handed in, and Mr. Burbidge stating the page of the book at which the particulars of the amount would be found.]

In 1830, under the head Town Clerk and Solicitor, the first item on your paper is 157*l.* 2s. 10d. (disbursements 4*l.* 4s. 6d.)?

That is my Annual General Bill.

The next item is £24 18s. (disbursements, £13 7s.). There is here a charge for the prosecution of two men: was it your duty to prosecute?

In cases of assaults upon constables, I was sometimes instructed by the Magistrates to prosecute.

Was it not the province of the prosecutor to select his own attorney?

That is a matter for argument. When peace-officers were assaulted, the Magistrates thought it their duty to protect them.

The next item is £84 10s. (disbursements £21 2s. 6d.)?

That was for leases.

Was not this charge for business performed previous to 1830?

I don't know: very likely it may; but the bill was not made out or paid before the period to which the calculation applies.

Were not these leases prepared before the year 1830—they appear from the bill to have been prepared some years before?

I don't know at all.

Have you, in your calculations, included all your receipts within the five years, whether the business was performed within that period or not?

I can't speak positively: perhaps I may; but that will be best ascertained by going through the bills. The question whether all I have received in the time is included in the statement, whether the work was then performed or not, will form matter for investigation.

And expunging?

There will be expunging enough, I dare say.

Can you say whether the business charged for in this item was or was not performed before 1830?

Not now; but I will ascertain, and if it was, the charge can be struck off.

The Council will require you to furnish copies of the bills for their own examination?

I am anxious to go into this inquiry fairly and candidly; but I hope that the Council will not put me to any unnecessary trouble, if they do not intend to deal with my claim, with an intention to assess the amount of my compensation.

I am not prepared to say what the Council will do. The next item is £2 2s. od.: is this for Charity business?

Yes.

In the calculation which you have made, have you included your profits as Solicitor to the Charity Trustees?

Yes, where they apply to the period.

The next item is £17 3s. od.: (disbursements, £1 10s. od.) Does not the whole of this charge relate to Sir Thomas White's Charity?

Yes, it does.

The next item is £22 15s. 6d.: (disbursements, £2 4s. 6d.) Does this form part of the bills referred to Mr. Mills?

I don't know.

The next item is £13 2s. 6d. To what does this relate?

I have omitted to note down a reference to the folio in the bill book where the particulars are entered: the item must stand over for future investigation.

The next item is £45 16s. od. (disbursements, £10 7s.)?

That is one of the bills submitted to reference.

For leases, I believe?

Yes.

Were these leases ever executed? [The names of the lessees were read.]

The bill forms part of those submitted to reference, and I must abide the issue.

Were the leases executed?

I don't know: some of them were not, certainly.

Part of the charge is for affixing the seals?

Well, the matter will remain for investigation: you brought the subject up in London, and there is no necessity to go into it now.

Where are the leases?

I don't know where they are, if they have not been sent to you.

They have not been sent to me.

Well, then, they have not been found yet: the offices will be further searched, and when the leases are found they will be sent to you.

You are not prepared to produce them at the present time?

No; they were made certainly, but whether they were executed or not I cannot say.

You can positively say that they were prepared?

Oh, yes.

Of that you are quite positive?

I can only say from their being entered and charged: they were ordered to be made by the South Fields Committee, and I have no doubt they were made. I shall probably be able to find them soon.

Has not the whole amount of the stamps been entirely lost?

Yes.

Then the leases have answered no beneficial end?

That is assuming they were not executed.

Did you not state in a letter I received from you that they had not been executed?

I don't know: part of them were not.

We have now gone through the items which, in addition to your stated salary of £200, you have set down on your paper to make out the first gross sum in your claim. What duties did your salary include?

They were not clearly defined. I had to attend upon the Corporation; and the salary was for my time, clerks, &c.: it included no professional business.

Did it include attendance at meetings of the Corporation and of Committees?

Corporation meetings, but not meetings of Committees: it included attendance on meetings of the Corporation as a body, and other matters, for which I made no special charge.

The amount stated in your claim under the first head—your receipts as Town Clerk and Solicitor in 1830—is £625 14s. 10d.; while the items on your paper, with the salary of £200, make little more than £500. Have you any other items to add?

Yes; there were many receipts which were omitted to be entered in any book, and I estimate the profit on these at £100 per annum.

Then the charge is not founded on any accurate calculation? Have you nothing to show for it?

No; but I have no doubt that I had receipts not entered to that extent.

Then you put down the item merely because you have no doubt that receipts to the amount of £100 have not been entered in your bill books?

Yes.

On what do you found your estimate?

On conjecture of bills not made out.

How not made out?

Services performed and no bills made out.

Had you any documents to refer to when you made your estimate?

No; but I believe that I am fully warranted in estimating the amount at £100 per year, and that I come within the extent of the receipts not entered.

Does the same item occur in each of the five years?

Yes, I took the sum as an average.

Is that the only explanation of the charge which you wish to give?

Yes; it was desirable that I should make a claim, and I put in a sum as near to the mark as I could.

You have put it in that you might claim enough?

Certainly.

There is here an item of £24 3s. 0d. for attendance at the hustings. This is an Election bill?

Yes.

On your paper you say £24 3s. 0d., but in your bill-book the sum is £13 2s. 6d.?

Then the other was Mr. Ellis's share.

Did Mr. Evans pay you the £10?

Yes, I believe he did: it remained due for some time, I dare say.

Was not the money paid to you as Assistant to the Returning Officer?

Yes.

Not as Town Clerk, but as Adviser of the Returning Officer?

Yes; it was a fee usually paid on such occasions: it was £20 in better times than these we now live in. There used to be such things as compliments then, but there are very few nowadays.

Did Mr. Evans pay you the compliment in 1830?

I dare say he did, if he has not forgotten it.

Mr. Ellis's is marked paid, but Mr. Evans's is not?

I think he did pay it in 1830. I have no doubt there was a great deal to do to get it.

Has the fee been paid at any subsequent Elections?

No, I think not: I'm not sure. If not, it should go into the £100 a-year.

Was it not a mere gratuity?

It was a compliment always paid at an Election.

Voluntarily?

Voluntarily, till of late years.

Do you make a charge to the Corporation independently of the fee from the Members?

No, except when it was not paid by the Members, and then I charged it to the Corporation.

And they rejected it.—The first item in 1831 is your General Annual Bill, £271 6s. 10d. (disbursements, £18 4s. 0d.). One item is for preparing a History of Leicester, in answer to articles in the *Leicester Chronicle*, called "Local Politics." There are also various other documents charged for in these bills. Can you furnish the documents?

Have you any wish to see them?

The Council are entitled to have all that you charge for. Do you object to furnish them?

Not if I have them.

In this Annual General Bill are there any items relating to Charities?

Yes, but not to any great amount. As I have said before, I shall be glad to go into all the details with a Committee.

I notice in this bill an item of £3 for correspondence with Mr. Bicknell, the solicitor of Mr. Sergeant Taddy, and also with the Learned Sergeant himself. Was not this after the passing of the Corporate Funds Bill?

I am not aware. It is astonishing how quickly you catch your eye on an item of that sort.

The next item on your paper is £63 9s. 0d. (disbursements, £13 2s. 0d.) Does this form part of the accounts referred to Mr. Mills?

Yes, I think it does.

The next is £6 9s. 8d. (disbursements, 12s.)?

That is a Charity bill: Alderman Newton's.

The next is £22 8s. 0d. (disbursements, £1 8s. 0d.)?

That also is a Charity bill: Sir Thomas White's.

The next is £21?

That is an Election bill.

You admit that this is altogether an Election bill?

Yes.

Was the money paid by Messrs. Evans and Ellis, or by any party?

When not paid by the parties, I charged it to the Corporation.

Have you received it?

It forms part of the excluded bill, I believe.

The money has not come into your pocket?

Yes, but it must come out again.

You have no profit on the bill?

I shall get very little profit by any of the bills which have been referred.

The next item is £65 1s. 4d. (disbursements, £3 7s. 0d.) Does this form part of the bills referred?

I don't know: very likely it does.

Are your conveyancing bills made out according to the usual rate of professional remuneration?

The charges are such as I used to make in days gone by. If such bills were made out by the scale of taxation, no solicitor could live by his profession; and, as a friend, I would not advise you to introduce the practice here.

Then the bills are not made out according to the usual and allowed professional charges?

They are not regulated by the strict tables of taxation. I am sure you must be surprised that I have charged so little.

Have you charged according to folio and sheet?

No, in gross sums. Instead of charging in detail for attendances, drawing, fair copies, &c., I put down one sum for all. If I had thought that any of the bills would have come under taxation, I should have set forth the details; because I believe that I have injured myself by charging in the gross.

Can you give us any account of the number of your attendances in any one of the cases included in the bill now under our notice—for instance, this one of a conveyance of land to the Leicester and Swannington Railway Company?

No, not now; perhaps not at all. I know that I had frequently to attend upon Messrs. Miles. But the bill has been referred to Mr. Mills, and there is no need to bring it before two tribunals: the tribunal there is sharp enough, without adding to it another—I know that I shall have little justice by the reference, whatever the Council may have.

You have not charged by the folio, nor on the scale allowed in taxation?

I have not charged on the principle of taxation.

The next item is £7 12s. 8d. (disbursements, £1 14s. 6d.) At what page does this bill occur?

That is one of the bills referred.—[Mr. B. mentioned the page, and the Town Clerk turned to the bill.]

It is a lease to Charles Mann: was it ever executed?

As to Mann, I don't know.

As to the Corporation?

I don't know: I believe not. I may here as well explain to the Council what I have before explained to you, with regard to these leases. It was agreed that the tenants should bear half the expense of the leases; but they got into possession, and then refused to execute the leases, to save the cost: they had got possession, and then did not care about the leases. Latterly, a tenant was required to pay £5 before he had possession.

Can you produce the minute-book of the South Fields Committee, by whom you say these leases were ordered to be made?

Have not you got it?

No. There was a book containing the proceedings of the South Fields Committee?

Yes.

Who has it?

I thought you had.

No. Did you attend the meetings of the Committee?

Yes; I made a rough draft of the proceedings at each meeting, and subsequently entered them in a book.

Who kept that book?

I did.

Who has it now?

I don't know: I thought you had.

No, I applied for it, but could not get it. Are the rough drafts you speak of in your possession?

I think not, but I will search.

Who usually kept the book?

I did generally: occasionally Mr. Firmadge and Mr. Parsons had it.

When did you see it last?

I can't say: it is some years since the Committee had a meeting.

Who was the Chairman of the Committee?

The Mayor for the time being.

Did you see the book in 1835?

I don't recollect.

Did you see it previously to the sales in December, 1835?

No, the Committee had nothing to do with those sales: they have not met for five or six years.

Then by whose authority were deeds prepared in cases of sales in that period?

There have been no conveyances executed lately, except in 1835. Mr. Firmadge had a general authority to sell land at 5s. per yard; and if he had sold, I should have prepared a conveyance.

Who gave instructions for leases when the Committee ceased to act?

Instructions would come from the Steward—always.

Was there any other book containing entries of sales, besides that of the South Fields Committee?

Not that I am aware of.

When did the book commence?

At a very ancient date. Meetings of the Committee have been held as far back as I can recollect.

It was an ancient book?

There were divers books.

Were their proceedings recorded in these books all this time?

Yes.

Were the contracts of sale entered in the books?

No, only the general authority.

What kind of books were they—like the Hall Books?

No, smaller—like an account book.

You don't know where the last book is?

No.

Nor when you last used it?

No; it has not been used for five or six years.

Have you seen it within the last two years?

I don't know.

Three?

I am not aware.

You are not able to say in whose possession it is at this time?

No.

Were any of the sales in 1835 ordered by the South Fields Committee?

No—certainly not.

By order of whom, then?

Of a Finance Committee, appointed by the Corporation.

Where is their minute book?

There were no minutes kept in reference to the sales. You have their books kept at the time when they were trying to put the finances of the Corporation on a different footing. Afterwards the Finance Committee was constituted a Secret Committee, and no entries were then made of their proceedings.

For purposes of secrecy?

It was not necessary—they only related to negotiations for the sale of property.

Were contracts of sale not entered in any book?

I never saw any.

Was any account kept of the purchase-money owing to the Corporation?

An account was kept by Mr. Firmadge, who reported at different periods to the Corporation, and his reports were entered on the Hall Books.

Was there any account of the kind entered in the Hall Books since 1824?

I don't know.

Do you intend to say that no account was kept independently of Mr. Firmadge's?

None—except the entries in the Hall Books, as I said before.

By what means did the Corporation ascertain the balances due to them from individuals?

I don't know: it was Mr. Firmadge's department to furnish that information, and latterly the Steward's.

Have you any record of Mr. Firmadge's accounts?

No, I have not.

Again I ask you, how would the Corporation ascertain the balance due to them from purchasers, principal and interest?

I had nothing to do with that department.

How would the Corporation?

By Mr. Firmadge's reports, and latterly Mr. Parsons'.

Were written reports presented?

No, except in some instances.

Then was no account kept of sales, showing the amounts received and the amounts due, for the last twenty years?

There are accounts entered in the Hall Books.

These accounts furnish only the receipts, not the balances due. There was a purchase completed by Mr. Barston in 1835—how was it ascertained what was owing from him?

I should think Mr. Barston would know.

To whom were accounts submitted before balances were accepted?

Mr. Firmadge would ascertain, and his report would be received.

Have you Mr. Firmadge's reports for the last 20 years?

No.

Who examined and settled the balance due from Mr. Rawson, on the completion of his purchase?

I cannot say.

Are there no documents in existence showing balances due from individuals?

Not to my knowledge.

The last account I find in the books is a copy of a South Fields sale-account in 1824: is there no subsequent account existing?

I can't say, without referring to the books.

Do you mean to say, that when Mr. Rawson executed his conveyance, no written account was produced, showing the balance due from him to the Corporation?

I don't know—there might be: it did not pass through my hands.

Was there a bank book kept?

Yes; Mr. Rawson, I believe paid his balance into the bank.

MR. WHETSTONE: There were balances paid by Mr. Rawson and others, at the close of 1835, we know—we wish to be informed from what account those balances were made out?

I don't know.

TOWN CLERK: How did the Corporation satisfy themselves that the sums paid were the sums due to them?

I don't know. The Finance Committee might ascertain: it was not in my presence.

Who received sale monies?

Mr. Firmadge generally.

Did he receive them in the last five or six years?

No; there were no sales in that time, except in 1835.

When he received such monies, did he not report his receipts and payments?

Yes, generally.

Are his reports preserved?

I don't know at all. They were not in account-books—generally separate accounts.

Then the books of the Corporation did not furnish the means of ascertaining what was due to them?

No, except Mr. Firmadge's accounts.

Have you a copy of his accounts?

No.

When a general release was given to Mr. Firmadge, in 1835, what accounts were audited?

None: his accounts had been audited and settled long before, as the release, I believe, recites.

You mean to say that Mr. Firmadge had nothing to do with these matters for the last five or six years?

Yes.

Who examined the accounts of Mr. Barston and Mr. Rawson, if Mr. Firmadge had ceased to act?

Mr. Barston's was a settled amount, long before. As to Mr. Rawson's, I don't know, unless the Committee did.

In an account furnished by Mr. Firmadge, and entered in the Hall Books in 1824, there is an item of £65 interest paid by you on purchase-money?

Yes, the residue of purchase-money.

What was the rate of interest?

Five per cent.

When was the conveyance executed to you?

In 1826, I think.

To whom was the £1,300 paid?

To the Corporation.

To what member of the Corporation?

I settled the account with Mr. Firmadge.

To whom was the money paid?

I paid through Mr. Firmadge, partly in money, and partly in bills I had against the Corporation.

Do you mean in bills which appear in the Chamberlains' books, or other bills?

Other bills.

What was the sum you paid to Mr. Firmadge?

I cannot tell.

In what account will the £1,300 appear?

Not in the Chamberlains', but in Mr. Firmadge's, as money received from me and partly repaid to me.

What was the nature of the bills?

Large conveyancing bills, and old matters, standing for some time. They are not included in my statement of claim.

Who examined the bills before Mr. Firmadge settled the account?

A Committee of the Corporation.—But this matter is foreign to the present inquiry.

I put these questions, because it appears from the books given up by the late Corporation to the Council, that in 1824 you paid £65 interest on purchase-money; and there is no subsequent entry showing that the principal has been paid: we therefore wished to know if the account was settled.

But this inquiry is not the medium through which you can legally arrive at that knowledge; and the Council will not let you travel out of the statements made in my claim.

Certainly the point in question affects your compensation. The Corporation Books show you to have been indebted a certain sum of money in the year 1824, and there is no subsequent entry acknowledging the receipt of the sum due. We therefore wish to be satisfied on this head.

It has no connection with the present investigation.

Yes, as affecting your compensation.

It is an old affair, brought to a conclusion long antecedent to the date of the bills now under examination. The account was settled, I dare say, in 1826.

Have you any account of the settlement?

I may have.

Will you furnish an account?

No; it was settled ten years ago, and I will not revive it now.

In whose custody are the bills which formed part of the consideration for the purchase?

I believe Mr. Firmadge had them: I handed them over to the South Fields Committee.

In whose possession are they now?

I cannot say.

We ask these questions, because, so far as our books show, the account is unsettled.

It is settled.

Can you satisfy the Council by any documents that the £1,300 has been paid?

No, I think I cannot. But I think that my having the conveyance, and there being nothing to produce to prove that the money is not paid, ought to be sufficient.

Did not the Corporation occasionally part with conveyances before the purchase-money was paid?

No, I believe not.

Not in Mr. Rawson's case?

I think not.

Then have you no further account to give relating to the payment of the money—do you object to furnish any account?

Yes, on principle; because the affair is not relevant to the present inquiry.

You say that no accounts of Mr. Firmadge's were audited in December, 1835?

None.

Were no papers given up by him at that time?

No; they were given up when he left Leicester.

To whom?

To Mr. Parsons, I believe, as successor to the agency.

Mr. Firmadge would have the accounts as to all sales under his direction?

I don't know: I did not see them.

Did he cease to act when he left Leicester for Leamington?

Yes.

Has Mr. Parsons the sale accounts of the last thirteen years?

I don't know.

The last item on your paper in this year is £65 1s. 4d. (disbursements, £3 7s. 0d.) The first item in 1832 is your General Annual Bill, £234 13s. 8d. (disbursements, £8 2s. 6d.) One charge is for a variety of Petitions to the House of Lords against the passing of the Reform Bill: is this charge according to the folio?

No; they were worth more than the charge allowed by the folio: I should be sorry to sell my brains by the folio.

Are they charged for according to the ratio of the bills submitted to reference?

They were charged what I thought then, and still think reasonable: they are not charged by the folio—they are worth more than that.

I am speaking of copies?

Oh, copies.

Are your charges now under consideration on the same scale as those submitted to Mr. Mills?

On that point I think I must take the benefit of your observation before Mr. Mills, that the charges in the bills before him appeared to be higher than those which I had made in former bills.

In your own opinion, are the charges in both made according to one ratio?

They were all meant to be fair and reasonable.

Do you mean to say that they were all made according to the same scale?

Yes, very likely they were: I charged what I thought fair and reasonable at the time.

Part of this Annual Bill is for Charity business?

Very little: my General Bill seldom contained much Charity business.

The next item is £397 15s. 3d. (disbursements £2 7s.) This is for the first Registration under the Reform Bill. I see there is a charge for the attendance of yourself and two clerks for twenty-six days, while the Freemen's claims were under revision: did you attend yourself personally during the whole of this time?

Yes; I was fully occupied during the whole twenty-six days. I should have almost thought it was six weeks: the claims were very numerous, and took a long time to revise.

The next item is £81 8s. 10d.?

That is one of the bills referred: it is one of the alehouse-keepers' bills.

There are no disbursements here?

No, they are included in the agencies, and taken off elsewhere.

The next item is £4 4s. 0d.?

That is a Charity bill.

The next is £21 13s. 0d. (disbursements, £1 10s. 0d.)?

That also is a Charity bill.

The next £261 13s. 0d. (disbursements, £214 15s. 0d.)?

That is an Election bill.

The fees here charged for the return of Members do not appear to be paid—were they paid?

I can't charge my memory—I should think they were—I am not certain.

The next is £29 7s. 4d. (disbursements, £1 18s. 0d.)?

That is one of the alehouse-keepers' bills.

Next, £45 16s. 0d. (disbursements, £10 7s. 0d.)?

That is for leases.

Were any part of them executed?

What were they?

[Here the Town Clerk read the names of the lessees from the bill-book, and Mr. Burbidge said]—

I should think part of them were executed: several of them were not.

And the stamps were entirely lost?

Yes.

In the item of £29 7s. 4d., there are charges included for drawing a declaration, payments to Mr. Sergeant Goulburn, &c. and you have only taken off £1 18s. 0d.?

Then I have taken off an additional sum elsewhere—in a gross total at the last.

In this year there is only a deduction of 13s. 4d. as agents' charges, while in the bills there are charges for various matters which could only be transacted by agents?

You will find a deduction made further on.

Then how do you make £836 18s. 11d. independently of salary?

It makes that sum with the £100.

In 1833, the first item is your Annual General Bill, £331 5s. 8d. (disbursements, £24 8s. 6d.) I understood you to say, in reply to former questions, that the South Fields Committee had not met for five or six years: I find here a charge for attending a meeting of the Committee, preparing resolutions, and making copy of six orders for the Steward?

Then I was in error: I knew that it was a long time since they had met.

Here is a charge of £3 18s. 8d. for preparing answers to several false charges circulated by the Radicals?

A very moderate sum, I think.

The next items are, £164 8s. 4d. for the Registration under the Reform Act; and one of £352 15s. 6d. for prosecuting Mr. Thompson?

This last bill is referred.

The next is £371 6s. 8d. This is for the prosecution of Mr. Cockshaw, and is referred?

Yes.

The next item is £14 (disbursements, £7 14s. 0d.)?

That is a bill for a prosecution.

The next, £134 18s. 6d.?

A Charity bill.

You have not taken off the agents' charges?

No; I have made a deduction of upwards of £300, including agency on the bills of several years, as you will find presently.

How do you know that that deduction is accurate?

It is done accurately, I have no doubt.

Why not make the deduction from each bill?

That would have been difficult, and this mode will make no difference in the result.

The next item is £365 18s. 2d. (disbursements, £54 10s. 6d.) This is for business done in connection with the Corporation Commissioners' Inquiry. There is a charge for a journey to London of £73 10s. 0d. at three guineas and a half per day?

Yes, we were expecting an application to be made for a criminal information, on the refusal of the Corporation to produce their books, and I went to London to consult the Recorder.

This was in November: is not the same journey also charged for in your bill against Messrs. Thompson and Cockshaw?

No, I believe not.

The rule came on in November, and you charge for the whole time. Was it not the same time?

No, I think they were distinct.

Can you give us the dates of your departure and return?

Not now.

You charge your absence all that term?

You will have a deduction made in the bills submitted to reference.

Yes, but you will be allowed by the arbitrator for ten days, and you charge them here too. Can you ascertain how the fact stands?

No, not now.

In Trinity term, 1833, don't you charge your journey to London both in the libel case and in the alehouse-keepers' bills?

No, I think not: but if so, the error shall be corrected.

I think you will find that you have charged half the expense as against Cockshaw and half against Thompson, and the whole in the alehouse cases?

Well, I'll see: I think not, but I will ascertain.

The next item is £47 5s. 0d.?

That is an excluded bill.

It is for the poll-books at an Election: it is not excluded, but referred, and only likely to be excluded, perhaps.

Oh, I thought it was one of the excluded bills.

The next item is £201 0s. 8d. (alehouse-keepers). This contains a charge for your journey to London in Trinity term, attending consultations, &c.?

Yes, I think you will find that you are wrong in supposing that the same journey is twice charged.

I think not.—The next item is £68 10s. 10d.?

That is the second beerhouse bill: one of the bills referred.

The next, £213 1s. 2d. (disbursements, 16s. 9d.)?

That also is referred: a conveyancing bill.

The next is £15 5s. 4d. (disbursements, £3 9s. 0d.)?

That also is referred: one of the bills for leases.

A charity bill?

No, leases.

Charity leases?

Some of them may be: I can't say.

[On investigation, it was found that one or more of the leases related to Charities.]

You have here, I see, deducted £339 16s. 4d. for agents' charges: does this apply to the year 1833 only?

I believe so; but that we can investigate afterwards: the amount includes counsel's fees, &c.

Is not the sum intended for the years 1831, 1832, and 1833?

Oh yes, they are.

Were there no agents' charges in 1830?

I should think not, as they don't appear in that account.

In the calculation you have made as to your profits, have you made any deduction for clerks?

No, I have not.

What amount of salary would you be obliged to give to clerks employed in the different duties to which your bills relate?

I can't say. I have gone on the principle that it was necessary for me to have a certain number of clerks, whether the work was more or less.

Shall you require as many clerks now as you did before?

I am afraid not: I have not made much difference at present.

What difference in the expense?

I have only parted with one at present. You can object that a deduction should be made on the score of clerks: I admit that it is a fair ground for argument, but I contend that no deduction should be made.

If a deduction should be made, would £300 a-year be too much?

Yes.

£250?

My opinion is that nothing should be deducted, if that will please you. I believe that it has been generally agreed that no deduction should be made on the ground of clerks.

Generally agreed by claimants, and as generally objected to by Councils. Would £250 be too much?

I must have clerks for different departments, if I have not full work for them. I can't have half a clerk. If they have not full employment, I must pay them the same as if they had.

Admitting that a deduction should be made, would £250 be too much?

Yes.

How much do you think should be deducted?

Nothing.

You think £250 would be too much?

It would be more than I would like to deduct. I think I should include compensation to such clerks as I may have to part with, as they will be thrown out of situations by the change. It is, I admit, fair matter for discussion, but I thought it better not to make any deduction myself.

What would you have to give for a clerk to act as Clerk to the Magistrates?

That depends on luck: sometimes you may get a good clerk cheap, and you may also have to pay dear for a bad one.

Would £100 a-year be too much?

I don't know; but his duties would be various—he would have to attend to other matters as well as being Clerk to the Magistrates.

It appears by the Report of the Corporation Commissioners, that you stated to them that your annual bills amounted on an average to three hundred guineas, in addition to your salary: how does this agree with your claim?

I should think I never said so—I could never make so wild a statement.

The Report states that you furnished the Commissioners with a Return to that effect?

Then the three hundred guineas merely included my General Annual Bill, and the average as to that is not so much, as you see.

The Return in the Report professes to give the whole expenses of the Corporation?

Oh no, it does not.

It says so here?

It was only my General Annual Bill as Town Clerk: I had other bills as Solicitor, &c.

It appears here as if it covered the whole: is it not correct?

You may see that it can't be so.

The first item in 1834 is £323 2s. 5d., your General Annual Bill, (disbursements, £7 19s. 11d.) Here is a charge for a declaration of trust and draft of conveyance, and for consultations thereon with Sir Edward Sugden and Mr. Preston the conveyancer?

Oh, that was to see if the Corporation Estate could not be managed without troubling you gentlemen with it.

When was the conveyance prepared?

When was it that the first rumour of this revolution went abroad? Oh, in 1834.

What was the nature of the trust deed?

It was a very cleverly drawn thing, I assure you, if you wish for a precedent.

What was the object of it—will you hand it over?

You had better let it alone: it won't give you much comfort. It was to place the property of the Corporation in the hands of certain individuals.

To transfer it from the Corporation as a body to the members as individuals?

It was not practicable, and so it was not done.

Are the declaration of trust and draft of conveyance in your possession, and will you hand them over?

If you pay me for them.

Do you object to give them up?

No; I will see what you pay me, and then think about it.

The next item is £233, (disbursements, £75 10s. 0d.)?

That is what is to be excluded—an Election bill.

Do you intend it to stand as part of your claim?

I suppose not—that will depend on the result of the reference: I have put it in.

[Having gone through the remaining items of 1834, which elicited no remarks of any consequence, the Town Clerk said]—

The next head in your claim refers to your office of Clerk of the Peace.

477

Have you not had enough for one day?

THE MAYOR: We won't detain you much longer today, Mr. Burbidge.

TOWN CLERK: On what have you made your calculation as Clerk of the Peace?

On my fees and law-bills.

Have you the bills and an account of the fees with you, as before?

Yes.

How do you show that the fees have been received?

By extracts from my bill-books, except that I put down a certain sum to cover fees omitted to be entered.

Like the £100?

No, only £20 in this case. I don't know how you find it, but I know that my fees very often did not get into the books; so I have guessed at the amount omitted.

Are the fees charged according to the table?

Yes, according to the usual practice. I believe they are according to the table: I did not often see the table.

[Here Mr. Burbidge produced a portion of what he had to show in support of his claim as Clerk of the Peace.]

You propose to show documents of this kind in support of every charge?

Yes.

Why do you assume that any fees were omitted?

Because I know that many were, and to a larger amount than my estimate.

Will these bills which you produce correspond with the Abstract of the Borough Account, as published by the Treasurer of the Borough Rate?

Yes, they all appeared there, no doubt.

What have you to show as Clerk to the Magistrates?

Exchange-books, cash-books, and parish-bills.

[Mr. Burbidge here handed up for inspection several books and papers.]

You have put down £25 a-year for fees omitted?

Yes; that is very moderate, I think.

Will you furnish the Council with a copy of the particulars on which you found your claim?

What! of all these sort of things?

Of the bills?

I don't know that I shall—you have made such a bad use of what you have already got.

We must go through them item by item?

You have no need: I have done that already. I will meet Mr. Hudson, and Mr. Whetstone, and any other gentlemen, and go through the whole with them in detail.

Before you go I may as well apprize you, that it is most likely the Council will send you a notice, calling upon you to furnish copies of the particulars upon which you found your claim.

I shall be glad to receive any notice from the Council; though I must say that your notices generally give me more pain than pleasure.

If you do not furnish copies to the Council, the Lords of the Treasury, in the event of an appeal to them, will be sure to require copies from you.

You should have copies, if you did not make so bad a use of the particulars I furnish you.

Mr. Burbidge having retired—

Resolved unanimously,

Moved by MR. ALDERMAN WHEATLEY,

Seconded by MR. ALDERMAN RICHARDS,

That, the Town Clerk be directed to give notice to Mr. Burbidge, that the Council will require copies of all bills, vouchers and accounts upon which he founds any claim for compensation; and that he be required to furnish as many as practicable by Wednesday next.

The Council adjourned to Wednesday, February 8, at 11 o'clock in the forenoon.

WEDNESDAY, FEBRUARY 8.

PRESENT:

THOMAS PAGET, ESQ. MAYOR.

ALDERMEN.

MR. JOHN BAILEY.
MR. SAMUEL CARTWRIGHT.
MR. JAMES CORT.
MR. JOSEPH CRIPPS.
MR. HENRY HIGHTON.
MR. THOMAS PAGET.
MR. JAMES RICHARDS.
MR. SAMUEL SPURRETT.
MR. JOSEPH WHEATLEY.

COUNCILLORS.

MR. JOHN ALLEN.
MR. ROWLAND AUSTIN.
MR. JOHN BANKART.
MR. JOHN BAXTER.
MR. JOHN BIGGS.
MR. ROBERT BREWIN.
MR. JOS. CHAMBERLAIN.
MR. JOHN COLTMAN.
MR. JOHN COOPER.
MR. WILLIAM DALTON.
MR. WILLIAM DRAYTON.
MR. JOSEPH FIELDING.
MR. RICHARD HARRIS.
MR. SAMUEL S. HARRIS.
MR. ISAAC HODGSON.

MR. JAMES HUDSON.
MR. CHARLES INMAN.
MR. JOHN KIRBY.
MR. JOHN MANNING.
MR. JOHN MELLOR.
MR. JOHN MOORE.
MR. JOHN NICHOLS.
MR. WILLIAM ROWLETT.
MR. JAMES SARGEANT.
MR. R. J. SMITH.
MR. JOHN P. STALLARD.
MR. THOMAS STOKES.
MR. EDWARD WESTON.
MR. JOSEPH WHETSTONE.
MR. JOSEPH F. WINKS.

MR. BURBIDGE took the same oath as at the previous Meeting of the Council, and the TOWN CLERK proceeded with the examination:—

Have you made any further search for the minute book of the South Fields Committee, Mr. Burbidge?

No.—It will perhaps be right, in the present stage of the proceeding, to state the course which I intend to pursue during the remainder of this inquiry. It will have been perceived, from the public papers, that I have laid myself open to misconception, from being willing to extend the examination to particulars into which you have here no legal authority to inquire. It is therefore my intention to object to any question you may be directed to put, which does not substantially and literally apply to the statements in my claim. To all extraneous questions I shall object, on the ground of their relating to matters which you have no legal authority to investigate here, whatever power you may have in another shape. Without meaning any disrespect to the Council, I hope I may be allowed to stand upon my right as an individual, and that you will not press upon me questions foreign to the Act of Parliament. As to other matters other courses are open to the Council: I am here only to reply to questions touching the statements in my claim. On that ground I shall object to answer any questions upon other subjects.—[Mr. Burbidge now handed over papers, stating that they comprised an analysis of each year's accounts, and showed the mode in which he had computed his compensation.]

TOWN CLERK: Of course, Mr. Burbidge, we have no power to compel you to answer questions. If we put questions to you which we think apply to your claim, and you decline to answer them, we cannot compel you, but we shall feel at liberty to make any comments on your refusal to do so.

MR. BURBIDGE: Of course—but I think that it will not be generous to press me beyond the Act of Parliament.

No questions will be put to you by the Council which they do not think have a bearing on this investigation.

Touching my claim?

As to your right to compensation.

That question I do not stand upon here. I have that right by Act of Parliament.—I had better now state, that I have not yet been able to make up my mind as to your right to require copies of my bills. I am at present advised that you have not the right; but if, on further consideration and advice, I come to a different conclusion, I will let you know my determination as early as possible, and furnish the copies as soon as they can be prepared.

As you have not decided whether you will furnish copies, will you inform us where are the original bills?

In my bill-books——Oh, the original bills—I thought you had them all: they were placed in the hands of the Corporation, and all deposited with the vouchers of the Chamberlains' accounts of the particular years to which they apply.

After they were delivered and paid, were they left in your custody?

No; I scarcely ever saw them afterwards. Sometimes I kept them a while. They were made up into bundles, and put with the Chamberlains' vouchers.

Who had the custody of the Chamberlains' vouchers?

That is one of the questions foreign to the inquiry.

In whose custody were the bills now in my possession, and those which form the subject of reference?

R*

I don't know: they were delivered to the Committee, and who kept them afterwards I don't know, except one: one was a subsequent bill altogether.

What Committee?

The Committee appointed by the Corporation to settle their affairs before the Election of the new Council.

Do you mean the Finance Committee, appointed in April, 1835?

No, long subsequent to that—not that Committee.

Was it that which consisted of the Magistrates and the Finance Committee?

And other individuals added to them, so far as my memory goes.

Was it the Committee appointed in July, 1835?

I think additions were made after that date.

Was it the Committee appointed at that time, with power to add to their number?

Yes, I believe it was.

That was the Committee you referred to?

Yes, I think it was.

From whom were the bills received which were sent to me in June last?

I don't know.

Whom did you inform that it was necessary the bills should be given up?

That is foreign to the inquiry: I don't know at all.

Were not the Council compelled to take legal proceedings to obtain those bills, and also the Chamberlains' books from 1820?

You can answer that question as well as myself: it has nothing to do with my claim, I apprehend.

Were the Corporation aware they were indebted to you to the extent of the bills you presented in 1835, when you retained in your hands the purchase-money from the sales then completed?

Yes, I believe they were: they knew they were indebted to me to an indefinite amount—they did not know the exact sum.

Why were the bills not presented in the usual course, and entered in the Chamberlains' Books, instead of being kept back for twelve or fourteen years after the business was performed?

They had stood over, and probably would have stood longer, if this change had not taken place.

You said at the last meeting that the South Fields Committee had not met for five or six years?

No, not for a long time, so far as I could remember: you referred to an item which showed that I was in error.

I find that in April, 1835, a resolution was passed that a Report then made be referred to the South Fields Committee: was it not in existence at that time?

It was always in existence—it was a permanently subsisting Committee, composed of the Mayor for the time being, the Aldermen, and the twenty-four senior Common Councilmen.

You said that you entered the minutes in the Committee's book?

No: I said that when I attended the meetings I took down the proceedings on a sheet of paper, and that they were afterwards copied into the book.

Are you still unable, or do you decline, to give us any information as to who has the custody of the book?

I object to the question. I shall have no objection to tell you individually, out of doors, what I know of the matter; but I object to it as a subject for interrogation here.

You said that you included in your claim your profits as Solicitor to the Charities?

As Solicitor to the Corporation, whether they acted as Trustees of Charities or in any other way.

When were you appointed Solicitor to the Corporation, in respect to the Charities?

I never had a distinct appointment in that capacity. I was Solicitor to the Corporation, and acted for them as such in all their characters, no matter what.

When did you cease to act as Solicitor to the Charities?

I don't recollect the time: it was not till after the new Corporation was elected.

Can you state the month?

No.

By whom were you removed?

I was not removed at all, that I am aware of.

Do you mean to say that you continued to act as Solicitor to the Ex-Corporators till the appointment of the new Charity Trustees?

No, certainly not.

By whom were you removed?

I was never aware that I was removed at all by any party: I had no notice, nor have I any knowledge of any such thing.

When was the last meeting held at which you attended as Solicitor to the Ex-Corporators in their character of Trustees of Charities?

I can't say: I seldom attended any meeting as Solicitor.

When was the last meeting held at which you attended in any character?

Some months ago: I can't say exactly.

Was it not before the 1st of August, 1836?

I can't charge my memory——Oh, that was the time they ceased to act—yes, previous to that time, certainly.

Did not Mr. Adcock act as their Solicitor some months previous to the 1st of August?

I think he did: I don't know how long.

Was he not entrusted with all their legal business from April, 1836?

I can't give you any information about that, at all: I am not at all acquainted with dates.

Did you transact any of their legal business after April?

There is none included in my claim.

There can't be: I am speaking of 1836?

Then I object to the question.

Will you state the reason why you ceased to act as their Solicitor?

No: I object to the inquiry.

I will tell you why I ask:—You claim for compensation as Solicitor to the Trustees of Charities; but if you were not removed by the Council or under the Act, you can have no claim.

That is a matter of judgment.—I claim as Solicitor to the Corporation: there was no such thing as Solicitor to the Charities separately.

Were you removed from your appointment as Solicitor by the Council, or by the Ex-Corporators themselves?

Neither by the one nor the other, that I am aware of; only so far as my removal from that office was included in my removal from the office of Town Clerk: I had no express removal in any shape.

Did you not continue to act as Solicitor some time after your removal from the office of Town Clerk?

I am not aware that I did in any instance—not at all.

Did you attend any meetings of the Ex-Corporators in reference to Charities, after you ceased to be Town Clerk?

Yes—not as Solicitor though.

In what character or capacity?

As Receiver, in one instance; and generally as Ex-Town-Clerk, so long as the old Trustees continued to administer the Charities.

Did you not cease to act as their Solicitor in consequence of their dissatisfaction at some part of your conduct?

I decline to answer that question: I object to it as irrelevant.

Did you at any time receive a notice to deliver up your papers to Mr. Adcock as their Solicitor?

I don't recollect that I did—I had interviews with Mr. Adcock, and did deliver up some papers—not as Solicitor in any way.

How do you mean not as Solicitor in any way? Did you not deliver them up to Mr. Adcock as their Solicitor?

Yes—I don't know in what character he acted—I did not attend their meetings as their Solicitor. But this inquiry does not arise out of my claim.

Yes, if you claim as Solicitor to the Charities?

But I do not claim as Solicitor to the Charities—as Solicitor to the Corporation.

Solicitor in respect of Charities?

484

No part of my claim touches upon the period you are speaking of.

Did you not cease to act in consequence of your having in your hands £5,000 belonging to Sir Thomas White's, and £3,000 belonging to Alderman Newton's Charity?

Not that I know of; but the question is quite foreign to the subject of inquiry, I think.

Who kept the accounts of Alderman Newton's Charity?

I object to the question: I should have no difficulty in answering it, but I object to the whole of this line of examination.

Then do you decline to state by whom the accounts were kept?

I object to the question, and to the inquiry altogether.

In the accounts of Alderman Newton's Charity, are there not entries of dividends received on stock years after that stock was sold out?

I have already said that I decline to answer any questions on the subject.

Were you not asked, at the last meeting you attended of the Trustees of Alderman Newton's Charity, whether the stock had been sold out; and did you not say that it had not, although, in fact, the stock had been sold out, and the money had been received by you?

This is grossly irregular—a gross abuse of the Act of Parliament. Your questions involve serious imputations upon me, while the principle upon which I stand here obliges me to decline replying to them. It is an ungenerous abuse of the Act to put such questions.

I will tell you why I put them: it is to show that you were not removed by the Council or from the operation of the Act, but by the Ex-Trustees themselves.

But such questions can have nothing to do with my claim as Solicitor to the Corporation; and having told you that I do not feel at liberty to answer inquiries of such a nature, it is unfair to persist in framing questions conveying serious imputations upon me, when you know that they will appear unaccompanied by any explanations of mine.

THE MAYOR: To clear Mr. Stone from any suspicion of being actuated by personal feelings, I wish you, Mr. Burbidge, and also the public, to understand, that the questions put by him are so put by direction of the Finance Committee, and not with any view to wound your feelings, but to protect the interests of the town, and for that purpose only.

MR. BURBIDGE: But, Mr. Mayor, you and the Council, allow me to say, should bear in mind that you stand between me and the town—that you are appointed, not only to protect the town from the payment of too large an annuity, but also to award to me what you judge to be an adequate compensation for the loss of an office which I held in the nature of a freehold for life. It is a mistaken view of your duty to suppose that the town is the exclusive object of your care. I have a claim to compensation under an Act of Parliament; and that Act constitutes you the judges of the amount to which in justice and equity I am entitled. As to the inquiry which has been entered into, and to which I have objected, I do not impute any personal feeling to Mr. Stone; yet I must say, that the framing of questions on a subject whereon my mouth is closed by the Act, is fraught with gross personal injustice, and I hope that such a course will not be persevered in.

TOWN CLERK: As to the office of Under Bailiff, what do you produce?— [Mr. Burbidge handed over a paper.]—This is the amount of your fees as Under Bailiff?

As Steward of the Borough Court and Under Bailiff.

You say, "Fees per annum, £20"?

It is a mere conjecture: the amount was small.

What fees did the Under Bailiff receive?

On the execution of writs issued by the Borough Court.

What were the fees?

If an execution, a poundage; if a writ, 2s. or 2s. 6d. or something of that sort. There were also fees for recording fines, &c. The office was so mixed up with that of Steward of the Borough Court, that it is difficult to separate the profits exactly; but, to the best of my judgment, I have taken a fair average.

You have no accurate account of the fees received in each year?

No, not as to the office of Under Bailiff.

How many writs do you suppose were issued out of the Borough Court in each of the five years, on an average?

I don't know: my calculation does not enable me to say. I have had reference to fees and perquisites received in Election matters, considering them as a warrantable portion of the profits of my appointment.

What fees in Election matters?

Fees on the return of Members, and there were formerly profits arising from the materials of the hustings.

Have you not also calculated your Election fees in your claim as Town Clerk?

I think I have included them in some instances.

On the return of Members?

Yes.

Then in point of fact you have calculated these fees twice—once as Under Bailiff, and once as Town Clerk?

The £20, I told you, is a conjectural amount: if objected to, I am not prepared to furnish documents in support of it. I have taken the sum as a fair average of my profits: the other parts of my claim are founded on bills; but this office is so mixed up with that of Steward of the Borough Court, that I don't know how to separate them. As to the recording of fines, whether I did that as Town Clerk or Under Bailiff, I don't know. I believe that I have taken a fair average.

Did the number of writs exceed fifteen in a year?

I don't know: the business did not come under my own personal management at all.

As Steward of the Borough Court, is your calculation made from fees or conjecture?

The estimate is furnished to me by Messrs. Dalby and Weston, and is founded upon the actual receipts, as entered in their books: it is, I have no doubt, accurate to a shilling. I can send for the books, if you wish: Mr. Weston was here with the books last Wednesday, for the purpose of producing them.

This is the amount furnished to you by Mr. Dalby as the clear profits in each year?

Yes, the clear profits.

You are not able to give us any information personally?

No, I am not: you can have Mr. Dalby or Mr. Weston.

We have no power to summon Mr. Dalby.

No, but I will send for him, if you choose: many of my own statements depend on my clerks.

Mr. Dalby, I believe, conducted the business of the office?

Yes: I attended on Court days, when there were any trials: the details were managed by him, and by persons in his office.

Is this calculation made without allowing any deduction for the expense of carrying on the business?

Yes, I believe so.

What do you produce as Assessor to the Coroners and Clerk to the Visitors of Lunatic Asylums? You put down £20 a-year: is this a conjecture?

Yes, it is pretty much a conjecture. The estimate includes charges for attending inquests, and four or five guineas a-year as Clerk to the Visitors of Asylums. My fee at each inquest was 11s. 8d.

In what bills was your salary as Clerk to the Visitors included?

In no bills at all: the sum paid by Dr. Hill on taking out his license was applied in payment of the Clerk's fee and the physician's fee.

In the calculation of your profits as Clerk to the Magistrates, have you included the fees remitted on account of the poverty of the parties?

No; it is founded entirely on my cash-books, except as to the sum I have put down for fees received but omitted to be entered. I will show you the mode of it.—[Here Mr. Burbidge handed over what he called the Exchange Book.]—That is the manner in which the Exchange receipts were kept; and from that and other books, including the parish-book, I have made my calculation.

In your calculation as Clerk to the Magistrates, do you include your fees on freedoms?

Yes, in some instances.

Have you also, as Clerk to the Magistrates, included your fees on indentures, or do you calculate them as Town Clerk?

I received these fees in a mixed character, as Clerk to the Magistrates and as Town Clerk. Besides what appears in the calculation before you as Clerk to the Magistrates, I have put down £25, which includes indentures prepared at my office, and executed in the presence of the Mayor. The calculation before you is simply confined to what was done at the Exchange.

Have you the Exchange Book?

That is it.

No, this is only an account of the receipts: I mean the book in which the depositions are entered?

I have not the deposition-books: the depositions did not get into that book at all.—You will find here a separate account of the fees received at Sessions and Assizes.

[Mr. Burbidge handed over a paper.]

I see here an item for prosecutions at Sessions and Assizes: do you mean the fees included in the Magistrates' certificate?

Yes.—At Sessions they were included in the costs, and there was no separate order; but at Assizes, there was a separate order.

Are there any charges for conducting prosecutions?

No.

Were these included in your calculations as Town Clerk?

Yes; that is the mode.—[Mr. Burbidge showed a book.]

What was the cause of the great difference between the years' profits of your office as Clerk to the Magistrates—in one year the amount is stated at £561 7s. 6d. and in another only £426 2s. 2d.?

I don't know, except the difference arises from the greater or less amount of business in the years to which you refer.

Is there any particular description of business charged in the one year which did not occur in the other?

No——Oh yes, I see—the difference arises from an extra number of freedoms taken up before the enrolment.

Previous to an Election?

Yes; there is an item of £120 for stamps.

Will the items in your parish-books correspond with those in the books of the parish-officers?

Yes.

Will you state in what books the accounts of the money borrowed by the Corporation will appear?

Borrowed about my compensation?

No, by the Corporation?

I can't answer any questions which do not arise out of my claim.

Is there any book in which the balance due from you or any other party would appear?

That is not a matter that I know any thing of: there may be. I can't answer the question in the character in which I now appear: what information I may be able to give you afterwards is another matter.

Was there any balance due from you when you retained in your hands part of the purchase-monies arising from the sales in December, 1835?

I can't think it right to answer a question of that nature in this attendance.

Who had the disbursement of the £10,000 borrowed of Mr. Palmer in 1829, on mortgage of the Town Estate?

That question, of course, I decline to answer.

By whom was the £500 received which was borrowed of Messrs. Clarke & Philips, and included in the list of payments handed to me?

That falls under the same principle: I can't answer such a question on this examination, without breaking down the principle on which I have determined to act. You know full well, I believe: and, therefore, you have no need to ask by whom the money was borrowed.

Perhaps you will be glad of an opportunity to give an explanation:—For what purpose was it borrowed?

You see the latitude we should get into, if we were to deviate from the legal line of inquiry.

Was any part of the £500 received by you for any purpose?

I have the same objection to that question. Besides, I have told you before, so that it cannot be for the purpose of information you ask me here.

Were accounts kept of the receipt and appropriation of the £500; and where will they appear?

There were no accounts kept, that I know of.

I ask you again if there be any balance owing from you to the Corporation?

I decline to answer the question. Not from any difficulty that I have, but because it is foreign to the present inquiry.

Was there no account kept by any person of the receipt and appropriation of the £500 and £10,000?

I will talk with you about that at any other time you like: but such an inquiry does not come within the Act of Parliament, and I will not enter upon the subject here.

Assuming any balance to be owing from you, would not the Council, in your opinion, be entitled to set it off against any compensation which may be awarded to you?

When the amount of my compensation is finally settled, no doubt they would; but this examination is not to ascertain the state of my accounts, but only to inquire into the statements in my claim.

Will you state whether there are any accounts from which it can be

ascertained whether or not a balance is due from you, or point out any mode
of arriving at the fact except by your examination in person?

I decline to answer any questions except such as strictly relate to my
claim.

MR. WHETSTONE now rose and said—Mr. Burbidge, as the course which
you have determined to adopt renders further inquiry useless, and as I
consider it necessary that I should make one or two observations before the
close of this meeting, I rise now for that purpose, choosing rather to make
them in your presence than in your absence. Mr. Stone has put no questions to you which were not directed by the Finance Committee, and
sanctioned by the Council. It is due to him to state this, because the discharge of his duty must have been rendered doubly painful by your remark
that the questions which he put were, in your opinion, unfair and ungenerous.—[Mr. BURBIDGE: I did not mean to impute any personal feeling
to Mr. Stone.]—I can assure you, Sir, (continued Mr. Whetstone,) it was
extremely painful to me, personally, and I may say to the Committee, and
to the Council at large, to ask you the questions which we have done this
day; but we considered it to be a duty we owed to the town, as the guardians
of its interests, and, however disagreeable to us, felt bound to perform it.
We have considered your claim, not only as to its legal, but also its moral
grounds, and we felt it to be imperative upon us to take the course we have
done. You have appealed to us as judges, not only in law, but also in justice
and equity. We take you, Sir, on your own ground: we look to your moral
as well as your legal title to compensation for the loss of your office, which
you have designated as being of the nature of a freehold for life, but which
we regard as of a different tenure. Before the Lords of the Treasury the
Council will most probably meet you on the ground that your past conduct
has been such as to bar your claim to any compensation at all; and our
questions have been so shaped as to make you aware of the line we are likely
to pursue, and to give you this public opportunity of explaining whatever at
present appears dark or mysterious. We regard you as the legal adviser of
the late Corporation, under whose direction their affairs were almost entirely conducted, and as, therefore, in a great measure responsible for their
acts. We look upon you, however you may blink the fact, as the *custos* of all
their books, papers, and other things, which we require for the public
benefit, and many of which are studiously kept back from us. Until these
are given up, we, as the chosen trustees of the public, will not rest satisfied.
Corporate property, to an immense amount, has been alienated, and of the
proceeds we have no account later than 1824. We have given you an opportunity for explanation: that opportunity you have refused to accept.
For myself and for the Council I disclaim the inclination to deal harshly or
unfairly with you. I repeat, that our duty has been most painful to us. You
have refused to answer our inquiries—you demur to furnish us with copies

of your bills. You state that you have been advised upon this question: that you have been rightly advised, it is not for me to say—that you have consulted your own interests by adopting such a course, is, I think, very doubtful. As to the light in which you place yourself before the public, I give no opinion. We have put to you questions on grounds affecting your right to any compensation at all; but instead of replying to these questions, and meeting us on these grounds, you have determined to stand upon a narrow interpretation of the Act, while you have altogether disregarded its spirit. It is quite clear, to my mind, that we have the power, and that it is our duty, to investigate your right to any compensation at all; and if we had meditated taking such ground before the Lords of the Treasury, without making you acquainted with our intention, or giving you an opportunity of establishing your right, we should have been more truly chargeable with unfairness and harshness than we now are, when we have dealt openly with you, and enabled you to be the better prepared to meet us. I have thought it right to say thus much in your presence: I intended to speak to the same effect before the Council adjourned, and would rather that it was spoken in your hearing than in your absence.

MR. BURBIDGE: Mr. Mayor, I hope that I may be permitted to say a few words in reply. And first, I would state, that, since the change took place in the Borough, in all my communications and intercourse with Mr. Whetstone, and Mr. Stone, and the Mayor, and other gentlemen connected with this body, I have experienced the greatest kindness, courtesy, and friendly feeling. I do not impute to the Council, individually or collectively, any desire wantonly and unnecessarily to pain and annoy me, or any wish to do me an injury. But I do think that more is expected from me, than, considering the situation in which I was placed, and the numbers for whom I acted, can fairly be required. You are visiting upon me more of the sins of others (if I may use the expression) than it is reasonable that you should do. It is not to be supposed that my individual power and authority could regulate and control, to the extent which you seem to presume, so large a body as that for which I acted. The responsibility, I think, is cast upon me more fearfully than, looking to the circumstances of my situation, is just and reasonable.—If to-day I have taken a wrong course, I regret it. I had no wish to refuse to answer your questions; but the experience of the irregularities which at the last meeting flowed from a departure from a strictly legal line of inquiry, induced me on this occasion to abide more closely by the Act. Unaware of the line of inquiry which would be pursued, I have had to answer at the spur of the moment. If in any respect I have erred, I hope that I shall be judged charitably and candidly. The Council will bear in mind, that I have not only to consult my own feelings, but that I owe a duty to those for whom I have acted in past years. In declining to answer questions put to me by the Council, I intended them no disrespect, and I hope that none will be imputed to me. I shall be happy to attend at any other time, though, from the turn which the inquiry has taken, I suppose that it will not formally be continued further. I shall, nevertheless, be ready to give what information I can, in any other way, to any gentleman of the Council.

TOWN CLERK: Mr. Burbidge, before you go, can you inform us whether you intend to furnish copies of the bills on which your claim is founded?

MR. BURBIDGE: If, on further consideration and advice, I determine to furnish copies, I will instantly let you know.

MR. WHETSTONE: Then your answer as to the bills is not yet final, Mr. Burbidge?

MR. BURBIDGE: No, Sir.

Mr. Burbidge having retired, it was moved by Mr. FIELDING, seconded by Mr. SARGEANT, and unanimously resolved:—

"That in case Mr. Burbidge should hand over copies of his bills before the next Meeting of the Council, the Finance Committee be empowered to take such steps as they may think proper in reference thereto, and that they be requested to report whether it would be in their opinion desirable to continue the examination of Mr. Burbidge."

Moved by Mr. JOHN BIGGS, seconded by Mr. CARTWRIGHT, and unanimously resolved:—

"That the Examination of Mr. Burbidge be printed, and a copy sent to each member of the Council; and that the Council at its rising do adjourn to Wednesday, the 22d instant, at 11 o'clock."

CENSUS ABSTRACTS

Town of LEICESTER								
BAPTISMS				BURIALS			MARRIAGES	
Years	Males	Females	Total	Males	Females	Total	Years	Mar-riages
1700	83	80	163	61	59	120	1754	76
							1755	83
1710	65	59	124	42	44	86	1756	78
							1757	67
1720	67	70	137	73	67	140	1758	76
							1759	77
1730	103	78	181	88	96	184	1760	83
							1761	83
1740	98	89	187	109	76	185	1762	70
							1763	92
1750	98	111	209	109	138	247	1764	74
							1765	81
1760	93	97	190	137	171	308	1766	82
							1767	75
1770	164	128	292	147	124	271	1768	94
							1769	111
1780	141	137	278	135	121	256	1770	96
							1771	77
1781	157	149	306	214	171	385	1772	83
							1773	69
1782	132	135	267	120	158	278	1774	88
							1775	95
1783	135	141	276	134	142	276	1776	105
							1777	103
1784	151	134	285	135	151	286	1778	82
							1779	107
1785	142	152	294	128	139	267	1780	82
							1781	84
1786	153	144	297	138	143	281	1782	91
							1783	77
1787	154	149	303	126	115	241	1784	100
							1785	118
1788	163	153	316	180	175	355	1786	116
							1787	123
1789	185	143	328	145	124	269	1788	120
							1789	107
1790	159	149	308	156	151	307	1790	114
							1791	108

TABLE I continued

Town of LEICESTER								
BAPTISMS				BURIALS			MARRIAGES	
Years	Males	Females	Total	Males	Females	Total	Years	Mar-riages
1791	165	179	344	161	137	298	1792	143
							1793	114
1792	171	156	327	162	157	319	1794	98
							1795	94
1793	188	162	350	127	147	274	1796	105
							1797	130
1794	181	165	346	167	193	360	1798	120
							1799	124
1795	141	147	288	162	177	339	1800	116
1796	132	130	262	127	128	255		
1797	140	149	289	141	136	277		
1798	151	151	302	145	177	322		
1799	186	153	339	139	145	284		
1800	155	179	334	143	155	298		

The above ABSTRACT is collected from the Registers of
All-Saints, St Leonard, St Martin's, St Mary, and of St Nicholas, all
in the Town of Leicester.

REGISTER of Baptisms and Burials of
St Leonard, ... defective in 1720.

OBSERVATION.
The Vicar of the Parish of St. Mary observes, "that the Increase of Burials
in 1781 was owing to the Small-Pox;" and also, "that an Infirmary, and an
Hospital for aged and infirm Persons, occasion the Burials of that Parish to
bear a larger Proportion in the Register."

1801 CENSUS FIGURES

HUNDRED, &c.	PARISH, TOWNSHIP, or Extra-parochial Place		HOUSES		
			Inhabited	By how many Families occupied	Uninhabited
Town of LEICESTER }	Newark Liberty	Parish	33	35	—
	All Saints	Parish	486	620	18
	Leonard, St	Parish	73	79	13
	Margaret, St	Parish	1,152	1,225	20
	Martin, St	Parish	591	691	2
	Mary, St	Parish	654	780	25
	Nicholas, St	Parish	191	209	4
	Liberty of the Friars	Liberty	25	29	3
			3,205	3,668	85

TABLE II

PERSONS		OCCUPATIONS			
Males	Females	Persons chiefly employed in Agriculture	Persons chiefly employed in Trade, Manufactures, or Handicraft	All other Persons not comprized in the Two preceding Classes	TOTAL of PERSONS
83	136	—	105	114	219
1,334	1,504	60	684	30	2,838
196	194	32	353	5	390
2,761	3,049	339	5,453	18	5,810
1,471	1,696	39	872	2,256	3,167
1,566	1,888	22	3,454 [sic]	14	3,454
456	491	5	285	657	947
54	74	2	124	2	128
7,921	9,032	499	11,330 [sic]	3,096	16,953

1811 CENSUS   FIGURES FROM 1801–1810   TABLE III

	Town of LEICESTER						
YEARS	BAPTISMS			BURIALS			MARRIAGES
	Males	Females	Total	Males	Females	Total	
1801	250	241	491	287	316	603	191
1802	256	293	549	251	285	536	225
1803	336	329	665	219	210	429	348
1804	331	329	660	152	147	299	237
1805	326	320	646	197	193	390	188
1806	307	312	619	230	221	451	179
1807	344	310	654	249	241	490	198
1808	309	278	587	180	189	369	231
1809	400	338	738	328	284	612	218
1810	352	367	719	266	272	538	240

The above Abstract is collected from the Registers of,—All-Saints V. St Leonards V. St Margaret V. St Martin V. St Mary V. St Nicholas V.

497

1811 CENSUS FIGURES

HUNDREDS, &c.	PARISH, TOWNSHIP, Or, Extra-Parochial PLACE		HOUSES			
			Inhabited	By how many Families Occupied	Building	Uninhabited
Borough of LEICESTER:						
All Saints	Parish		664	791	3	9
Leonard, St with Abbey & Woodgate }	Parish		93	94	—	1
Margaret, St with Bishop's-Fee (z) }	Parish		2,064	2,138	56	26
Martin, St	Parish		598	635	1	23
Mary, St	Parish		816	823	10	11
Nicholas, St	Parish		337	355	3	4
Newark (a)	Liberty		37	37	—	—
			4,609	4,873	73	74

(z) Containing Knighton.—(a) Castle-View is entered in Guthlaxton Hundred.

TABLE IV

OCCUPATIONS			PERSONS		
Families chiefly employed in Agriculture	Families chiefly employed in Trade, Manufactures, or Handicraft	All other Families not comprized in the Two preceding CLASSES	MALES	FEMALES	TOTAL of PERSONS
39	697	55	1,549	1,813	3,362
17	77	—	212	211	423
293	1,672	173	4,835	5,323	10,158
24	549	62	1,446	1,808	3,254
25	768	30	1,951	2,128	4,079
30	300	25	721	868	1,589
—	27	10	87	194	281
428	4,090	355	10,801	12,345	23,146

1821 CENSUS   FIGURES 1811–1820   TABLE V

BOROUGH OF LEICESTER								
BAPTISMS				BURIALS			MARRIAGES	
Years	Males	Females	Total	Males	Females	Total	Years	Marriages
1811	426	384	810	308	238	546	1811	257
1812	463	280	743	261	239	500	1812	245
1813	393	359	752	269	263	532	1813	264
1814	388	373	761	274	294	568	1814	305
1815	447	475	922	278	304	582	1815	379
1816	513	461	974	317	288	605	1816	329
1817	447	410	857	373	320	693	1817	317
1818	470	456	926	317	289	606	1818	333
1819	472	364	836	304	279	583	1819	354
1820	482	431	913	333	353	686	1820	367

The above Abstract is collected from the Registers of,—All-Saints V. St Leonard V. (k) St Margaret V. St Martin V. St Mary V. and of St Nicolas V. (k) There is no Church at St Leonard's.

1821 CENSUS FIGURES

PARISH, TOWNSHIP, or EXTRA-PAROCHIAL PLACE		HOUSES			
		Inhabited	By how many Families Occupied	Building	Un-Inhabited
Borough of LEICESTER.					
All-Saints	Parish	655	680	3	67
Black-Friars	Extra-P.	129	134	9	6
Leonard, St with Abbey and Woodgate	Parish	105	108	—	4
Margaret, St (part of) with Bishop's Fee (r)	Parish	3,148	3,313	60	242
Martin, St	Parish	560	568	—	53
Mary, St	Parish	1,086	1,157	17	57
New Works or Newark (s)	Liberty	38	40	—	2
Nicholas, St	Parish	316	340	—	20
White-Friars	Extra-P.	48	49	—	2
		6,085	6,389	89	453

(r) The Parish of St Margaret is partly in Guthlaxton Hundred; and a considerable portion of the Parish called "Bishop's Fee," is locally situate in Gartree Hundred. The increase of Population is partly attributed to the return of discharged and disembodied soldiers, together with a continuance of public tranquillity. The entire Parish contains 15,409 Inhabitants; one male upwards of 100 years of age in St Margaret with Bishop's Fee Parish.—(s) The difference in the number of Females in Newark Liberty, between the Returns of 1811 and 1821, is accounted for by the removal of a large female boarding school; and the large proportion of old persons in so small a place, is in consequence of an hospital containing upon an average forty aged persons of both sexes.

TABLE VI

	OCCUPATIONS			PERSONS		
Families chiefly employed in Agriculture	Families chiefly employed in Trade, Manufactures, or Handicraft	All other Families not comprized in the Two preceding Classes	MALES	FEMALES	TOTAL of PERSONS
24	596	60	1,728	1,712	3,440
15	109	10	277	320	597
19	88	1	241	249	490
70	3,148	95	7,340	7,686	15,026
7	527	34	1,487	1,713	3,200
50	908	199	2,546	2,860	5,406
1	30	9	88	131	219
28	281	31	760	780	1,540
6	36	7	95	112	207
220	5,723	446	14,562	15,563	30,125

1831 CENSUS   FIGURES 1821–1830   TABLE VII

LEICESTER BOROUGH								
BAPTISMS				BURIALS			MARRIAGES	
Years	Males	Females	Total	Males	Females	Total	Years	Marriages
1821	485	472	957	339	356	695	1821	405
1822	581	469	1,050	323	305	628	1822	467
1823	619	570	1,189	361	329	690	1823	420
1824	624	564	1,188	406	367	773	1824	393
1825	646	534	1,180	466	415	881	1825	483
1826	615	603	1,218	464	415	879	1826	384
1827	610	564	1,174	401	425	826	1827	448
1828	647	578	1,225	377	346	723	1828	481
1829	611	560	1,171	359	313	672	1829	396
1830	570	544	1,114	470	461	931	1830	469

1831 CENSUS   ANALYSIS OF HOUSES AND OCCUPATIONS

PARISH, TOWNSHIP, or EXTRA-PAROCHIAL PLACE	AREA	HOUSES			
	English Statute Acres	Inhabited	Families	Building	Uninhabited
LEICESTER Borough					
All-Saints Parish ⎫		656	677	—	118
Black-Friars (t) Extra-Par.		248	264	—	15
Leonard, St with ⎫ Parish Abbey and Woodgate ⎭		86	94	—	15
Margaret, St (part of) ⎫ Parish with Bishop's Fee (u) ⎭	3,960	5,020	5,210	27	256
Martin, St Parish		544	564	—	39
Mary, St (w) Parish		1,398	1,441	23	114
New-Works or Newark Liberty		39	41	—	—
Nicholas, St Parish		314	359	5	43
White-Friars Extra-Par. ⎭		43	45	—	—
	3,960	8,348	8,695	55	600

(t) The great increase of Population (555 Persons) resident in Black-Friars, Extra Parochial, is attributed partly to the increase in Building, and also to the erection of a Lying-in Hospital.—(u) The Parish of St Margaret is partly in Guthlaxton Hundred; and a considerable portion of the Parish, called Bishop's-Fee, is locally situate in Gartree Hundred; the great increase of Population (8,928 Persons) is attributed to the extension of Factories. The entire Parish contains 24,356 Inhabitants. Rail Roads are mentioned as a source of employment for a few Labourers.— (w) The Liberty of South-Fields (part of St Mary's Parish) extends into Guthlaxton Hundred, and is so entered. The entire Parish of St Mary contains 6,776 Inhabitants.

TABLE VIII

OCCUPATIONS			PERSONS		
Families chiefly employed in Agriculture	Families chiefly employed in Trade, Manufactures, and Handicraft	All other Families not comprised in the two preceding Classes	Males	Females	Total of Persons
9	566	102	1,639	1,645	3,284
8	232	24	540	612	1,152
17	70	7	221	223	444
168	4,058	984	11,759	12,195	23,954
3	421	140	1,444	1,590	3,034
65	1,238	138	2,483	2,685	5,168
—	19	22	72	122	194
8	314	37	716	778	1,494
1	33	11	84	96	180
279	6,951	1,465	18,958	19,946	38,904

[continued overleaf]

TABLE VIII continued

Males Twenty Years of Age	AGRICULTURE			Employed in Manufacture, or in making Manufacturing Machinery	Employed in Retail Trade, or in Handicraft as Masters or Workmen	Capitalists, Bankers, Professional and other Educated Men
	Occupiers employing Labourers	Occupiers not employing Labourers	Labourers employed in Agriculture			
848	1	4	20	397	190	42
270	1	—	6	59	153	6
123	3	1	17	54	16	2
5,856	4	74	119	1,954	2,515	216
774	—	—	3	22	537	92
1,687	18	10	51	806	516	50
54	1	—	—	12	5	10
375	1	—	9	92	208	15
43	—	—	2	11	19	1
10,030	29	89	227	3,407	4,159	434

TABLE VIII continued

Labourers employed in Labour not Agri- cultural	Other Males 20 Years of Age (except Servants)	Male Servants		Female Servants	PARISHES, TOWNSHIPS, &c.
		20 Years of Age	Under 20 Years		
					LEICESTER
130	57	7	—	69	All-Saints
30	11	4	1	10	Black-Friars
25	4	1	—	8	Leonard, St &c.
636	233	105	39	376	Margaret, St &c.
6	65	49	28	347	Martin, St
90	136	10	8	183	Mary, St
—	21	5	2	21	New Works
24	21	5	—	37	Nicholas, St
1	8	1	—	3	White-Friars
942	556	187	78	1,054	

1831 CENSUS   ANALYSIS OF OCCUPATIONS   TABLE IX

COUNTY OF LEICESTER.—Males (Twenty years of age) employed in Retail Trade, or in Handicraft, as Masters or Workmen; distinguishing the Borough of *Leicester* and Town of *Loughborough*, but not excluding them from the County Total.

Specification	Leicester Borough	Loughborough Town	Leicester County
Auctioneer or Appraiser, Sheriff's Broker	12	4	31
Baker, Gingerbread, Fancy	133	26	479
Barber, or Hair-dresser, Hair-dealer	47	6	127
Basket-maker	17	6	96
Blacksmith, Horse-shoes	72	39	578
Boat-builder, Ship-wright	50	7	63
Bookbinder	2	—	10
Bookseller, or Vendor	20	2	40
Brass-worker, Tinker	14	3	41
Brewer	17	8	48
Broker	20	—	26
Brush-maker	5	—	7
Coachmaker	15	2	38
Coach-owner, Driver, Grooms, &c.	90	—	173
Coal Merchant, Fuel	21	12	75
Cooper	32	8	101
Copper-plate Printer, Engraver	6	—	8
Corn-dealer	11	2	27
Currier	23	8	63
Cutler	12	1	21
Drysalter, Colouring Materials	—	—	1
Dyer	202	14	228
Earthenware, China, Pottery	12	2	82

Occupation			
Builder	19	6	66
Land-jobber	1	—	2
Bricklayer	158	32	582
Brickmaker	59	8	283
Lime Burner	20	—	32
Plasterer	18	1	47
Slater	2	2	15
Mason or Waller	31	10	120
House-painter	54	10	121
Butcher, Flesher	116	40	672
Carpenter	236	60	1,036
Cabinet-maker	68	18	125
Wheelwright	26	12	267
Sawyer	42	11	152
Carrier, Carter	36	4	214
Carver and Gilder	9	—	13
Cattle-dealer	—	4	12
Caulker	—	—	—
Chair-maker	—	—	4
Cheesemonger	5	—	12
Chemist and Druggist	24	6	64
Clock and Watchmaker	22	6	65
Clothier	18	10	47
Linen-draper, Haberdasher	85	22	181
Silk Mercer, or Dealer	1	—	25

Occupation			
Farrier, Cow-doctor, Cattle-doctor	1	2	44
Feather-dresser	—	—	—
Fellmonger	13	5	53
Fish-dealer	6	2	17
Flax-dresser	—	—	2
Fruiterer	5	—	16
Furrier	1	—	3
Glazier, Plumber	31	6	125
Glover	3	2	17
Grocer, Green-grocer	111	39	340
Gun-maker	2	1	7
Harness-maker, Collar-maker	180	4	65
Hatter, and Hosier	—	13	278
Horse-dealer, Stable, Hackney Coach, or Fly-keeper	2	6	42
Huckster, Hawker, Pedlar, Duffer	50	16	271
Indigo Extract-maker	3	—	3
Ironfounder	87	1	90
Ironmonger	17	6	42
Jeweller	8	1	11
Lace-dealer	109	6	162
Maltster	29	10	144

TABLE IX continued

Specification

Specification	Leicester Borough	Loughborough Town	Leicester County
Marble Cutter, Statuary	7	1	15
Mat, Mop, Net-maker	—	2	7
Milkman, Cowkeeper	33	1	87
Miller	33	8	272
Millwright	1	—	17
Nailor	5	3	9
Nightman, Scavenger	—	—	10
Old Clothes-dealer, Rag-dealer	7	1	24
Optician	2	—	2
Paper-maker	—	—	8
Pastrycook, Confectioner	17	9	36
Pattenmaker	11	—	23
Pawnbroker	6	2	10
Pipe-maker	—	9	9
Plough-maker	—	—	1
Poulterer	4	—	10

Specification	Leicester Borough	Loughborough Town	Leicester County
Sinker-maker	8	—	12
Soap-maker	—	—	1
Soot, and Chimney Sweeper	12	3	30
Spirit Merchant, Spirit Shop	13	7	35
Stationer	8	1	15
Stay-maker	2	3	9
Stockbroker	—	—	—
Stone-dealer	—	—	4
Straw-plait and Bonnets	8	—	20
Tailor, Breeches-maker	210	60	829
Tallow-chandler, Wax-chandler	9	4	41
Tanner	6	—	21
Tawer	—	—	1
Tea-dealer	75	5	95
Tinman	17	—	42
Tobacconist	1	—	5
Toyman	2	—	6
Turner	24	6	60

Printer	35	3	44
Printseller	1	—	7
Publican, Hotel, or Innkeeper, Retailer of Beer	212	60	979
Ropemaker	17	3	51
Saddler	20	3	58
Shoe and Bootmaker, or Mender	425	121	1,585
Shop-keeper {Dealer in sundry necessary Articles, such as are sold in a Village Shop}	167	10	535
Sieve-maker	—	—	1
Undertaker of Funerals	2	—	13
Upholsterer	9	—	10
Wharfinger	2	—	13
Whitesmith	50	42	113
Wine-dealer	1	—	16
Woolcomber	147	—	216
Worsted-maker	—	—	4
Defective Specification	—	—	103
Total employed in Retail Trade or Handicraft	4,159	899	13,772

The Manufacture of Stockings in the County of Leicester is of considerable importance, employing upwards of 10,000 Males, upwards of Twenty years of age. The Town of Leicester contains 3,400 Manufacturers, of whom probably 3,000 are Stocking-makers. Loughborough contains 900, Hinckley 700, Sheepshead 500 Stocking-makers; Great Wigston and Earl Shilton, about 280 each; Sileby 200; Southfield, Burbage, Thurmaston, Kegworth, Barwell, Anstey, Whitwick, Blaby, Mountsorrel, Oadby, contain from 180 to 130 each;—after these, in order, may be reckoned Countes-thorpe, Cosby, Whitstone, Enderby, Narborough, Sapcote, Long Stratton, Syston, as containing above 100 each. Less than 100, but more than 50, Desford, Belgrave, Woodhouse, Gilmorton, Thungston, Great-Glenn, Quorndon, Stoke-Golding, Lutterworth, Wykin, Smeeton and Westerby. About 750 Men are employed in Lace-making, most of them probably at Leicester, several at Melton-Mowbray and Quorndon: Frame-smiths and Makers of Machinery are of course frequent in all these places. In the County are mentioned about 40 Weavers of Linen, 40 Carpet-makers, as many workers in Silk Goods; and Needle-makers, Worsted-spinners and Hatters, exist in small numbers in various parts of the County. [Editor's Note: "Long Stratton" may be Long Whatton, and "Thungston" may be Thurmaston.]

BRITISH SESSIONAL PAPERS

BRITISH SESSIONAL PAPERS,

HOUSE OF COMMONS,

1828 (367),–vol. XX, pp. 707–38

BOROUGH OF LEICESTER

A RETURN

Of the Amount of Assessments made upon the several Parishes within the
Precincts of the Borough of Leicester, for the Maintenance of the Gaol,
Bridewell, Police, &c. specifying, in separate Sums, the amount of
Salaries paid in each Year, to the Gaolers, Maintenance of the Prisoners,
Expense of Prosecutions and Police Establishments, commencing from
the Year 1810 to the present time, and distinguishing the several
Quarterly Payments of each Parish; also, a Return of the number of
Prisoners committed within the same period to the Borough Gaol,
stating the date of the offence, age of the offender, conviction or acquittal,
with the name of the place in which the offence was committed, and
whether in the Borough or County of Leicester;—viz.

1st.—THE Amount of Assessments made upon the several Parishes within
the precincts of the Borough of Leicester, for the maintenance of the
Gaol, Bridewell, Police, &c.; distinguishing the several quarterly Payments of each Parish, commencing with the year 1810.

2d.—THE Amount of Salaries paid in each Year to the Gaolers; maintenance of Prisoners; maintenance of Gaol; expense of Prosecutions and
Police Establishments; commencing from the same time.

3d.—THE Number of Prisoners committed within the same period to the
Borough Gaol: stating the date of the offence, age of the offender, conviction or acquittal; with the name of the place in which the offence was
committed, and whether in the Borough or County of Leicester.

Ordered, by The House of Commons, to be Printed,
23 May 1828.

s*   513

PART I.—Being the Amount of Assessments made upon the several Parishes within the Precinct of the Borough of Leicester, for the maintenance of the Gaol, Bridewell, Police, &c.;—distinguishing the several quarterly Payments of each Parish commencing with the year 1810.

NAME OF PARISH	1810 TOTAL	1811 TOTAL	1812 TOTAL	1813 TOTAL	1814 TOTAL	1815 TOTAL
	£ s. d.	£ s. d.	£ s. d.	£ s. d.	£ s. d.	£ s. d.
St. Martin's	209 6 –	145 12 –	300 6 –	436 16 –	382 4 –	418 12 –
St. Margaret's	218 10 –	152 – –	313 10 –	456 – –	399 – –	437 – –
St. Mary's	180 11 –	125 12 –	259 1 –	376 16 –	329 14 –	361 2 –
All Saints	80 10 –	56 – –	115 10 –	168 – –	147 – –	161 – –
St. Nicholas	27 12 –	19 4 –	39 12 –	57 12 –	50 8 –	55 4 –
St. Leonard's	13 16 –	9 12 –	19 16 –	28 16 –	25 4 –	27 12 –
£	730 5 –	508 – –	1,047 15 –	1,524 – –	1,333 10 –	1,460 10 –

NAME OF PARISH	1816 TOTAL			1817 TOTAL			1818 TOTAL			1819 TOTAL			1820 TOTAL			1821 TOTAL		
	£	s.	d.	£	s.	d.	£	s.	d.	£	s.	d.	£	s.	d.	£	s.	d.
St. Martin's	581	—	—	581	17	6	581	—	—	726	5	—	435	15	—	726	5	—
St. Margaret's	365	2	—	365	2	—	365	2	—	456	7	6	273	16	6	456	7	6
St. Mary's	292	12	—	292	12	—	292	12	—	365	15	—	219	9	—	365	15	—
All Saints	216	6	—	216	6	—	216	6	—	270	7	6	162	4	6	270	7	6
St. Nicholas	93	16	—	93	16	—	93	16	—	117	5	—	70	7	—	117	5	—
St. Leonard's	12	8	—	12	8	—	12	8	—	15	10	—	9	6	—	15	10	—
Black Friars	21	4	—	21	4	—	21	4	—	26	10	—	15	18	—	26	10	—
White Friars	17	12	—	17	12	—	17	12	—	22	—	—	13	4	—	22	—	—
£	1,600	—	—	1,600	—	—	1,600	—	—	2,000	—	—	1,200	—	—	2,000	—	—

NAME OF PARISH	1822 TOTAL			1823 TOTAL			1824 TOTAL			1825 TOTAL			1826 TOTAL			1827 TOTAL		
	£	s.	d.	£	s.	d.	£	s.	d.	£	s.	d.	£	s.	d.	£	s.	d.
St. Martin's	653	12	6	798	17	6	944	2	6	1,162	—	—	1,452	10	—	1,743	—	—
St. Margaret's	410	14	9	502	—	3	593	5	9	730	4	—	912	15	—	1,095	6	—
St. Mary's	329	3	6	402	6	6	475	9	6	585	4	—	731	10	—	877	16	—
All Saints	243	6	9	297	8	3	351	9	9	432	12	—	540	15	—	646	18	—
St. Nicholas	105	10	6	128	19	6	152	8	6	187	12	—	234	10	—	281	8	—
St. Leonard's	13	19	—	17	1	—	20	3	—	24	16	—	31	—	—	37	4	—
Black Friars	23	17	—	29	3	—	34	9	—	42	8	—	53	—	—	63	12	—
White Friars	19	16	—	24	4	—	28	12	—	35	4	—	44	—	—	52	16	—
£	1,800	—	—	2,200	—	—	2,600	—	—	3,200	—	—	4,000	—	—	4,800	—	—

PART II.—Being the Amount of Salaries paid in each year to Gaolers, Maintenance of Prisoners, Maintenance of Gaol, Expenses of Prosecutions and Police Establishments; commencing with the Year 1810.

	GAOLER'S SALARY			Maintenance of PRISONERS			Other GAOL EXPENSES			COSTS of PROSECUTIONS			POLICE ESTABLISHMENTS, including Expenses of Vagrants, &c.			TOTALS		
	£	s.	d.	£	s.	d.	£	s.	d.	£	s.	d.	£	s.	d.	£	s.	d.
1810	70	14	8	94	18	7	46	2	11	41	7	4	145	17	3	399	–	9
1811	89	9	8	149	2	2	143	16	2	173	17	1	308	6	4	864	11	5
1812	120	–	–	179	18	11	93	9	8	57	14	–	353	8	3	804	10	10
1813	120	–	–	108	18	6	134	19	10	95	7	10	151	13	4	610	19	6
1814	120	–	–	152	19	–	172	3	5	156	12	4	344	13	–	946	7	9
1815	120	–	–	116	11	11	99	14	11	112	4	8	466	10	1	915	1	7
1816	120	–	–	199	8	9½	724	11	8	306	–	5	415	4	11	1,765	5	9½
1817	200	–	–	295	1	8	556	2	5	284	13	11	300	11	4	1,636	9	4
1818	200	–	–	243	16	7	346	7	10	473	9	9	350	–	8	1,613	14	10
1819	200	–	–	212	14	–	588	8	2	405	16	9	268	12	6	1,675	11	5
1820	200	–	–	233	19	6	342	1	1	222	18	10	272	10	2	1,271	9	7
1821	320	–	–	263	18	–	652	5	10	306	9	4	209	3	6	1,751	16	8
1822	320	–	–	235	19	11	400	14	3	422	7	4	260	16	5	1,639	17	11
1823	345	–	–	218	18	8	523	8	1	566	6	6	587	–	6	2,240	13	9
1824	390	–	–	241	11	5	326	5	4	304	3	10	705	11	11	1,967	12	6
1825	390	–	–	190	17	6	620	8	6	716	15	4	394	17	9	2,312	19	1
1826	390	–	–	236	–	2	351	13	9	514	1	8	1,622	8	–	3,114	3	7
1827	390	–	–	266	2	3	984	15	2	911	12	2	1,570	10	1	4,122	19	8

PART III.—Being an Account of the total Number of Prisoners committed to the Gaol of the Borough of Leicester, in each Year, commencing with the Year 1810.

in 1810		157	
1811		141	
1812		148	
1813		154	
1814		124	
1815		183	
1816		233	
1817		271	
1818		311	
1819		318	
1820		334	as far as can be ascertained
1821		344	
1822		330	
1823		440	as far as can be ascertained
1824	(from Michaelmas 1823 to Michaelmas 1824)	539	
1825	(from Michaelmas 1824 to Michaelmas 1825)	653	
1826	(from Michaelmas 1825 to Michaelmas 1826)	755	
1827	(from Michaelmas 1826 to Michaelmas 1827)	670	

May 23d, 1828.   (signed)   Mr. Gregory, Mayor.

BRITISH SESSIONAL PAPERS

HOUSE OF COMMONS,

1829 (304),–vol. XVIII, pp. 335–41

BOROUGH OF LEICESTER

AMENDED RETURN

OF the amount of the ASSESSMENT made upon the several Parishes
within the Precincts of the Borough of Leicester, for the Maintenance of
the Gaol, Bridewell and Police; with all Items of the CORPORATION
ANNUAL RECEIPT and EXPENDITURE from the Year 1810 to the
Year 1828.

Ordered, by the House of Commons, to be printed,
2 June 1829.

1.—AN ACCOUNT of the Amount of ASSESSMENTS made upon the
several Parishes within the Precincts of the Borough of Leicester, for
the maintenance of the Gaol, Bridewell and Police; together with all
the other Items of the TREASURER'S RECEIPTS.

2.—AN ACCOUNT of the EXPENDITURE of the Treasurer of the
Borough; containing all the Items of Expenditure which were not
enumerated or set forth in the former Return, and which were not in
fact required by the former Order.

1.—AN ACCOUNT of the Amount of the ASSESSMENTS made upon the several Parishes within the Precincts of the Borough of Leicester, for the Maintenance of the Gaol, Bridewell and Police; together with all the other Items of the Treasurer's Receipts.

Note.—FOR particulars of the Assessments, the Mayor and Magistrates refer to their former Return presented to the House, which they beg to be considered as a part of their present Return; and they enumerate and particularize only in this Return the items which they did not include, and were not required to include, in their said former Return.

	£	s.	d.
TOTAL of Assessments for the year 1810, as particularized in the former Return	730	5	–
Other items of receipt, viz.			
Corn Returns	10	–	–
Total Amount of Assessments for the year 1811, as particularized in the former Return . . .	508	–	–
Other items of receipt, viz.			
Balance of Gaol Account	377	9	9
Corn Returns	10	2	–
Total Amount of Assessments for the year 1812, as particularized in the former Return . . .	1,047	15	–
Other items of receipt, viz.			
Corn Returns	5	4	–
Total Amount of Assessments for the year 1813, as particularized in the former Return . . .	1,524	–	–
Other items of receipt, viz.			
Fines for false Weights	2	–	–
Corn Returns	4	16	–
Total Amount of Assessments for the year 1814, as particularized in the former Return . . .	1,333	10	–
Other items of receipt, viz.			
Corn Returns	5	2	–
Total Amount of Assessments for the year 1815, as particularized in the former Return . . .	1,460	10	–
Other items of receipt, viz.			
Corn Returns	5	–	–

Total Amount of Assessments for the year 1816, as particularized in the former Return . . .	1,600	–	–
Other items of receipt, viz.			
Corn Returns	5	4	–
Total Amount of Assessments for the year 1817, as particularized in the former Return . . .	1,600	–	–
Other items of receipt, viz.			
Balance of Militia Account	100	–	–
Corn Returns	4	18	–
Total Amount of Assessments for the year 1818, as particularized in the former Return . . .	1,600	–	–
Other items of receipt, viz.			
Corn Returns	5	–	–
Total Amount of Assessments for the year 1819, as particularized in the former Return . . .	2,000	–	–
Other items of receipt, viz.			
Corn Returns	5	4	–
Total Amount of Assessments for the year 1820, as particularized in the former Return . . .	1,200	–	–
Other items of receipt, viz.			
Corn Returns	5	–	–
Total Amount of Assessments for the year 1821, as particularized in the former Return . . .	2,000	–	–
Other items of receipt, viz.			
Corn Returns	5	2	–
Total Amount of Assessments for the year 1822, as particularized in the former Return . . .	1,800	–	–
Other items of receipt,			
—None.—			
Total Amount of Assessments for the year 1823, as particularized in the former Return . . .	2,200	–	–
Other items of receipt, viz.			
Fines for false Weights and Measures . .	52	10	–
Total Amount of Assessments for the year 1824, as particularized in the former Return . . .	2,600	–	–
Other items of receipt, viz.			
Fines for false Weights, &c.	45	5	–
From Sale of false Weights	4	2	4

Total Amount of Assessments for the year 1825, as particularized in the former Return . . .	3,200	–	–
Other items of receipt,			
—None.—			
Total Amount of Assessments for the year 1826, as particularized in the former Return . . .	4,000	–	–
Other items of receipt, viz.			
Fines for false Weights	48	15	2

Total Amount of Assessments for the year
1827, as particularized in the former
Return . . . . . . £4,800 – –
    Deduct, Rate laid at Michaelmas Ses-
    sion 1827, but not receivable by the
    Treasurer till Epiphany Session 1828   1,200 – –

	3,600	–	–
Other items of receipt, viz.			
Fines for false Weights and Measures .	19	6	1

2.—AN ACCOUNT of the Expenditure of the Treasurer of the Borough, containing all the Items of Expenditure which were not enumerated or set forth in the former Return, and which were not in fact required by the former Order.

    Note.—FOR the particulars of the Items of Expenditure stated in the former Return, the Mayor and Magistrates refer to such former Return, which they pray may be considered as a part and parcel of their present Return.—They abstain from recopying the same, to avoid unnecessary repetition.

	£	s.	d.
1810. AMOUNT of Expenditure in this year, as particularized in the former Return	399	–	9
Other items of expenditure, viz.			
Militia	77	8	8
Paving, Bridges, &c.	18	3	–
Balance due to the Treasurer, on the last Account	358	11	5
1811. Amount of Expenditure in this year, as particularized in the former Return	864	11	5

Other items of expenditure, viz.

Militia	53	6	6
Treasurer's Salary	6	6	–
Inquests	27	11	6

1812. Amount of Expenditure in this year, as particularized in the former Return 804 10 10

Other items of expenditure, viz.

Militia	70	6	7
Treasurer's Salary	6	12	–
Inquests	37	13	9

1813. Amount of Expenditure in this year, as particularized in the former Return 610 19 6

Other items of expenditure, viz.

Militia	36	18	1
Bridges, &c.	8	3	9
Inquests, and Corn Returns	42	14	–

1814. Amount of Expenditure in this year, as particularized in the former Return 946 7 9

Other items of expenditure, viz.

Militia	55	17	10
Bridges, &c.	128	16	3
Inquests, and Corn Returns	61	3	–

1815. Amount of Expenditure in this year, as particularized in the former Return 915 1 7

Other items of expenditure, viz.

Bridges	5	14	10
Law Expenses in Trials with the County . .	200	–	–
Inquests	39	4	–
Corn Returns	4	–	–
Sessions Advertisements, &c. . . .	20	15	–
Treasurer	4	4	–

1816. Amount of Expenditure in this year, as particularized in the former Return . . . . .   1,765 5 $9\frac{1}{2}$

Other items of expenditure, viz.

Bridges	2	–	6
Law Expenses in Trials with the County . .	248	–	–
Damage by Rioters	35	9	$7\frac{1}{2}$
Inquests	27	2	–
Corn Returns	6	10	–
Poor Returns	4	10	–

Printing	3	7	6
Treasurer	4	4	–

1817. Amount of Expenditure in this year, as particular-
ized in the former Return . . . . . | 1,636 | 9 | 4 |

Other items of expenditure, viz.

Militia	28	19	–
Paid County Magistrates on account of Law Costs	200	–	–
Corn Returns	5	4	–
Inquests	21	16	–
Miscellaneous	33	7	2
Treasurer	21	–	–

1818. Amount of Expenditure in this year, as particular-
ized in the former Return . . . . . | 1,613 | 14 | 10 |

Other items of expenditure, viz.

Treasurer's Salary	21	–	–
Corn Returns	5	4	–
Inquests	20	8	–
Printing, and Incidentals	48	5	11

1819. Amount of Expenditure in this year, as particular-
ized in the former Return . . . . . | 1,675 | 11 | 5 |

Other items of expenditure, viz.

Corn Returns	5	4	–
Inquests	24	18	–
Printing, and Incidentals	53	3	4
Treasurer's Salary	21	–	–

1820. Amount of Expenditure in this year, as particular-
ized in the former Return . . . . . | 1,271 | 9 | 7 |

Other items of expenditure, viz.

Treasurer's Salary	21	–	–
Corn Returns	5	4	–
Inquests	42	11	6
Printing	18	4	11
Collecting Rates	42	–	–

1821. Amount of Expenditure in this year, as particular-
ized in the former Return . . . . . | 1,751 | 16 | 8 |

Other items of expenditure, viz.

Treasurer's Salary	21	–	–
Clerk of Peace's Bill	122	17	4
Corn Returns	5	4	–
Inquests	53	8	6

Printing and advertising	46	1	3
Collecting Rates	61	8	–

1822. Amount of Expenditure in this year, as particularized in the former Return . . . . . | 1,639 | 17 | 11

Other items of expenditure, viz.

Bridges	110	9	7
Lamps, &c.	28	5	7
Treasurer's Salary	21	–	–
Corn Returns	5	4	–
Inquests	43	16	–
Printing, &c.	11	7	–
Collecting Rates	60	14	6

1823. Amount of Expenditure in this year, as particularized in the former Return . . . . . | 2,240 | 13 | 9

Other items of expenditure, viz.

Bridges	128	2	11
Clerk of the Peace's Bill	64	12	10
Inquests	28	7	6
Corn Returns	5	4	–
Advertising, &c.	35	17	10
Collecting Rates	10	13	3
Miscellaneous	69	11	4
Treasurer's Salary	21	–	–

1824. Amount of Expenditure in this year, as particularized in the former Return . . . . . | 1,967 | 12 | 6

Other items of expenditure, viz.

Bridges	57	19	6
Inquests	33	5	6
Corn Returns	5	4	–
Advertisements, &c.	47	5	6
Collecting Rates	13	3	–
Miscellaneous	3	10	–
Clerk of the Peace's Bill	312	18	–
Treasurer's Salary	21	–	–

1825. Amount of Expenditure in this year, as particularized in the former Return . . . . . | 2,312 | 19 | 1

Other items of expenditure, viz.

Bridges	8	16	6
Law Bill	42	4	7
Paid Clerk of the Peace, on account of Law Expenses	400	–	–

Inquests	48	14	6
Corn Returns	2	12	–
Printing, &c.	14	9	–
Collecting Rates	10	–	–
Miscellaneous	5	5	–
Treasurer's Salary	21	–	–

1826. Amount of Expenditure in this year, as particularized in the former Return **3,114 3 7**

    Other items of expenditure, viz.

Bridges	211	2	3
Treasurer's Salary, two years. . . .	42	–	–
Inquests	18	13	4
Corn Returns	7	16	–
Advertisements, &c.	8	11	–
Collecting Rates	13	17	6
Damage done by Rioters	63	18	–

1827. Amount of Expenditure in this year, as particularized in the former Return **4,122 19 8**

    Other items of expenditure, viz.

Bridges	106	14	6
Inquests	45	5	6
Corn Returns	10	8	–
Advertisements	46	10	8
General Miscellanies	23	16	–
Treasurer's Salary	21	–	–

Omissions in the former Return of Payments, occasioned by dissecting the different Payments under the several heads required by the former Order . . 118 19 7

LISTS OF HONORARY FREEMEN

LISTS OF HONORARY FREEMEN

Those offered the Honorary Freedom of the town in 1768, 1777 and 1822–4. Those marked with an asterisk actually took up their Freedom. Blanks in the list indicate that the forename or place of residence has never been filled in.

Common Hall held 3 May 1768

The Earl of Huntingdon

*The Earl of Denbigh

*The Lord Viscount Wentworth

*The Hon. Thomas Noel Esq. of Kirkby Mallory in this County

Sir Thomas Cave Baronet of Stanford Hall in Leicestershire

Sir John Palmer of Carlton in Northamptonshire Baronet

*Sir Charles Halford Baronet of Wistow

Sir Wolstan Dixie Baronet of Bosworth Park

Sir Charles Sedley Baronet of Nuthall in Nottinghamshire

Sir Robert Burdett Baronet of Foremark in Derbyshire

Sir Roger Newdigate Baronet

*The Hon. Robert Shirley Esq. of Belgrave

*Rowney Noel D.D. of Kirkby Mallory in this County

*Thomas Cave Esq. of Stanford Hall aforesaid

Charles Cave Esq. of the same place

Willoughby Dixie Esq. of Bosworth Park aforesaid

Francis Burdett Esq. of Foremark aforesaid

Thomas Skipwith of Newbold in Warwickshire Esq.

Samuel Phillipps of Garrendon in Leicestershire Esq.

*Thomas Babington of Rodeley Temple in Leicestershire Esq.

Peter Leigh of Lime in Cheshire Esq.

Edward Palmer of Withcott in Leicestershire Esq.

Charles Jennings of Gopshall in Leicestershire Esq.

Francis Mundy of Martin in Derbyshire Esq.

Charles James Parke of Prestwould in Leicestershire Esq.

*Edward William Hartopp of Little Dalby in Leicestershire Esq.

*Edward Rooe Yeo of Normanton Turvile in Leicestershire Esq.

Thomas Boothby of Potters Marston Leicestershire Esq.

*Thomas Boothby Jun. of the same place Esq.

*Francis Wheeler Esq. of Coventry

*Charles Dashwood of Stanford in Nottinghamshire Esq.

*John Hungerford of Dingley in Northamptonshire Esq.

*William Herrick (of Beaumannor in Leicestershire Esq.) the Younger

*Edward Farnham of Quorndon in Leicestershire Esq.

*Justinian Raynsford of Bricksworth in Northamptonshire Esq.

*James Harryman of New Sleaford in Lincolnshire Esq.

*Richard Dyott of Freeford in Staffordshire Esq.

William Inge of Thorpe Constantine in Staffordshire Esq.

*John Cave Brown Esq. of Stretton in the Fields in Derbyshire Esq.

529

John Benskin of Stony Stanton in Leicestershire Esq.

Thomas Hodgkin of Allexton in Leicestershire Esq.

Robert Hodgkin of South Luffenham in Rutland Esq.

Richard Farrer of Market Harborough in Leicestershire Esq.

*Richard Farrer Jun. Gent. of the same

*John Farrer of the same Clerk

Nathaniel Palmer Johnson of Loughborough in Leicestershire Esq.

*Thomas Allsopp of the same Esq.

*William Reeve of Melton Mowbray in Leicestershire Esq.

William Shalcross Mason of Burton on the woulds in Leicestershire Esq.

Francis Mundy of Derby Esq.

James Shuttleworth of Aston in Derbyshire Esq.

*Lebeus Humphrys of Kibworth in Leicestershire Esq.

*Thomas King of Sileby in Leicestershire Esq.

*Samuel Steele Perkins of Orton on the Hill in Leicestershire Esq.

*Joseph Boultbye of Coleorton in Leicestershire Esq.

*William Belgrave of North Kilworth in Leicestershire Gent.

Joseph Boultbye Jun. of Baxterly in Warwickshire Gent.

*Thomas Boultbye of Staughton Grange in Leicestershire Gent.

*Thomas Holled of Lutterworth in Leicestershire Gent.

John Piddock of Ashby de la zouch in Leicestershire Gent.

Holled Smith of Lutterworth in Leicestershire Gent.

*John Kirkland Gent. the Bailiff of this Borough

*Thomas Kirkland of Ashby de la zouch in Leicestershire Gent.

*John Noon Gent. of Mountsorel in Leicestershire

*George Buckley of Thornton in Leicestershire Gent.

*William Wartnaby of Market Harborough in Leicestershire Gent.

*John Smart of Thurlston in Leicestershire Gent.

*Thomas Major of Blaby in Leicestershire Gent.

*John Lambert of the City of London Gent.

*Robert Hames of Great Glen in Leicestershire Gent.

*James Bickham of Loughborough in Leicestershire Clerk

*John Liptrott Clerk of Broughton Astley in Leicestershire

*Isaac Liptrott Clerk of Oadby in Leicestershire

James Liptrott Clerk of Broughton Astley in Leicestershire

Henry Wigley Clerk of Pensham Hall in Worcestershire

*Henry Baseley Clerk of Beeby in Leicestershire

*John Fenwick Clerk of Hallaton in Leicestershire

*John Kerchival Clerk of Scraptoft in Leicestershire

*Edward Griffin Clerk of Dingley in Northamptonshire

*Charles Dickeson Clerk of Pickwell in Leicestershire

*Samuel Chambers Clerk of Higham on the Hill in Leicestershire

*James Piggott Clerk of Newmarket

*William Farnham Clerk of Sheepshead in Leicestershire

Thomas Mould Clerk the second master of Appleby School in Leicestershire

Thomas Greasley Clerk of Nether Seal in Leicestershire

*Peter Shuter Clerk of Kibworth in Leicestershire

*James King Wragge Clerk of Galby in Leicestershire

*James Chambers Clerk of Lullington in Derbyshire

*John Ledbrooke Clerk of Bosworth in Leicestershire
*Joseph Boyer of Loughborough in Leicestershire Gent.
*John Brown Clerk of Little Dalby in Leicestershire

Robert Power of Barleston in Leicestershire Gent.
John Davys of Loughborough in Leicestershire Gent.
*John Watkinson of the same Gent.
*John Cooper Clerk of Stony Stanton in Leicestershire

Common Hall held 1 July 1768

The Right Honourable William Lord Craven
*William Tilly Gent., Steward of this Borough
Mundy Musters of Collett in the County of Nottingham Esq.
Peter Burgh M.D. of Coventry
*Benjmn Bewick of London Esq.
Calverley Bewick Jun. Esq. of Lime Street London
*John Statham Esq. of Saint James's Street Westminster
Phillip Harley Bainbrige Esq., of Lockington in Leicestershire
*Anthony Burleton of Shaftesbury in Dorsetshire Esq.
Thomas Charlton of Chilwell Esq. in Nottinghamshire
Noah Thomas M.D. of old Burlington Street London
Lewis Palmer Clerk of Carlton in Northamptonshire
*Richard Palmer Gent. of the Six Clerks office in London
John Weston of Hatton Garden London Esq.
Richard Green of Rollston in Leicestershire Esq.
Joseph Greaves of Aston in Derbyshire Esq.
Robert Whatcock Avery of Sloleyhill in the parish of Arley in Warwickshire Esq.
*Edward Aspinshaw of Ashby de la Zouch in Leicestershire Gent.
*William Ebboral of Atherstone in Warwickshire Gent.

*Richard Banbury of North Kilworth in Leicestershire Gent.
*John Barnet of the Minories London Gent.
*William King of Stoke Golding in Leicestershire Gent.
*Edward King of Daventry Northamptonshire Gent.
*Henry Browne of Hoby in Leicestershire Clerk
*William Brown of Little Dalby in Leicestershire Gent.
*William Boss of Narborough in Leicestershire Gent.
*James Oldershaw of Emanuel Colledge Cambridge Gent.
*John Bird of Congeston in Leicestershire Clerk
Richard Cowlishaw of Ashley in Northamptonshire Gent.
John Cowlishaw of the same Clerk
*William Reeve the younger of Meltonmowbray in Leicestershire Gent.
*Richard Raworth of Knawston in Leicestershire Gent.
*Richard Raworth the younger of Owston in Leicestershire Gent.
*John Cooper of Lutterworth in Leicestershire Gent.
William Craven of Ashton Park in Berks Esq.
*George Clerke Esq. of Ashby de la Zouch in Leicestershire
John Needham of the same place Gent.

*Josiah North of Burton Lazars in Leicestershire   Gent.

*Thomas Chapman of Ashby de la Zouch in Leicestershire   Gent.

William Cradock of Loughborough in Leicestershire   Gent.

John Davys the younger of the same place   Gent.

*Michael Darker of Stoughton in Leicestershire   Gent.

*Joseph Iliff of Hinckley in Leicestershire   Gent.

*Ross Jennings of Newnham Paddox in Warwickshire   Gent.

John Dabbs of Gopshall in Leicestershire   Clerk

Thomas Dabbs the Elder of Seckington in Warwickshire   Gent.

Thomas Dabbs the younger of the same place   Gent.

*William Dickinson of Gopshall in Leicestershire   Gent.

William Major of Lawton in Leicestershire   Clerk

*John Major of Blaby in Leicestershire   Gent.

*Roger Dutton of Grafton in Cheshire Esq.

*Henry Fosbrooke of Hoton in Leicestershire   Gent.

*John Foster of Old Swinford in Worcestershire   Gent.

*Thomas Flavell of Ashby de la Zouch in Leicestershire   Gent.

*George Foxton of Upper Kibworth in Leicestershire   Gent.

Thomas Gamble of Willoughby Waterless in Leicestershire Gent.

John Gamble of the same place Gent.

*John Haycock of East Norton in Leicestershire   Gent.

John Mynors of Ashby de la Zouch in Leicestershire   Gent.

*Edward Muxloe of Pickwell in Leicestershire   Gent.

*Thomas Godfary of Scraptoft in Leicestershire   Gent.

*John Bowater of Portsmouth in the County of Hants Esq.

*Mansfield Gregory of Scraptoft in Leicestershire   Gent.

*William Holmes of Trinity Colledge in Cambridge   Gent.

*Robert Holmes of Sleaford in Lincolnshire   Gent.

Thomas Moore of Appleby in Leicestershire   Clerk

*George Moore of the same place Gent.

Richard Strey of Nottingham   Gent.

*John Watchorn of Lubbenham in Leicestershire   Gent.

*William Watchorn of Warwick Gent.

Miller Sadler of Over Whittaker in Warwickshire   Gent.

Joseph Sturgis of Sibbertoft in Northamptonshire   Gent.

Edward Taylor of Ansty in the County of the City of Coventry Esq.

*William Tompson of Houghton on the Hill in Leicestershire   Gent.

*William Tompson the younger of the same place   Gent.

*Olliver Wrighte of Lutterworth in Leicestershire   Gent.

*John Wrighte of Lubbenham in Leicestershire   Gent.

*Edward Stokes the younger of Melton Mowbray in Leicestershire   Gent.

*Thomas Sansome the younger of Hinckley in Leicestershire Gent.

*Thomas Wade of Clipston in Northamptonshire   Gent.

*William Wade of the same place Gent.

Thomas Thacker of the City of Coventry   Gent.

*John Vincent of Ashby de la Zouch in the County of Leicester   Gent.

*Richard Swinfen of Hinckley in Leicestershire   Gent.

*Richard Turville of North Kilworth in Leicestershire   Gent.

*Erasmus Turville of the same place Gent.

*William Willson of the Minories London Gent.

*Robert Willson of Birmingham Gent.

George Tompson of Northampton Gent.

*Henry Tompson of Northampton Gent.

Christopher Hatton Walker of Market Harborough in Leicestershire Clerk

*John Walker of Frolesworth in Leicestershire Gent.

Charles Vann of Nottingham Gent.

William Vann the younger of Evington in Leicestershire Gent.

*Richard Vann of the same place Gent.

*Richard Oxley of Bread Street London Gent.

William Brown Allsopp of Stretton in the Fields in Derbyshire Gent.

William Biddle of Atherstone in Warwickshire Clerk

Peter Cowper Clerke of Ashby de la Zouch Leicestershire

Thomas Baker of Atherstone in Warwickshire Clerk

*Thomas Frewin of Sapcoate in Leicestershire Clerk

*Joseph Fowler of Hugglescoate in Leicestershire Clerk

Davonport Gamble of Willoughby Waterless in Leicestershire Clerk

*Farmerie Law of Sibson in Leicestershire Clerk

*Thomas Liptrott of Nuneaton in Warwickshire Clerk

*John Liptrott of the same place Clerk

*Francis Harris of Whitwick in Leicestershire Clerk

John Binnion of Charlton in Cheshire Gent.

*Daniel Iliff of Kilby in Leicestershire Clerk

Robert Mearson of Carlton Curlieu in Leicestershire Clerk

John Levett of Willoughby Waterless in Leicestershire Clerk

*William Langford of Eaton in Berks Clerk

*Robert Marriott of Cottesbach in Leicestershire Clerk

*Thomas Hudson of Quorndon in Leicestershire Clerk

*Henry Newman of Hinckley Leicestershire Clerk

*John Simpson of Mountsorel in Leicestershire Clerk

*William Waterman of Burbage in Leicestershire Clerk

Joseph Whittingham of Bilsdon in Leicestershire Clerk

*Isaac Whyley of Witherly in Warwickshire Clerk

Cornelius Belgrave of Ridlington in Rutland Clerk

*Thomas Brown of Hinckley in Leicestershire Gent.

*Matthew Simons of Gumbley in Leicestershire Gent.

*William Brown of Hinckley in Leicestershire Gent.

Richard Clutton of Tinkwood in Cheshire Gent.

*Edward Morpett of Turlangton in Leicestershire Gent.

*John Meadows of Asfordby in Leicestershire Gent.

*Francis Goode the younger of Cussington in Leicestershire Gent.

Common Hall held 22 October 1776

*Sir William Gordon Knight of the Bath of Garrendon Park in Leicestershire

*Ralph Milbank Esq. of Halnaby in Yorkshire

*William Burleton Jun. Esq. of Donnhead in Wilts

Philip Burleton Esq. of the same place

*Thomas Levett Esq. of Whittington in Staffordshire

Samuel Hartopp Esq. of Little Dalby in Leicestershire

*Thomas Wilson of Scraptoft in Leicestershire Esq.

Francis Newman of Burbage in Leicestershire Esq.

*John Green of Owston in Leicestershire Gent.

*William Turner of Hinckley in Leicestershire Gent.

*Charles Loraine Smith Esq. of Enderby in Leicestershire

*Chamberlain Goodwin the Elder of the City of London Gent.

*Chamberlain Goodwin Jun. of the same place Gent.

Common Hall held 5 September 1777

*Richard Parry D.D. of Market Harborough in Leicestershire

John Topp Esq. of Whitton in Shropshire

Levett Hanson of Emanuel College in Cambridge Esq.

*The Hon. William Cockayne of Rushton in Northamptonshire

Col. William Fielding of the first Regiment of foot guards

*William Dades of South St. Westminster Gent.

*John Dobbins of South St. aforesaid Gent.

*Ellis Shipley Pestell of Hinckley in Leicestershire Gent.

*Charles Pestell of Ashby de la Zouch in Leicestershire Gent.

*John Green of Hinckley aforesaid Hosier

John Turner of the same Woolcomber

Common Hall held 18 December 1822

The Earl of Denbigh

The Earl of Stamford & Warrington

Robert Shirley Earl Ferrers

The Earl of Aylesford

Earl Howe

Lord Charles Manners of Belvoir Castle

Lord Robert Manners of Belvoir Castle

Lord Grey of Groby

Lord Brudenell

Viscount Tamworth

Robert Peel, one of His Majesty's principal Secretaries of State

Henry Goulburn, Chief Secretary to the Lord Lieutenant of Ireland

The Hon. Mr Fielding

*Sir George Crewe of Calke Abbey Baronet

Sir William Brown Cave of Stretton-en-le Fields Baronet

*Sir John Henry Palmer of Carlton Curlieu Baronet

Sir Willoughby Wolstan Dixie Baronet

Sir George Howland Beaumont of Coleorton Baronet

*Sir Lawrence Vaughan Palk Baronet

Sir Charles Payne of Belgrave Baronet

Sir Robert Peel Baronet

General Sir Charles Hastings of Willersley Hall Baronet

Sir Henry Halford of Wistow Baronet

*Sir Frederick Gustavus Fowke of Lowesby Baronet

*Poyntz Owsley Adams, of Harborough Esq.

Richard Astley of Odstone Esq.

Edward Abney of Measham Hall Esq.

*James Astlett of Loughborough Gent.

Nathaniel Atcheson of Great Winchester Street, London Esq.

*William Allen of Uppingham

Richard Arkwright, the elder, of Crompton Esq.

*Richard Arkwright, the younger, of Ashbourne Esq.

Robert Arkwright Esq.

Peter Arkwright Esq.

John Arkwright of Hampton Court Esq.

*John Atkins, Alderman, of London Esq.

*John Arthur Arnold of Lutterworth Esq.

*The Reverend Frederick Apthorpe of Gumley Clerk

The Reverend Charles Alsop of Sheepshead Clerk

Charles Alsop of Woodhouse

Francis Alsop of Humberstone

*The Reverend Thomas Adnutt of Broughton Clerk

Thomas Adnutt Jun. of Esq.

*Thomas Gisborne Babington of Rothley Temple Esq.

*The Reverend John Babington of Cossington Clerk

*Matthew Babington of Rothley Temple Esq.

*George Gisborne Babington of London Esq.

*The Reverend Matthew Drake Babington of Clerk

Thomas Black of Melton Gent.

Daniel Baker of Barlestone Gent.

John Baker of do. Gent.

*J. D. Barnard of Owston Esq.

*William Baker of Melton Schoolmaster

Ambrose Brewin of Loughborough Gent.

*The Revd Thomas Belgrave of North Kilworth Clerk

*The Revd Gilbert Beresford of Aylestone Clerk

*The Revd James Beresford of Kibworth Clerk

Thomas Bent of Gilmorton Gent.

*Allen Bent of Queneborough Gent.

*Thomas Berridge of Dunton Gent.

*[Edward] Bright of Melton

*[Edward] Bright Jun. of Melton

The Revd Bright of Skeffington Clerk

*John Bright of Skeffington Esq.

*George Billings of Galby

Thomas Billings of Illstone

*John Billings of Illstone

*James Thomas Bishop of Melton Gent.

Thomas Bishop of Grimstone

Joseph Bishop of Grimstone

Joseph Bishop of London

The Revd J. W. Boyer of Quorndon Clerk

Thomas Boyer of Quorndon

John Boyer of Quorndon

*Thomas Bosworth of Beeby

Brown of Northampton

*James Brookes of Croft

*Charles Bloomar of Hugglescote Esq.

Joseph Brown of Burton on the Wolds

*John Dick Burnaby of Rotherby Esq.

*The Revd Thomas Burnaby of Misterton Clerk

*John Myners Bulstrode of Worthington Esq.

*Marston Buszard of Lutterworth Esq.

*Francis Burgess of Lutterworth

*Thomas Burkhill of Loughborough

John Burgess of Barrow upon Soar Esq.

*James Williams Buchanan of Nuneaton Gent.

*The Reverend Henry Bullivant of Marston Trussell Clerk

John Bullivant of North Kilworth Gent.

*Thomas Roby Burgin of Shardlow

*The Reverend Dean Judd Burdett of Gilmorton Clerk

*William Burbidge of Great Packington

Thomas Burbidge of Coleshill

Joseph Burbidge of Shirchill near Coventry

John Burbidge of the city of Coventry

The Revd Henry St. John Bullen of   Clerk

*The Revd Thomas Buckley of Kegworth Clerk

*John Buckley of Normanton

Gilbert Brydges of Narborough Surgeon

*John Clarke of Little Peatling Esq.

John Clarke of New Parks Gent.

*John Brown Cave of Stretton-en-le-fields Esq.

John Cradock of Stanford Esq.

John Cradock the younger of Loughborough Gent.

*Thomas Cradock of Loughborough Gent.

Joseph Cradock of Loughborough Gent.

Ferdinando Cradock of London Gent.

Otway Cave of Stanford Esq.

*John Caldecott of Holbrook Grange Esq.

Chambers of Kilworth

*The Revd Joseph Cragg of Owston Clerk

*John Craddock of Nuneaton Gent.

*John Hood Chapman of Atherstone Esq.

*Robert Capes of Holborn Court Grays Inn London

*John Plomer Clarke of Wolton Place, near Daventry Esq.

William Ralph Cartwright of Aynho, Northamptonshire Esq. M.P.

*Richard Cheslyn of Langley Esq.

*Richard Cheslyn the younger of Langley Esq.

John Cheslyn of Loughborough Gent.

Cheslyn of Diseworth

The Revd William Cleaver of Wanlip Clerk

*Edward Hawkins Cheney of Gaddesby Esq.

*Robert Cresswell of Ravenstone Esq.

Robert Cresswell the younger, of Ravenstone Esq.

*Richard Cresswell of Ravenstone Esq.

Edward Cresswell of Burton on the Wolds

John Cresswell of Hoton

John Cooke of Hothorpe Esq.

The Revd Cooke of Theddingworth Clerk

*The Revd Sherrard Coleman of Houghton Clerk

*John Cooper of Bond Street London Esq.

Henry Cooper of Drakelow

Thomas Cooper of Castle Greasley

*Henry Coleman of Clipstone Esq.

*Henry Davie Coleman of Oadby Esq.

*The Revd Francis Thomas Corrance of Great Glen Clerk

Robert Coleman of Queneborough Gent.

*John Crowder of Ashby Magna
The Revd Cocker of Bunney   Clerk
*Thomas Cox of Harborough
The Revd Collyer of Hambleton,
  Rutland   Clerk
*Samuel Cook of Moor Barns
Samuel Cook of Sheet Fields
The Very Revd William Cockburn,
  Dean of York
    Curtis of Illstone
*George John Danvers Butler Danver
  of Swithland Esq.
*The Revd John Dalby of Castle
  Donnington   Clerk
The Revd Samuel Dashwood of
  Clerk
The Revd Davis of Glooston   Clerk
George R. Dawson Esq. M.P.
Thomas Denning of Ulverscroft
  Esq.
*John Deverell of Shoby
William Dent of Hallaton Esq.
*The Revd Dent of Hallaton   Clerk
*William Dewes of Ashby-de-la-
  zouch   Gent.
*Alexander Dixie of   Esq.
John Driver of Harborough   Gent.
*Edward Thomas Dicey of   Esq.
William Dickenson of Twycross
  Gent.
*William Duncan of London Esq.
*[Andrew Robert] Drummond of
  London Esq.
*Major General Dyott of Freeford
*John Philip Dyott of Lichfield Esq.
*James Ella of Wimeswould Esq.
*William Ella of do. Esq.
*William Eagleston of Comberford,
  near Tamworth Esq.
Thomas Elliott of Burton Overy
    Farnell of Snarestone
*Edward Farnham of Quorndon Esq.
*Robert Faulks of Flanborough
*The Revd [Richard] Farrer of Ashley
  near Harboro'   Clerk
Daniel Farrow of Loughborough
  Farmer
*John Franks of Burton Overy

*The Revd Thomas Farmer of
  Aspley, Woburn   Clerk
*George Freer of Enderby
*The Revd Thomas Cotton Fell of
  Sheepy   Clerk
    Fell of (Leicester Militia) Esq.
The Revd John Fisher of Cossing-
  ton   Clerk
Robert Fisher of   Esq.
Edward Fisher of Higham Esq.
The Revd John Fisher the younger
  of Higham   Clerk
*The Revd John Fisher the elder of
  Hiam   Clerk
*[George] Finch of Burleigh Hall Esq.
The Revd Finch of Oakham   Clerk
*Sir John Fowler, Knight, Burton
  upon Trent
Robert Foster of Wolvey Esq.
The Revd John Fry of Desford
  Clerk
John Fry of Desford Esq.
The Revd Grantham of Hungerton
  Clerk
*Thomas Gamble of Scraptoft   Gent.
*John Gamble of Lowesby
*John Davenport Gamble of Wil-
  loughby Waterless   Gent.
*Henry Green of Rollestone Esq.
*Valentine Green of Normanton Esq.
Edward Green of
*Thomas Geary of Old Hayes
*John Geary of Dadlington
*The Revd William Greasley of
  Netherseal   Clerk
The Revd William Whitmore Green-
  way of Newbold Verdon   Clerk
*George Greenway of Attleborough
  Hall Esq.
*John Gregory of Loughborough
  Draper
*William Gillson of Ullesthorpe Esq.
*Edward Gillson of Ullesthorpe Esq.
*William Gillson, Jun. of Hambleton
*John Cole Gillson of Burleigh Esq.
John Giles of Sheepshead
*The Revd [John] Girardot of
  Stanford   Clerk

T   537

*John Goodacre of Ullesthorpe Esq.
John Goodacre the younger of Ullesthorpe Esq.
*Richard Gough of Misterton Esq.
*The Revd Jeremiah Goodman of Kibworth   Clerk
John Goodman of Gumley
Richard Goodman of Smeeton
*[John] Goodacre of Lutterworth Gent.
*The Revd [Robert] Gutch of Seagrave   Clerk
*The Revd Evans Hartopp of Thurnby   Clerk
*Robert Haymes of Great Glen Esq.
Robert Haymes Jun. of do. Esq.
Henry Halford of Wistow Esq.
*The Revd Dr Hardy of Loughboro'
William Harris of Overseal Esq.
William Harris of Castle Hayes Esq.
Thomas Harris of Throwley Hall Esq.
William Haymes of Kibworth Esq.
The Revd Samuel Hartopp of
*John Hall of Countesthorpe Farmer
The Revd Thomas Hanbury of Langton   Clerk
*Charles Hastings [of Willesley Hall]
William Hall of Tempe
*Thomas Hall of Middleton, Derbyshire
*The Revd James Harrington of Sapcote   Clerk
*John Henson of Walton
Thomas Henton of Hoby
*William Hill of Melton   Gent.
John Hill of Appleby
Joseph Hill of Cottesbach
*The Revd Thomas Holditch of Maydwell   Clerk
Hungerford Holditch of   Esq.
*Thomas Howcutt of Willoughby
*Samuel Holt of Northampton Esq.
*The Revd T. Hoe of Long Clawson Clerk

The Revd James Hodges of
Abraham Hoskins of   Near Burton upon Trent Esq.
The Revd Hoskins of Rempstone Clerk
The Revd Charles Hope of Derby Clerk
John Samuel Hudson of   Esq.
William Fisher Hulse of Cossington Esq.
*John Benjamin Humphrey of Kibworth Esq.
Richard Humphrey of
*Lebeus Charles Humphrey of Lincoln Chambers, Lincoln's Inn Fields London Esq.
*Saville John Hyde of Quorndon Esq.
*Edward Phillips Jackson of Quorndon
Charles Jervis of Hinckley Esq.
William Jervis of do. Esq.
William Inett of Great Dalby
*[William] Jones of Lutterworth Surgeon
The Revd Thomas Jones of Appleby Fields   Clerk
        Jones of Measham Fields Esq.
*John King of Knighton Esq.
*Jonathan Gilbert King of Beeby
*Newbold Kinton of London
*Peter Augustus Lafargue of Husbands Bosworth Esq.
        Lafargue Jun. of do. Esq.
George Lakin of Lutterworth
*John Lea of Kirkby
*Thomas   Leadbetter   of   Little Dalby
John Lee of Ravenstone
William Lee of Burton Lazars
*James Lee of Lutterworth
*John Lucas of Walton by Kimcote
*William Marvin of Frowlesworth
The Revd William Marvin of Frolesworth   Clerk
*Robert Marston of Enderby
*John Marston of Enderby
General Colin Macaulay of

John Marriott of Kibworth Grazier
*Hayes Marriott of [Kibworth Harcourt]
*John Marriott the younger of Kibworth [Beauchamp]
*[Roger] Manners of Goadby
*The Revd Dr Spencer Madan of Ibstock
The Revd Madan of Seal Clerk
*Edward Mammatt of Ashby-de-la-Zouch Esq.
*John Heyrick Macaulay of Plymouth Gent.
*Thomas Macaulay of London Surgeon
*William Marshall of Shelford
*John Marshall of Shelford
William Marston of Goadby
*James Martin of Whetstone
*The Revd Henry John Maddock of Huddersfield Clerk
*The Revd Benjamin Maddock of Wimeswold Clerk
*Edward Meeson of Ashby-de-la-Zouch
*The Revd George Mettam of Barwell Clerk
*The Revd Francis Merewether of Coleorton Clerk
*William Middleton of Loughboro' Esq.
George Miles of Atherstone
Joseph Miles of Calcote
Joseph Miles of Atherstone
*William Morris Middleton of Loughborough Esq.
*James Morpott of Lutterworth Gent.
*The Revd [Hugh] Monkton of Seaton Clerk
*The Revd Nathaniel Morgan of Rearsby Clerk
John Morpott of Langton Esq.
James Morpott of Kibworth
The Revd William McDouall of Ashby de la Zouch Clerk
*Charles Godfrey Mundy of Burton on the Wolds Esq.

*Francis Nedham of Hungerton Gent.
John Nethercoat of Haselbeach Esq.
John George Norbury of Snareston Esq.
*The Revd [Samuel] Noble of Frolesworth Clerk
*The Revd Thomas Norris of Harby Clerk
William Owen of Atherstone Esq.
*The Revd James Ord of Langton Clerk
*James Pickering Ord of Langton Esq.
The Revd Thomas Ord of
George Osborne of Northampton Esq.
George Osborne Jun. of do.
The Revd Orton of Kegworth Clerk
*Thomas Parr of Wanlip
William Page of
The Revd Joseph Wilton Pawsey of Leir Clerk
*The Revd Henry Palmer of Carlton Curlieu Clerk
James Park of Melton
*Joseph Pratt of Huncote
*Joseph Pratt Jun. of Croft
*John Pratt of Marston Hall
James Parsons of Walcote
Thomas Parsons of Walcote
Thomas Parry of Shipstone on Stour Esq.
*The Revd George Peake of Enderby Clerk
William Yates Peel of Tamworth Esq. M.P.
*Jonathan Peel of Drayton Manor Esq.
The Revd John Peel of Drayton Manor Clerk
Lawrence Peel of Drayton Esq.
*Thomas Penford of Galby
*Robert Peake of Burrow
*Shirley Farmer Steele Perkins of Sutton Coldfield Esq.
George Peake of Birstall Esq

*The Revd Dr [William] Pearson of South Kilworth
William Perkins of Laughton
John Perkins of
Leonard Piddocke of Ashby-de-la-Zouch Gent.
*Leonard Piddocke Jun. of do. Gent.
*Thomas Piddocke of do. Gent.
*The Revd John Piddocke of [Ashby de la Zouch]
*Robert Piper of Breedon Esq.
Thomas Prior of Desford
Edmund Piercy of Leamington
    Princep of Newton Thistles near Tamworth Esq.
*George Pochin of Barkby Hall Esq.
The Revd James Powell of Bitteswell Clerk
The Revd Proctor of Aylestone Clerk
*John Power of Hinckley Esq.
The Revd Reynolds of Little Bowden Clerk
    Reynolds Jun.
*The Revd [John] Roby of Congerstone Clerk
*Bradshaw Roby of Ansty Gent.
*Benjamin Rowland of Hoton
*Thomas Rowland of Hoton
*John Rowland of Stanford
Benjamin Sadler of Leeds Esq.
*Michael Sadler of Leeds Esq.
*Thomas Sansome of Hinckley Esq.
*[Thomas] Samwell of Upton, Northamptonshire Esq.
*Richard Spencer of Snarestone
*Edward Stephens of Manchester Esq.
Thomas Stephens of Coventry
*Thomas Asheton Smith of [Tedworth, Hants] Esq.
The Revd Loraine Loraine Smith of Northamptonshire Clerk
Benjamin Simpkin of Hoby
*John Simpkin of Little Glen
*The Revd Thomas Smith of Catthorpe near Lutterworth Clerk

*John Bainbrigge Storey of Lockington Esq.
    Stokes of Clifton Hall, near Tamworth Esq.
*Nathaniel Shuttleworth of Harborough
*Henry Shuttleworth of Harborough
Henry Shuttleworth of Great Bowden Esq.
*Robert Shuttleworth of do.
Thomas Sykes of Pilton
*Isaac Taylor of Somerby
    Taylor of Manchester
    Taylor Jun. of do.
*John Tebbs of Gilmorton
Thomas Thorpe of Loughborough Esq.
John Thorpe of do. Esq.
The Revd Thomas Thorpe of Burton Overy Clerk
The Revd Thomas Thorpe of Notts. Clerk
John Thorpe of Overseal Esq.
*The Revd Dr [Edward] Thomas of Billesdon
Robert Thornley of Ashby-de-la-Zouch
*William Toone the younger of Belton
William Thomas of London Esq.
William Thomas the younger of London Esq.
*William Tupman of Somerby
*The Revd William Richardson Tyson of Thurcaston Clerk
Dr Peter Vaughan
Charles Richard Vaughan Esq.
*Thomas Vowe of Hallaton
William Wartnaby of Clipstone
*William Wartnaby Jun. of do.
*Dr John Kenworthey Walker of [Huddersfield]
Joseph Samuel Walker of   Esq.
Joseph Walker of Lascelles Hall Esq.
*Richard Watson of Lutterworth Esq.
Richard Watson Jun. of do. Gent.
*The Revd Richard Walker of Galby Clerk

The Revd Thomas Wartnaby of Kibworth   Clerk

John Wartnaby of Hothorpe

The Revd William Henry Walker of Great Wigston   Clerk

The Revd Thomas Walker of Standon, Staffordshire   Clerk

*Thomas Ward of Church Langton

*Philip Waterfield of Woodeaves, Derbyshire

Watkinson of Woodhouse

*[Wannom Langham] Watson of Walton by Kimcote Esq.

John Warner of Leeds

*Dr [William] Webb of Clare Hall, Cambridge

Thomas West of Coptall Court, London

*John West of Little Bowden

The Revd Wm Wilkinson of South Croxton   Clerk

Wilson of Allexton

*George Williamson of Gaddesby Esq.

*Christopher Williamson of do.

Williamson of do.

*The Revd [Charles] Wright of [Market] Bosworth   Clerk

The Revd Henry Wright of Stockport   Clerk

*William Wright of Earl Shilton Farmer

Robert Wildbore of Tilton   Grazier

*Frederick William Wollaston of Shenton Esq.

Revd George Woodcock of

Thomas Worthington of New Parks

Richard Worthington of Cadeby

*The Rev. Henry Rushworth Woolley of [Middleton, Warwickshire]

*John Young of Narborough

Common Hall held 20 January 1823

*Isaac Barnes, Gent., Deputy Town Clerk of this Borough

Thomas Alsager of Wilncote near Tamworth Esq.

Samuel Adams of Nottingham Hosier

George Allen of Earl Shilton

*James Attenborough of Braybrook Lodge

*Robert Attenborough of Braybrook Lodge

*Henry Attenborough of Nottingham Grocer

John Andrews of Turlangton

William Ades of Oakham Esq.

Armfield of Northampton

William Armfield of Northampton

John Iliffe Atkins of Northampton

*John   Atkins of London Esq.

Thomas Arnold of Stamford M.D.

George Ashton of Lubenham

The Revd Robert W. Almond of Nottingham   Clerk

*Daniel Acomb of Nottingham Hosier

William Alsop of Thorpe Arnold

Thomas Alsop of Garthorpe

*Thomas Ayre of Coleorton

*George Bramley of Bushby

*John Bramley of Bushby

*Norman Bramley of Sheepshead

Bramley of Sheepshead

*John Blakesley of Hinckley Esq.

The Revd Joseph Bray of Hinckley Clerk

*Thomas Bray of Hinckley

Edmund Bland of East Farndon

George Bland of Theddingworth

Edmund Bland of Theddingworth

John Baguley of Cossington Grazier

*Richard Baxter of the Crescent, Wisbeach

Thomas Baker of Melton

Thomas Bradshaw of Barrow

Thomas Black of Frisby

Thomas Black of Ashby Folville
William Black of Frisby
*John Balguy Jun. of [Wiverton Hall]
  Nr Nottingham Esq.
    Bates of Ansty
Samuel Barker of Lindon Hall, near
  Uppingham Esq.
Edward Barnard of Burrow Gent.
Major   Bamford of Wilncote near
  Tamworth
Thomas Francis Philip Hutchinson
  Barber of Lamb Close House, Nr
  Nottingham
*John Storer Beaumont of Barrow
John Breedon of Rotherby
Thomas Beasley of Thrussington
*John Beasley of do.
*Thomas Beale of Ashby Magna
  Bird of Houghton on the Hill
*Harry Brierley of Brinklow Gent.
James Birdsall of Northampton
Robert Birdsall of do.
*William Birdsall of Syston Surgeon
*   Thomas Bishop of Thurnby
The Revd John Bright of Pickwell
  Clerk
*John Biddle of Thringstone
Thomas Brombley of Goadby
*Samuel Bonner of Hinckley
The Revd George Boulton of
  Oxendon Clerk
Henry Boulton of Oxendon
    Boulton of   Surgeon
George Bosworth of Lubenham
*John David Brown of Loddington,
  Northamptonshire
Samuel Bolton of Nottingham Esq.
*Gervas Bourne of Bramcote Grove,
  Nr Nottingham
*The Revd Robert Boon of Stocker-
  stone Clerk
*Joseph Bostock of Breedon
*Richard Broughton of Blaston
*Henry Hind Browne Jun. of
  Melton
*John Bonnett of Whitwick
The Revd John Cave Brown of
  Stretton Clerk

Robert Cave Brown of Fazeley
  Surgeon
Richard Burdett of Kimcote
The Revd John Buckley of Gilsboro'
  Clerk
    Buckley of do.
Henry Burgess of Illstone Lodge
Robert Buswell of Arthingworth
*Charles Buswell of Marston Trussell
William Stanford Burnside of
  (Plumtree) Nottingham Esq.
The Revd John Burnside of do. do.
  Clerk
Thomas Butcher of Northampton
  Esq.
Richard Beaumont Burnaby Esq. of
  the Royal Artillery
Charles Herrick Burnaby Esq. of the
  Royal Artillery
*Dr Sherrard Burnaby Doctor's
  Commons
Alpheus Buck of Loughborough
  Bookseller
    Buck of Holwell
Thomas Burbidge, High Street,
  Borough, London
William Astley Browne Cave of
  Stretton-en-le-fields Esq.
*Thomas Browne Cave of do. Esq.
    Cantrell of Ashby-de-la-Zouch
*John Carpendale of Melton
    Capenhurst of Netherseal
William Carver of Ingarsby
*[Dr William] Calvert of Melton
*The Revd Richard Cragg of Wy-
  mondham Clerk
*David Chapman of Swithland
William Chamberlain of Lowesby
Henry Chamberlain of Desford
The Revd Samuel Charlton of
  Chilwell
George Charlton of Breedon
Thomas Clarke of Melton Esq.
*William Clarke of Great Bowden
*William Clarke Jun. of do.
*Israel Chamberlain of Red Hill
John Chamberlain of do.
James Chamberlain of Northampton

*Thomas Carter of Waltham
*Samuel Caldecott of Melton
*John Thomas Caldecott of do.
*Martin Callow of Melton Uphol-
sterer
*[John] Chambers of Northampton
Andrew Chambers of Northampton
The Revd John Chambers of Elwall
near Derby Clerk
The Revd Leonard Chapman of
Nottingham Clerk
*Nathaniel Goodwin Clarke of
[Handsworth] near Birmingham
Esq.
Nathaniel R. Clarke Jun. of do.
Esq.
*John Sanderson Chapman of Key-
thorpe
*William Chapman of Keythorpe
George Chapman of Keythorpe
Robert Chessher of Hinckley Esq.
Henry Robert Crewe of Trinity
College, Cambridge Esq.
Samuel Cheetham of Nottingham
Hosier
William Cheetham of Nottingham
Hosier
Thomas Cheetham of Nottingham
Grocer
William Clifford of Cold Newton
James Clifford of Cold Newton
William Clifford Jun. of South
Croxton
Frederick Clifford of South Crox-
ton
    Clifford of Baresby
    Christey of Quenby Esq.
*William Cowdell of Hinckley Gent.
*Robert Cort of Smeeton
James Cort of Great Bowden
*John Henry Cooke of London
Charles Cox of Wilford near Not-
tingham Gent.
*John Cox Jun. of do.
    Coventry of Wistow Esq.
John Corby of Medbourn
The Revd J. B. Copestakes of
Kettleby Clerk

William Wylde Churchill of Sheeps-
head
*John Clutton of the High Street,
Borough [of Southwark] Esq.
Samuel Cullen of Nottingham
Draper
*John Davenport of Ashby-de-la-
Zouch
Thomas Reginald Davenport of
Harboro'
Thomas Dainty of Northampton
    Dale of Ashbourne Esq.
Major Thirstan Dale of do.
William Daulby of Loughboro'
Grocer
*William Draycott of Kilby
*Dr John Dean, Principal of St Mary
Hall, Oxford
Robert Dickenson of Nottingham
Draper
    Dorman of Dunton Bassett
*James Ley Douglass of Harboro'
Gent.
Charles Dodd of Northampton Esq.
*The Revd Dr Doncaster of Oakham
Strafford Dugdale Dugdale M.P. of
Merevale Hall, Nr Atherstone Esq.
William Dugdale Jun. of do. Esq.
John Earl of Quorndon
*The Revd Edward Evans of Shawell
near Lutterworth Clerk
*[James] Eaton of Knipton
*Sommersby Edwards of Warwick
Gent.
Sir Henry Every, Baronet, of Egg-
ington Hall
Henry Every Esq. of do.
Thomas Webb Edge of Shelley,
Notts Esq.
The Revd John Webb [Edge] of do.
Clerk
William Elliott Elliott of Gedling,
Notts Esq.
The Revd   Eddowes of Belton
Clerk
Thomas Exton of Eastwell
John Exton of do.
Thomas Eyre of Coleorton

The Revd Eddy of Gilsborough Clerk

John Fabling of Stapleford

Major William Fawcett of Clipstone

The Revd G. D. Faithful of Eastwell Clerk

Col. Featherstone of   near Bosworth

*Peter Fearnhead of Nottingham Gent.

Charles Fletcher of   do. Grocer

*Thomas Ferneley of Thrussington

Charles Frisby of Cold Newton

Thomas Finn of Nottingham Draper

*Thomas Ford of London

*Joseph Ford of Coventry

James Flore of Rearsby

*George Fludyer of Ayston Hall, near Uppingham Esq.

*George Fludyer Jun. of Ayston Hall, near Uppingham Esq.

*William Fludyer of do. Esq.

*William Farbrace Gramshaw of Hinckley

*[William Hoey] Gatliffe of Leeds

Henry Gatty of Harborough Surgeon

*Richard Garratt Jun. of Thorpe Malson

The Revd Garratt of Thorpe Malson

*William Gates of Northampton Esq.

The Honorable Henry Booth Grey

Thomas Gearey of Atterton near Atherstone

John Gee of Arthingworth

Michael Gedling Jun. of Nottingham

Thomas Gilbert of Peckleton

*Marshall Thompson Goude of Cossington

*Marshall Goude of Barrow

Henry Goude   Beds.

*The Revd George Gordon Rector of Muston

*The Revd George Gordon D.D. Dean of Lincoln & Rector of Sedgebrook

*Thomas Hatton of Ashby-de-la-Zouch

John Hayes of Hinckley

*Richard Hack of Burton Lazars

Charles Hazard of Nottingham

John Hardy of Nottingham

John Hackett of Breedon

*George Hackett of do.

Sampson Hackett of Newbold Hackett of Barrow Hill Lodge

*Gratian Hart of London Esq.

Captn Hart

John Hassall of Shelford, Notts

The Revd George Ludford Hervey of Diseworth   Clerk

The Revd Herbert of Bulwell   Clerk

Samuel Henton of Orton

*William Hind of Swithland

*Thomas Hind of Quorndon

*James Hind of do.

*Robert Hind of Harborough

*John Hind of Loughborough

Hugh Higgins of Northampton

John Knight Higgins of do.

*John Hilton of Adbolton, near Nottingham

*John Hickinbotham of Ratcliffe on Soar

The Hon. and Revd Augustus Edward Hobart of Walton Houghton of Lutterworth Wine Merchant

Henry Hoskins of Newton Park near Burton on Trent

Green Hodgkin of Great Glenn

William Howkins of Frowlesworth

*William Holloway Jun. of Harboro' Builder

Richard Hootton of Nottingham Gent.

*[John] Hall Hoyle of Kirby Bellars

*William Holwell Jun. of Melton

John Holt of Northampton

*William Cave Humfrey of Laughton Esq.

*Samuel Huskinson of Tugby Huskinson of South Croxton Huskinson of Rollestone

*The Revd John Hutton of Sproxton
Clerk
*William Hutchinson of Whitwick
John Jackson of Derby
*Henry Jackson of Mountsorrel
George Jackson of do.
John Jackson of Manchester
The Revd John James of Oundle
Clerk
*William Robert James of Ely Place,
London Gent.
Gibson Jalland of Nottingham
Wine Merchant
Sir Justinian Isham, Baronet of
Lamport
The Revd Henry Isham of Lamport
Clerk
The Revd Vere Isham of do. Clerk
*John Jennell of Gaddesby
William Johnson of Hinckley
John Johnson of Nottingham Lace
Manufacturer
Jones of Northampton
*The Revd John Jones of Burley
Clerk
*[Robert] Judd Jun. of Melton
*Thomas Kay of Nottingham Lace
Manufacturer
Stephen Kendall Jun. of Cosby
*Edward Knight of Coleorton
Thomas Kidger of Coleorton
John Kilby Sen. of Queneboro'
William Kilby of do.
John Kilby Jun. of do.
Charles King of Husband's Bos-
worth
Robert King of Melton
*Thomas Kirby of Ashby-de-la-
Zouch
Charles Lacey of Loughboro' Gent.
Richard Lacey of Wimeswould
Farmer
Edward Lacey of do.
John Lathbury of Hungerton
Charles Lacey of Standard Hill,
Nottingham Esq.
Daniel Langley of Nottingham
Grocer

*Thomas Lewin of Beeby
*Luke Lewin of Barkby
John Lewin of Thrussington
James Lefevre of Great Bowden
Grazier
*John Leadbeater of Melton
John Lingford of Nottingham
Jeweller
Thomas Lingford of do.
The Revd John V. Lindsay of
Swinford Clerk
Dr Lloyd of Appleby
William Morpott Marriott of Kib-
worth Surgeon
The Revd William Madan of Poles-
worth Clerk
Lord Viscount Maynard
*[Stephen] Mash Sen. of Lutter-
worth
William Mash of Warwick
William Mash of Southam
Mash of Dunchurch
*Thomas Marris of Copthall Court,
Throgmorton Street, London
*William Marris of Gray's Inn,
London
*John Higginson Marvin of Froles-
worth
*Thomas Marshall of Kettering
Gent.
Thomas Maltby of Nottingham Esq.
David Melville of Wood Street,
London
Meldrum of Lutterworth
John Mills of Nottingham Hosier
*John Morley of West Bridgeford,
near Nottingham
*Thomas Morris of Nottingham
Gent.
*Joseph Morris of do. Gent.
The Revd John Morris of Nether
Broughton Clerk
Thomas Morris of Cotgrave, Notts
William Neale of Stoke Golding
Jonathan Nethercoat of Thedding-
worth
Newby of Northampton
John Newbold of Breedon

T*

Edward Newbold of Near Ashby-Zouch

John Needham of Queneboro'

*Charles Needham of do.

*John Nicholls of Melton

The Revd H. H. Norris of Hackney, London Clerk

*William Nurse of Little Ashby

*Abraham Nurse of Sapcote

*William Nursey of Sutton Bassett in the County of Northampton Grazier

The Revd John Owesly of Blaston Clerk

*John Orton of Kegworth Surgeon

Robert Newland Orton of Atherstone Gent.

*John Patrick of Harborough Inn-keeper

Robert Padley of Burton Joyce Notts Esq.

Robert Wilkinson Padley of do. Esq.

The Revd Alfred Padley of Bulwell House, Notts Clerk

John Place Jun. of Nottingham Sadler

George Payne of Sulby Esq.

*The Revd [John Thomas] Parker of Newbold on Avon, Nr Rugby Clerk

*Walton Pell of Clipstone

John Pettifor of Northampton

John Pearson of Nottingham Gent.

*Benjamin Perkins of Sapcote

Marshall Pickard of Bagworth Park

The Revd Prior of Quorndon Clerk

*John Pocklington of Hallaton

*Francis Potter of Coleorton

*John Potter of Thringstone

William Potter of do.

*Joseph Pocklington of Smithfield, London Banker

John Power of Little George Street, London M.D.

Lieut. Col. Reeve of Leadenham, Lincolnshire

The Revd William Reeve of Clare Hall, Cambridge Clerk

*Joseph James Ward Rigley of Nottingham Gent.

*James Rickett of Oundle

Launcelott Rollestone of Wotnall Esq.

*The Revd Isaac Robinson of Stoke Golding Clerk

William Roe of Nottingham Hatter

George Robinson of Mansfield Esq.

*John Rose of Cransley near Kettering Esq.

*Richard Sarson of Loughborough Grocer

*William Sharrad of Knossington Gent.

John Fisher Sharpe of Coleorton

John Shaw of Northampton

Durham Sharpe of do.

Francis Paul Stratford of Thorpe Lubenham Esq.

H. Sandy of Holmepierrepoint Esq.

*The Revd Thomas Stafford of Doddington Clerk

*John Sharpe of Melton

R. Sharpe Jun. of Melton

Edward Sarson of Stoughton

*The Revd John Stanton, Rector of Scaldwell, Northamptonshire Clerk

William Sherrard of Knossington Esq.

*William Spencer Sen. of Knossington

Francis Spencer of Normanton Turville

James Severn of Nottingham Wine Merchant

*The Revd Dr William Boulton Sleath of Repton

*The Revd John Sleath of Saint Paul's

Abraham Seward of Newgate Street, London Esq.

  Sheppard of Melton

*William Sills of Hinckley

John Sills of do.

John Swingler of Lubenham

*William Sibley of Harrington

Samuel Sibley of Thorpe Underwood

John Sibley of Maidwell

Charles Smith of Northampton
Esq.

Smithson of Northampton

William Parker Sibson of Thrussington

William Tyler Smith of Northampton Esq.

*Ascough Smith of Leesthorpe Hall
Esq.

John Simpson of Brentingby

John Smith of Huncote Lodge

The Revd John Stoddart Sen. of
Northampton Clerk

*John Stones of Nottingham Coach-
maker

Storer of East Farndon

*Gabriel Sutton of Dunton

*Charles Shuttleworth of Leadenhall
Street, London Druggist

Robert L. Sykes of Nottingham
Gent.

The Revd Thomas Sykes of Gilsborough Clerk

*William Tailby of Humberstone

Thomas Taylor of Northampton

*John Tailby Jun. of Welham

Tailby of Turlangton

John Theobald of London

*John Theobald Jun. of London

*Thomas Theobald of London

William Theobald of London

William Trentham of Nottingham
Gent.

John Tebbs of Arnesby

Tresham of Oulde near Lamport

Henry Tillard of Wiln Mills near
Nottingham

*William Thornton of Rothley Plain
Farmer

*Henry Thornton of Cropstone
Farmer

*William Thorpe of Dingley Gent.

William Thomas of Daybrook near
Nottingham Lace Manufacturer

John Townsend of Nottingham
Haberdasher

*William Toone of Loughboro'
Grocer

Joseph Toone of do. Grocer

*Henry Toone of do. Gent.

*Samuel Vanderplank of Long Buck-
by Gent.

Vellum of Twyford

John Veasey of Northampton

Jonathan Ward of Hinckley

*William Zouch Lucas Ward of
Gilsborough Esq.

*William Ward of Gilsboro' Esq.

*John Ward of Brownsover, near
Rugby

*George Watkinson of the Bank of
England

*James Watson of Kensington Esq.

*Thomas Warner of Loughborough
Timber Merchant

*Robert Alexander Wallace of Oxford
Esq.

John Walton of Queneboro'

*Thomas Ward of Melton

*The Revd [Daniel] Wagstaffe of
Goadby Clerk

John Waite of Burton Lazars

George Webster of Desford

John Webster of do.

*Sir William Earl Welby, Baronet, of
Denton Hall Nr Grantham

*Charles Cope Earl Welby Esq. of do.

*Thomas Earl Welby Esq. of do.

*Daniel Webster of Deanthorpe

*Thomas Willey of Walton Surgeon

The Revd William Willson of
Harrington, Northamptonshire
Clerk

Henry White of Cold Newton

Thomas White of do.

Willows of Hoby

Reuben Whitchurch of Melton

John Whitchurch of do.

Robert Wilcock of Fazeley

William Wilcock of do.

Thomas Wright of Nottingham
Draper

The Revd Dr Wright of Great Billing Nr Northampton
Wright of Lenton Esq.
*Edward Whittle of Melton
George Woodcock of Hinckley

Thomas Woods of Branstone Rutland Esq.
John Wood of Great Wigston
*John Worth of Evington

Common Hall held 5 March 1823

*John Adams of Loughborough Druggist
*The Rev. Henry Atlay of Wakerley
*The Rev. [Charles] Atlay Sen. of the Grammar School Stamford
The Revd Atlay Jun. of Stamford Clerk
Edward Abney Jun. of Measham Hall Esq.
*The Revd John Taylor Allen of High Leigh, Knutsford Clerk
*George Abbey of Northampton Esq.
*Thomas Atkinson of Peterboro' Esq.
*Thomas Abbott of Harboro'
John Arnold of Birmingham Gent.
The Right Honorable Arbuthnot of Northamptonshire
Thomas Barrs of Mountsorrel
*Robert Baxter of Wisbeach Ironmonger
The Revd Wm Baker of Lyndon Clerk
The Revd De Foe Baker of Greetham Clerk
William Bradshaw of Maidwell
*John Braithwaite of Dean Gent.
*David Brake of Stoughton
*John Brake of Carlton Curlieu
*Ralph Blackwell of Nottingham
*Charles Henry Bland of Flawboro'
John Barratt of Northampton Esq.
William Baker of Northampton M.D.
*Joseph Berridge of Broughton
The Revd Beetham of Costock Nr Loughboro' Clerk
The Revd John Beetham of do. Clerk
George Beaumont of Winthorpe Cottage near Newarke Gent.

William Beddington of Camp Hill Birmingham
George Beeby of Upton, near Atherstone
John Beeby of Atherstone Draper
*Thomas Calvert Beasley of Harston near Belvoir Castle
*Edward Brewster of Ratcliffe, Nottingham
*John Beauclerck of Whittlebury Esq.
Birdsall Sen. of Northampton
William Billings of Illston
*John Billings Jun. of do.
Thomas Billings Jun. of do.
*Richard Briggs of Grantham Chymist
*John Brown of Mountsorrel
*Benjamin Brown of Mountsorrel
The Revd Edward Brown of St Mary's Row, Birmingham Clerk
*The Revd Dr Bloxam of Rugby
The Venble Henry Keye Bonney, Archdeacon of Bedford, King's Cliffe near Wainford
John Brown of Ketton near Stamford
John Bonnett Jun. of Ratby
Sir Richard Brooke de Capel Brooke, Baronet, Great Oakley
*John Booth of Glendon Hall Esq.
Busby of New Street, Birmingham Esq.
*Marston Buszard Jun. of Lutterworth Esq.
The Revd M. Butcher of Northampton Clerk
George Burnham of Wellingboro' Esq.
*Edmund Singer Burton of Daventry Gent.

548

Robert Clarke of Nottingham
Cabinet maker

*Robert Carver of Leicester Forest
Farmer

*John Clarke of Beske Abbey near
Waltham   Farmer

John Chamberlain of Sapcote

*William Chandler of Potter's Mar-
ston

*The Revd [John] Chamberlain of
Elwall near Derby   Clerk
Campion of Newbold Near
Leamington

Joseph Clay of Burton upon Trent
Esq.

Henry Clay of do. Esq.

*The Revd Richard Carey of Barrow-
den

*Captn Thos Cradock of Lough-
boro'

*William Clark of Melton   Auction-
eer

*Thomas Cartwright of Bewdley Esq.

William Chaplin of Ratby

W. T. Catlett of Grantham
Surgeon

Thomas Carter of Edgcott Esq.

John Chetwode of Fillongly Lodge,
Nr Atherstone Esq.

*Chevallier Temple M.A. Catherine
Hall, Cambridge

Thomas Chettle of Grantham

Charles Fynes Clinton, Esq., Deputy
Recorder of Grantham

The Revd Thos Collins of Thed-
dingworth   Clerk
Crofts of Church Lawford,
Warwickshire

Sir Montague Cholmeley   Baronet

Montague Cholmeley Esq.

*The Revd Henry Cornie of Harring-
worth near Rutland   Clerk

*The Revd George Elwes Cornie,
Fellow of Catherine Hall

*Thomas Cox of Willford, Notts
Gent.

*Thomas Cook of Northampton Esq.

William Church of Maidwell

The Hon. & Revd Thomas Dawney
Rector of Ashwell near Oaks

James Alexander Diswell of Nottingham   Gent.

The Revd John Giles Dimmock of
Uppingham   Clerk

John Dunmore of Goadby

Thomas Duffty of Oakham   Draper

John Duffty of Oakham

*John Eames of Ashby-de-la-Zouch

William Everard of Maidwell
Eyre of   Derbyshire

Adml Eyles of Loddington

George Farrand of Basford

Edward Freer of Dale end, Birmingham   Grocer

*John Fleetwood of [New Ormond
St.] London

Thomas Finn of Nottingham

*The Hon. Dr. Finch,   Tanfield
Court, Temple, London

Major the Hon. John Finch, Burley
on the Hill

*George Finch of Burley on the Hill,
Rutland Esq.

The Hon.   Finch of

*John Foster of Market Harborough

*Job Foster of do.

The Revd Foster of Ayston, Rutland

Francis Forrester Esq. M.P. 28
Sackville Street, Piccadilly

Lord Forrester

*Henry Flower Jun. of Scarrington,
Notts.

*Jacob Watson Fowler of Thorpe
Arnold near Melton

John Garrard of Olney, Bucks

*Lieut. Col. Wm Gray of Barrow

Francis Robinson Gray of Loughboro'   Surgeon

*Benjamin Gabb of Park Street,
Birmingham

*John Gates of Peterboro' Esq.

*The Revd [Henry] Green of Bristol
Clerk

*Robert Green of Normanton

John Gilbert of Evington

Thomas Gill of Harboro'   Draper

The Revd Gill of Scraptoft   Clerk

*Jonathan Gibbons of Uppingham Esq.

The Revd Edward Griffin of Dingley Clerk

The Revd Edward Griffin Jun. of Weston   Clerk

John Griffin of Dingley Esq.

*The Revd Dr Gilbert, Principal of Brazen Nose College, Oxford

John Glover of Potlock near Derby Grazier

John Gutteridge of Hinckley

William Guilford of Keyham

J. E. Harrison of Nottingham

George William Finch Hatton of Kirby, Northamptonshire

*The Revd Daniel Hatton, Rector of Weldon, Northants.

Samuel Haines of New Street, Birmingham   Silversmith

William Haines of Birmingham Gent.

*The Revd Wm Hardyman, Rector of North Luffenham, Rutland

*Charles Hall of Uppingham   Gent.

*Henry Bagshaw Harrison of Bugbrooke, Northamptonshire

*Capt. Francis Hawkesley Hall of Arnold, Nottingham

Thomas Harper of Tamworth Esq.

*Thomas Harvey of Grantham Draper

B. Heathcote of   near Derby Esq.

*William Healey of Freeby near Melton

Capt. Hewlett Northampton

Joseph Hill of Stanford Hall

Charles Hitchcock, St George's Hotel, Albermarle Street

Richard Hitchcock of Albany, London   Gent.

William Hickinbotham of Newton Harcourt

The Revd John Hinman of Market Overton, Rutland   Clerk

Thomas Hind of Gonalstone near Nottingham

Temple Hillyard of Northampton Esq.

Clarke Hillyard of Thorpe Lands Esq.

*William Hobson of Stretton

*Thomas Hobson of Little Stretton

Thomas Hodson of Burton on Trent

Edwin Hodson of do.

Hodson of Wellingborough Esq.

*Henry Hodson of Spring Cottage nr Burton-upon-Trent Esq.

Thomas Peach Holdich of Maidwell Esq.

William Holdich of Marston Trussell

William Hopkins of Bury St Edmonds Esq.

John Holmes of Tamhorn nr Tamworth

*John Holroyd of Catherine Hall, Cambridge, M.A.

Thomas Howes of Northampton Esq.

John Howes of Irthlingboro' Esq.

The Revd Thomas Hornsby of Ravenstone

William Hubbard of Great Ashby Farmer

*John Huskisson of Norton   Grazier

*John Hunter of Fazeley   Gent.

*William Hulton of Hulton Park, Lancashire Esq.

Henry Hughes of Northampton Esq.

John Jackson of Mountsorrell

Matthew Jackson of Harby   Grazier

*William Jammison of Wilford, Notts

William Jamison of Burton Joice, Notts Esq.

George Jamison Jun. of North Reston Lowth

*Revd Mr Charles Inge of Ibstock

Revd Dr Jenkins Master of Baliol College

Edmund Ivens of Flecknoe near Dunchurch

John Ivens of Granboro' near do.

Samuel Isted of Eaton Esq.

William Tiffin Iliffe of London Surgeon

*Revd Nath. Palmer Johnson of Aston Rectory Derbyshire

Revd Hugh Johes of Burton on Trent

Joseph Johnson of Evington Farmer

*James Kewney of Nottingham

John King of Loughborough Gent.

William Kirton of Sleaford Esq.

*John Kipling of Overstone Esq.

Sir Charles Knightley of Fawsley Bart

George Lant of Coventry Esq.

Wedman Lant Allesley nr Coventry

William Lant of Berkswell nr do.

Joseph Lathbury Sen. of Burton on Trent

John Lambert Sen. of Middleton

*John Lambert Jun. of do.

*Joseph Silvester Langwish of Grantham

Edward Lewin of Keyham

Joseph Lenton Jun. of Peek Lane Birmingham

John Lees of Burton on Trent

Revd Dr Lee President of Trinity College

*Thomas Legh of Lime Park Stockport Esq.

Edward John Littleton of Yedderley Hall Staffordshire

*Hon. Col. Lowther Cecil Lowther of Cottesmore

*William Lowe of Basingfield nr Nottingham Grazier

*John Lowe of Holme Grange nr Nottingham do.

William Ludlow of Dale End, Birmingham

John Marriott of Beeby

Francis Marriott Malster of Newark

*Joshua Mann Jun. of Stragglethorpe nr Nottingham

*Stephen Mash of Lutterworth

*George [Aulay] Macaulay of Bury St Edmonds Surgeon

*[Thomas Philip] Maunsell of Thorpe Malsor nr Kettering

*Thomas Manners of Grantham Attorney

Revd Dr Marlow of Saint Johns College [Oxford]

John Marshall Esq. nr Hackney Shipbroker

*Robert Mather of Grantham Surgeon

Charles Markham of Northampton Esq.

*Christopher Markham of do. Esq.

George Mettam; N. J. Crowthers Esq. Nottingham

John Mercer of Northampton Esq.

John Meadows of Thorpe Malsor

Thomas Mills of Stamford Druggist

John Moore Old Club Melton Esq.

*Thomas Mowbray of Loughborough Schoolmaster

*Charles Campbell Morris of Broughton, Northants Esq.

Mr Moorehouse Sloane Street

Frederick Mortlock of Oakham

*Joseph Montgomery St Pauls Church Yard [London] Mrcht

Thomas Munton of the Swans Inn Harborough

*Francis Munday of Markeaton Derbyshire Esq. M.P.

    Nadin of Stanton nr Burton Esq.

Francis Nalder of London

Thomas Nalder of do.

*Frederick Newcome of Grantham

*Thomas Newcome of Braunstone Lodge Grazier

*Revd John Newling Canon Residentiary of Lichfield

Nicholas Needham of Knossington Gent.

Charles Neale of Alverton, Notts

George Newton of Disby nr Buxton Esq.

*Joseph Neale Jun. of Grantham

Thomas Norton of Maidwell

Revd Charles Oakover of Atherstone

Oakover of Oldbury Hall nr Atherstone

*William Henry Osborn High St Birmingham Liquor Mercht

William Osborne of Burton upon Trent

Revd George Osborne Rector of Stainby

George Osborne Esq. (son of do.)

*Revd Joseph Parsons Prebendary of Peterborough

Revd Pratt Prebend of do.

Thomas Parkins of Ullesthorpe

Charles Perkins of Sinai Park nr Burton Esq.

*Revd Fredk David Perkins of Sow nr Coventry

*Edmund Peel of Bonehill nr Tamworth Esq.

Revd Charles Hendrick Prescott Rector of Stockport

Revd Kelshall Prescott of Stockport

*Sir George Pigott of Potshull nr Birmingham Bart

*Revd Dr Joseph Proctor Master of Catherine Hall Cambridge

*Revd William Potchett of Grantham

*William Pougher of Ashby Shrubs nr Kirby Muxloe

*Wm Power of Barwell Gent.

James Powell of Hackney Esq.

Baden Powell of same Esq.

*Charles Rattray of Daventry Esq.

Captain Rattray of same

John Rawden of Chard Somersetshire

*William Rather of Grantham Solicitor

Richard Renshaw of Nottingham Hosier

Rupert Renshaw of same Lacemaker

Samuel Renshaw of same Hosier

*James Reynolds of Loughborough Esq.

*William Reeve of Rugby Ironmonger

*Samuel Ridge of Grantham Stationer

Revd Roberts of Wolston nr Coventry

James Roberts of Whitby Brook Esq.

*Revd John Rose of Wilton nr Daventry

Thomas Rowlett Jun. of Great Bowden Grazier

William Robinson of Tamworth Gent.

Joseph Swain of Huncote Sale Draper

Thomas Seagrave of Carlton

Joseph Sheppard of Wimeswould

George Skelton of Nottingham Hosier

John Spencer of Burton on Trent Esq.

*William Spencer of Sapcote

John Ruding Stephens Man Street Hackney

Joseph Smith of Sapcote Smith of Houghton on the Hill

Edward Smith of Burton on Trent Esq.

*William Simons of Ullesthorpe

John Smith 540 Oxford Street London

George Smith of Northampton Esq.

*Revd Henry Shield of Preston nr Uppingham

*Robert Shipman of Grantham Ironmonger

*William Shipman of Sedgebrooke Lincolnshire Farmer

*Stephen Smith of Knighton

Revd Dr Smith of Daventry

Thomas Slow of Waltham Gent.

Captain Thomas Scott (Artillery)

The Venerable Dr Strong Archdeacon of Peterboro'

Revd Dr Stone Wootton Rivers nr Marlborough

Thomas Sutton of Levi

Thomas Sutton of Dunchurch Esq.

William Sutton of do. Esq.

Henry Sutton of Thurlaxton nr Dunchurch

Charles Sutton of do.

*John Sturton of Sleaford

Revd   Spry of Edgbaston nr Birmingham

*Benjamin Tabberer of Repton Derbyshire Surgeon

Dr Richard Taylor of Bath

*Richd Thos Wilson Taylor of Wadham College Oxford Esq.

*Henry Terry of Northampton Esq.

*Joseph Tindall of Grantham Farmer

*George Frewen Timberlake of London Esq.

Samuel Tibbitts of Northampton Esq.

Thomas Toone of Loughborough Plumber

James Torkington of Stukeley nr Huntingdon Esq.

*Thomas Tompson of Ashby-de-la-Zouch Tanner

*William Tomlinson of Hinckley

Revd Dr Tournay Warden of [Wadham College, Oxford]

Wm James Thompson of London

Wm Turner Jun. of Snow Hill Birmingham

Thomas Turton, B.D., Catherine Hall, Cambridge

Wm Turner of Grantham M.D.

*Robert Turner of do.   Chymist

Revd Wm Thursby Abingdon Thursby Esq.

Thomas Tryon of Bulwick Esq.

*Thomas Tryon Jun. of same Esq.

Revd John Tryon Rector of Bulwick

*John Valentine of Coleshill, Warwicks.

*Thomas Vincent Jun. of Bottesford nr Grantham

*Robert Vincent of Orston nr Bingham

William Wade of Stonton Wyville

Richard Ward of Nottingham

James Ward of Great Bowden

Joseph Ward of the Market Place Nottingham

*Richard Warner of Coventry

*Henry Warner of do.

Richard Warner Weston nr Nuneaton

Thomas Warner Germany nr do. Sons of do.

William Watlington Jun. of Burton on Trent Esq.

William Walcott of Oundle Esq.

*Edmund Walker of Lincolns Inn Fields Esq.

Francis Walker of Charing Cross Optician

Benjamin Ward of Whitwick Grocer

Henry Pilkinton Ward of Nottingham Druggist

Joseph Watson of Clapton Middlesex Esq.

Revd Edwd Watkin of Cucknoe

Revd   Wetherall of Rushton Wetherall of do. Esq.

William Wright of Systonby nr Melton

Revd Thomas Wilson of Barrow on Soar

*Samuel Wilson of Flawborough Notts.

*Revd Charles Wright of Bosworth

Revd Matthew Wilt of Repton

Revd Thomas Winfield Rector of Teigh Rutland

William Wiggins of Draughton (Northants.)

Thomas Wickham of Nottingham Lace-maker

*Jno Wm Burton Wilkins of Grantham Gunsmith

Charles Whitworth of Northampton Esq.

Revd   Williams of Daventry

Willm Worthington Senr of Burton on Trent Esq.

Captain Henry Worthington of do.

*James Woodhouse of Lutterworth Grocer

John Wooley of Wellingborough
Charles Wynne Griffith Wynne Esq.
*Lawrence Wyles of Grantham
    Grocer
*Joseph Wyles of Grantham   Miller

William Wyman of Kettering Esq.
Revd Edmund Yeadon of Nottingham
    Young of Orlingbury Esq.

Common Hall held 25 April 1823

Adams Rev. Thomas Coker of
    Anstey near Coventry   Clerk
Adams   Esq. of Do.
*Anderson Rev. Edward of Hickling
    Notts.   Clerk
*Archer Matthew of Harby   Farmer
Barton Mr Ashton of Coventry
Barton Lieutenant Samuel of Do.
Barker Edward of Nottingham
    Hosier
*Branson Josiah of Osgathorpe
    Currier
Blackwell John of Nottingham
    Hosier
Berridge Matthew of Frisby on the
    Wreake
Beaufoy Benjamin of Meredew
    Surgeon
*Berkley Charles Paul of Cotterstock
    Hall Esq.
Bellairs Rev. Henry of Bedworth
    Clerk
*Briggs Samuel of Grantham
    Draper
*Briggs William of Grantham
    Plumber
Boycott William of Hill Grove near
    Kidderminster
*Bunney John of Coventry
Bunney Captain Robert of Do.
Bury Mr of Coventry   Surgeon
Cherrey Edward of Coventry
    Surgeon
Cheetham Henry of Nottingham
    Druggist
Creswell Mr of Coleorton
*Cook Thomas of Nottingham
    Grocer
Cox John of Kilby   Farmer
Cross Thomas of Woodboro'

Cornfield George of Gold Street
    Northampton
Cooch John Jun. of Arlestone near
    Do.
Cox John
*Cox Thomas } Merchants of Derby
Cox George
*Cust Hon. and Rev. Richard of
    Belton near Grantham
*Cust Hon. Peregrine Francis
*Cust Hon. Edward
Douglass Mr William of Coventry
*Duffield Christopher of Little
    Gonerby near Grantham
Dyson James of Newark   Wine
    Merchant
*Evans Mr John [Southam] of
    Coventry
Evans John at Mr Kites Park Street
    Nottingham   Hosier
*Eaton Thomas of Derby   Surgeon
Flamstead Rev.   of Spondon
    near Derby
Flamstead J. Jun. of Lambley Notts.
Freer Rev. Thomas Lane of Hands-
    worth near Birmingham
*Freer William of Liverpool
*Freake Joseph Frederick of Nor-
    thampton
*Fisher John Morris of Grays Inn
    London Esq.
Fitche George of Derby
Fowler Cornelius of Belgrave
Fryer James of Bewdley Esq.
*Gamble William of Grimstone
    Gent.
Gayfere Mr Thomas of Abington
    Street Westminster
*Gadsby John of Lockington   Grazier
*Gates Edward of Northampton

Gresham William Weekday Cross Nottingham

Gresham Richard Farmer Chicksands Lodge near Shelford Beds.

Gresham Robert Do.

*Hand Robert of Woolsthorpe Lincolnshire Farmer

*Hand Henry of Scottlethorpe Do.

*Harrison James Harwood of Lincolns Inn Esq.

Hassard Joseph Duston near Northampton

Hackett Francis Benyon Esq. Moor Hall near Sutton Coldfield

Hassall John of Shelford Manor near Nottingham Grazier

Hewitt John of Northampton Music Maker

Hobbs Captain John Thomas of Coventry

Hopkins Thomas of Belgrave

Hoe Thomas Crabtree, 42 Gutter Lane London

Hulbert George Redman Aston Lodge Derbyshire Esq.

*Humpston Joseph of Derby Merchant

Hyde William of Barnsley

Jackson P. D. of Kearsley Coventry

*Jeffery Christopher of Peterboro' Merchant

Jebbs William Francis Lieutenant of Thrapstone R.N.

John Johnson of Gosford Street, Coventry

*Johnson Thomas of Osgathorpe

Jordan Joseph of Coventry

Jordan   Sons

Kayes Lieutenant William of Nottingham 73rd Regiment

Kirk St John, Burrow on the Hill

Laxton William of Coventry Surgeon

Laing John of Coventry Attorney

Lant Richard of Berkswell near Coventry

*Leeson Rev. William of Clare Hall, Cambridge

Linney John of South Witham, Lincolnshire

*Loggin Rev. George of Rugby

*Maunsell Captain Robert of Thorpe Malsor R.N.

*Maunsell Captain John of Do.

Marshall William John Frederick of Kettering

*Manton John of Grantham Malster

Mellor Dr George of Coventry, M.D.

Mills Rev. Thomas of Peterboro'

Morris   of Coventry

*Morton George of Grays Inn, London

Moore Benjamin of Nottingham

*Mountnay Mr Barclay of London

*Musson Francis Jun. of Hough on the Hill Lincolnshire Farmer

*Musson William of Burton Cogles Lincolnshire Farmer

*Musson John Jun. of Corby Lincolnshire Tanner

Need Major General of Fountain Dale near Mansfield

Ormond George of Coventry

Parker Benjamin of Coventry

Pratt Thomas Sen. of Do.

Pratt Thomas Jun. of Do.

*Palmer Philip of East Bridgford Notts.

Pardoe Robert of Bewdley Esq.

Pears Abijah of Coventry Ribbon maker

*Pepper Thomas Coventry Clerk to Lamb & Co.

Pridmore George of Coventry

*Phillips Edward of Do.

Pimm George of Coleorton

*Pimm Thomas Stanley of Do.

*Power [Edward] Esq. of Stretton under Foss near Lutterworth

*Reader William of Coventry Printer

Rew Sir Skears of Coventry

*Reynardson Major General Birch of Holywell near Stamford

*Reeve Thomas of Uppingham
Sharpe Thomas of Coventry
*Sharpe William Jun. of Cranford
  near Kettering Woolstapler
Stanton Dr of Northampton M.D.
Stephens John of Coventry Silver-
  smith
*Stevenson William of Grantham
Simpson Rev. Robert of Coventry
*Shipman John of Belvoir Inn
Smith George Sen. of Northampton
  Esq.
Smith George Jun. of Do.
*Simpson James Blythe of Derby
  Solicitor
Slott George of Coventry
*Sollery James of Bridlesmith Gate
  Nottingham Glazier
*Storer Mr Robert Ayre of Coleorton
Storer Mr   of Coleorton
Summers Mr William of Coventry
Taylor John of Coventry Silk
  merchant
*Taylor Edward of Somerby
  Grazier
*Tallents William Edward of New-
  arke Esq.
Tempest John of Belgrave
Twist John of Coventry (Attorney)
Thirlby George of Ibstock Lodge
Troughton Rev. James of Coventry
Thorald Thomas of Eaton near
  Belvoir

Vale Alderman S. of Coventry
Vale   Jun. of Coventry
Vaughan Robert of Wall near
  Lichfield Esq.
*Walker Thomas of Nottingham
  Lacemaker
Warren Captain Francis of Notting-
  ham
Watkin William of Daventry Esq.
Weare James of Coventry
Wedge Charles of Coventry
Wedge Francis of Bicknell, War-
  wickshire
*Williamson Joseph of Coventry
Wilmot Thomas of Do. Attorney
Wilson James William of Do.
  Carrier
Wright Samuel of Over Broughton
  Esq.
*Wilson Rev. John of Do.
*Winter Richard Jun. of Grantham
*Winter Thomas of Do. Gent.
Woodcock John Jun. of Coventry
  Attorney
Woodhouse Christopher of Coven-
  try
*Woodhall Rev. William of Braun-
  stone Leicestershire Clerk
Wyley John of Coventry
Wyles Thomas of Honington Lin-
  colnshire Farmer

Common Hall held 6 August 1823

Aston Thomas of Upper Guilford
  Street London
Baguley Richard of Southwark
*Branson William of Osgathorpe
Backhouse John of 2 Adam Court
  Road
*Berridge John of Tower Street
  London
*Betts Thomas of Seagrave
Billing John of Derby
*Blower William Senr of Rotherby
  Grazier

Bushwell William of Portland
  Square Esq.
Cuttley Stephen Wildman of Toot-
  ing Surrey Esq.
*Calvert Edward   Bank Derby
*Carlisle John of Bristol
Crawley Revd John Lloyd of Hey-
  ford nr Daventry
Clarke Robt of Nottingham Cabi-
  net Maker
*Charlesworth John of Ashby de la
  Zouch Woolstapler

*Chouler Timothy of Nottingham Bankers Clerk

Davis Henry of Berkeley Square Bristol

Deacon Mr of Towcester Surgeon

Evans Revd Arthur Benion Gloucester

Elliott Mr of Towcester Attorney

Eustice Chetwynd of Portman Square Esq.

Eddy Revd   of Guilsboro' Northamptonshire

*Elwyn Wm Brame Barrister of Clifton nr Bristol Esq.

*Flavell John Gutteridge of Loughborough Grocer

Fletcher Revd   of Tiffield nr Towcester

*Freeman Charles of Northampton

*Freeman Richard of Gold Street Northampton Attorney

Gamble Thomas of Cottesmore Rutland

*Green Revd Valentine of Aylestone

Gutch John Matthew of Redland nr Bristol Esq.

Heathcote Simon Oakley of Knipton Surgeon

Herrick   Esq. of Lincolns Inn

*Hurd Philip Kentish Town House nr London

*Jackson John Beetham of Saint Pauls Church yard

*Jenner George of Doctors Commons London Esq.

Ives Revd Mr of Braddon nr Towcester

Ives Cornelius of do.

Johnson George 7 Kings Bench Walk Temple London

Johnson Charles Genl Post office London Esq.

*Kirby [John] Matsbury of Towcester

Kinton Mr W. C. Chittem of Keytsbury

Kinton Robert 21 Lambs Conduit Street London

King Sir Abraham Bradley of Dublin Bart

*Lees James Senr of Nottingham Surveyor

Lees James Junr of do. do.

Lister John of Ashbourne Gent.

Lloyd Revd John Crawley of Heyford nr Daventry

Lovell Mr of Towcester Attorney

Lovett Mr James of Coventry Druggist

Machin Joseph of Nottingham Gent.

Manton Gildon Mr Joseph Manton's Hanover Square London

Manton Mr Henry of St John's College Cambridge

*Newman Henry Wenman of Thornbury Park Glos.

*Orton Henry of Derby Tobacconist

*Palmer John of Lockington Farmer

*Pigeon Alfred Staines of Southwark

Pigeon Henry of Throgmorton Street London

*Pigeon Richard Hotham do.

*Reynolds Joseph of Loughboro' Currier

Richardson William of Kensington

Riddlesdon William of Ashbourne Gent.

Rose Wm of Brampton nr Northampton Esq.

Rose Revd Henry of Whilton nr Daventry

Rose Revd Charles of Lincoln College Oxford

Roberts William of Freeby

*Rouse Henry of Montague St Russell Square London Esq.

Swann Revd Charles of Ridlington Rutland

Sharpe Richd of Grantham

Stanton Daniel of Berkeley Square Bristol Esq.

*Sherrer John Walter of Harringworth Esq.

Spencer Robert of Southwork

Stephenson   of Ketton nr Stamford Esq.

*Smith Sampson Mesman of Nottingham   Attorney

Singleton Wm Junr of Witham nr Coltsworth Lincolnshire Esq.

*Smith Revd Thomas of Stanton on the Wolds nr Nottm

*Simpson Charles of Derby   Cheesefactor

Still Peter of Lincolns Inn London Esq.

Taylor Revd William of Lichboro' nr Daventry

*Thorald Richard of Eaton nr Belvoir Miller

Tunnard Joseph Bradley of Grantham   Innkeeper

*Vincent Francis of Barrowby nr Grantham   Farmer

Walker Thomas of Stockerstone Esq.

*Watts William of Belvoir   Farmer

*Walkington [William] of Grantham Bankers Clerk

Welch Revd Thomas of Pattishall nr Towcester

Wildgoose John of Daventry

Wildgoose Robert of do.

White Revd Mr of Maidford near Towcester

*Wright John Junr of Derby   Merchant

*Williams   Reverend   Richard   of Markfield

Young Charles Allen of Southwork Esq.

Young Florence Thomas of Montague Street Russel Square Esq.

Common Hall held 3 September 1824

*George Allen Little Gonerby Grantham

*Michael Ashwell, Barrowby, Lincolnshire   Grazier

John Bland of Flawboro' near Newarke

Edward Brierly of Kings Newnham nr Coventry

Sparrow   Bodychen   Esq.   Great George Street Westminster or Leamington

*Charles Clarke Lieut of Life Guards, Barracks Regents Park

  Chamberlain Esq. Derby

*Benjamin   Carter   Pepper   Street Nottingham   Lacemanufacturer

Thomas Church Ratcliffe

*Arthur Church do.

*Matthew Maurice George Dowling Smith Street Chelsea

The   Honble   and   Revd   James Douglass, Broughton, Kettering

*Edward Edman of Lincoln   Grocer

*John Eminson of Barrowby Lincolnshire   Grazier

*John William Fleetwood Gent. 23 New Ormond Street London

*William Gray 45 Portman Place, Edgeware Road

*James Gray do. do.

Philip Gates of Stanground nr Peterboro'   Tanner

*William Gilson Junr of Uppingham Gent.

*Jonas Kewney   Veterinary Surgeon Nottingham

*John Lawrence Esq. Grantham

The Revd John Leete of Bletsoe Bedfordshire

C. Lowe Stamford

John Mason 151 Fleet Street London   Seedsman

Thomas Mills High Street Stamford Druggist

*Thomas Anthony Negus 13 Henry Street Pentonville   Stock Broker

Philip Hall Palmer Esq. East Bridgford Nottingham

    Pochin of Morcott Leicester Militia

*Fredk Fowler Robertson of Little Gonerby nr Grantham   Tanner

Edis Spencer Stamford   Grocer

*[Richard] Turnill St Peters Hill Stamford   Maltster

*Thomas Hall Vaughton Fillongley Lodge nr Atherstone Esq.

George Webster 16 Poland Street, Oxford Street London

Edward Henry Wilks Grantham Yeoman

William Wright Peckleton House Gent.

Lawrence Wright of Peckleton, Gent.

*Thomas Winterton, Earl Shilton

INDEX OF PEOPLE

Abbey, George, 548
Abbott, John, 221, 225; Thomas, 548; William, 162, 163
Abell, Isaac, 227; Thomas, 183, 184
Abney, Edward, 535, 548; John, 86; Philip, 33; Ald. 27, 31, 58, 59, 61–3, 69; ——, 19, 63
Acham, Anthony, 398
Acomb, Daniel, 541
Adams, John, 104, 548; Poyntz Owsley, 535; Samuel, 541; Thomas Coker, 554
Adcock, Henry, 180; John, 61, 176; Thomas, 85, 106; ——, 483, 484
Ades, William, 541
Adison, John, 43; Philippa, 43
Adnutt, Thomas, 535
Agar, Edward, 179, 209, 210; ——, 300–2
Alcock, Daniel, 84, 85, 112, 115
Alfray, Suzanna, 148
Allamand, John Peter, 156, 159; ——, 240
Allen, Amey, 91; Ann, 211, 212; Benjamin, 52; George, 541, 558; James, 74; John, 164–6, 454, 480; John Taylor, 548; Judith, 210; Simon, 67; William, 106, 107, 211, 212, 535
Allen alias Johnson, John, 184
Almey, William, 126
Almond, Robert W. 541
Alsager, Thomas, 541
Alsop, Allsopp, Benjamin, 35; Charles, 535; Edward, 51; Francis, 535; John, 91, 130; Mary, 91; Nicholas, 30; Thomas, 530, 541; William, 91, 135, 541; William Brown, 533
Alston, Messrs. Miles, —— & Miles, 311
Anderson, Abraham, 13, 204, 205; Andrew, 91; Edward, 554; George, 86; Robert, 91
Andrew, Richard, 32
Andrews, John, 541; Thomas, 103; ——, 285
Annis, James, 60, 86; John, 284, 285; Ald. 81, 90
Anslip, William, 48
Ansty, Elizabeth, 109
Appleby, William, 75
Appleton, Teavil, 101
Apthorpe, Frederick, 535
Arbuthnot, Rt Hon. 548
Archer, Matthew, 554
Arkwright, John, 535; Peter, 535; Richard, 535; Robert, 535
Armes, James, 171; Mary, 171
Armfield, William, 541; ——, 541
Armston, James, 23, 24; Robert, 39; Widow, 98
Arnold, Allen Robert, 140; Edward, 213;

John, 548; John Arthur, 535; Thomas, 160, 541; William, 147; Dr, 154
Ashby, John, 139
Asher, Francis, 163; Henry, 211; William, 213
Ashton, George, 541; John, 161
Ashurst, Justice, 243
Ashwell, Benjamin, 61; James, 219; Josiah, 53; Michael, 558; Sarah, 219
Aslin, John, 79
Aspinshaw, Edward, 531
Astill, Francis, 223
Astle, Thomas, 108; William, 133, 146
Astlett, James, 535
Astley, Richard, 535
Aston, Thomas, 556
Astwell, John, 61, 68, 89; see also Hastwell
Atcheson, Nathaniel, 535
Atherstone, Jonathan, 221, 222; Lucy, 221
Atkins, John, 535, 541; John Iliffe, 541; Joseph, 68; Robert, 182; Thomas, 206; William, 220
Atkinson, Thomas, 548
Atlay, Charles, 548; Henry, 548
Attenborough, Henry, 541; James, 541; Robert, 541
Aumey, Robert, 5, 240
Austin, Rowland, 454, 480; ——, 297, 298
Avery, Robert Whatcock, 531
Axson, James, 150, 151
Aylesford, Earl of, 534
Ayre, Ayres, John, 86; Thomas, 58, 65, 83, 85, 86, 88, 541; Ald. 63, 66, 81, 103; see also Eyre

Babington, George Gisborne, 535; John, 535; Matthew, 535; Matthew Drake, 535; Thomas, 529; Thomas Gisborne, 535; ——, 408
Backhouse, John, 556
Baggerly alias Mahone, Judith, 220
Bagnall, Margaret, 100; Robert, 80; William, 100
Baguley, John, 541; Richard, 556
Bailey, Bayley, Elizabeth, 180, 182, 207, 209; John, 104, 120; Samuel, 55
Bainbridge, Philip Harley, 531
Bainbrigg, James, 70
Baines, James, 274
Baker, Daniel, 535; De Foe, 548; John, 535; Junius, 169, 171; Thomas, 533, 541; William, 67, 535, 548
Bakewell, Robert, 117
Bales, Robert, 226
Balguy, John, 542
Ball, Mary, 124; Richard, 109
Bamford, Major, 542

INDEX OF SUBJECTS AND PLACES